GT511 .F375 2007

Fashion theory : a reader

2007.

2007 11 30

DATE DUE	RETURNED
SEP 2 4 2012	
OCT 3 1 2012	OCT 3 1 2012
	NOV 0 2 2012
SEP 1 3 2013	SEP 1 3 2013

Fashion Theory

What is fashion theory? Do we need it? Can we avoid it?

From its beginnings in the fifteenth century, intensified interest in fashion and the study of fashion over the last thirty years has led to a vast and varied literature on the subject. There is now barely a discipline in the humanities or social sciences that does not take a position on what fashion is, what it does and how it works.

This collection of essays surveys and contextualises the ways in which a wide range of disciplines (including sociology, cultural studies, anthropology, fashion history, gender studies and cultural history) have used different theoretical approaches to explain, and sometimes to explain away, the astonishing variety, complexity and beauty of fashion. Themes covered include individual, social and gender identity, clothes and the body, the erotic, consumption and communication.

Each extract is introduced, placed in its historical and theoretical context and its significance for fashion theory is explained.

By collecting together some of the most influential and important writers on fashion and exposing the ideas and theories behind what they say, this unique collection of extracts and essays brings to light the presuppositions involved in the things we think and say about fashion.

Fashion Theory: A Reader is a timeless and invaluable resource for undergraduate students across a range of disciplines including sociology, cultural studies and fashion.

Malcolm Barnard is Senior Lecturer in the History and Theory of Art and Design at the University of Derby.

Routledge Student Readers

Series Editor: Chris Jenks, Vice Chancellor, Brunel University

160201

Fashion Theory

A Reader

Edited by Malcolm Barnard

LONDON AND NEW YORK

First published 2007
by Routledge
2 Park Square, Milton Park, Abingdon, Oxon OX14 4RN

Simultaneously published in the USA and Canada
by Routledge
270 Madison Ave, New York, NY 10016

Routledge is an imprint of the Taylor & Francis Group, an informa business

Typeset in Perpetua and Bell Gothic by
RefineCatch Limited, Bungay, Suffolk
Printed and bound in Great Britain by
The Cromwell Press, Trowbridge, Wiltshire

British Library Cataloguing in Publication Data
A catalogue record for this book is available from the British Library

Library of Congress Cataloging in Publication Data
Fashion theory: a reader / Malcolm Barnard.
    p. cm.
  Includes bibliographical references and index.
  ISBN13: 978–0–415–41339–8 (hardcover)
  ISBN13: 978–0–415–41340–4 (paper cover) 1. Fashion. I. Barnard, Malcolm, 1958–
  GT511.F37 2007
  391—dc22
                                                          2006031748

ISBN10: 0–415–41339–7 (hbk)
ISBN10: 0–415–41340–0 (pbk)

ISBN13: 978–0–415–41339–8 (hbk)
ISBN13: 978–0–415–41340–4 (pbk)

Contents

PART SIX
Fashion: identity and difference

Sex and gender

Social class

Ethnicity and race

Culture and subculture

PART SEVEN
Fashion, clothes and the body

PART EIGHT
Production and consumption

PART NINE
Modern fashion

Series editor's preface

I am pleased to welcome readers to this, the sixth in our series of *Routledge Student Readers* and one that is most timely in providing an analytical spectrum onto our times. Social life is multi-layered and sociologists, anthropologists and cultural theorists have long been aware of the necessity to address the ways in which all kinds of social relations, both historically and comparatively, express themselves in material forms, through symbolic manifestations and as conventions and processes. Thus, even though the term *fashion* has come to be regarded as a particular hyperbole of contemporary Western capitalism its broader remit can be applied to all demonstrations of either collective or individual identification and differentiation. Fashion is, of course, a modern industry but that huge enterprise itself is, in turn, merely one more realisation and formalisation of humankind's infinite range of capacities to adorn, to decorate, to present, to membership, to belong, to eroticize, to both artfully stabilize and de-stabilize. We can begin to regard fashion as not merely the prerogative of celebrity and footballer's wives but as an expressive playground for creative social practice.

As Malcolm Barnard has demonstrated in his careful and imaginative selection of extracts for this book fashion is a social phenomenon that has not failed to escape the interest and attention of theorists from a whole range of disciplines within the arts, the humanities and the social sciences and across an equally wide range of theoretical perspectives from materialist Marxism to hermeneutics and semiology. Clearly fashion speaks more than it says at any moment, it can simultaneously signify exploitation, beauty, class, gender, ethnicity, age and so on. Fashion communicates and mediates between the individual and the collectivity but it also enables a sense of identity.

If we take the issue of body modification and let us focus on perhaps its most common form, that of tattooing. To my parents generation this was an almost exclusively class and gender-specific activity. It carried strong associations with mass conscription and the armed forces. In post-War years it claimed an even more specific alignment with a sense of a seedy underclass and the criminal fraternity – hard men, gangsters, boxers and thugs were always depicted as wearing tattoos. To a young and perhaps over-sensitive sociologist developing through the same period such adornment assumed a repugnance to me, it offered no compelling image of camaraderie or strength but rather resonances with slavery and concentration camps. Now and for almost two decades tattoos have been a chosen means of expression across such conventional categories as class, age and gender – but particularly for the young (and footballer's wives). But how ethnocentric! My anthropological colleagues will show me evidence of such bodily adornment stretching back through time and across a whole range of cultures and signifying statuses that I have hardly attended to.

Malcolm Barnard is the ideal person to provide us with a guide to and a critical appraisal of these important themes running through societal forms and to assemble for us a collection of the most important and penetrating insights provided by 'fashion theory'. He has been researching and publishing and teaching in this area of work for over a decade and has established a firm reputation, both nationally and internationally, based on his seminal contribution to the field. I believe this Reader will soon establish itself as an important and well-regarded landmark in this area of social and cultural analysis.

The way this work is organized will surely provoke the reader's critical awareness. It is certainly important that those of us who are living through a period where fashion is realised as a predominant statement of being and self-identity, increasingly so in less developed societies through the less benign elements of globalization, that we become more reflexive about what we are achieving, both consciously and unconsciously, through such routine action. We need to ask how we become positioned through markets, how our chosen forms of differentiation are both potentially highly divisive but, at the same time, ironically conventional. We need to address the ways in which our very senses of beauty, our self images and, perhaps more significantly, our perceptions of others become ascribed by forces outside of ourselves often merely commercial forces.

You may, of course, regard fashion as a trivial epiphenomenon of an increasingly facile world – I will be more persuaded of that position when young women stop suffering and dying from anorexia.

Chris Jenks
Brunel University

Acknowledgements

I would like to thank Gill Braley (Hi Gill!), Mark Durden, Jo Entwistle, Chris Jenks and Josie Walter for suggestions, advice and sending me stuff. I would also like to thank the staff of the LRC at the University of Derby for procuring inter-library loans, inter-site copies and for helping me to work the copier. And I must thank Jo Fenoulhet for scanning the illustrations.

Although all the contributors deserve my gratitude for giving me permission to use their work, some demand special thanks: they are Zandra Rhodes and Alice Rawsthorn for permission to use the *Observer* article, Professor Richard Sennett for permission to use material from *The Fall of Public Man* and Erica Lennard for permission to use her words and pictures.

Finally, I owe quite a lot to the anonymous reviewers of Routledge, without whom none of my proposals would ever get commissioned, for their usual maturity, good sense and wide reading.

The publishers would like to thank the following for permission to reprint material:

Elizabeth Wilson (1985) 'Explaining It Away', in *Adorned in Dreams: Fashion and Modernity*. © 1985 I. B. Tauris. Reprinted by permission of I. B. Tauris.

Gilles Lipovetsky (1994) 'Introduction' from *The Empire of Fashion: Dressing Modern Democracy*. © 1994 Princeton University Press, 2002 paperback edition. Reprinted by permission of Princeton University Press.

Edward Sapir (1931) 'Fashion'. Reproduced from *Encyclopedia of the Social Sciences*, Palgrave Macmillan, 1931.

A. B. Young (1937) 'Fashion Has Its Laws'. Reproduced from A. B. Young: *Recurring Cycles of Fashion 1760–1937*, Harper and Brothers Publishers/Cooper Square Press, 1937.

Ann Rosalind Jones and Peter Stallybrass (2000) 'Introduction' from *Renaissance Clothing and the Materials of Memory*, Cambridge University Press. Reprinted by permission of Cambridge University Press.

Gilles Lipovetsky (1994) 'A Century of Fashion' from *The Empire of Fashion: Dressing Modern Democracy*. © 1994 Princeton University Press, 2002 paperback edition. Reprinted by permission of Princeton University Press.

Fred Davis (1992) pp. 3–15, 168–86 in *Fashion, Culture and Identity*. © 1992 University of Chicago Press. Reprinted by permission of University of Chicago Press.

Zandra Rhodes and Alice Rawsthorn (2003) 'Is Fashion a True Art Form?', *Observer*, July 13. Reprinted by permission of Zandra Rhodes and Alice Rawsthorn.

Mary Ellen Roach and Joanne Bubolz Eicher (1979) 'The Language of Personal Adornment', in J. M. Cordwell and R. A. Schwartz (eds) *The Fabrics of Culture: The Anthropology of Clothing and Adornment*. © 1979 Mouton de Gruyter. Reproduced by permission of Mouton de Gruyter.

Elizabeth Rouse (1989) 'Why Do People Wear Clothes?', in *Understanding Fashion*. © Blackwell Publishing. Reprinted by permission of Blackwell Publishing.

John Flügel (1950) 'Protection'. Reproduced from J. C. Flügel: *The Psychology of Clothes*, Hogarth Press, 1950; reprinted by International University Press, 1971.

Umberto Eco (1973) 'Social Life as a Sign System', in D. Robey (ed.) *Structuralism: An Introduction — Wolfson College Lectures 1972*. © 1973 Oxford University Press. Reprinted by permission of Oxford University Press.

Colin Campbell (1997) 'When the Meaning is Not a Message', in M. Nava, A. Blake, I. MacRury and B. Richards (eds) *Buy This Book: Studies in Advertising and Consumption*, © 1997 Routledge. Reproduced by permission of Taylor & Francis Books UK.

Malcolm Barnard (2007) 'Fashion Statements: Communication and Culture', in *Fashion Statements*. © 2007 SUNY Press. Reprinted by permission of SUNY Press.

Tim Edwards (1997) Extracts from *Men in The Mirror*, London, Cassell. Reprinted by permission of Tim Edwards.

Lee Wright (1989) 'Objectifying Gender: The Stiletto Heel', from J. Attfield and P. Kirkham (eds) *A View from the Interior: Feminism, Women and Design*, London, Women's Press. Reprinted by permission of Lee Wright.

Joanne Entwistle (1997) 'Power Dressing and the Construction of the Career Woman', in M. Nava, A. Blake, I. MacRury and B. Richards (eds) *Buy This Book: Studies in Advertising and Consumption*. © 1997 Routledge. Reproduced by permission of Taylor & Francis Books UK.

Angela Partington (1992) 'Popular Fashion and Working-Class Affluence'. Reproduced from Elizabeth Wilson and Juliet Ash: *Chic Thrills: A Fashion Reader*, Pandora Press, 1983.

Herbert Blumer (1969) 'Fashion: From Class Differentiation to Collective Selection', *Sociological Quarterly*. © Blackwell Publishing. Reprinted by permission of Blackwell Publishing.

Emil Wilbekin (1999) 'Great Aspirations: Hip Hop and Fashion Dress for Excess and Success', from *The Vibe History of Hip Hop*, edited by Alan Light, copyright © 1999 by Vibe Magazine. Used by permission of Three Rivers Press, a division of Random House, Inc.

Elizabeth Wilson (1985) 'Oppositional Dress', in *Adorned in Dreams: Fashion and Modernity*. © 1985 I. B. Tauris. Reprinted by permission of I. B. Tauris.

Dick Hebdige (1979) Extracts from *Subculture: The Meaning of Style*. © 1979 Routledge. Reproduced by permission of Taylor & Francis Books UK.

Joanne Entwistle (2000) 'Addressing the Body', in *The Fashioned Body*. © 2000 Polity Press. Reprinted by permission of Polity Press.

Paul Sweetman (1999) 'Anchoring the (Postmodern) Self? Body Modification, Fashion and Identity', in *Body and Society* 5:2–3, 51–76. © 1999 Sage Publications. Reprinted by permission of Sage Publications.

Umberto Eco (1998) 'Lumbar Thought', from *Faith in Fakes* by Umberto Eco, published by Secker & Warburg. Reprinted by permission of the Random House Group Ltd.

Ruth Holliday (1999) 'The Comfort of Identity', in *Sexualities* 2:4, 475–91. © 1999 Sage Publications. Reprinted by permission of Sage Publications.

Thorstein Veblen (1992) 'Dress as an Expression of the Pecuniary Culture', in *The Theory of The Leisure Class*. © 1992 Transaction Publishers. Reprinted by permission of the publishers.

Karl Marx (1990) 'The Fetishism of the Commodity and its Secret', in *Capital*, Volume 1, Penguin Books in association with New Left Review. Reprinted by permission of Penguin Books and New Left Review.

Peter Braham (1997) 'Fashion: Unpacking a Cultural Production', in P. du Gay (ed.) *Production of Culture / Cultures of Production*. © Sage Publications 1997, in association with the Open University. Reprinted by permission of Sage Publications and the Open University Press Publishing Company.

Tim Dant (1999) Extracts from *Material Culture in the Social World*. © 1999 Open University Press. Reprinted with the kind permission of the Open University Press Publishing Company.

Elizabeth Wilson (1985) 'Introduction', in *Adorned in Dreams: Fashion and Modernity*. © 1985 I.B. Tauris. Reprinted by permission of I. B. Tauris.

Kurt Back (1985) 'Modernism and Fashion'. Reproduced from M. R. Solomon (ed.) *The Psychology of Fashion*, Lexington Books, 1985.

Richard Sennett (1988) Extracts from *The Fall of Public Man*, London, Faber and Faber. Reprinted by permission of Richard Sennett.

Ulrich Lehmann (2000) 'Benjamin and the Revolution of Fashion in Modernity', in *Tigersprung: Fashion in Modernity*. © 2000 MIT Press. Reprinted by permission of MIT Press.

Jean Baudrillard (1981) Extracts from *For a Critique of the Political Economy of the Sign*, St Louis, Mo., Telos Press.

Jean Baudrillard (1993) 'The Enchanting Spectacle', in M. Gane (ed.) *Symbolic Exchange and Death*. © Sage Publications 1993. Reprinted by permission of Sage Publications.

Kim Sawchuk (1988) 'A Tale of Inscription: Fashion Statements', in A. Kroker and M. Kroker (eds) *Body Invaders: Sexuality and the Postmodern Condition*. © 1988 Macmillan. Reproduced with permission of Palgrave Macmillan.

Alison Gill (1998) 'Deconstruction Fashion', *Fashion Theory*, Volume 2, Issue 1, pp. 25–50, reprinted by permission of the publisher. © 1998 Berg. All rights reserved.

Roland Barthes (1983) 'Fashion Photography'. Reproduced from Roland Barthes: *The Fashion System*, Trans. by M. Ward and R. Howard, University of California Press, 1990.

Rosetta Brookes (1992) 'Fashion Photography. The Double-Page Spread: Helmut Newton, Guy Bourdin & Deborah Turbeville'. Reproduced from Elizabeth Wilson and Juliet Ash: *Chic Thrills: A Fashion Reader*, Pandora Press, 1983.

Erica Lennard (1980) Extract from C. Di Grappa (ed.) *Fashion: Theory*, New York, Lustrum. Reprinted by permission of Erica Lennard.

Tamsin Blanchard (2004) Extracts from *Fashion and Graphics*. © 2004 Laurence King. Reprinted by permission of Laurence King Publishing Ltd.

Sigmund Freud, 'Fetishism' (1927), from *The Standard Edition of the Complete Psychological Works of Sigmund Freud*, Vol. XXI, translated and edited by James Strachey. © copyrights the Institute of Psycho-Analysis and the Hogarth Press. Reprinted by permission of the Random House Group Ltd.

David Kunzle (2004) 'The Special Historic and Psychological Role of Tight-Lacing', in *Fashion and Fetishism*. © 2004 Sutton Publishing. Reprinted by permission of Sutton Publishing.

Valerie Steele (2001) 'Fashion and Fetishism', in *The Corset: A Cultural History*. © 2001 Yale University Press. Reprinted by permission of Yale University Press.

Lorrain Gamman and Merja Makinen (1994) Extracts from *Female Fetishism: A New Look*. © 1994 Lawrence & Wishart. Reprinted by permission of Lawrence & Wishart.

Roland Barthes (1975) *Pleasure of the Text*. Reproduced from Roland Barthes: *The Pleasure of the Text*, Trans. by R. Miller, Hill and Wang, 1975.

Every effort has been made to contact copyright holders for their permission to reprint selections in this book. The publishers would be grateful to hear from any copyright holder who is not here acknowledged and will undertake to rectify any errors or omissions in future editions of this book.

Introduction

■ Malcolm Barnard

What is this book about?

IT IS ABOUT THE THEORIES (or organised ideas) behind what we think, write and say about the things we wear. When, for example, we mock our male friends for wearing a shirt that is a bit 'girly', complex theories of gender, social status and communication lie behind what we say, usually without our knowing it. When we say that one of our friends has an endearingly retro style but that another is locked in some ghastly 1980s time warp, we are using theories about what history is and how fashion relates to history. This book is about these theories and ideas in a way that makes us think about what ideas or theories are and how they colour or even make possible the things we think, write and say about the things we wear. And it is about these ideas in a way that makes us think 'Who is this "we", this "us" that is doing the thinking, writing and saying?' How does what we wear make us a group, an 'us' or a 'we'? When we say 'fashion', do we mean the same thing as when we say 'clothing', or 'dress' and is saying 'the things we wear' any different from saying 'fashion', 'clothing' or 'dress'? What ideas and theories lie behind these words and how might they affect the meaning of what we think and say about fashion? It is not impossible that we are thinking and saying things we don't actually understand. So, if we don't know what we're talking about, how will anyone else? This book, then, is an attempt to identify and explain some of the ideas and theories behind what we think and say about what we wear. In order to begin this task, the following sections of this Introduction will consider three questions, 'What is fashion?', 'What is theory?' and 'What is fashion theory?' They will look at some of the ideas and theories that people have had about what fashion, theory and fashion theory might be.

What is fashion?

At first glance, the question 'What is fashion?' is an easy one to answer. Fashion is either one of the crowning achievements of western civilisation or it is incontrovertible evidence of consumer culture's witless obsession with the trivial and the unreal. It is either creative to the point of being an 'art', enabling individuals and cultures to express their inner feelings and personalities, or it is exploitative to the point of criminality, forcing people to work and spend more than is healthy for them or society. For H. G. Wells's extinct uncle, fashion was 'the foam on the ocean of vulgarity . . . the vulgar – blossoming' (Wells 1895: 17). For William Hazlitt, fashion was merely the sign of 'folly and vanity' (quoted in Bell [1947] 1992: 112). However, for James Laver, fashion and clothing are 'the furniture of the mind made visible' (quoted in Lurie 1981: 3), and for Susan Ferleger Brades, art and fashion 'overlap' and pursue a common set of visual discoveries (Ferleger Brades, in Hayward Gallery 1998: Preface). Taking a more practical approach, one may point to one's coat and say 'This Balenciaga coat is fashion', or one may suggest that 'Fashion is what people wear'. Answers such as these would suffice for most people in most situations most of the time. However, most people are not routinely occupied in the analysis and critical explanation of fashion, and some people never involve themselves in such activities. For those of us that are so engaged, the question 'What is fashion?' demands our full attention: how are we to analyse and explain fashion if we do not know what fashion is?

Answers such as the one just given, in which a particular example (the Balenciaga coat) is given as a definition of a concept (fashion), will not do. Such responses assume that one already knows enough about what fashion is to identify Balenciaga coats as examples of it, but they do not actually tell us anything about what fashion is. They are therefore said to 'beg the question'. They also hide or obscure the way in which the meaning of 'fashion' drifts in and out of the sense of the 'fashionable': while this Balenciaga coat may be fashionable now it will be unfashionable next year – and yet it will still be an example of fashion. Answers such as the one above in which it is suggested that fashion is simply what people wear will not do either. It, too, presupposes that one already knows what fashion is (how could one identify people wearing it otherwise?). Also, some people do not wear fashion in the sense that what they have on is fashionable, or 'in fashion' at the moment, and others wear things that are simply not fashion items. This drifting or slippage of 'fashion' in and out of the sense of 'fashionable' is something that requires explanation.

The *Oxford English Dictionary* provides nine different senses of the word 'fashion', and Princeton University's WordNet Search engine (http://wordnet.princeton.edu) offers five senses. Between them they offer a range of meanings and definitions, from 'the action or process of making', 'dress', 'manner', 'a particular shape or cut', 'characteristic or habitual practice' and 'form' through to 'consumer goods in the current mode and "the latest and most admired style"'. However, both distinguish "fashion" as a noun from "fashion" as a verb. As a noun, "fashion" means "kind", "sort", "style" or "manner" and as a verb it indicates the action of making or doing something.

It is as a noun that the word 'fashion' is probably most familiar to us and it is as a noun that the word leads us into more or less confusion. As such, 'fashion' may apparently be used interchangeably with words such as 'dress' and 'style', as in 'the latest and most admired style' noted. Consumer goods in general also appear to be synonymous with 'fashion', as in 'consumer goods in the current mode', also already mentioned. (It will be observed that these senses also introduce the notions of consumption and the admiration of others into our understanding of what fashion might be.) Ted Polhemus and Lynn Procter add other words for which 'fashion' might be substituted when they point out that 'in contemporary western society, the term "fashion" is often used as a synonym of the terms "adornment", "style" and "dress" (Polhemus and Procter 1978: 9). Adding "adornment" to the definition or understanding of the word "fashion" as "style" and "dress" complicates the definition even more.

Two things are happening here. Firstly, fashion is being defined in relation to various other phenomena ('dress', 'adornment' and 'style', for example). Entwistle points out that 'dress' and 'adornment' have an anthropological pedigree and are used because anthropology is looking for an 'all-inclusive term that denotes all the things that people do to their bodies' (Entwistle 2000: 40). 'Fashion' is more specific than 'dress' or 'adornment' and denotes a particular 'system of dress that is found in western modernity' (ibid.). Secondly, fashion seems to invite or include the sense of 'in fashion'. This is the same move as found in the word 'style', where the meaning of style as 'the manner or way of doing something' slides into 'a socially or culturally approved way of doing something', and it is probably just as unavoidable.

While neither of these things helps us to find a simple or once-and-for-all definition of fashion, neither actually prevents us from gaining an understanding of what fashion is. Defining fashion in terms of a network or structure of other elements is inevitable: it is the way language works and we should get used to it. And the second thing, the inclusion of being in fashion into the meaning of fashion, is probably also unavoidable.

We seem to end up with Anne Hollander's definition of fashion:

> everybody has to get dressed in the morning and go about the day's business . . . [w]hat everybody wears to do this has taken different forms in the West for about seven hundred years and that is what fashion is.
>
> (Hollander 1994: 11)

This may sound, ironically enough, as though we are back where we started, with 'fashion is what people wear' – but 'what people wear' should be understood to include (but not be exhausted by) all instances of what people wear, from catwalk creations, through High Street and outlet purchases, to police and military uniforms. Consequently, this volume will not concentrate exclusively on fashion: it is interested in what people wear, and, insofar as what people wear in modern western countries is fashion, then it is interested in fashion. Another problem that arises here is that fashion sounds as though it is different from clothing: while clothing sounds like, or has connotations of, the sort of thing one wears everyday and is mundane, fashion connotes glamour and sounds somehow special and different from clothing. However, if fashion is what people wear to go about their everyday lives, as Anne Hollander says, then fashion has to include what we would usually want to call clothing or 'what people wear'.

Such a definition, however useful it is here, invites challenges as to what counts as 'western' and what counts as 'modern'. It may presuppose 'modernity' and 'western-ity'. In response, it can be argued that it is simply the case that the existence of fashion in a society is a good test of whether that society is modern, or western. A society in which there are no different classes, no social structure, and in which upwards mobility in a class structure is neither possible nor desirable has no need of fashion, and it might reasonably be described as being neither modern nor western.

Similarly, while fashion may be about the body, as Joanne Entwistle says, it is also, as she also says, about the 'fashioned' body (Entwistle 2000: 1). By 'the fash-ioned body' one is obliged to understand not a natural or Edenic body but a 'pro-duced' and therefore 'cultured' body. This is partly because one of the meanings of fashion (as a verb) is 'to make' or 'to produce', and partly because there can be no simple, uncultured, natural body. (Babies are probably as close as one gets, but, unlike their parents, they tend not to be interested in fashion.) Even when naked, the body is posed or held in certain ways, it makes gestures and it is thoroughly meaningful. To say that the fashioned body is always a cultured body is also to say that the fashioned body is a meaningful body, and that it is therefore about communication. This is because saying that fashion is meaningful is to say that fashion is a cultural phenom-enon. The reason for this, in turn, is that culture is about shared meanings and the communication and understanding of those meanings. The sharing of meanings and being in communication is what makes a cultural group a cultural group 'in the first place' (Cherry 1957: 4). Given this, we can say that differently cultured bodies com-municate different things (meanings), by means of the different things (clothes, fash-ion) that they wear. Fashion is thus defined as modern, western, meaningful and communicative bodily adornments, or dress. It is also explained as a profoundly cultural phenomenon.

What is theory

It is probably not unreasonable to suggest that common, everyday or non-specialist accounts of theory include the ideas that it involves the use of highly abstract and often needlessly difficult conceptual frameworks to provide complex explanations of phenomena that are actually quite simple and straightforward. Playing a series of crunchy, satisfying power chords on an electric guitar does not need (and sounds no better for knowing) the music theory that concerns perfect fifths. Checking one's change at the store is no less accurate for not knowing the theory of real numbers. It may come as a surprise, therefore, to learn that our word 'theory' derives from an ancient Greek word (*theoria*) meaning nothing more abstract or complicated than 'looking' or 'vision': '*theorein*' means 'to look at' and '*theoros*' means 'spectator'. The abstraction, complexity and difficulty associated with theory and conceptual activity appear to be entirely absent from what is experienced everyday in the simple practices of seeing, looking at, and spectating or beholding something.

However, this surprise should be short-lived if we consider the well-known story concerning the farmer, the general and the art student standing together in a field. Asked to describe what they see, each gives an entirely different account. The farmer sees a profitable unit with good drainage, which would be easy to plough and would support arable crops. The general sees an exposed killing field that would be impossible to defend. And the art student sees a pastoral scene that would make a delightful watercolour if the trees on the left were a darker shade of green and moved a little to the right. Looking at the field, each sees something different, according to the conceptual frameworks they adopt: to this extent, what they see is a product of the theories they are accustomed to using. The farmer is employing a combination of economics, biology and geology to produce what one might call agricultural theory; the general is employing military theory; and the student is employing aesthetic theory. As a result of the different theories, the different conceptual and abstract resources each has at their disposal, each 'sees' something different. A theory, then, might be thought of as a set or framework of concepts, the purpose of which is to describe and explain a specific phenomenon.

This story introduces a problem that is relevant to all theory, theories and theorising. The problem concerns the extent to which the object being studied is a product of the theory employed to study it and is known as the 'theory-ladenness' of 'facts' or the theory-dependency of what is ostensibly innocent observation. To the farmer, it is true, or a fact, that the field will support arable crops; to the general, it is a true fact that the field is impossible to defend; and to the art student it is a fact that the imagined watercolour would be improved by moving the trees. Each of the 'facts', however, is a product of the theory that is being used, or dependent upon it.

Paradoxically, then, while theory may be the use of abstract, conceptual frameworks in the explanation and analysis of phenomena, theory is also necessary in order to see those phenomena 'in the first place'. The derivation of our word 'theory' from the Greek 'theoria' ('vision' or 'looking') should therefore alert us to the role of conceptual work in constructing our visual experience. Everything we see is the product of conceptual frameworks, or what amount to theoretical constructs, being applied to the so-called raw data that is supplied by the eyes to the brain. The derivation might also help us to appreciate the metaphorical drift in the meaning of the word 'see' from seeing as a visual experience to seeing as understanding. This drift is well understood in the everyday English phrase 'I see what you mean', where a word used to describe a visual experience (seeing) is used to represent an experience which is not visual (understanding). Seeing is already understanding because it is a product of the application of conceptual frameworks (theories) to visual experience; consequently, the everyday and apparently straightforward activities of 'seeing' and 'looking at' involve a good deal more abstraction and are a good deal more complicated than was implied above. In short, they involve more conceptual or theoretical activity than is commonly appreciated.

The story also introduces a significant difference between the sorts of theories that are appropriate to, and the kinds of accounts that might be expected from, the study of fashion. The farmer used theories from biology and geology to construct and describe what s/he saw, and the art student used aesthetic theory to construct and describe what s/he saw; the difference to be noted is that between the natural sciences on the one hand and the social sciences and humanities on the other.

The natural sciences are concerned with the explanation and predictability of natural phenomena – the 'mastery' of the physical universe. And in the natural sciences it was long thought that theory was the product of the observation of those phenomena. Francis Bacon (1561–1626) was one of the first scientists to depart from medieval traditions and to 'emphasise the role of positive science and its observational character' (Larrain 1979: 19). Positive science stresses the role of facts, and a science that begins with the observation of phenomena is called empirical science. The idea is that the scientist observes the phenomena and then constructs a theory to explain the facts. This is known as the inductive method and it was thought to be a description of the scientific method used by the natural sciences: in other words it was believed to be a description of what happened in the natural sciences. The empirical natural sciences were developing rapidly in the eighteenth and nineteenth centuries, and Giddens, for example, writes of the 'sensational illumination and explanatory power' of the natural sciences at this time (1976: 13). The methods used to such tremendous effect by the natural sciences at this time, then, were positivist (stressed the objective existence of facts) and empiricist (stressed the role of observation).

The social sciences of the eighteenth and nineteenth centuries were in need of a method that would guarantee them the same levels of explanatory and predictive success that were being enjoyed by the natural sciences. In the social sciences and humanities, however, idealist and interpretative traditions that are absent from the natural sciences come into play. Idealist traditions insist on the predominant role of thought, or theory, in investigation; interpretative traditions emphasise the part that an individual's or actor's understanding of what is happening plays in human knowledge. It is over the nature of facts and observation, and the roles of positivism and empiricism, that some of the major methodological debates in the social sciences have occurred. One debate concerns whether observations and facts in the social sciences are the same kinds of thing as observations and facts in the natural sciences.

Another has been to do with whether empiricism is the best way of understanding social actors; the social sciences want to provide true explanations of social phenomena but an additional claim, to understanding, is also made on their behalf. Consequently, the predicting and controlling functions of the natural sciences are often received rather poorly by social scientists, but the notion that understanding social phenomena is key is often stressed. Bauman, for example, says that 'social phenomena . . . demand to be understood in a different way than by mere explaining' (1978: 12). 'Mere explaining' is found in the natural sciences, but understanding social phenomena 'must contain an element missing from the explanation of natural phenomena'. What is missing from natural phenomena is the actor's purpose or intention, the fact that what people do is meaningful to those people and to the people around them, and the social sciences must therefore pay attention to understanding that meaning. This extra dimension that is present in the social sciences and humanities is an interpretative or 'hermeneutic' dimension.

What is fashion theory?

Having explained what fashion is and having explained what theory is, this Introduction should now be perfectly placed to explain what fashion theory is. It would appear to be simply a matter of adding the one to the other. Unfortunately, the situation is not quite as simple as that. There is no one set of ideas or no single conceptual framework with which fashion might be defined, analysed and critically explained. Consequently, there is no single discipline, approach or discrete body of work that can be identified and presented here as fashion theory. Rather, there are theories about fashion or, to put it another way, there are fashion theories. What one finds is that various and diverse academic disciplines apply themselves or are applied to the practices, institutions, personnel and objects that constitute fashion. Each discipline has its own set or sets of ideas and conceptual frameworks in terms of which it defines, analyses and explains fashion. Each discipline, then, comes with its own theory, or theories, in terms of which it goes about the task of studying fashion. This Introduction therefore needs to ascertain which disciplines and which theories might be applied to fashion in order to explain, analyse and understand it.

In his (1981) *The Structures of Everyday Life*, Fernand Braudel says that the history of costume is 'less anecdotal than would appear. It touches on every issue – raw materials, production processes, manufacturing costs, cultural stability, fashion and social hierarchy' (Braudel 1981: 311). By 'less anecdotal' he means less dependent on random or accidental observations and more the product of sustained theoretical or idea-driven inquiry. The idea-driven inquiries he has in mind here are academic disciplines, and they include economics and cultural and social theory. Lisa Tickner also stresses the way in which many different academic disciplines are required for the study of fashion. Fashion is 'a rich and multi-disciplinary subject, and a point at which history, economics, anthropology, sociology and psychology could be said to meet' (Tickner 1977: 56). To this list could be added art history, for, as Elizabeth Wilson says, the 'serious study of fashion has traditionally been a branch of art history' (Wilson 1985: 48, and see Lipovetsky 1994: 64–74). Fashion and dress history may indeed be said to have 'followed' the methods of some of the more traditional or 'old' art histories in their interest in the dating of costume, the attribution of 'authorship' and in preserving the distinction between high art and popular art.

It is interesting to note at this point that the fashion historian Valerie Steele (1998) and the dress historian Lou Taylor (2002: 69), who both support the idea of an 'object-based' history, also propose a three-part 'method' for the study of those objects that is based on the work of Jules Prown, Professor of Art History at Yale. Prown said that

> analysis proceeds from description, recording the internal evidence of the object itself; to deduction, interpreting the interaction between the object and the perceiver; to speculation, framing hypotheses and questions which lead out from the object to external evidence for testing and resolution.
>
> (Prown 1982: 1, quoted in Steele 1998: 329)

According to Steele, Prown cites the earlier work of Fleming as a 'model' for his own work, and she describes it as a 'supplement'. Fleming (quoted in Steele 1998) suggests a four-part method:

1   Identification (factual description).
2   Evaluation (judgement).
3   Cultural analysis (relationship of the artefact to its culture).
4   Interpretation (significance).

This method is proposed by Steele as a way of investigating or 'reading' items of dress. The first step, that of factual description, relies heavily on observation. Steele provides an example of such factual description or observation by using a dress from the Wadsworth Atheneum in Connecticut; she says that it was a 'woman's dress . . . [and] consisted of a bodice and a skirt . . . a shirred apron overskirt covered most of the front of the skirt which was full and backswept with a train' (1998: 330). Steele says that 'the next stage, speculation' involves the framing of hypotheses that are then tested against external evidence and, in the case of the dress, these hypotheses are 'inextricably connected with cultural perceptions of sexuality and gender' (ibid. 331).

As pointed out previously, there are various problems with this method, which contains elements of both empiricism (in its emphasis on observation and description) and positivism (in its emphasis on a split between facts and hypotheses). The most significant problem is that the notion of 'identification' or factual description presupposes that it is possible to give an 'objective' account of the 'object itself' without the influence of any cultural preconceptions. Any words that one uses to describe the object will exist and be meaningful within a language, and that language will inevitably contain and communicate any number of cultural preconceptions. There are no 'neutral' or 'passive' descriptions of what is observed: even observation is not passive or neutral in this sense (see Williams 2000: 34). Consequently, to describe the object as a 'woman's dress' is to use two culturally loaded words that depend on one's membership of a certain culture in order to be understood. These words are only meaningful within an existing conceptual framework of beliefs and values, a cultural perspective, and to that extent are already the product of theoretical (conceptual) activity. The cultural phases are therefore already present in the first phase and, no matter how careful one is, one cannot undertake the method strictly in sequence and keep the stages discrete as Prown urges (Steele 1998: 329).

There are many academic disciplines, then, that take an interest in the history, analysis, and critical explanation of fashion. Each discipline will have its own idea, or theory, of what fashion is and of what sorts of activities count as analysis and explanation. It is the task of this book to try to represent the range of those disciplines and to give some idea of what sorts of things they say about fashion.

There are also many different accounts of the relations between those disciplines and their theories and fashion. As noted above, theory may be seen as an unnecessary and unnecessarily difficult detour or diversion from the main activity. Alternatively, theory may be conceived as a necessary evil, something that one is obliged to pay lip-service to in the obtaining of educational qualifications. In her (1985) *Adorned in*

Dreams, Elizabeth Wilson employs the metaphor of spectacles to describe the relation between fashion and academic study:

> The attempt to view fashion through several different pairs of spectacles simultaneously – of aesthetics, of social theory, of politics – may result in an obliquity of view, or even of astigmatism or blurred view, but is seems we must attempt it.
>
> (Wilson 1985: 11)

Appropriately enough (given the Greek derivation of '*theoria*' as 'looking'), theories are conceived here as various different pairs of spectacles through which one may view or study fashion. Also appropriate is the insistence on the necessity of using different theories in order to see, however obscurely, and study the phenomenon that is fashion. What is less welcome in this metaphor is the (slightly inconsistent) implication that, as spectacles may be taken off, so theory might be dispensed with: the argument here has to be that, in the absence of some form of theory or set of ideas, the phenomenon that is fashion would not even appear. Fashion theory is therefore inevitable; it cannot be avoided and there is a sense in which one is always already engaged in theoretical activity when commenting on or studying fashion. As noted in the very first paragraph of this Introduction, calling a friend's shirt 'girly' or 'endearingly retro' is already to have employed theories of gender, history and communication, for example. Fashion theory is not an evil, necessary or otherwise, and it is not something that can be escaped: we are doing it all the time, whether we recognise it, or like it, or not.

It will have been noted that the theories in terms of which it is suggested that fashion is to be studied are all from the humanities and social sciences rather than the natural sciences. This is not to say that natural science disciplines (such as chemistry, physics and biology, for example) do not or cannot have interesting and useful things to say about fashion and clothing. Some fashionable clothing would not exist were it not for the knowledge of certain chemical processes that are used in constructing synthetic fabrics, for example, and an explanation of that clothing would strictly be incomplete without an account of those processes. Nor is it to deny the fascination of such projects as Wills and Christopher's (1973) attempt to apply mathematical stochastic approaches to fashion trends. Stochastic models are concerned with calculating the probability of events occurring and Wills and Christopher apply the techniques involved in Markov chain processes and Epidemic Theory to try to explain the movement or transition from one fashion state to another (1973: 17ff.). It is, however, to recognise that this volume is concerned with explaining *and* understanding (the meanings) of fashion: it is therefore a humanities/social science reader. The essays that are collected here are all from the disciplines that make up the humanities and social sciences because they all deal, in their own ways, with the explanation and understanding of the objects, institutions, personnel and practices of fashion.

Bibliography

Barnard, M. (2001) *Approaches to Understanding Visual Culture*, Basingstoke: Palgrave.

Bauman, Z. (1978) *Hermeneutics and Social Science*, London: Hutchinson University Library.

Bell, Q. ([1947] 1992) *On Human Finery*, London: Allison and Busby.

Braudel, F. (1981) *Civilisation and Capitalism 15th–18th Century*. Volume One: *The Structures of Everyday Life*, London: Collins/Fontana.

Cherry, C. (1957) *On Human Communication*, Cambridge, Mass. and London: MIT Press.

Entwistle, J. (2000) *The Fashioned Body*, Cambridge: Polity Press.

Giddens, A. (1976) *New Rules of Sociological Method*, London: Hutchinson University Library.

Hayward Gallery (998) *Addressing the Century: 100 Years of Art and Fashion*, Exhibition Catalogue, London: Hayward Gallery Publishing.

Hollander, A. (1994) *Sex and Suits: The Evolution of Modern Dress*, New York: Kodansha International.

Larrain, J. (1979) *The Concept of Ideology*, London: Hutchinson.

Lipovetsky, G. (1994) *The Empire of Fashion: Dressing Modern Democracy*, Princeton: Princeton University Press.

Lurie, A. (1981) *The Language of Clothes*, London: Bloomsbury.

Polhemus, T. and Procter, L. (1978) *Fashion and Anti-Fashion: An Anthropology of Clothing and Adornment*, London: Thames and Hudson.

Steele, V. (1998) 'A Museum of Fashion is More Than A Clothes Bag', *Fashion Theory* 2, 4: 327–36.

Taylor, L. (2002) *The Study of Dress History*, Manchester: Manchester University Press.

Tickner, L. (1977) 'Women and trousers', *Leisure in the Twentieth Century*, London: Design Council Publications.

Wells, H. G. (1985) *Conversations With An Uncle Now Extinct*, London: John Lane.

Williams, M. (2000) *Science and Social Science: An Introduction*, London: Routledge.

Wills, G. and Christopher, M. (1973) 'What Do We Know About Fashion Dynamics?' in G. Wills and D. Midgley (eds) *Fashion Marketing*, London: George Allen and Unwin.

Wilson, E. (1985) *Adorned in Dreams: Fashion and Modernity*, London: Virago.

PART ONE

Fashion and fashion theories

THE INTRODUCTION TRIED TO ANSWER the questions 'what is theory?', 'what is fashion?' and 'what is fashion theory?' This section looks in more detail at the relation between fashion and fashion theories.

One of the problems referred to in the Introduction concerned the extent to which the object of study was the product of the theory employed to study it. Standing in a field and asked to describe what they see, the general saw the exposed killing field and the art student saw the pastoral idyll – at least partly because they were using different theories. Another problem that arises is the extent to which any explanation that is given using such theories are partial, or reductive: the farmer's description or explanation of the field as a profitable unit does not exhaust the account that might be given of that field. These problems also affect the ways in which theories describe and explain what fashion is and how it works. There is a sense in which any conception and explanation of fashion is the product of the theory used to describe, explain and understand it. For example, if the theory is that fashion is about expression of gender identity, then any and all examples of fashion will be constructed and explained in terms of gender and identity. And there is a sense in which any theory used to explain and understand fashion will inevitably reduce the phenomenon of fashion to its own terms. The explanation of fashion as the expression of gender identity, for example, will not be interested in those aspects of fashion that are not about gender identity and to that extent will be open to accusations of reductionism. This section will introduce the relation between fashion and fashion theories by considering the ways in which theories construct and explain fashion.

The artist and art historian, Quentin Bell, writing in 1947, is quite explicit on these matters, devoting an entire chapter of *On Human Finery* to 'Theories of Fashion'. At the end of this chapter, he sets out what he believes 'the facts' to be and he says that 'any theory' of fashion must 'fit those facts' ([1947] 1992: 105). In Bell's account 'the facts' pre-exist the theories that are to explain them, and the force behind his critical review of the four types of theory is based upon them not fitting the facts. The facts, then, exist independently of the theories that are to explain them in Bell's account, rather than being the products of those theories. The second problem noted concerns reductionism and is to do with the way in which a theory or an explanation of fashion reduces fashion to the terms of that theory and that explanation. All the theories that Bell discusses in this chapter are presented as attempts to answer the following questions: 'What sets this incredibly powerful evolutionary process [fashion] into motion, what maintains and increases its velocity, gives it its vast strength and accounts for its interconnected phenomena?' (ibid.: 90).

Bell identifies four types of theory that are proposed in the attempt to explain the changes of fashion. The first sees fashion as the work of individuals. The second proposes fashion as the 'product' of human nature. The third explains fashion as the 'reflection' of political or spiritual events. And the fourth suggests 'the intervention of a Higher Power' ([1947] 1992: 90). What Bell finds, however, is that 'the facts' do not fit these theories. Fashion is not the work of individuals because individuals such as Beau Brummel and Paul Poiret were, in fact, often 'unable to stand against the current of taste'. This form of theory also provides no account of why anyone should wish to 'obey' these individuals (ibid.: 93). Fashion is not the product of human nature because 'as a rule' men and women have been happy to wear what their parents wore: only recently and only in Europe have people worn 'fashion' (ibid.: 94). Neither is fashion the reflection of great historical and political events. Bell cites numerous wars and economic crises in which fashion conspicuously failed to 'mirror' events, and he discusses various histories of religion and nationalism in which what people wear also does not reflect events (ibid.: 79–102). Bell uses Heard's account of evolution in fashion as an example of fashion being explained in terms of a Higher Power. Evolution fails as an explanatory theory because evolution in living things 'is one in which the fittest survive and the claims of utility are inexorable' (ibid.: 104). Exactly the opposite is true of fashionable dress, according to Bell, in that utility is often the last thing one thinks of when one thinks of fashion.

Despite his arguments concerning fashion and natural selection, Bell still wants to think of fashion as an 'evolutionary process' and he appears committed to the idea that it can and will be explained in terms of its motive force ([1947] 1992: 89–90). Bell says that fashion is the 'grand motor force of taste', and the way in which he explains it turns out to have much in common with Veblen's concept of consumption, a socialised account of class emulation and class distinction (see Part Eight, 'Production and Consumption', for more on this). Clearly, there are other definitions of fashion (as a sequence of random differences, or as the expression of inner psychological states, for example) and there are other questions that could be asked of it ('What pleasure does it afford?' or 'How does it relate to consumption?', for example). To the extent that other quite legitimate definitions and other entirely appropriate questions exist, Bell's account may be said to be reductive.

This is essentially Elizabeth Wilson's thesis in her chapter on fashion theories in *Adorned in Dreams*, tellingly entitled 'Explaining It Away'. She looks at economic and anthropological theories of fashion; her argument is that all are reductive, or 'simplist', as she puts it (1985: 54). While she is not explicitly concerned with the ways in which facts are produced from within theories, rather than existing objectively or independently of them, the ways in which economic and anthropological theories presuppose the nature of the thing they are to explain (fashion) is of concern to her. Baudrillard's (economic) account of fashion consumption, for example, is said to be 'oversimplified and over-deterministic' because it reduces fashion to class emulation through consumerism and 'grants no role to contradiction . . . or pleasure' (Wilson 1985: 53). That is, Baudrillard's theory, which owes much to Marx and Veblen, presupposes a definition of fashion and it ignores anything that does not 'fit' into that definition. The definition of fashion here is that it is about class emulation; contradiction and pleasure are ignored here because they do not fit easily into that definition. It will be noted that this is the same move as that made by Bell when he marshals 'the facts' and tries to find a theory that will 'fit' them.

Gilles Lipovetsky (1994) provides an argument that sounds as though it is in almost complete disagreement with both Wilson and Bell. Writing from a philosophical perspective, he says that fashion has 'provoked no serious theoretical dissension' (1994: 4). This is quite a claim. However, it is not to say that there is no such thing as fashion theory; it is to say that there are theories, but that there is no conflict between them. There exists within fashion theory a profound 'critical unanimity' and that unanimity is not produced by accident but is 'deeply rooted in the thought process that underlies philosophical reflection itself' (ibid.: 9). What Lipovetsky is getting at here is that all critics of fashion, all fashion theorists, have agreed that fashion is fickle or superficial and that it may be fully explained in terms of fashion's role in 'class rivalries' and in the 'competitive struggles for prestige that occur among the various layers and factions of the social body' (ibid.: 4). In this, Lipovetsky is essentially in agreement with Wilson (if not with Bell), who says that '[f]ashion writers have never really challenged Veblen's explanations' (Wilson 1985: 52). This is because Veblen is one of the first writers to suggest that fashion is to be explained in terms of struggles over prestige between different social classes.

Lipovetsky's account of the relation between fashion and theory is a version of the argument that theory (in this case western philosophy) produces the phenomenon to be studied. The argument is that since Plato western thought has operated with a conception of truth and knowledge that distrusts and devalues images and surface appearance. In Plato's cave, humans are misled by the play of shadows on the wall: they do not see, and therefore cannot know what actually causes them. Fashion is thought to be like the play of shadows in this argument and as a result western thought mistrusts fashion, seeing it as distracting and superficial. Consequently, fashion theorists are only following some of the most basic tenets of western thought when they construct fashion as enchanting and condemn it for its triviality and superficiality. This is the 'ruse of reason' (Lipovetsky 1994: 9) that operates in all fashion theorising as far as Lipovetsky is concerned. The notion that knowledge is like light in some way, and that light may be used as a metaphor for knowledge (as in 'enlightenment', for example), is one of the founding metaphors of western thought and it is hardly surprising that it plays a profound role in western theory, including western theories about fashion.

So, in the light of these considerations (to follow the Platonic metaphor again) it seems insufficient to suggest that, if all theory is tied to disciplines and therefore reductive, then as many disciplines and theories as possible should be employed in order to try to escape the charge of reductionism. That is, if any one theory concerning what fashion is and how it should be explained and understood is likely to be reductive, then interdisciplinarity is required to avoid oversimplifying and reducing fashion to the terms of that discipline's theory. It may sound insufficient, but this interdisciplinarity is precisely what theorists such as Wilson, Tickner and Braudel were seen to suggest in the Introduction. All were agreed that fashion, perhaps uniquely, demanded the use of a number of disciplines in order to define, explain and understand it. If it is the nature of disciplinary theory to pre-construct its object (and thus to be reductive) then many disciplines, many theories, many constructions and many different types of explanation and understanding are necessary in order to minimise (if not escape) the less helpful consequences of fashion theorising.

Bibliography

Bell, Q. ([1947] 1992) *On Human Finery*, London: Allison and Busby.

Lipovetsky, G. (1994) *The Empire of Fashion: Dressing Modern Democracy*, Princeton: Princeton University Press.

Tseëlon, E. (2001) 'Fashion Research and Its Discontents', *Fashion Theory* 5, 4: 435–52.

Wilson, E. (1985) *Adorned in Dreams: Fashion and Modernity*, London: Virago.

Chapter 1

Elizabeth Wilson

EXPLAINING IT AWAY

[. . .]

BECAUSE FASHION is constantly denigrated, the serious study of fashion has had repeatedly to justify itself. Almost every fashion writer, whether journalist or art historian, insists anew on the importance of fashion both as cultural barometer and as expressive art form. Repeatedly we read that adornment of the body pre-dates all other known forms of decoration; that clothes express the mood of each succeeding age; that what we do with our bodies expresses the *Zeitgeist*. Too often, though, the relationship that of course exists between social change and styles of dress is drawn out in a superficial and cliché-ridden way. The twenties flapper becomes the instant symbol of a revolution in manners and morals after the First World War; the New Look symbolizes women's return to the home (which anyway didn't happen) after the Second World War; the disappearance of the top hat signals the arrival of democracy. Such statements are too obvious to be entirely true, and the history they misrepresent is more complex.

The serious study of fashion has traditionally been a branch of art history, and has followed its methods of attention to detail. As with furniture, painting and ceramics, a major part of its project has been accurate dating of costume, assignment in some cases of 'authorship', and an understanding of the actual process of the making of the garment, all of which are valid activities.[1] But fashion history has also too often been locked into the conservative ideologies of art history as a whole.

The mid twentieth century was a prolific period for the investigation of fashion. Doris Langley Moore, one of the few women then known for her writings on the subject, commented that the subject matter was women, the writers almost exclusively men.[2] Their acceptance of prevailing conservative attitudes towards women led to a tone sometimes coy, sometimes amusedly patronizing, sometimes downright offensive, and itself fundamentally *unserious*, as if the writer's conviction, often stated, of the transcendent importance of his subject matter was subverted from within by his relegation of women to a denigrated sub-caste. Because fashion has been associated with all that is feminine, these writers wrote about it as they would write about women; indeed, Cecil Willett Cunnington, author of many books about dress, even contributed a book to a series called 'Pleasures of Life' — the subject matter *Women*.[3] Other 'pleasures of life' included cricket and gardening!

Art history has also tended to preserve the élitist distinction between high art and popular art. Fashion then becomes essentially *haute couture*, and the disintegration of this tradition, the decline of the Dress Designer as Artist, together with the ascendancy of the mass clothing industry, are alleged to have brought about the end of 'true' fashion. Once we are all in fashion, no one can be, so the hallmark of both bourgeois democracy and socialism is said to be uniformity of dress, that 'grey sameness' by which all fashion writers are haunted. So Cecil Willett Cunnington sighed for the Edwardian glamour of lace and chiffon, and the charm of bustle and crinoline, regretful that

> The modern woman no longer finds costume a sufficient medium for the expression of her ideals . . .
> As the twentieth century lunges on towards the accomplishment of its destiny it is natural that it should discard those forms of art which have ceased to suffice. This is Progress and part of its price is the Decline and Fall of the Art of Costume.[4]

Quentin Bell, on the other hand, while he comes to the same conclusion, does so for the opposite reason, since he foresees that if abundance became universal

> class distinctions would gradually be swamped from below and the pecuniary canons of taste would slowly lose their meaning; dress could then be designed to meet all the needs of the individual, and uniformity, which is essential to fashions, would disappear.[5]

Those who have investigated fashion, finding themselves confronted with its apparent *irrationality*, have tried to explain this in *functional* terms. The most bizarre styles and fads, they argue, must have some function; there must be a rational explanation for these absurdities, if only we could find it. Yet this gives rise to a dilemma, for how can what is irrational have a function?

This line of argument seems to assume that because fashionable dressing is an activity that relates directly to the human body, as well as being a form of art, it must therefore be directly related to human biological 'needs'. Furthermore, because when human beings dress up they often make themselves uncomfortable and even cause themselves pain, there has been a tendency to explain this 'irrational' behaviour in terms that come from outside the activity itself: in terms of economics, of psychology, of sociology. We expect a garment to *justify* its shape and style in terms of moral and intellectual criteria we do not normally apply to other artistic forms; in architecture, for example, we may all have personal preferences, yet most of us can accept the pluralism of styles, can appreciate both the austerity of the

Bauhaus and the rich convolutions of rococo. When it comes to fashion, we become intolerant.

Because the origins and rise of fashion were so closely linked with the development of mercantile capitalism, economic explanations of the fashion phenomenon have always been popular. It was easy to believe that the function of fashion stemmed from capitalism's need for perpetual expansion, which encouraged consumption. At its crudest, this kind of explanation assumes that changes in fashion are foisted upon us, especially on women, in a conspiracy to persuade us to consume far more than we 'need' to. Without this disease of 'consumerism' capitalism would collapse. (Doris Langley Moore argued that this is simply not true of the fashion industry, since the men's tailoring trade, where fashion changed more slowly, has proved far more stable than the fluctuating women's fashion market, where undue risks have to be taken since it is never known in advance which fashions will catch on and which will expire as fads.[6]

Underlying such arguments is a belief that human individuals do have certain unchanging and easily defined needs. The attempt to define and classify such needs has proved virtually impossible, however, and in fact even such biological needs as the need for food and warmth are socially constructed and differentially constructed in different societies. The concept of need cannot elucidate fashion.

Another, related, argument explained fashion in terms of the fight for status in capitalist societies. In such societies costume became one arena for the continuous social struggle of each individual to rise by dint solely of merit and ruthlessness. The old, rigid boundaries of feudal life dissolved, and all were now free to copy their betters. Unfortunately, as soon as any fashion percolated down to the middling ranks of the bourgeoisie, or lower, it became disgusting to the rich. They moved on to something new. This in turn was copied. According to this argument, fashion became an endless speeded-up spiral.

The most sophisticated version of this explanation was Thorstein Veblen's *Theory of the Leisure Class*. Veblen argued that fashion was one aspect of the conspicuous leisure, conspicuous wealth and conspicuous waste he held to be characteristic of an acquisitive society in which the ownership of wealth did more to confer prestige on its owner than either family lineage or individual talent. Veblen, like Engels, also argued that the women of the bourgeoisie were effectively the property of their men:

> It has in the course of economic development become the office of the woman to consume vicariously for the head of the household; and her apparel is contrived with this object in view. It has come about that obviously productive labour is in a peculiar degree derogatory to respectable women, and therefore special pains should be taken in the construction of women's dress, to impress upon the beholder the fact (often indeed a fiction) that the wearer does not and cannot habitually engage in useful work . . . [Women's] sphere is within the household, which she should 'beautify' and of which she should be the 'chief ornament' . . . By virtue of its descent from a patriarchal past, our social system makes it the woman's function in an especial degree to put in evidence her household's ability to pay . . .

The high heel, the skirt, the impracticable bonnet, the corset, and the general disregard of the wearer's comfort which is an obvious feature of all civilized women's apparel, are so many items of evidence to the effect that in the modern civilized scheme of life the woman is still, in theory, the economic dependent of the man – that, perhaps in a highly idealized sense, she still is the man's chattel.[7]

Veblen argued that conspicuous waste accounted for change in fashion, but he also believed in a 'native taste' (that is, some kind of essential good taste) to which conspicuous wastefulness was actually abhorrent. It is abhorrent, he argued, because it is a 'psychological law' that we all 'abhor futility' – and to Veblen the stylistic oddities of fashion were manifestly futile. He explained fashion changes as a kind of restless attempt to get away from the ugliness of the imposed, irrational styles, which everyone instinctively *did* recognize to be ugly. For Veblen, then, the motor force of fashion was a wish, forever frustrated, finally to *escape* the tyranny of irrational change and perpetual ugliness.

Fashion writers have never really challenged Veblen's explanations, and his analysis still dominates to this day. Yet his theory cannot account for the form that fashion changes take. Why did the bustle replace the crinoline, the leg of mutton sleeve the sloping shoulder? Theodor Adorno, a Marxist cultural critic, exposed deeper inadequacies in Veblen's thought, arguing that for Veblen

progress means, concretely, the adaptation of the forms of consciousness and of . . . economic consumption to those of industrial technology. The means to this adjustment is science. Veblen conceives of it as the universal application of the principle of causality, in opposition to vestigial [magical thinking]. Causal thinking is for him the triumph of objective, quantitative relations, patterned after industrial production, over personalistic and anthropomorphic conceptions.[8]

In other words, Veblen, according to Adorno, has succumbed to the nineteenth-century obsession with the natural sciences. In Veblen's ideal world there was no place for the irrational or the non-utilitarian; it was a wholly rational realm. Logically, pleasure itself must be futile since it is unrelated to scientific progress. This was the measure of Veblen's utilitarian, clockwork universe, and he therefore hated pursuits such as fashion and organized sport. This ideology led him to reduce *all* culture to kitsch, and to see leisure as absurd in itself. This utilitarian ideology fatally marked the movements for dress reform.

The persistence of Veblen's theories is curious. They have not only continued to dominate discussions of dress by a variety of writers in the fashion history field, but have also influenced recent, supposedly 'radical' critics of 'consumer culture'. In America, Christopher Lasch and[9] Stuart and Elizabeth Ewen[10] have condemned modern culture, including fashion; in France Jean Baudrillard has explicitly made use of Veblen's theory to attack consumerism. Like Veblen, Baudrillard condemns fashion for its ugliness:

Truly beautiful, definitively beautiful clothing would put an end to fashion . . . Fashion continually fabricates the 'beautiful' on the basis of a radical denial of beauty, by reducing beauty to the logical equivalent of ugliness. It can impose the most eccentric, dysfunctional, ridiculous traits as eminently distinctive.[11]

and he regards fashion as a particularly pernicious form of consumerism, since it

embodies a compromise between the need to innovate and the other need to change nothing in the fundamental order. It is this that character-izes 'modern' societies. Thus it results in a game of change . . . – old and new are not relative to contradictory needs: they are the 'cyclical' paradigm of fashion.[12]

Such a view is oversimplified and over-deterministic; that is, it grants no role to contradiction, nor for that matter to pleasure. Baudrillard's vision is ultimately a form of nihilism. The attack on consumerism perceives our world as a seamless web of oppression; we have no autonomy at all, but are the slaves of an iron system from which there is no escape. All our pleasures become, according to this view, the narcotics of an oppressive society; and opera, pop music, thrillers and great literary 'masterpieces' should therefore logically be condemned along with fashion.

What is especially strange about Baudrillard's analysis is that he appears to reject Marxism, while accepting this most conspiratorial of Marxist critiques of capitalism. He furthermore suggests that there is some ultimate standard of 'authen-tic' beauty, while elsewhere he rejects the idea of such rationalistic standards and seems to suggest that desire, which after all creates 'beauty', in a sense, is necessarily contradictory and divided, implying that artefacts would reflect this ambivalence. Where then does the notion of 'true beauty' come from?

One type of economic explanation of fashion interprets it in terms of techno-logical advance, and it is of course true that without the invention of the sewing machine (which Singer patented in 1851), for example, the mass fashion industry could not have come into being. This, though, does not explain the parade of styles of the past 135 years.

A more complex economic explanation would include the cultural con-sequences of expanding trade and expanding economies in western Europe. Chandra Mukerji argues that Europe was already a 'hedonistic culture of mass consumption' in the early modern period. According to her, this contradicts the prevailing view, elaborated by the sociologist Max Weber and popularized in Britain by R. H. Tawney, that the 'Protestant Ethic' which fuelled capitalist expansion was one of 'ascetic rationality', that the early capitalists were thrifty, 'anal' character types who saved rather than spent, and that only with the arrival of industrial capitalism, and especially in our own period, did modern consumerism begin. Even the English Puritans, she suggests, wore costly and elaborate clothes – and in any case, their clothes were influenced as much by the sober but fashionable wear of the Dutch as by religious considerations.[13]

Economic simplism was matched by nineteenth-century anthropological sim-plism. So long as the biblical account of the Creation was accepted, the wearing of clothes might be not only a sign of vanity, but paradoxically might also reflect humankind's consciousness of its fallen state. However remote the first figleaf of Adam and Eve from the peculiarities of Victorian dress, it could be argued that women and men wore clothes out of modesty, to hide their nakedness and the sexual parts that reminded them of their animal nature.

This naive view was shattered as the truth of Genesis began to be questioned. In addition, the explorations of early European anthropologists, the discovery of lost worlds and 'primitive' societies, contributed to a gradual, but radical questioning of the nature of European culture in general and of European costume in particular (although this was usually still in supremacist terms). Anthropology undermined the belief that clothes are 'needed' to shield us from the excessive heat and cold of the climate.

Already in 1831 Thomas Carlyle was writing:

> The first purpose of Clothes . . . was not warmth or decency, but Ornament . . . for Decoration [the Savage] must have clothes. Nay, among wild people we find tattooing and painting even prior to clothes. The first spiritual want of a barbarous man is Decoration, as indeed we still see among the barbarous classes in civilized Countries.[14]

Later such views were further confirmed by Charles Darwin's description of the people of the Tierra del Fuego. This people, although living in one of the most inclement regions of the world, near the Falklands Islands, wore little clothing:

> The men generally have an otter skin, or some small scrap about as large as a pocket-handkerchief, which is barely sufficient to cover their backs as low as their loins. It is laced across the breast by strings, and according as the wind blows, it is shifted from side to side. But these Fuegians in the canoe were quite naked, and even one full-grown woman . . . It was raining heavily, and the fresh water, together with the spray, trickled down her body.

Later, Charles Darwin commented:

> We were well clothed, and though sitting close to the fire were far from too warm; yet these naked savages, though farther off, were observed, to our great surprise, to be streaming with perspiration at undergoing such a roasting.[15]

and when given pieces of cloth large enough to have wrapped themselves in, they tore it into shreds and distributed the pieces, which were worn as ornaments. Darwin, whose writings on this subject were permeated with the racism of his time, poured scorn on the 'savages' and for him this behaviour was merely further evidence of their idiocy. What it actually suggests is that dress has little or nothing to do with the 'need' for protection.

It has as little to do with modesty. As Havelock Ellis, a pioneer sexologist pointed out: 'Many races which go absolutely naked possess a highly developed sense of modesty.'[16]

The growing importance of anthropology in the twentieth century, and its usually imperialist assumptions, had an impact on western fashion and on the way in which fashion was perceived. On the one hand designers could rifle 'primitive' societies for exotica to give a new flavour to jazz age dress, matching the 'primitivism' of 'Negro music' with African designs and ornaments. (Nancy Cunard always wore an armful of ivory bangles.) On the other hand, the diversity of ways of dressing found in distant lands could make western fashion appear completely relativistic. This implied another kind of conservative explanation. The bizarre varieties of dress could all be seen as reflecting the *sameness* of 'human nature', at all times and in all places. The abstract entity 'human nature', it was argued, always loves novelty, dressing up, self importance and splendour. This cliché reduces all social and cultural difference to a virtually meaningless surface scribble; but actually dress and styles have specific meanings. 1980 mass-produced fashion is not at all the same as Nuba body painting, the sari or Ghanaian robes.

Anthropological discussion of dress tends to blur the distinctions between adornment, clothing and fashion, but is interesting because when we look at fashion through anthropological spectacles we can see that it is closely related to magic and ritual. Dress, like drama, is descended from an ancient religious, mystical and magical past of ritual and worship. Many societies have used forms of adornment and dress to put the individual into a special relationship with the spirits or the seasons in the enactment of fertility or food-gathering rites, for war or celebration. The progression from ritual to religion, then to secular seriousness and finally to pure hedonism seems to have been common to theatre, music and dance – the performing arts – and dress, itself a kind of performance, would seem to have followed this trajectory from sacred to secular. Fashion, too, contains the ghost of a faint, collective memory of the magical properties that adornment once had.

Even today garments may acquire talismanic properties, and both children and adults often become deeply and irrationally attached to a particular item. Billie Jean King, for example, wore a favourite, sixties-style mini-dress for her big tennis matches in the belief that it brought her luck; during the Second World War British Spitfire pilots used to attach their girlfriends' bras to their cockpits for the same reason.

Fashion offers a rich source of irrational and superstitious behaviour, indispensable to novelist and social commentator. And, as Quentin Bell has pointed out, 'there is . . . a whole system of morality attached to clothes and more especially to fashion, a system different from, and . . . frequently at variance with that contained in our law and religion'.[17] He suggests that this has to do with a whole covert morality, and is symptomatic not of conformity but of commitment to another, hidden and partly unconscious world, a hidden system of social, collective values.

Alison Lurie sees clothes as expressive of hidden and largely unconscious aspects of individual and group psyche, as forms of usually unintentional non-verbal communication, a sign language.[18] Her vignette interpretations of the sartorial behaviour of both groups and individuals are sharp and amusing, but although dress is, among other things, a language, it is not enough to assume that our choice of dress makes unintended statements about self image and social aspiration. Alison Lurie is always the knowing observer, treating others to put-downs from some height of sartorial self knowledge and perfection; she assumes that even those who most knowingly use clothes to 'make a statement' are letting their psychic slips show in spite of themselves. Her use of the metaphor of language (for it is only a metaphor), far from explaining the 'irrationality' of dress, merely reinforces the view that it is irrational.

Roland Barthes[19] uses linguistics and semiology (the science of signs) in a more sophisticated way, but equally takes it for granted that fashion is irrational. In fact his theory of fashion is based entirely on the idea of irrationality, since for him the sign, like language, is a system of arbitrarily defined differences. He suggests that language works in the following way: the words used to name objects (dog/*chien* and so on) are arbitrary, but the objects named have significance only in terms of their differences from other objects — ultimately our conception of a dog is based on its *difference* from a cat or a cow. Barthes argues that all sign systems work in this way, and like language, fashion is for Barthes an enclosed and arbitrary system, the meanings it generates entirely relative. His exhaustive analysis of the 'rhetoric of fashion' (captions and copy in fashion magazines) places fashion in a vacuum. Fashion has no history and no material function; it is a system of signs devoted to 'naturalizing the arbitrary'.[20] Its purpose is to make the absurd and meaningless changes that constitute fashion *appear* natural.

Barthes, therefore, is not, like Veblen, a functionalist; his theory depends on the belief that fashion has no function. Yet, like Veblen, he does see fashion as morally absurd, as in some way objectionable, and this leads him to argue that at another, ideological, level, fashion does have exactly the conspiratorial function assigned to it by Veblen:

> [The discourse of] fashion describes certain types of work for women
> . . . . woman's identity is established in this way, in the service of Man
> . . . of Art, of Thought, but this submission is rendered sublime by being
> given the appearance of pleasant work, and aestheticized.[21]

He analyses fashion from a hostile point of view that at heart believes fashion to be an unnecessary aberration. Women who like fashion, his analysis implies, suffer from false consciousness. But to banish fashion from the realm of truth in this way is to imply that there exists a wholly other world, a world in which, contrary to his own theory, meaning is *not* created and recreated culturally, but is transparent and immediately obvious. But not only would this be a world without fashion, it would be a world without discourses, a world, that is, without culture or communication. Such a world cannot, of course, exist, or if it did it would be a world without human beings in it.

Even psychoanalysis, which seems to offer a richer understanding of fashion than other psychologies, and which I shall discuss in relation to sexuality, still explains it in terms of its function for unconscious impulses. This is an important dimension. All functionalist arguments nevertheless miss fashion's purposive and creative aspects.

Of all those who have written about fashion, René König[22] has come as close as any to capturing its tantalizing and slippery essence. He sees fashion's perpetual mutability, its 'death wish', as a manic defence against the human reality of the changing body, against ageing and death. Fashion, Barthes' 'healing goddess', substitutes for the real body an abstract, ideal body; this is the body as an idea rather than as an organism. The very way in which fashion constantly changes actually serves to fix the idea of the body as unchanging and eternal. And fashion not only protects us from reminders of decay; it is also a mirror held up to fix the shaky boundaries of the psychological self. It glazes the shifty identity, freezing it into the certainty of image.

Fashion is a branch of aesthetics, of the art of modern society. It is also a mass pastime, a form of group entertainment, of popular culture. Related as it is to both fine art and popular art, it is a kind of performance art. The concept of 'modernity' is useful in elucidating the rather peculiar role played by fashion in acting as a kind of hinge between the élitist and the popular.

Even the society of the Renaissance was 'modern' in its tendency towards secular worldliness, its preoccupation with the daily, material world, and its dynamism. Characteristic of that world was its love of the changing mode, and a wealthy middle class that already competed in finery with the nobility. From its beginnings fashion was part of this modernity.

[. . .]

Notes

1   Newton, Stella Mary (1975), 'Fashions in Fashion History', *Times Literary Supplement*, 21 March, argues that fashion history lags behind other branches of art history, and is 'unlikely to catch up'.

2   Moore, Doris Langley (1949), *The Woman in Fashion*, London: Batsford. 'As it happens all the psychological enquiries into fashion are predominantly concerned with feminine fashion, and the band of theorists has without exception been male.' (p. 1.)

3   Cunnington, Cecil Willett (1950), *Women* (Pleasures of Life Series), London: Burke.

4   Cunnington, Cecil Willett (1941), *Why Women Wear Clothes*, London: Faber and Faber, pp. 260–61.

5   Bell, Quentin (1947), *On Human Finery*, London: The Hogarth Press, p. 128.

6   Moore, Doris Langley, op. cit.

7   Veblen, Thorstein (1957), *The Theory of the Leisure Class*, London: Allen and Unwin, pp. 179–82. (Originally published in 1899.)

8   Adorno, Theodor (1967), 'Veblen's Attack on Culture', *Prisms*, Cambridge, Ma.: The MIT Press; translated by Samuel and Sherry Weber, p. 77.

9   Lasch, Christopher (1979), *The Culture of Narcissism*, New York: Warner Books.

10   Ewen, Stuart and Ewen, Elizabeth (1982), *Channels of Desire: Mass Images and the Shaping of the American Consciousness*, New York: McGraw Hill.

11   Baudrillard, Jean (1981), *For a Critique of the Political Economy of the Sign*, St Louis, Mo.: Telos Press, p. 79; translated by Charles Levin.

12   ibid., p. 51n.

13   Mukerji, Chandra (1983), *From Graven Images: Patterns of Modern Materialism*, New York: Columbia University Press, pp. 2, 188.

14   Carlyle, Thomas (1931), *Sartor Resartus*, London: Curwen Press, p. 48. (Originally published in 1831.)

15 Darwin, Charles (1959), *The Voyage of the Beagle*, London: J. M. Dent and Sons, pp. 202–3, 210. (Originally published in 1845.)

16 Quoted in Laver, James (1969), *Modesty in Dress: An Enquiry into the Fundamentals of Fashion*, London: Heinemann, p. 9.

17 Bell, Quentin, op. cit., p. 13.

18 Lurie, Alison (1981), *The Language of Clothes*, London: Heinemann.

19 Barthes, Roland (1967), *Système de la Mode*, Paris: Éditions du Seuil.

20 Culler, Jonathan (1975), *Structuralist Poetics*, London: Routledge and Kegan Paul.

21 Barthes, Roland, op. cit., p. 256.

22 König, René (1973), *The Restless Image*, London: George Allen and Unwin.

Chapter 2

Gilles Lipovetsky

THE EMPIRE OF FASHION: INTRODUCTION

THE QUESTION OF FASHION is not a fashionable one among intellectuals. This observation needs to be emphasized: even as fashion goes on accelerating its ephemeral legislation, invading new realms and drawing all social spheres and age groups into its orbit, it is failing to reach the very people whose vocation is to shed light on the mainsprings and mechanisms of modern societies. Fashion is celebrated in museums, but among serious intellectual preoccupations it has marginal status. It turns up everywhere on the street, in industry, and in the media, but it has virtually no place in the theoretical inquiries of our thinkers. Seen as an ontologically and socially inferior domain, it is unproblematic and underserving of investigation; seen as a superficial issue, it discourages conceptual approaches. The topic of fashion arouses critical reflexes even before it is examined objectively: critics invoke it chiefly in order to castigate it, to set it apart, to deplore human stupidity and the corrupt nature of business. Fashion is always other people. We are overinformed about fashion in terms of journalistic accounts, but our historical and social understanding of the phenomenon leaves much to be desired. The plethora of fashion magazines is matched by the silence of the intelligentsia, by its forgetfulness of fashion as both infatuation with artifice and the new architecture of democracy.

Many studies have been devoted to the subject, of course. We have masterful histories of costume, and an abundance of detailed monographs on the trades associated with fashion and its creators; we do not lack statistical information about its production and consumption, or historical and sociological studies of shifting tastes and styles. However, we must not allow these bibliographical and iconographical riches to obscure the most important thing about fashion: the profound, general, largely unconscious crisis that actually holds the key to an overall understanding of the phenomenon. The case of fashion may be unique in the universe of speculative thought. Here is an issue that has stirred up no real battles over its problematics; it has provoked no significant theoretical dissension. As a matter of fact, the question accomplishes the feat of bringing about a meeting of virtually all minds. For the last hundred years or so, the enigma of fashion has seemed by and large resolved. There has been no major dispute over its interpretation; the corporation of thinkers, with admirable collective momentum, has adopted a common credo on the subject. In this view, fashion's fickleness has its place and its ultimate truth in the existence of class rivalries, in the competitive struggles for prestige that occur among the various layers and factions of the social body. This underlying consensus leaves room—according to the theoreticians, of course—for interpretive nuances, for slight inflections, but with only a few exceptions the inconsistent logic of fashion and its assorted manifestations is invariably explained in terms of social stratification and social strategies for achieving honorific distinction. In no other realm is scholarly knowledge so firmly ensconced in the untroubled repetition of a single all-purpose recipe available for exploitation by lazy minds. Fashion has become a problem devoid of passion, lacking in theoretical stakes, a pseudo-problem whose answers and explanations are known in advance. The capricious realm of fantasy has managed only to impoverish the concept and reduce it to monotony.

The study of fashion needs new impetus, renewed questioning. Fashion is a trifling, fleeting, "contradictory" object par excellence; for that very reason it ought to provide a good stimulus for theoretical argument. The opacity of the phenomenon, its strangeness, its historical originality, are indeed considerable. How has an institution structured by evanescence and aesthetic fantasy managed to take root in human history? Why in the West and not elsewhere? How can an age dominated by technology, an age in which the world is subjugated by reason, also be the age of fashion in all its unreasonableness? How are we to conceptualize and account for the establishment of shallow instability as a permanent system? Once we resituate fashion within the vast life span of societies, we cannot see it as the simple manifestation of a passionate desire to be admired and to set oneself apart; it becomes an exceptional, highly problematic institution, a sociohistorical reality characteristic of the West and of modernity itself. From this standpoint, fashion is less a sign of class ambition than a way out of the world of tradition. It is one of the mirrors that allow us to see what constitutes our most remarkable historical destiny: the negation of the age-old power of the traditional past, the frenzied modern passion for novelty, the celebration of the social present.

The schema of social distinction that has come to be viewed as the sovereign key for understanding fashion, in the realm of objects and modern culture as well as dress, is fundamentally unable to account for fashion's most significant features: its logic of inconstancy, its great organizational and aesthetic mutations. This idea is the basis for the overall reinterpretation I propose here. By insisting on the idea of social distinction, theoretical reason has set up as the motive force of fashion what is actually its immediate, ordinary acceptation. Theoretical reason has remained in the thrall of the lived meaning of the actors on the social stage, positing as fashion's origin what is merely one of its social functions. This identification of origin with function lies behind the extraordinary simplification that characterizes genealogical explanations of the "invention" of fashion and its transformations in the West. A kind of epistemological unconscious underlying discourse on fashion, the problematics of social distinction has become an obstacle to a historical understanding of the phenomenon, an obstacle accompanied by an ostentatious play of conceptual whorls capable of concealing the deficiencies of scholarly discourse on the subject. A theoretical face-lift is in order. It is time to detach analyses of fashion from the heavy artillery of social class, from the dialectic of social distinction and class pretensions. Countering the imperialism of schemas of symbolic class struggle, I seek to show that, in the history of fashion, modern cultural meanings and values, in particular those that elevate newness and the expression of human individuality to positions of dignity, have played a preponderant role. These are the factors that allowed the fashion system to come into being and establish itself in the late Middle Ages; in an unexpected way, these same factors allow us to trace the major stages in fashion's historical evolution.

What I offer here, then, is an interpretive history of fashion: a conceptual and problematic history, governed not by a desire to set forth its inexhaustible contents but by a desire to present a general interpretation of the phenomenon and its metamorphoses over time. I shall not provide a chronological history of styles and social elegance; instead, I shall focus on the defining moments, the major structures, the organizational, aesthetic, and sociological modulations that have determined the centuries-long course of fashion. I have deliberately opted here for a clear and comprehensive overview at the expense of detailed analyses: what we lack most is not specific knowledge, but the global meaning, the underlying economy, of the dynamics of fashion. This book, then, has two goals. On the one hand, I seek to understand the emergence of fashion in the late Middle Ages and its principal lines of evolution over the centuries. In order to avoid psychosociological generalizations about fashion that manifest little historical understanding, and in order to resist resorting to broad parallelisms of a kind that are all too often artificial, I have chosen to confine my attention here to a relatively homogeneous object that best exemplifies the phenomenon in question: clothing and its accessories, the archetypal domain of fashion. On the other hand, I attempt to comprehend the rising power of fashion in contemporary societies, the central, unprecedented place it occupies in democracies that have set out along the path of consumerism and mass communications. For the dominant feature of our societies, one that has played a major part in my decision to undertake this book, is precisely the extraordinary generalization of fashion: the extension of the "fashion" form to spheres that once lay beyond its purview, the advent of a society restructured from top to bottom by the attractive and the ephemeral—by the very logic of fashion. Hence the unevenness in this book's organization, as measured by the yardstick of historical time. Part One [of Lipovetsky's book], which deals with fashion in the narrow sense, covers more than six centuries of history. Part Two analyzes fashion in its multiple networks, from industrial objects to the culture of the mass media, from advertising to ideology, from communication technologies to the social sphere; it focuses on a much briefer historical period, the era of democratic societies oriented toward mass production, consumption, and communication. This difference in the way historical time is treated and explored is justified by the new, highly strategic place now occupied by the fashion process in the workings of free societies. Fashion is no longer an aesthetic embellishment, a decorative accessory to collective life; it is the key to the entire edifice. In structural terms, fashion has completed its historical trajectory; it has reached the peak of its power, for it has succeeded in reshaping society as a whole in its own image. Once a peripheral phenomenon, it is now hegemonic. In the pages that follow, I seek to shed some light on the historical rise of fashion, in an attempt to understand how its empire was established, how it evolved and reached its apogee.

In our societies, fashion is in the driver's seat. In less than half a century, attractiveness and evanescence have become the organizing principles of modern collective life. We live in societies where the trivial predominates, societies that constitute the last link in the centuries-old capitalist-democratic-individualist chain. Should we be dismayed by this? Does it announce the slow but inexorable decline of the West? Must we take it as the sign of the decadence of the democratic ideal? Nothing is more commonplace or widespread than the tendency to stigmatize—not without cause, moreover—the consumerist bent of democracies; they are represented as devoid of any great mobilizing collective projects, lulled into a stupor by the private orgies of consumerism, infantilized by "instant" culture, by advertising, by politics-as-theater. The ultimate reign of seduction annihilates culture, it is said, and leads to a general brutalization, to the collapse of a free and responsible citizenry: no intellectual tendency is more widely shared than the tendency to condemn fashion. The contradictory and paradoxical interpretation of the modern world I propose here, however, points in quite a different direction. Looking beyond fashion's "perversions," I attempt to reveal its globally positive power with respect both to democratic institutions and to the autonomy of consciousness. Fashion holds more surprises in store: whatever deleterious influence it may have on the vitality of minds and democracies, it appears above all as the primary agent of the spiraling movement toward individualism and the consolidation of liberal societies.

To be sure, the frivolous new deal is apt to provide fodder for a certain number of anxieties. The society it outlines does not look much like the democratic ideal, and it does not offer the best conditions for getting out of the economic slump into which we have slid. On the one hand, our citizens take little interest in public affairs. Lack of motivation and indifference to politics prevail more or less everywhere; the voter's behavior is beginning to resemble the consumer's. On the other hand, isolated, self-absorbed individuals are not much inclined to consider the general good, to give up acquired privileges; preparing for the future tends to be sacrificed by individuals and groups to immediate satisfactions. Citizens' behavior is just as problematic where the vitality of the democratic spirit is concerned—that is, the capacity of our societies to take themselves in hand, to make timely conversions, to win the new market war.

All these weaknesses are well known, and they have been abundantly analyzed. The same cannot be said, however, for the future prospects of democracies. To put it succinctly, late-twentieth-century democracies, inconstant as they seem, do not lack weapons with which they can confront the future. The resources they now have at their disposal are priceless, although they are not measurable and not very spectacular: they consist of a human "raw material" that is more flexible than we used to think. This raw material has come to terms with the legitimacy of peaceful change; it has given up revolutionary and Manichean worldviews. Under fashion's reign, democracies enjoy a universal consensus about their political institutions; ideological extremes are on the wane and pragmatism is on the rise; the spirit of enterprise and efficiency has been substituted for prophetic incantation. Should these factors of social cohesion, of institutional solidity, of modernist "realism," be completely disregarded? Whatever social conflicts and corporatist reflexes may hinder modernization, the process is under way, and it is gathering steam. Fashion does not do away with the demands and defensive tactics of special-interest groups, it makes them more negotiable. Conflicts of interest and selfishness remain, but they are not obstacles; they never reach the point of threatening the continuity or the order of the republic. I do not share the gloomy outlook of some observers about the future of the European nations. These pages have been written with the idea that our history has not played itself out that in the long run the consummate fashion system represents an opportunity for democracies. Now that they are free from the fervor of extremists, the democracies have been by and large won over to change, to perpetual reconversion, to the need to reckon with national and international economic realities. Here are the first paradoxes of our societies: the more seduction is used as a tool, the more people face up to reality; the more triumphant the element of playfulness becomes, the better the economic ethos is rehabilitated; the more progress the ephemeral makes, the more stable, profoundly unified, and reconciled with their pluralist principles the democracies become. Although these factors cannot be quantified, they constitute immense assets for the construction of the future. To be sure, on the level of short-term history, the data are not always encouraging; to be sure, not everything will be accomplished all at once, without collective effort, without social tensions, and without a political will to change. Still, in an age recycled by the fashion form, history is more open than ever. Modernism has won such a measure of social legitimacy that the recovery of Western European nations is more probable than irreversible political decay. Let us avoid reading the future solely in the light of quantified schemas of the present. An age that functions in terms of information, the seductive power of novelty, tolerance, and mobility of opinions, is preparing us, if only we can take advantage of its strong points, for the challenges of the future. We are going through a difficult passage, but we are not at an impasse. The promises of fashion society will not yield their fruits right away; we need to let time do its work. In the short run, we may see little beyond rising unemployment, a precarious labor market, weak growth rates, a flabby economy. If we fix our gaze on the horizon, however, reasons for hope are not entirely lacking. The mature phase of fashion is not the road to oblivion. Considered with a certain detachment, it leads to a dual view of our destiny: pessimism about the present, optimism about the future.

The denunciation of the consummate stage of fashion has taken on its most virulent tones in the domain of the life of the mind. In analyzing media culture as a reason-destroying machine, a totalitarian enterprise designed to do away with autonomous thought, the intelligentsia has made common cause, speaking with one voice to stigmatize the degrading dictatorship of the consumable, the infamy of the culture industries. As long ago as the 1940s, Theodor Adorno and Max Horkheimer were inveighing against the "monstrous" fusion of culture, advertising, and industrialized entertainment that led to the manipulation and standardization of consciousness. Later, Jürgen Habermas analyzed media-oriented consumer products as instruments designed to reduce people's capacity for critical thinking, while Guy Debord denounced the "false consciousness," the generalized alienation induced by the pseudo-culture of the spectacular. And today, although Marxist and revolutionary thought are no longer in season, the offensive against fashion and media-induced brain rot is again in full swing: new times bring new ways of saying the same old thing. In place of Marx-as-joker, out comes the Heidegger card. The dialectic panoply of merchandising, ideology, and alienation is no longer brandished; instead, we find musings on the dominion of technology, "the autonegation of life," or the dissolution of "life with the mind." We are invited to open our eyes, then, to the immense wretchedness of modernity. We are condemned to the degradation of a media-dominated existence. A soft totalitarianism, we are told, has infiltrated our democracies: it has successfully sown contempt for culture; it has generalized regression and mental confusion. We are fully ensconced in "barbarianism," according to the latest jingle of our antimodern philosophers. They fulminate against fashion, but they are quick to follow its lead, adopting similar hyperbolic techniques, the sine qua non of conceptual one-upmanship. There is no way around it: the hatchet of apocalyptic war has not been buried; fashion will always be fashion. Denunciation of fashion is no doubt consubstantial with its very being; such denunciation is part and parcel of the crusades of lofty intellectual souls.

The critical unanimity provoked by the empire of fashion is anything but accidental. It is deeply rooted in the thought process that underlies philosophical reflection itself. Ever since Plato's day we have known that the play of light and darkness in the cavern of existence blocks progress toward truth. Seduction and evanescence enchain the human spirit, and they are the very signs of its captivity. According to Platonic philosophy, rational thinking and progress toward truth can only come about through a fierce effort to root out appearances, flux, the charm of images. No intellectual salvation is to be found in the protean universe of surfaces; this is the paradigm that presides even today over attacks on the rule of fashion. Ready access to leisure, the ephemeral nature of images, the distracting-seductiveness of the mass media—these phenomena can only enslave reason, beguile and disorder the mind. Consumption is superficial, thus it makes the masses childlike; rock music is violent and nonverbal, thus it does away with reason; the culture industries deal in stereotypes, thus television abuses individuals and creates couch potatoes, while "feeling" and "zapping" produce airheads. Superficiality is evil in any event.

Whether they see themselves as followers of Marx or Heidegger, our intellectual clerks have remained moralists trapped in the froth on the surfaces of phenomena; they are completely unable to fathom the way fashion actually works—what we might call the ruse of fashion's irrationality. Here is fashion's greatest and most interesting historical lesson: at the other extreme from Platonism, we need to understand that seduction now serves to limit irrationality; that the artificial facilitates access to the real; that superficiality permits increased use of reason; that playful displays are springboards to subjective judgment. Fashion does not bring about the definitive alienation of the masses; it is an ambiguous but effective vector of human autonomy, even though it functions via the heteronomy of mass culture. The paradoxes of what is sometimes called postmodernity reach their apogee here: subjective independence grows apace with the empire of bureaucratic dispossession. The more ephemeral seduction there is, the more enlightenment advances, even if it does so in an ambivalent way. At any given moment, to be sure, the process is hard to detect, so compelling are the negative effects of fashion. The process comes into its own only by comparison over the long term with the evils of earlier eras: omnipotent tradition, triumphant racism, religious and ideological oppression. The frivolous era of consumption and communication has been caricatured to the point of delirium by those on the right and the left alike who hold it in contempt; it needs to be reinterpreted from start to finish. Fashion cannot be equated with some gentle new realism. Quite to the contrary, fashion has allowed public questioning to expand; it has allowed subjective thoughts and existences to take on greater autonomy. Fashion is the supreme agent of the individualist dynamic in its various manifestations. In an earlier work I sought to identify the contemporary transformations of individualism; here I have tried to understand what paths the process of individualization has taken, what social mechanisms it has used in order to enter the second cycle of its historical trajectory.

Let me attempt to set forth briefly the idea of history implied by an analysis that takes fashion as the ultimate phase of democracy. Clearly in one sense I have returned to the philosophical problematics of the ruse of reason: collective "reason" advances in fact through its contrary, distraction; individual autonomy develops through the heteronomy of seduction, the "wisdom" of modern nations is constructed through the folly of superficial tastes. What is at issue is not the classic Hegelian model, the disorderly game of selfish passions in the achievement of a rational city, but a formally equivalent model: the role of the frivolous in the development of critical, realistic, tolerant consciousness. The erratic progress of the exercise of reason is brought about, as in Hegel's and Marx's philosophies of history, by the action of its opposite. But my complicity with theories of the ruse of reason ends here. I shall limit my purview to the dynamics of contemporary democracies alone; I shall not proceed to develop a global conception of universal history, nor do I intend to imply any metaphysics of seduction.

To avoid misunderstandings, I need to add two further remarks. First, the fashion form that I analyze is not antithetical to "rationality": seduction is already in itself, in part, a rational logic that integrates the calculations, technology, and information that characterize the modern world. Consummate fashion celebrates the marriage of seduction and productive, instrumental, operational reason. What is at stake is not at all a vision of modernity that would affirm the progress of rational universality through the dialectical play of individual tendencies, but the autonomy of a society structured by fashion, where rationality functions by way of evanescence and superficiality, where objectivity is instituted as a spectacle, where the dominion of technology is reconciled with play and the realm of politics is reconciled with seduction. Second, I do not subscribe unreservedly to the idea of the progress of consciousness. In reality, as enlightenment advances it is inextricably mingled with its opposite; the historical optimism implied by my analysis of fashion must be confined within narrow limits. Human minds taken collectively are in fact better informed but also more disorderly, more adult but also more unstable, less subject to ideologies but also more dependent on fashions, more open but also more easily influenced, less extremist but also more dispersed, more realistic but also more *fuzzy*, more critical but also more superficial, more skeptical but also less meditative. An increase in independent thinking goes hand in hand with increased frivolity; tolerance is accompanied by an increase in casualness and indifference among thinkers. Neither theories of alienation nor theories of some optimal "invisible hand" offer an adequate model for fashion, and fashion institutes neither the reign of ultimate subjective dispossession nor the reign of clear, solid reason.

Even though it has links with theories of the ruse of reason, the model for the evolution of contemporary societies that I propose does not make the intentional initiative of human beings any less significant. Insofar as the ultimate order of fashion produces an essentially ambivalent historical moment of consciousness, the lucid, voluntary, responsible action of human beings is more possible than ever, and more necessary for progress toward a freer, better-informed world. Fashion produces the best and the worst, inseparably: news around the clock, and zero-degree thinking. It is up to us to stand our ground and challenge myths and presuppositions; it is up to us to limit the harmful effects of disinformation, to bring about the conditions for a more open, freer, more objective public debate. To say that the universe of seduction contributes to the dynamics of reason does not condemn us to nostalgia for the past; it does not mean that "everything is the same in the end"; it does not amount to a smug apology for generalized show business. Fashion is accompanied by ambiguous effects. Our job is to reduce its "obscurantist" dimension and enhance its "enlightened" dimension—not by seeking simply to eradicate the glitter of seduction, but by putting its liberating potential at the service of the greatest number. Consummate fashion calls neither for unconditional defense nor for unqualified rejection. If the terrain of fashion is propitious for the critical use of reason, it also makes manifest the exile and confusion of thought: there is much to correct, to regulate, to criticize, to explain ad infinitum. The ruse of fashion's irrationality does not rule out human intelligence and free initiative, or society's responsibility for its own future. In the new democratic era, collective progress toward freedom of thought will not occur apart from seduction; it will be undergirded by the fashion form, but it will be seconded by other agencies, reinforced by other criteria: by the educational establishment, by the openness to scrutiny and the ethical standards proper to the media, by theoretical and scientific works, and by the corrective system of laws and regulations. In the slow, contradictory, uneven forward movement of free subjectivities, fashion is clearly not alone on the slopes, and the future remains largely undetermined insofar as the specific features of individual autonomy are concerned. Lucidity is always hard-won; illusion and blindness, like the phoenix, are always reborn from their own ashes. Seduction will fully accomplish its democratic work only if it succeeds in allying itself with other parameters, if it avoids stifling the sovereign rules of truth, facts, and rational argument. Nevertheless, contrary to the stereotypes in which it is clothed, the age of fashion remains the major factor in the process that has drawn men and women collectively away from obscurantism and fanaticism, has instituted an open public space and shaped a more lawful, more mature, more skeptical humanity. Consummate fashion lives on paradox. Its unconscious is conducive to consciousness; its madness is conducive to the spirit of tolerance; its frivolity is conducive to respect for the rights of man. In the speeded-up film of modern history, we are beginning to realize that fashion is the worst scenario, with the exception of all the others.

PART TWO

Fashion and history/fashion in history

IT WILL COME AS NO SURPRISE to anyone to hear that fashion has a history, nor that the related areas of textiles and dress also have histories. It may come as something of a surprise to learn that 'the history of dress and fashion was not studied seriously in academic circles before the 1960s' (Jarvis 1998: 299; and see Breward 1998: 303). And Lou Taylor says that 'old' universities in the UK deemed object-based dress and textile history to be improper subjects of academic study until as recently as 1990 (2002: 64–5). What was until relatively recently, then, the 'largely male academic world of "real" history' took the attitude that fashion, textiles and dress were too trivial, frivolous and ephemeral to be fit for 'serious' academic study: indeed, it was even held that the study of these areas would 'trivialise history itself' (ibid.: 1–2). At the beginning of the twenty-first century the idea that the study of the history of fashion and clothing could spoil an entire discipline probably strikes us as preposterous. Eric Hobsbawm takes quite the opposite view. In his *The Age of Extremes*, he suggests that

> [w]hy brilliant fashion-designers, a notoriously non-analytic breed, some-times succeed in anticipating the shape of things to come better than professional predictors, is one of the most obscure questions in history; and, for the historian of culture, one of the most central.
>
> (Hobsbawm 1994: 178)

In an only slightly backhanded Wellsian compliment, it is implied that fashion designers foresee the future better than professional historians and the reason for this is so untrivial that it is one of the central problems of the discipline.

History is, as Lisa Tickner says (1977: 56), one of the disciplines in terms of which fashion may be studied. Taylor concurs, suggesting that economic, social and cultural history are the names of some of the sub-disciplines in terms of which fashion may be approached and studied (2002: 64ff.). Tickner's essay is itself an example of how social and cultural history may be used in the study of fashion. In that she is concerned with the cultural construction of gender in the late nineteenth and early twentieth centuries, she is writing a cultural history of women and trousers; her essay is about the ideas and beliefs that groups of people have about what sorts of beings women are. In that she is also concerned with the ways in which women's roles in society and the ways in which leisure and work opportunities changed, she is also writing a social history of women and trousers; her essay is about the social roles or functions of women. However, noting that fashion has a history and that history is one of the disciplines that may be used to explain it does not exhaust the account of the relation between fashion and history.

There are three basic positions that may be taken on the relation between fashion and history: history as a backdrop to fashion; history as a context for fashion, and history as a product of fashion. There are also two fairly radical alternative positions that may be adopted, arguing either that fashion has and can have no relation to history or that fashion is historically ineffective. The first of the former positions is that history forms a backdrop to fashion, occurring or going on 'behind' fashion, in the manner of the scenery in a theatre. This is the position often adopted by James Laver (1969) in his book *Costume and Fashion, a Concise History* for example. In this book, history is regularly reduced to a chronological series of dates, and when historical events are mentioned they have the simplest and most direct effects on what people are wearing. For example, writing of women's fashions at Longchamps in 1930, Laver says that 'The skirts are on the eve of going long again and the waist is about to resume its normal place' (1969: 237). Fashion here is a simple sequence. When he writes 'As the clouds of World War II began to gather, it became obvious that the fashionable silhouette was beginning to be modified' (1969: 246), the historical event that was the Second World War is just something happening in the background while 'fashionable silhouettes' change. And, when he says that the French Revolution 'had a profound effect on the dress of both men and women. The dress of the Ancien Régime was swept away' (1969: 148), the explanation is given in terms of 'anglomania' and a desire to dress in 'English country clothes' (1969: 151). The social, political and cultural identities of these 'anglomaniacs' are not revealed, and the idea that it is only aristocratic 'English country clothes' that are desirable (and not the clothes of the peasantry) is assumed without question.

The second position, and possibly the most common or prevalent, is that history is a context for fashion: history on this sort of account is either something that fashion reflects or to which it points, or it is something from which fashion derives its significance. According to this position, history is one of the ways in which fashion itself appears: fashion is itself a historical concept insofar as a particular example of fashion is utterly meaningless if extracted from its place in a temporal or chronological sequence. As Sapir says, the qualities of fashion 'depend on a context' (Sapir 1931: 139). A popular example of this position may be found at ⟨http://www.yale.ws/ynhti/curriculum/units/2001/4/01.04.11.x.html⟩, where the author says that '[t]he French Revolution brought on outlandish fashions, reflecting the unrest of the times'.

Laver also sometimes adopts this position. Writing of the nineteenth-century fashion for crinolines, he says that the garment 'symbolises' the 'supposed unapproachability' and actual seductiveness of Victorian Englishwomen (1969: 184). It also symbolises the prosperity and extravagance of Second Empire France in which the Empress Eugénie wore crinolines that reflected her style 'to perfection' (ibid.: 185). The connection between historical periods of economic prosperity and female fashions is also regularly made by popular journalists. In the *San Diego Source* for 5 September 2002, for example, John Patrick Ford proposes just such a link, suggesting that there is 'historical basis' for the theory he attributes to George Taylor of the University of Pennsylvania in the 1920s (www.sddt.com/Commentary/article.cfm? Commentary_ID=12&SourceCode=20020905tza June 2006). The connection is supposed to be that when hemlines rise the economy improves and when hemlines go down the economy declines. Unfortunately, as Lindsey Rosenberg points out, there is a theory that proposes exactly the opposite: according to this theory, 'hemlines go up when fabric prices rise because it prevents designers from purchasing as many textiles' (www.usc.edu/org/InsightBusiness/archives/fall2005/TheNation.htm June 2006).

And the third position is that fashion is productive or transformative of history; on this sort of account, fashion makes history possible. John Styles suggests that this third position is a relatively recent development in dress history and one that is itself made possible by three factors. The first is the rise of feminist scholarship, the second is the emergence of cultural studies, and the third is a 'shift in interest across the social sciences from production to consumption' (Styles 1998: 385). Where the histories of fashion and dress had been ignored before the 1960s, feminist thought and the 'new women's history', along with a concomitant interest in 'identity, autonomy and resistance' and in consumption, led to the serious study of the ways in which 'mass-produced goods could be appropriated and used by working class consumers to contest established authority' (ibid.). Lou Taylor takes a slightly different approach, suggesting that the work of Veblen and Simmel at the turn of the nineteenth century, and of Flugel in the 1930s, had no impact for sixty years (Taylor 2004: 46). Dick Hebdige's (1979) work on working-class youth cultures and Angela Partington's (1992) essay on working-class women and the New Look are examples of this third position on the relation between fashion and history. In both of these works, fashion and dress are being used by subcultural groups to contest traditional identities and politics and to construct new identities and politics.

The first of the latter positions (according to which fashion either has no relation to history or is historically ineffective) is represented by Nathalie Khan's (2000) essay 'Catwalk Politics'. Under the slightly misleading heading 'The social and political context of fashion', Khan identifies a few examples of fashion 'reflecting' the 'wider social landscape' – Katharine Hamnett's '58% don't want Pershing' t-shirts, Benetton's controversial HIV advertising and the early 1990s anti-fur campaigns (2000: 115–16). These examples are ostensibly radical and political: Hamnett wore the t-shirt (the slogan of which was protesting against the use of American nuclear weapons on British soil) to meet Margaret Thatcher, who was then the UK prime minister; Benetton's advertising was known for pushing the limits of acceptability and aesthetics at the time, and a group of 'supermodels' famously posed nude in order to protest against the use of fur in fashion. However, Khan argues that these confrontations are or were 'ephemeral, lasting no more than the duration of a particular fashion season' (ibid.: 115). Hamnett's anti-Pershing t-shirts were a part of the 1983–4 'Choose Life' collection and the supermodels were back in fur as soon as the industry discovered the 'profitability of a new trend' (ibid.: 116).

Khan's point is that 'fashion can do little more than reflect upon that which is current' and that, therefore, fashion can 'reflect, but it cannot renew, society' (2000: 116). The metaphor of reflection indicates the ineffectiveness of fashion with regard to society. As a result, fashion is also ineffective with regard to history on Khan's account. She says that 'fashion can . . . only promote a particular set of values if those values reflect current trends' (as the anti-fur/pro-fur supermodels attest) and fashion's 'fickle' nature thus prevents it from 'creating history' (ibid.). So fashion is historically ineffective (and therefore, it must be said, politically conservative or even quietist) in Khan's account: it has no part to play in creating history and all it can do is reflect current trends, values and tendencies.

The second of these positions would be to argue that fashion has no relation to history, or, to put it another way, that it has no history. This position is not incompatible with Baudrillard's position, as found in his (1981) *For a Critique of the Political Economy of the Sign*. The argument here begins from Baudrillard's claim that the logic of fashion is a logic of differentiation (1981: 67). What he means by this is a radicalised version of Saussure's account of linguistic structure. For Saussure, a language is a structure in which there are no positive terms: the linguistic sign is what it is by virtue of its differences from (its relations to) all other signs. In Baudrillard's account of fashion, the fashion sign operates in much the same way. In fashion there are no positive terms (nothing is naturally 'beautiful', or indeed 'fashionable'), and beautiful or fashionable items of dress are what they are because of the differences between them and all the other items and objects in the world of fashion. As Baudrillard says, in fashion it is only the difference between items that creates meaning (1981: 79). This is what he means by the 'logic of differentiation'. One of the consequences of this logic is that it strips away the fashion object's 'substance and history' (1981: 93) so that the fashion item functions only as a marker of difference. If the fashion sign is what it is only by virtue of its relations to all other fashion signs, then the reference to history is 'outlawed' as inappropriate: there is and can be no historical reference when meaning and values are the product of the present (and fashionable) moment. While Baudrillard does not say it, it would not be inaccurate to suggest that, on this account, fashion may have a memory but it has no history.

Ann Rosalind Jones and Peter Stallybrass set themselves the task of understanding the significance of clothes in the Renaissance (2000: 2). This project immediately raises a number of hermeneutic problems. How are twenty-first century people to understand the ways in which fourteenth- and fifteenth-century people thought? Their answer begins with the idea that 'we need to undo our own social categories' and try to understand the 'world-view' of Renaissance men and women (ibid.). 'Our' social categories include the ideas that 'subjects are prior to objects' and wearers are prior to what is worn, and among those alien and antique views that we must try to understand are the ideas that the superficial has its own depth and that clothes mould and shape people 'both physically and socially, [constituting] subjects through their power as material memories' (ibid.). These are utterly fascinating and very difficult problems, but Jones and Stallybrass are insisting that fashion is situated in a different time and they are explaining that it is precisely the beliefs about clothes and fashion held by people at the time that make the Renaissance a different time. Fashion and clothing are explicitly constitutive of historical epochs or periods of time in Jones and Stallybrass's work: history is not a reflection of people's ideas, beliefs and practices concerning fashion, nor is it some inert backdrop to those ideas, beliefs and practices; rather, those beliefs and values constitute Renaissance subjects as subjects and constitute the Renaissance as a different time from 'ours'. The Jones and Stallybrass extract is also of interest because it provides a perspective on the Renaissance notion of fetish, which can be usefully contrasted with the more modern accounts found in Part Twelve.

Fashion's role in the production of history is also the subject of Lipovetsky's (1994) *The Empire of Fashion*. Lipovetsky's argument is that fashion has an essential part to play in the historical development of modern democratic societies: by emphasising the trivial, the ephemeral and the superficiality of individual appearance, fashion has cut traditional society's ties with ancient caste traditions and religious affiliations, thus enabling people to 'get along', as Richard Sennett puts it, in a new world of democratic individualism (in Lipovetsky 1994: viii). To simplify Lipovetsky's case slightly, there are two phases in the history of modern fashion. The first phase lasts from the mid-nineteenth century to the 1960s and the second phase lasts from the 1960s to the present (1994: 55). During the first phase fashion is organised around two industries, *haute couture* and 'industrial clothing manufacture'. The second phase is characterised by the emergence and development of '*prêt-à-porter*', or ready-to-wear fashions. These two phases are not separate, distinct or discrete units of time: rather, the second phase extends and deepens the developments of the first. In the first phase, for example, *haute couture* contributed to the democratisation of fashion by encouraging the 'cult of individuality' (ibid.: 85) and by making the latest styles easier to imitate (ibid.: 59). And, in the second phase, couture is still active, though much reduced (ibid.: 89), and it 'aims much more at perpetuating the great tradition of luxury' (ibid.: 90).

Agnes Brooks Young's thesis is that between 1760 and 1937 there were three fundamental types or 'contours' of women's dress fashion and that these three contours rotated in cycles that lasted approximately thirty years. The contours are labelled 'back-full', 'tubular' and 'bell-shaped'. History here is likened to the repertoire of a barrel-organ that plays only three tunes but whose tunes are so long that, by the time the organist has passed down the street, the people in the next street have yet to hear the tunes for the first time, with the result that the tunes are perceived by everyone as new and interesting (1937: 29).

Bibliography

Baudrillard, J. (1981) *For a Critique of the Political Economy of the Sign*, St Louis, Mo.: Telos Press.

Breward, C. (1998) 'Cultures, Identities, Histories: Fashioning a Cultural Approach to Dress', in *Fashion Theory* 2, 4: 301–13.

Brooks Young, A. (1937) *Recurring Cycles of Fashion: 1760–1937*, New York: Harper Brothers.

Hebdige, D. (1979) *Subculture: The Meaning of Style*, London: Routledge.

Hobsbawm, E. (1994) *The Age of Extremes: 1914–1991*, London: Abacus.

Jarvis, A. (1998) 'Letter from the Editor', *Fashion Theory* 2, 4: 299–300.

Jones, A. R. and Stallybrass, P. (2000) *Renaissance Clothing and the Materials of Memory*, Cambridge: Cambridge University Press.

Khan, N. (2000) 'Catwalk Politics', in S. Bruzzi and P. Church-Gibson (eds) *Fashion Cultures: Theories, Explorations and Analysis*, London: Routledge.

Laver, James (1969) *Costume and Fashion: A Concise History*, London: Thames and Hudson.

Lipovetsky, G. (1994) *The Empire of Fashion: Dressing Modern Democracy*, Princeton: Princeton University Press.

Partington, A. (1992) 'Popular Fashion and Working Class Affluence', in J. Ash and E. Wilson (eds) *Chic Thrills*, London: Pandora.

Sapir, E. (1931) 'Fashion', *Encyclopaedia of the Social Sciences* 6: 139–144, New York: Macmillan.

Styles, J. (1998) 'Dress in History: Reflections on a Contested Terrain', in *Fashion Theory* 2, 4: 383–90.

Taylor, L. (2002) *The Study of Dress History*, Manchester: Manchester University Press.

—— (2004) *Establishing Dress History*, Manchester: Manchester: University Press.

Tickner, L. (1977) 'Women and Trousers', *Leisure in the Twentieth Century*, London: Design Council Publications.

Chapter 3

Edward Sapir

FASHION

THE MEANING OF THE term fashion may be clarified by pointing out how it differs in connotation from a number of other terms whose meaning it approaches. A particular fashion differs from a given taste in suggesting some measure of compulsion on the part of the group as contrasted with individual choice from among a number of possibilities. A particular choice may of course be due to a blend of fashion and taste. Thus, if bright and simple colors are in fashion, one may select red as more pleasing to one's taste than yellow, although one's free taste unhampered by fashion might have decided in favor of a more subtle tone. To the discriminating person the demand of fashion constitutes a challenge to taste and suggests problems of reconciliation. But fashion is accepted by average people with little demur and is not so much reconciled with taste as substituted for it. For many people taste hardly arises at all except on the basis of a clash of an accepted fashion with a fashion that is out of date or current in some other group than one's own.

The term fashion may carry with it a tone of approval or disapproval. It is a fairly objective term whose emotional qualities depend on a context. A moralist may decry a certain type of behavior as a mere fashion but the ordinary person will not be displeased if he is accused of being in the fashion. It is different with fads, which are objectively similar to fashions but differ from them in being more personal in their application and in connoting a more or less definite social disapproval. Particular people or coteries have their fads, while fashions are the property of larger or more representative groups. A taste which asserts itself in spite of fashion and which may therefore be suspected of having something obsessive about it may be referred to as an individual fad. On the other hand, while a fad may be of very short duration, it always differs from a true fashion in having something unexpected, irresponsible or bizarre about it. Any fashion which sins against one's sense of style and one's feeling for the historical continuity of style is likely to be dismissed as a fad. There are changing fashions in tennis rackets, while the game of mah jong, once rather fashionable, takes on in retrospect more and more the character of a fad.

Just as the weakness of fashion leads to fads, so its strength comes from custom. Customs differ from fashions in being relatively permanent types of social behavior. They change, but with a less active and conscious participation of the individual in the change. Custom is the element of permanence which makes changes in fashion possible. Custom marks the highroad of human interrelationships, while fashion may be looked upon as the endless departure from and return to the highroad. The vast majority of fashions are relieved by other fashions, but occasionally a fashion crystallizes into permanent habit, taking on the character of custom.

It is not correct to think of fashion as merely a short lived innovation in custom, because many innovations in human history arise with the need for them and last as long as they are useful or convenient. If, for instance, there is a shortage of silk and it becomes customary to substitute cotton for silk in the manufacture of certain articles of dress in which silk has been the usual material, such an enforced change of material, however important economically or aesthetically, does not in itself constitute a true change of fashion. On the other hand, if cotton is substituted for silk out of free choice as a symbol perhaps of the simple life or because of a desire to see what novel effect can be produced in accepted types of dress with simpler materials, the change may be called one of fashion. There is nothing to prevent an innovation from eventually taking on the character of a new fashion. If, for example, people persist in using the cotton material even after silk has once more become available, a new fashion has arisen.

Fashion is custom in the guise of departure from custom. Most normal individuals consciously or unconsciously have the itch to break away in some measure from a too literal loyalty to accepted custom. They are not fundamentally in revolt from custom but they wish somehow to legitimize their personal deviation without laying themselves open to the charge of insensitiveness to good taste or good manners. Fashion is the discreet solution of the subtle conflict. The slight changes from the established in dress or other forms of behavior seem for the moment to give the victory to the individual, while the fact that one's fellows revolt in the same direction gives one a feeling of adventurous safety. The personal note which is at the hidden core of fashion becomes superpersonalized.

Whether fashion is felt as a sort of socially legitimized caprice or is merely a new and unintelligible form of social tyranny depends on the individual or class. It is probable that those most concerned with the setting and testing of fashions are the individuals who realize most keenly the problem of reconciling individual freedom with social conformity which is implicit in the very fact of fashion. It is perhaps not too much to say that most people are at least partly sensitive to this aspect of fashion and are secretly grateful for it. A large minority of people, however, are insensitive to the psychological complexity of fashion and submit to it to the extent that they do merely because they realize that not to fall in with it would be to declare themselves members of a past generation or dull people who cannot keep up with their neighbors. These latter reasons for being fashionable are secondary; they are sullen surrenders to bastard custom.

The fundamental drives leading to the creation and acceptance of fashion can be isolated. In the more sophisticated societies boredom, created by leisure and too highly specialized forms of activity, leads to restlessness and curiosity. This general desire to escape from the trammels of a too regularized existence is powerfully reenforced by a ceaseless desire to add to the attractiveness of the self and all other objects of love and friendship. It is precisely in functionally powerful societies that the individual's ego is constantly being convicted of helplessness. The individual tends to be unconsciously thrown back on himself and demands more and more novel affirmations of his effective reality. The endless rediscovery of the self in a series of petty truancies from the official socialized self becomes a mild obsession of the normal individual in any society in which the individual has ceased to be a measure of the society itself. There is, however, always the danger of too great a departure from the recognized symbols of the individual, because his identity is likely to be destroyed. That is why insensitive people, anxious to be literally in the fashion, so often overreach themselves and nullify the very purpose of fashion. Good hearted women of middle age generally fail in the art of being ravishing nymphs.

Somewhat different from the affirmation of the libidinal self is the more vulgar desire for prestige or notoriety, satisfied by changes in fashion. In this category belongs fashion as an outward emblem of personal distinction or of membership in some group to which distinction is ascribed. The imitation of fashion by people who belong to circles removed from those which set the fashion has the function of bridging the gap between a social class and the class next above it. The logical result of the acceptance of a fashion by all members of society is the disappearance of the kinds of satisfaction responsible for the change of fashion in the first place. A new fashion becomes psychologically necessary, and thus the cycle of fashion is endlessly repeated.

Fashion is emphatically a historical concept. A specific fashion is utterly unintelligible if lifted out of its place in a sequence of forms. It is exceedingly dangerous to rationalize or in any other way psychologize a particular fashion on the basis of general principles which might be considered applicable to the class of forms of which it seems to be an example. It is utterly vain, for instance, to explain particular forms of dress or types of cosmetics or methods of wearing the hair without a preliminary historical critique. Bare legs among modern women in summer do not psychologically or historically create at all the same fashion as bare legs and bare feet among primitives living in the tropics. The importance of understanding fashion historically should be obvious enough when it is recognized that the very essence of fashion is that it be valued as a variation in an understood sequence, as a departure from the immediately preceding mode.

Changes in fashion depend on the prevailing culture and on the social ideals which inform it. Under the apparently placid surface of culture there are always powerful psychological drifts of which fashion is quick to catch the direction. In a democratic society, for instance, if there is an unacknowledged drift toward class distinctions fashion will discover endless ways of giving it visible form. Criticism can always be met by the insincere defense that fashion is merely fashion and need not be taken seriously. If in a puritanic society there is a growing impatience with the outward forms of modesty, fashion finds it easy to minister to the demands of sex curiosity, while the old mores can be trusted to defend fashion with an affectation of unawareness of what fashion is driving at. A complete study of the history of fashion would undoubtedly throw much light on the ups and downs of sentiment and attitude at various periods of civilization. However, fashion never permanently out-runs discretion and only those who are taken in by the superficial rationalizations of fashion are surprised by the frequent changes of face in its history. That there was destined to be a lengthening of women's skirts after they had become short enough was obvious from the outset to all except those who do not believe that sex symbolism is a real factor in human behavior.

The chief difficulty of understanding fashion in its apparent vagaries is the lack of exact knowledge of the unconscious symbolisms attaching to forms, colors, textures, postures and other expressive elements in a given culture. The difficulty is appreciably increased by the fact that the same expressive elements tend to have quite different symbolic references in different areas. Gothic type, for instance, is a nationalistic token in Germany, while in Anglo-Saxon culture the practically identi-cal type known as Old English has entirely different connotations. In other words, the same style of lettering may symbolize either an undying hatred of France or a wistful look backward at madrigals and pewter.

An important principle in the history of fashion is that those features of fashion which do not configurate correctly with the unconscious system of meanings charac-teristic of the given culture are relatively insecure. Extremes of style, which too frankly symbolize the current of feeling of the moment, are likely to find themselves in exposed positions, as it were, where they can be outflanked by meanings which they do not wish to recognize. Thus, it may be conjectured that lipstick is less secure in American culture as an element of fashion than rouge discreetly applied to the cheek. This is assuredly not due to a superior sinfulness of lipstick as such, but to the fact that rosy cheeks resulting from a healthy natural life in the country are one of the characteristic fetishisms of the traditional ideal of feminine beauty, while lipstick has rather the character of certain exotic ardors and goes with flaming oriental stuffs. Rouge is likely to last for many decades or centuries because there is, and is likely to be for a long time to come, a definite strain of nature worship in our culture. If lipstick is to remain it can only be because our culture will have taken on certain violently new meanings which are not at all obvious at the present time. As a symbol it is episodic rather than a part of the underlying rhythm of the history of our fashions.

In custom bound cultures, such as are characteristic of the primitive world, there are slow non-reversible changes of style rather than the often reversible forms of fashion found in modern cultures. The emphasis in such societies is on the group and the sanctity of tradition rather than on individual expression, which tends to be entirely unconscious. In the great cultures of the Orient and in ancient and medi-aeval Europe changes in fashion can be noted radiating from certain definite centers of sophisticated culture, but it is not until modern Europe is reached that the familiar merry-go-round of fashion with its rapid alternations of season occurs.

The typically modern acceleration of changes in fashion may be ascribed to the influence of the Renaissance, which awakened a desire for innovation and which powerfully extended for European society the total world of possible choices. Dur-ing this period Italian culture came to be the arbiter of taste, to be followed by French culture, which may still be looked upon as the most powerful influence in the creation and distribution of fashions. But more important than the Renaissance in the history of fashion is the effect of the industrial revolution and the rise of the common people. The former increased the mechanical ease with which fashions could be diffused; the latter greatly increased the number of those willing and able to be fashionable.

Modern fashion tends to spread to all classes of society. As fashion has always tended to be a symbol of membership in a particular social class and as human beings have always felt the urge to edge a little closer to a class considered superior to their own, there must always have been the tendency for fashion to be adopted by circles which had a lower status than the group setting the fashions. But on the whole such adoption of fashion from above tended to be discreet because of the great importance attached to the maintenance of social classes. What has happened in the modern world, regardless of the official forms of government which prevail in the different nations, is that the tone giving power which lies back of fashion has largely slipped away from the aristocracy of rank to the aristocracy of wealth. This means a psychological if not an economic leveling of classes because of the feeling that wealth is an accidental or accreted quality of an individual as contrasted with blood. In an aristocracy of wealth everyone, even the poorest, is potentially wealthy both in legal theory and in private fancy. In such a society, therefore, all individuals are equally entitled, it is felt, so far as their pockets permit, to the insignia of fashion. This universalizing of fashion necessarily cheapens its value in the specific case and forces an abnormally rapid change of fashion. The only effective protection possessed by the wealthy in the world of fashion is the insistence on expensive materials in which fashion is to express itself. Too great an insistence on this factor, however, is the hall mark of wealthy vulgarity, for fashion is essentially a thing of forms and symbols not of material values.

Perhaps the most important of the special factors which encourage the spread of fashion today is the increased facility for the production and transportation of goods and for communication either personally or by correspondence from the centers of fashion to the outmost periphery of the civilized world. These increased facilities necessarily lead to huge capital investments in the manufacture and distribution of fashionable wear. The extraordinarily high initial profits to be derived from fashion and the relatively rapid tapering off of profits make it inevitable that the natural tendency to change in fashion is helped along by commercial suggestion. The increasingly varied activities of modern life also give greater opportunity for the growth and change of fashion. Today the cut of a dress or the shape of a hat stands ready to symbolize anything from mountain climbing or military efficiency through automobiling to interpretative dancing and veiled harlotry. No individual is merely what his social role indicates that he is to be or may vary only slightly from, but he may act as if he is anything else that individual phantasy may dictate. The greater leisure and spending power of the bourgeoisie, bringing them externally nearer the upper classes of former days, are other obvious stimuli to change in fashion, as are the gradual psychological and economic liberation of women and the greater opportunity given them for experimentation in dress and adornment.

Fashions for women show greater variability than fashions for men in contemporary civilization. Not only do women's fashions change more rapidly and completely but the total gamut of allowed forms is greater for women than for men. In times past and in other cultures, however, men's fashions show a greater exuberance than women's. Much that used to be ascribed to woman as female is really due to woman as a sociologically and economically defined class. Woman as a distinctive theme for fashion may be explained in terms of the social psychology of the present civilization. She is the one who pleases by being what she is and looking as she does rather than by doing what she does. Whether biology or history is primarily responsible for this need not be decided. Woman has been the kept partner in marriage and has had to prove her desirability by ceaselessly reaffirming her attractiveness as symbolized by novelty of fashion. Among the wealthier classes and by imitation also among the less wealthy, woman has come to be looked upon as an expensive luxury on whom one spends extravagantly. She is thus a symbol of the social and economic status of her husband. Whether with the increasingly marked change of woman's place in society the factors which emphasize extravagance in women's fashions will entirely fall away it is impossible to say at the present time.

There are powerful vested interests involved in changes of fashions, as has already been mentioned. The effect on the producer of fashions of a variability which he both encourages and dreads is the introduction of the element of risk. It is a popular error to assume that professional designers arbitrarily dictate fashion. They do so only in a very superficial sense. Actually they have to obey many masters. Their designs must above all things net the manufacturers a profit, so that behind the more strictly psychological determinants of fashion there lurks a very important element due to the sheer technology of the manufacturing process or the availability of a certain type of material. In addition to this the designer must have a sure feeling for the established in custom and the degree to which he can safely depart from it. He must intuitively divine what people want before they are quite aware of it themselves. His business is not so much to impose fashion as to coax people to accept what they have themselves unconsciously suggested. This causes the profits of fashion production to be out of all proportion to the actual cost of manufacturing fashionable goods. The producer and his designer assistant capitalize the curiosity and vanity of their customers but they must also be protected against the losses of a risky business. Those who are familiar with the history of fashion are emphatic in speaking of the inability of business to combat the fashion trends which have been set going by various psychological factors. A fashion may be aesthetically pleasing in the abstract, but if it runs counter to the trend or does not help to usher in a new trend which is struggling for a hearing it may be a flat failure.

The distribution of fashions is a comparatively simple and automatic process. The vogue of fashion plates and fashion magazines, the many lines of communication which connect fashion producers and fashion dispensers, and modern methods of marketing make it almost inevitable that a successful Parisian fashion should find its way within an incredibly short period of time to Chicago and San Francisco. If it were not for the necessity of exploiting accumulated stocks of goods these fashions would penetrate into the remotest corners of rural America even more rapidly than is the case. The average consumer is chronically distressed to discover how rapidly his accumulated property in wear depreciates by becoming outmoded. He complains bitterly and ridicules the new fashions when they appear. In the end he succumbs, a victim to symbolisms of behavior which he does not fully comprehend. What he will never admit is that he is more the creator than the victim of his difficulties.

Fashion has always had vain critics. It has been arraigned by the clergy and by social satirists because each new style of wear, calling attention as it does to the form of the human body, seems to the critics to be an attack on modesty. Some fashions there are, to be sure, whose very purpose it is to attack modesty, but over and above specific attacks there is felt to be a generalized one. The charge is well founded but useless. Human beings do not wish to be modest; they want to be as expressive—that is, as immodest—as fear allows; fashion helps them solve their paradoxical problem. The charge of economic waste which is often leveled against fashion has had little or no effect on the public mind. Waste seems to be of no concern where values are to be considered, particularly when these values are both egoistic and unconscious. The criticism that fashion imposes an unwanted uniformity is not as sound as it appears to be in the first instance. The individual in society is only rarely significantly expressive in his own right. For the vast majority of human beings the choice lies between unchanging custom and the legitimate caprice of custom, which is fashion.

Fashion concerns itself closely and intimately with the ego. Hence its proper field is dress and adornment. There are other symbols of the ego, however, which are not as close to the body as these but which are almost equally subject to the psychological laws of fashion. Among them are objects of utility, amusements and furniture. People differ in their sensitiveness to changing fashions in these more remote forms of human expressiveness. It is therefore impossible to say categorically just what the possible range of fashion is. However, in regard to both amusements and furniture there may be observed the same tendency to change, periodicity and unquestioning acceptance as in dress and ornament.

Many speak of fashions in thought, art, habits of living and morals. It is superficial to dismiss such locutions as metaphorical and unimportant. The usage shows a true intuition of the meaning of fashion, which while it is primarily applied to dress and the exhibition of the human body is not essentially concerned with the fact of dress or ornament but with its symbolism. There is nothing to prevent a thought, a type of morality or an art form from being the psychological equivalent of a costuming of the ego. Certainly one may allow oneself to be converted to Catholicism or Christian Science in exactly the same spirit in which one invests in pewter or follows the latest Parisian models in dress. Beliefs and attitudes are not fashions in their character of mores but neither are dress and ornament. In contemporary society it is not a fashion that men wear trousers; it is the custom. Fashion merely dictates such variations as whether trousers are to be so or so long, what colors they are to have and whether they are to have cuffs or not. In the same way, while adherence to a religious faith is not in itself a fashion, as soon as the individual feels that he can pass easily, out of personal choice, from one belief to another, not because he is led to his choice by necessity but because of a desire to accrete to himself symbols of status, it becomes legitimate to speak of his change of attitude as a change of fashion. Functional irrelevance as contrasted with symbolic significance for the expressiveness of the ego is implicit in all fashion.

Chapter 4

Agnes Brooks Young

FASHION HAS ITS LAWS

[. . .]

IF IT IS REALLY TRUE that the changes of fashion in women's dress follow well-defined rules, there must be some good explanation to account for the fact that these rules were not discovered long ago. The explanation needs to cover much more than our prolonged tardiness in discovering the rules or the laws which govern the changes in fashion; it needs to show convincingly the possibility that such laws can exist. During all our modern period, and even in ancient times, the literatures of many nations have expressed the general belief of mankind that the fashions of women's dress are fickle, disorderly, capricious, and utterly unpredictable. The evidence here presented seems to show that these almost universally accepted beliefs are not valid. And so we need to consider just how the illustrations of dresses reproduced in this book differ as evidence from those scores of previous volumes.

The illustrations in this book, showing the dresses worn year by year over a century and three quarters, have been most carefully selected as representing the most fully typical dresses of each year. This sort of selection has not been attempted in previous studies, which have instead mainly shown dresses that were striking examples of those worn in selected periods, or costumes of notable people, or modes chosen to exemplify some particular feature of the fashions of a period. Probably it is true that most of the illustrations in the published histories of fashion really represent exceptional styles of their years rather than typical ones. And it may well be that the almost universally accepted beliefs in the lawlessness of fashion have tended to influence students toward selecting exceptional costumes as subjects of discussions.

Perhaps the distinction may be made clearer if we consider the analogy of the studies that economists make of the movements of stock prices. Here is a field of activity in which change is going on constantly, and in which the numbers of individual changes are almost limitless. Every day the prices of great numbers of individual securities advance, while those of numerous others decline, and still others remain unchanged. Nevertheless, there is in reality a general average change over long periods, first in one direction and then in the other. And these general tendencies produce the long advances which stock traders call bull markets, and the declines which they term bear markets. Economists call them market cycles.

The individual declines are numerous even while general prices are advancing in bull markets. And there are many advances throughout the periods of generally decreasing prices in bear markets. But the long term trends cannot be judged or studied by noting these exceptions. We have in this country detailed records of millions of changes in security prices extending back over more than one hundred years, but it is only during the past forty years or so that students of such matters have learned how to use the average price changes of selected typical stocks to measure the central tendencies of the long term changes. By studying these typical movements instead of the individual ones they have identified the cycles, and almost all economic knowledge of these matters has been developed in recent years since these new methods were employed.

This study of typical fashions in women's dress, arranged in unbroken annual sequence for 178 years, reaches conclusions which may well be stated here at the outset in brief outline. These conclusions are that in modern times the changes in prevailing fashions in women's dress have moved through a series of recurring cycles lasting for about a third of a century each; that during each cycle the annual fashion changes have been variations and modifications from one central type fashion; and finally that there have been in all only three of these central types of fashion, which have succeeded one another in unchanging sequence over the past two centuries.

[. . .]

The concept of the existence of typical fashions in women's dress in a given year is implicit in the very nature of fashion itself. Many women can tell at a glance which ones among the other women they meet at a social gathering are wearing this year's dresses. They can tell it as surely as the automobile dealer can recognize at a glance this year's Buick and last year's model, without needing to examine the serial numbers. The reason why the woman who is keenly interested in fashion, and well informed about it, can immediately recognize this year's fashions is that there is always a typical annual fashion, as well as numerous modifications of it and many variants from it.

The controlling factor in changes in women's dress is that all women desire to wear each year dresses which are sufficiently different from those of last year so as to be unmistakably recognizable by the initiated as being of the latest mode, and yet at the same time neither identical with those of other women, nor so different from them as to be undesirably conspicuous. This governing principle in fashion has long been recognized, and more than a century ago the English critic, Hazlitt, made the penetrating observation that the two things which fashion abhors most are vulgarity and singularity. He also wrote that fashion was gentility fleeing from vulgarity.

Fashion in dress is a process of continuous slow change of typical annual modes, accompanied each year by innumerable slight variations from the dominant type. The changes must be continuous, for otherwise the fashion would promptly cease to be fashionable. It must be sufficiently rapid to out mode previous fashions every year, but it must be sufficiently slow to prevent the leaders from outdistancing their followers. It follows from these inexorable conditions, which control the evolution of fashions in women's dress, that the annual change which outmodes annually the styles of the year before must be a slight but significant alteration in the central type of generally accepted costume, from which the numberless modifications are restricted variations. If we can surely identify these most truly typical styles year by year over a long period of time, we shall have the material for studying and comparing them, and for tracing and even measuring their changes. That is what this book undertakes to do.

The continuous process of change which we call fashion is not handicapped by any compulsion to make progress. In a real sense, fashion is evolution without destination. The world generally considers that progress in material things consists in changes that make them more useful, or better looking, or less expensive. In the long run fashion never attains these objectives. Its ideal is slow continuous change, unhampered by the restrictions of either aesthetics or practicality.

This piece of research began to assume its present form when the writer first realized that it would not be possible for annual fashion changes regularly to out-mode existing styles unless practically all the fashionable dresses of each year possessed in common certain rather definite characteristics. It is because they do possess in common those particular characteristics that they belong to the mode of that year, and not to that of some other year. And it is the alteration of those essential style characteristics by the annual fashion change which outmodes them and replaces them by a new set of characteristics which constitute the style of the next year.

We may well restate this for emphasis. We know that fashion outmodes previous styles each year, so there must be a continuous change under way. We know this continuous change must be relatively slow because only the initiated can recognize the differences from one year to the next Finally, if fashion in dress is a slow continuous change, outmoding each year that which had general acceptance, and substituting for it something slightly different, then there must of necessity always exist a typical expression of fashion, or a typical style, on which the changes are operating. If there were numerous types, no one change could outmode them all, and if there were numerous annual changes, there could be no accepted fashion. The conclusion must be that the process of fashion is a process of slow continuous change of typical costumes. Fashion always tolerates, encourages, and even requires each year numerous variations from the central type. But the typical fashion exists and it is on it that the annual changes that are essentially significant and controlling take place.

It is because the dresses that are in fashion in a given year do possess in common certain features which might be technically termed their differentiating fashion characteristics that it becomes possible to identify a typical fashion for each year. These typical dresses, illustrated in later chapters, are the ones selected from the available costumes of each year as most fully combining in themselves the differentiating fashion characteristics of their years. In the following chapter there is a description of the method by which these selections of the annual typicals were made. The methods were the product of much experimenting and careful testing, and though they now appear relatively simple, it is believed that they are reliable and produce adequately accurate results.

The final outcome of this part of the undertaking was the assembling of the continuous annual series of illustrations of the typical yearly fashions prevailing in women's daytime dresses from 1760 to the present time. These illustrations should show, and it is believed that they do faithfully show, what really happened during that long span of years in the prevailing trends and dominant currents of fashion change. In this series the illustrations for the first thirty years or so are less surely typical of the fashions which prevailed in those years than are the illustrations for the later periods, when the material available for selection is much more ample in volume, and so affords better evidence to tell us what the fashions and their changes actually were.

After considerable experimenting, it was decided to make up the series wholly from street and daytime dresses, and to exclude evening gowns. The reason for this was partly that only a small proportion of the feminine population ever wears evening gowns, and partly because evening dresses always tend to be extreme in their rendering of the current modes, and often feature fashion trends which are short-lived. The daytime dresses from which the selections of the annual typicals were made may be decribed as being the kinds of dresses which women wore in each year for daytime calls and for shopping.

As this long series of illustrations was being worked over and having its gaps filled in, and being improved as new material became available in collections of fashion prints and in the stacks and files of libraries here and abroad, it gradually became apparent that change in women's dress has not only been going on constantly during the past 178 years, but also that the changes have moved in a series of well-defined cycles, each of which has lasted for something more than thirty years.

In some ways the fact that fashions move in cycles is not a novel idea. Everyone who has given even the slightest attention to the history of modern dress knows that at about the time of our Civil War, and for a good many years before that, hoop skirts were in fashion and constituted the most dominant feature of women's dress. Again, the older people among us can remember that after the Civil War and for a long period extending perhaps to about the turn of the century, women commonly wore dresses with skirts which were extended backwards by the use of bustles, or by some substitute arrangement having the same effect.

Finally, we all realize that since about the beginning of this century prevailing dress fashions have excluded both hoops and bustles and have dictated that dresses should be more nearly form-fitting. Here we have then in modern times three periods of not greatly unequal duration in which prevailing fashions were dominated by the forms and contours of the skirts. In their aggregate those three periods cover something more than one hundred years. This book considers that each one of these three periods may properly be termed a fashion cycle, because each is clearly a well-defined entity possessing in its own right an individuality that entitles it to such a designation.

We are all accustomed to discussions of fashion which emphasize its lawlessness, its fickle character, its changeability, and the impossibility of predicting what it will do next. Nevertheless, it is clear that such characterizations are valid only in most restricted degrees, for we may always be safely confident that there are many changes that fashion will not make. It will not dictate that hoop skirts shall be worn in one year, skirts with bustles in the following year, and form-fitting skirts in the third year. In point of fact, it never in modern times has made any sudden changes. Fashion changes continuously, but always slowly, and as we shall see, its changes during the past two centuries have been in a series of well-defined cycles that have followed one another in regular and unchanging order.

In these three simple distinctions or classifications, which do not need to be substantiated by any extended historical research, we have a hint of the possible existence of cycles in fashion changes. It was in part this very hint which led to the conclusion that there has been under way ever since 1760 a succession of well-defined style cycles and that the distinguishing characteristic by which these cycles have been marked has been the shape of the skirts.

In the long process of selecting the illustrations of the most truly typical fashions for each of the 178 years, the procedure was adopted of arranging the tracings or photostats of the fashion plates on long rows of card tables, and then comparing, assorting, discarding and substituting in accord with the statistical evidence that was being compiled concerning them. When the series of typical skirts was nearing final form, it became evident to anyone who would walk to and fro along the tables on which the pictures were arranged in chronological order, year after year, and decade after decade, that minor fashion changes had taken place every year in the long period of over a century and three quarters, but that major changes in the types of dresses approved by fashion had occurred only every three or four decades.

For example, the hoop skirt was not a fashion of short, sporadic occurrences, but the dominating factor in the typically accepted fashions of every year from about 1830 to 1870. Clearly that span of almost four decades was a hoop-skirt period in women's fashions, and all the numerous changes and variations in other features or details of accepted costumes are subordinate facts compared with this major and dominating one. It may be noted in passing that this is referred to as a hoop-skirt period in a popular use of that term, rather than in a technically accurate one, for many of the dresses of that time did not, in fact, have hoops.

Continued analysis and inspection, based on this observation of the characteristics of the hoop-skirt period, showed that a classification based on the types of skirts would be equally valid for the entire period from 1760 to date. During the first four decades of that long span of years the typical fashions were those of dresses having bustles, or at least extended backward much as they would have been if actually supported behind by bustles. American women of our Revolutionary War period wore gowns of that sort. There followed a period of several decades when dresses were generally tubular in form, much as are those to which we are accustomed today. Next came the hoop-skirt period, then the dresses with bustles or back-fullness, which were worn up to and even beyond the time of the War with Spain, and finally this present period of tubular skirts.

The conclusion which was borne in upon one who walked back and forth in front of the tables on which were arranged the pictures showing the typical fashions for the 178 years was that the only really major fashion changes were those in the types of skirts. This was clear in spite of the fact that change of some sort was continuous, and constantly bringing about such alterations as that of sleeves from long and tight to short and full, or neck lines from deep v-shaped to high, or repeated shifts in the waist line. Moreover, during this entire span of years there had been only three of these skirt types.

Each type, when definitely established, had maintained its dominance for three or four decades, and then had given way to one of the other two types. If these general inferences can be fully supported by the evidence, they lead to the conclusions that the determining factor in major fashion types is the general form of the skirt, and that the period of years during which one definite type of skirt characterizes the accepted fashions of dress may properly be termed one fashion cycle.

The three types of skirts are illustrated in [Figure 4.1, which shows] figures in solid line and the three types of skirts in dotted outline. The first figure stands squarely in the center of a large bell, which is wide at the base; the second stands at the front of a skirt with all the fullness at the back; and the third stands in a cylinder, which has almost the same width at top and bottom.

The classification of fashions on the basis of the skirt is not new. It was primarily to skirt structure that Grand-Carteret referred when he wrote: "The two conceptions of fashion; the one is built out from the woman's body by all sorts of contrivances; the other more or less follows its lines." Outside of these two principles, he points out, there can only be half-measures.

Clearly his division is both valid and important, but it would be more so if he had noted that fashions of one type persist for long periods of years, and that the supporting framework which forms the basis of one of his classifications is of two distinct sorts. Though his figure-conforming group yields to no logical subdivision, the built-out class may readily be divided into skirts which are held away from the figure all the way around, after the manner of the hoop, and those which protrude only in back. As each of these styles completely dominated fashion for approximately a third of the last century, there seems good reason to regard them both as major fashions.

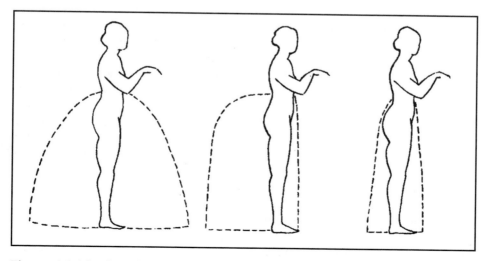

Figure 4.1 The three fundamental skirt contours

If we could have the 178 pictures of typical fashions reproduced on as many cards, which we could hold in our hands like playing cards, we would find that they could easily be sorted into the three groups. The principle which would govern the sorting would be the relation of the mass of the skirt to the figure beneath. When the sorting was finished and the resulting three piles examined, they would be seen to contain dresses like those which appear in silhouette [in Figures 4.2, 4.3 and 4.4.]

The first of these illustrations . . . represents dresses in which the figure stands at the front of the skirt with the bulk in the back. This sort of contour has been referred to as the bustle type, but since for the student of costume the term "bustle" has a special and restricted connotation, it may be wiser to call this the back-fullness type. It will then include any dress having this characteristic structure, whether the dress has an actual bustle beneath or is made to protrude simply by its own bulk, for obviously dresses having this shape belong to this group, no matter how they are made.

The little silhouettes show, in fact, that the back-fullness effect was achieved in a number of ways . . . They show a good deal of variety in the size of this back-fullness, which was sometimes enormous and protruded like a shelf from the waist, as in 1790, 1875 and 1885, and sometimes small and rather lower down, as in 1880. Now and again the dresses were somewhat short, as that of 1780, and at other times they developed trains, as in 1875 and 1895 The differences between the little figures are, in fact, considerable, but it is interesting to observe that the back-fullness effect which is common to them all loses nothing thereby. On the contrary, it seems to emerge all the more clearly as a fundamental structural principle.

The next group of illustrations [Figure 4.3] represents the tubular type . . . There are more illustrations on this page because their slimness makes it possible, not because there were more variants of this type of skirt. They comprise Grand-Carteret's group of dresses, which follow more or less the natural lines of the figure without an attempt to create an artificial form. Many of these dresses we can remember from our own experience.

The chief difference between dresses in this group is in the length of the skirts, which range all the way from the extremely short skirts, which were in fashion between 1925 and 1930, to those which touch the floor. Great as this difference is, however, it does no damage to the characteristic appearance of the type. This is true of short skirts in the other two types as well, and might be illustrated by pictures of little girls in their short dresses at the time of hoops, of bustles, and the present day. The three typical contours would be, in fact, as clearly marked as in adult clothing, though the little girls wear dresses reaching only to their knees.

A similar comment might be made about trains, in that they may be added to any of the three types without destroying the type characteristic. Understandably enough, trains were seldom so universal as to be worn on the majority of daytime dresses and so only appear occasionally in the series of typical fashions, but neverthe-less they were worn during the dominance of each of the three types. That even tubular skirts may have trains without losing their tubular form, every woman knows who can remember them on the hobble-skirted evening dresses in 1913 and 1914.

In width, the skirts in this tubular group range all the way from the extremely tight hobble to the fashion of 1825, which is almost as full as it can be and still be

Figure 4.2 Recurring examples of the back-fullness contour

1805   1810   1815

1820   1825   1910   1915

1920   1925   1930   1935

Figure 4.3 Recurring examples of the tubular contour

Figure 4.4 Recurring examples of the bell-shaped contour

classed as tubular. This last, in fact, represents the skirt as it looked when on the verge of discarding altogether the tubular form and taking on the bell-shaped contour, which is illustrated [in Figure 4.4].

This third page of silhouettes represents skirts which form a wide circle at the bottom and taper upward to the waist. This cannot correctly be called the hoop-skirt type, because actual hoops were worn only for a part of the long period during which this type was popular, nor can we name it after the crinoline for the same reason. Long ago such skirts were occasionally referred to as bee-hive skirts, because they were similar in outline to the plaited straw hives of a former day The simile is a good one, but the name is perhaps too unfamiliar for modern use, and for this reason it might be well to substitute the less descriptive term "bell-shaped." The dresses on this page are all so similar that little need be said about them beyond noting that there are slight differences in length and width and location of waist line.

The illustrations on these three pages with their accompanying dates show that though each type dominated fashion for long periods, no one of them retained an absolutely static form. Examination of the yearly typicals brought out the further interesting fact that the variants which each type produces were great enough to keep fashion constantly changing. In fact, during the whole 178 years women were under the constant necessity of renewing their wardrobes in order not to be out of fashion, exactly as they are today, and the change was so fast for those who could afford the pace that clothes had continually to be discarded long before they were worn out. In this way the variants within the types fed the endless craving for novelty and provided for the perpetual change which has been recognized since ancient times as an outstanding characteristic of fashion. It is no contradiction, but a generalization which fits all three types, to say that though fashion retained given structural characteristics for long stretches, fashion never stood still. A type might then be defined as a given structural characteristic including numerous variants.

The evidence which was furnished by the bringing together of the year-by-year fashions which were the actual prevailing typical dresses of women in Europe and America for the past 178 years might be summarized by saying that during this long period feminine dress was of three main types and may be classified into three basic groups. The classification is guided by the skirt, and in reality by the contour and mass of the skirt in its relation to the figure beneath.

Each of the three types, back-fullness, tubular and bell, lasted for long periods of time, during which its characteristic structure completely dominated fashion. During these periods of dominance a regular and steady change occurred annually— and almost it might be said, seasonally—but in such a way as to preserve the dominant form of the type, the change taking place, as it were, within the boundaries of the dominant silhouette. Fashion in modern times has consistently followed this pattern of evolutionary change based on the contour of the skirt.

The conclusion that fashion has followed a regular course conflicts with ancient and firmly held beliefs in the lawlessness of style. Probably it is true that the literatures of all modern nations contain somewhat bitter and cynical expressions of the general conviction that it is futile to apply the rules of reason to the vagaries of women's dress. Modern civilization has accepted as axiomatic the proposition that women's fashions could not be judged or compared or even discussed in any common-sense terms and so the attempt to do so ought not to be made. We know that it is not merely a modern attitude, for we find it as clearly expressed in the literature of classic antiquity in the Roman dictum that differences in taste must not even be discussed, *de gustibus non disputandum est.*

Despite this record of age-old conviction this book maintains that, during the past two hundred years at least, changes in women's fashions have conformed to the almost rigid rules outlined in this chapter, and that the changes have moved in cycles which have, so far, been more nearly uniform in length and more closely constant in character than any of the cycle series in business and industry that have been charted by the economists.

If this is true, it is clear that changes in women's styles are not arbitrarily created by a little set of fashion dictators in Paris. Each season the Paris designers present a number of variations on the mode, which become fashionable only if women all over the world approve them, and disappear rapidly into oblivion if they do not. There seems to be no doubt that the Paris designers are themselves swayed by and subject to the great cycle trends, and that their preëminence in their field depends on their ability to follow Chandler's recipe for leadership, "Look to see where the people are going and lead them where they drive you."

The fact that women's fashions appear to be in their major characteristics a series of steadily evolving variations of only three principal types, which have so far succeeded one another in an unvarying sequence, has much significance. The existence of typical styles carries the implication that fashion changes can be accurately recorded, studied and measured. The presence of a pattern in the change insures that fashion changes can profitably be charted and in some important respects can even be predicted.

Chapter 5

Ann Rosalind Jones and Peter Stallybrass

RENAISSANCE CLOTHING AND THE MATERIALS OF MEMORY: INTRODUCTION

Fashion

"**F**ASHION**,**" Elizabeth Wilson writes, "is dress in which the key feature is rapid and continual changing of styles. Fashion . . . *is* change."[1] Wilson is writing about modernity, but it was in the late sixteenth century that the word "fashion" first took on the sense of restless change. Indeed, "the fashion" as referring to "the mode of dress . . . adopted in society for the time being" is first recorded in the *Oxford English Dictionary* from 1568. As "fashion" begins to define the rapid shifting of styles in clothing, it does so largely negatively: fashion is "vnconfirmed"; it is "a deformed theefe"; it makes the wearer turn about "giddily." And yet its demands are inexorable. Not to obey fashion is to become oneself "stale, a Garment out of fashion."[2]

The innovative force of fashion was associated both with the dissolution of the body politic and with the exorbitance of the state's subjects. And this too was registered linguistically. "Fashion" extended its semantic field to include the sense of mere form or pretence ("worshipping God slyghtly for fashyon sake"). And at the very end of the sixteenth century, to "fashion" acquired a new meaning: to counterfeit or pervert. The Englishman's clothes, Thomas Dekker claimed, were not merely perverse but the epitome of treason:

> An English-mans suit is like a traitors bodie that hath beene hanged, drawne, and quartered, and set up in seuerall places: the collar of his doublet and the belly in France; the wing and narrow sleeue in Italy; the shorte waist hangs over a Dutch botchers stall in Utrich; his huge sloppes speakes Spanish; Polonia gives him his bootes; the blocke for his head alters faster than the feltmaker can fit him.[3]

As the clothes themselves condensed the geography of England's trading relations, they dismembered the body of the English subject. Critics of fashion nostalgically conjured up the "russet yeas, and honest kersie noes"[4] that had supposedly preceded the "traitor's body" constituted by foreign luxury goods.

There is nothing particularly surprising to us about this association of "fashion" with the world of expensive imports. But there was something surprising about the connection in the Renaissance. For "fashion" did not have changing styles of clothing as its naturalized referent; rather, it commonly referred to the act of making, or to the make or shape of a thing, or to form as opposed to matter, or to the enduring manners and customs of a society. It was thus the goldsmith's "fashion" (what would later be called "fashioning") which added value to the raw material that he worked upon. One could marvel at the "fashion" (form) of the earth and sky. One could note that "the seed . . . receiueth not *fashion* presently vpon the conception, but remaineth for a time without any figure."[5] Above all, in its verbal form, "fashion" had Biblical resonance. In the Geneva translation, Job says: "Thine hands haue made me, and facioned me wholy rounde about, and wilt thou destroye me?" And the Psalms repeat the notion that God's work is a work of fashioning: "Thine hands haue made me and facioned me"; "He facioneth their hearts euerie one."[6] The spelling of the Geneva Bible ("facion") emphasizes the derivation of "fashion" from the Latin *facio, facere*, to make.

But why, we should ask, did the notion of making come to bear both the glamor and the opprobrium of shifting styles of clothing? "Thine hands haue made me" – Job's response to God, but also and increasingly the response of the fashionable man or woman to his or her tailor. It has become a cliché that "the clothes make the man." Yet modern analysts of "fashion" have found it hard to think through the contradictory implications of the term. Focusing upon "fashion" as the rapid transformation of clothing styles, they have seen it above all as a dazzling play of surfaces. In doing so, they have repeated, even if to critique, the antithesis between clothes as the surface/outside and the person as the inside/depth. That antithesis is certainly not a new one. Indeed, it is embedded in classical theories of rhetoric in which the logic of the argument was its "body" and the figures of speech its "ornament" or "clothing." But this opposing of clothes and person was always in tension with the social practices through which the body politic was composed: the varied acts of investiture. For it was investiture, the putting on of clothes, that quite literally constituted a person as a monarch or a freeman of a guild or a household servant. Investiture was, in other words, the means by which a person was given a form, a shape, a social function, a "depth."

At the end of *Henry IV Part 2*, Hal, even before he is crowned, imagines the assumption of monarchy as the assumption of clothes: "Maiesty" is, he says, a "new, and gorgeous Garment" (5.2.44 [TLN 2930]). And then, seeing his brothers' sorrow at their father's death, he assumes that, too, as if it were a garment: "I will deeply put the Fashion on, / And weare it in my heart" (5. 2. 52 [TLN 2938–9]). One could, of course, take this as a sign of Hal's emotional shallowness. But such a reading effaces what is so challenging about the passage to a modern perspective: the notion that "Fashion" can be "*deeply* put on" or, in other words, that clothes permeate the wearer, fashioning him or her within. This notion undoes the opposition of inside and outside, surface and depth. Clothes, like sorrow, inscribe themselves upon a person who comes into being through that inscription.

To understand the significance of clothes in the Renaissance, we need to undo our own social categories, in which subjects are prior to objects, wearers to what is worn. We need to understand the animatedness of clothes, their ability to "pick up" subjects, to mold and shape them both physically and socially, to constitute subjects through their power as material memories. Memories of subordination (e.g. of the livery servant to the household to which he or she "belongs"); memories of collegiality (e.g. of the member of a livery company with his or her guild); memories of love (e.g. of the lover for the beloved from whom he or she receives a garment or a ring); memories of identity itself. For it is through the coronation service – the putting on of a crown and of coronation robes – that the monarch becomes a monarch. It is through the eldest son's ritual inheritance, publicly staged in church, of his father's armor, sword, and shield that the son "becomes" his father (the dead Earl of Arundel transformed into the living Earl of Arundel). It is through the putting on of tire and mantle that the boy actor becomes Cleopatra.[7]

Clothing is a worn world: a world of social relations put upon the wearer's body. "I will deeply put the Fashion on, / And weare it in my heart," says Hal. Sorrow is a fashion not because it is changeable but because fashion fashions, because what can be worn can be worn deeply. That the materials we wear work as inscriptions upon us is an insight more familiar to pre- or proto-capitalist societies than to fully capitalist ones. Anthropologists often have to learn how to understand their own latent care for such materials if they are to understand the cultures they analyze. Panetan, a Tubetube man, asked the anthropologist Martha Macintyre to explain the ring she was wearing, which had been her grandmother's; in response, he said:

> When it was her ring it was to show that she was engaged, but you hold that ring to remember your Grandmother. You can look at it every day and keep her in your mind. It is the same with *mwagolu*, the hair necklaces our ancestors wore during mourning. You wear your ring and it shows people [something]. Our widows wore a *mwagolu* and it shows – it reminds – herself and others who look at it.[8]

Clothing (by which we understand all that is worn, whether shoes or doublet or armor or ring) reminds. It can do so oppressively, of course. Why, for instance, should women alone have to recall the dead? But, whether oppressively or not, memory is materialized. Both ring and hair necklace are material reminders, working even when what is recalled is absent or dead. And if they remind others, they also remind the wearers themselves. This is the significance of Hal's "put[ting] on" of sorrow: sorrow will permeate him only if it acts with as much force as mourning clothes.

It is Hal's view, not Hamlet's, that we need to understand if we are to make sense of the constitutive function of clothes in the Renaissance. Hamlet, in a saying which is all too familiar, "know[s] not seems."[9] His mourning garments "seem" but he has that within, he claims, which passes show. But even Hamlet has been misheard in our haste to find a modern subject, untrammeled by the objects that surround him. " 'Tis not *alone* my inky cloak," says Hamlet, that shows grief. His grief nonetheless takes the material form of that very cloak. If he claims something in addition to his mourning clothes, those clothes are still a necessary part of his memorializing of his father. But Hamlet's appeal to inner depth, because of its very "obviousness," has less to tell us about clothes in the Renaissance than Hal's notion of "deep" wearing.

In *The Anatomie of Abuses*, Phillip Stubbes captures both Hamlet's sense of the literal superficiality of clothing and Hal's insistence upon the depth of the super-ficial. Stubbes reviles extravagant apparel as superfluous, a waste of money, a drain upon the English economy. But he dedicates such passion to apparel because it is a superfluity that has the power to constitute an essence. The physical presence of clothes makes them, in his view, more dangerous (more inward, one might say) than the inward workings of corruption. He writes:

> Pride is tripartite, namely, the pryde of the hart, the pride of the mouth, & the pryde of apparell, which (unles I bee deceiued) offendeth God more than the other two. For as the pride of the heart & the mouth is not opposite to ye eye, nor visible to the sight, and therefor intice not others to vanitie and sin . . . so the pride of apparel, remaining in sight, as an exemplarie of euill, induceth the whole man to wickednes and sinne.

Pride of the mouth, Stubbes continues,

> is not permanent (for wordes flye into the aire, not leauing any print or character behinde them to offend the eyes.) But this sinne of excesse in Apparell, remayneth as an Example of euyll before our eyes, and as a prouocatiue to sinne.[10]

Clothes, unlike the working of the spirit, leave a "print or character" upon observer and wearer alike. And, when excessive, they visibly imprint "wickednes and sinne." Through its ability to "print or character" the wearer, exotic clothing "*transnatureth*" English gallants, "making them weake, tender, and infirme."[11] Clothes give a nature to what previously had no nature; they take an existing nature and transnature it, turning the virtuous into the vicious, the strong into the weak, the male into the female, the godly into the satanic.

Not understanding this "transnaturing" power of clothes, modern commenta-tors (pursuing the purified "spiritual" logic of a later culture) have been puzzled and embarrassed by the central Protestant conflict of Elizabethan England: the vestiarian controversy. According to this later logic, reformers should have been worrying about theology and the nature of the sacraments, not about what clothes the priest should or should not wear. Yet it was precisely the latter question that most exer-cised radical reformers in later sixteenth-century England. For the priest's clothes were not a matter of indifference, a question of social decorum; rather, the surplice and square cap that Archbishop Parker insisted upon were attacked as the material-izations of the Whore of Babylon at the heart of the Church of England. Such vestments were, according to Miles Monopodios, the soldier-hero of a dialogue written by the puritan Anthony Gilby, "worse than lowsie: for they are sybbe [closely related to] the sarcke of Hercules, that made him teare his owne bowels a sunder."[12] Like Hercules's shirt, vestments would poison the wearer, corrupting his inner faith at the same time as they branded him with "the popes liverie."[13] Dr. Turner not only argued that no parishioner should listen to a priest who wore such livery; he also made an adulterer do penance wearing a "popish" square cap and trained his dog to bite the caps of visiting bishops off their heads.[14]

If the radicals believed that Catholics and Satanists placed "all their religion in hethen garments, & Romish raggs,"[15] they themselves saw such clothing as a form of transnaturing. They thus agreed with those whom they opposed on the animating and constitutive power of clothes.[16] As Edmund Spenser observed in *A View of the State of Ireland*: "mens apparrell is commonly made according to their conditions, and their conditions are oftentimes governed by their garments . . . there is not a little in the garment to the fashioning of the minde and conditions."[17] For Milton, the "free" and reformed subject could come into being only if one first discarded the "polluted cloathing" of Catholic ceremony.[18] And in *Areopagitica*, he wrote:

> I fear yet the iron yoke of an outward conformity hath left a slavish print
> upon our necks; the ghost of a linnen decency yet haunts us.[19]

Clothing has the force of an iron yoke, enforcing conformity; clothing has the ability to leave a "slavish print"; clothing is a ghost that, even when discarded, still has the power to haunt.

The rapid development of "fashion" (as we now understand that term) in the Renaissance has obscured the sense in which clothes were seen as printing, charactering, haunting. The centrality of clothes as the material establishers of identity itself is apparent in the early modern institution of livery, the custom whereby people were paid for their services not in cash but in goods, especially clothing. Livery included food and drink; livery cupboards, also known as "dole cabinets," were built to contain the allowance of food and drink given to people working in a household each night. (One from about 1500, now at the Victoria and Albert Museum, has an openwork wooden front to allow air to circulate around the edibles inside.) But cloth or clothes were so essential a part of such payments that the term came to have the predominant meaning of clothing that identified its wearer as the servant of a particular household or member of a particular liveried group.

Livery acted as the medium through which the social system marked bodies so as to associate them with particular institutions. The power to give that marking to subordinates affirmed social hierarchy: lords dressed retainers, masters dressed apprentices, husbands dressed their wives. But livery, as it dignified the institutions to which it identified people as belonging, also dignified the participants in such institutions. This mutually supportive interplay of loyalties is what was seen as being at risk by writers attacking sartorial anarchy, the tendency of modern Englishmen (and women) to dress as free-floating individuals rather than as representatives of groups defined by shared labors or loyalties. When Stubbes's Spudeus denounces vestimentary disguise, he does so because it is adopted to elevate single agents rather than to affirm the corporate entities that confer genuine social identity:

And as for . . . priuat subjects, it is not at any hand lawful that they should weare silks, veluets, satens, damasks, gould, siluer, and what they list . . . except they being in some kind of office in the common wealth, do vse it for dignifying and innobling of the same. But now there is such a confuse mingle mangle of apparrell in *Ailgna* [anagrammatically, Anglia], and such preposterous excesse thereof, as every one is permitted to flaunt it out, in what apparell he lust himselfe, or can get by anie kind of meanes.[20]

Stubbes wants to reserve sumptuous dress as the proper dignity of high office. He deplores the existing situation in which

it is very hard to knowe, who is noble, who is worshipfull, who is a gentleman, who is not: for you will have those, which are neither of the nobylitie gentilitie nor yeomanry, no, nor yet anie Magistrat or Officer in the common welth, go daylie in silkes, veluets, satens, damasks, taffeties and such like, notwithstanding that they be both base by byrthe, meane by estate, & seruyle by calling.

Stubbes wants clothes to place subjects recognizably, to materialize identities for onlooker and wearer alike. But he is forced to recognize what he deplores: that clothes are detachable, that they can move from body to body. That is precisely their danger and their value: they are bearers of identity, ritual, and social memory, even as they confuse social categories.

We began by noting that "fashion" as it is now conceived is above all about change. The connection between fashion and change emerged in the Renaissance, and was registered in such phrases as "shifting fashion" and "changing fashion." But fashion-as-change was in tension with the concept of fashion as "deep" making or as enduring cultural pattern. Renaissance "anthropology" developed as the collecting of the manners and customs of other societies. In 1520, Johann Boemus published a small but highly influential book entitled *Omnium gentium mores, leges, & ritus*; in 1555, this was translated into English as *The fardle of façions, conteining the aunciente maners, customes, and lawes, of the peoples enhabiting the two partes of the earth, called Affrike and Asie.*[21] To write about "aunciente" manners and customs was to write about "*façions.*" And what characterized such fashions was the supposed fact that, far from shifting, they endured. These "deep" fashions were portrayed in terms both of customs and of costumes. The travel writer recognized the alien by their clothes. But that, of course, presumed that the alien had a particular style of clothing. A society remembered itself visually and tactilely through what it distinctively wore, through its habits.

"Habit" (both clothes and "habitual" behavior) is at the furthest remove from the emergent meaning of "fashion." While the latter came to characterize the lability of an elite, the former suggested the persistence of cultural patterns. As Daniel Defert argues:

To confuse the meaning of habit [*l'habit*] in the sixteenth century with that of fashion [*la mode*] is an anachronistic illusion. Habit has the original connotation of *habitus*, which implies work upon the body. The serious expression of a judge or the reticence of a virgin, the hairlessness or the tattoos of an Indian, body piercing or asceticism, are all part of the *habit-habitus* which defines the mode of being of established groups and not the free choice of individuals.[22]

Clothing, as "habit," implies a cultural way of life. This was perfectly clear in relation to the "habits" that monks wore. As Defert notes:

> No sixteenth-century French dictionary defines [*habitus monasticus*] simply as "garment." The *habitus monasticus* designates the rule, the way of life, from which the garment cannot be disassociated: *l'habit-habitus* makes the monk . . . The garment is a rule of conduct and the memory of this rule for the wearer as well as for others.[23]

Indeed, anticlerical proverbs warning against the equation of monks' gowns with their behavior (for example, Rabelais's "L'habit ne faict poinct le moine" in his first Prologue, or Queen Katherine's "They should be good men . . . But all Hoods make not Monkes," in Shakespeare's *Henry VIII*[24]) made their point only by denying the antithetical assumption that costume and custom were mutually determining.

One can locate the determining features of "habit" in many early modern societies. Jennifer Wearden, for instance, has fascinatingly traced the clothing of Siegmund von Herberstein, sent by Ferdinand I, the Holy Roman Emperor, as an ambassador to Süleyman the Magnificent in 1541, after most of Hungary had been annexed to the Ottoman Empire. At the Ottoman court, von Herberstein was given a special gown of cloth of gold in which to be presented to the sultan. The gown was both a mark of honor and "a pledge of security." It thus points to the significance of clothing in the constitution of the social, since it was given to him as a gesture of incorporation. Such gowns had traditionally been worn by the sultan himself, so the transfer of the gown was an assimilation of the recipient to the body politic through the medium of the sultan's own body. In a book published in Vienna in 1560, von Herberstein memorialized this transfer by including a woodcut of himself in the gown that the sultan had given him.[25]

But in von Herberstein's gown, one can see the complex intertwining of fashion-as-social-incorporation with fashion-as-transformation. The gown was of Turkish cut, so von Herberstein was being reshaped by the *habitus* of the Ottoman court. Yet the gown itself was hybrid, since it was made from red Italian velvet dating from about 1500. An almost identical piece of velvet is now displayed in the Victoria and Albert Museum. The Ottomans had, indeed, been trading with Genoa since the fourteenth century and ambassadors from the West brought European velvets to Istanbul where they were highly valued. Two splendid kaftans of the late sixteenth and early seventeenth centuries in the Topkapi Sarayi Museum are made of Italian velvet. A kaftan attributed to Osman II (1604–22) is made from a velvet of about 1540, which is probably Italian although influenced by Spanish design, and a similar fabric appears in the gown worn by Eleanora of Toledo when she was painted by Bronzino about 1544. The history of von Herberstein's gown reminds us of the limitations of a European-focused history that, even as it traces the hybridization of

Europe itself through colonialism and trade, imagines its "Others" as "uncontaminated," without history. The latter view was, indeed, the founding myth of anthropology and was in turn to become the founding myth of tourism. The Other is imagined as eternally itself (Turkish, or Navaho, or Ashanti), subject to the mobile and restless observation of the European observer: the Other is changeless, outside of fashion; the European is the marker and bearer of fashion and of historicity itself. Against such an opposition, the gown that Süleyman presented to von Herberstein simultaneously records both the workings of fashion that brought Italian velvets to the Ottomans even as they brought silks, carpets, and other textiles from the Ottoman empire to Europe, and the rituals of incorporation, obligation, and memory.[26]

But such relatively equal gift-exchanges between powerful allies and antagonists were not, of course, the only models of exchange. Conquest, colonization, and slavery also provided the material base for radically unequal "exchanges," in which the appropriated goods were deliberately stripped of their "memories," memories that testified to violence and oppression. In place of such memories, the European colonizers manufactured their own myths of the "exotic," myths which memorialized the supposed heroism of the merchant adventurers (often, like Drake, pirates and slave traders) even as they purified the appropriated goods of the "unheroic" labors of their manufacture.[27] These unequal "exchanges," which tainted and haunted materialization, were one of the causes of an increasing uneasiness among the colonizing powers toward materiality itself. For paradoxically, as Europe imported goods from Asia, Africa, and the Americas in ever greater quantities, it increasingly asserted the detachment of the European subject from those goods. From this new perspective, to attach too much signficance to the power of clothes was to fetishize them — to endow "mere" objects with a power that would increasingly be appropriated as the sole prerogative of subjects.

Fetishism

In the introduction to his important book on *Material Culture and Mass Consumption*, a book that attempts to restore the significance of things to the making of culture, Daniel Miller writes: "an approach to modern society which focuses on the material object always invites the risk of appearing fetishistic, that is of ignoring or masking actual social relations through its concern with the object *per se*."[28] It is extraordinary that, in a book about the necessity and inevitability of objectification, Miller still seems embarrassed before actual objects. We are here at the end of a long trajectory that situates us as subjects (or rather, "individuals") whose interest in objects (including clothes) is characterized by disavowal. To care about things is to appear "fetishistic." Nowhere have antithetical political positions had more in common than in the denunciation of the materialism of modern life and of our supposed obsession with "mere" things. The force of that denunciation depends upon the assumption of a place before the fall into materialism, a society where people are spiritually pure, uncontaminated by the objects around them.[29]

The denunciation often draws either explicitly or (as with Miller) implicitly upon Marx. For was it not Marx who analyzed how an obsession with "material objects" effaced "actual social relations"? The answer is: no. No one has been less embarrassed by material makings than Marx. Marx's critique of capitalism is not a critique of "materialism."[30] Marx, of course, famously developed a theory of fetishism, but it was a theory of the fetishism of the *commodity*, not of the *object*. For Marx, the commodity comes to life through the death of the object. What defines a commodity always lies outside any specific object, and depends upon the equating of a specific quantity of paper cups with a specific quantity of coal or diamonds or academic books. Only if one empties out the "objectness" of the object can one make it readily exchangeable on the market. A shoe manufacturer who is obsessed with the particular shoes that he makes is almost certainly a failed capitalist. Capital needs to pursue profit and thus to detach itself from any particular object so as to transfer itself (to adopt Marx's animistic language) from one style of shoe to another, or from shoes to paper cups or armaments, as the market dictates. Capitalism could, indeed, be defined as the mode of production which, in fetishizing the commodity, refuses to fetishize the object. In capitalist societies, to love things is something of an embarrassment. Things are, after all, "mere" things. To accumulate things is not to give them life. It is because things are not fetishized that, in capitalist societies, they remain theoretically lifeless.[31]

To oppose the materialism of modern life to a non-materialist past is not just wrong; it actually inverts the relation of capitalism to prior and alternative modes of production. As Marcel Mauss puts it in *The Gift*, his founding book on pre-capitalist exchange, objects in such exchanges can be "personified beings that talk and take part in the contract. They state their desire to be given away." Things-as-gifts are not "indifferent things"; they have "a name, a personality, a past."[32] Similarly, in the livery economy of Renaissance Europe, things took on a life of their own. That is to say, one was paid not only in the "neutral" currency of money but also in material that was richly absorbent of symbolic meaning and in which memories and social relations were literally embodied. Yet new forms of trade, colonial conquests, and political and religious conflict within Europe put increasing strain upon these forms of embodiment, finally leading to the radically dematerialized opposition between the "individual" and his or her "possessions." As Igor Kopytoff notes, "this conceptual polarity of individualized persons and commoditized things is recent and, culturally speaking, exceptional."[33]

One aspect of this dematerializing polarity was the development of the concept of the "fetish." In a series of brilliant articles, William Pietz has traced the etymology and the function of the concept in early modern Europe.[34] Pietz argues that "the fetish, as an idea and a problem, and as a novel object not proper to any prior discrete society, originated in the cross-cultural spaces of the coast of West Africa during the sixteenth and seventeenth centuries."[35] The word "fetish" derives from the pidgin *fetisso*, which may be traced to the Portuguese *feitiço* (meaning "magical practice" or "witchcraft"). *Feitiço* has its root in the Latin *facticius*, meaning a manufactured as opposed to a natural object. "Fetish," like "fashion," is derived from the Latin *facere*: to make.[36] There was, as Pietz argues, a long history of distrust of the "made"; Pliny used the term *facticium* to mean "artificial" in the sense of "made to deceive," "factitious." This distrust was elaborated and reinforced by the Church Fathers, who associated *facticii* with idolatry, and hence, by extension, with witchcraft. Pietz notes, though, that the prior history of *facticium* cannot account for its specific emergence within Portuguese West Africa in the Renaissance to define "the problem of the social and personal value of material objects."[37] For the *fetisso* marks less the earlier distrust of false manufactures (as opposed to the "true" manufactured wafers and images of the Catholic Church) than a suspicion both of material embodiment itself and of "the subjection of the human body . . . to the influence of certain significant material objects that, although cut off from the body, function as its controlling organs at certain moments."[38] The *fetisso* thus represents "a subversion of the ideal of the autonomously determined self."[39]

Moreover, the fetish (in contrast to the free-standing idol) was from the first associated with objects worn on the body – leather pouches, for instance, worn around the neck, containing passages from the *Koran* (37). In 1625, the Cape Verdean trader Andre Donelha met a young African, whom he called Gaspar Vaz, on the Gambia river. To the "distress" of Donelha, Vaz, "a good tailor and button-maker," was wearing "a Mandinga smock, with amulets of his fetishes around his neck." Vaz claimed to be doing so because he wanted to inherit from his uncle, who believed in "the Law of Mohammed." To show his own belief in "the Law of Christ Jesus," he "took off his smock, beneath which he wore a doublet and shirt in our fashion, and from around his neck drew out a rosary of Our Lady" (38). No doubt, the clothes functioned as livery for Vaz, who became Donelha's interpreter. The contrasting garments materialized conflicting cultural and religious identities. Yet there is a surprising overlap between the so-called "fetishes" and the Catholic rosary. Both focus power in a worn object. At the same time, the naming of the the African amulet as fetish disavows the "fetishistic" quality of the rosary. The concept of the "fetish" was thus developed literally to demonize the power of "alien" worn objects (through the association of *feitiço* with witchcraft), while at first preserving the notion of the sacramental object. It was not, in Donelha's view, mistaken to attribute spiritual powers to an object; rather, it was necessary to distinguish between legitimate and illegitimate objects.

By the late 1590s, the Dutch began trading with the Guinea coast and, after the organization of the Dutch West Indies Company in 1621, they displaced the Portuguese. But the Dutch were Protestant. For them, there was no distinction between African fetish and Catholic sacramental object. In 1602, Pieter de Marees wrote of the Akans as having "divers Wispes of straw about their Girdles, which they tie full of Beanes, and other Venice Beades, esteeming them to be their Fetissos, or Saints."[40] Marees called the beads "*Paternosters*," explicitly conflating African "fetish" and Catholic rosary. Marees also refers to the "Ceremonies of their Idolatrous Fetissos":

> they hang a Net about the bodie [of their children], like a little shirt, which is made of the barke of a tree, which they hang full of their Fetissos, as golden Crosses, strings with Coral about their hands, feet, and neckes, and their haire is filled full of shels.[41]

The Dutch thus attacked "fetishes" for being, like the objects of Catholic worship, "idolatrous." That is, the fetish was said to personify and spiritualize "dead" matter (although in doing so it might indeed incorporate the demonic). At one level, then, the critique of the fetish became an extension of Protestant attacks upon

Catholicism. There had been an extraordinarily intense period of iconoclasm in the Netherlands in 1566, and iconoclasm, like the attack upon vestments, was central to Protestantism throughout Europe.[42] "Idols" were pulled down in churches, the Catholic sacrament itself derided as idolatrous.

Protestants saw idolatry as permeating everday life in the "over-reverence" for "mere" things.[43] The extreme form of such reverence was the devotion to relics, many of which took the form of "fetishes" that had been and could be worn. In 1535, the English reformers disposed of "the vincula S. Petri, which women put about them at the time of their delivery"; "S. Thomas of Canterbury's penneknyff and his bootes"; the Virgin's girdle "which women with chield were wont to girde with"; the "singulum of S. Bernard . . . sometimes lent for pregnant women"; the combs of St. Mary Magdalen, St. Dorothy, and St. Margaret.[44] In 1604, John Reynolds denounced the wedding ring as itself an idol.[45] There was a potentially democratizing impulse in these attacks upon the church's materializations, since they were aimed at the power of an elite to embody its own powers and memories to the exclusion of all others. For it was only the church that could sacramentalize an object, as it was only the priest who could "make" the sacraments themselves. But the attack upon such elite sanctifications slid into a critique of the animating powers of *all* objects. Moreover, as such animations were attributed to a corrupt ecclesiastical hierarchy, they were also and increasingly attributed to the "fetish"-worshipping African. The concept of the "fetish" thus emerged as the colonizing subject simultaneously subjugated and enslaved other subjects and proclaimed his own freedom from material objects.

This disavowal of the object has often been read as merely a ruse. In this view, colonial entrepreneurs proclaimed their detachment from objects, while "fetishistically" collecting them. But this constant repetition of "fetishism" as a category of abuse repeats rather than illuminates the problem. For colonial entrepreneurs did not, at least after the early stages, fetishize objects; on the contrary, they were interested in objects only to the extent that they could be transformed into commodities and exchanged for profit on the market. We need, then, to understand the economic, as much as the religious, motivation of the concept of the fetish. The Dutch, like the Portuguese before them, were intent above all upon finding gold in Africa. As Pietz notes, they discovered it in three states: as gold dust, as lumps of ore, and as the golden *fetissos* worn on the body. It was above all in relation to these latter forms of gold among the Akan ("cast into elaborate and varied animal, vegetable, and mythic forms") that European "fetish" discourse developed. What the concept of the "fetish" marked in economic terms was the site of a crisis in value. For, on the one hand, these fetishes were viewed by Europeans as "trifles" or "toys" and even as peculiarly valueless. Thus Nicolas Villault claimed that the fetishes of the Gold Coast were "inanimate things, and most often so filthy and vile that one would not wish to touch them."[46] On the other hand, if they were made out of gold, they were precisely what the Europeans were in search of. And yet the Akan did not distinguish between their fetishes primarily on the basis of "market value" (gold as against beads or leather). Their interest in the power of the inanimate did not, indeed, seem to be about "value" at all as Europeans understood the concept. Hence, Akan fetishes, even when they were golden, were often composed of a mixture of metals of which gold was only one. As a result, " 'Fetiche Gold' became associated with 'false gold' used in commercial fraud."[47]

The "fetish," then, came into being as a term of religious and economic abuse. As a term of economic abuse, it posited the Akan as a people who worshiped "trifles" ("mere" fetishes) and "valuable" things (i.e. gold) alike. This meant that they could be "duped" (goods that the Europeans considered valueless – beads, for instance – could be exchanged for "valuable" goods). But it also implied a new definition of what it meant to be European: that is, a subject unhampered by fixation upon objects, a subject who, having recognized the true (i.e. market) value of the object-as-commodity, fixated instead upon the transcendental values that transformed gold into slaves, slaves into ships, ships into guns, guns into tobacco, tobacco into sugar, sugar into gold, and all into an accountable profit. What was demonized in the concept of the fetish was the possibility that history, memory, and desire might be materialized in objects that are touched and loved and worn.

A by-product of this demonization of the fetish was the impossible project of the transcendental subject, a subject constituted by no place, no object – by nothing worn. "The Word *Fetish*," John Atkins wrote in 1737, "is used in a double significa-tion among the *Negroes*: It is applied to dress and ornament, and to something reverenced as a Deity."[48] The transcendental subject of modernity, on the other hand, "knew the value of things" – that is, disavowed any but a financial investment in objects. Clothes could be "fashion" – detachable and discardable goods – but they were less and less likely to be fashionings, the materializations of memory, objects that worked upon and transformed the body of the wearer. The sixteenth and seventeenth centuries, the period of our study, are of particular interest in the history of clothing because clothes were still material mnemonics in metropolitan centers even as they were becoming the commodities upon which international capitalism was founded.

Renaissance clothing

Renaissance Clothing and the Materials of Memory explores the contradictory implica-tions of "fashion" as "deep making" and as circulating goods. The first part of this book, "Material subjects," explores the function of clothes in the constitution of Renaissance subjects. In chapter 1, "The currency of clothing," we explore clothes as payment and as stored and circulated wealth. Servants, whether aristocratic attend-ants upon the monarch or the poor workers for a yeoman, usually received less of their income in cash than in material goods and benefits: lodging, food, cloth and clothing. Payment in cloth and clothing was a form of bodily mnemonic, marking the wearer's indebtedness to master or mistress. The liveried body, even though the livery was rarely marked as such, stitched servants' bodies to their households. Such clothes were "habits" in the sense that they were persistent material reminders of status and of incorporation. But because of their economic value, clothes could be traded for cash at the pawnbroker or fripper. The value of clothes, then, pointed in antithetical directions: on the one hand, they materialized social status and indebtedness; on the other, they were circulating commodities.

In chapter 2, "Composing the subject: making portraits," we return to the value of clothes to argue that portrait paintings were often supplements to the specific clothes that the sitter wears. That is, whereas portraits have often been seen as founding the interior self, we contend that they display a self that is constituted through investiture. At the simplest, aristocratic clothes were commonly far more expensive than even a full-length portrait by Van Dyck, and portraits were frequently painted to commemorate an occasion, such as a wedding, for which new and costly clothing had been bought. Moreover, the faces of the sitters were often sketched in haste, whereas the clothes were sent to the studios, where they exhibited a patience that their sitters had rarely if ever shown. If the sitters' clothes materialized their status, though, they also inscribed other forms of memory: the memory of the dead, marked by the mourning clothes of the living; family memories (such as the "C4" jewel that Queen Anne so often wore to commemorate her father, Christian IV); the memory of the beloved (through a glove worn in the hat or a locket held open); religious memory (such as an inherited cross, materializing the sitter's Catholicism); memories of incorporation (such as the "livery" that marked Sir Robert Shirley as Persian ambassador). The sitters are permeated by what they wear.

In "composing the subject," the act of material memorialization is arrived at through a collaboration between sitter and artist that itself depends upon a range of hybrid material forms (paints made from Mexican beetles or from lapis lazuli; clothes made from a variety of imported textiles). In chapter 3, "Yellow starch: fabrications of the Jacobean court," we turn to the fears that such material fabications engendered. If a person could be permeated by the material memories of what he or she wore, how could one construct a national subject from "foreign" materials? In the violent attacks upon yellow starch in the early seventeenth century, we trace the xenophobic fear of a subject undone by the contagion of foreign fashion, a fashion that is depicted as Catholic, effeminate, demonic, and poisonous. The poison of yellow starch is above all attributed to the manufacture of women.

In the second part, "Gendered habits," we turn to the relations between women's manufactures — spinning, weaving, needlework — and the attempts to produce "femininity" through the repeated habits of the body. We move here from "habits" in the sense of what is worn to "habits" in the sense of embodied disposition. In chapter 4, "Arachne's web," we explore the tension between the social insistence that women play a crucial part in the production of textiles, above all through spinning, and the fears that women will weave their way into the social fabric, a fear that we explored in the previous chapter. In Velázquez's painting, commonly known as *Las Hilanderas* ("The Spinners"), what is the relation between the plebeian spinners in the foreground and the mythological splendor of the tapestried room in the background? And what do Renaissance commentaries on the myth of Arachne and Minerva tell us about both the relegation of female labor to the uncelebrated work of spinning (Arachne as spider) and the creation of social memory in the narrative weavings of Minerva?

Chapter 5, "The fate of spinning: Penelope and the Three Fates," analyzes transformations of the story of Penelope in the Renaissance as a means of exploring the changing relations between spinning and weaving as forms of women's work. As weaving became dominantly a male profession, Penelope was recast as a spinner rather than a weaver. As a consequence, her woven narrative was displaced by praise for her spinning, the repetitive habit through which she came to embody a wifely industry both virtuous and meaningless. But the fate of Penelope in these retellings is contradicted by the myth of the Three Fates, in which spinning, far from being meaningless work, is the foundation of the social fabric.

In chapter 6, "The needle and the pen: needlework and the appropriation of printed texts," we analyze comparable tensions within needlework. Like spinning for poor women, needlework was the expected labor of aristocratic women, a supposed cure for idleness. But while needlework was often imagined, like spinning, as a bodily habit that inculcated virtue through meaningless repetition, elite women stitched their own versions of the social and political realm into the textile narratives they made. These narratives were usually taken from engraving and pattern books, but in choosing specific models (such as Judith and Holofernes or the Gunpowder Plot) women reworked and transformed the imagined boundaries of the domestic and the political, the private and the public.

In the third part, "Staging clothes," we bring together the preoccupations of the first two parts of the book in an examination of the function of clothing in the English professional theaters. On one hand, we return to the concerns of chapter 1, exploring the relations between livery and the circulation of clothes; on the other, we explore how gender, class, and memory are materialized through worn habits. In chapter 7, "The circulation of clothes and the making of the English theater," we argue that the accumulation and circulation of clothes were constitutive features of the professional theater. The professional companies also offer us an extraordinary insight into the significance of the trade in secondhand clothes, since they recycled clothes from the court, the church, and the city. But while the companies partici- pated in the profitable circulation of clothes, they staged plays that as frequently emphasized clothing as forms of material memory. The companies spent large sums of money on clothes, but again and again they staged the haunting power of a ring, a handkerchief, a detached piece of clothing to connect the present to the past, the living to the dead, the present to the absent. The theater embodied the antithetical possibilities of clothing: as commodities which, in the form of props, took on only temporary meaning during the life of a performance and which could be discarded and replaced; as the imagined materials of memory itself.

In chapter 8, "Transvestism and the 'body beneath': speculating on the boy actor," we turn to the question of the dressing and undressing and the naming, unnaming, and renaming of the boy actor. It is as if the clothes literally re-member the actor's body, "transnaturing" it, as the anti-theatricalists claimed. Indeed, on the professional stage, the gender of the boy actor is usually marked by the donning of specific clothes. In a woman's clothes, he becomes Viola; in a man's, Cesario. Names emerge from prosthetic parts, the clothes that gender and regender the imagined body beneath. The theater plays with the problem of that body, above all in undress- ing scenes where the attachable parts that constitute a gendered identity begin to be detached. But if the body beneath can be imagined as male, it is also portrayed as permeable, open to transformation by the materials which it assumes and which, in turn, shape it.

In chapter 9, "(In)alienable possessions: Griselda, clothing, and the exchange of women," we address in a different context the problem of dressing and undressing. We here examine what it means to be clothed by the hands of another. The story of

Griselda was probably the most popular story of the Renaissance, told by Boccaccio, retold by Petrarch and Chaucer, and performed on the stage. Griselda, a poor peasant, is married by Walter, a prince. But this is possible only because he has first "translated" her, reclothing her as a suitable bride. Later dismissing her, he strips her of her courtly clothes and sends her home in her own undergarment. Dressing and undressing are embodied forms of naming and unnaming. But in the Admiral's Men's staging of *The Pleasant Comodie of Patient Grissill*, Griselda's gray gown, the garment of which she was stripped to reclothe her in courtly livery, hangs upon the stage as a counter-livery, a material mnemonic of her former self.

These material mnemonics are at the center of chapter 10, "Of ghosts and garments: the materiality of memory on the Renaissance stage." We here explore the persistence of the clothes of the dead as material forms of haunting. This is related to the wills in which the dying bequeathe gowns, doublets, petticoats, hose, rings to the family, the friends, the lovers they leave behind. What is the burden of these material memories? Who receives them? How do the living step into the shoes or assume the mantle of the dead? At the same time, the dead themselves return to the stage either in the "ghostly" clothes that they now wear, the sheets which are the shrouds in which they were buried, or, like Achilles and Hamlet's father, in the armor in which they lived. We conclude by looking at the ways in which memory itself is figured as and through permeable cloth and impermeable metal, torn shroud and burnished armor.

Throughout *Renaissance Clothing*, we focus on the making of the human subject through the worn things that shape the body and work as material mnemonics. Yet these worn things can be transferred from body to body; they can be appropriated or stolen. As memories, their meaning is neither given nor fixed. Even crown jewels, the symbols of royal splendor, can lose their magic by being turned back into pawnable commodities. But at the same time, the most worn-out piece of clothing can materialize an absent lover. Our argument is that fabrics were central both to the economic and social fabrication of Renaissance Europe and to the making and unmaking of Renaissance subjects.

Notes

1   Elizabeth Wilson, *Adorned in Dreams: Fashion and Modernity* (Berkeley: University of California Press, 1987), 3.

2   All quotations from Shakespeare are from *The First Folio of Shakespeare: The Norton Facsimile*, ed. Charlton Hinman (New York: Norton, 1968) and are followed by act, scene, and line numbers keyed to *The Riverside Shakespeare*, ed. G. Blakemore Evans (Boston: Houghton Mifflin, 1974) and then to the through line numbers (TLN) of Hinman's *First Folio*. William Shakespeare, *Loues Labour's Lost*, 4. 2. 18 (TLN 1169); *Much Adoe About Nothing*, 3. 3. 124 (TLN 1450), 3. 3. 141 (TLN 1457); *The Tragedie of Cymbeline*, 3. 4. 53 (TLN 1722).

3   Thomas Dekker, *The Seuen Deadly Sinnes of London* (1606) in *The Non-Dramatic Works of Thomas Dekker*, ed. Alexander Grosart (London: privately printed, 1885), vol. 2, 59–60.

4   Shakespeare, *Loues Labour's Lost*, 5. 2. 413 (TLN 2345).

5 William Tyndale, trans., *The New Testament* (1526), St. Luke 12.56; Thomas Bowes, *De La Primaudayes French academie* (London, 1594), vol. 2, 394.

6 *The Bible* (Geneva, 1560), Job 10. 8; Psalm 119.73; Psalm 33.15. On "fashioning," see also Stephen Greenblatt, *Renaissance Self-Fashioning: From More to Shakespeare* (University of Chicago Press, 1980), 2–3.

7 As Stephen Orgel observes: "What allows boys to be substituted for women in the theater is not anything about the genital nature of boys and women, but precisely the costume and more particularly, cultural assumptions about costume" (*Impersonations: The Performance of Gender in Shakespeare's England* [Cambridge University Press, 1996], 103–4. We are deeply indebted to Orgel's insights and suggestions.

8 Quoted in Nicholas Thomas, *Entangled Objects: Exchange, Material Culture, and Colonialism in the Pacific* (Cambridge, Mass.: Harvard University Press, 1991), 21.

9 *Hamlet* 1. 2. 76–7 (TLN 257–8). See also Hal's later disavowal of the significance of investiture in *Henry V* (4. 3. 26–7 [TLN 2270–1]): "It yernes [grieves] me not, if men my Garments weare; / Such outward things dwell not in my desires."

10 Phillip Stubbes, *The Anatomie of Abuses* (London, 1583), sigs. B6, B7v.

11 Stubbes, *The Anatomie of Abuses*, sig. G1.

12 Anthony Gilby, *A Pleasaunt Dialogue betweene a Souldior of Barwicke and an English Chaplaine* (London?, 1566), sig. K4v. Gilby was one of the translators of the Geneva Bible. For the controversy, see M. M. Knappen, *Tudor Puritanism: a chapter in the history of idealism* (Gloucester, Mass.: P. Smith, 1939), 187–216; Patrick Collinson, *Godly People: Essays on English Protestantism and Puritanism* (London: Hambledon Press, 1983), 325; and *The Elizabethan Puritan Movement* (London: Cape, 1967), "That Comical Dress," 71–83 and "The People and the Pope's Attire," 92–7.

13 Gilby, *A Pleasaunt Dialogue*, sig. C4v. Miles insists that the surplice, stole and tippet that Parker attempted to impose must be cast away as "a menstruous cloth" and as "Anti-christes Garmentes" that imprint "Idolatricall slauerie" (sig. K5, 15, K6v). "Christes lieuerie garmentes," in contrast, are the preaching of the word and purity of life (sig. K8v).

14 Knappen, *Tudor Puritanism*, 214, 205, 187.

15 Stubbes, *The Anatomie of Abuses*, sig. C5v.

16 For a later denial that the wearing of vestments and other "superstitious practices" were things indifferent, and therefore could be imposed by the state, see George Gillespie, *A dispute against the English-popish ceremonies obtruded vpon the Church of Scotland* (London?, 1637). Gillespie attacks the surplice and other forms of "idolatry" as "the wares of *Rome*, the baggage of *Babylon*, the trinkets of the Whoore, the badges of Popery, the engines of Christs enemies, and the very Trophies of Antichrist" (Part 3, 35).

17 Edmund Spenser, *A View of the State of Ireland*, ed. Andrew Hadfield and Willy Maley (Oxford: Blackwell, 1997), 72–3.

18 John Milton, *The Reason of Church Government* (London, 1641), 247.

19 John Milton, *Areopagitica*, in *John Milton: Complete Poems and Major Prose*, ed. Merritt Y. Hughes (New York: Macmillan, 1957), vol. 4, 348.

20 Stubbes, *The Anatomie of Abuses*, sigs. C1^{v}–C2^{v}.

21 The significance of Boemus's book may be gauged from the fact that between 1536 and 1611 it went through twenty-three reprints and revisions in five languages (nine in Latin, five in Italian, four in French, three or four in English, and one in Spanish). See Margaret T. Hodgen, *Early Anthropology in the Sixteenth and*

Seventeenth Centuries (Philadelphia: University of Pennsylvania Press, 1964), 131–43.

22   Daniel Defert, "Un Genre éthnographique profane au xvie: les livres d'habits," in *Histoires de l'Anthropologie (XVIe-XIXe Siècles)*, ed. Britta Rupp-Eisenreich (Paris: Klincksieck, 1984), 27 (our translation).

23   Defert, "Un Genre éthnographique," 28.

24   These instances of the anticlerical proverb are cited under "Cowl" in *The Oxford Dictionary of English Proverbs*, 3rd edn. (Oxford: Clarendon Press, 1982), 152. See Shakespeare, *The Life of King Henry the Eight* (3. 1. 23 [TLN 1643]).

25   For an account of the "excellencyes" of Eastern textiles, see the instructions which Charles I gave to the painter Nicholas Wilford when he was sent to Persia. He was particularly requested to "take notice" of the manufacture of "Cloth of Gould Silke with its colors and dies" (R. W. Ferrier, "Charles I and the Antiquities of Persia: The Mission of Nicholas Wilford," *Iran* 8 [1970]: 51).

26   All the materials for these three paragraphs are drawn from Jennifer Wearden, "Siegmund von Herberstein: An Italian Velvet in the Ottoman Court," *Costume* 19 (1985): 22–9. See also John Nevinson, "Siegmund von Herberstein: Notes on Sixteenth-Century Dress," *Waffen und Kostümkunde* (1959): 86–93, and Patricia L, Baker, "Islamic Honorific Garments," *Costume* 25 (1991): 25–35 on the presentation of clothes as honorific gifts. Baker notes that Muhammad supposedly gave his own cloak to a poet as a mark of respect. This cloak was used by the Abissad caliphate (750–1258) as the caliphal investiture robe. "After the 1517 Ottoman conquest of Mamluk Egypt and Syria, such a garment passed into the royal Ottoman treasury. On the fifteenth day of Ramadan each year, the garment was washed and the water, now containing *baraka* (blessings), was saved to fill phials for imperial distribution as gifts" (25).

27   It is perhaps surprising that trade with Asia, Africa, and the Americas was ideologically so prominent, given that the majority of trade was still between different regions of Britain and between Britain and Europe.

28   Daniel Miller, *Material Culture and Mass Consumption* (Oxford: Blackwell, 1987), 18.

29   Our thinking on subjects and objects in the Renaissance has been deeply shaped by Margreta de Grazia. See also the introduction to *Subject and Object in Renaissance Culture*, ed. Margreta de Grazia, Maureen Quilligan, and Peter Stallybrass (Cambridge University Press, 1995), 1–13.

30   See Karl Marx, "The Fetishism of the Commodity and Its Secret," in *Capital*, vol. 1, trans. Ben Fowkes (New York: Vintage, 1976), 163–77. For Marx's assertion of the *necessity* of "alienation" in the positive form of the imbuing of objects with subjectivity through our work upon them and of the imbuing of the subject with objectivity through our materializations, see his *On James Mill*, in *Karl Marx: Selected Writings* (Oxford University Press, 1977), ed. David McLellan, 114–23.

31   On the movement of objects in and out of commodification, see Igor Kopytoff, "The Cultural Biography of Things: Commoditization as Process," in *The Social Life of Things: Commodities in Cultural Perspective*, ed. Arjun Appadurai (Cambridge University Press, 1986), 64–91.

32   Marcel Mauss, *The Gift: Forms and Functions of Exchange in Archaic Societies*, trans. Ian Cunnison (New York: Norton, 1967), 55, 22. For developments and critiques of Mauss's theory, see Chris Gregory, "Kula Gift Exchange and Capitalist Commodity Exchange: A Comparison," in *The Kula: New Perspectives on Massim Exchange*

(Cambridge University Press, 1983), 103–17; Annette Weiner, "Inalienable Wealth," *American Ethnologist* 12 (1985), 210–27; Appadurai, *The Social Life of Things*, "Introduction: Commodities and the Politics of Value," 3–63; Marilyn Strathern, *The Gender of the Gift: Problems with Women and Problems with Society in Melanesia* (Berkeley: University of California Press, 1988); Thomas, *Entangled Objects*; Jacques Derrida, *Given Time: 1. Counterfeit Money*, trans. Peggy Kamuf (University of Chicago Press, 1992), 34–70.

33   Kopytoff, "The Cultural Biography of Things," 64.

34   William Pietz, "The Problem of the Fetish, 1," *Res* 9 (1985), 5–17; "The Problem of the Fetish, II," *Res* 13 (1987), 23–45; "The Problem of the Fetish, IIIa," *Res* 16 (1988), 105–23. See also his "Fetishism and Materialism: The Limits of Theory in Marx," in *Fetishism as Cultural Discourse*, ed. Emily Apter and William Pietz (Ithaca: Cornell University Press, 1993), 119–51.

35   Pietz, "Fetish, I," 5.

36   Pietz, "Fetish, II," 24–5.

37   Pietz, "Fetish, II," 35.

38   Pietz, "Fetish, I," 10.

39   Pietz, "Fetish, II," 23.

40   Pieter de Marees, "A Description and Historicall Declaration of the Golden Kingdome of Guinea," in Samuel Purchas, *Hakluytus Posthumus, or Purchas His Pilgrimes* (Glasgow: MacLehose, 1905), vol. 6, 280–1, quoted in Pietz, "Fetish, II," 39. De Marees' "Description" was published in Dutch in 1602 and published in English translation in 1625.

41   De Marees, "A Description," 319, quoted in Pietz, "Fetish, II," 43–4.

42   For attacks upon images in the Netherlands, see P. Mack Crew, *Calvinist Preaching and Iconoclasm in the Netherlands, 1544–1569* (Cambridge University Press, 1978) and David Freedberg, *Iconoclasm and Painting in the Revolt of the Netherlands, 1566–1609* (New York: Garland, 1987); for England, see J. Phillips, *The Reformation of Images: Destruction of Art in England, 1535–1660* (Berkeley: University of California Press, 1973); Margaret Aston, *England's Iconoclasts*, vol. 1, "Laws Against Images" (Oxford: Clarendon Press, 1988); and Eamon Duffy, *The Stripping of the Altars: Traditional Religion in England, c.1400–c.1580* (New Haven: Yale University Press, 1992).

43   On Protestantism and (de)materialization, see Stephen Greenblatt, "Remnants of the Sacred in Early Modern England," in *Subject and Object in Renaissance Culture*, ed. Margreta de Grazia, Maureen Quilligan, and Peter Stallybrass (Cambridge University Press, 1995), 337–45.

44   Duffy, *The Stripping of the Altars*, 384.

45   Aston, *England's Iconoclasts*, vol. 1, 467.

46   Nicolas Villault, *Relation des Costes d'Afrique, Appellées Guinée* (Paris: Thierry, 1669), 261, quoted in Pietz, "Fetish, IIIa," 110n.

47   Pietz, "Fetish, IIIa," 110.

48   John Atkins, *A Voyage to Guinea, Brasil, and the West Indies* (London, 1737), quoted by Pietz, "Fetish, IIIa," 110.

Chapter 6

Gilles Lipovetsky

A CENTURY OF FASHION

FASHION AS WE UNDERSTAND IT TODAY emerged during the latter half of the nineteenth century. Not everything about it was brand-new, of course; far from it. Still, it is clear that an unprecedented system of production and diffusion appeared during that period and was maintained with great consistency for a century. This historical phenomenon is what I want to emphasize here: technological progress and its own endless stylistic reversals or revolutions notwithstanding, fashion has not escaped what might be called a long-term structure. From the mid-nineteenth century to the point in the 1960s when the system began to crack and to transform itself to some extent, the organization was so stable that it is legitimate to speak of a fashion that lasted a hundred years. This was the first phase of the history of modern fashion, its sublime, heroic moment. A century of fashion: doubtless this is one way of saying that a cycle has ended, while stressing everything that continues to connect us most deeply to the phase that instituted a durable organization of the ephemeral. Of this hundred years' fashion, one might say without exaggeration what Tocqueville said of America: [1] more than a fashion, it is a metaphor for the advent of modern bureaucratic societies. More than a page in the history of luxury, class distinctions, and rivalries, it is one facet of the ongoing "democratic revolution."

Fashion and its double

Modern fashion is articulated around two new industries that might seem to have little in common. Their goals and methods, the articles they produce, and the prestige they earn are undeniably incommensurate; nevertheless, these two industries together form a single configuration, a homogeneous system in the history of the production of ephemera. *Haute couture*–initially known as *couture*–on the one hand, industrial clothing manufacture (*confection*) on the other: these were the two keystones of the century of fashion. The system was bipolar: at one extreme there were luxury items and made-to-order creations, while at the other there were inexpensive, mass-produced, ready-to-wear articles that imitated more or less closely the prestigious "labeled" models of haute couture. The creation of original models coupled with the industrial reproduction of copies the emerging fashion system was characterized by a marked differentiation in techniques, prices, reputations, and objectives, as befitted a society itself divided into classes with quite distinct life-style and goals.

The system as thus described is only a partial transcription of a more complex historical reality. There have always been intermediate organizations, low-level and middle-level couture, between the two poles. In France in particular, during the period in question, large numbers of women (60 percent in the 1950s) continued to use dressmakers or made their own clothes from patterns sold in stores or through fashion magazines. At the same time, especially in the highly industrialized countries (the United States, for example) where haute couture models could be reproduced legally and rapidly, manufacturing was not limited to low-priced production; manufacturers diversified their offerings and produced articles across a wide quality range, from modest to near luxury. Still, the overall schema can fairly be characterized as one in which haute couture had a monopoly on innovation and set the annual trends; clothing manufacturers and related industries followed along, producing goods inspired more or less directly and more or less immediately by haute couture but in any event offered at very different prices. If modern fashion was undergirded, then, by two principal axes, it nevertheless became for the first time clearly monocephalic.

To the extent that haute couture can be described as an unrivaled laboratory for novelty, the hundred years' fashion was essentially synonymous with feminine fashion. This does not mean that a parallel masculine fashion did not exist; however, the latter was not rooted in any institution comparable to that of haute couture, with its illustrious houses, its seasonal renewals, its parades of fashion models, its bold strokes, and its "revolutions." Compared to couture fashion, masculine fashion could be characterized as slow, moderate, steady, "egalitarian," even if it was also articulated according to the opposition between made-to-order and ready-to-wear. Haute couture is without question the most significant institution in modern fashion. No other fashion institution has had to keep on mobilizing a legal arsenal to protect itself against plagiarists and imitators; no other has given rise to passionate debates or enjoyed worldwide fame; no other has benefited from the steady, intense publicity of a specialized press. Extending a phenomenon that was already visible in the eighteenth century, modern fashion is feminine in essence.

The two-tiered order of fashion was not structured around an explicit objective; it did not even arise within an entirely synchronous time frame. Industrial manufacturing came before haute couture. Starting in the 1820s in France, following England's example, an industry for producing new, inexpensive, ready-to-wear clothing was established; it was flourishing by 1840, even before the age of mechanization inaugurated around 1860 with the advent of the sewing machine. As department stores gained a foothold as technology progressed and production costs were lowered, manufacturers diversified the quality of the goods they offered the lower and middle bourgeoisie. After the First World War, manufacturing was profoundly transformed under the influence of an increased division of labor, improved machinery, breakthroughs in the chemical industry allowing richer colors, and—as of 1939—new textiles based on synthetic fibers. But despite this progress, the organization of fashion remained unchanged; until the 1960s, all fashion industries were subject to the dictates of haute couture.

In the winter of 1857–58, Charles-Frédéric Worth set up his own fashion house in Paris in the rue de la Paix. This was the first in the line of houses that would soon be known as haute couture. Worth advertised "ready-made dressed and coats, silk goods, top-notch novelties"; however, his real originality—to which contemporary fashion is still heir—lay in the fact that for the first time brand-new models, prepared in advance and changed frequently, were presented to clients in luxurious salons, then made to measure according to the client's choice. This revolution in the process of creating fashion was accompanied, moreover, by a major innovation in sales technique that was also initiated by Worth: the models were worn and presented by young women, prototypes of today's mannequins or fashion models, known then as *sosies*, "doubles." Fashion became an enterprise involving not only creativity but also advertising spectacles. In France, dozens of fashion houses sprang up following Worth's example and organized along similar lines. The 1900 World's Fair included twenty houses of haute couture, including Worth, Rouff (established in 1884), Paquin (1891), and Callot Soeurs (1896). Doucet, which later hired Poiret, opened its doors in 1880; Lanvin was founded in 1909, Chanel and Patou in 1919. The 1925 decorative arts show welcomed seventy-two fashion houses; in 1959, some fifty were registered with the Chambre syndicale de la Couture parisienne. These houses, many enjoying illustrious reputations, employed from one hundred to two thousand people, depending on their size and on the year, but their impact on the national economy was clearly out of all proportion to the number of their employees. The luxury industry represented by haute couture came to play a major role in the French economy, above all in clothing exports; owing to the prestige of the great Paris houses, this sector occupied second place in France's external trade in the mid-1920s.[2] During that period, an exceptionally prosperous one to be sure, prior to the Great Depression and its severe impact on high fashion, haute couture accounted single-handedly for one-third of France's export sales in clothing.[3] Haute couture sales represented at that point roughly 15 percent of all French exports.[4] Nevertheless, by the mid-1950s the situation had already changed significantly: the House of Dior, which accounted all by itself for more than half the total sum of visible and invisible haute couture exports, represented no more than .5 percent of all France's visible exports.

Although it came into being in the mid-nineteenth century, not until the beginning of the twentieth century did haute couture adopt the rhythm of creation and presentation that is familiar today. At the outset there were no collections to be presented at fixed dates, for models were created throughout the year, varying only according to the season. Nor were there organized fashion shows: these began in 1908 and 1910 and became authentic spectacles, presented at a fixed hour of the afternoon in the great fashion house salons. After the First World War, as foreign professional buyers acquired more and more models, the seasonal shows began to be organized at more or less fixed dates. From then on, twice a year, in late January and early August, every great fashion house in Paris presented its summer and winter collections; later, in response to pressure by foreign buyers, fall and spring (half-season) collections were presented in April and November. Collections were first shown to foreign agents, especially American and European buyers; private clients were admitted two or three weeks later. The foreign professionals bought models of their own choosing, generally with the right to reproduce them in major lines in their own country. Supplied with models and reference slips that provided the information needed to reproduce the garment, manufacturers—except for those in France, who, for obvious reasons of exclusivity, did not have immediate access to the season's novelties—could reproduce simplified versions of the Parisian creations very rapidly; in just a few weeks, their foreign clients could thus be dressed in the latest haute couture craze at reasonable cost, sometimes even at very little cost, depending on the manufacturing techniques used. As a result, and contrary to widespread belief, the effect of haute couture was not so much to accelerate fashion change as to regularize it. In fact, the tendency to rapid change in fashion did not arrive simultaneously with haute couture but preceded it by more than a century: by the end of the Old Regime in France, fashion had already acquired its frenetic rhythm. But prior to the haute couture period, the rapidity of change in fashion had remained a random phenomenon, driven somewhat chaotically by one variable arbiter of elegance or another. With the age of haute couture, however, renewal in fashion was for the first time institutionalized and orchestrated. Fashion became for the most part a biennial affair: the half-season collections did little more than offer hints of the fashion to come. In place of a fortuitous logic of innovation, we find a normalization of change in fashion, an obligatory renewal brought about at fixed dates by specialized groups. Haute couture brought discipline to fashion at a time when fashion was giving rise to an unprecedented process of innovation and creative fancy.

Fashion's decrees originated in Paris. With the hegemony of haute couture, a hypercentralized fashion appeared, entirely indigenous to Paris and yet at the same time international: Parisian fashion was followed by all the "up-to-date" women in the world. In this respect, moreover, fashion bears some resemblance to modern art, for its pioneers were concentrated in Paris and they developed a style from which national characteristics were expunged. The phenomenon is certainly not an entirely new one: from the seventeenth century on, France was increasingly recognized as the beacon of fashion in Europe. Dealings in "fashion dolls," those earliest ambassadors of fashion, became commonplace in the eighteenth century, betraying both the tendency toward uniformity of dress in Europe and the tendency for Paris to serve as the pole of attraction. Nevertheless, throughout this entire period the way people dressed continued to present certain recognizable traits characteristic of their respective countries: like painting, fashion retained a certain national character. Aided by manufacturing, haute couture on the contrary allowed fashion to break loose from the national grip by leaving intact only the model and its many copies, which were identical in all countries. Thus even though it remained subject to the luxurious authority of haute couture, modern fashion stands out as the earliest manifestation of mass consumption: homogeneous, standardized, indifferent to frontiers. Under the Parisian aegis of haute couture, fashion approached worldwide uniformity, a homogenization in space with a parallel diversification in time linked to the regular cycles of the seasonal collections.

As fashion was centralized and internationalized, it was also *democratized*. The rise of industrial dressmaking on the one hand and of mass communications on the other, the dynamics of modern life-styles and values, led not only to the disappearance of diverse regional folk costumes but also to the attenuation of heterogeneous class differences in dress: dressing in the fashion of the day become possible for an increasingly broad social spectrum. The most remarkable thing about this whole process is the contribution made by haute couture–a luxury industry par excellence–to the democratization of fashion. From the 1920s on, with the simplification of women's clothing that was symbolized, in a way, by Chanel, fashion indeed became less inaccessible because it was easier to imitate: the gap between dress styles inevitably narrowed. As soon as the display of wealth became a sign of poor taste, as soon as true elegance required discretion and the absence of show, women's fashion entered the era of democratic appearances. In 1931, the journalist Janet Flanner noted that Chanel inaugurated the "poor" style, introduced the apache sweater to the Ritz, lent elegance to the housemaid's shirt collar and sleeves, exploited the workman's scarf, and dressed queens in mechanics' overalls. Clear separations continued to set apart the dress styles of the various social strata, but what matters is that it was no longer obligatory for the upper classes to dress with ostentatious luxury. Such dress was legitimate only if it was discreet or even imperceptible; a certain "impersonal" and apparently standardizable simplicity took over the scene of feminine elegance. "Here is Chanel's Ford": the American edition of *Vogue* came to that conclusion in 1926 about a simple long-sleeved black dress. At the opposite extreme from aristocratic emphasis, the modern democratic style was incarnated in simplified, supple lines, in ostensibly unostentatious "uniforms." While the first revolution instituting the look of the modern woman can be traced to Poiret's suppression of the corset in 1909–10, the second and unquestionably more radical one arrived in the 1920s under the impetus of Chanel and Patou. Paul Poiret abandoned the corset and gave feminine allure a new suppleness, but he remained faithful to the taste for elaborate ornamentation, to a traditional sumptuousness in dress. Chanel and Patou on the contrary repudiated the strident look of luxury; they stripped away frills and affectations from women's clothing. Women would henceforth wear simple sheaths, cloche hats, pants, and sweaters. Chanel managed to dress society women in tailored jersey suits and grey, black, or beige pullovers. Patou created sweaters with geometric motifs and straight pleated skirts. From that point on it was chic not to appear rich. What Brummell's aesthetic claimed for men in the nineteenth century had won over the feminine universe in an entirely different way: flamboyant display was eclipsed in favor of the democratic aesthetic of purity, restraint, and comfort.

The heterogeneity of dress styles characteristic of the aristocratic order, in which ostentatious display was a social imperative intended to mark human and social differences in no uncertain terms, was replaced at the beginning of the twentieth century by a fashion that was "homogeneous" in tendency, based precisely on a rejection of the principle of lofty, majestic exhibition of hierarchy. "Before," according to Poiret, "women were architectural elements, like ships' prows, and they were beautiful. Now they resemble underfed little telegraph operators."[5] Social difference, no longer oversignified by dress, was now obscured by the decline in marks of visible sumptuousness. This dissolution of symbols of social distance clearly cannot be detached from the imagined democratic ideal of equality of conditions: in the long run, creatures recognized as being of the same essence cannot help offering self-images from which extreme disparities, blatant marks of a hierarchical gulf, are absent. At the deepest level of this revolution in women's clothing, following on the heels of an earlier revolution in men's dress, we find the advent of a society governed by the ideal of democratic equality.

The process was not lacking in a certain ambiguity, however. Indeed, luxury did not disappear, but it had to be treated euphemistically, as an irreplaceable value of taste and class refinement at the heart of haute couture. The democratization of fashion did not mean that appearances had to be uniform or equalized; new signs, more subtle and more nuanced, particularly in the realm of labels, shapes, and fabrics, ensured that dress would continue to mark social distinctions and social excellence. Democratization signified a lessening of the marks of social distance, a muting of the aristocratic principle of conspicuous consumption, along with the new criteria of slenderness, youth, sex appeal, convenience, and discretion. The fashion system that lasted for a century did not eliminate signs of social rank, but it attenuated them by promoting values that stressed more personal attributes.

Nor did the restrained democratic style carry the day with perfect uniformity. Alongside simple, lightweight daytime outfits, haute couture went on creating sumptuous, elaborate, hyperfeminine evening attire. The hundred years' fashion deepened the gulf between the types of women's clothing. On the one hand, there were daytime fashions for city and sports, governed by discretion, comfort, and functionality. On the other hand there were enchanting evening fashions designed to bring out the seductiveness of femininity. The democratization of fashion was accompanied by a *disunification* of feminine appearance: women's dress became much more varied in form, much less homogeneous. It could play on a greater number of registers, from the voluptuous woman to the relaxed woman, from the "schoolgirlish" woman to the professional woman, from the sportswoman to the sexy woman. The rejection of showy signs brought the feminine into the cyclic play of complete metamorphosis, the coexistence of disparate and sometimes antagonistic images.

More directly than the idea of equality, cultural and aesthetic factors sports, in particular–played a primordial role in the democratic revolution of feminine appearance. Even though they were not widely practiced, activities such as golf, tennis, cycling, swimming, mountain climbing, hiking, hunting, winter sports, and automobile driving helped modify the shape of women's clothing, slowly at first, then much more quickly after the First World War.[6] The cardigan sweater came in with golf; around 1890, the bicycle allowed for bouffant pants drawn in below the knee and, in 1934, summer shorts; at the turn of the century, swimming gave impetus to the innovation of sleeveless bathing suits with a rounded décolleté, followed in the 1920s by one-piece suits with bare legs and arms. In the 1930s, two-piece bathing suits left backs completely exposed. Skirt lengths grew shorter for hockey, skating, and tennis starting in the 1920s; in 1921, Suzanne Lenglen caused a sensation by playing tennis for the first time in a sleeveless white cardigan and a pleated skirt that came just below the knee. From the end of the nineteenth century on, sports clothes proliferated: in 1904, Burberry devoted a 254-page catalog almost entirely to ready-made sportswear. In the early 1920s, haute couture plunged into the sportswear sector: in 1922, Patou offered a first showing of sportswear and outdoor outfits; he opened his shop, "Le Coin des Sports," in 1925. Sports wear made its first "classy" appearance in that era: it was considered chic even for walking about town and eating in restaurants. Going out in shorts, exposing one's legs, arms, back, or midriff, gradually became acceptable: the bikini appeared in the late 1940s. The new supple, functional, sexy styles cannot be detached either from the growing popularity of sports or from the democratic-individualist universe affirming the primordial autonomy of individuals; these two things together set off a process that bared the female body and reduced the rigid constraints of clothing that had hampered the free expression of individuality. Sports lent dignity to the natural body; they allowed it to be displayed more directly, relieved of the excessive armature and trappings of dress.

Sports not only prompted an evolution in specialized dress, they made a crucial contribution to the changing lines of women's clothing in general by creating a new aesthetic ideal of femininity. Through the cult of sports, the prototype of the slim, svelte, modern woman who plays tennis and golf took over from the sedentary woman hobbled by her flounces and lace. The simplification of clothing in the 1920s, the elimination of gathers and frills in favor of restrained, clean lines, was a response to this new idea of lightness and energy drawn from sports. Between 1924 and 1929, Patou created all his designs on the same principles as his outdoor clothing and sportswear: "My clothes are made to practise *le sport* . . . I have aimed at making them pleasant to the eye and allowing absolute liberty of movement."[7] Forty years later, Courrèges's futurist lines of the 1960s, the "Courrèges effect," did nothing more than radicalize this process in the name of the identical values of physical comfort and well-being: "I have sought a dynamic fashion, with constant concern for freedom of movement . . . Today's woman is liberated. She must also be liberated physically. She cannot be dressed as a static, sedentary figure" (Courrèges).

In addition, it is impossible to ignore the considerable influence of trends in modern art on the democratic transformation of fashion following the First World War. The straight, flat-chested figure of the 1920s woman harmonizes perfectly with the cubist pictorial space comprising planes and angles, vertical and horizontal lines, geometrical contours and flattenings; it echoes Léger's tubular universe, the stylistic austerity introduced by Picasso, Braque, and Matisse in the wake of Manet and Cézanne. Feminine voluminousness and roundness yielded to a purified, simplified appearance analogus to the work of the artistic avant-gardes. Fashion learned a lesson from the modernist project that began with Manet, a project characterized, according to Georges Bataille, by the "negation of eloquence," by the rejection of "grandiloquent verbiage," and by the majesty of images. By abandoning the poetics of ornamentation and glittering display, couture fashion worked to desublimate and deidealize the female figure, in part; it democratized clothing styles in the climate of the new modernist aesthetic values that tended toward the purification of forms and the rejection of the decorative.

The democratization of appearance was matched by the extension and eventual generalization of a *desire for fashion*, a desire previously confined to the privileged strata of society. The hundred years' fashion not only brought divergent ways of dressing closer together, it also turned frivolous ephemera into objects of desire for the masses as it gave tangible form to the democratic right to fashion. Although increasingly broad strata of society had been gaining access to fashion over the centuries, it was only after the two world wars that the "right" to fashion gained a real foothold and won mass-market legitimacy. Earlier, when members of the lower classes imitated aristocratic dress they had been subject to sarcasm; that time had long since passed. What was deemed ridiculous in the democratic age was not so much imitation in fashion (apart from manifestations of snobbery) as being out-of-date; that was the new mass "taboo." The hundred years' fashion simultaneously freed personal appearance from traditional norms and imposed on all and sundry the ethos of change, the cult of modernity. Fashion was more than a right; it had become a social imperative. Through the magic of haute couture, fashion magazines, and fashion-plate celebrities, the masses were trained in the code of fashion, in the rapid variations of the seasonal collections, while at the same time the code of originality and personality was becoming sacred. One defining characteristic of the hundred years' fashion lies in the way an increasing demand for originality was accompanied by a synchronized, uniform, compulsory obedience to the codes of haute couture. Just as novelties were regularly prescribed for every season, immediately making everything that was done earlier out-of-date, fashion was followed step-by-step, as closely as possible; gaps, challenges, and antifashions began to be significant only in the 1960s. On the one hand, homogeneous trends were imposed and an "official" fashion was proclaimed every season; on the other hand, the public at large conformed and submitted to uniform standards of dress. Despite its organizational specificity, the moment just described was related to the rigid and standardized age of the fashion trades.[8] The fashion system that had been constituted in the name of the principle of individuality managed to spread only by imposing uniform, standardized norms, swallowing up the free play of personal difference. Along with disciplinary organizations and democratic institutions, the hundred years fashion helped detach our societies from the holistic, traditional order; it contributed to the establishment of universal centralized standards, and to the institution of the first phase of modern, authoritarian, individualist societies.

[. . .]

Notes

1   Alexis de Tocqueville, *Democracy in America*, ed. J.P. Mayer and Max Lerner, trans. George Lawrence (New York: Harper and Row, 1966), vol. 1, intro., p. 12.

2   Germaine Deschamps, "La Crise dans les industries du vêtement et de la mode à Paris pendant la période de 1930 à 1937," Ph.D. diss., Paris, 1937.

3   Philippe Simon, "Monographie d'une industrie de luxe: La haute couture," Ph.D diss., Paris, 1931, p. 102.

4   Jean-Charles Worth, "A propos de la mode," *La Revue de Paris* (15 May 1930): 295–311.

5   Cited in Edmonde Charles-Roux, *Le Temps Chanel* (Paris: Chêne-Grasset, 1979), p. 211.

6   A good deal of information about this phenomenon is provided by Bruno du

Roselle in *Le Mode* (Paris: Imprimerie nationale, 1980); see also Marylène Delbourg-Delphis, *Le Chic et le look* (Paris: Hachette, 1981).

7   Cited in Meredith Etherington-Smith, *Patou* (New York: St. Martin's/Marek, 1983), p. 55.

8   The 1960s, characterized by rapid and abrupt variations, especially in skirt lengths (mini, maxi), represent the last phase of that "directed" mass unanimism.

PART THREE

What fashion is and is not

Art and anti-fashion

HAVING INVESTIGATED the similarities and differences between fashion, clothing, dress and other near-synonyms of fashion in the Introduction, this section will take a slightly different approach to the question as to what fashion is and is not. It will begin to consider the relations between fashion and art and present some accounts of anti-fashion.

The question as to whether fashion is art or not is regularly raised in any number of forms by any number of media, from popular newspapers and magazines, to art galleries and academic journals. (See www.glamourmagazine.co.uk/fashion/chicest_link/Fashion_as_art/verdict.html (2001), 'Chic Clicks' exhibition 2002 at Boston ICA and Winterthur Museum of Photography, for example.) It is also raised by Yves Saint Laurent's 1965 cocktail dress, which is usually described as being 'inspired' by the modernist paintings of Piet Mondrian (see Laver 1969: 266, for example). Wilson's point (noted in the Introduction), that the study of fashion has often been seen as a branch of art history, could be interpreted as lending support to the idea that fashion is art. This is because fashion, like art, may be approached in terms of style, attribution and the accurate dating of artefacts. Also, the practice of exhibiting examples of fashion in art galleries goes some way to countering the suspicion that while art is eternal, fashion is ephemeral: the display of fashion items in glass cases, for example, lends them an air of permanence and suggests that they are worth keeping for longer than a season. And Richard Martin notes that the Dutch conceptual artists Viktor & Rolf have produced numbered, limited edition plastic shopping bags, white dresses, dresses made from collage and Modernist dresses, for example (Martin 1999: 111, 113, 114). Such 'artistic' engagement with the paraphernalia and objects of fashion serving, Martin suggests, is to show that fashion and art 'are similar if not identical impulses' (ibid.: III). And finally in this connection, it was noted in the Introduction to this book that Susan Ferleger Brades argues that art and fashion 'overlap' and pursue a common set of visual discoveries (Ferleger Brades in Hayward Gallery 1998: Preface). The idea that fashion is like art, or even the same as art, is one that is regularly posed, even if it is also one that is not regularly answered in any satisfactory manner.

The Rhodes/Rawsthorn confrontation from the *Observer* that is reproduced here introduces many of the usual suspects in the fashion/art case. Rhodes uses the ideas of 'artistic expression', 'beauty' 'museums', and 'practicality' to argue that fashion is a 'true art form'. And Rawsthorn uses the ideas of 'practicality', 'beauty' and museums, along with a funny story about Donna Karan, to argue that fashion is not a true art form. For Rhodes, having a useful, practical function is no bar to fashion being considered art, but for Rawsthorn it is precisely fashion's practicality that distinguishes it from art. Where Rhodes sees fashion's artistic nature as deserving of exhibition in museums, Rawsthorn considers that the 'best' fashion could be included in museums. And Rhodes believes that art and fashion are about 'artistic expression', while Rawsthorn argues that fashion is about exploring modern life and reflecting changes in contemporary culture. Finally, where 'beauty' is at best a by-product of fashion in Rawsthorn's account, fashion is 'always about' beauty for Rhodes. Expression, beauty and practicality are the foundational ideas for theories of whether fashion (or any other branch of 'design') is art or not, and Rhodes and Rawsthorn employ them in exemplary ways in the extract.

In her (1998) essay 'Is Fashion Art?', Sung Bok Kim attempts to address this very question. She notes that Diana Vreeland, one time editor of *Harper's Bazaar* and *Vogue*, for example, has no doubt that fashion is not art and argues that art is 'extraordinary' and that fashion is not (Sung Bok Kim 1998: 53). Her account of art also includes the ideas that art is something '*spirituelle*' and that it possesses an 'intangible vitality' (ibid.) while fashion is not and does not. While words like 'extraordinary', '*spirituelle*' and 'intangible' are of little help here (they possess and are given little useful sense), it is clear that her conclusion that fashion is not art is not inconsistent with the account of fashion being 'what people wear' that was advanced previously. If fashion is what modern, western people wear to go about their everyday lives, then it seems unlikely that those people would consider it art. The idea that the everyday can be art is one that many people are resistant to. Michael Boodro also argues that while fashion and art are similar in some ways and have often been closely linked, fashion is not art, because fashion is an industry and art is not (in ibid.: 54). However, it is difficult to uphold the idea that art is not an industry for very long. After all, artists may be said produce goods for sale to consumers in a market. The difference, which has remained unaddressed thus far, is one of whether artistic and fashionable production and reproduction are the same things.

Although it is not reproduced here, and despite that fact that it is about photography, Walter Benjamin's essay 'The Work of Art in the Age of Mechanical Reproduction' actually provides a more useful way of beginning to make sense of whether fashion is art or not. Writing in 1936, Benjamin argues that art possesses what he calls 'aura' and that mechanical reproduction destroys aura. Aura is the sense of uniqueness and authenticity that one feels before a work of art and it is a product of the piece of art's place in ritual and tradition (Benjamin 1992: 214, 217). Mechanically reproducible art-works are not in fact art because they do not possess 'aura'.

Being mechanically reproducible, they are available in many copies and this very availability destroys 'aura', the sense of uniqueness and the potential role of the artwork in ritual and tradition. On this account, fashion is not art for the most part because art is one-offs and fashion and clothing are potentially or in principle reproducible. However, we appear to be obliged to consider clothing one-offs, such as a bespoke suit or a handmade dress, as art because and to the extent that they are not mechanically reproducible in the same way that a Ford car or a pair of Levi 501s are mechanically reproducible. And it has to be said that some aspects of being measured for a suit – the repeated visits, one's belief in the truth of the tailor's pronouncements, and the sense that this suit is a unique product of a unique set of circumstances, for example – could well be interpreted as ritual and as part of a venerable tradition.

Another aspect pertaining to what fashion is and is not concerns what some analysts call 'anti-fashion'. This phenomenon does not refer to wearing green when blue is in, or to wearing flowery prints when geometric shapes are the rage. Ted Polhemus and Lynn Procter's account of fashion and anti-fashion (Chapter 8) may be traced back to Georg Simmel's 1904 essay 'Fashion'. Simmel argues that 'two social tendencies are essential to the establishment of fashion' and that if one or other of these tendencies is lacking in a society then fashion will 'not be formed' in that society (1971: 301). These two social tendencies are the need for isolation (the 'differentiating impulse') and the need for union (the 'socialising impulse'). What Simmel calls 'primitive societies' have no fashion because in such societies the socialising forces are much stronger than the need for isolation (ibid.). In more complex societies possessing well-defined and segregated social or class groups the differentiating impulses are stronger and fashion can develop. As Simmel says, 'segregation by means of differences in clothing . . . is expedient only where the danger of absorption and obliteration exists': where members of a society feel that their individuality is at risk, there will be a need for fashion (ibid.).

John Flügel also relates the existence of fashion to different forms of social organisation, different types of society. Where Simmel distinguishes between the presence and the absence of fashion Flügel's distinction is between 'fixed' and 'modish (or fashionable)' types of clothing. The difference between the two can be explained in terms of their opposite relations to time and space. Where 'fixed' costume 'changes slowly in time . . . but varies greatly in space', modish costume or fashion 'changes very rapidly in time . . . but varies comparatively little in space' (Flügel 1930: 129–30). What this means is that simple forms of society, lacking hierarchical class structures for example, will adopt fixed costume and more complex forms of society that possess hierarchical class structures, and will adopt fashionable or modish costume. This is because a simple social group existing outside the sphere of western influence will be geographically isolated and their clothing will remain much the same from year to year, although it is likely to be very different from that of another social group living in another place. Modish or fashionable clothing, however, will change very quickly in time, but will not change much in place because styles are rapidly diffused throughout that world (ibid.).

Polhemus and Procter use the terms 'fashion' and 'anti-fashion' instead of 'modish' and 'fixed' clothing, and they develop the account of the political relations between fashion, anti-fashion and different social groups; but, like Simmel, they are trying to explain the differences between clothing that is fashion and clothing that is not fashion. And, like Flügel, they use different conceptions of time to begin to explain these differences. Following the anthropologist Evans-Pritchard, Polhemus and Procter argue that time is a concept that 'reflects and expresses a society's or a person's real or ideal social situation' (Polhemus and Procter 1978: 13). A society or a person will understand time differently, according to the way they see their (political) situation, and that understanding will be manifested in the presence or absence of fashion. So, for Polhemus and Procter, 'traditional, anti-fashion adornment is a model of time as continuity (the maintenance of the status quo) and fashion is a model of time as change' (ibid.). On this account, politically conservative people and societies who have an interest in things staying the same will not have an interest in fashion (because it suggests a model of time as change); politically radical people and societies who have no interest in things staying the same will have an interest in fashion (for the same reason).

Bibliography

Bell, Q. ([1947] 1992) *On Human Finery*, London: Allison and Busby. The appendix deals with fashion and the fine arts.

Benjamin, W. (1992) 'The Work of Art in the Age of Mechanical Reproduction', in *Illuminations*, London, Fontana.

Flügel, J. C. (1930) *The Psychology of Clothes*, London: Hogarth Press and Institute of Psychoanalysis.

Hayward Gallery (1998) *Addressing the Century: 100 Years of Art and Fashion*, Exhibition and Catalogue, London: Hayward Gallery Publishing.

Laver, J. (1969) *Costume and Fashion: A Concise History*, London: Thames and Hudson.

Martin, R. (1999) 'A Note: Art and Fashion, Viktor and Rolf' *Fashion Theory* 3, 1: 109–20.

Polhemus, T. and Procter, L. (1978) *Fashion and Anti-Fashion: An Anthropology of Clothing and Adornment*, London: Thames and Hudson.

Rawsthorn, A. (2003) 'Is Fashion a True Art Form?', in the *Observer*, Sunday, 13 July.

Rhodes, Z. (2003) 'Is Fashion a True Art Form?' in the *Observer*, Sunday, 13 July.

Simmel, G. (1971) 'Fashion', in *On Individuality and Social Forms*, Chicago: University of Chicago Press.

Stern, R. (2004) *Against Fashion: Clothing as Art, 1850–1930*, Cambridge, Mass., MIT Press.

Sung Bok Kim (1998) 'Is Fashion Art?', *Fashion Theory* 2, 1 (March): 51–72.

Taylor, L. (2004) *Establishing Dress History*, Manchester: Manchester University Press. Pages 283–6 contain a sustained critique of Wollen's 1998 V&A exhibition 'Addressing the Century' on the relation between fashion and art.

Chapter 7

Fred Davis

ANTIFASHION: THE VICISSITUDES OF NEGATION

[. . .]

Varieties of antifashion

ANTIFASHION ASSUMES MANY FORMS and springs from diverse cultural sources.[1] Doubtlessly more forms can be delineated than I shall discuss here, but among the prevalent ones I would give names to are these: utilitarian outrage, health and fitness naturalism, feminist protest, conservative skepticism, minority group disidentification, and counterculture insult. Clearly, some of these (e.g., minority group disidentification and counterculture insult, health-fitness naturalism and feminist protest) overlap to an extent, while others are quite distinct.

Utilitarian outrage

This is perhaps the most familiar, numerous versions of which are to be found in "famous quotations" on fashion.[2] These go far back in literature and include even biblical maxims and aphorisms decrying the vanities of egoistic dress and adornment.[3] Briefly, this attitude castigates the wastefulness, frivolity, impracticality, and vanity associated with fashion, with its changes from season to season, with the invidiousness it occasions and the fickleness it induces. In modern times the American economist-sociologist Thorstein Veblen stands as the foremost exemplar of this viewpoint. His *Theory of the Leisure Class* (1899) not only points to fashion as class-based capitalism's principal channel of conspicuous consumption and waste but as altogether contrary to the instinct of workmanship, which Veblen saw as one of the few redeeming traits of humans. Analogous sentiments, though in a more heavily ironic vein, are to be found in the 1836 work of Thomas Carlyle *Sartor Resartus: The Life and Opinions of Herr Teufelsdröckh.*

Of course, a near-identical form of fashion resistance is evidenced in everyday lay attitudes as well, as when persons object to the waste, expense, and inconvenience entailed in casting aside perfectly wearable old garments to make room for the new fashion. Given the greater fashion pluralism abroad today, this happens, perhaps, somewhat less often today with women's apparel than it did as recently as the 1940s and 1950s. Still, it is by no means uncommon to come upon outraged commentary and letters in newspapers and magazines denouncing some new fashion for the economic (and aesthetic) waste it would engender. A spate of these appeared most recently (1988) when designers sought to put women back into 1960s-style miniskirts.[4]

In what must at first glance seem a case of biting the hand that feeds one, it is by no means rare for designers themselves to fulminate against the profligacies and impracticalities of fashion. Championing the virtues of simplicity, functionality, and durability, Chanel at one time produced clothes whose appeal derived mainly from their antifashion posture, as have such American designers as Claire McCardell, the late Rudi Gernreich, and, more recently, Liz Claiborne. Other designers have from time to time given greater scope to utilitarian outrage by coming up with what is termed "modular" or "surplice" dressing for women, and sometimes on a unisex basis for men as well. Reminiscent of Russian 1920s constructivist design or of what one can easily imagine issuing from a Bauhaus studio in its heyday, these consist typically of an array of very simply styled, usually loose-fitting, single-color garments (e.g., separate tops, tunics, leggings, jumpsuits, skirts, scarfs, wraps, pants), which can be combined in a great variety of ways to comfortably carry their wearers through the purposes and places of the day and, within limits, from one season to the next as well.[5] Needless to say, despite comfort, practicality, and comparative low cost, modular dressing has not proved particularly successful in the marketplace.

Health and fitness naturalism

A distinguishable yet closely related antifashion posture to that of the above is health and fitness naturalism. This form places much less emphasis on matters of economy, choosing instead to direct its ire at the deleterious health consequences of much fashion and at the unnatural demands it makes upon the human physique, especially that of women: shoes that pinch and do battle with the natural contour of the foot, and high heels that make walking unsteady and cause back pain; skirts and dresses that inhibit movement because they are either too short, too tight, or too voluminous; undergarments that constrict; fabrics that chafe and are either too warm in summer or too cool in winter; cosmetics and bleaches that damage the skin and hair; coiffures and jewelry that hamper head and arm movement; sports clothes designed more for bodily display than for the putative activity of swimming, skiing, bicycling, tennis, or whatever.[6] These comprise but a fragment from the litany of complaints laid at fashion's door over the centuries.

Similar complaints are by no means unheard of in the case of men's clothing: the physical confinement and weather unadaptability of the man's business suit, especially its three-piece version; button-secured collars and throat-grasping ties; at business places, the mandated white shirt, which easily shows dirt and requires frequent laundering; abdomen-clenching trouser belts or, alternatively, tight shoulder-straddling suspenders to prevent pants from sagging; head cover of one kind or another (e.g., bowlers, homburgs, slouch and straw hats), which is generally too warm in summer and ill adapted to the inclemencies of rain, wind, and cold; etc. The list of health and fitness delicts is almost as long as that assembled for women's clothes. Revealingly, remedies that have appeared over the years have in large part been consigned to that special category of men's dress known as "leisure wear."

Yet, perhaps precisely because men's clothing has since the eighteenth century resisted the dictates of fashion to a much greater extent than women's, these objections have never acquired the ideological force that was evidenced, for example, in the women's dress reform movement of the mid-nineteenth century or in today's women's movement (Wilson 1985). For the nineteenth-century dress reformer,

> fashion was the enemy. They [physical culturists] lamented the dangers of long skirts and bemoaned styles that inhibited movement, but, most of all, they declared war on tightly laced corsets. "By far the most frequent difficulty with our women [according to a physical culturist of the time] arises from uterine displacement and . . . the utter disuse of the muscles . . . which are kept inactive by the corset."
>
> (Schreier 1989, 97–98)

It is as if the "cultural bargain" struck between the sexes during the late eighteenth and early nineteenth centuries—i.e., a fashion-exempted men's dress code attesting to work and sobriety; a fashion-driven women's code in behalf of sexual attractiveness, dependency, and, with marriage, domesticity . . .—could come unstuck too easily were men, in search of greater comfort, to tamper self-indulgently with the terms enjoined by their side of the contract.[7] Dominant groups are nearly always prepared to suffer some discomfort and inconvenience for the sake of the status quo.

Not so, however, for subordinate groups who come to think themselves disadvantaged under the terms of the cultural contract. As modest and ladylike as surviving sketches of it look to late-twentieth-century eyes, the "radical" and "licentious"—and, of course, roundly condemned and markedly unsuccessful—(Amelia) Bloomer costume of the mid-1850s grew directly out of the reform movement against the confining, constricting, voluminous, and complicated apparel worn by middle-class women of the time (Lauer and Lauer 1981). As Foote (1989, 147) explains:

> This small group of reformers believed in the contemporary rhetoric about the innate natures of men and women. And they used these beliefs in their writings and lectures to gain support for dress reform among a larger audience. They stressed the unhealthy and unsuitable aspects of fashionable attire for women to fulfill their role as mothers. They contended that the Bloomer Costume made women healthier and, thus,

better mothers. They also ascribed part of the mortality and sickness of newborn children to the unhealthy attire of their mothers.

Repeated attempts since Amelia Bloomer's time to revive wear like hers have intermittently proven somewhat more successful than did the original. At that, the tendency has been to segregate such attire to women's exercise and team sportswear. One is forced to conclude, then, that Bloomer's mid-nineteenth-century call for total reform of women's dress in the name of health and fitness has, at best, been only partially realized in the succeeding century and a half.

Health naturalism's advocacy of women's dress reform was, to be sure, part of a larger nineteenth-century, utopianlike social movement, which believed the corruptions, contaminations, and depredations of an expanding industrial order could only be overcome by a return to all things "natural": in food, clothing, shelter, recreation, the arts and crafts. Strong echoes of it were to be heard in the public hygiene movement at the turn of the century. Much nearer today, its lingering spirit infuses the post-1960s physical fitness vogue that has swept North America and parts of Europe with its associated life-style emphases on jogging, nonsmoking, weight reduction, exercising, and nutritional asceticism (Glassner 1989; Gusfield 1987). Evocative of its earlier incarnation, the contemporary fitness vogue, too, has given rise to certain antifashion manifestations in apparel, albeit of a sometimes contradictory tendency: loose, baggy, and underdesigned (e.g., cotton sweats, baggy jeans, Chi pants with gusset inserts), on the one hand, and sleek, extremely close-fitting (i.e., "a second skin"), and vividly patterned, on the other (e.g., leotards, bodysuits, and bicycling pants made of synthetic Lycra stretch fiber). A main difference, however, between contemporary fitness-inspired antifashion and that of earlier eras is that nowadays its dissents and innovations are adopted much more quickly, even avidly, by fashion per se than was the case up until about the time of the second World War. Indeed, in the instance of certain apparel, spandex sportswear for example, it is almost impossible to say whether it began as antifashion or fashion. But that it is unmistakably "fashion" within a very short time there can be no doubt.

Wishing to signal an ideological attachment to health and fitness, many persons have, as Kron (1984) reports, taken to wearing such garments to work, to school, and in town. (In some quarters the running shoe has virtually replaced the dress shoe.) Devotion of this kind notwithstanding, it must be granted that the antifashion impact of contemporary health and fitness apparel is probably a good deal less than that registered by the "scandalous" Bloomer costume of a century and a half ago. Nowadays, fashion, as we have seen, stays in much closer touch with antifashion impulses abroad in the land. No sooner, then, had the health and fitness vogue begun to take hold in the mid-1970s than fashion appropriated, "styled," and claimed for its own the mishmash of apparel seen in gyms and on jogging paths and bicycle trails (Fraser 1981). With characteristic shamelessness, fashion represented itself as much beholden to health and fitness as would the most dedicated 10K runner and habitué of health food stores. So far has this trend gone that many fashion-conscious women now complain of fashion no longer affording them the bodily "little white lies," coverups, and distractions that once made them "look good" (Brubach 1990).

Feminist protest

The antifashion of feminist protest not only concurs fully with that of health and fitness naturalism, and nearly as much with utilitarian outrage, but carries its objections to fashion even further. Beyond considerations of economy, bodily health, and comfort, it sees in fashion and, for that matter, in the clothing code of the West generally, a principal means, as much actual as symbolic, by which the institutions of patriarchy have managed over the centuries to oppress women and to relegate them to inferior social roles. With polemical roots going well back into the nineteenth century, the arguments to this effect are many and, by now, quite familiar; it is only possible to touch on them here.[8]

Given fashion's invidiousness and conformism, women are constantly under pressure to supplant one wardrobe with another. The unending succession of styles devised for them (usually by male designers) is rarely functional. As a rule, fashion's garments and accessories call for great amounts of time and attention when dressing. They are costly to have cleaned and require much attention to keep presentable. All of this is seen as investing women's lives with a fastidiousness bordering at times on the comically frivolous (Foltyn 1989).

In addition, modern fashion's fixation on youth, slenderness, sexuality, and eroticism serves mainly to diminish other aspects of woman's person while reinforcing those favored by men, i.e., such traditionally sanctioned roles as sexual object, wife, mother, and homemaker. Large-framed and obese women in particular are made to feel the sting of fashion's obsession with the young and the lean (Millman 1980). Not only do the fashion media hide such women from view, but their chances for finding suitable "in fashion" garments in either regular apparel stores or those catering to "large sizes" are almost nonexistent given modern fashion's idealization of the slimmed-down, lean female figure. It might be noted that only very obese men encounter similar obstacles in finding appropriate apparel that can pass for being more or less "in fashion."

The relative freedom from fashion's dictates granted men in contrast to the coercion they exert on women is further evidence of how aptly fashion serves the ends of male domination. In sum, fashion has in Western society been a quintessential component of the societal machinery—or ruling discourse, as Foucault (1980) would have it—by which women have been kept "in their place."

While feminists would, I suspect, agree in all essential respects with such an analysis, there appears to be less agreement among them on what can and should be done as far as women's clothing is concerned. Indeed, something approximating a condition of "structural strain" (Smelser 1963) in regard to the issue seems to have developed within the feminist social movement. Some feminists enjoin women to spurn fashion and its associated habits and attitudes altogether. They decry women's fear of not being in fashion, their absorption with the drivel of fashion magazines, their obsessive concern for proving oneself sexually attractive to men, their profligate purchase of advertised beauty products that perpetuate sexual and romantic stereotypes, etc. Advocates of this position often urge women to dress essentially as men.[9] This, it is said, would to a significant extent act to symbolically diminish the gender gap. It would encourage women to bring forth from themselves qualities and abilities customarily obscured, if not actually submerged, through the everyday activation of a patriarchal gender code.

Other feminists believe the adoption of men's clothing by women would lend tacit legitimation to the patriarchic representation of the world. Rather than sycophantic surrender to men's dress codes, they wish for some new, more fashion-resistant, dress for women, which neither perpetuates the role inferiorities and infirmities of traditional women's dress nor subscribes tacitly to the notion that men's construction of social reality, as symbolized in their dress code, is the only viable one. Implicit in this stance is the conviction that Western society has systematically suppressed a range of distinctive values and attitudes anchored in *feminine* experience (Foucault 1980), which, if permitted to surface, could contribute greatly to human welfare. Women's clothes in this view should strive to symbolically represent such values and attitudes and by so doing help animate them in society at large. In light, however, of the alleged submergence of these values and attitudes in contemporary society, one has at this point only the vaguest inkling of what such clothes might look like. Quite possibly, harbingers have already appeared among us without our being quite aware of them. As with many cultural products, more time and social definitional processing may be required before they acquire a recognizable and distinctive form.

In the meantime, the fashion industry itself has, since the 1920s, not been altogether unresponsive to the complaints and protests issuing from feminist quarters. Certainly, the voluminous, elaborate, and physically burdensome clothing of the Victorian era has long since fallen prey to women's demands, led in large part by turn-of-the-century feminists, for more functional clothing. Since Chanel some seventy years ago down to the present, designers have been proclaiming their belief in the "modern active woman" who has neither the patience nor the means to loll about all day in elaborate finery. Since the 1950s they have even come to laud the woman who earns her own living, who picks up and travels near and far on her own unencumbered by chaperons or overly solicitous males, who eschews coquetry and feigned frailty and is as straightforward in her romantic pursuits as men are in theirs.

Two designers I interviewed (one a woman well known in California, the other a man of international reputation) expressed revulsion over the frou-frou and other frilly impediments that traditionally have been part of women's dress. The man was known for his advocacy of unisex clothing. The woman went on to say she foresees the "end of fashion" due to the changing social position of women brought about by the contemporary women's movement. Although the woman designer qualified her opinion somewhat later in the interview, their attitudes reflect the degree to which feminist views have, I believe, penetrated the ranks of fashion creation itself. Even though wary of translating feminist precepts into actual women's clothing designs—as, indeed, the fashion industry by and large still shows itself to be—no designer of stature nowadays can pretend indifference to the antifashion sentiments emanating from feminist quarters.[10] Short of an "end to fashion," these sentiments, too, shall in time have to be accommodated within fashion's symbolic sphere.

Conservative skepticism

While perhaps the blandest from an expressive standpoint, the form of antifashion that I have termed conservative skepticism is economically, through its sheer massiveness, the most powerful. By the term I mean that sort of garden variety resistance to a new fashion millions upon millions of women exercise from time to time, often to the point of killing off the new fashion altogether or causing it to be so modified as to greatly neutralize its symbolic intent and visual impact. The examples, as noted in several connections, are many and are known to have wreaked financial havoc throughout the women's clothing industry: e.g., the mid-1920s attempt to drop hemlines to pre-World War I heights, the midiskirt of the mid-1970s, the abrupt 1987 try at reintroducing sixties-style miniskirts.

What is noteworthy about conservative skepticism is that it is not ideologically driven, as is, for example, health and fitness naturalism or feminist protest. And unlike these other forms, it posits no dress alternatives other than remaining wedded to the established style of the day. The conservative skeptics are women not against fashion per se, only against that which the fashion industry, the fashion press, and other assorted "authorities" are trying at a particular time to foist on them. On the contrary, they believe in remaining "in fashion" and worry lest what they deem objectionable will soon "triumph" and require them to overhaul their wardrobes. Their resistance derives usually from some ill-defined sense that the new fashion "is not them" and would, if adopted, entail so pronounced a redefinition of presentational self as to clash with what they feel to be more enduring, less malleable images of self.[11] Their skepticism is buttressed by a belief, half hope and half conviction, that a great many others feel as they do and that the propaganda of the fashion industry will fail to convert a number sufficient to put the style over, thus sparing them the disgrace of being thought unfashionable.

It is mainly at these women that the batteries of fashion publicity are aimed: promises, enticements, reassurances, and consolations, etc., all designed to detach resistors from the view the new fashion "is not them." This makes for a style of discourse I refer to elsewhere as the rhetorical consolations of fashion. Illustrative of such rhetoric are the many statements, blatant contradictions notwithstanding, one comes across in fashion media to the effect that the proffered fashion is "not nearly so extreme as it first appears"; or that it will "highlight the fascinating you obscured by the reticent styles of yesterday"; or that it is "meant for everyone" because it offers "a new freedom to be your real self, unshackled from others' ideas of who you are and can be." The quotes, I confess, are made-up paraphrases of a thousand and one statements of this genre I have encountered in the fashion press. Those that follow, though, are actual:

> "It's a wonderful new balance," says Ronaldus Shamask [a New York designer], whose spare, clean collection combined Oriental and architectural elements. "People don't want to be fashion victims or classic. The only way to dress now is to look like it just happened," he says. "It's a more nonchalant fascination. Pomodoro [another New York designer] calls it "a not-thinking-about-clothes-attitude." (Gross 1988)
> "Clothing is a visual feast," he [Geoffrey Beene] continued. "Fashion

should be beautiful, not necessarily newsworthy. Changes should evolve slowly. I have never admired revolutionary changes."

Esthetically, Mr. Beene feels comfortable with two different styles: ornate and simple.

"Both are wonderful," he said. "There is no need to make a choice; that is what freedom is all about."

He believes it does not matter whether jackets are short or long, or whether clothes are fitted or full. Those are details. What is important is individual style.

(Morris 1988)

The writer Jamie Wolf (1980, 44), in her biting appraisal of fashion's late-1970s "retro look," manages to parody this rhetorical genre to a turn.

> In this land of fashion-ese, after all, last year was always the year when things were in flux, clothes lacked a certain element of fantasy, clothes had perhaps a touch too much fantasy, styles were a little overpowering, styles were a little dull; and this year is always the year when the dust has settled, fantasy has finally returned but in appropriate measure, the kinks have been worked out, there is a whole new spirit of finesse and refinement, and the new clothes are once more exciting—as exciting as they've ever been—but above all, eminently wearable.

At first conservative skeptics are, I suspect, as disinclined to attend to the rhetoric as they are to accept the new fashion itself. Still, should resistance cave in, the rhetoric allows the rationalization that the switchover, while perhaps not welcome, was inevitable.

Minority group disidentification

Yet another kind of antifashion that, in America at least, has come to the fore with the rise of ethnic consciousness, the gay movement, and the women's movement is that of minority group disidentification. Varying from group to group in the degree of deliberate consciousness entailed in the construction of a distinctive group identity, the intent of this type of antifashion is quite straightforward: to differentiate via clothing and other behaviors one's subgroup from the culturally dominant segments of a society. In disidentifying thus with the cultural mainstream, members of such groups also mean to proclaim a new found sense of pride in those very attributes (e.g., blackness, homosexuality, fatness) mainstream society devalues and denigrates, as indeed had many from the minority group itself before having their "consciousness raised" or before "coming out of the closet."

In some special cases of minority group disidentification, as, for example that of Hassidic [sic] Jews living in large American cities, the group's distinctive dress has remained essentially unchanged for hundreds of years. In these instances, as with such separatist, rural-based religious denominations as the Amish and Mennonites, not only does dress serve as testimony to the group's solidarity and oneness with their religious beliefs, but it quite purposefully erects a barrier to interaction with others in the society, thus keeping the group relatively isolated and safe from secular and other forms of moral contamination.

This subspecies of antifashion, however, is at best a marginal case. Hasidic Jews, for example, are much less interested in challenging the dominant dress codes of a society than they are in guarding their own, well-delineated, historic identity. This is not quite the case, however, with other racial and ethnic minorities who lack the same sort of self-imposed barriers to assimilation and whose ethnic identities, therefore, are less well fortified against the onslaught of mainstream cultural influences. In such cases, differentiating dress styles have to be invented, or possibly resurrected from a nearly forgotten group past. The Afro hairstyle and dashiki of militant, racially conscious blacks in America is a good example of the latter; the zoot suit, dangling trouser chain, and exceptionally wide-brimmed slouch hat of young Mexican-American men in the 1940s is an example of a more or less indigenously invented ethnic dress style.[12] Both these styles carry more of a (perhaps transitory) aura of cultural challenge about them than does the dress of such insular religious groups as the Amish, Mennonites, and Hassids. Perhaps because of this—i.e., their sociological proximity to the mainstream allows them to enter into the fashion/antifashion dialectic more readily than can the dress styles of insular religious groups—the styles emanating from black and various Hispanic enclaves in the American city have been known to "float upward" (in modified form, to be sure) into mainstream fashions (Field 1970). Today's gay subculture lies in still closer proximity to branches of the fashion world.[13] This allows its particular antifashions (e.g., men's earrings, exaggerated western wear, certain leather stylings, tight T-shirts) to be assimilated even more readily into mainstream fashions.[14]

The tacitly ideological imposition of distinctive antifashion dress styles can, of course, pose numerous problems of identification for some members of the minority group or subculture. It poses related problems of identification and interaction for majority group members as well. For the former the problem hinges on the issue of whether the identity sustained by some distinctive dress style will at the same time result in others "keeping their distance, 'thus denying minority group members the equality of access, recognition, and recompense that, in democratic society, they are likely to regard as their due (see Davis 1961). For some majority group members the problem is the obverse: overcoming the social distance and "strangeness" implied by the other's distinctive ethnic dress and interacting with him or her "as an equal."

Given, then, the interactional tension experienced in these not unfamiliar encounters, it may be the case that even diluted borrowings of minority group and subculture antifashions by mainstream social groups can help further a democratization of social relations. (At the same time, of course, it may also attenuate the distinctive social identities that other minority group members seek to promote.) Many years ago George Herbert Mead (1934) wrote of how the sharing of significant symbols among diverse groups and peoples could in time bring about an enlightened democratic world order. In that quest, dress constitutes as much of a significant symbol as do law and language and much else that is culture.

Counterculture insult

Moving beyond the stance adopted by racial, ethnic, and certain other minority entities, the antifashion of a counterculture aims at more than just designating via dress a distinctive identity for some self-defined subcultural group. Counterculturists seek as well to distance themselves from, diminish, and even scandalize society's dominant cultural groups, i.e., those usually, if somewhat vaguely, referred to in modern times as the bourgeoisie or the middle classes (Davis 1971). Fifties beatniks, sixties hippies, and present-day punkers (with their various stylistic subdivisions of skinheads, hard rockers, heavy metalists, etc.) are the most obvious recent examples of the category, although *épater le bourgeois* unconventional dress and other forms of outrageous behavior have been generally associated with bohemianism in Europe and America for the better part of the last two centuries.

The long hair, beads, bracelets, floral prints, fringed garments, and other folkloric allusions of hippie ware were in their way as determinedly oppositional to middle-class dress (Davis 1967) as are the torn jeans, heavy leather, chain-festooned jackets, pierced cheek, and spiked and pastel-color-dyed hair of the 1980s punker. Both proclaim a disdain for the middle-class values of the workaday world, although whereas the former accomplished this through a kind of romantic pastoralism the latter is more partial to dystopian postures of sadomasochistic nihilism. In either case, as intended, many "ordinary people" respond with revulsion to the outlandish representations of self that hippie and punk dress parade before them.

Of the various forms of antifashion tolerated in modern Western democracies, that of the counterculture is symbolically the most potent. The reasons for this appear to be several. First, of the several antifashions it most directly confronts and challenges the symbolic hegemony of the reigning fashion. It injects itself headlong into the dialogue of fashion by attempting through its iconoclasms to debunk and deride the dominant mode rather than to merely propose some group-specific alternative as do other antifashions discussed here.

Second, while counterculture antifashion often originates with working-class, ethnic, socially deviant, and other more or less disadvantaged and disenfranchised groups in society, its main thrust typically comes from disaffected and rebellious middle-class youth (Levine 1984). The hippie and punk counterculture manifestations afford dramatic evidence of this (Kopkind 1979, Hebdige 1979).

Despite, then, the condemnation such blasphemous behavior elicits from middle-class parents and other authorities, the fact remains that these youths exist on closer terms with mainstream culture than do, for example, members of ethnic minority or socially deviant marginal groups. This means that the antifashion affront of wayward middle-class youth carries with it more cultural point and poignancy than that issuing from other quarters. (It smacks more of subversion from within than opposition from without.) But, given the close social proximity of counterculture youth to mainstream middle-class society, it should not be surprising, for example, that certain select hippie paraphernalia (e.g., men's beaded necklaces, granny glasses, embroidered jeans, high-top shoes) had by the early 1970s come to be worn by adult middle-class men and women as well. Similarly, modifications of certain punk modes (e.g., men's earrings, disheveled and spiked hair, "black everything") have already made their way into mainstream fashions (Gross 1987).

Counterculture "purists" are likely to look askance at these borrowings and at those from within their ranks who cater to this sort of "bourgeois frivolity"; charges of "selling out" and "commercialism" are promptly leveled.[15] However, from another vantage point the borrowings do represent a kind of symbolic appeasement of the severe intergenerational strife that periodically engages Western society.

A third reason for the special saliency of counterculture antifashion for mainstream fashion was alluded to earlier: Parts of the fashion world have since about the turn of the century come more and more to overlap with demimonde, arty, bohemian, socially deviant, radical, and other counterculture formations.[16] Simmel had already astutely noted this in his famous 1904 essay on fashion. The interweaving of the worlds of fashion and the arts was especially pronounced in Paris during the period 1910 to 1940, roughly. Friendships and work ties between the pre-World War I designer Paul Poiret and the ballet master Diaghilev, between Chanel and the poet-dramatist Jean Cocteau, between Schiaparelli and the surrealist painter Salvador Dali are extensively recorded in chronicles of the time. The important synchronist painter Sonia Delaunay also designed fashionable clothing during the 1920s and 1930s.

This is not to say that the influence flowing between prominent fashion designers and leading artists of an era is the same as commanding special access to the antifashions of counterculture groups. Still, as accounts of artistic avant-gardes since the late nineteenth century attest (Poggioli 1968), the boundaries separating various "nonconventional" groupings in present-day Western society are quite fluid and permeable.

Either, then, through firsthand experience of the dissenting currents of thought and practice that flow through these sectors, or through peripheral, though not infrequent, association with persons from within them, designers, especially younger ones wishing to make a name for themselves by "doing something different," will draw upon the off-beat cultural products and attitudes that germinate in an era's countercultures. Add to this modern fashion's near-institutionalized tendency to accord a place for antifashion in its very own domain—conspicuous in the case of such contemporary designers as Jean-Paul Gaultier, Franco Moschino, and Vivienne Westwood; more subdued in that of Claude Montana and Romeo Giglio— and the resort to counterculture antifashion is almost inevitable.

[. . .]

Notes

1   Again, unlike Polhemus and Procter (1978), I exclude from this rubric non-fashion, which phenomenologically is of a very different order.

2   See, for example, the two dozen or so indexed under *fashion* in *The Oxford Dictionary of Quotations*.

3   The most famous of these is from Isaiah 3:16–24, the first lines of which read: "Then the Lord said: Because the women of Zion hold themselves high and walk with necks outstretched and wanton glances moving with mincing gait and jingling feet, the Lord will give the women of Zion bald heads, the Lord will

strip the hair from their foreheads. In that day the Lord will take away all finery."

4   An op-ed column by National Public Radio's legal reporter, Nina Totenberg (Totenberg 1988), received wide notice and soon became something of a banner under which popular protest against the miniskirt rallied. The column, in part, read: "For many American women, the big news a couple of weeks ago was made not in the Middle East or the Super Tuesday primaries but in our own home towns, where the fashion industry is taking a major bath on the miniskirt. Many professional women simply refuse to buy the mini, so retail clothing sales are the worst since the 1982 recession. In short, the mini is a fashion disaster. . . . Every moment of the fashion industry's misery is richly deserved by the designers, retail clothiers and newspapers and magazine poltroons who perpetuate this absurd creation. . . . It's simple justice that miniskirt promoters are being rewarded with empty cash registers. But beware, ladies, the battle is not yet won. Many in the fashion industry haven't given up yet. They figure we'll quit first. Hold the line. Don't buy. And the mini will die."
Its death, however, turned out to be more like a coma. Within two years it experienced a remarkable recovery and was to become the preferred skirt length of younger women.

5   The Los Angeles designer Harriet Selwyn introduced such a line in the early 1980s. More recent attempts at marketing modular dress have come from designer-led firms variously named Singles, Multiples, and Units. According to Hochswender (1988c), these firms' collections "promise freedom from the ironing board as well as from the dictates of fashion."

6   As in the case, in the opinion of some (Janovy 1991), of the close-fitting spandex uniforms to be worn by the women players of the newly organized women's professional basketball league, the Liberty Basketball Association.

7   It may be sociologically significant that less confining, environmentally adaptable clothing (e.g., open-collared short-sleeve shirts, jacketless business wear, loose fitting garments) is commonly worn by men in Israel, where an egalitarian ideology of socialist zionism placed great emphasis on the elimination of sexual stratification and segregation. Rejoinders to the effect that relaxed men's dress in Israel is due solely to the country's hot climate are contradicted by the mainten-ance of relatively rigid men's dress codes in much of British-influenced Africa and Asia.

8   See Wilson (1985) and Steele (1985) for fuller discussions of feminism and fashion, although both take issue with a number of feminist arguments on the question.

9   [W]omen's fashions since the latter part of the nineteenth century have frequently traded, rather avidly at times, on the antifashion possibilities attaching to the borrowing of men's items of apparel. From the perspective of a strongly ideo-logical feminist such cautious flirting with cross-gender dress has amounted to little more than what the political scientist Harold Lasswell once termed "defeat through partial incorporation."

10   Even Yves Saint Laurent, probably the most famous designer alive today, is credited with a feminist coup by some feminists because in the late 1960s he legitimated pants as high fashion for women.

11   Almost by definition, a new fashion, as noted in chapter 6, nearly always triggers some clash of presentational and more or less fixed images of self (Stone 1962).

The social psychological issue for clothes wearers is more one of degree than of occurrence per se.

12   Though not concerned with dress as such, the recent vogue among West Coast Chicano youth for converting used, factory model Detroit cars into baroque "low rider" automotive chariots, replete with antiqued velvet interiors and chainlink steering wheels, can be counted as an identity-defining equivalent of the 1940s zoot suit. As might be expected, the "low rider" creation derives much of its symbolic force from the fact that it stands in exact opposition to the "high rider" vehicular conversions popular among non-Hispanic white youth.

13   Tragic evidence of the close linkage is that the death toll from AIDS in the fashion world is believed to be especially high. It is not surprising, therefore, that since the mid-1980s the American and French fashion industries have been exceptionally active in fund-raising for AIDS research and in extending help and support to those suffering from the disease.

14   Andrew Kopkind (1979) supplies a particularly vivid example of one such manifestation: "When Ralph Lauren introduced his hardcore western clothes collection earlier this month, several stores constructed complete western environments to complete the mystique of the designs. Bloomingdale's version for Lauren's western women's wear was done in rough pine boards, decorated with harnesses and yokes for horses and cattle, ropes, spikes in the wall, and antique posters from California fruit and produce companies. Boots were placed at random as adornments; there was a colorful display of western kerchiefs in an array of colors. No store anywhere in the real West ever looked like that: in fact, the Bloomingdale's boutique was a perfect replica of a "western" gay men's bar, from the spikes to the colored kerchiefs. What was the message conveyed? Perhaps only the store's set designer can tell."

15   The outcry from the faithful is structurally the same as that from members of ethnic minority groups who take umbrage at the easy borrowing of their distinctive identity tags by mainstream elements. Reporting on a symposium held at New York's Fashion Institute of Technology on the topic of punk-style dress, Hochswender (1988) writes: "The 300 or so students who packed the auditorium seemed to care deeply about the issues raised, which ranged from modern merchandising to the 'commodification' of art to clothes as a form of free speech. When Mr. [Stephen] Sprouse, who synthesizes influences from punk rock and pop art in his clothes, showed a video with excerpts from his past collections, he was criticized by an F.I.T. student who said he commercialized punk and had shown an 'advert' for his own fashions. Mr. Sprouse replied: 'I have a big company behind me, which is great. I'm no authority on punk. I just think it's cool the way it looks.' Mr. Sprouse's business is owned by CSI Associates."

16   The coterie that formed around the late Andy Warhol is a well-publicized instance of the overlap of fringe elements from mainstream culture and counterculture groups.

References

Brubach, H. (1990) 'In Fashion, Retroactivity', *New Yorker*, 31 December.

Davis, F. (1961) 'Deviance Disavowal, the Management of Strained Interaction by the Visibly Handicapped', *Social Problems* 9, 2: 120–32.

—— (1967) 'Why All of Us May be Hippies Someday', *Transaction* (December).

—— (1971) *On Youth Subcultures: The Hippy Variant*, New York: General Learning Press.

Field, G. A. (1970) 'The Status Float Phenomenon, the Upward Diffusion of Fashion', in G. B. Sproles (ed.) (1981) *Perspectives of Fashion*, Minneapolis: Burgess.

Foltyn, J. L. (1989) 'The Importance of Being Beautiful', Unpublished Ph.D., University of California, San Diego.

Foote, S. (1989) 'Challenging Gender Symbols', in C. B. Kidwell and V. Steele (eds) *Men and Women: Dressing the Part*, Washington: Smithsonian Institution Press.

Foucault, M. (1980) *Power/Knowledge: Selected Interviews and Other Writings*, New York: Pantheon.

Fraser, K. (1981) *The Fashionable Mind*, New York: Knopf.

Glassner, B. (1989) 'Fitness and the Postmodern Self', *Journal of Health and Social Behaviour* 30, 2: 180–91.

Gross, M. (1987) 'Effervescent Betsey Johnson', *New York Times*, 3 November.

—— (1988) 'Changing of the Guard', *New York Times*, 28 November.

Gusfield, J. (1987) 'Nature's Body, Metaphors of Food and Health', Unpublished.

Hebdige, D. (1979) *Subculture: The Meaning of Style*, London: Routledge.

Hochswender, W. (1988) 'Punk Fashion Revisited', *New York Times*, 23 September.

Janovy, J. (1991) 'The Spandex League', *New York Times*, 6 March.

Kopkind, A. (1979) 'Dressing Up', *Village Voice*, 30 April.

Kron, J. (1984) 'Sneakers Gain as a Symbol of Commuting', *Wall Street Journal*, 17 October.

Lauer, R. and Lauer, J. (1981) *Fashion Power*, Englewood Cliffs, N.J., Prentice-Hall.

Levine, B. (1984) 'Tale of Two Cities: Who Wears What?', *Los Angeles Times*, 1 April.

Mead, G. H. (1934) *Mind, Self and Society*, Chicago: University of Chicago Press.

Millman, M. (1980) *Such a Pretty Face*, New York: Norton.

Morris, B. (1988) 'For Geoffrey Beene, 25 Years at the Top', *New York Times*, 10 May.

Poggioli, R. (1968) *The Theory of the Avant-Garde*, Cambridge, Mass.: Harvard University Press.

Polhemus, T. and Procter, L. (1978) *Fashion and Anti-Fashion*, London: Thames and Hudson.

Schreier, B. A. (1989) 'Sporting Wear', in C. B. Kidwell and V. Steele (eds) *Men and Women: Dressing the Part*, Washington: Smithsonian Institution Press.

Smelser, N. (1963) *Theory of Collective Behaviour*, New York: Free Press.

Steele, V. (1985) *Fashion and Eroticism*, New York: Oxford University Press.

Stone, G. P. (1962) 'Appearances and the Self', in A. M. Rose (ed.) *Human Behavior and Social Processes*, Boston: Houghton Mifflin.

Wilson, E. (1985) *Adorned in Dreams*, London: Virago.

Wolf, J. (1980) 'Retro Babble', *New West*, 14 January.

Chapter 8

Zandra Rhodes and Alice Rawsthorn

IS FASHION A TRUE ART FORM?

ACCLAIMED DESIGNER ZANDRA RHODES and the director of the Design Museum, Alice Rawsthorn, go head to head.

Yes: Zandra Rhodes

I think fashion is an art form – you might call it decorative or applied art as opposed to fine art, but what's the distinction? Because the same amount of artistic expression goes into clothes, a piece of pottery or a painting. I've founded a museum on the basis that I think it's an artistic form that should be remembered. I think fashion galleries – such as the one at the V&A (Victoria and Albert Museum, London) and the one at the Metropolitan Museum in New York – are very relevant.

Fashion can tell you what people wore at a certain period just as pottery can tell you what their tea parties were like. I don't think the fact that these things were designed to be practical distinguishes them from fine art. You could say a painting is designed to go on the wall, but if it were made as a fresco, where it was part of the wall, would you say it was not art because it was practical?

Fine art at the moment is no longer particularly concerned with beauty, so you could say that fashion – which is always about a concept of beauty, whether or not everyone agrees on the concept – is more relevant, more artistic, than the garbage they put out as conceptual. If you look at it that way, fine art may go by the wayside, and fashion, which has a bit more effort put into it, will take over.

Some designers are directly influenced by fine art – a lot of Bill Gibb's things were influenced by the slashed panels in dresses in, say, Flemish paintings. I myself once designed something called the Venus dress which was somewhat influenced by Botticelli, though I haven't really gone too much in that direction. But when I see my clothes in my museum I don't feel any differently from how I felt about them at the time – I see that I believed in what I did with them, that they were the right thing to do.

Ossie Clark would have argued that fashion was art – he definitely thought his contribution was worthwhile, and his clothes were being shown in museums even at the time. He certainly would have expected them to be in museums now.

[. . .]

No: Alice Rawsthorn

On a trip to Paris, the New York fashion designer Donna Karan was dragged off to the Picasso Museum by her late husband, Stephen Weiss. He hoped that his wife would love it as much as he did. Instead, or so he told American *Vogue*, she dashed at speed from gallery to gallery barely pausing to look at the works.

Suddenly Weiss heard Donna screaming with glee in another gallery. At last, he thought, she has finally found a Picasso that inspires her. He ran into the gallery only to discover his wife gazing at a bare expanse of green wall. This particular shade of green, she explained breathlessly, would be perfect for next season's lingerie.

Now, this story tells us a great deal about Donna Karan, not least that she is refreshingly free from pretentiousness and pomposity when it comes to her chosen field. You can't help wondering whether, if you asked Donna 'Is fashion art?', her response would be the style slut's equivalent of former Liverpool manager Bill Shankly's proclamation: 'Some say football is a matter of life and death – I'd say it's much more important than that.'

Quibbling over whether fashion is more or less important than art is just as pointless as questioning whether or not it is art. Of course it's not, it's fashion. That is not to say that fashion, at its best, is not a suitable subject for museums or that it cannot share some of the attributes of art. On the contrary, an exquisite *haute couture* dress – like the ones that Cristóbal Balenciaga created in his 1950s heyday – can look as perfect as a beautiful painting or sculpture.

Yet only an old-fashioned aesthete would argue that the role of the artist is to create beauty. Sometimes artists do, but for most of them beauty tends to be a by-product of their quest to explore the complex, messy, ambiguities of modern life. Think of Wolfgang Tillmans's photographs of aeroplane wings and window sills now on display at Tate Britain. Beautifully composed they may be, but with a forlorn beauty too subtle to be replicated in fashion.

Similarly, fashion is adept at fulfilling another traditional function of art by reflecting changes in contemporary culture, but only up to a point. Think of how the Ossie Clark dresses in the V&A's exhibition evoke the desire for escapism at the turn of the 1970s. Yet, unlike art, fashion rarely expresses more than the headlines of history.

And fashion has a practical purpose, whereas art does not. The result may be as gorgeous as a vintage Balenciaga ballgown or an eloquent political metaphor for its time, but it is still an item of clothing intended to be worn. Why pretend that it is anything else?

Alice Rawsthorn is the design correspondent of the *International Herald Tribune* and a columnist for the *New York Times*.

PART FOUR

What fashion and clothing do

HAVING EXAMINED what fashion is in the previous section, this section must begin to account for what it does. This section, then, is about the function, or functions, of fashion and clothing. A preoccupation with the functions of fashion is characteristic of what might be called 'early' treatments of the subject. As Joanne Entwistle says, 'early explanations of fashion and dress ... tended to start from "why" questions: why do we wear clothes?' (2000: 57). And much of the material that deals with the answers to these 'why' questions, with the functions of fashion and clothing, comes from anthropology. The answers anthropology provides are predominantly to do with basic human needs and begin with the need for protection from the elements: we wear clothes because the human body needs to be protected from extremes of heat and cold and from the wet.

The question of function, and of how function relates to fashion and clothing, however, is not relevant to only early treatments or explanations of fashion and clothing. A flick through any fashion magazine, or a survey of internet shopping pages, will quickly bring up a wide range of products, from cycling clothing, nurses' uniforms, mobile phones and sunglasses to basketball shoes, all of which are marketed using the strapline 'Fashion and Function!'. The exclamation mark, presumably, signals that the manufacturers think that they and only they have, for the first time, managed to produce something that looks okay and also works. The juxtaposition of fashion and function in straplines such as this raises three questions that this Introduction must explain. The first is whether fashion is properly thought of as even having a function. The second is that, if fashion may be said to behave functionally, then what is the relation or priority between fashion and function? And the third concerns whether the explanation of fashion and clothing in terms of function is reductive.

At this point the difference between fashion and either clothing or dress begins to be pertinent and of interest again. Following the discussion of these differences in the

Introduction, it is worth pointing out that questions about the functions of fashion and clothing, and proposing answers that are based on protection and modesty, sound more appropriate to clothing and dress than they do to fashion. Suggesting that one might be interested in the protective function of a silk blouse worn to a cocktail party seems to miss the point in a way that the same suggestion made regarding a fishing jacket worn to a rainy riverbank does not. The connotations of the former as a glamorous, high-status and therefore fashionable item seem to render the question about its protective functions improper, but the connotations of the latter, as a piece of functional clothing, do not. Similarly, the question of modesty seems to require a different sort of answer depending on whether it is asked of a strappy party frock or a tailored suit for work. No one expects the latter, as a piece of clothing worn for everyday, functional purposes, to be seductive in the way that most people would expect the former to be, and the question of modesty does not arise in the same form. None of this is to deny that silk blouses may protect one (very poorly) from the rain, or that fishing jackets may exert a (minimal) seductive charm, but it is to suggest that cultural prejudices will determine that these functions of these garments are probably not worth pursuing very far.

Carlyle suggests that the first function of clothing was ornament and that clothes then developed other functions: 'clothes . . . began in foolishest love of ornament' (1987: 31). Clothes subsequently gave rise to 'Increased Security, and pleasurable Heat' (ibid.) and then came shame and modesty. Lastly, clothes enabled 'individuality, distinctions [and] social polity' (ibid.: 32). There seems to be a sliding scale from the simple to the complex, or from the biological/natural to the social/cultural, here, as 'foolishest' (or 'most natural'?) decoration leads into protection ('Security' and 'Heat', which then develops into shame and modesty (involving religion and belief systems) before finally becoming what is effectively a version of socio-cultural identity and difference and a concomitant politics. This latter suggestion is followed up later in the book when Carlyle has Professor Teufelsdrockh twice present the idea that society is founded on cloth. He introduces the matter on p. 41, only to say that it would be a mad ambition to try to explain the professor's presentation, but returns to the matter on pp. 47–8, where the example of the hanging judge and the criminal is discussed. In this example, one person is dressed in fine Red and one in 'coarse threadbare Blue'; Red says to Blue 'Be hanged and anatomised' and Blue marches to the gallows, where he is duly hanged, brought down and made into a 'skeleton for medical purposes'. Carlyle's point is that it is what Red is wearing, the squirrel fur and the horsehair wig, that constructs him in a position and a role as a judge and, along with that identity, gives him the authority to thus order Blue to be hanged. Consequently, he says that society is 'founded upon cloth'.

Two of Carlyle's other suggestions will be followed up here: that of security and that of modesty. Maybe everyone has a favourite winter coat, which they can wrap around themselves and in which they feel safe from the worst the weather can throw at them; the US Army extreme cold weather parka certainly seems designed to make its wearers feel totally bombproof and as though they personally could invade and take over any country with absolute impunity. And both Poll (1965: 146) and Roach Higgins et al. (1995: 221–35) note the case of the Hasidic Jew who described how wearing traditional Hasidic clothing left him feeling more secure: it 'serve[d] as a guard and a shield from sin and obscenity', he said. In his section on modesty, Rene Koenig refers to Isaiah iii, 16–24, which reports the Lord's threat to punish the haughty, mincing, wanton women of Zion for what appears to be their fashionable dress (Koenig 1973: 29–30). He will take away their bracelets, mufflers, bonnets, headbands, rings, earrings and nose-jewels, as well as their fine linens and they shall be made to wear sackcloth. While it is arguably the wives' 'wanton eyes' and 'bravery' – that is, their lack of modesty – that the Lord objects to, the list of their finery given in these six verses is indeed impressive.

The tension between the way an item of fashion looks (its form) and the job it is here to perform (its function) has long been debated. However, the tension is actually a priority and there are two possible ways that priority can be organised. The first way is expressed in Louis Sullivan's (1896) so-called law of modern design – 'form follows function'. Sullivan is actually writing about tall buildings, but the principle may be applied to any and all items of design. He is expressing the idea that the way a piece of design looks is or should be secondary to its function, its job or purpose. The function of the object 'drives' or determines the way the thing looks on this account. And the second way is to say that form has priority over function: that is, no matter what the item's function is, the most important thing is for it to look good or stylish or, indeed, fashionable. This 'law' has much in common with another principle of modern design – that ornament is a crime. This principle is attributed to Adolf Loos, the modernist architect. To suggest that ornament is a crime is to suggest that any and/or all decoration should be avoided, and Loos says this because he thinks that decoration and ornament cause items to go out of style (or fashion) too quickly. Modernism is not interested in here-today-gone-tomorrow fads, but wants to make a long-lasting, if not eternal impression on art and design. Both of these laws or principles, however, agree that function comes first, that it has priority over form – the ways things look. Now, if fashion involves an emphasis on the formal and decorative, on the ways things look (as opposed to the functional), and if modernism would eschew the decorative and non-functional, then either fashion cannot be modern or, if it is modern, its function will be subordinate to its form. These ideas are revisited in Part Nine, on modernism.

The third question raised was whether the discussion of fashion and clothing in terms of functions entails the reduction of fashion and clothing to a series of 'causes and effects' (Entwistle 2000: 57). It has to be said at the outset that to explain all the things that people wear in terms of either modesty/display, protection or decoration does seem to invite accusations of reduction. What of the things that we wear without intending to be either modest or immodest? What, precisely, of what we think we're doing when we wear clothes *per se*? There is no obvious place for the agent's own accounts of what they are doing if it is already decided in advance that what is happening when we wear clothes is either modesty/display, protection or decoration.

Consequently, the readings collected here present three classic sources for the account of what it is that fashion and clothing do. Mary Ellen Roach and Joanne Eicher's chapter, written in 1979, is a comprehensive account of the things that clothing does. The authors cover an enormous range of functions and provide examples of each. Elizabeth Rouse's account of how fashion and clothing provide a certain level of modesty and concealment, and also allow for various forms of immodesty and display, is also included here. Finally, John Flügel's 1930 description of the protective functions of clothes, including spiritual protection, is also included.

Bibliography

Carlyle, T. (1987) *Sartor Resartus*, Oxford: Oxford University Press.

Entwistle, J. (2000) *The Fashioned Body*, London: Polity.

Koenig, R. (1973) *The Restless Image*, London: George Allen and Unwin Ltd.

Poll, S. (1965) 'The Hasidic Community', in M. E. Roach and J. B. Eicher (eds) *Dress, Adornment and the Social Order*, New York: John Wiley and Sons.

Roach, M. E. and Eicher, J. B. (eds) (1965) *Dress, Adornment and the Social Order*, London and New York: John Wiley and Sons.

—— (1979) 'The Language of Personal Adornment', in J. M. Cordwell and R. A. Schwartz (eds) *The Fabrics of Culture: The Anthropology of Clothing and Adornment*, The Hague: Mouton Publishers.

Roach-Higgins, M. E., Eicher, J. B. and Johnson, K. K. P. (eds) (1995) *Dress and Identity*, New York: Fairchild Publications.

Sullivan, L. (1896) 'The Tall Office Building Artistically Considered', *Lippincott's Magazine*, New York, March.

Chapter 9

Mary Ellen Roach and Joanne Bubolz Eicher

THE LANGUAGE OF PERSONAL ADORNMENT

PERSONAL ADORNMENT is characteristic of all societies, whereas coverings that protect are not. For many people, dressing oneself can be an aesthetic act, and all aesthetic acts are acts of speaking, through which an individual may speak as an individual, what is said having meaning only because of relationships with other people. Aesthetic acts do not grow out of a vacuum, but from what is learned from others. For example, no one individual invents fine dress, instead, the language of personal adornment is acquired from others. Personally unique inventions embellish or modify the "tongue" learned from human associates, but do not represent a new language of dress.

The form of a society's language of personal adornment depends upon environmental resources, technical developments, and cultural standards for judging what is fine or beautiful; and an individual may speak the dialect of a specific sub-group within a society. Beautiful dress or finery in one group may be represented by clean and neat dress, in another by a jewel-studded crown, in still another by an array of body scars. The form of what is *most* or *least* "fine" also depends upon the social group from which the standards for judging "fineness" emerge. Clean and neat dress may be a maximum standard for beauty in dress among those in American lower economic levels for example, but only a minimum standard for middle levels.

Adornment as aesthetic experience

The individual can derive aesthetic pleasure from both the act of creating personal display and from the contemplation of his own display and that of others. In either the creative or contemplative act a person is concerned with the characteristics of body and dress that prompt aesthetic responses. The body itself has its aesthetically describable qualities — color, texture, shape, and dimension — and the added materials of adornment modify the total arrangement displayed by an individual.

Reactions to the three-dimensional, and mobile, presentation of body and dress on the basis of its aesthetic qualities alone are almost impossible; for as human beings receive stimuli they continually process and respond to these stimuli attributing meaning to them. Thus, what is seen may stimulate an aesthetic response, but it also carries a number of other messages, frequently of social and psychological significance.

Individualistic expressions through personal adornment

MOOD. Personal adornment may reflect inner emotional states called mood. It may also reinforce, disguise, or create mood. An individual caught up in a certain mood may wish to externalize it so it can be conveyed to and shared with others. Perhaps an individual feels light-hearted and energetic. In America, a culturally recognized way to create this effect is to choose constume with colors and linear arrangements that show contrast rather than sameness. Typically, color contrast can be attained by using a number of different colors together, by using bright colors that contrast with a somber background, and by using sharp differences in lightness and darkness of color. Linear contrast occurs if lines suddenly change direction or intersect when proceeding in different directions. The culturally encouraged interpretation is that the redirection of eye movements required by line contrasts is symbolic of a dynamic inner state within the wearer. Thus, at least for Americans, contrasting line and color in costume can express exuberant mood to others and also reinforce the same mood in the wearer.

Dressing in a certain way, however, may contradict rather than support mood. To banish depression and melancholy, an individual may deliberately wear dress of color and design which is thought to express opposite feelings, the joyful and buoyant, for example. Success in changing mood may depend also on other environmental changes, such as change in activity or human company. A more complex kind of mood change can come with the putting on of new clothes. Part of the reorientation of mood that some people receive from new clothes results from response to crisp new textures and the unblemished quality of the color and design that has not been altered by wear. A new item may affect mood by reinforcing an individual's feeling of uniqueness and providing a break from the sameness of appearance that an individual had been presenting for a period of time. However, the reaction of an individual is also likely to be highly social in reference. New clothes may be a way of acquiring the confidence that comes with "good" timing within the fashion cycle. The anticipation is that new clothing places one more surely within the range of the most admired appearances of the moment and, therefore, in a position of social approval. Thus mood change may grow out of adjustments to social environment as well as aesthetic responses.

Dress may be used to hide feelings from others with no expectation of trans-forming one's mood. If the disguise of mood is to be convincing, gesture, body stance, and voice tones must complement dress, otherwise associates will not be deceived.

An individual who consciously decides to "dress up" or "dress down" perceives the possibility of creating mood through dress, particularly if the act of "dressing up" or "dressing down" is isolated from any particular social event or occasion. In the theater and in dance performances, such conscious use of dress is the rule, for performers are expected to use dress to create a mood that can be communicated to and participated in by their audience. The dress is a cue that communicates mood from performers to audience, a mood which may in turn be conveyed back to performers.

Dress used in ceremonial rites contributes to the creation of mood. For example, because of sentiments attached to traditional bridal attire, it can add to the solemnity or joy inspired by the traditional music, precise movements, and recitations of a wedding ceremony. The lively spirit of festivals may be promoted by clothing clearly designated to be festival dress and not everyday attire. Festive dress ordinarily presents colors, materials, accessories, and designs that are different from dress worn every day.

DIFFERENTIATION FROM OTHERS. Complementing, yet opposing, forces that influence people's lives are those that provide feelings of individual worth and those that assure social value. Preservation of some kind of balance between these forces contributes to emotional survival. Although one learns the language of personal adornment from peers, and thus may be expected to conform somewhat to their patterns of dress, one can also show determination to be an individual and declare uniqueness through dress. Differentiation of one's self from others on the basis of dress relates to rarity. Acquiring the most expensive clothing is often a way of achieving differentiation through rarity, which usually commands social admiration. Rarity, however, sometimes has quite an opposite social effect. The least expensive clothing may be comparatively rare within a society with widely dispersed economic resources, and may be owned by the poor. The type of clothing may be their possession exclusively, but its quality of rarity does not automatically bring social value; instead, it is more likely just the opposite. For those who reject the expensive, or wish to identify with the poor, the inexpensive (like bib overalls) may express individual philosophy and ethical stance.

The new and fashionable also has the quality of rarity for a time and may set one apart. The position of a form of dress within the fashion cycle, from introduction to obsolescence, has interesting effects on rarity. An item just out of fashion may be relatively rare but, because of its recent descent into the realm of the unfashionable, socially unpopular. However, given sufficient age, an out-of-date fashion takes on the aura of the antique and it may become a device used to show uniqueness. English and American youth discovered this route to individual expression in the 1960s and early 1970s. The display of attic discoveries or secondhand store finds were sources of unique expressions of dress by youth, regardless of their economic level.

Individual differentiation also depends on reference group. Thus individual differentiation from general societal norms for dress is different from subgroup differentiation in that the individual who is differentiated in appearance from general society may still be conforming to group code, that of the subgroup. The individualist looks for differentiation no matter what group he is in. Thus "hippies" of the 1960s sought individuality within the accepted code of dress of their peers, whereas Liberace or Tiny Tim in their early careers were truly individuals.

Contrary to popular belief, widespread mass production of clothing does not eliminate possibilities of dressing uniquely. It places its own peculiar limitations on forms produced, but the high volume of goods produced, in America at least, allows room for greatly varied combinations of clothing, especially in color and texture, and in type of combinable items. For some observers this can be a confusing variety, since the communicative efficiency of dress is reduced as the possible types of expected appearance multiply in number.

Adornment as definition of social role

Adornment is communicative of many subtleties in social relations. It suggests the behaviors (roles) expected of people on the basis of their various and sometimes multiple connections with each other and can, therefore, distinguish the powerful from the weak, the rich from the poor, the hero from the outcast, the conformer from the nonconformer, the religious from the irreligious, the leader from the follower. It *can* make these distinctions, but not necessarily so. Just as verbal language can be deceptive, so can the language of dress. Individuals can assume disguises to deceive the observer. Such a disguise usually involves dress, but requires correlation of dress with other style-of-life symbols. We can seldom be fooled by people we know, but we can be deceived by strangers because we depend almost entirely upon external cues of dress and grooming, facial expression, tone of voice, and conversational style, plus props such as automobiles or furnishings in living quarters to identify them.

Not all disguise via dress is deception: in the theater, players deliberately dress to fit a role, choosing costume that helps the audience identify the age, social class, sex, or occupation of the character being portrayed, and the audience knows that the dress used is intended to transform the actor temporarily into the stage character and obliterate for the moment the real-life identity of the person playing the part.

Beau Brummell remains a classic example of someone who used clothing and other props purposely to establish a role for himself in a situation that was not make-believe or deceptive. The careful way in which he prepared the setting for his entrance into society suggests that his arrival as leader of the fashionable elite of London was more than fortuitous circumstance (Franzero 1958). Brummell's education at Eton and the opportunity to meet the Prince of Wales helped him establish a foothold in society, as did a modest inheritance from his father. But more important was the astuteness with which he chose his acquaintances and put his inheritance to work. He bought several good horses in order to transport himself in "correct" style. He chose his apartment carefully so that it would be in the "right" location. He hired a cook who could prepare exquisite meals for dinner parties and invited groups of carefully chosen guests. Within the security of the "right" setting he practiced the art of personal dress to its fullest and established a unique image for himself in a position between the florid elegance of the earlier part of the eighteenth century and the neglect in dress affected by some fashionable Englishmen in the latter part of the century. The lingering legend of Beau Brummell after more than a century is proof that his uniqueness aided him in establishing his role as fashion leader.

In times of great social unrest and rapid change, an individual's approach to dress is likely to reflect general social upheaval. The hypothesis that variability in dress reflects conflict concerning content of social roles (Bush and London 1960) appeared to be substantiated in the late 1960s and the early 1970s. Racial roles, the roles of rich and poor, the roles of male and female, were questioned and efforts made, particularly by the young, to articulate new roles within all these categories, and to wear dress that reflected these new roles. Sometimes during a time of testing new roles the language of dress becomes a jumbled code, difficult to decipher. For example, a study of college students in the late 1960s showed that variation in style of dress was a weak indicator of radicalness of political ideas, even though the general public was interpreting forms of dress that deviated greatly from the traditional as indicating political radicalism (*Life* 1970).

Adornment as statement of social worth

Evaluations of social worth are often made on the basis of personal adornment. In some societies valued kinds of adornment are widely available to all, with perhaps some restrictions placed on age. Among the Andamans, when studied by Radcliffe-Brown (1933) scarification was a mark of added value generally available to all boys and girls who were at the threshold of adulthood. The kind of value it bestowed and the incentives to acquire them were thus described:

> The explanation of the rite [scarification] would therefore seem to be that it marks the passage from childhood to manhood and is a means by which the society bestows upon the individual that power, or social value, which is possessed by the adult but not by the child. . . . The individual is made to feel that his value — his strength and the qualities of which he may be proud — is not his by nature but is received by him from the society to which he is admitted. The scars on his body are the visible marks of this admission. The individual is proud or vain of the scars which are the mark of his manhood, and thus the society makes use of the very powerful sentiment of personal vanity to strengthen the social sentiments (1933:315).

In societies with sharp social divisions of caste or class, adornment that represents the most desirable symbols of social worth may be exclusive to an upper-class elite. The elite maintain a monopoly on these symbols as long as they maintain a monopoly on wealth, for lack of economic resources prohibits lower classes from adopting adornment that could proclaim for them a social worth equal to that of the upper class. However, when wealth becomes more available to the common man, as happened in the Late Middle Ages, the upper classes cannot automatically keep "fine dress" exclusive to their class. Enactment of sumptuary law is one way a social group may try to stave off obliteration of the outward distinctions of class that exclusive access to finery provides them. In the late seventeenth century in Nuremberg, where four ranks of society were recognized, the paternalistic government regulated the amount that citizens of all ranks could spend on clothes, weddings, christenings, and burials. Regulation on dress included top-to-toe specifications. Specifically, a late fourteenth-century Nuremberg ordinance indicated that "no burgher, young or old, shall wear his hair parted; they shall wear the hair in tufts as it has been worn from of old" (Greenfield 1918:109). An order of the mid-fifteenth century directed cobblers "on pain of a definite penalty henceforth to make no more peaks on the shoes" (1918:110). Equally intriguing is that even horses had differential access to adornment, for they also had to abide by the sumptuary laws that bound their masters. In the upper class the horse that drew a bride's coach might have his forelock, mane, and tail tied with a colored ribbon; in the second class only his forelock and tail; in the third class nothing but his forelock (1918:128).

Earlier in origin, much more explicit and detailed, and more restrictive, were sumptuary laws in Japan (Hearn 1904:183–185). However, they reached their peak at about the same time as in Europe, that is, about the seventeenth century. During the Tokugawa period (1600–1867) the regulations for the farmer classes varied according to their income and described in great detail the limitations placed on the exact length of houses, the kinds of foods to be served, and the fibers to be used in the thongs of sandals. In the family of a farmer worth 20 *koku* of rice, no one was allowed to wear leather sandals: only straw sandals or wooden clogs were permitted and throngs of the sandals or the clogs were to be made of cotton. In the family of a farmer assessed at 10 *koku* the women of the family were required to wear sandals with thongs of bamboo grass.

When wealth is widely enough dispersed for lower classes of people to afford finery in dress similar to that worn by those in the upper classes, but they are prevented from doing so by strict enforcement of sumptuary laws, they may spend money on adorning themselves in ways unique to their own social level and not competitive with other classes. Some regional dress in Europe is such a phenomenon, and represents a phase in the long transition from feudalism to capitalism. Davenport (1948:376) suggests that much of European regional dress emerged in the sixteenth century when the bourgeoisie costume became differentiated on the basis of provinces or sometimes cities. These differentiations became a basis for the later peasant regional costume. As the well-to-do bourgeoisie climbed the social ladder to become gentry, the peasantry were also rising, and well-to-do peasants could afford to adopt the regionally unique costume of the former bourgeoisie.

Adornment as indicator of economic status

Adorning oneself can reflect connections with the system of production characteristic of the particular economy within which one lives. Clothing worn at work can identify the productive, that is, occupational role of an individual. A uniform and badge indicate services expected from a policeman; a pin, cap, and white uniform the services expected from a nurse. Other costumes place individuals in general occupational categories: white-collar apparel (suit with shirt and tie) is, for example, associated with many levels of office work and the professions. Blue-collar apparel of denim or work twill is associated with some kind of manual labor.

In America, women's dress is generally more ambiguous in its symbolism of occupational role than is men's. This ambiguity stems partly from the tendency of industrial societies to recognize only occupational roles that produce money income and partly from traditions established during the nineteenth century. Thus, because they do not receive money income for work, the large number of women who are exclusively homemakers, performing many productive tasks within their households and communities, do not have clearly perceived positions within the American occupational structure, and correspondingly no form of dress that clearly distinguishes them as belonging to a particular occupational category. However, persistence of nineteenth-century traditions concerning male and female roles is probably what more strongly limits symbolic association between women's dress and occupation; for nineteenth-century society developed an expectation of women to indulge in personal display through dress, contrasted with an expectation of men to eschew such display and to garb themselves in somber symbols of the occupations provided by an industrializing society. In the twentieth century, women continue to fulfill the display role, exhibiting a great deal of variety in their dress, as they are homemakers and also as many of them are workers in a number of different occupations. Among white-collar women workers, who represent the largest percentage of women in the labor force, relatively little consistency in dress has developed to symbolize the occupational category, despite occasional drifting in that direction. At the turn of the century, for instance, a costume consisting of a dark skirt and a shirtwaist seemed destined to become a standardized type of dress for female white-collar workers since it was widely used by them and in a general way resembled the type of dress that had become standard wear for male white-collar workers. But, as time passed, competing forms brought variety into the dress of female white-collar workers and the shirtwaist and skirt did not emerge as long-lasting symbols for the group. A trend in the 1970s toward use of so-called career clothes by female as well as male workers in some business institutions such as banks may indicate that occupational dress symbolizing white-collar work for females has simply been slow in coming, or it may represent one more drifting toward consistency that will disappear as variety reasserts itself.

As far as economic symbolism is concerned, women's dress probably indicates ability to consume more clearly that occupational role since consumption is dependent on money available, no matter what the source. This is not to say that type of work, and the skill with which it is done, does not affect dress, for occupation affects income, and income, in turn, directly affects ability to consume, hence the opportunity for both men and women to indulge in personal display. In some societies, because of religious conviction or moral precept, conspicuous display in dress is at a minimum no matter what level of income. In others display is confined to class levels that can afford it. In still others ability to display is widely available and actual display largely a matter of personal values and philosophy.

Adornment as political symbol

Adornment has long had a place in the house of power. It may show the position of a person in a hierarchial system of authority; it may be visible proof of affiliation with a particular political party, or dedication to one political ideology and opposition to another. If political power passes from one ideological group to another, sometimes the entering group will adopt the symbolic dress of their predecessors. Napoleon reintroduced types of dress that were symbols of state from the old regime to support the legitimacy of his empire visually and to unite the old and new elite. At other times a group will institute its own symbols of dress, as did Castro and his followers when they adopted drab fatigue uniforms. At yet other times, subtle modifications in dress, rather than radical change, may occur among the politically sensitive. For example, the military coups in Nigeria in the 1960s resulted in de-emphasis of the Nigerian "national" dress among the Ibo politicians and civil servants of eastern Nigeria, because the "national" dress symbolized the peoples of the west and north, that is, their political opposition.

An occasional political figure may have unique adornment that helps set him apart in his elevated position of leadership. Moshe Dayan, defense minister of Israel in the 1960s and 1970s made a black eye patch more than a cover: it was his particular ornament and mark of identification. The brown derby was the personal identification mark of Al Smith, New York politician and Democratic party leader, who ran for president of the United States in 1928, whereas the ten-gallon hat symbolized Lyndon B. Johnson in the 1970s.

Traditional ceremonial costume of royalty has become less common in the world, but the investiture of Prince Charles in 1969 as Prince of Wales gave opportunity for traditional costume to mix with the contemporary. Queen Elizabeth dressed in twentieth-century fashions but her son, the prince, was bedecked in eighteenth-century splendor. The 1970 wedding of the crown prince of Nepal was another occasion for much traditional ceremonial display. In both cases fineness in dress indicated the elevated political status of the participants (*Newsweek* 1970).

Military and police uniforms with various kinds of ornamentation call attention to those who stand ready to exert force in maintaining social order according to the authority delegated to them by those in positions of power. Police uniforms adorned with brass buttons, badges, buckles, and insignia announce the policemen whose job is to help with law enforcement. Identification of police uniforms as symbols commanding respect was sometimes challenged in America in the 1960's, as sentiments were expressed against what was considered the dehumanized, impersonal nature of police authority within America's mass society. This loss of respect for the uniform sometimes encouraged its abandonment, apparently in the hope that removal of the uniform would also remove hostility it might symbolically stimulate in encounters between police and the public. In 1969 *Newsweek* reported that a growing number of police forces were moving into civilian clothes in an effort to reduce a military image which had become unpopular and to encourage people to regard policemen as "friends" (*Newsweek* 1969).

Decorative emblems frequently accompany planned political activities. Pins, badges, armbands, and hats often declare political affiliation and support. American political conventions are usually made colorful by these kinds of identification. In protest marches against the war in Vietnam in 1969, black armbands identified those voicing their protest.

During the reign of Queen Anne in Britain in the early years of the eighteenth century, preferences for political parties could be indicated by beauty patches. Whig women patched the right cheek, the Tories the left, and those who were neutral, both cheeks. Out of either vanity or political fervor, one woman in 1771 stipulated in her marriage contract that she be permitted to patch on the side she pleased no matter what her husband's political stand was (Andres 1892:192).

The seriousness with which people may take the ideological symbolism of dress was probably never so clear as during the French Revolution, when fine dress and powdered hair identifying the aristocracy placed them at the risk of being arrested by the revolutionaries (Davenport 1948:653). Trousers also were an important symbol of political differentiation: to be a *sans-culotte* was to be a revolutionary who wore tubular trousers; knee-breeches (*culottes*) belonged to the aristocracy.

Powdered hair lasted longer in England than in France but there, too, met political opposition. When a flour shortage hit England, anyone using hair powder was required to purchase a license at one guinea per year (Ashton 1885:60–61, 73). In angry opposition to the legislation, the Whigs in 1795 entreated men to abandon hair powder. Some organized the Crop Club, a group that cut off their hair and made a ceremony of combing out the powder.

A twentieth-century social movement with strong political intent is the women's liberation movement that gained momentum toward the end of the 1960s. The members of this movement did not have physically restricting dress to protest against as did their nineteenth-century predecessors, but they followed in the spirit of their feminist forebear by protesting against the social restraints of their clothing. Rejection of cosmetics, elaborate hairstyles, foundation garments, and of the practice of removing body hair was a symbolic demand for freedom from customs that placed women in a position of dependency upon rather than equality with men.

Adornment as indicator of magico-religious condition

An individual's approach to self-adornment may reflect affiliation with a religious sect or denomination. In addition, it may show position within a religious group and possibly indicate the intensity of a person's religious participation. Some dress showing religious affiliation or position was once common, fashionable dress of laymen, but, as the dress of the laymen changed, the dress of the religious did not — perhaps as a symbolic reinforcement of belief in the everlasting value of the tenets of the religion to which they subscribed. Sometimes the dress used was formerly the clothes of the poor people, at other times the dress of the well-to-do. In either case, the antique appearance of forms of dress characteristic of an earlier time sets apart the religious individuals or groups who are wearing them so that they can readily be distinguished. The Roman Catholic church has retained examples of dress that typify the poor and the rich of bygone days — some of the vestments of the priests take their form from the everyday costume of well-to-do Romans. From the fourth century, while Roman dress changed steadily, church dress changed little if at all. The male monastic orders, however, adopted and kept the everyday dress of the poor people of the Middle Ages. For example, St. Benedict, in the sixth century, prescribed the scapular, which had been a farm-laborer's apron, as the work garment of his monks (Davenport 1948:99; Norris 1947:172). The women's orders, evolving later than the men's, wore tunics or frocks similar to those worn by the male orders but with added draped head coverings similar to those of widows and married women of the Middle Ages.

The dress of the Roman Catholic clergy shows how clothing can indicate position and rank within a religious structure, with different dress prescribed for different clerical ranks such as priest, bishop, cardinal, and pope. Outstanding distinctions in clerical dress are the tiara of the pope and the scarlet costume of the cardinal. These items and others identify relative positions in a hierarchial system of prestige, responsibility, and power.

The dress of the Hasidic Jews is considered by them to be apparel once worn by all Jews (Poll 1962:65). Since most present-day Jews dress similarly to non-Jews, the costume worn by the Hasidim is an exclusive symbol of their sect. Hasidic men and women in America utilize systems of dress related to other American dress but with distinguishing differences. The dress of the Hasidic men indicates for them their degree of religious intensity. The greater the number of rituals and the more intensely these are observed, the greater the esteem accorded a person, and costume makes known to the individual and to others this degree of intensity. The less the fervor of a man's religious observance, the more his appearance resembles that of a man in modern Western dress. The most religious class, the Rebbes, have the greatest quantity of Hasidic elaborations in dress. The Yiden class wear the fewest of the Hasidic symbols and are the least religious and also least ritualistic (Poll 1962:59–69).

The relation of adornment to the individual as a religious figure may differ. Adornment may protect the religious individual in his encounter with the supernatural; it may prepare him to act as celebrant of a religious rite; it may symbolize his leadership in acts of petition or meditation; and it may also be a means for his assuming the power of the supernatural, as he puts on the clothes of God.

Adornment as a facility in social rituals

In many rituals of social life, such as weddings, funerals, feasts, and dance, dressing up in garb with more fineness than that used in routine day-to-day existence is expected. Dress used for such events may range between the best dress one has to a very explicitly prescribed type of dress, Donning the dress generally marks "putting on a mood": ritual cheerfulness and gaiety or ritual sadness and gloom may, for example, be required. In Western society the traditional black garb of the widow identifies her as the chief mourner. How well an individual can assume the required mood may determine how socially at ease the person will be in the ritual situation.

Adornment as reinforcement of belief, custom, and values

Adornment, or rejection of adornment, may serve as a means for symbolically tying a community together. Agreement on bodily adornment reinforces common consciousness and a common course of action that holds people together in a closely knit group. This unifying function of adornment is easier to identify in a small, homogeneous society than in heterogeneous mass society, because not all groups within the latter type of society have the same beliefs, attitudes, and values. In the small Amish community, for example, a very clear-cut symbolism can be observed within their very restricted definition of finery (Hostetler 1963:131–148). Amish dress admits individuals into full participation with the society of the Amish and clarifies the part each plays. Hats thus distinguish the Amish from outsiders, but variations do exist in hats for young boys, bridegrooms, grandfathers, and for bishops. Their dress stands as an ever-present reminder of the Amish position in society and of the individual duties associated with Amish life.

The Hasidim are also aware that their religious dress may protect them from the disunifying effect of outside influences, as illustrated by the following remark of a Hasidic Jew:

> With my appearance I cannot attend a theater or movie or any other place where a religious Jew is not supposed to go. Thus my beard and my sidelocks and my Hasidic clothing serve as a guard and a shield from sin and obscenity (Poll 1962:65).

Adornment as recreation

For people who have leisure time available as well as the opportunity for display, acquiring materials for personal adornment or adorning oneself may be recreational activities, that is, they may provide respite from regular routines, responsibilities, and work. As the recreational purpose is achieved, however, other functions may also be served. For instance, in societies where leisure is a scarce resource monopolized by a social elite, personal display that is recreational may become an indicator of social class.

During the nineteenth and twentieth centuries American society has generally allotted more discretionary control of time to women than to men; therefore, dressing as a recreational activity has been more characteristic of the former. For the same reason — available time — male and female adolescents in the twentieth century have used dress as a recreational outlet more often than older age groups. An aspect of the entertainment value of dress was also identifiable among the youth in the 1960s and early 1970s who used unique adornment to authenticate that they were "doing their own thing" — really joining in a popular search for identity.

Adornment as sexual symbol

Male and female have historically been differentiated by their dress. However, bodily adornment of the sexes has not only been used to distinguish one sex from the other but also for the purpose of sexual enticement. Obviously, emphasizing the genital area by special ornamentation or type of clothing focuses attention on that area. The codpiece, a decorated covering for the male genitals, is one example. The "pasties" over the nipples of a burlesque dancer is an example for females. Padding of men's shoulders and women's breasts and hips emphasizes differences in male and female body contours.

Dress used to entice members of the opposite sex may be considered within two settings: private and public. Private or intimate settings are best exemplified by

the bedroom or boudoir where undergarments, sleeping garments, or lack of garments, are used to lure one's spouse, lover, or momentary companion into sexual
involvement. These liaisons may represent legal or illegal relationships between the
sexes or between members of the same sex. Historically, adorning the body has
been an integral symbol of sexual enticement. Public settings such as the street,
restaurants, and theaters are places where dress can be a public announcement of
sexual identity and an enticement to private settings. Prior to enticement, whether
for heterosexual or homosexual involvement, sexual identification must occur.
Dress and ornamentation may emphasize body characteristics and mannerisms that
have been culturally defined as symbolic of sexual enticement. Emphasizing body
characteristics beyond what the mode in dress prescribes has often provided the
additional variable necessary for enticement. Thus, micro-miniskirts during the time
of the miniskirt, the tightest sweaters during the era of the sweater girl, or the most
sleekly fitting trousers for males, may publicly announce the availability of the
wearers for sexual pursuits. Films have stereotyped the dress of the prostitute in
Western society so that red high-heeled shoes and a matching handbag worn with
tightly-fitting clothing and heavy makeup are common symbols.

In countries, ordinarily tropical, where a completely or partially nude body is
the norm in public, the nude body with its obvious sexual distinguishing characteristics is seldom used for sexual enticement purposes, while ornament may. In special
nude enclaves within clothed societies, such as in Europe and America, nudist-
colony members claim the nude body is less enticing than the clothed body. Some
analysts of behavior in these colonies explain the differences as essentially cultural.
Interaction patterns are altered among the nudists so that more controls are placed
on touching and looking at each other and on verbalization with sexual references
than among nonnudists (Weinberg 1968:217–219).

Summary

Adornment is a communicative symbol that serves crucial functions within human
lives. Individual satisfaction may be derived from pleasurable emotional experiences
prompted by both display and observation of the adornment provided by dress,
whether extensively or minimally developed. Adoring oneself supports the individual in his endeavors to speak as a unique individual and provides him a way of
expressing, reinforcing, initiating, or camouflaging mood. At the same time that
adornment offers a way for individual expression and for dealing with life aesthetically, it serves a number of useful functions within society. It can be used to indicate
social roles, to establish social worth, as a symbol of economic status, as an emblem
of political power or ideological inclination, as a reflection of magico-religious
condition, as a facility in social rituals, and as a reinforcement of beliefs, custom, and
values. Furthermore, adornment can be elaborated into a recreational activity and
utilized in sexual enticement.

References

Andres, William (1892) *Bygone England*, London: Hutchinson.

Ashton, A. John (1885) *Old times*, London: J. C. Mimmo.

Bush, George, Perry London (1960) "On the Disappearance of Knickers: Hypothesis for the Functional Analysis of the Psychology of Clothing," *Journal of Social Psychology* 51: 359–366. (Reprinted in *Dress, Adornment and the Social Order*, edited by Mary Ellen Roach and Joanne Bubolz Eicher, New York: John Wiley and Sons, pp. 64–72.)

Davenport, Millia (1948) *The Book of Costume*, New York: Crown.

Franzero, Charles Marie (1958) *Beau Brummell: His Life and Times*, New York: John Day.

Greenfield, Kent Roberts (1918) *Sumptuary Law in Nürnburg: A Study in Paternal Government*, Baltimore: Johns Hopkins University Press.

Hearn, Lafcadio (1904) *Japan*, New York: Macmillan.

Hostetler, John A. (1963) *Amish Society*, Balimore: Johns Hopkins University Press. *Life* (1970) Which Would You Pick Up? Guess Again, *Life* 68 (March 13): 61–62. *Newsweek* (1969) Out of the Blue, *Newsweek*, 74, 13 (September 29): 79.

(1970) Nepal: "Come, Let Us Marry," *Newsweek* 75, 11 (March 16): 14–15.

Norris, Herbert (1947) *Costume and Fashion*, London: J. M. Dent and Sons.

Poll, Solomon (1962) *The Hasidic Community of Williamsburg*, New York: Free Press of Glencoe.

Radcliffe-Brown, A. R. (1933) *The Andaman Islanders*, Cambridge: Cambridge University Press.

Weinberg, Martin S. (1968) "Sexual Modesty and the Nudist Camp," in *Deviance: The Interactionist Perspective*, edited by Earl Rubington and Martin S. Weinberg, New York: Macmillan, pp. 217–219.

Chapter 10

Elizabeth Rouse

WHY DO PEOPLE WEAR CLOTHES?

[. . .]

Modesty

IT IS QUITE commonly believed that we wear clothes because certain parts of our bodies are shameful and need to be covered. Attitudes of this kind have their origins in the religious mythology of Judaeo-Christian tradition, in particular in the story of Adam and Eve.

> And they were both naked, the man and his wife, and they were not ashamed . . . And when the woman saw the tree was good for food, and that it was pleasant to the eyes, and a tree to be desired to make one wise, she took of the fruit thereof, and did eat, and also gave unto her husband with her; and he did eat. And the eyes of both of them were opened, and they knew that they were naked; and they sewed fig leaves together, and made themselves aprons . . . Unto Adam also and to his wife did the Lord God make coats of skins and clothed them.[1]

For a long time this allegory was accepted as literal fact, and it has had a tremendous influence on our attitudes to our bodies and on our feelings about nakedness. Were clothes invented then as a result of feelings about nakedness. Were clothes invented then as a result of feelings of shame and a sense of sinfulness?

The theory of evolution has done much to undermine the general acceptance of the Genesis story, and naturist and nudist groups have attempted to challenge the notion that the naked human body is sinful, or something to be ashamed of. But, there are very few amongst us who would not feel embarrassed if we found ourselves sitting on a bus, or walking down our local high street stark naked. However, we are not experiencing the same kind of shame as Adam and Eve. It is not just a matter of covering certain prohibited areas of the body as the Genesis story implies. Even if we wear our underwear and, therefore, are theoretically decent, we would still be embarrassed. *This is because modesty or shame is relative.* The amount and type of clothing varies according to social context and we feel embarrassed if we are not wearing the appropriate type and number. We are quite happy to appear in minimal clothing on a beach but not in a bus queue. All over the world people have different ideas about what one should be modest about. An Australian Aboriginal woman for example has only the minimal attire of a belt round her waist and necklace whereas a Muslim woman will reveal nothing of her face and figure . . . These examples undermine the view that covering certain parts of the body is universal in mankind. In Britain, a study of fashionable dress in the last hundred years would show quite dramatic shifts in standards of modesty. In the Victorian period, women concealed their ankles but displayed their shoulders and breasts; in the twenties women exposed more of their legs than ever before; and in the thirties they exposed their backs in evening dress cut to the waist. Today, we are witnessing changes in ideas about decency as nudist beaches become more popular and topless sunbathing for women becomes popular in the Mediterranean, if not in Britain.

It seems then that our sense of embarrassment and modesty comes not from shame of particular parts of the body but the loss of what we are accustomed to wearing or feel is required in a particular situation. A Muslim woman would be embarrassed without her veil, the Victorian lady without her long skirts, and the conventional English holidaymaker without her bikini top. Embarrassment is not necessarily linked to lack of clothes. As Marilyn Horn points out: 'Among the Suya Indians of Brazil, for example, neither men nor women are the least bit embarrassed by their naked bodies, but are humiliated if caught without their lip disks.'[2] A lip disk is the customary form of body decoration among the Suya, an essential part of normal appearance.

People do not have an innate sense of shame; young children are conspicuously lacking in a sense of modesty. As they grow up, they are taught which parts of their bodies should be concealed. They learn this along with many other kinds of knowledge and behaviour necessary for life amongst the group of people in which they live. A child is not embarrassed by a lack of clothing until he has become accustomed to wearing them. Children brought up in groups where very little clothing is worn are not embarrassed by their near-nakedness. *It must be said that modesty or shame was not a causal factor in the initial development of clothes, but is merely a result of the habit of wearing them.*

Attraction

The modesty theory has been attacked from another point of view. Clothing, it has been suggested, does not draw attention away from the body, or reduce an awareness of it as is implied in the term 'modesty'. Rather, the converse is true. Clothing actually serves to display the body and exhibit it in order to gain admiration. One writer, Rudofsky, compares the wearing of clothes to the sexual displays of birds and animals:

> It seems that man's and animals' clothes serve much the same purpose – sexual selection. Only the roles of the sexes are reversed. In the animal kingdom it is the male who infatuates the female with his gorgeous garb. She falls for his looks rather than his strength and aggressiveness. In human society, on the other hand, the burden is on the woman. Hers is the first move; she has to track and ensnare the male by looking seductive. Being devoid of anything comparable to the extraordinary antennae and giant legs that serve animals for prehending a partner she exerts her powers by way of artificial plumage. To prevent the male from escaping, she has to keep him perpetually excited by changing her shape and colours by every means, fair and foul. In the traditional battle of the sexes, dress and its accessory arts are her offensive weapons.[3]

James Laver makes a similar point:

> It would seem, in fact, that our clothes are dictated to us by the deepest unconscious desires of the opposite sex. Throughout the greater part of history and prehistory, men have chosen their partners in life by their attractiveness as women. Therefore, women's clothes are intended to make their wearers as attractive, as women, as possible. Women, on the other hand, have, for the greater part of human history, instinctively chosen their husbands for their capacities to maintain and protect a family.
>
> Women's clothes are governed by what might be called the Seduction Principle – that is, they are sex-conscious clothes. Men's clothes, on the other hand, are governed by the Hierarchical Principle – that is, they are class-conscious clothes.
>
> In general the purpose of clothes for women has been to make them more sexually attractive and the purpose of men's clothes has been to enhance their social status.[4]

The implications of Rudofsky's argument is that clothing is necessary for the maintenance of sexual interest and therefore, implicitly, to the future of the human species. Laver contends that the dominant function of women's clothing is that of sexual attraction. For both of them, it is universally true that it is the role of the female to attract, and to be chosen on the criterion of her attractiveness, and that clothes are a key factor in this process. Their views rest on quite dubious assumptions about 'human nature' and 'instincts'. *They play down the role of culture in both shaping sexuality and dress styles, and show a considerable disregard for historical accuracy.* Their ideas may describe some uses of clothing in sexual relationships in our society during specific periods in history but they do not constitute an adequate explanation of all forms of clothing nor do they represent accurately human behaviour in all periods and places. For example, at various times in our own society men have worn decorative clothes. They have worn jewellery, rich fabrics, extravagant trimmings and lace. . . . They have worn make-up, wigs and perfume. Can we assume that the attraction of these objects only operated in one direction and only served to attract men to women, even when they were wearing these objects themselves?

However, this is certainly not to deny that some clothes worn by women are designed to be sexually attractive. To take one example, women's eveningwear is often made of silky or sensuous fabrics; it is designed to reveal the shape of the body, or to reveal certain parts such as the breasts or legs. Many women possess some garments which are intended to attract attention to or show off the body. This is the case because it is the custom in our society at present for people to select their partners on the grounds of finding them sexually attractive. Along with face, figure and personality, clothing can play a part in such an assessment. The dominance of the idea of romantic love in our society as a basis for marriage has led to the notion that sexual attractiveness is an essential ingredient for a successful match. In particular, it has been seen as a woman's duty to be sexually attractive and this has had implications for the clothes women wear. But this is not part of the human condition: in other societies, and at other periods in our own history, partners were selected on quite different criteria. The dress of women in strict Islamic societies is not a form of sexual display; it is not intended to provoke desire. In fact, it has quite the opposite intention. In some Islamic societies, the sexual partnership of marriage is arranged by relatives and not by the couple concerned, who may not necessarily know each other. Laver's assertion that 'Throughout the greater part of history and prehistory, men have chosen their partners in life by their attractiveness as women' does not hold true for many non-European societies. How people select their sexual partners is not merely a matter of instinct as is implied by Laver, and by Rudofsky's comparison with animals – it is controlled and constructed by a complex of learned cultural attitudes and norms. *Clothing cannot be reduced to a mere trigger for a biological mating instinct.*

Even in our own society, it just does not make sense to explain all the clothing worn by women in these terms. Women do wear clothes which are designed to be *not* sexually attractive; their purpose may be entirely different. One example is that of nun's clothing; other perhaps more commonplace examples these days are the uniforms of the female traffic warden and policewoman. If these uniforms were seen as 'sexy', the authority and respect required by these women to do their jobs effectively would be undermined. They would find it difficult to exert the control necessary in their dealings with the public.

[. . .]

Notes

1   Genesis 2: 5, and 3: 6, 7, 21.
2   Horn, M. (1968) *The Second Skin*, Boston: Houghton Mifflin Co., pp. 3–4.
3   Rudofsky, B. (1971) *The Unfashionable Human Body*, New York: Doubleday and Co., pp. 12–13.
4   Laver, J. (1969) *Modesty in Dress*, Boston: Houghton Mifflin Co.

Chapter 11

John Flügel

PROTECTION

Nay, now when the reign of folly is over, and thy clothes are not for triumph but for defence, hast thou always worn them perforce and as a consequence of Man's Fall; never rejoiced in them as in a warm, movable House, a Body round thy Body, wherein that strange THEE of thine sat snug, defying all variations of Climate? Girt with thick, double-milled kerseys; half-buried under shawls and broadbrims, and overalls and mud boots, thy very fingers encased in doeskin and mittens, thou hast bestrode that 'Horse I ride'; and, though it were in wild winter, dashed through the world, glorying in it as if thou wert its Lord. . . . Nature is good, but she is not the best; here truly was the victory of Art over Nature.

Thomas Carlyle, *Sartor Resartus*, ch. ix

THE PROTECTIVE FUNCTION OF CLOTHES might seem at first sight to be simple enough. Nevertheless it shows itself, upon examination, to be much more diverse and complex than our casual and somewhat one-sided habits of thought upon this matter might lead us to expect.

The most obvious form of protection afforded by clothes is that against **cold**. Indeed, in a cold climate, there is considerable risk that it might be taken to be the only one. There seems little doubt that, in the later developments of dress, at any rate, it has played a more important part than any other protective function. It is probable that many of the higher developments of the tailor's art (such as that involved in the change from a loose-fitting 'gravitational' costume to a more tight-fitting and form-following 'anatomical' costume) would never have occurred in a warm climate, and that they owe their existence to the migration of certain portions of the human race from southerly into more northerly regions. Nevertheless it is possible, as we have seen, for human beings to exist in a practically unclothed state even in one of the most inclement portions of the inhabited world; and this should warn us against the danger of exaggerating the importance of the motive of protection as compared with the motives of decoration and of modesty. Especially so, since the motive of protection appears in certain ways more 'rational', more adapted to reality, than the other motives, and man is always inclined to indulge in 'rationalisation' of his motives. There is a good deal of unwillingness to admit the full force of the tendencies towards decoration and modesty, and, in consequence, man has probably exaggerated his need of covering himself to shut out the cold. At any rate, most medical authorities are to-day agreed that, from the point of view of hygiene, Europeans wear too many, rather than too few, clothes (though there has admittedly been a great improvement in women's clothes during recent years).[1] And the same applies *a fortiori* to clothing during the last few hundred years or so, when, except for brief periods, it was generally more ample than at present.

But clothing can protect not only against uncomfortably low temperature, but also against **heat**, in so far as this is due to the direct rays of the sun. Few Europeans, at any rate, could live in tropical countries without the protection to the head afforded by their sun helmets, and many of us have had occasion during a warm summer to regret dispensing for too long with the protection that our clothes afford against the rays of the sun upon other parts of the body; for sun-bathing, if indulged in too suddenly and without due habituation, can—as many have discovered—have very painful consequences.

Clothes can also protect us against enemies, both human and animal. The desire for protection against **human enemies** has led to the development of quite a special kind of clothing, known as armour. Armour, in western countries, has usually been of metal; in this form it underwent an immense development in the Middle Ages and, as the standard professional clothing of the knight, became intimately symbolic of the whole martial spirit of that time. The gradual disappearance of armour was doubtless due to the improvements in fire-arms, which eventually made it useless for its real purpose. But, as a ceremonial garment, a few vestiges of it have remained to the present day; for instance, the steel breastplate which forms a part of the uniform of the Guards, that most sumptuous of all military costumes. And, curiously enough, modern warfare, though in other respects it has made armour obsolete, has yet led to the revival of a very mediaeval-looking steel helmet, as well as to certain entirely new features of protective clothing, e.g. the gas mask. In some places, however, materials other than metal have been used for armour, as in the case of certain African tribes who wear large woollen pads covering the whole body.

Apart from regular warfare, armour or other special forms of protective clothing may, of course, protect against sudden or isolated attacks from fellow human beings. At one time a good many persons who had reason to suppose that their lives were in danger wore a metal tunic under their ordinary clothes, and, if report be true, quite a number of them succeeded in prolonging their lives in this way. Even ordinary clothing, if sufficiently thick or voluminous, may sometimes serve this purpose, and, quite recently, under the heading 'Passion and Petticoats', the *Observer* reported such a case. A girl in a Slovakian village was shot at with a revolver by a jealous lover, but fortunately she was wearing the traditional peasant costume of the district and, being in consequence 'armoured with some ten starched petticoats, the bullet only slightly injured her hip'.

Passing from deliberate attacks to unintentional injuries, certain forms of special clothing, mostly made of relatively soft and yielding material, are worn to protect from the **accidents** incidental to dangerous occupations or sports. Witness the goggles of the stonebreaker, the padded costumes of dirt-track racers and baseball players, the protective face-covering of the fencer and leg-covering of the wicket-keeper. The top hat of the rider to hounds, though doubtless primarily used because it has become part of the correct equipment for this sport (just as most sports have become associated with a certain uniform which only permits of small individual variations), is often justified—how reasonably I know not—on the ground that it lessens the danger of injury to the head in case of a fall.

Of the **animal foes** against which man has sought to protect himself by clothes, insects are probably the most important, and indeed some writers e.g. Knight Dunlap consider that the wearing of clothes for protection against insects has played an important part in the origin of human dress. We ourselves sometimes clothe horses for protection against flies, and it seems not impossible that loose garments that would flap against the limbs when in movement, may have been of immense utility in many countries and led to the permanent adoption of garments of this kind.

All the functions of clothing which we have so far considered in this chapter are connected with protection against **physical** dangers and inconveniences. They are indeed, for the most part, sufficiently simple and obvious. Much more subtle in their operation and more easy to be overlooked are the ways in which clothing can reassure us against various real or imaginary dangers which are primarily **psychological** in origin and nature.

The most important of this second class of protective functions of clothing (especially in the early stages of the history of clothes) is undoubtedly that which has to do with the supposed influence of **magic** and of **spirits**. To the primitive mind the cause of all evils, whose source is not immediately obvious, is to be found, not in the physical properties and interactions of things, but rather in the influence of magical or spiritual agencies. To such a mind the whole universe is continuously permeated by these influences, and the disasters which befall human beings—such as accidents, disease, and death (for death is not attributed to 'natural causes')—are supposed to be due, either to hostile magic set into operation by other men, or to the working of ghosts or other discarnate psychical forces. The only protection that is possible against these multitudinous and maleficent influences is the use of counter-magic, and, as it is impossible to be perpetually engaged in exercising this counter-magic by actual magical practices (even supposing that the requisite procedure is known, for the more potent formulae are often the property of certain professionals or specialists), it is extremely convenient to carry about some amulet which can be trusted to ward off the evil influences without the necessity of active intervention. For this purpose various objects, supposed to possess magical properties, were hung or otherwise attached to the body, and some authorities are inclined to believe that this magical purpose of articles carried on the person preceded even the ornamental purpose, and therefore constituted the real motive for the first beginnings of clothing. Such a view is of course in harmony with the opinion now coming to be widely held among anthropologists, that in general the earliest forms of art served utilitarian (i.e. magical) rather than purely aesthetic ends. If this is true with regard to clothes, it may be said that the motive of decoration in dress, in its earliest manifest-ations, gradually grew out of the magical utilitarian motive, in much the same way that, in later forms of art, instruments and other objects, originally constructed to serve some useful purpose, became decorative, and eventually, in certain cases, persisted as decorations, even when the advance of culture had reduced or abolished their utilitarian function. And, certainly, what we are able to trace of the later history of clothes supports this view, for there are numerous features in the clothes we wear to-day which are now purely ornamental, but which were once useful; we shall find many instances of this in the chapter dealing with the evolution of garments.

If this view of the priority of magic over ornamentation be correct, the opinion held by the majority of writers that decoration was the original motive underlying clothing will need revision; not decoration but protection will have to be given the honour of first place—but, of course, protection against agencies other than those with which we chiefly associate it at the present day. Be this as it may, it is safe to assume that the magical and the decorative functions developed to some extent concurrently, both finding satisfaction in the same objects; and that the motive of decoration gradually acquired an increasing independence, so that eventually the magical purpose fell into the background and tended to disappear. But it never disappeared entirely, and even to-day we can appreciate something of the attitude of the savage in this matter, for we still use objects that are believed by the superstitious (and few of us can boast that we have entirely cast off the thralls of superstition) to bring good luck or avert ill luck. Not a few people have, at some time or other in their lives, worn a necklace, ring, jewel, or other decorative trinket which was supposed to have defensive properties, such as the ability to prevent disease or accident; indeed, there exists quite an extensive magical lore about some of the precious stones that are in use as ornaments to-day.

In somewhat more primitive cultures the function of such amulets is usually considered to be that of warding off 'the evil eye' (much as, in the Middle Ages, the cross was supposed to have the power of driving off the Devil and his minions). Now this belief may help us to realise something of the deeper meaning that would seem to underlie a great many (perhaps indeed all) of these superstitions concern-ing the protective value of certain ornaments. Psycho-analytic and anthropological observations have made it clear that one of the chief ways in which the 'evil eye' was supposed to harm its victims was by damaging their reproductive powers or reproductive organs. The doctrine of the evil eye seems in fact to be intimately connected with the castration complex.[2] In harmony with this view is the fact that most of the amulets used to ward off the evil eye appear to be symbols of the reproductive organs—male or female; the psychological principle involved being, apparently, in the nature of an assurance that potency and reproductive power are still intact.

Here we are brought back to the general subject of phallic symbolism. . . . It would appear that the general sexual symbolism of clothes, in virtue of which clothes seem to form an unconscious substitute for crude sexual display, is reinforced by the magical exhibition of sexual symbols as a defence against the fear of infertility. How far the actual widespread occurrence of genital symbolism is due to an active, aggressive tendency of sexual pride, how far it is a defence-mechanism against sexual fears connected with the castration complex, it is impossible to say with certainty in the present state of our knowledge. Here, as in many similar cases, the positive and negative elements are so intimately intertwined that it is difficult or impossible to disentangle them.

Closely similar, both in its ultimate psychological nature and in its tendency to become associated with phallic symbolism, is the function of clothes as a means of protection against **moral danger.** The monk protects himself in his plain, but all-enveloping, habit against the lures and temptations of this wicked world, and clothing is a help to many others in attempting to avoid distracting influences that might lead them away from the straight and narrow path of virtue. To be of service for this end, clothing must be ample, thick, tight, stiff, or unprovocative in colour; or, better still, possess several or all of these qualities. But these qualities (especially the last four) are not purely negative in their protective value; they are in most cases at the same time a symbol of the resistive strength within. From the more simple and purely protective functions there is a continuous transition to a more positive reaction to moral dangers, through the assurance of moral strength that clothing can afford. Thus it is that certain garments can become symbolic of inflexibility of character, severity of moral standard, and purity of moral purpose—an ethical symbolism that plays a very considerable rôle in the more austere and formal of the costumes of modern men. In the thickness of material and solidity of structure of their tailored garments, in the heavy and sober blackness of their shoes, in the virgin whiteness and starched stiffness of their collars and of their shirt-fronts, men exhibit to the outer world their would-be strength, steadfastness, and immunity from frivolous distraction. Thus it is that garments of this kind have come to signify seriousness of mood and devotion to duty, and are associated with all the more responsible forms of professional and commercial work. Tightly gripping garments, also, have their moral significance; and women too have, at one time or another, enjoyed their share of this by means of corsets, bone collars, and bodices whose tightness was only matched by their rigidity.

All garments of this kind contrast with the gayer, looser, softer, and lighter clothes that are considered to befit a holiday. Soft collars are often thought unsuitable for business wear, the assumption being that their lack of rigid form betokens a corresponding 'slackness' in the wearer; while a dressing-gown and slippers, on the other hand, have become almost proverbial signs of ease and relaxation.

Various sources have contributed to the growth of associations of this kind, of which the most important seem to be:

(1) **Colour.**—The universal connection (into the origin of which we cannot enter here) of black with seriousness and white with innocence and moral purity, as distinct from the spectral colours—especially the brighter ones—which signify a freer play of the emotions.

(2) **Amplitude.**—The ascetic notion of the body as a source of evil passions, which can best be forgotten or controlled by as complete a covering as possible.

(3) **Thickness** (and stiffness).—The real protective value of thick clothes against certain physical dangers, this protection being unconsciously extended to the moral sphere. It is possible that the former use of armour and its associations with the moral traditions of chivalry have helped in this association.

(4) **Stiffness.**—The symbolic equation of physical stiffness and 'uprightness'

(note the word) with moral probity and firmness, and of 'loose', 'slack', and 'sloppy' clothes with corresponding ways of life.

(5) **Tightness.**—The association is doubtless primarily due to the actual support of tightly fitting garments, a support which is largely physical, but which is easily and frequently transferred to the moral sphere.[3] Tightness, by its firm pressure on the body, may symbolise a firm control over ourselves e.g. 'keeping a tight rein' on our passions), the opposite of that 'looseness' or 'dissoluteness' that we associate with immorality.[4]

Both stiffness and tightness are, however, liable to be over-determined by phallic symbolism. The stiff collar, for example, which is the sign of duty, is also the symbol of the erect phallus, and in general those male garments that are most associated with seriousness and correctness are also the most saturated with a subtle phallicism. Here, again, we find the compromise-formation between moral and instinctive factors which psycho-analysis has shown us to be characteristic, not only of so many neurotic manifestations, but also of so many aspects of our culture.

There is, I believe, still one other and more general way in which clothes exercise a protective function. Like the last-mentioned functions of protection from magical and moral danger, it is psychological in nature; like these functions, too, it seems to depend in the last resort upon unconscious symbolism. The kind of protection to which we are now referring is, just because of its generality, more difficult to describe than are the previous kinds. Perhaps it can best be said to be a protection against **the general unfriendliness of the world as a whole; or,** expressed more psychologically, **a reassurance against the lack of love.** If we are in unfriendly surroundings, whether human or natural, we tend, as it were, to button up, to draw our garments closely round us. On a chilly day, when we leave our warm house and enter shudderingly into the inhospitable street, we turn up our collars and settle down as snugly as possible into our coats. Under the friendly influence of the sun, on the other hand, we throw off our outer coverings, or carry them more loosely, so that they no longer envelop us and isolate us from the external world. These influences are, I think, not to be accounted for entirely by the temperature. In the one case there is a sort of general unfriendliness which prompts us to withdraw our innerselves into the protection of our clothes, much as a tortoise may withdraw its head into the protecting armour with which Nature has provided it. In the other case there is a general kindliness with which we want to get intimately into touch, and to which we expand and open our arms (often literally) as if in welcome; there is no need here of protective layers; on the contrary we feel a longing to bring our inmost being into contact with the friendly elements.

It is much the same with regard to our human environment. If we find ourselves among unsympathetic people—people to whom we feel ourselves superior, with whom we have nothing in common, or of whom we are afraid—in this case also we tend to draw our clothes tightly around us, as if they somehow kept us apart or protected us from these people with whom we desire no intimacy. Writers on clothes have already noticed that certain forms of clothing, e.g. a high neckband or a high-cut coat collar, have, in the past, symbolised 'unapproachableness', 'stand—offishness', and resistance to democratic principles. Examples of this same general tendency from present-day life are not difficult to find. Thus, for instance, a man in a dress suit will often wear an overcoat while walking in the street, even in warm weather. He may not need it for protection against the climate, but he wears it because he feels that the other people in the street, who are probably most of them not in evening dress, are somehow different from himself, and, from the mere fact of being dressed as it were in different mood, will regard him with a certain degree of suspicion or hostility. He reserves the vision of his inner splendour for his own, similarly dressed, associates whom he will meet at the termination of his journey.[5]

With women similar tendencies are at work, though perhaps more tinged with an erotic element. Even more than with men (with whom it is often a mere sign of respect) the removal of outer garments signifies a condition of friendliness and of being 'at home'. Furthermore, there would seem to be a correspondence between democratic sentiments, sexual freedom, and the public exhibition of female beauty. In Mohammedan countries, where the sexual freedom of women was reduced to a minimum, women were apt to be carefully concealed from the public gaze, the very sight of their faces being jealously reserved for their husbands. In Europe, after the French Revolution, when 'liberty, equality, fraternity' was the slogan of the day, women wore the lightest of costumes in the street, where *décolleté* was regarded as no less appropriate than in the ballroom. In the period of prudishness and of greater social snobbery and differentiation that came later in the nineteenth century, such exposure became reserved for indoor occasions with friends and social equals. At the present day, when democratic views and greater sexual liberty are once more triumphant, women again unhesitatingly expose a larger portion of their bodies to the general view.

I am inclined to think that the same correspondence holds in individual cases, and that, for instance, the readiness with which a woman will remove her cloak when she is in evening dress at a theatre or other public function is to some extent diagnostic of her general friendliness and willingness to invite sexual admiration. If she throws off her outer wrap promptly, she is socially and sexually in sympathy with her environment; so long as she retains it, she preserves a certain aloofness, either because she is diffident about her own capacities or charms, or because she feels out of harmony with her surroundings and does not desire to invite the intimacy of those about her.

It will of course be said that, even supposing this is true, the situation here is complicated by the existence of individual differences in the sensibility to cold and in the consequent willingness to dispense with covering over bare arms and shoulders. I admit this to some extent; but, as I am endeavouring to show, this very matter of the sensitiveness to cold is itself far from being independent of the psychological factors here under consideration. The fact that we protect ourselves both from cold and from unfriendliness by clothing is surely not unconnected with the further fact that we naturally tend to symbolise love and friendliness by warmth and unfriendliness by cold. 'Coldness' is a universal metaphor for lack of love, as when we speak of sexual frigidity or of a person's manner being icy, just as, on the other hand, we speak of a fiery passion or a warm embrace. Now it seems probable that this connection, like so many other linguistic associations, is pretty deeply embedded in our mental structure, and that our reaction to, and even our feelings of, cold and heat are to a large extent unconsciously determined by these psychological identifications. I think it is even possible that some people are more generally sensitive to cold than others because they feel a lack of love in their lives. Others again perhaps dislike warmth, because they are afraid of giving free vent to their feelings of love. At any rate, there is definite evidence that in certain individuals periods of depression, anxiety, loneliness, or homesickness may coincide with a desire to be more warmly clad than usual. Thus a woman who, during the rest of her life, has made a special point of wearing the lightest clothes she could, continually wore a coat, even for playing tennis, at one particular period of adolescence, during which she passed through a phase of depression and was contemplating suicide. A boy who at home refused to wear an overcoat, at boarding-school, when he was homesick, would insist upon always going about in his overcoat, in spite of the teasing remarks of his companions. A student from America, studying in London, writes: 'It may be that homesickness calls for more clothes, for I have noticed that a steamer rug and gas fire . . . will do wonders for an attack of self-pity.' A special investigation on this point was recently carried out in a city of south-western England by Eve Macaulay. A group of fifty students were asked the question: 'Are there any circumstances (other than temperature) or states of mind in which you feel the need of more clothes than you usually wear?' Out of the fifty, twenty-four stated that purely mental conditions of the kind just mentioned did have this effect. Of course it is possible that this need for warmer clothing is entirely a secondary result of the influence of depression, anxiety, etc., upon the circulation. But it is noteworthy that only three of the twenty-four referred to 'lowered vitality' or other physical conditions in this connection, and in view of our general ignorance as to the real causal interrelations between body and mind in cases of this sort, and of the indubitable fact of the existence of a psychic association between cold and lack of love (as revealed, for instance, by the above-mentioned linguistic usages), it would be rash to neglect the possible existence of a purely (or primarily) psychic determinant of the need of more clothes. Thomas Carlyle—the writer of what is probably the most famous of all books on clothes—has admirably expressed in a few words the analogy between a protecting love and a protecting garment (an analogy which, by the way, was said by the above quoted homesick American student to be 'quite perfect'). Speaking of his dead wife, he says, 'She wrapped me round like a cloak to keep all the hard and cold world off me'.[6]

This last example gives, I think, the clue to the unconscious symbolism which (in some cases, at any rate) underlies the substitution of clothes for love. Carlyle's words almost irresistibly call up the thought of a mother. Deep down in the heart of mankind is the longing for a mother who will protect us, cherish us, and warm us with her love—a longing which seems to take us back to the very earliest stages of our being. One of the most astonishing discoveries of psycho-analysis was that concerning the importance and frequency of 'womb phantasies', *i.e.* phantasies of a return to the warm, enveloping, and protecting home, where we spent the first nine months of our existence. Concerning the precise significance of this phantasy, its causes, its importance for normal development and for psycho-pathology, there is still much doubt and much dispute. The fact that it has some considerable importance is beyond all reasonable doubt. The aspect of the phantasy that concerns us here is that the womb, or its symbol, is regarded as a refuge both from a generally hostile environment and from cold. That the womb is, in this phantasy, treated as a place of safety, to which one can retire from the dangers and difficulties of the world, has been very amply shown by many psycho-analytic studies. Recently Ernest Jones . . . has endeavoured to show that the unconscious foundation of the fear of cold is derived from the fear of separation from the mother. From this it is but one step to the idea that a return to the womb would constitute a refuge at one and the same time, both from cold and from the dangers incidental to separation from the beloved mother. Since clothes obviously protect us from cold, it is not surprising that they frequently become symbols of this aspect of the protective function of the mother, and then, by extension, of the other aspects also—the aspects in virtue of which she becomes a refuge from 'the hard and cold world' in general.

This extension is rendered easier by the fact that, with the majority of individuals, the mother is, for external reasons, associated with clothes from a very early age. It is she who usually dresses and undresses the child, or at least superintends these operations. And for many years after this (often indeed throughout her own life) the mother, as if prompted by an intuitive understanding of the symbolism here in question, tends to show her love by manifesting an anxiety lest her children should be inadequately clothed. It is seldom indeed that a mother warns her son or daughter against the danger of being overclothed—but how innumerable are the occasions on which she may be heard urging the putting on of warmer undergarments, or the taking of an extra wrap! Indeed, her anxiety in this matter often becomes a considerable source of worry and annoyance to her children, and may rouse in them a spirit of rebellion, which, by contra-suggestion, manifests itself in a desire to wear as little covering as possible. But this is a matter which we must reserve for the next chapter.

We may close the present chapter by pointing out a parallelism, to which we shall also have to allude again in another connection, but which is peculiarly germane to the matter we have just been discussing. The parallelism in question—one to which many writers on clothing have drawn attention—is that between the protective functions of clothes and of the house respectively. Both protect against cold and other inclemencies of the weather. In fact their functions are to some extent complementary; in cold weather we divest ourselves of our outer garments on entering the house and put them on again when leaving. Clothes, like the house, are protective; but, being nearer the body and actually supported on it, they are (unlike the house) portable. With their help, we carry—like snails and tortoises—a sort of home upon our backs, and enjoy the advantages of shelter without the disadvantage of becoming *sessile*. We have even invented a number of objects which are in the nature of transitions between clothes and houses. The roofed-in car or carriage is, as Gerald Heard has pointed out, one type of such an object. The umbrella is another. As regards this little instrument with its emergency roof, it is difficult to say whether it corresponds more to a miniature transportable house or to a temporary outer garment.[7]

Now it is interesting to note that the house,[8] with which clothes have so much in common and with which they have so often been compared, has been shown by psycho-analysts to be a frequent symbol of the mother and of the mother's womb. In fact, it is one of the clearest and one of the most indubitable of this class of symbols. This must surely strengthen our conviction of the reality of the occurrence of this same symbolism with regard to clothes.

Notes

1   In the words of Knight Dunlap, 'Woman, long the worst offender, has suddenly outstripped man, both literally and in the line of progress.'

2   See, e.g., J. C. Flügel, 'Polyphallic Symbolism and the Castration Complex', *Inter. Jour. of Psycho-analysis*, 1924, vol. v, p. 188.

3   While on the way to his death (to be shot as a spy) Sergeant Grischa, in Arnold Zweig's well-known story, found that 'the only thing that comforted him was the feel of the broad leather belt round his middle, that kept him stiff and erect. Pride, sad, splendid liar, that forced him to preserve his honour in the face of his enemies by a brave death in a far country, was like that belt of his: it too held him together.'

4   The moral protection of tight corsets, for instance, is interestingly brought out in the case of a lady who admitted that she 'would risk an encircling arm' when defended in this way, though she would not allow it under other circumstances; while the more active moral implications are shown by another lady who put on a stiff corset as soon as she became engaged. To the remonstrances of her somewhat disconcerted fiancé, she replied: 'I mustn't flop about now but *you* can see me without them'. Actually the donning of this garment coincided with a change from a very free flirtatiousness to a distinctly rigid monogamous moral standard.

5   In confirmation of this it may be noted that where there is less sense of a hostile or unsympathetic environment, there is less objection to walking abroad in evening dress. Thus, in a small region of the 'west end' of London, where it is understood that occasions demanding evening dress abound, men may sometimes be seen in the streets thus clad and without overcoats. The same holds true in even greater degree in the case of students at Oxford and Cambridge. Here the feeling is that the University forms the most important body of the population, a body for which, and round which, the other inhabitants exist; the undergraduate is therefore master of the situation and need fear no criticism from hostile outsiders.

6   Quoted in *One Thousand Beautiful Things* (edited by Arthur Mee), p. 37.

7   If, as regards protection, clothes may be said to take over the functions of the house, as regards modesty, our houses, obviously to some extent, take the place of clothes. Within our own rooms, at any rate, most of us can divest ourselves of our clothes without feeling immodest. Mohammedan ladies are, as we [have] remarked, for the most part confined to their houses away from the gaze of the public, but . . . when they leave their houses the protection thus abandoned can, to a very large extent, be made good by clothing. In this particular case, the lady from Tunis is almost as completely sheltered from the eyes of the indiscreet as she would be in the privacy of her own apartments. This shows us that the complementary function of house and clothes holds good in the sphere of modesty as it does in that of protection.

8   And the room. Compare the German word *Frauenzimmer*.

PART FIVE

Fashion as communication

THIS SECTION CONTINUES AND DEVELOPS the account in the previous section of what fashion does. It will argue that, whatever else fashion and clothing do (protection, decoration, preserving/abandoning modesty, for example), they are always already performing a communicative function. Bodily protection, decoration and modesty may be of concern to all cultures, but each different culture will inevitably consider different levels of exposure to be suitably protective or modest. Similarly, each will consider different garments or coverings to be adequate to protect the body or to preserve its modesty. The notoriously hardy Yaghans of Tierra del Fuego, who astonished Charles Darwin by allowing snow to melt on their bare flesh (see Flügel 1930: 16–17), clearly possessed a different sense of bodily protection from many Europeans and Americans, who don cosy down-filled jackets on moderately frosty mornings. And the anthropologist's tales of near-naked women fleeing in shame because they were not wearing the correct labrets or ear-rings (see, for example, Roach and Eicher 1965: 16–17; Rouse 1989: 9), suggest that alternative senses of modesty are commonplace. That different cultural groups consider different levels of clothing to afford sufficient protection and appropriate modesty is clear. The argument here is that those differences are also meaningful.

So, what constitutes exposure, what counts as sufficient protection or modesty and the garments used to achieve those levels of protection or modesty are always going to be different in or to different cultural groups. They will differ because they are the products of the values and beliefs of different cultures: in a sense they *are* the values and beliefs of the different cultures. People will always require some protection from the elements and they will usually need to be properly (modestly) dressed; what they wear to achieve these requirements will change from culture to culture, and it is these differences that are meaningful and hence communicative. Insofar as these things are different, they are also meaningful: they are the different ways in which different cultures make sense of their experience, thus constituting themselves as a culture and communicating that experience. Fashion and clothing are therefore indicative/constitutive of a culture and so they are always going to perform a communicative function. The debate in this section therefore surrounds the conception of communication that is best suited to explain fashion and clothing. Two central questions arise. The first is 'what sort of communication are fashion and clothing?' The second is 'what is communicated in or through fashion and clothing?'

There are usually reckoned to be two schools of thought on the matter of what communication is (see Fiske 1990). There are those who believe communication to be the sending and receiving of messages and there are those who believe that communication is the cultural negotiation of meanings. The former may be referred to as the 'process' school of thought because communication is thought of as a process, in which someone (the sender) sends a message (the meaning) to someone else (the receiver) via some medium (the channel). The classic presentation of this model of communication is found in the work of Shannon and Weaver (1949) — see the diagrammatic representation following.

Information source → Transmitter (encoder) → Signal → Receiver (decoder) → Destination

↑

Noise

The 'information source' produces the raw information that is to be transmitted and the transmitter (the encoder), puts the information into a signal appropriate to the channel. The signal is sent in the channel, to be received and decoded as a message by the receiver. At all points, the signal or the message is subject to noise, the distortion of or interference with that message. The origins of this model of communication in telecommunications are probably quite clear and it is already difficult to understand how fashion and clothing can be explained using it.

There are plenty of problems involved in applying this model to fashion and clothing. Colin Campbell's (1997) essay explains them clearly, but the following questions will give some idea of what these problems might be. Is the fashion designer the information source or the transmitter? Or is the item of fashion itself the transmitter? Who or what is the receiver — the purchaser of the item of fashion or the spectator, or both? What would count as 'noise' when considering fashion as communication in this way? Given that fashion designers ('senders'?) already know their market and take that market's preferences into consideration, and given that it is possible that the purchaser of the garment is a potential 'receiver', there is a sense in which the receiver determines the nature of the message. The design careers website wetfeet.com explains it in the following way:

> as a designer you'll need to be able to understand who will use your design as well as how they will use it. In other words, you'll need to know what the market you're designing for wants and needs in the products you're designing.
>
> (http://www.wetfeet.com/Content/Careers/Design.aspx May 2006)

If this is the case, then the receiver is effectively producing or generating the message to be sent and this is surely a problem for the 'sender/receiver' model of communication.

Although it is very attractive and seductive, there are a number of other problems involved with this model. Most people will naturally think of spoken and written languages when they think of communication and it is probably to be expected that speaking and writing will provide many metaphors of how fashion might communicate. Alison Lurie, for example, famously uses the metaphor of fashion and clothing as spoken/written language in her *The Language of Clothes* (1981). Here it is explained that items of fashion and clothing are words and that there are clothing equivalents of archaic, slang and foreign words, for example, and that, where a fashion leader may have several hundred words at their 'disposal', a sharecropper's 'vocabulary' may be limited to a few 'words' or garments (1981: 5). That Lurie manages to keep up this conceit for nearly three hundred pages is itself surely testament to the fecundity and attractiveness of this metaphor.

The second of the two schools noted, is often called the 'semiotic' or 'structural-ist' school because, as Fiske says, 'semiotics . . . defines social interaction as that which constitutes the individual as a member of a particular culture or society' (1990: 2–3). Communication through or by means of fashion and clothing, therefore, is a social interaction that produces or constitutes the individual as a member (or not) of a culture. On this account of communication, meaning is not a 'thing' or 'content' that is expressed and sent from one place to another, it is more the unstable and changeable effect of an ongoing negotiation. Meaning on this account is not dissimilar from Barthes' (1977) version of connotation in that it is a set of associations or feelings that are the product of the individual's cultural location. It is the interaction between the individual's cultural values and beliefs (the product of him/her being a certain age, nationality, class, gender, and so on) and the item of fashion or clothing that generates the meaning of that item. Given that different people will be members of different cultural groups they will possess different beliefs and values, and the meanings of items of fashion will therefore differ between them. It should be clear that, on the semiotic account of meaning and communication, communication is not a sending/receiving and meaning is not the sort of thing that can be sent/received. Rather, it is one of the ways in which an individual is (or is not) constructed as a member (or not) of a cultural group: if an individual does not share the beliefs and values of a group, s/he will not be constructed as a member of that group when the beliefs are used in generating the meaning of items of fashion and clothing. If your values and beliefs lead you to understand that short skirts and skimpy tops are decadent and corrupting then you are unlikely to be constructed as a member of any modern western youth group. It is the sharing (or not) of the cultural beliefs and the application of them in the interpretation of items of fashion and clothing that make the individual a member (or not) of the cultural group.

The second question raised, concerning what is communicated in or through fashion and clothing, has been dealt with less convincingly in theories of fashion in that many analysts are clear about what kind of thing is not or cannot be communicated but less clear about what kind of thing is communicated. In Fred Davis's extract

(Chapter 3) he uses Roz Chast's New Yorker cartoon to make his point that the things we wear do not communicate our preference for tuna or our guilt at not visiting our mothers more often. Specific information about taste in food and personal feelings are not the kind of things communicated by what people wear. The cartoon also satirises or critiques the sender – receiver model of communication in that it pretends to 'decode' Rhonda's 'fashion statements': as well as being funny, the preposterousness of the 'messages' and the patent absence of any shareable codes completely undermine the idea that what could ever be going on here is a 'decoding'. In the extract Davis is less clear about the kind of thing(s) fashion and clothing might communicate, suggesting that they are perhaps more like 'art' or music when they communicate what they communicate. Colin Campbell is also clear as to what kinds of thing are not communicated. The kind of thing that is not communicated in Campbell's account is a 'single unambiguous meaning' (Campbell 1997: 348). And this is followed up in the extract from my own essay, where what is communicated by the things people wear are neither single nor unambiguous messages and meanings in the manner proposed by the sender – receiver model, but depend upon and therefore vary between the cultural locations of people wearing and observing them for any meanings they have.

It is probably worth noting how persistent are the metaphors involved in the sender – receiver model of communication, even when other aspects of that model have correctly been abandoned. In her essay 'Projecting an Image and Expressing Identity: T-shirts in Hawaii', for example, Marjorie Kelly (2003) deliberately uses the metaphors of 'projecting' and 'expressing' to describe communication. To project something is to throw or cast it from one place to another, and we speak of 'projectiles' and image-projection in these senses. Expression is the pressing out of material from one place to another. Communication conceived in these terms is the movement of some (already-formed) thing from one place to another place. And meaning conceived in these terms is the already-formed 'thing' that is moved or 'transmitted' from one place to another. These are the terms of the sender – receiver model of communication. Now, the terms and metaphors themselves are never explicitly discussed or thematised in the essay and, to be fair, on reading the essay it becomes clear that the process of communication described there actually bears little relation to projection, expression, sending or receiving. It is actually much more to do with the construction of cultural membership (or not) by means of shared (or not) values and beliefs as communicated (or not) in the T-shirts. However, that 'projection' and 'expression' are used to describe the process of communication is a sign of how certain models of communication have become taken for granted and remain unquestioned in the analysis and explanation of fashion.

Given that communication and meaning are about the sharing or not of values, ideas and beliefs, and given that what makes different cultures is the existence of different values and meanings, it is the case that all of the topics to be discussed in the following chapters will be to do with values and ideas. Consequently, there is a sense in which all of the following sections are elaborating on some or other communicative aspect of fashion and clothing.

The brief extract from Umberto Eco's 1972 Wolfson College Lecture, 'Social Life as a Sign System', introduces the ideas that a sign, a meaningful thing, can be anything at all and that culture is to be understood as a sign system. Eco's insistence on the presence of 'codes' may strike some as overly confident or even scientific these days (even if he says that fashion codes are 'less articulate than linguistic codes'), but the idea that it is the meanings, the 'ideological connotations' of what he is wearing, that are of interest to him is of the profoundest significance. Fred Davis is also concerned with the differences between the sorts of communication that are represented by fashion and other arts such as painting and music. Whilst they are all performing communication, he says, they are not the same kind of communication. In his essay, 'When the Meaning is Not a Message', Colin Campbell takes issue with the sender – receiver model of communication and comprehensively exposes its presuppositions and attendant weaknesses. The model of communication that is most often used to explain fashion as communication is severely criticised here. In my own contribution, I suggest that the sender – receiver model is indeed inadequate to the task of describing the sorts of communication the fashion is, and I try to suggest a more fruitful account of meaning (based on Barthes' version of what one might also call 'ideological connotation') in which meanings are constructed by members of cultural groups rather than sent and received by pre-existent individuals.

Bibliography

Barnard, M. (2007 forthcoming) 'Fashion Statements: Communication and Culture', in R. Scapp and B. Seitz (eds) *Fashion Statements*, New York: SUNY Press.

Barthes, R. (1977) 'Rhetoric of the Image', in *Image–Music–Text*, Glasgow: Fontana/Collins.

Campbell, C. (1997) 'When the Meaning is Not a Message', in M. Nava *et al.* (eds) *Buy This Book: Studies in Advertising and Consumption*, London: Routledge.

Davis, F. (1992) *Fashion, Culture and Identity*, Chicago: University of Chicago Press.

Eco, U. (1973) 'Social Life as a Sign System', in David Robey (ed.) *Structuralism: An Introduction*, Oxford: Clarendon Press.

Fiske, J. (1990) *Introduction to Communication Studies*, London: Routledge.

Flügel, J. (1930) *The Psychology of Clothes*, London: Hogarth Press and Institute of Psychoanalysis.

Kelly, M. (2003) 'Projecting an Image and Expressing Identity: T-shirts in Hawaii', *Fashion Theory* 7, 2: 191–211.

Lurie, A. (1981) *The Language of Clothes*, London: Bloomsbury.

Roach, M. E. and Eicher, J. B. (eds) (1965) *Dress, Adornment and the Social Order*, New York: John Wiley.

Rouse, E. (1989) *Understanding Fashion*, Oxford: Blackwell.

Shannon, C. and Weaver, W. (1949) *The Mathematical Theory of Communication*, Champaign: University of Illinois Press.

Chapter 12

Umberto Eco

SOCIAL LIFE AS A SIGN SYSTEM

I **AM SPEAKING TO YOU**. You are understanding me, because I am following the rules of a precise code (the English language), so precise that it also allows me to make use of it with a lot of phonetic and grammatical variations. Its strong underlying structure in some way acts like a loadstone which magnetizes and attracts my deviations from the norm. You understand me because there exists a code (a sort of inner competence shared by you and me) and there exist possible messages, performed as concrete utterances and interpretable as a set of propositions.

I am using signs. The code (the *langue*, according to Saussure) couples a sign-vehicle (the *signifiant*) with something called its meaning or its sense (the *signifié*), something to be better defined later. As a semiotic entity the sign is—according to Peirce[1]—'something which stands to somebody for something (else) in some respect or capacity'. Let us accept these two definitions as two unquestionable starting-points for the following discourse.

However, Peirce has said more: 'A sign is anything which determines something else (its *interpretant*) to refer to an object to which itself refers (its *object*) in the same way, the interpretant becoming in turn a sign, and so on ad infinitum.'[2] If the interpretant is not, as many so-called semioticists believe or sometimes believed, the interpreter, but if it is a sign which translates, makes clear, analyses, or substitutes a previous sign, then the world of semiosis proceeds from sign to sign *in infinitum regressum* (but is it *regressum* or *progressum*?) In this continuous movement semiosis transforms into signs everything it encounters. To communicate is to use the entire world as a semiotic apparatus. I believe that culture is that, and nothing else.

When I said that I was speaking to you, I meant that I was speaking by means of verbal devices, recognized and classified by linguistics. But I am also speaking (if you prefer, communicating) through my voice inflections. I am musically, or 'tonemically', using my voice in order to become persuasive, interrogative, provocative, shocking—in order to underline my attitudes, to emphasize my understatements or my paradoxes. Maybe I do not properly perform the tonemic code used by an English speaker: I should like to express irony, you detect a shadow of perplexity, or vice versa. I do not share completely the English *paralinguistic code*. Until a few years ago linguists maintained that they were not entitled to theorize concerning such types of behaviour as voice qualities, ranges, pitches, dispositions of accents, purely emotional interjections; for this reason they put all these features into a sort of no-man's-land, that of free variants and of idiosyncratic performances. Paralinguistics is now able (when possible) to systematize, and (always) to classify in repertoires this kind of behaviour.

I am speaking through my gestures. Not only as an Italian; from my point of view Anglo-Saxons also have a very articulated gestuality, as emphatic as the Latin one, maybe less conceived as a substitute for words and rather more intended to underline abstractions, but anyway a gesticulation subject to a complete theorization. A new branch of communication theory called *kinesics* deals with this important topic.

I am speaking through my facial expressions. I could state some important ideas, and yet I could underline them with calculated movements of my eyebrows, tongue in cheek, biting my lips, or with ironic smiles, which could subdue or destroy the conceptual force of my statements. Kinesics, again, deals with these forms of behaviour and has proposed a complex and strongly organized kind of shorthand in order to note every significant feature of facial muscular movements.

I am speaking through my body position in respect to other bodies interacting in a given space. If I were speaking standing up instead of sitting, if I moved towards you, if I were walking among you instead of remaining hierarchically fixed in my place, the very sense of my words would be changed.

I am speaking through my collocation in a public space; I am connoting my discourse by the fact that I speak here and my audience is sitting in front of me, and we are not all sitting together around a table or co-involved in a revolutionary sit-in. You would agree with me that spatial forms in this room (in every building and town) are conceived in order to suggest, to induce types of behaviour. A new branch of semiotics, *proxemics*, assumes that this is not a matter of suggestion or mere stimulation, but that it is a process of signification, any spatial form being a precise conventional message conveying social meanings, on the basis of existing codes.

I am speaking through my clothes. If I were wearing a Mao suit, if I were without tie, the ideological connotations of my speech would be changed. Obviously fashion codes are less articulate, more subject to historical fluctuations than linguistic codes are. But a code is no less a code for the fact that it is weaker than other stronger ones. Gentlemen button their jackets, shirts, and coats from left to right, ladies from right to left. Suppose I were speaking of semiotics, standing in front of you, buttoned from right to left: it would be very difficult for you to eliminate a subtle connotation of effeminacy, in spite of my beard.

I could continue to list the various ways in which we are communicating and exchanging information. The fact is that communication neither has to do with verbal behaviour alone, nor involves our bodily performances alone; communication encompasses the whole of culture.

Several decades ago Ferdinand de Saussure composed a passage of his *Cours* that at that time was purely utopian and to many readers sounded rather paradoxical:

> La langue est un système de signes exprimant des idées et par là comparable à l'écriture, à l'alphabet des sourds-muets, aux rites symboliques, aux formes de politesse, aux signaux militaires, etc. etc. Elle est simplement le plus important de ces systèmes. On peut donc concevoir une science qui étudie la vie des signes au sein de la vie sociale. Elle formerait une partie de la psychologie sociale et par conséquent de la psychologie générale. Nous la nommerons sémiologie—du grec *semeion*, signe—Elle nous apprendrait en quoi consistent les signes, quelles lois les régissent. Puisqu'elle n'existe pas encore, on ne peut pas dire ce qu'elle sera. Mais elle a droit à l'existence, sa place est déterminée d'avance.[3]

Now let me quote another definition, given by C. S. Peirce, one of the founders of the semiotic discipline: 'I am, as far as I know, a pioneer, or rather a backwoodsman, in the work of clearing and opening up what I called semiotic, that is, the doctrine of the essential nature and fundamental varieties of possible semiosis.'[4] Peirce was the first to list the various possible kinds of signs. Among his various triadic classifications, there are an enormous number of proliferating ramifications (I shall spare you them because I believe that their use during a lecture is not admitted by the Geneva Convention). Peirce listed:

(a) *symbols*—that is arbitrary devices such as the words of verbal language;
(b) *indexes*—that is either *symptoms*, natural events from which we can infer other events (for instance, the footprints which revealed to Robinson the presence of Friday on the island), or the so-called *deictic* signs, such as a finger pointed towards an object, or a pronoun or an adjective in the context of a phrase (for instance: 'Once upon a time there was a girl living in a forest. THAT girl was named Little Red Riding Hood.');
(c) *icons*—a very large category of signs supposed to possess some of the properties of their referent, which now are increasingly revealed to be less homogenous [sic] than common opinion believed, and are being submitted to an intensive criticism and to new attempts at description, classification, semiotic foundation.[5]

Peirce and Saussure were the first to foresee the existence of a new discipline, linked to linguistics only in so far as linguistics is the most developed communication science and entitled as such to furnish blueprints for any other approach. It is difficult to maintain that the entire set of linguistic categories can be applied to the other sign systems. The basic assertion which links semiotics to linguistics is only this: that all sign processes can be analysed in the same sense in which linguistics can, that is as a dialectic between codes and messages, *langue* and *parole*, competence and performance. The task of semiotics is to isolate different systems of signification, each of them ruled by specific norms, and to demonstrate that *there is* signification and that *there are* norms. Nevertheless semiotics aims to become able to describe, to structure, and to legitimate its entire field using a unified set of theoretical tools. To assert that semiotics is not a branch of linguistics does not mean that semiotics has neither autonomy nor unity. It may signify simply that linguistics is one of the branches of semiotics.

I cannot now explore the whole challenging and exciting landscape of these identities and differences. I can only limit myself to listing the different paths of research that semiotics foresees or actually recognizes as its own proper field: *zoosemiotics*, the study of *olfactory and tactile communication, culinary codes, medical semiotics* (becoming a branch of a general semiotics), *musical codes, formalized languages, secret alphabets, grammatology* (as the study of writing) *visual communications* in general, *graphic systems, iconic signs, iconography* and *iconology, card games, riddles, divination systems, systems of objects* and *architectural forms, plot structures, kinship structures, etiquette systems, rituals,* the *typology of cultures,* and so on, as far as the upper levels of *rhetorical systems* and *stylistic devices.*

The wish of Saussure seems now crowned with success. Semiotics covers the entire field of culture (or social life). But Saussure only wished to see a discipline able to study the life of signs 'au sein de la vie sociale'. He did not say—as semiotics today claims (and as the title of my lecture suggests)—that the whole of social life could be viewed as a sign process, or as a system of semiotic systems. The recognition of a great number of sign repertoires cannot convince one that those repertoires *are systems*, nor can we take for granted that any cultural phenomenon *is a sign*. Nevertheless, in order to adopt a semiotic approach one must assume that any cultural manifestation *can be viewed* as a communication process. The task of this lecture, then, will be neither to demonstrate the possibility of a general, complete, and satisfying formalization of the entire semiotic field, nor to demonstrate that any sign repertoire is necessarily a system. My purpose is more basic: I have, above all, to demonstrate that any cultural phenomenon is *also* a sign phenomenon.

Please note that I could propose two hypotheses. One of them is more radical, a sort of unnegotiable demand on the part of semiotics: that *the whole of culture must be studied as a phenomenon of communication*. Then there is a second more moderate hypothesis: *all aspects of a culture can be studied as the elements of content of communication.*

[. . .]

This process is possible from the moment that culture exists. But culture exists only because this process is made possible. Culture presupposes the semiosic use of any one of its items: sounds, images, actual objects, bodies. If we read attentively the first book of *Das Kapital* by Karl Marx we shall see that an object, endowed with use value, in so far as it acquires an exchange value, becomes the sign vehicle of other objects. Marx not only shows how commodities, in the general framework of economic life, may become sign vehicles referring to other goods; he also shows that this relationship of mutual significance is possible because the commodity system is precisely a system, structured by means of oppositions, as semiotic systems are. It is only because a commodity acquires a position within the system that it is possible to establish a code of commodities, in which one semantic axis is made to correspond to another semantic axis, and the goods of the first axis become the sign vehicle for the goods of the second one, which become in turn their meaning. Marx indicates this process saying that commodities possess an exchange value IN WHICH is expressed the value of another commodity, the value OF WHICH is the meaning of the former. The relationship is reversible.

Similarly, at the level of the sign vehicles of verbal language, /automobile/ can be the significant form expressing the meaning /voiture/, or /whale/ can be the significant form expressing as its meaning the Hebrew equivalent /tâg/—these two relationships being equally reversible. Similarly in the process of signification, the sign vehicle /whale/ can be the significant form expressing a complex semantic unit subjected to many definitions, but the entire set of these definitions may in turn be understood as the organized expression of a lexical content which is the word /whale/. Similarly the presence of a real /whale/ may be understood as the significant form referring back to a sememic unit, or maybe to the lexical entry /whale/.

C. S. Peirce defined the sign as 'anything which determines something else (its *interpretant*) to refer to an object to which itself refers . . . in the same way, the interpretant becoming in turn a sign, and so on ad infinitum'.[6] The interpretant is another sign (or something assumed as a sign) which explains or translates, or substitutes, the first sign, in order to make the world of unlimited semiosis progress, in a sort of spiral movement, actual objects never being touched as such, but always transformed into significant forms. This process of unlimited semiosis is the result of the humanization of the world by culture. In culture any entity becomes a semiotic phenomenon. The laws of communication are the laws of culture. Culture can be studied completely under a semiotic profile. Semiotics is a discipline which must be concerned with the whole of social life.

Notes

1   C. S. Peirce, *Collected Papers* (Harvard University Press, Cambridge, Mass., 1931–5), ii. 228.

2   Ibid., ii. 303.

3   F. de Saussure, *Cours de linguistique générale* (Payot, Paris, 1960), iii. 3.

4   C. S. Peirce, *Collected Papers*, v. 488.

5   Cf. Umberto Eco, *La Structure absente* (Mercure de France, Paris, 1972), section B; 'Introduction to a Semiotics of Iconic Codes', *VS-Quaderni di studi semiotici*, ii (1972) (and the whole of issues ii and iii, with several articles on this topic); *Communications*, xv (1970) (special issue on 'L'analyse des images').

6   C. S. Peirce, *Collected Papers*, ii. 303; cf. W. Wykoff, 'Semiosis ad Infinite Regressus', in *Semiotica*, ii. 1 (1970).

Chapter 13

Fred Davis

DO CLOTHES SPEAK? WHAT MAKES THEM FASHION?

THAT THE CLOTHES WE WEAR make a statement is itself a statement that in this age of heightened self-consciousness has virtually become a cliché. But what is the nature of the statements we make with our clothes, cosmetics, perfumes, and coiffures, not to mention the other material artifacts with which we surround ourselves? Are such statements analogous to those we make when we speak or write, when we talk to our fellows? In short, as the novelist Alison Lurie (1981) has recently claimed, though hardly demonstrated, is clothing not virtually a visual *language*, with its own distinctive grammar, syntax, and vocabulary? Or are such statements more like music, where the emotions, allusions, and moods that are aroused resist, as they almost must, the attribution of unambiguous meanings such as we are able to give the objects and actions of everyday life: this chair, that office, my payment, your departure? If the latter is the case, it is perhaps incorrect to speak of them as statements at all. Or can it be that clothes sometimes do one and sometimes the other, or possibly both at the same time—that is, make clear reference to who we are and wish to be taken as while alternatively or simultaneously evoking an aura that "merely suggests" more than it can (or intends to) state precisely?[1]

Cultural scientists must address these questions (as they have not thus far) if they are ever to make sense of a phenomenon that has periodically intrigued them, less for its own sake, unfortunately, than for the light they thought it could shed on certain fundamental features of modern society, namely, social movements, social stratification, and mass-produced tastes. I speak, of course, of fashion and some of its many facets: its sources in culture and social structure, the processes by which it diffuses within and among societies, the purposes it serves in social differentiation and social integration, the psychological needs it is said to satisfy, and, not least of all, its implications for modern economic life. But oddly, one facet sociologists have not fastened on—nor for that matter have psychologists or anthropologists to any appreciable extent—is that which joins the makers, purveyors, and consumers of

fashion, namely, its meaning. By meaning, I refer to the images, thoughts, sentiments, and sensibilities communicated by a new or old fashion and the symbolic
means by which this is done (Davis 1982). Such analytic neglect strikes me as
analogous to watching a play whose dialogue is kept from us but whose gross
gestural outlines, scenery, and props we are permitted to observe. Although we are
likely to come away with some sense of what is going on—whether it is comedy,
tragedy, or melodrama; whether it concerns love, murder, or betrayal—we would
have only the vaguest idea of the whys and wherefores. In the case of the sociological
interest in clothing and fashion, we know that through clothing people communicate
some things about their persons, and at the collective level this results typically in
locating them symbolically in some structured universe of status claims and life-style
attachments. Some of us may even make so bold as to assert what these claims and
attachments are—"a tramp presuming the hauteur of a patrician," "nouveau riche
ostentation masking status anxiety"—but, as in the voiceless play, the actual
symbolic content the elicits such interpretations eludes us. Lacking such knowledge,
we can at best only form conclusions without quite knowing how we derived them;
this is something we often have to do in everyday life, but by itself it hardly satisfies
the requirements of a science.

The clothing code

In the past decade or so certain newer intellectual currents in the social sciences and
humanities have begun to offer hope for penetrating this gap in the sociological
analysis of fashion, if not for altogether filling it. I refer to the burgeoning—some
would say, not altogether unjustifiably, omnivorous—field of semiotics, in particular
to its seminal notion of *code* as the binding ligament in the shared understandings
that comprise a sphere of discourse and, hence, its associated social arrangements.
Following Eco (1979), then, I would hold that clothing styles and the fashions that
influence them over time constitute something approximating a code. It is a code,
however, radically dissimilar from those used in cryptography; neither can it be more
generally equated with the language rules that govern speech and writing. Compared
to these clothing's code is, as the linguist would have it, of "low semanticity."
Perhaps it can best be viewed as an incipient or quasi-code, which, although it must
necessarily draw on the conventional visual and tactile symbols of a culture, does so
allusively, ambiguously, and inchoately, so that the meanings evoked by the combinations and permutations of the code's key terms (fabric, texture, color, pattern,
volume, silhouette, and occasion) are forever shifting or "in process."[2] The anthropologist and linguist Edward Sapir (1931, 141) with characteristic insight noted this
about fashion more than fifty years ago:

> The chief difficulty of understanding fashion in its apparent vagaries is
> the lack of exact knowledge of the unconscious symbolisms attaching to
> forms, colors, textures, postures, and other expressive elements of a
> given culture. The difficulty is appreciably increased by the fact that
> some of the expressive elements tend to have quite different symbolic
> references in different areas. Gothic type, for instance, is a nationalistic

token in Germany while in Anglo-Saxon culture, the practically identical type known as Old English . . . [signifies] a wistful look backward at madrigals and pewter.

Clearly, while the elements Sapir speaks of do somehow evoke "meanings"—moreover, meanings that are sufficiently shared within one or another clothes-wearing community—it is, as with music, far from clear *how* this happens.[3] Associative linkages to formal design elements (e.g.: angularity = masculine; curvilinear = feminine) are obviously involved (Sahlins 1976, 189–92), as are linkages to occasions (e.g.: dark hue = formal, serious, business; light hue = informal, casual, leisure) and to historical frames of reference (e.g.: bindings, stays, and corseting = Victorian, pre-female emancipation; loose fit, reduced garment volume, exposed skin = the post—World War I modern era). There are, though, as McCracken (1985) has so tellingly demonstrated in his research, no fixed, rule-governed formulas, such as exist for speech and writing, for employing and juxtaposing these elements. The correspondence with language is at best metaphoric and, according to McCracken, misleadingly metaphoric at that. Schier (1983) states the matter nicely in his criticism of Roland Barthes's *The Fashion System*: "There is certainly something to the idea that we say things with what we choose to wear, though we must not press toohard to find a set of rules encoded in every choice."[4] Chast's cartoon drawing [Figure 13.1] lights on the same point even more tellingly.

Temporally, too, there is reason to be cautious about ascribing precise meanings to most clothing. The very same apparel ensemble that "said" one thing last year will

Figure 13.1 Drawing by R. Chast. © The New Yorker Collection 1988 Roz Chast from ⟨cartoonbank.com⟩.

"say" something quite different today and yet another thing next year. Ambiguity, therefore, is rife in what could be considered the contemporary dress code of Western society and is, as we shall see, becoming even more so.

To this condition of awesome, if not overwhelming, ambiguity, I would add three other distinguishing features of the clothing-fashion code, although many more could in fact be cited.[5] Enninger (1985), for example, lists as many as thirty-one, First, it is heavily context-dependent; second, there is considerable variability in how its constituent symbols are understood and appreciated by different social strata and taste groupings; and third, it is—at least in Western society—much more given to "undercoding" than to precision and explicitness.

Context-dependency

Even more so, perhaps, than the utterances produced in everyday face-to-face interaction, the clothing-fashion code is highly context-dependent. That is, what some combination of clothes or a certain style emphasis "means" will vary tremendously depending upon the identity of the wearer, the occasion, the place, the company, and even something as vague and transient as the wearer's and the viewers' moods. Despite being made of identical material, the black gauze of the funeral veil means something very different from that sewn into the bodice of a nightgown. Similarly, the leisure suit that "fits in so nicely" at the outdoor barbecue will connote something quite different when worn to work, especially if you happen not to live in southern California.

High social variability in the signifier–signified relationship

While the signifiers constituting a style, an appearance, or a certain fashion trend can in a material sense be thought of as the same for everyone (the width of a lapel, after all, measures the same in Savile Row as in Sears) what is *signified* (connoted, understood, evoked, alluded to, or expressed) is initially at least, strikingly different for different publics, audiences, and social groupings: for the conservative as against the experimentally inclined, for the fashion-wise as against the fashion-indifferent, for the creators of fashion and their coteries as against its consumers, including even relatively sophisticated consumers. In short, while certainly not rigidly castelike in its configuration, the universe of meanings attaching to clothes, cosmetics, hairstyles, and jewelry—right down to the very shape and bearing of the body itself (Fraser 1981, 215–19; Hollander 1980)—is highly differentiated in terms of taste, social identity, and persons' access to the symbolic wares of a society.

Indeed, as the first social scientists who wrote on the subject were quick to declare (Sapir 1931; Simmel 1904; Tarde 1903; Veblen 1899), it is precisely the differentiated, socially stratified character of modern society that fuels the motor of fashion and serves as the backdrop against which its movements are enacted. In my opinion these writers, Veblen and Simmel in particular, placed *too* exclusive an emphasis on social class differentiation as the basis for fashion motivation. Still, they must be credited for their lively recognition that clothing styles and fashions do not mean the same things to all members of a society at the same time and that, because of this, what is worn lends itself easily to a symbolic upholding of class and status boundaries in society.

That the same cultural goods connote different things for different groups and publics applies equally, of course, to almost any expressive product of modern culture, be it the latest avant-garde painting, a high-tech furniture piece, an electronic music composition, ad infinitum. In the symbolic realm of dress and appearance, however, "meanings" in a certain sense tend to be simultaneously both more ambiguous and more differentiated than in other expressive realms. (This holds especially during the first phases of a new fashion cycle, as I shall illustrate in a moment.) Meanings are more ambiguous in that it is hard to get people in general to interpret the same clothing symbols in the same way; in semiotic terminology, the clothing sign's signifier-signified relationship is quite unstable. Yet the meanings are more differentiated inasmuch as, to the extent that identifiable thoughts, images, and associations crystallize around clothing symbols, these will vary markedly, most certainly at first, between different social strata and taste subcultures (Gans 1974).

Take, for example, the rather masculine, almost military styles that were fashionable among some women in the mid-1980s: exaggerated shoulder widths tapering conelike to hems slightly above the knee. It is, I believe, difficult even now to infer quite what this look meant to the broad mass of fashion consumers. Several different interpretations were possible initially, and it was only after the fashion was well launched that some partial synthesis seemed to emerge from among competing interpretations as symbolically dominant, i.e., an appropriation of masculine authority, which at the same time, by the very exaggeration of its styling, pointedly undercut any serious claim to masculinity as such.

But whatever consensus may have been arrived at eventually, the broad shoulder-inverted cone look was bound to be perceived and responded to quite differently by the coteries, audiences, and publics to which it was exposed. For cosmopolitan fashion elites it appears to have signified a kind of gender-inverted parody of military bearing. Suburban, fashion-conscious socialites, on the other hand, were repelled at first by the severity of the silhouette, which was seen as a visual affront to the conventions of femininity. Many professional and career women, however, took favorably to the style because it seemed to distance them from unwelcome stereotypical inferences of feminine powerlessness and subservience. Judging by lagging retail sales, though, many mainstream middle-class homemakers regarded this same 'look' as irrelevant at best, ugly and bizarre at worst. What meaning the style held for women factory and clerical workers is hard to infer. Assuming they became aware of it at all, it may have been devoid of meaning for them altogether, although nonmeaning in something that for others is pregnant with meaning is itself a kind of meaning in absentia.

Undercoding

That clothing styles can elicit such different responses from different social groups points to yet another distinguishing feature of the clothing code and the currents of fashion to which it is subject. That is, except for uniforms, which as a rule clearly establish the occupational identity of their wearers (see Joseph 1986), in clothing, as in the arts generally, undercoding (the phonetic proximity to *underclothing* here is perhaps not altogether infelicitous) is especially important in how meanings are communicated. According to Eco (1979, 135–36), undercoding occurs when in the absence of reliable interpretative rules persons presume or infer, often unwittingly, on the basis of such hard-to-specify cues as gesture, inflection, pace, facial expression, context, and setting, certain molar meanings in a text, score, performance, or other communication. The erotic message we carry away from the poet Herrick's 'erring lace,' 'careless shoe-string,' and 'cuff neglectful' is perhaps as good an example of undercoding in dress as can be found.[6]

At the same time it would be a mistake to assume that the undercoding of clothing and fashion is necessarily inadvertent or the product of an inherent incapacity of the unit elements constituting the code (fabric, color, cut, texture) to signify as clearly as do words or icons. (Again, the wearing of uniforms attests to clothing's ability to register clear meanings for persons wishing to establish an unambiguous role identification for themselves.) Rather, the point is that in the main the clothing-fashion code much more nearly approximates an aesthetic code than it does the conventional sign codes, such as information-oriented speech and writing, semaphore, figures and charts, or road and traffic signs, employed in ordinary communication. As Culler (1976, 100) has so trenchantly observed:

> The reason for the evasive complexity of these [aesthetic] codes is quite simple. [Conventional sign] codes are designed to communicate directly and unambiguously messages and notions which are already known. . . . But aesthetic expression aims to communicate notions, subtleties, [and] complexities which have not yet been formulated, and therefore, as soon as an aesthetic code comes to be generally perceived as a code (as a way of expressing notions which have already been articulated), then works of art tend to move beyond it. They question, parody, and generally undermine it, while exploring its mutations and extensions. One might even say that much of the interest of works of art lies in the ways in which they explore and modify the codes which they seem to be using.

What Culler does not say, and what is of special interest to the sociologist, is that such code modifications do not occur spontaneously, as if wholly and mysteriously dependent on some magical ferment called 'aesthetic expression.' Beyond the purely technical opportunities and limitations affecting an art or craft's ability to initiate some rather than other code modifications (Becker 1982) there also are the manufacturers, publicists, critics, merchandisers, and innovators (some of whom truly are artists) in whose interests it is to launch, inhibit, or otherwise regulate the transmission of code modifications from creators to consumers. Not that, as some Marxists would have it, all that happens in this connection can be attributed reductionistically to some conspiratorial, self-serving, profit-driven alignment of structurally interdependent economic interests. Still, to overlook the impress of such interests on what goes on from the moment of creation to that of consumption would be tantamount to attributing a persistent efficacy to free-floating ghosts.[7]

That undercoding is powerfully implicated in aesthetic expression would seem irrefutable. And to the extent that the fashion aspect of clothing can be viewed as aesthetic expression, which by and large it must, it is incumbent on us to try to understand better how fashion as such does and does not relate to what I have more generally termed the 'clothing code.'

Fashion and the clothing code

Thus far I have claimed that, vague and elusive as its referents ('signifieds' in semiotic talk) may be when compared to ordinary speech and writing, what we wear, including cosmetics, jewelry, and coiffure, can be subsumed under the general notion of a code. This means that within that broad are termed 'contemporary Western culture,' a great deal of sign conventionalization obtains in clothing as it does in the arts and crafts generally. Hence, different combinations of apparel with their attendant qualities are capable of registering sufficiently consistent meanings for wearers and their viewers. (In today's world, a tennis outfit will never be mistaken for formal dress or a Nehru jacket for laborer's attire, much as the occasional eccentric may insist she or he means it to be taken that way.)

In referring to qualities, I have in mind such clothing features as fabric, color, texture, cut, weight, weave, stitching, transparency, and whatever else makes a difference in how the garment or its surrounding ensemble of apparel is responded to in a community of clothes-wearers. What qualities do and do not make a difference in how clothing is responded to in a 'clothes community' can, up to a point, be conceptualized in terms analogous to the phonetic/phonemic distinction in linguistics. The essential distinction, however—what most distinguishes clothing as a mode of communication from speech—is that *meaningful* differences among clothing signifiers are not nearly as sharply drawn and standardized as are the spoken sounds employed in a speech community (see Hawkes 1977, 23–28).

To formulate matters as I have here is essentially to say no more or less than that clothing's meanings are cultural, in the same sense that everything about which common understandings can be presumed to exist (the food we eat, the music we listen to, our furniture, health beliefs, in sum, the totality of our symbolic universe) is cultural. Or as George Herbert Mead (1934) might have phrased it, the clothing we don calls out essentially, if not precisely (the difference is significant, though I shall not dwell on it here), the same images and associations in ourselves as it does in others, even granted that from time to time and from group to group different values will attach to them. For example, the shoulder-length hair of the male hippie, which for him and his friends connoted unisex liberation, for his more conventional contemporaries signified perverse androgyny and ostentatious slovenliness. But even such varying interpretations of the same grooming item or overall look are meaningful, provided each party understands where, in the vernacular, 'the other is coming from,' as most often each does.

If, then, there exists among a society's members a sufficiently shared perception of 'how to read' different items, combinations, and styles of clothing, where does fashion come into the picture? Is *fashion* merely another way of designating some distinctive style or, more generally yet, as Robert and Jeanette Lauer (1981, 23) define it, 'simply the modal style of a particular group at a particular time . . . the style which is considered appropriate or desirable?' The problem with these definitions and a host of others like them is their failure to differentiate adequately fashion per se from the consensually established clothing code (conventionalized signifiers, accepted canons of taste, etc.) operative in a society at a particular time. That some sort of difference exists between the operative code and those elements we term 'fashion' is, to be sure, hinted at in even these definitions when they speak of a modal or prevalent style, implying thereby some succession of styles over time. But the implication for fashion is lost through the failure to discriminate between what happens during the last phases of a fashion cycle, when a style has already become part of the common visual parlance, and what happens at the beginning of the cycle, when the new style typically jars, or at least bemuses, us. Precisely this difference, of course, underlies the familiar insight that a fashion that has been accorded wide acceptance is, ironically, no longer fashionable.

Clearly, any definition of *fashion* seeking to grasp what distinguishes it from style, custom, conventional or acceptable dress, or prevalent modes must place its emphasis on the element of *change* we often associate with the term. (The word itself, according to the *Oxford English Dictionary*, derives from the Old French and originally meant, as it still does today in one of its usages, 'to make' in the sense of 'fabricate.') And at the level of communication, by *change* we necessarily imply, as the linguist Saussure insisted (MacCannell and MacCannell 1982, 10), some shift in the relationship of signifier and signified, albeit always bearing in mind that in dress the relationship between *signifiers* and the referents, attributes, or values thereby *signified* is generally much less uniform or exact than in written or spoken language. In any case, *fashion*, if it is to be distinguished from *style* and numerous other of its neighbor terms, must be made to refer to some alteration in the code of visual conventions by which we read meanings of whatever sort and variety into the clothes we and our contemporaries wear. The change may involve the introduction of wholly new visual, tactile, or olfactory signifiers, the retrieval of certain old ones that have receded from but still linger in memory (Davis 1979), or a different accenting of familiar signifiers; but change there must be to warrant the appellation *fashion*.

This, I concede, skirts the issue of exactly how extensive such changes must be for us to speak of fashion rather than, for example, a modal style or the accepted dress code. Do the apparently slight modifications from season to season in hem length, waist or hip accenting, shoulder buildup, or lapel width represent code modifications of sufficient magnitude to justify the designation *fashion*? Our intuition says no, but it would be unwise to be too arbitrary with respect to the question. In the lived world of everyday dress, clothing design, and merchandising there is, perhaps inevitably, a good deal of uncertainty in the matter depending in no small part on whose interests are served by proclaiming the code modification a new fashion and whose by resisting such a proclamation. Among those coteries and publics for whom it is terribly important to be thought of as fashion trendsetters, the tendency will, of course, be to invest even minor changes with fashion significance. Among those more indifferent to fashion and those who cultivate a fashionably out-of-fashion stance (Kinsley 1983), the tendency will be to deny or discount those code modifications that manage to steal into one's wardrobe. Ideally, from a phenomenological as well as sociological point of view, one would want to restrict the word *fashion* to those code modifications that, irrespective of their apparent character, somehow manage on first viewing to startle, captivate, offend, or otherwise engage the sensibilities of some culturally preponderant public, in America the so-called middle mass. It is their acceptance or rejection of a code modification that will determine whether it succeeds as fashion or merely passes from the scene as a futile symbolic gesture.

[. . .]

Notes

1   No finer rendering of dress's capacity to suggest a good deal more than it states exists than Robert Herrick's (1579–1674) poem "Delight in Disorder":

> A sweet disorder in the dress
> Kindles in clothes a wantonness:
> A lawn about the shoulders thrown
> Into a fine distraction:
> An erring lace, which here and there
> Enthrals the crimson stomacher:
> A cuff neglectful, and thereby
>
> Ribbands to flow confusedly:
> A winning wave, deserving note,
> In the tempestuous petticoat:
> A careless shoe-string, in whose tie
> I see a wild civility:
> Do more bewitch me, than when art
> Is too precise in every part.

(Taken from *The Oxford Book of English Verse*, edited by Sir Arthur Quiller-Couch. New York: Oxford University Press, 1941.)

2   Levine (1985) argues that Western social thought and social science have over the centuries developed an almost institutionalized aversion toward dealing in analytically constructive ways with ambiguity. This may help account for the proclivity of many social scientists, in particular modern structuralists like Lévi-Strauss and Barthes, to so readily assimilate clothing communication into the axiomatic structure of Saussure's linguistic model.

3   Some indication of how such meanings are accomplished, albeit within a rather narrow sphere of apparel accessory design, is given by Brubach (1989, 67) in her report on fashions in sunglasses: "Mikli [a sunglasses designer] has just finished designing a collection for Ray-Ban's international division—five sunglasses frames intended as a feminine alternative to the Macho classics. The shapes are upswept and less severe, suggestive of the way the eyes turn up at the corners when a person smiles; the lines are curved rather than straight; and the contours are sculptural, not flat like those of the Wayfarer [an earlier, highly successful, "masculinized" Ray-Ban style]. Mikli says it's possible to change *le regard* altogether, to give a face an entirely different expression—an expression of violence, of sensuality, of sweetness, or whatever one chooses. So that, even though the eyes are hidden, by the act of reproducing the shape of the eye in some exaggerated form sunglasses can reconstitute *le regard* and remodel the face."

4   Like Barthes, Descamps (1979) creates elaborate taxonomic schemes to decode, with spurious precision I would hold, exactly what clothing and fashions "mean."

5   For example, whereas speech messages unfold continuously as the speaker moves from one utterance to another, a clothing ensemble is capable of but a single message, however complex, until such time as the wearer decides to change clothes. Viewed differently, speech, unless captured in writing, fades quickly,

whereas clothing holds its meaning over the duration of an encounter. Moreover, as the late Herbert Blumer (1984) reminded me in response to an early version of this chapter I had sent him, "while clothing may 'speak,' it seems rarely to engage in dialogue. The give and take in the adjustment of meaning (which is the mark of dialogue) does not seem to take place in the presentations of clothing; while clothing may say something, it is scarcely involved in conversation."

6 Another charming example of undercoding in the realm of clothing and its capacity to imply a great deal on the basis of minimal cues is offered by Gisele d'Assailly in her book *Ages of Elegance* (Paris: Hachette, 1968). There she reports that Marie Antoinette and her entourage would often refer to items of dress in such metaphors as 'a dress of *stifled sighs* covered with *superfluous regrets*; in the middle was a spot of *perfect candour come-and-see* buckles; . . . a bonnet decorated with *fickle feathers* and streamers of *woebegone eyes*' (italics in original, 139; quoted in Rosencranz 1972, 287.)

7 Consider in this connection the many flops recorded in fashion history, that is, failed attempts by designers, manufacturers, publicists, etc., to foist a new style on the public. The most recent of some notoriety was perhaps that of the publisher of *Women's Wear Daily*, John Fairchild, to marshal the considerable authority of his publication in behalf of the decisively rejected 'midi look' of the early 1970s.

Bibliography

Becker, H. S. (1982) *Art Worlds*, Berkeley: University of California Press.

Blumer, H. (1984) Letter to Author, 14 August.

Brubach, H. (1989) 'In Fashion, Visionaries', *New Yorker*, 28 August.

Culler, J. (1976) *Ferdinand de Saussure*, Glasgow: Collins.

Davis, F. (1979) *Yearning for Yesterday: A Sociology of Nostalgia*, New York: Free Press.

Deschamps, M.-A. (1979) *Psychosociolozie de la Mode*, Paris: Presses universitaires de France.

Eco, U. (1979) *A Theory of Semiotics*, Bloomington: Indiana University Press.

Enninger, W. (1985) 'The Design Features of Clothing Codes', *Kodias/Code* 8, 1–2: 81–110.

Fraser, K. (1981) *The Fashionable Mind*, New York: Knopf.

Gans, H. (1974) *Popular Culture and High Culture*, New York: Basic Books.

Hawkes, T. (1977) *Structuralism and Semiotics*, Berkeley: University of California Press.

Hollander, A. (1980) *Seeing Through Clothes*, New York: Avon.

Joseph, N. (1986) *Uniforms and Nonuniforms*, New York: Greenwood Press.

Kinsley, M. (1983) 'Dressing Down', *Harpers*, February.

Lauer, R. and Laner, J. (1981) *Fashion Power*, Englewood Cliffs, N.J.: Prentice-Hall.

Levine, D. N. (1985) *The Flight from Ambiguity*, Chicago: University of Chicago Press.

Lurie, A. (1981) *The Language of Clothes*, New York: Random House.

MaCannell, D. and MacCannell, J. F. (1982) *The Time of the Sign*, Bloomington: Indiana University Press.

McCracken, G. (1985) 'Clothing as Language: An Object Lesson in the Study of the Expressive Properties of Material Culture', in B. Reynold and M. Stott (eds) *Material Anthropology*, New York: University Press of America.

Mead, G. H. (1934) *Mind, Self and Society*, Chicago: University of Chicago Press.

Rosencrantz, M. (1972) *Clothing Concepts*, New York: Macmillan.

Sahlins, M. (1976) *Culture and Practical Reason*, Chicago: University of Chicago Press.

Sapir, E. (1931) 'Fashion', *Encyclopedia of The Social Sciences* 6, New York: Macmillan.

Schier, F. (1983) 'Speaking Through Our Clothes', *New York Times Book Review*, 24 July.

Simmel, G. (1904) 'Fashion', Reprinted in *American Journal of Sociology* 62 (May 1957): 541–58.

Tarde, G. (1903) *The Laws of Imitation*, New York: Henry Holt.

Veblen, T. (1899) *The Theory of The Leisure Class*, New York: Macmillan.

Chapter 14

Colin Campbell

WHEN THE MEANING IS NOT A MESSAGE

A critique of the consumption as communication thesis

Introduction

IT HAS BECOME QUITE USUAL for sociologists to suggest that when individuals in contemporary society engage with consumer goods they are principally employing them as 'signs' rather than as 'things', actively manipulating them in such a way as to communicate information about themselves to others. It is also commonly assumed that these individuals, in their capacity as consumers, engage with goods in order to achieve 'self-construction' (Langman 1992: 43), or as Bauman expresses it, for the purpose of 'fashion[ing] their subjectivity' (Bauman 1988: 808). Consequently it is not unusual to encounter claims like that made by John Clammer to the effect that 'Shopping is not merely the acquisition of things: it is the buying of identity' (Clammer 1992: 195), or Beng Huat Chua's assertion that clothing 'is a means of encoding and communicating information about the self (Chua 1992: 115). In other words, the perspective regards consumption as an activity in which individuals employ the symbolic meanings attached to goods in an endeavour both to construct and to inform others of their 'lifestyle' or 'identity', and hence that 'consumption' is, in effect, best understood as a form of communication.

In essence, this thesis consists of five linked assumptions. First, that in studying the activity of consumption sociologists should focus their attention, not on the instrumentality of goods, but rather upon their symbolic meanings. Second, that consumers themselves are well aware of these meanings (which are widely known and shared) and hence that the purchase and display of goods is oriented to these rather than the instrumental meanings of goods. Third, and following on from this, that these activities should be regarded as being undertaken by consumers with the deliberate intention of 'making use' of these meanings, in the sense of employing them to 'make statements' or 'send messages' about themselves to others. Fourth, the content of these 'messages' that consumers send to others through their purchase and use of goods are principally to do with matters of identity (or 'lifestyle'). Fifth and finally, the reason for sending messages to others is to gain recognition or confirmation from them of the identity that consumers have selected.

This argument has become virtually taken for granted by many sociologists, who therefore automatically adopt a communicative act paradigm when focusing on consumption. This results in consumer actions being studied, not as physical events involving the expenditure of effort, or for that matter as transactions in which money is exchanged for goods and services, but rather as symbolic acts or signs, acts that do not so much 'do something' as 'say something', or perhaps, 'do something through saying something'. This communicative act paradigm – in which talk, or language more generally, is the model for all action – is widely employed throughout sociology, being common to theorists as diverse in other ways as Veblen, Goffman, Bourdieu and Baudrillard. Hence it is this perspective, especially as applied to consumption, that I wish to examine in this paper. I intend to examine each of the above five assumptions in turn, and in order to give the thesis a fair test, I shall take as an illustration of it a genre of products in relation to which this argument is more commonly advanced than any other, that of clothing. In other words, I shall consider the thesis that, when it comes to the selection, purchase and use of clothing, these activities are best viewed as efforts by consumers to communicate messages about themselves (especially about their identity) to those who are in a position to observe them.[1]

Consumers and the symbolic meaning of goods

The consumption as communication thesis clearly requires that sociologists should demonstrate first that consumer goods possess symbolic as well as instrumental meanings, second that consumers have a common understanding of these meanings, and third that their consumption activities are guided by them. In other words, to speak of the symbolic meanings carried by clothes is to presume the existence of a shared system of symbols; one known to wearer and observer alike, and hence one that allows the acts of selecting and displaying certain items of clothing to serve as a means of communication, such that a message is passed between the wearer and observer(s). Such assumptions are, of course, necessarily implied in any reference to a 'language of clothing' (Lurie 1981). If it is assumed that consumer goods do possess symbolic meanings the first issue to be confronted is the question of whether whatever symbolic meanings or associations goods possess can be said to be shared to the extent that successful communication of messages is indeed possible.

One of the first difficulties here is that of the sheer variety of languages which it has been suggested clothing constitutes or 'carries'. The issue is less that consumer goods, such as clothing, may constitute *a* language, but rather that they may constitute multiple or even overlapping languages or language codes. For example, Veblen (1925) was one of the first theorists to suggest that an act of consumption might be intended to send a message and he was very explicit about what that might be. He considered that it indicated something about the consumer's 'pecuniary strength'. In other words, observers, because of their knowledge of how much things cost, would be able to assess an individual's wealth – and hence their social status – from the purchased goods that he or she displayed. This could be said to be one 'language' – the language of wealth – since the price of a good is a symbolic attribute like any other, even if it does have a direct connection with material resources.[2]

But there have been other claims concerning the nature of the language of clothes. There is, for example, the obvious suggestion that one may 'read' someone's clothes in terms of their fashion status or style, qualities which may be relatively independent of wealth. Then there is the increasingly common assumption (as mentioned above) that clothing can be 'read' in terms of the 'lifestyle' it manifests and hence for the 'identity' that the wearer has selected. Finally, one might mention the fact that several writers, often inspired by the work of Freud, have claimed that clothing constitutes a language of sexuality, such that one may 'read' particular fashion phenomena and styles of dress as indicators of sexual assertiveness or submission, availability or non-availability, or of gender ambiguity (Konig 1973) (although here there is often the suggestion that the wearer is not fully aware of the message he or she is sending to others). It follows from this that before any observer can hope to begin 'reading' whatever message a particular individual may be 'sending' by means of his or her clothing, it is first necessary to correctly identify the 'language' that is being 'spoken'.[3]

However, where there are grounds for assuming that speaker and listener (that is to say, wearer and observer) are 'speaking the same language', there is still the question of how conversant each might be with that particular tongue. For obviously sender and receiver need to have sufficient knowledge to 'interpret', and to 'send', a message in that language. It is not enough to know which language is being spoken; it is also necessary to be a competent speaker. Thus, in the Veblen example, if a successful message is to be communicated, both sender and receiver of the message must be familiar not merely with the product concerned but also with its price. The same thing obviously applies to the other 'languages' mentioned; hence one must be knowledgeable and up to date concerning the ever-changing world of fashion in order to send and receive messages successfully in that language.

How reasonable is it to assume that the necessary linguistic competence is widely shared? Research has yet to be undertaken to provide all the data needed to answer this question, but what information is available does suggest grounds for scepticism. For example, it would appear that it is not unusual for there to be a lack of agreement among the public at large of the sort necessary before a 'language' of fashionability could be said to exist; that is to say, concerning those items of clothing (or features of clothing) that are actually 'in fashion' or 'out of fashion' at any one time. Thus Gallup, in their *Social Trends* survey for June 1991, found that 45 per cent of people interviewed thought that turn-ups on men's trousers were 'in fashion' at that time, whilst 43 per cent thought that they were actually 'out of fashion'. This suggests that, in that year, few observers of male attire would be in a position to make a confident interpretation of the 'message' they were receiving. Similar sizable differences of opinion were found when consumers were questioned about other items of clothing.[4] Admittedly, the same survey did suggest a degree of consensus on some items. Thus two-thirds of respondents thought that mini-skirts were in fashion, whilst 80 per cent thought that this was also true of blue jeans. However, even in these cases sizable minorities disagreed, or claimed not to know. What this suggests is either that the world of fashion is itself confused, with 'experts' in disagreement with one another (unfortunately Gallup did not back up this survey with questions directed at the gurus of fashion), such that, in this respect at least, clothing represents a 'tower of Babel'; or, alternatively, that most people are simply not sufficiently conversant with the 'language of fashion' to be successful in either sending or receiving a message in that language.

One could claim that this overall lack of agreement about fashionability is somewhat misleading, as the figures given are for the population at large, whilst those items deemed to be 'in fashion' at any one time will vary from one social group or subculture to another. Unfortunately Gallup did not break their results down in this way. However, if this is true, then it does constitute a significant modification to the general thesis that consumer behaviour should be understood as an attempt to convey messages to others by means of the symbolic meanings attached to goods. For if one accepts that the 'meaning' of any one particular item of clothing displayed will differ depending on who witnesses it – and may indeed be 'meaningless' to some observers – then the scope of the theory is significantly modified. For the general thesis includes the assumption that everyone in society is equally conversant in the 'language of clothes', and consequently that this constant 'talk' is understood by all who 'hear' it. That is to say, what is being 'said' is capable of being interpreted by everyone and in approximately the same way. If, however, we now have to admit that this is not true, and that only those who share the values and attitudes of the wearer speak the same 'language', then much of what is being 'said' is necessarily the equivalent of double-Dutch to many who 'hear' it. Or, at least, even if the majority of 'hearers' do profess to 'understand' what the wearer is 'saying', there would be good reason to believe that this does not coincide with what the wearer believes that he or she is 'saying'. Successful communication to some people – presumably the target audience for one's 'message' – is thus only likely to be achieved at the expense either of a lack of communication with others, or of sending them a message which is not what was intended.

Of course, people may try to overcome this problem by only wearing the message-carrying clothes when in the company of their target audience. Occasionally this may be possible. On the other hand, such successful segregation of audiences is often not easy to achieve, as one may need to travel by public transport to the opera, or wear to work what one is going to wear that evening to the party, etc. In these cases the 'meaning' of one's ensemble is necessarily ambiguous. If, however, the meaning cannot be read successfully without knowledge of the context in which the clothing is intended to be worn, then the analogy with language breaks down. For although the meaning of particular words and phrases may also change with context, here what one needs to know is not simply the context of use, but rather the *intended* context of use. For example, we see a man on the underground in evening dress. Is he perhaps a waiter on his way to or from work, a guest going to or from a formal social occasion or a musician on his way to perform in an orchestra? The context in which we see him wearing these clothes – making use of public transport – does not help us resolve these questions. For what we need to know is the *intended* context of use. Finally it should be noted that what such spatial and temporal segregation of clothes display suggests is not merely that the 'meaning' of clothes is typically situated, but that it is crucially dependent on the *roles* that people occupy. What the observer tends to 'read' is less the clothes themselves than the wearer's role.

Sending a message

In assessing the claim that the clothes people wear should be 'read' as if they constituted a 'text' containing a message, it is profitable to consider the issue from the perspective of the would-be communicator. How exactly would individuals set about 'sending a message' to some one or more other people by means of clothes alone, should they wish to do so? What kind of messages could they hope to send, and how indeed would they know whether or not they had succeeded? Now there are situations in which people often want to do just this. The typical job interview is a case, in point. Individuals may indeed spend some time prior to such an occasion thinking about the impression that their clothes (and the manner in which they are worn) might make on a prospective employer. The 'message' they might want to get across may well vary, but it will probably focus on conveying the idea that the applicant is a 'smart', 'tidy' or at least 'respectable' person; someone who 'cares about their appearance'. It is important to note three things about this example. First, there is little possibility of conveying any very detailed or specific message – only a vague 'impression' is possible. Second, in most cases the applicant will have little idea of how successful, if at all, they have been in getting their message across. They may discover this if they get the job (although success in itself would not prove that their exercise in 'impression management' played a critical part in the outcome), as they may be told that they 'made a good impression' with their clothes at the interview. Alternatively they may learn this in those organisations where interview de-briefings are held for unsuccessful candidates. But often the applicant will have no feedback at all and hence have little idea whether successful 'communication' occurred. Third, the 'language' that individuals are attempting to use in such cases is not one of those mentioned earlier; indeed it is not one sociologists usually discuss at all. Typically a job applicant is not attempting to convey wealth, status or even fashion-consciousness to prospective employers, but personal qualities of ethical or moral significance. In other words these occasions represent attempts to use clothes as a 'language of character'.

A rather better example of a situation where an individual attempts to convey a specific message through clothing would be that of the prostitute, or, more precisely perhaps, what used to be called the street-walker. Here we have a situation in which there is a need to convey a very specific message – that sexual services are available for a price – largely by means of clothes alone and virtually at a glance. In reality of course make-up, demeanour and general appearance all contribute to the sending of this message. One must presume that most of those individuals who do attempt this have a high degree of success in conveying the message or they would not continue long in their chosen profession. Interestingly, this need to succeed means that the typical dress of a prostitute virtually approximates to a 'uniform', and is relatively unchanging over time in its fundamentals (high-heeled shoes, black stockings, short skirts, etc.). Even here, however, mistakes in reading this 'language' are still common enough, as is witnessed by the well-known phenomenon of 'respectable women' who live in or near a red-light district, regularly being accosted by men who mistake them for prostitutes; a mistake that one would assume should be rare if there was such a thing as an unambiguous 'language of clothes'.[5]

Not sending a message

We can also profitably invert this imaginary exercise and ask ourselves what individuals would do who do not wish to send messages to others via their clothing at all: where they desire, in fact, to be inconspicuous. Classic examples might be the undercover policeman, the spy, or even the pickpocket. Here the ambition is less to convey a given message than for observers to treat the individual as so much 'part of the scenery' that they do not really register their presence. One way to do this might be to hide behind a uniform (that of a postman or traffic warden, for example), but where this is not possible then a suitably universal, which is to say, 'anonymous', form of dress will be adopted. The extent to which this is actually possible might be considered a good guide to whether there really is a 'clothing language' in society.

Yet there is a more important point here. For the ability to 'send a message' in any true language is critically dependent on the possibility of *not* sending one. In order to be able to say something meaningful it is essential to be able to stay silent. Such a contrast is essential to all forms of communication. Consequently one of the most forceful objections against the claim that goods (and especially clothes) can be used to send messages is the fact that this possibility rarely exists. For it is a strange feature of this so-called 'language' that you are only allowed to pause for breath when you no longer have any listeners. Unlike language proper, the so-called 'language of clothes' is one that consumers are only able to stop speaking when they are no longer observed; or, when in the company of others, if they take the drastic step of removing all their clothes (although one suspects that in practice this would actually be 'read' as a statement of some significance). In other words, not only is it impossible to have 'nothing to say', but most of the time individuals are simply repeating themselves endlessly to anyone who is in a position to 'hear' them.[6]

It is clear from this discussion that there are few grounds for claiming that clothing constitutes a 'language', and that such assertions should really be regarded as purely metaphoric. The claim is inappropriate as there are no fixed, rule-governed formulas, such as exist for speech and writing. That is to say, there is no grammar, syntax or vocabulary. What is more, the essentially fixed nature of a person's appearance renders any 'dialogue' or 'conversation' through clothes an impossibility, with the consequence that individuals typically 'read' clothing as if it were a single gestalt, whilst they employ a very limited range of nouns and adjectives to categorise those portrayed. In addition, no one ever attempts to 'read' outfits in a linear sense or to detect novel messages. Indeed, as Grant McCracken's research has shown, the more individuals try to employ clothing as a language, that is by making their own combinations of items to construct a personal 'ensemble', the less successful it is likely to be as a means of communication (McCracken 1990: 55–70). It is only when individuals wear conventional outfits of the kind that correspond to existing social stereotypes (such as, for example, 'businessman', 'beggar' or 'prostitute') that anything approaching a 'language code' can be said to exist at all. If one adds to this the fact that whatever 'meanings' or associations an item of clothing may have are themselves highly context-dependent as well as subject to rapid temporal change, then it becomes quite clear that there simply cannot be a 'language of clothes'. Indeed, even Davis' (1992) suggestion that clothing should be seen as a 'quasi-code' in which ambiguity is central is probably claiming too much.[7]

Davis goes on to suggest that, when viewed as a vehicle for communicating meaning, clothing is rather like music in possessing the ability to convey powerful associations while being utterly unable to communicate anything resembling a precise message. Hence, whilst it is impossible to agree on what 'meaning' should be attributed to the fact that a particular individual has purchased a pair of blue jeans or chooses to wear them to go shopping – in the way, for example, that in British society, the decision of a bride to wear a white dress on her wedding day can be said to have a specific and widely understood meaning – this is not to say that blue jeans do not carry a range of cultural associations. Indeed market researchers devote a good deal of time and effort to discovering precisely what these might be. Thus, just as music could be said to convey moods (such as sadness, melancholy or joy, for example), so one might claim that clothes could 'indicate' such qualities as informality, restraint or exuberance. However, such an analogy hardly supports the consumption as communication thesis; rather it supports the suggestion that clothing functions as a means of personal expression, and hence should be regarded as an art form.

This should serve to remind us that language and the arts are designed to fulfil rather different functions. Consequently if clothes are used as a means of 'expression' (artistic or not), they can hardly be employed at the same time to convey a message that others will understand. For in choosing items to meet their emotional needs individuals are unlikely to be abiding by the standardised requirements of a social code. Nor is this objection overcome by assuming that if clothes perform an expressive function then it must follow that what they express is the self, and hence can be regarded as indicative of a person's identity. For what clothes may well express could be no more than a mood, whim or temporary need, largely unrelated to the basic personality, let alone the social identity, of the wearer. Thus, just because an individual dons casual clothes one weekend, an observer would be mistaken in assuming from this that he or she is a 'casual' sort of person. For all it might indicate is that he or she experienced a need to relax that particular weekend.

In fact whilst clothing may reasonably be compared with an art form, music is not a good parallel. In the first place, although there is no agreed language for translating sounds into ideas, there is in Western music a very precise musical language, that of notation, one which any musician working in this tradition must be able to read. There is no similar agreed system of abstract symbols for translating ideas about clothing into garments. More important, since music is a temporal art it is possible to say nothing – that is to have silence – using this medium. Finally, music is usually purely expressive in character, whilst clothing does fulfil an important instrumental function. Hence a better parallel might be architecture, for houses, shops and offices serve instrumental functions while also having expressive properties; but here too there is no commonly accepted 'language' that would enable these artifacts to be interpreted as messages.

The puzzling question which arises from this discussion is why, given such powerful objections, does the clothing as language argument, as well as the consumption as communication thesis more generally, still continue to find favour among sociologists? One possibility is that it stems from a common tendency to link three doubtful assumptions in such a manner as to construct an attractive yet specious argument. These assumptions are first, because people generally find an individual's appearance 'meaningful' it is presumed to have *a* meaning. Second, since it is generally assumed that people choose to wear what they wear, it is assumed that this 'singular' meaning is intended. Third, since clothing is usually displayed, in the sense of being worn in public, it is assumed that individuals must be 'making a statement', or 'conveying a message' to those in a position to observe them.

In reality of course objects can be meaningful without having a symbolic meaning (that is, like a paper-clip, their meaning is effectively equivalent to their use), just as they can be regarded as symbolically meaningful without having a single unambiguous meaning (as is the case with most works of art, for example). Yet the biggest mistake in this chain of reasoning is the tendency to infer conscious intent from the apparent presence of design. In this respect, the problem here is reminiscent of the nineteenth-century 'argument from design' that was popular among those keen to defend Christianity from the attacks of atheists and sceptics. The proponents of that argument suggested that the presence of what looked very much like 'design' in the natural world implied not merely the work of a conscious designer, but of a 'purpose' behind all things: in other words, God and God's purpose. We now know that the apparent 'design' in nature owes nothing to the conscious actions of a divine being, but is actually the product of the interaction of processes of mutation and natural selection operating over millions of years. A similar false inference is commonly drawn with respect to the clothes people wear. An observer scrutinises an individual's outfit, perceives a 'meaning' of some sort and thus infers that the wearer must be the 'creator' of that meaning, and what is more, must have created it for some purpose. Consequently they go on to infer that the outfit represents a 'message' that the wearer intends to send to whoever happens to be in a position to receive it. Yet here too the inference of purpose (if not entirely that of design) is frequently unwarranted.

The critically important point is that, as noted above, since consumers cannot avoid wearing clothes they are unable to prevent others from 'reading' meanings into the clothes they wear. Now they may be well aware of this: that is to say, they may anticipate that the wearing of an old, worn suit is likely to lead others to assume that they are relatively poor. But it does not follow from this that because they wear it they therefore *intend* to send such a message. Other considerations may have dictated the choice of clothes on this occasion. In this context it is important to remember the criticism that has been made of Merton's famous manifest-latent function distinction, which is that he failed to distinguish the separate dimensions of intention and awareness (Campbell 1982). For individuals may intend to send a message and be aware that this is what they are doing; they may, however, be aware that they are sending a message, even though it is not their intention to send one, just as they may succeed in sending a message even though they neither intend to do so nor are aware that they have done so. In addition, some individuals may intend to send a message and indeed believe that they have succeeded when in fact this is not the case.

We can end by noting that the belief that people's clothes can be 'read' for the intended 'messages' they contain will probably continue to persist as long as no attempt is made to falsify it. Like most dubious beliefs it is not abandoned simply because it is rarely if ever put to the test. One can be quite certain that if clothing were a true language, and consequently individuals had to understand and respond correctly, then they would quickly discover the full extent of their failure to 'read' the clothing of others. As it is, individuals can be confident in asserting that they 'understand' the meaning of someone else's ensemble, secure in the knowledge that their understanding is unlikely to be challenged. In a similar fashion sociologists can continue to assert that acts of consumption constitute 'messages' until such time as this thesis is put to the test.

Notes

1   This is not intended as a critique of semiotics. It is clear that goods can be analysed as if they constituted 'texts'. Although I am doubtful of the value of any analysis that does not make reference to the views of consumers, it is possible that there is something to be gained from treating commodities and consumption acts as if they were plays, poems or paintings. The object of this critique is the thesis that includes the presumption that individual consumers *intend* their actions to be interpreted by others as 'signs' or 'signals'. For this is necessarily to suggest the presence of communicative intent and hence to imply that consumption activities should be understood as constituting 'messages'. In other words, it is one thing for academics to 'discover' symbolic meanings attached to products; it is another to assume that the conduct of consumers should be understood in terms of such meanings. Apart from the fact that this latter claim requires evidence (and is hence refutable) in a way that the former does not, it also begs a series of important questions.

2   Unlike many of the other proposed clothing 'languages' there are reasonable grounds for believing that many people will be familiar with this one, as it is usually displayed on products themselves at the point of sale.

3   A *nouveau riche* person may be 'speaking' the language of pecuniary strength, attempting to send the message 'I am a wealthy person', only to have his or her 'listeners' 'hearing' the language of fashionability, and concluding that he or she is 'old-fashioned'. Or, a young person in a nightclub may be trying to speak the language of sexuality, attempting to send the message of youthful virility, only to have the other clubbers 'hearing' the language of pecuniary strength, and reading the message 'poor' and 'not well-off'.

4   Bermuda shorts and lace tights were among the other items mentioned. Up to a third of respondents admitted that they did not know whether these items were fashionable or not.

5   It is interesting to note that when it is necessary to convey something about a person quickly through clothes alone, as is often the case on the stage, this is done by making use of long-established, generally unchanging and simple, traditional 'codes' or understandings, such as the colourful and ill-fitting trousers that denote a clown, or the black cloak and hat that indicate a villain.

6   If clothing alone can be used to communicate a message, one wonders why

beggars find it necessary to place pieces of cardboard on the pavement in front of them announcing that they are 'unemployed and homeless', or 'hungry and homeless'. Should they not be able to communicate these facts through their clothes alone?

7   Davis observes that the 'fashion-code' in modern Western societies is heavily context-dependent, in 'having considerable variability in how its constituent symbols are understood and appreciated by different strata and taste groupings', and by being 'much more given to "undercording" than to precision and explicitness' (1992: 8). What is surprising, having admitted all this, is that he still seems to believe that an identifiable 'code' exists.

References

Baudrillard, Jean (1975) *The Mirror of Production*, St Louis, Mo.: Telos Press.

Baudrillard, Jean (1981) *Towards a Critique of the Political Economy of the Sign*, trans. C. Lewin, St Louis, Mo.: Telos Press.

Baudrillard, Jean (1983) *Simulations*, New York: Semiotexte.

Baudrillard, Jean (1988) 'Consumer Society', in M. Poster (ed.) *Jean Baudrillard: Selected Writings*, Oxford: Polity Press.

Bauman, Z. (1988) *Sociology and Modernity*, Cambridge: Polity.

Bauman, Z. (1992) *Intimations of Postmodernity*, London: Routledge.

Bourdieu, P. (1984) *Distinction: A Social Critique of the Judgement of Taste*, translated by R. Nice, London: Routledge and Kegan Paul.

Bowlby, R. (1985) *Just Looking: Consumer Culture*, London: Methuen.

Campbell, Colin (1982) 'A Dubious Distinction? An Inquiry into the Value and Use of Merton's Concepts of Latent and Manifest Function', *American Sociological Review*, 47, 29–44.

Campbell, Colin (1987) *The Romantic Ethic and the Spirit of Modern Consumerism*, Oxford: Blackwell.

Campbell, Colin (1992) 'The Desire for the New: Its Nature and Social Location as Presented in Theories of Fashion and Modern Consumerism', in Roger Silverstone and Eric Hirsch (eds) *Consuming Technologies: Media and Information in Domestic Spaces*, London: Routledge.

Chua, Beng Huat (1992) 'Shopping for Women's Fashion in Singapore', in Rob Shields (ed.) *Lifestyle Shopping: The Subject of Consumption*, London: Routledge.

Clammer, John (1992) 'Aesthetics of the Self: Shopping and Social Being in Contemporary Urban Japan', in Rob Shields (ed.) *Lifestyle Shopping: The Subject of Consumption*, London: Routledge.

Davis, Fred (1992) *Fashion, Culture and Identity*, Chicago: University of Chicago Press.

Dittmar, Helga (1992) *The Social Psychology of Material Possessions: To Have Is To Be*, Hemel Hempstead: Harvester Wheatsheaf.

Douglas, Mary (1992) 'In Defense of Shopping', *Monograph Series Toronto Semiotic Circle* no. 9.

Goffman, E. (1990) *The Presentation of Self in Everyday Life*, London: Penguin.

Langman, Lauren (1992) 'Neon Cages: Shopping for Subjectivity', in Rob Shields (ed.) *Lifestyle Shopping: The Subject of Consumption*, London: Routledge.

Lurie, Alison (1981) *The Language of Clothes*, New York: Random House.

McCracken, Grant (1985) 'Dress Colour at the Court of Elizabeth I: An Essay in Historical Anthropology', *Canadian Review of Sociology and Anthropology* 22, 4.

McCracken, Grant (1990) *Culture and Consumption: New Approaches to the Symbolic Character of Consumer Goods and Activities*, Bloomington, Ind.: Indiana University Press.

Rudmin, Floyd (ed.) (1991) *To Have Possessions: A Handbook on Ownership and Property*, a special issue of the *Journal of Social Behavior and Personality* 6, 6.

Shields, Rob (ed.) (1992) *Lifestyle Shopping: The Subject of Consumption*, London: Routledge.

Veblen, T. (1925) *The Theory of the Leisure Class*, London: George Allen and Unwin.

Warde, A. (1990) 'Introduction to the Sociology of Consumption', *Sociology* 24, 1.

Chapter 15

Malcolm Barnard

FASHION STATEMENTS
Communication and culture

Introduction

MODERN, WESTERN PEOPLE are accustomed to the way in which the clothes they wear begin their lives as 'trendy' or 'stylish', but then start to age, become 'stale' and are no longer trendy or stylish. We are used to the idea that clothes come, or go, in and out of fashion, and the English phrase 'old hat' would appear to describe a well-understood drift from literal to metaphorical usage. Thus, fashion, the idea that what people wear may or may not be the current or latest style, is clearly understood in modern and western cultures. Also, modern, western people are familiar with the idea that the clothes they and others wear are meaningful. Clothes are selected for purchase, and for wearing, according to the meaning we believe them to have, or the messages we believe them to send. A novelty tie or a strappy frock worn to a job interview in the city, for example, 'sends out all the wrong messages'. The English phrase again appears to give away an entire culture's implicit understanding of fashion's communicative function. Both fashion itself and the communicative function of fashion are perceived as being unproblematic and well understood in modern western cultures, as evidenced by the title of the current volume.

However, while the conception of fashion as a temporal sequence of 'looks' or styles that is taken for granted by certain cultures may be relatively uncontroversial, the conceptions of meaning and communication that are presupposed in the notion that fashion or clothing are meaningful or communicative phenomena certainly are not. For example, presupposed in the apparently unproblematic and well understood accounts of the sort of meaning that items of fashion and clothing possess is the idea that meaning is a message. Meaning here is conceived as the 'sending out', or expression, of a 'message', which is itself conceived as some form of inner mental content or statement. Similarly, presupposed in the above accounts of the sort of communication that fashion performs is the idea that communication is the conveying or transmission of that message from one place to another. This paper will try to define and explain the nature of fashion statements; it will investigate the presuppositions of the conceptions of meaning and communication noted above, outline what is problematic about them and attempt to suggest a more accurate and productive way of thinking about them.

In order to do these things, the rest of this essay will be divided into four sections. The first section will outline a brief definition and explanation of fashion. In this section, fashion and clothing will be defined and explained as meaningful and cultural phenomena. The second section will consider the notion of meaning that is presupposed by many accounts of fashion and clothing. In this section, meaning will be established as a profoundly cultural phenomenon. The third section will explain the notion of communication. It will argue that communication is not the sending receiving of messages, but that it is the cultural construction of meaning and, thereby, identity. The fourth section will take two examples of fashion and clothing and show how they may be explained in terms of meaning and communication.

Fashion

I am not proposing a particularly sophisticated, overly technical or calculatedly controversial definition of fashion in this section. However, even to follow Anne Hollander's deceptively simple definition of fashion as what modern 'western' people wear,[1] is already to offer an all-inclusive definition of fashion, which includes everything that people wear, not just that which is 'up to the minute'. It is also to court challenges as to what is to count as 'western' and as 'modern'. So, the definition of fashion offered here includes, but is not exhausted by, all instances of what people wear, from catwalk creations, through High Street and outlet purchases, to police and military uniforms. And it insists on both the modernity and 'westernity' of fashion. Indeed, the existence of fashion in a society may be a good test of whether that society is either modern or western: a society that is classless, with no social structure, and in which upwards mobility is neither possible nor desirable has no need of fashion and might reasonably be said to be neither modern nor western.

While fashion may be about bodies, as Joanne Entwistle says,[2] it is also, as Entwistle also says, about 'fashioned' bodies. And by 'fashioned' bodies I understand produced, cultured bodies, because one of the meanings of fashion (as a verb) is 'to make' or 'to produce'. The fashioned body is therefore a made or produced body. To that extent there can be no such thing as 'the body': the body is always already a constructed and meaningful body; it is a cultured or cultural body, because differently cultured bodies wear different fashions. Another way of putting this is to say that fashion is meaningful (as was said above), and that it is therefore about communication. This is because saying that fashion is meaningful is to say that fashion is a cultural phenomenon. The reason for this, in turn, is that culture is about shared meanings and the communication and understanding of those meanings. Given this, and in the light of what Entwistle says about the fashioned body, we can say that differently cultured bodies communicate different things (meanings) by the different things (clothes, fashion) that they wear.

Fashion has been established as being meaningful and as communicative. It has also been established as a profoundly cultural entity. Therefore, the next problem for this paper is explaining (a) what sort of meaning fashion communicates and (b) what sort of communication fashion is. Now, I also want to argue that fashion is one of the ways in which people are constructed as members (and/or non-members) of cultural groups. The reference to culture was a significant part of the definition or explanation of what fashion is and that definition inevitably refers to culture. So the third problem for this essay is (c) how fashion as meaningful communication constructs people as members, or non-members, of cultural groups.

By way of light-hearted relief, the Roz Chast cartoon [shown in Figure 15.1] gives some idea of the sort of meanings that fashion does not communicate and illustrates one of the ways in which it does not communicate those meanings. Fashion statements are not like spoken statements, or the speech bubbles in cartoons, and they are not about such things as not forgetting to send your Aunt Hilda a thank-you note. Similarly, meanings are not 'messages' in any simple sense, and fashion does not communicate messages in terms of a 'speaker/listener' or 'sender/receiver' model. These ideas will be discussed in more detail in what follows.

Figure 15.1 Drawing by R. Chast. © The New Yorker Collection 1988 Roz Chast from ⟨cartoonbank.com⟩.

Meaning

What this section requires is a definition of meaning that will be of use in the explanation of fashion and communication. It also needs an account of meaning and communication that will perform the tasks demanded in the explanation and analysis of what has become known as visual culture. It must be said that the account of meaning to be proposed here cannot even pretend to be entirely uncontroversial. There are many people who would argue that it is not entirely convincing. However, I am trying to avoid an account of meaning where meaning is a function of either individual intention (what is going on in someone's head) or of the item of clothing itself. In the first case, meaning is something that is expressed and conveyed; in the second, it is something like a natural or inherent property of the item of clothing itself (like colour or texture). Neither can be supported. Basically, I have in mind Roland Barthes' version of connotation, but without the sense that somewhere beneath connotation there is denotation. For Barthes, it will be recalled, denotation is the 'literal' or 'dictionary' definition of a word and connotation is the set of associations that accrue to it. Denotation can be correct or incorrect, precisely because it is thought of as being 'literal' or 'natural' in some way. Because it is 'cultural' and dependent on an individual's socio-historical location, connotation does not admit of being correct or incorrect. This essay will try to make a case for meaning being like connotation because and insofar as Barthes' version of connotation already refers to the work of culture. That is, meaning here is connotation 'all the way down' and not 'built' or 'based' on anything that is not connotation. This conception of meaning will be used because it already and explicitly depends upon culture: Barthes' connotational meaning is explicitly the product of culture. Meaning on this account is a product of cultural beliefs and values, and different beliefs and values generate different meanings.

In his famous account of the 'Panzani' advertisement in 'Rhetoric of the Image'[3] Barthes identifies five connotational meanings, or 'connotative signs', and he scrupulously explains each one in terms of the culturally specific knowledges (structures of ideas) needed to understand, or construct, those meanings. One, for example, is 'Italianicity', and he says that in order to be able to understand or construct that meaning one needs to be familiar with certain tourist stereotypes: members of a culture that has no tourist industry, or no stereotype of Italians, will not be able to understand that meaning. He also points out that Italians will also have a different take on the ad from non-Italians, precisely because they are Italian: membership or non-membership of the cultural group is here explicitly linked with the production of different meanings. On this account, then, meaning is a product of the interaction between the beliefs and values an individual holds as a member of a particular culture and some example of visual culture. In Barthes' case, the example of visual culture is the 'Panzani' ad; in our case it is fashion.

Such an account of meaning is not inconsistent with other (cultural studies-type) accounts of meaning in that meaning does not pre-exist the interaction between an individual member of a culture's beliefs and values and the example of visual culture. Meaning is sometimes said to be a product either of the item in question or of individual intention: a tweedy jacket may be said to signify 'rustic simplicity', for example, or an individual may say they are wearing a shirt because it means something unique to them. But on this account, a piece of fashion or clothing is not meaningful in itself and a piece of fashion or clothing is not meaningful because of any individual intention.

Of course, one may say that one is aware of, or indeed knows, the meaning an item of clothing has. But this formulation is surely a species of shorthand for saying that one knows the meaning an item of clothing has for, or within, a culture; it is therefore already to have interacted with that culture's values and beliefs. So, shared meaning constructs one as a member of a cultural group. If one does not share the meaning, then one is not constructed as a member of that social group. If you do not share or understand the meaning, then you are not produced or reproduced as a member of the culture.

Communication

The model of communication that is adopted in this essay is essentially a semiological/cultural studies type one, according to which communication is a negotiation of meaning through the interaction between items of visual culture and the values (beliefs and ideas) held by an individual as a member of a cultural group. It is also one with which those who believe that communication is expression, or reflection, or the sending and receiving of a message, are likely to disagree.

Fashion communication as expression is the idea that something going on inside someone's head, individual intention, is somehow externalised and made present in a garment or an ensemble. It may also be the idea that entire cultures can express themselves in or through what members wear. Joanne Entwistle, for example, says that clothes 'can be expressive of identity'.[4] She also says that clothing is 'part of the expressive culture of a community'.[5] Both individuals and cultural communities can use fashion to express or make externally visible what were 'internal' and invisible ideas and beliefs.

Fashion communication as reflection is the idea that what people wear is a reflection or mirroring of something else. That something else may be a society's social or economic structure, or it may be a culture's values, for example. On this model of communication, people may claim that Victorian women wear tight corsetry, voluminous bustles and tight-shouldered dresses because they are reflecting their culture's idea of women as weak and helpless. Other people may claim that upper-class Victorian women wear expensive dresses and their lower-class servants wear cheap dresses because they are reflecting their society's economic structure. However, the communication of gender in fashion is not the reflection of something else. It is not, for example, the reflection of a culture's values, for example. The Victorian women are not reflecting their culture's view of them as weak, dependent and immobile: they are weak, dependent and immobile. Similarly, upper-class Victorian women are not reflecting the economic structure: dress is one of the ways in which economic structure is produced and reproduced.

In the sender/receiver model of communication messages are encoded by a sender and sent, or transmitted, through a channel to a decoder or receiver. Following this theory's origins in telecommunications engineering, the paradigm case is that of telephony: the sender (encoder) is the speaking individual, the channel is the telephonic equipment and the receiver is the listener (decoder) on the end of the line. Should the message arrive at the receiver in a form other than that in which it was transmitted, communication theorists will speak of a communication problem or breakdown and appeal to concepts such as 'noise' to explain the unexpected form. Insofar as most analysts seem to agree that fashion is not a language in any straightforward sense, they may be taken to agree that a simple version of the sender/receiver model cannot explain fashion. But it is not difficult to find people who are happy to assert that fashion and clothing are used to convey or 'send messages'. Elizabeth Rouse, for example, uses this notion in her *Understanding Fashion* when she writes of fashion 'conveying' an impression.[6] And Eicher *et al.* (2000) suggest that 'individuals often select items of dress because of the personal or public meaning that it conveys'.[7]

Roz Chast's cartoon [see Figure 15.1], for example, explicitly mocks this conception of fashion communication, claiming to have 'decoded' the 'fashion statements of Rhonda Perlmutter III'. Fred Davis is more cautious and, while committed to the idea that fashion is some sort of communication, is wary of the idea that it is exactly like spoken or written language. Rather, he prefers to think of it in less 'precise' terms, in terms of 'aesthetics' or as being more like art or music.[8]

Such circumspection is to be distinguished from the approach of someone like Alison Lurie in *The Language of Clothes* (1992) where she becomes embroiled in a metaphor of clothing as a language and takes that metaphor literally, if that is possible.

I want to argue that if meaning is a cultural construction, in the manner of connotation, then it is not the sort of thing that can be reflected, expressed, sent, received, conveyed, or transmitted, and that communication cannot involve any of these things. So, I want to argue that communication through fashion is not reflection, nor is it either individual or cultural expression. The points made above also suggest that we need to be a little careful with this notion of expression. This is because the notion of communication as expression involves the idea of simply moving something from 'inside' someone's head, or a cultural community's 'unconscious' (a meaning, intention or value), to 'outside'. Expression, that is, is a metaphor: it is a metaphor of conveying or transmitting something from one place to another. The problem here, of course, is that metaphor is itself a metaphor, and one that is dependent on the notion of 'conveying' for any rhetorical power it possesses. The 'meta' in 'metaphor' means 'beyond' or 'over' and the 'phor' means 'to carry'. Communication as a conveying employs a transport metaphor, but metaphor is itself already a figurative use of the notion of transport; it is itself a transport metaphor. As a result, this essay suggests that there are problems involved in believing that meaning is expression and that communication is a transmitting or conveying of a meaning.

The notion of meaning that is being followed in this essay suggests that meaning is constructed in the interaction between an individual's values and beliefs (which they hold as a member of a culture) and the item of visual culture. If meaning works in this way, as an interaction, then it cannot simply be transported or conveyed in communication. Consequently, as the idea of expression uses a metaphor of transportation, neither cultures nor individuals can be said in any simple way to be 'expressing' themselves through what is worn; it is more accurate to say that identity is being constructed and reproduced.

Finally, it is worth nothing that there is one problem that is equally relevant to all the conceptions of communication discussed so far. It is that, according to the model of communication as conveying, something has to pre-exist the conveying or sending. As a passenger on a bus or train, for example, pre-exists their being conveyed by that train or bus, so meaning on this model pre-exists communication. Colin Campbell rightly and mercilessly takes issue with this model of communication in his essay 'When the Meaning is Not a message: A Critique of the Consumption as Communication Thesis'.[9] He is correct to critique the model of communication, but the notion of communication in or through fashion need not suppose that communication is the sending and receiving of a message. This paper is committed to arguing that communication through fashion is not a simple sending and receiving of messages. This is because meaning does not pre-exist the process of communication, the negotiation between an individual's beliefs and ideas and the example of visual culture. And because meaning does not pre-exist the members of cultures who are communicating, communication cannot be the sending or receiving of a pre-existing message. There is no meaning until the interaction between cultural values and items of fashion has taken place. This is why the argument is made here that fashion is not a vehicle for conveying messages.

Indeed, in order for any of these phenomena (expression, conveying or reflection) to happen it seems reasonable to suppose that there is something that exists prior to the expression, conveying or reflection of that thing. This is the origin of a major, if usually unacknowledged, difference between fashion theorists on these matters. There are those who believe either that something can meaningfully exist prior to representation or that something exists beyond representation, and there are those who believe that there can be no such priority or beyond. For the former, such things as 'the body', or 'individual intention' play the role of that which exists outside of, or prior to, representation. Taking this position, it is perfectly possible to say that something, a meaning, pre-exists the reflection, conveying or expression of that meaning. For the latter, such things as the body and individual intention literally make no sense unless they are represented. According to this latter position, it is impossible for meaning to pre-exist the process of communication. For what it is worth I don't think that there is a 'beyond' to representation. I am with Derrida here: when he says that there is nothing outside the text,[10] I take him to mean that in order for anything to be meaningful it must necessarily be represented. Similarly, I do not think that anything can pre-exist expression, or representation, even in experience or spoken/thought language. This is a question raised, and some would say answered, by Wittgenstein, when he argues in his *Philosophical Investigations*[11] that there are no private languages and nor can there be. Communication, then, is either not-private (that is, it is shareable) or it is not communication.

Rather, on the account presented in this paper, communication is the negotiation of meaning: it is the result or product of the interaction between cultural values (ideas and beliefs) and the visual. Communication is also the process in which an individual is, or is not, constructed as a member of a cultural group. If I may argue by analogy in order to illustrate what I mean here: when I watch *Sex and the City* or the football on TV, the values and beliefs I hold as a result of my social and cultural positions as a white, middle-class European male generate the meanings of the programmes for me. Meaning is a product of the interaction between culture –

cultural values, beliefs and ideas – and the visual. The meanings that I construct are shared with other white, middle-class European males. We are likely to agree in our interpretation of the show, or the inestimable value of football on TV, for example. It is the sharing of the values (and thus the meanings) that makes us into an identifiable cultural group; that is, it is this sharing that makes us into an 'us'.

Members of other cultural groups will construct the meanings differently. Non-European, or Muslim, or old, or working-class women, for example, will almost certainly construct entirely different meanings for *Sex and the City*. And this is because they will hold different beliefs and values. Those shared meanings are what construct and identify people as members of that group. Therefore, the meaning of items of fashion will likewise be produced through the interaction between cultural values and ideas and the visual appearance of the items of fashion.

Case studies

The first case study concerns what President Bush and Prime Minister Blair are wearing in the photograph of the meeting of the Euro-Atlantic Partnership Council in June 2004[12] [see Figure 15.2], and the second concerns 'hoodies' – short, hooded jackets that have recently acquired demonic status in some parts of the British news media.

In the photograph, Bush and Blair are wearing dark suits, light shirts and red ties. Notwithstanding the fact that this picture has been chosen to support an argument, the case against either man being engaged in any form of individualistic self-expression would appear already to be made. What is being claimed here is that

Figure 15.2 Tony Blair and George Bush at the meeting of the Euro-Atlantic Partnership Council, June 2004

neither man is sending a message, or using what they are wearing to convey a message. Both men know perfectly well some of the more dominant meanings that will be constructed by those viewing them and the photograph, and they put together an outfit or a 'look' accordingly. In the terms of the sender/receiver model, this is effectively to suggest that the receiver is determining the message to some extent; it is an odd message that is constructed by the receiver, but that is what the proponents of the sender/receiver model of communication are effectively suggesting. Both Bush and Blair already know that a dark suit, light shirt and contrasting tie mean 'middle class', 'serious', 'authoritative', 'businesslike' and, for that matter, 'masculine' to the people they will be dealing with at the meeting and that is why they have put together such similar outfits.

This is not to say that both men know all the meanings of their suits and ties that might be constructed by all cultural groups; they do not necessarily know all of the possible structures of beliefs and values that suits and ties may be interpreted in terms of. For example, given their particular situations in 2004, it is unlikely that either man would wish to offend Christians or Muslims, but some Islamic purists consider it *haram*, or prohibited, to wear ties made entirely of silk[13] and the frog (as featured on Blair's tie) has been a Christian symbol of uncleanliness. In this example, then, 'alternative' or 'new' interpretations of items of clothing may be explained as being constructed by people who either (a) know how the structure of cultural beliefs and values extends beyond the limits understood by the wearer or (b) are able to construct other parts of that structure.

Someone else who is neither expressing his individuality nor sending a message in the sense assumed by the sender/receiver model is Osama bin Laden in [Figure 15.3]. He knows very well that fellow Wahabite Muslims will know that the white robes and headgear mean purity, and he knows just as well that western audiences will know that the combat jacket and AK47 mean a certain level and form of military/technological threat and also a specific form of masculine identity.[14] His outfit is constructed already knowing the different meanings that will in turn be

Figure 15.3 Osama bin Laden

constructed for it by different cultural groups; this, clearly, is not to convey a message in any simple sense.

The second case study is that of the 'hoodie'. A 'hoodie' is a short, hooded jacket with or without a zipper on the front. Recently in the UK, 'hoodie' has also become the name given to those wearing such a jacket and it refers specifically to young people who are perceived by respectable, law-abiding middle-class observers and journalists as lower-class, drug-taking shoplifters. The meaning communicated by these garments is now so powerful in the UK that hoodie wearers are being denied access to shopping malls because they are perceived as a shoplifting threat. This constitutes a different kind of example in that here the structures of ideas and beliefs within which members of cultures construct meaning are being 'extended': new and different meanings are being made possible by 'continuing' or extending existing patterns of beliefs in order to make new meanings. This may be seen by considering previously existing structures within which hooded garments have been constructed in the past.

Hooded garments have a long history, and there is nothing about hooded garments that is inherently or naturally lower-class, or that inevitably indicates that the wearer is a delinquent and a threat to society. Academics, for example, have long worn hooded garments to communicate their status within a university. Certain religious orders are also in the habit of wearing hooded garments. And the humour in Neil Bennett's cartoon [Figure 15.4] is generated by the realisation that when

"Let's go and hang about on
the footbridge"

Figure 15.4 'Christopher Robin Hoodie' by Neil Bennett. Reproduced by kind permission of PRIVATE EYE magazine/Neil Bennett

Christopher Robin, the golden-haired goody-goody of A. A. Milne's poem "Vespers", pulls his hood right over his head so that nobody knows he's there at all, nobody even thinks of him doing it to conceal his identity whilst engaged in a bit of mindless vandalism. In these cases, 'learned', 'pious' and 'innocent childhood' are among the meanings constructed by and for certain cultural groups.

What is happening in the demonisation of hoodie-wearers is that the (British) print and television media are providing a new application of a set of values and ideas in terms of which certain cultural groups may construct the meaning of a particular garment. Those beliefs and ideas (shoplifting, young people as threat, for example) are already present in the culture, but they have never been associated with this particular garment. Consequently, the structure of beliefs and ideas is being extended to include this new garment and thus to construct new meanings. And when a particular cultural group (middle-class, middle-aged affluent consumers, for example) interprets hoodies as the latest evidence of moral decay, it is the result of the interaction between the values and ideas they hold and the garment they are looking at. Again, meaning here is not simply a message being sent to a receiver.

Conclusion

This essay has attempted to define and explain the nature of fashion statements. In order to do this, it has had to investigate meaning and communication and explain what sort of meaning it might be that fashion has and what sort of communication it can be that fashion accomplishes. Meaning and communication have been explained in terms of culture: neither makes any sense without reference to culture. Culture has been understood as structures of beliefs, ideas and values and as the communication of those beliefs, ideas and values in the construction (or not) of individuals as members (or not) of cultural groups. The construction of meaning by individuals, then, is one of the ways in which those individuals are themselves constructed as individuals. It is also one of the ways in which different, new or alternative meanings are constructed. Fashion statements, then, are one of the ways in which cultural structures and individual agency relate and in which they are both constructed and reproduced.

Notes

1   Hollander, Anne, *Sex and Suits*, New York: Alfred A Knopf, 1994, p. 11.
2   Entwistle, Joanne, *The Fashioned Body*, London: Polity, 2000, p. 1.
3   Barthes, Roland, 'Rhetoric of the Image', in *Image-Music-Text*. Glasgow: Fontana, 1977, p. 34.
4   Entwistle, *The Fashioned Body*, p. 112.
5   Ibid., p. 66.
6   Rouse, Elizabeth, *Understanding Fashion*, Oxford: Blackwell, 1989, p. 24.
7   Joanne B. Eicher, Evenson, Sandra Lee, and Lutz, Hazel A., *The Visible Self*, New York: Fairchild, 2000, p. 297.
8   Davis, Fred, *Fashion, Clothing and Identity*, Chicago: University of Chicago Press, 1992, p. 11.

9   Campbell, Colin, 'When the Meaning, is Not a Message: A Critique of the Consumption as Communication Thesis', in Mica Nava, Andrew Blake, Iain MacRury and Barry Richards (eds) *Buy This Book*, London: Routledge, 1997.

10   Derrida, Jacques, *Of Grammatology*, Baltimore and London: Johns Hopkins University Press, 1974, p. 158.

11   Wittgenstein, Ludwig, *Philosophical Investigations*, Oxford: Blackwell, 1953.

12   Image courtesy of NATO: www.nato.int/pictures/2004/040629f/b040629ag.jpg (accessed July 2005).

13   www.pakistanlink.com/religion/97/re05–23–97.html (accessed July 2005).

14   See Mansell, Philip, *Dressed to Rule*, New Haven: Yale University Press, 2005. See the 'Postscript' to Mansell for more on this.

Bibliography

Barthes, Roland (1977) 'Rhetoric of the Image', in *Image-Music-Text*, Glasgow: Fontana/Collins.

Butler, Judith (1990) *Gender Trouble: Feminism and the Subversion of Identity*, London: Routledge.

Campbell, Colin (1997) 'When the Meaning is Not a Message: A Critique of the Consumption as Communication Thesis', in Mica Nava, Andrew Blake, Iain MacRury an Barry Richards (eds) *Buy This Book*, London: Routledge.

Davis, Fred: (1992) *Fashion, Clothing and Identity*, Chicago: University of Chicago Press.

Derrida, Jaques (1974) *Of Grammatology*, Baltimore and London: Johns Hopkins University Press.

Eicher, Joanne B., Evenson, Sandra Lee and Lutz, Hazel A. (2000) *The Visible Self*, New York: Fairchild.

Entwistle, Joanne (2000) *The Fashioned Body*, London: Polity.

Hollander, Anne (1994) *Sex and Suits*, New York: Kodansha International.

Lurie, Alison (1992) *The Language of Clothes*, London: Bloomsbury.

Mansell, Philip (2005) *Dressed to Rule*, New Haven: Yale University Press.

Nava, Mica, Blake, Andrew, MacRury, Iain and Richards, Barry (eds) *Buy This Book*, London: Routledge.

O'Sullivan, Tim, *et al.* (1994) *Key Concepts in Communication and Cultural Studies*, 2nd edn, London: Routledge.

Rouse, Elizabeth (1989), *Understanding Fashion*, Oxford: Blackwell.

Wittgenstein, Ludwig (1953) *Philosophical Investigations*, Oxford: Blackwell.

PART SIX

Fashion

Identity and difference

PREVIOUS SECTIONS HAVE INVESTIGATED what fashion is and what fashion does. This section introduces four topics or concerns that will reappear in various guises in all of the following sections: sex/gender; social class; ethnicity/race and culture/subculture. It also introduces the notions of identity and difference, and some of the ways in which fashion and clothing mediate identity and difference will also reappear in all of the following sections. To some extent then, this section – and indeed the entire volume – is a product of the developments that were described in Part Two. It was noted here that the emergence of a radicalised feminist scholarship and of cultural studies in the 1960s, along with an increasing interest in the political economy of consumption, led to an interest in fashion *per se* and to a certain kind of fashion theorising in which fashion was studied in terms of identity/difference, autonomy and resistance. Everyday, ordinary activities such as fashion and clothing became the routine object of some fairly serious analytical and critical study. And certain forms of academic study, which were interested in social and gender identity and in power, for example, were brought to bear on fashion and clothing. To some theorists, the consumption of fashion and clothing was one of the ways in which stereotyped social and cultural identities, for example, could be investigated and challenged. Among those identities were race, ethnicity, class and gender: each became an arena in which difference and identity were negotiated through the consumption of fashion and clothing.

It is clear that fashion and clothing have parts to play in negotiating the relations between identity and difference, and various fashion theorists have argued that identity and difference are important concepts in the definition and explanation of what fashion and clothing are. In his 1904 essay 'Fashion', for example, Georg Simmel introduced the principles of 'union' and 'isolation' to the explanation of fashion. Fashion is a process in which the individual constantly compromises between 'socialistic adaptation to society and . . . departure from its demands' ([1904] 1971: 294). 'Individual differentiation' is desired and achieved through fashion in order to avoid being and acting like everyone else (ibid.: 295). What people wear is a way of managing to remain an individual, possessing a recognisable image or identity, while not becoming so different that one is isolated from society. And Elizabeth Wilson points out that, while we may want to look like our friends, we do not want to be clones of them (1992: 34). What we wear is a way of negotiating identity and difference in that the same outfit is used to construct an image (an identity) that is similar to that of our friends but also, crucially, different from them as well. This is what is meant by the 'negotiation' and 'mediation' of identity and difference by fashion and clothing, and the phenomenon will be seen in all of the examples given.

The ways in which fashion and clothing negotiate or mediate identity and differ-ence introduce a set of difficulties that have been referred to as the 'structure and agency' debate. From one direction, the problem is to explain human agency in a way that does not ignore the role played in human activity by cultural and social struc-tures: from the other direction, the problem is to explain cultural and social structures in a way that does not reduce human agency to the simple reproduction of those structures. In terms of fashion and clothing the problem is to explain the construction and communication of individual identity through fashion and clothing (agency) in a way that does not reduce that agency or identity to the predictable effect of existing structures or ignore the role of those structures entirely. In the first case, fashion is seen as the simple and predictable effect or reflection of social, cultural or economic structures; in the second case, fashion is seen as entirely outside or beyond those social, cultural or economic structures.

Agency is a product of structure in that individual actions are made possible by the existence of structures. Structure is a product of agency in that it is only through the actions of individuals that structures are constructed and reproduced. Fashion's relation to the problem and the roles of identity and difference here may be explained by saying:

(a)   that the construction of an individual identity in fashion or clothing is possible only by using the available different garments, and the different garments available at any one time form a structure, and

(b)   that structures of difference are generated only by the actions of individuals who are constructing identities for themselves.

Such are the paradoxes of identity and difference as they work their ways through the problems involved in structure and agency.

However, less clearly, there is a sense in which all of the extracted readings in this volume could be included in this section. This is the sense in which difference is essential to the construction and communication of any identity, meaning or experi-ence whatsoever, whether through fashion and clothing or not. This sense must be elaborated on briefly.

One of the central ideas of these forms of theorising is that identity is a product of difference. What this means is that identity is not to be thought of as a simple, self-sufficient and stable existence that enters into relations with other identities; it is, rather, the product of a series of relations to other non-fixed and non-stable 'identities'. In the Introduction, it was noted that there was no simple, stand-alone definition of fashion that did not refer to all kinds of other different activities and objects, such as adornment and style for example. There was no essence of fashion that could be appealed to as its identity: rather, what identity it possessed resulted from its relations to and differences from all the other terms.

Differing conceptions of the relation between identity and difference may also be used to explain the difference between those theorists who disapprove of fashion as trivial, deceitful or immoral and those theorists who celebrate fashion's apparently endless changes and novelties. Those who disapprove of fashion in these ways do so because they conceive fashion to be mere representation, one thing arbitrarily or capriciously standing for another thing, and because they think that an outside or beyond to representation is possible. Thus today gingham stands for spring and white jeans stand for middle-class youthfulness. Next year, or tomorrow, seersucker will stand for spring and chinos will represent the bourgeois young at heart. Identity here is a product of difference, and those who disapprove of fashion are those who conceive or desire an end to this play of differences. Their idea is that the relentless substitution of seersucker for gingham and of white jeans for khakis is both undesirable and may potentially be brought to an end by 'proper' or 'genuine' clothing, which really would be beautiful or appropriately respectable. The disapproval of fashion, then, is effectively to conceive or desire an end or beyond to representation itself, as it is to desire an end or beyond to the play of differences in which fashion and fashionable items are meaningful and fashionable. It is to desire a signifier that is outside or beyond the play of differences and that is not, therefore, defined or produced by its relations to all the things it is different from.

However, there are also those who do not think that there can be an end to, or an outside of, representation. Those who celebrate fashion, the eternal return of styles and differences, may be taken to understand that there is and can be no end, outside or beyond to the play of differences that generate meaning.

'Sex and' gender

Sex and gender are among the clearest, if also the most complicated and hotly debated examples of the ways in which identity and difference are mediated through fashion and clothing. The first thing to do here is to distinguish sex from gender. In theory, sex is to do with nature, physiological differences and biological reproduction: gender is to do with culture, behavioural differences and cultural reproduction. One is assigned a sexual identity on the basis of one's genitalia: physiological differences generate sexual identity and enable biological reproduction. Gender is the meaning that a culture assigns to sexual differences; masculinity and femininity are sets of meanings that a culture gives to behaviour and characteristics considered by that culture to be appropriate to men and women. Gender identities are the meaningful, culturally varying, behaviour and characteristics of men and women and they are the products of differences between those behaviours and characteristics. Gender identities and differences are culturally produced and reproduced.

Joanne Entwistle's essay studies the ways in which working women construct themselves as 'career women' by means of fashion and clothing. She uses ideas from the French philosopher Michel Foucault and the popular psychologist John T. Molloy to explain how a specific and recognisable gender identity for women in the 1980s was produced. There is no natural feminine 'essence', which is reflected or expressed in what is worn, in Entwistle's account: femininity is something that can be, and is to be, constructed.

Lee Wright's essay argues that women used the stiletto heel to construct an alternative gender identity for themselves in the 1960s. Where one of the existing patterns or stereotypes for women had been 'housewife', young women latched onto the stiletto and used it to construct a new and different gender identity, one that was energetic and independent. The item itself ends up as what Derrida would call undecidable, with various (gender-inflected) meanings being created for it as it appears in various discourses. The heel has no single easily identifiable meaning as it has a different meaning in each of the 'discourses' in which it appears. There is no 'end', then, to the generation of different meanings and the item is, strictly, undecidable.

Tim Edwards looks at masculinity and fashion in tshe extract from his book *Men in the Mirror*. Significantly, he sees the role of gender in the explanation of men and their relation to fashion as an episode in the 'politics of difference'. Gender identity is explicitly presented here as a product of difference. Edwards also introduces and explores the relation between fashion, masculinity and homosexuality in this extract.

Social class

This section in concerned with social identity and social difference, or class. Society may be thought of as a group of individuals forming a social system, with its own distinctive forms of relations, institutions and culture.

There are two main ways of conceiving these individuals, relations, institutions and cultures: Marxism and Functionalism. For Marxism, individuals are first of all members of social classes, and individual consciousness (what they think they know, and their values, for example) is determined by their membership of a social class. As members of social classes, they exist in hierarchical and political relations with members of other social classes. These relations are conceived as antagonistic in Marxist theory as they are the result of different relations to the means of production. Social identity (social class) is the result of economic difference: an individual's either owning or working with the factory, plant, machinery, and so on of industrial production generates that individual's class identity as either bourgeois or proletarian. Institutions function to produce and reproduce a social group's dominant position on this kind of account.

For Functionalism, the stress is on the sharing of values among members of groups, rather than on the antagonism between groups. People join together in social institutions in order to work together because they share the same values. In schools and universities, for example, the value of educating the young is shared by those working in the institutions that make up the education system. The analogy used is that of the human body: where the organs of the body function together for the continued survival of the body, social institutions function together for the continued existence and benefit of society. On a functionalist account, the sharing of values and the resulting order or balance is stressed, as opposed to the stress on different interests and class antagonisms that is a feature of Marxist accounts.

The relation between fashion or clothing and society may also be conceived in different ways. As noted in Part-Five, there are those who believe that fashion or clothing reflects, expresses or points to society and to the relations between (members of) social classes. James Laver, for example, says that 'clothes are never a frivolity; they are always an expression of the fundamental social and economic pressures of the time' (1968: 10). And there are those who argue that fashion is one of the ways in which society is (or social relations between members of social classes are) made possible and either reproduced or challenged. The extracts collected here fall into the second category insofar as they are interested in the ways in which fashion constructs and communicates social identity/difference.

Angela Partington's essay is about class, consumption and cultural critique. Partington argues against the idea that post-war working-class women were the passive consumers of fashion, and she disputes the idea that fashion 'reflects' socio-economic identities and differences. Rather, her essay examines the ways in which working-class women of her mother's generation used a mixture of 'officially sanctioned' good taste in fashion, their own tastes and proclivities and High Street patterns to construct an original and class-specific version of the New Look. Class is explicitly a matter of opposition here: the working-class women featured in the essay are challenging dominant views of themselves and proposing that a new visual identity be constructed out of an appropriation of available design and fashion material. These women used fashion and other goods actively to construct and communicate new class identities in new ways. Partington does not hold with the idea that fashion and clothing 'express' class experience or identity: she is describing the process in which fashion and clothing are used to construct and communicate an alternative class identity, one that challenges existing stereotypes and identities.

The extract from Herbert Blumer's 1969 essay also concerns class, but he is arguing that class is not the best way of explaining what fashion is or how it works. Rather, he suggests that Simmel's analysis in which styles are fashionable because a social elite associates itself with them be replaced by an account in which the fashionableness of the design allows or enables the social prestige of a social group to be attached to it. Simmel, on Blumer's account, gets things almost perfectly the wrong way round. Rather than class, then, Blumer proposes the notion of the 'collective' as part of his explanatory theory. There is less obvious class opposition in this account: the 'collective' that Blumer proposes seems, in fact, to be agreed on their interpretation of what is fashionable and to that extent follows a more functionalist account of society.

Ethnicity and race

Race and ethnicity present suspiciously low profiles in fashion and clothing studies. Like sex and gender they appear to be clear examples of the ways in which either naturally or culturally occurring identities are expressed or constructed and signalled in fashion and clothing. They should therefore be much-debated examples of the ways in which identity and difference are constructed, communicated and contested in and through fashion and clothing. However, Joanne Eicher points out that while 'ethnic dress has been noted as an aspect of ethnicity . . . it has been neglected analytically' (Eicher 1995: 1). John A. Walker makes a more general point to the effect that design history as a discipline does not deal as thoroughly as it might with notions of ethnicity or race (Walker 1989: 19). Neither, of course, is making the point that western fashion and clothing worn by whites is 'ethnic' fashion and clothing: it may be argued that to be white and western is to be a member of a race and an ethnic group. There is here an asymmetry in which the racial and ethnic aspects of whiteness and westernity are occluded and only the non-white and the non-western are thought of as requiring explanation in racial and ethnic terms.

Eicher points to the work of Manning Nash as providing a theory of how dress relates to ethnicity. Nash says that ethnicity represents a 'core', 'deep' or 'basic structure', which is visibly marked by 'secondary, surface pointers' such as dress and other 'items of apparel' (in Eicher 1995: 5). Ethnicity is a product of 'blood, substance and cult' and it is represented and implied by what people wear (ibid.). Clearly 'items of apparel' does not rule out fashion. Equally clearly, the notions of 'blood', 'substance' and 'cult' are quite useless in defining and explaining what ethnicity might be. It is not at all obvious what substance should be given to the notion of 'substance' here, and 'blood' and 'cult' are just as nebulous and meaningless. The problem here is that both ethnicity and race are 'socially produced concepts' that cannot be reduced to biological content (see Popeau 1998: 173). There are no 'natural' characteristics that can be identified and used to describe a racial or ethnic identity and consequently there can be no 'naturally occurring' racial or ethnic identities, as implied by the sentence above. Race and ethnicity, then, are attempts to distil an essence or identity from a range of shifting and unstable differences. This position is supported by Stuart Hall, who argues that specifically black subjectivity and experience are not the result of natural differences but are socially, culturally and historically constructed (quoted in Popeau 1998: 174). However, this is not to say that they are politically inert or that they can safely be ignored. It is precisely due to the fact that they are not politically inert that people believe them and act on the basis of them, which demands that we do not ignore them. As the United Nations website has it, racial and ethnic identities are not found in nature; they are 'artificial' or cultural productions (http://cyberschool bus.un.org/discrim/dh_print.asp June 2006). However, as cultural constructions, these ideas raise social and political issues, and it is as raising social and political issues that race and ethnicity should be understood here in relation to the Wilbekin extract.

Emil Wilbekin's essay considers the ways in which various hip-hop cultures have related to fashion. Many are hostile to the big fashion houses, either believing that those houses care nothing for black culture or rejecting the values they are perceived to hold. Others are more sympathetic to the notion of fashion, creating their own fashions and their own fashion houses. In both cases, identity is a product of differentiation. Wilbekin also notes the ways in which black hip-hop stars use the products of white fashion to identify with their less fortunate brothers and thereby subvert the meanings of those products. That Wilbekin's account is not describing the ways in which fashion expresses anything that might be called a 'black identity' is clear: the ironic use of chains and padlocks (signifiers of a dominant and offensive white culture's criminalisation of blacks and a reference to slavery) that is described in Wilbekin's essay is hardly to express a black essence. Rather, it is to challenge and oppose that dominant culture by means of appropriating and changing the meanings of signs that once appeared in a dominant political economy and now appear in an alternative economy.

Culture and subculture

Culture can mean the way of life of a given group; it can mean the beliefs, values and desires of a group; and it can mean the artefacts and practices produced and consumed by a group, along with the institutions necessary for the production of those artefacts and practices. Culture also refers us to notions of cultural identity and difference; our cultural identity is descriptive of who we think we are, which group(s) we are members of, and which groups we are not members of.

Fashion relates to cultures and subcultures in various ways, therefore. Fashion and clothing are among the artefacts produced and consumed by cultural groups; they represent one of the ways in which cultural identity is constructed and communicated; and they communicate and reproduce the beliefs and values of cultural groups. Fashion and clothing are also at least one of the ways in which cultural identity may be challenged or resisted.

There are various ways of distinguishing and signalling aspects of cultural behaviour that are common or dominant from those that are alternative or subordinate. 'Sub-', 'counter-' and 'contra-' are the prefixes that may precede the word 'culture' in order to indicate a difference between a culture and some distinct alternative aspect(s) of it.

The extract from Dick Hebdige's 1979 book *Subculture: The Meaning of Style* considers style as 'homology'. Homology is the 'fit' between the style (the fashions, music and characteristic dances and drugs, for example) of a subculture and the values it holds. Big boots and cropped hair, for example, are homologous with the values held by members of the skinhead subcultures of the 1970s: there is an appropriateness or fit between what is worn and what is thought and believed. The extract also introduces the idea of 'bricolage', where items and aspects of other, possibly alien, cultures are taken up and appropriated by subcultures. Thus, for example, neat suits and haircuts are purloined from the respectable world of middle-class employment in order to communicate something of the world-view of the 1960s Mod. Again, this is not to argue that punk or skinhead fashions express some essential punk or skinhead identity; it is to argue that fashion and clothing are some of the ways in which punk or skinhead values and beliefs are communicated, thus constructing one as a member (or not) of the cultural sub-group. The explanation of graphic design's role in the construction and communication of membership of subcultural groups in Hebdige's work can be compared with Blanchard's account of the same phenomenon in the extract from her work in the section on fashion and image (see Chapter 44).

Bibliography

Baizerman, S., Eicher, J. B. and Cerny, C. (1993) 'Eurocentrism in the Study of Ethnic Dress', *Dress* 20: 19–32.

Edwards, T. (1997) *Men in the Mirror*, London: Cassell.

Eicher, J. (ed.) (1995) *Dress and Ethnicity*, Oxford: Berg.

Eicher, Joanne B. and Sumberg, Barbara (1995) 'World Fashion, Ethnic and National Dress', in J. Eicher (ed.) *Dress and Ethnicity*, Oxford: Berg.

Hebdige, D. (1979) *Subculture: The Meaning of Style*, London: Routledge.

Laver, J. (1968) *Dandies*, London: Weidenfeld and Nicolson.

Popeau, J. (1998) 'Race/Ethnicity' in C. Jenks (ed.) *Core Sociological Dichotomies*, London: Sage.

Simmel, G. ([1904] 1971) 'Fashion', in *On Individuality and Social Forms*, Chicago: University of Chicago Press.

Walker, J. A. (1989) *Design History and the History of Design*, London: Pluto Press.

Wilbekin, E. (1999) 'Great Aspirations: Hip Hop and Fashion Dress for Excess and Success', in A. Light (ed.) *The Vibe History of Hip Hop*, London: Plexus Publishing.

Wilson, E. (1992) 'Fashion and the Meaning of Life', *Guardian*, 18 May, p. 34.

Chapter 16

Tim Edwards

EXPRESS YOURSELF
The politics of dressing up

[. . .]

FOR A LONG TIME, fashion has been seen as an apolitical phenomenon, outside of politics, and of little concern to politicians. It is still the case today that politicians rarely involve themselves in decision-making processes that impact on fashion – although the rise in VAT on adult clothing in the UK and the question of its introduction on clothing for children is one exception. (In addition, sales taxes in the US and similar policies in parts of Europe, plus the impact of interest and exchange rates, all have some effect.) Fashion is, however, now a very political phenomenon. This is due, for the most part, to the various social movements of the 1960s and 1970s that sought to politicize appearance as part of an overall politics of identity.

The perception of fashion as an apolitical phenomenon has always been a partial *mis*perception, as fashion and appearance have always played a key part in the politics of difference. The politics of difference here refers to those politics which affect, reinforce or even invent difference within groups and societies whether according to class, age, gender, race, sexual orientation or, more simply, the politics of bodily regulation. For example, sumptuary laws were used periodically – and particularly in the wake of the Reformation and later periods of Puritanism – to regulate perceived extravagance, which usually meant expenditure on personal appearance and fashion. This still persists today in the rather mixed series of attitudes towards fashion, and particularly haute couture, often seen as wasteful, unproductive and superficial. Often what is implied in such attempts to moralize against extravagance is a sense of social, as well as economic, control in maintaining class distinctions, an attempt to stop people 'putting on airs and graces' or 'getting ideas above their station in life'. Sumptuary laws were rarely applied at the top of the social ladder and were aimed primarily at the middle classes as a defensive gesture from the aristocracy (Barnard, 1996).

What is perhaps less apparent in the application of such legislation is the issue of gender. The stereotype of the extravagant and wasteful person spending plenty of time and money on their appearance and fashion was usually a woman. As with most stereotypes, this was not merely the production of myth as middle- and upper-class women *were* the primary consumers of their own or their menfolk's income. . . . If women of leisure were often mocked and portrayed as superficial and passive, then men who adopted similar modes of living were condemned with the vitriol of hell-fire and damnation. The primary example of this process at work were the dandies of the early nineteenth century who were seen as excessive, effeminate pansies in need of three years' hard labour (Laver, 1968). This often masked a reality of aristocratic wealth which meant these men did not need to work and, on occasions, a serious attempt to redress the dullness in some areas of men's dress. This sense of unease concerning dressed-up men continues into the present as very well-dressed men, unless pop or film stars, are often seen as narcissistic, silly, homosexual or all three; whilst their female counterparts are perceived as stylish, having good dress sense, and fit for the front cover. However, the situation concerning the interpretation of fashion increased in complexity in the 1960s when the politics of identity entered the scene and crashed the party.

The 1960s represent a rather mythic period in time that is open to misinterpretation. It is particularly apparent that the whole of the UK, France or the USA were not the same as swinging London, Paris or New York, although the seismic effects were felt throughout the countries in question. The difficulty lies in assessing the degree of continuity and change that took place at the time and, within that, the particular groups most affected. The 1960s in many ways represented a continuation rather than a disjunction from the 1950s, as the motors of postwar consumerism continued to accelerate and spread wider throughout society. Thus, in an economic sense, the rise of 1960s hippie and minority fashions followed on from, rather than broke with, the apparent stoicism of the 1950s. This popular perception of stoicism was centred on a notion of fashion as reinforcing a sense of a time when 'men were men and women were women', in other words when men *looked like* men in their sharp, shoulder-widening suits and slick hair-styles, and when women equally *looked like* women with their hour-glass figures, full skirts and high heels. However, the difficulty with this view is that although the gender differences in men's and women's appearances were rather rigidly reinforced through dress, it rather underestimates the sheer sexiness of the decade, later reconstructed in the 1980s. This was, after all, also the era of rock 'n' roll and the rise of Elvis-the-Pelvis Presley whose quiffed, suited and then sweat-leathered looks led not only to media hysteria as a thousand wet dreams came true, but also to the whole redefinition of men and masculinity as *the* sexy and looked-at gender. This notion was derived in many ways from the USA, which had also stormed the media and the UK with 'over-paid' and 'over-sexed' GIs in figure-hugging uniforms as well as floods of Hollywood idols. In addition, it was not a lot later that the Mods reinvented the sharp-suited looks of the 1950s and clashed with the Rockers' reconstruction of the frock coat.

However, politically, the 1960s did see a radical discontinuity with previous developments. This primarily came from a whole series of minority, and not so minority, movements: feminism, youth and student protests, peace campaigners, gay groups, civil rights, rising tensions around racism and, in particular, hippie culture which was also welded to the rise of youth culture and 'sex, drugs and rock 'n' roll'. Hippie culture was far and away the most influential of all the movements, as it was the most loosely focused and encompassed most groups and issues: free love, self-expression and spirituality were woolly concepts that could incorporate pacifism, youthism, homosexuality and even some forms of androgynous feminism all at the same time.

The impact of hippie culture on fashion was, as a consequence, immense. Jeans, cheesecloth, velvets, beads, bangles and lengthening hair ultimately, if briefly, became the uniform of almost the entire population under forty. The two or three groups left out, over-forties, stoic conservatives and corporatists, interestingly, were also the praying mantises waiting to take over in the 1980s. The significance of hippie culture upon fashion was, ultimately, threefold. Firstly, it fuelled a near revolution in casual clothing and undermined formal dress as for the middle-class, middle-aged and conservative only; secondly, it created an intense interest in dress and appearance that went hand-in-glove with a rapid increase in mass-produced cheap products and a second-hand market; and thirdly, it led indirectly to the creation of a very strong sense of politically correct dress centred particularly on an anti-middle-class and anti-formal rhetoric. This last factor is tied up with the simultaneous development of identity politics.

Identity politics at their most simple state that identity is not neutral, it is socially shaped and, most importantly, political (Edwards, 1994; Rutherford, 1990; Weeks, 1985). Identity itself is particularly tricky to define other than as a social sense of one's own individuality and location in the wider society, or as the process of self-definition and self-presentation in everyday life. There is an intense sense of conflict here as identity is often seen on the one hand as something of a fixed entity, something one is; whilst it is often equally experienced as contradictory and awkward like an ill-fitting shoe that pinches and slips, or something one may be, could be or would like to become. Identities also tend to multiply and change according to time and place; I am not the same here as there, or the same now as I was.

At the heart of all of this is the tension of the individual and the social, a sense of oneself as the same and yet different to others, as fitting in and as standing out, and as shaped and yet creative. It is, moreover, not surprising that the swirling world of fashion should have so strong a connection with the equally dynamic world of identity, and as the patterns and shapes of the clothes on models turn and mutate in front of us we are also confronted with the three-dimensional kaleidoscope of ourselves: here, now and me. For some, this is taken further to lead to connections to postmodernity and fashion as the epitome of a consumer-oriented, image-driven society where meanings are increasingly less fixed and more chaotic (Baudrillard, 1983; Evans and Thornton, 1989; Kroker and Kroker, 1988).

This current view of identity politics and its relationship to fashion is in many ways new and the result of a collapse in whatever sense of political unity existed previously. To unpack this further necessitates a detailed consideration of some of the unities and tensions concerning dress, appearance and fashion that existed within some of the political groups and movements of the 1960s and 1970s.

[. . .]

Drag, camp and macho: gay men and fashion

If feminism provided a powerful critique of femininity and fashion for women, then it was up to gay men as 'outsider men' to provide a similar set of insights into masculinity and fashion for men. These insights were distinctly mixed and heavily derived from the historical position of male homosexuality. Male homosexuality was, and to some still is, seen as almost synonymous with effeminacy: limp-wristed, lisping and dressy queens of high, and low, culture. This conception of homosexuality as masculinity 'in crisis' has a very long, if very varied, history starting with Greco-Roman and Muslim notions of passivity, developing through the molly-houses of the seventeenth and eighteenth centuries, and culminating in the very definition of homosexuality itself in the late nineteenth century as an 'inversion' or a 'feminine soul in a male body' (Bray, 1982; Edwards, 1994; Eglinton, 1971; Tapinç, 1992; Weeks, 1977).

The problematic relationship of homosexuality to masculinity and the part myth/part reality of effeminacy, although mixed up and undermined in various ways throughout the centuries, has never quite been severed. As a result, it was not entirely surprising that those asserting the positivity of gay culture from the late 1960s onwards should also assault the association of homosexuality with effeminacy. The difficulty lay, and still lies, in which way to shove it: a camp masquerade of self-parody typified in drag where effeminacy is pushed all the way into attempted femininity, or an attempt to prove once and for all that gay men are real men too, if not more so.

This latter position, on occasions, led to a sending-up of masculinity itself as the 'hyper' masculinity of clone culture, where leather biker jackets were slung across naked and muscled torsos or skin-tight white T-shirts, whilst button-fly Levis clung to well-defined and accentuated cocks and asses that practically screamed sexual availability. This ended up as something bordering on self-parody (Bersani, 1988; Blachford, 1981; Gough, 1989). The problem undermining this, though, was the very welding of masculinity to sexuality, on occasions literally, as the gay clone was not only the epitome of the appearance of masculinity, he was the epitome of masculine sexuality in concept and practice (Edwards, 1990, 1994). Quentin Crisp's dreams and desires for a 'dark man' were hardly dead, rather they were extolled and expanded upon as the muscular clone in cock-hugging jeans was precisely what many gay men desired and dreamed of and, what is more, this figure now cruised the streets inviting partners to revel in lookalike sex (Crisp, 1968; Lee, 1978; Rechy, 1977).

The difficulty in interpreting the degree of seriousness or silliness involved in all of this led to a series of unresolved discussions throughout the 1970s and the 1980s. For some, this intense masculinization of gay culture represented a triumph of sexual expression and political opposition to heterosexual ideology, whilst for others it meant attempted conformity to oppressive stereotypes of sexual attractiveness and practice. The difficulty lay partly in the interpretation of appearances as, for some, the macho gay clone was precisely a clone, an android, and not a 'real man' at all, only a man who *looked like* a man, hence the constant jokes concerning muscular men in leather jackets discussing cookery and Jane Austen (Bristow, 1989)!

The drag queens and effeminists, meanwhile, had lost out almost altogether. The advent of AIDS had also done little to challenge gay male imagery, if not worsen it in terms of a dreariness of clones without hair, sun-tans, moustaches, muscles and accentuated cocks: in short, clones without sex. However, drag queens regained significant attention in the late 1980s when the Vogue Movement was highlighted in the media. The Vogue Movement referred to an underground network of posing and impressionist dancers taking place in New York and some other major cities where young, gay and often black men would don the costumes and appearances of many cult icons, including Hollywood idols and some, more contemporary, hegemonic images of femininity and masculinity. These were then paraded in front of audiences on the street or in bars and nightclubs, as if in a fashion show, and often set to music as part of a particular contest or competition. The men were otherwise deeply oppressed as outsiders racially, sexually or simply in terms of their effeminacy and poverty, and the practice of voguing partly parodied and partly affirmed the aspirational dreams of the famous magazine and, in particular, their desire for the front cover.

Moreover, the matter of voguing gained media-wide attention and controversy when Madonna, herself an icon of pastiche and parody, released 'Vogue', a highly successful single and an even better video featuring black men dressed in 1940s suits voguing to the record whilst Madonna herself imitated a collection of cultural icons from Bette Davis to Marilyn Monroe via a series of stylized 'front cover' poses. This then spread, diluted, into discoland where dancers desperately tried to pull off the same effect with a series of hand-on-head dance routines. Controversy concerned whether the wealthy Madonna had exploited an oppressed minority movement or given it the media attention it deserved, as much of the original message was lost in a sea of hand gestures (Kellner, 1995; Patton, 1993; Schwichtenberg, 1993).

The potential of the Vogue Movement remains partially untapped, as an adherence to the parody and display of cultural icons has not generally led to an equal parody of the traditional styles of masculinity. This was particularly apparent in the 1980s when the proliferation of images of maleness – from naked torsos and Levi's 501s to 1950s iconography and pinstripe suits – was wide open to parody and take-off. However, there is some evidence for the idea that the impact of this movement has supplemented the slightly increasing diversity of styles displayed in the gay male community, which now include more sporting, work-related and design-led fashions in addition to the perpetual proliferation of fetish, leather and clone looks. As a consequence, the 1980s effected some continuity and change in the gay community's relations with fashion as the intense masculinization of gay culture finally gave way to some variations in style. Interestingly, drag has taken off again in the 1990s through the cult hit movies *The Adventures of Priscilla, Queen of the Desert* and *To Wong Fu, Thanks for Everything, Julie Newmar* and the current style situation represents a jostling sense of change and stasis.

[. . .]

Bibliography

Barnard, M. (1996) *Fashion as Communication*, London: Routledge.

Baudrillard, J. (1983) *Simulations*, New York: Semiotext(e).

Bray, A. (1982) *Homosexuality in Medieval and Renaissance England*, London: Gay Men's Press.

Bersani, L. (1988) 'Is The Rectum a Grave?', in D. Crimp (ed.) *AIDS: Cultural Analysis, Cultural Activism*, London: MIT Press.

Blachford, G. (1981) 'Male Dominance and the Gay World', in K. Plummer (ed.) *The Making of the Modern Homosexual*, London: Hutchinson.

Bristow, J. (1989) 'Homophobia/Misogyny: Sexual Fears, Sexual Definitions', in S. Shepherd and M. Wallis (eds) *Coming On Strong: Gay Politics and Culture*, London: Unwin Hyman.

Crisp, Q. (1968) *The Naked Civil Servant*, Glasgow: Collins.

Edwards, T. (1990) 'Beyond Sex and Gender: Masculinity Homosexuality and Social Theory', in J. Hearn and D. Morgan (eds) *Men, Masculinities and Social Theory*, London: Unwin Hyman.

—— (1994) *Erotics and Politics: Gay Male Sexuality, Masculinity and Feminism*, London: Routledge.

Eglinton, J. Z. (1971) *Greek Love*, London: Neville Spearman.

Evans, C. and Thornton, M. (1989) *Women and Fashion: A New Look*, London: Quartet.

Gough, J. (1989) 'Theories of Sexuality and the Masculinisation of the Gay Man', in S. Shepherd and M. Wallis (eds) *Coming on Strong: Gay Politics and Culture*, London: Unwin Hyman.

Kellner, D. (1995) *Media Culture: Cultural Studies, Identity and Politics between the Modern and the Postmodern*, London: Routledge.

Kroker, A. and Kroker, M. (1988) *Body Invaders: Sexuality and the Postmodern Condition*, London: Macmillan.

Laver, J. (1968) *Dandies*, London: Weidenfeld and Nicolson.

Lee, J. A. (1978) *Getting Sex: A New Approach – More Fun, Less Guilt*, Ontario: Mission Book Company.

Patton, C. (1993) 'Embodying Subaltern Memory: Kinesthesia and Problematics of Gender and Race', in K. Schwichtenberg (ed.) *The Madonna Connection: Representational Politics, Subcultural Identities and Cultural Theory*, Oxford: Westview.

Rechy, J. (1977) *The Sexual Outlaw: A Documentary*, London: W.H. Allen.

Rutherford, J. (ed.) (1990) *Identity: Community, Culture, Difference*, London: Lawrence and Wishart.

Schwichtenberg, K. (ed.) (1993) *The Madonna Connection: Representational Politics, Subcultural Identities and Cultural Theory*, Oxford: Westview.

Tapinç, H. (1992) 'Masculinity, Femininity and Turkish Male Homosexuality', in K. Plummer (ed.) *Modern Homosexualities: Fragments of Lesbian and Gay Experience*, London: Routledge.

Weeks, J. (1977) *Coming Out: Homosexual Politics in Britain from the Nineteenth Century to the Present*, London: Quartet.

—— (1985) *Sexuality and its Discontents: Meanings, Myths and Modern Sexualities*, London: Routledge.

Chapter 17

Lee Wright

OBJECTIFYING GENDER
The stiletto heel

THIS ESSAY WILL FOCUS on the notion of gender in relation to design. One reason for selecting the stiletto heel as a case study is that as an object it is seen as being exclusively female.[1] Even when worn by men it is with a view to constructing a female image. Gender specificity in object design exists on many levels. This essay attempts to equate the *process of making* with the *construction of meaning*. I will be discussing the stiletto heel in terms of its manufacture and production process alongside ideas concerning representation from its inception in the early 1950s to its demise as a mass fashion item a decade later.

The stiletto heel of the 1950s marks the culmination of an historical continuum: the high heel as representative of the female in footwear. At the same time it heralds a new era of shoe production and design. By focusing on this particular moment in the history of the high heel, this article identifies many of the issues concerning industrial manufacture in the 1950s, which, together with the particular social context of the period, explain the emergence of the stiletto as a new fashion item.

The stiletto is a particularly contentious case study in view of the interpretations which have caused its boycott since the 1960s. Feminists, in an attempt to express their reaction against traditional female roles, have often cast the stiletto as an object of exploitation, along with other items of clothing which appear to be inherently feminine. In the rejection of certain items belonging to the women's sartorial code, adoption of those thought inherently masculine has been sought: examples of the 1970s are flat-heeled shoes and dungarees.[2]

Using the stiletto as a focal point this study is part of a more general review which looks at how and why certain meanings become attached to objects and whether these meanings are inherent in the design criteria. An alternative reading of 'stiletto' may now be necessary in the light of a wider discussion in current fashion design of the manipulation of masculine and feminine aspects in clothing for both sexes. This reworking seems to centre on trying to redefine meaning rather than changing the form of clothes.[3]

The stiletto has been widely accepted as symbolising female subordination. It seems that this sort of theory is widely applied to female-gendered objects but not to those that are resolutely male. It would appear that the more 'female' an object, the more it is devalued. This implies that meanings are often based on an association already determined: that is, that *meaning* is subject to stereotyping, which results in the perpetuation of particular perspectives. With reference to gender it seems that all too often objects construed as male are equated with 'masculine' and are therefore active and assertive, while defining female is equivalent to 'feminine', indicating passivity and subservience.

Since the early nineteenth century conventional criteria of styling based on gender difference have been established in footwear. Before then, male and female fashions were closely allied in style.[4] The heel is the component of the shoe which has become the most visible expression of gender in that, in the nineteenth century, high heels became 'female' footwear and were disallowed in a male sartorial code.[5] Therefore, the high heel established itself as a part of female iconography and has since become a useful tool in the construction of a female image. The stiletto heel has evoked the most potent symbolism because, in design terms, it managed to reach the ultimate dimensions of its *genre*, combining thinness and height in a relationship never before attained. The stiletto is the peak of the career of the high heel, fulfilling all requirements of feminised styling at the same time as it *literally* reached its highest point. The extremity of such styling demands precipitated the technological innovation necessary to manufacture such shoes. In other words, the *idea* for the stiletto predated any means of producing it.

The stiletto was one of several objects created in the aftermath of the Second World War as deliberately feminine,[6] at a time when the role of women in society was particularly polarised. Much discussion has centred on the way women consumers were 'constructed' by specific traits in the design of clothes and other products. One can speculate on whether this was a conscious attempt to cast women in a more feminine mould or part of a less conscious social movement which objectified its ideals in a reinforcement of femininity.

Footwear cannot be isolated from fashion: it is an intrinsic element in the creation of a 'total look'. In this instance, the New Look launched by Christian Dior in 1947 provided the keynote in the design. Generally regarded as the most important fashion event in the immediate post-war period, the Corolle line, as the New Look was originally christened, became the fashion paradigm of the shoe industry. The high-fashion magazine *Harpers Bazaar* commented in May 1947:

> The New Look is a new shape and that shape follows the lines of the best possible figure, emphasising every feminine charm.

This reaction was one of many which stressed the expression of femininity as the prime motivating force in shaping the fashion of the time. Moreover, it stressed that the 'feminine' was determined by the female form itself rather than by an artificial form. It is obvious that the clothes were meant to be an extension of the female figure and *emphasise* it rather than *distract* from it.

The other essential ingredient was the need to appear contemporary. The creation of a 'new' design of a feminine nature was in contrast to the design philosophy of the Utility system, which was in operation during the war and for some time afterwards.[7] The Utility scheme was a system of rationed items specially designed to be functional and to save raw materials. Clothing had to be practical and durable and this led to forms of dress for women being based on menswear, which, since the nineteenth century, had tended to place novelty and fashion second in matters of design. Footwear manufacturers now used the stylistic guidelines of the new Paris fashions as a contrast to those of the Utility scheme.[8] This scheme emphasised function above any other design criteria, equating 'good design' with a non-ornamental style. A product which was lighter in weight would counteract the chunky practical Utility style, but the dilemma remained of how to oppose austerity plainness when new fashions were also demanding simplicity based on lack of ornament. However manufacturers resolved this, they were ultimately concerned with a concept of form rather than function in the late 1940s and early 1950s. The main issue was how to follow the French fashion dictate; as one journal put it in 1947,

> . . . whether heels should reach a new extremity of height or a new low; which is the most flattering line for the ankle and interprets best the revival of flourishing femininity which characterises the recent fashion change.[9]

A year later this was still under discussion: 'Everything points to an even greater development of femininity . . .'[10]

Footwear manufacturers started trying to produce shoes that met these criteria, but it was a number of years before they finally came up with a satisfactory solution. Discussions centred on a tailored, refined shoe which gave the impression of lightness by means of a slender form.[11] The approach adopted was typical of the fashion industry. In order to appear 'new' the design had to be not just different from previous styles but a complete contrast to them.[12]

> The new spring shoes will be more delicate, more ladylike, more flattering than ever before. The heavy bulky shoe is definitely OUT.[13]

In contemporary language the term 'stiletto' is often used to describe a type of heel *and* the type of shoe to which it is attached – the court shoe. The two have become synonymous. The name originally given to the heel has, since 1953, become a generic title often used to describe this particular style and heel type. The reasons for this are basic to an understanding of the making and the meaning of the heel. The court shoe suited the New Look concept in that it was a tailored shape which followed the natural line of the foot. This slim-fitting form indicated and determined a lighter-weight product than Utility styles. It was not a new style, but its reintroduction after the war coincided with a refinement in last-making,[14] so it appeared updated even though it was a pre-war design. The plain court shoe shape, therefore, both *followed* and *broke* with the concepts of Utility footwear design. Just like the whole of the New Look the 'modernising process' was in some ways based on pre-war values. More importantly, its 'graceful' qualities apparently suited the new ethos determining what femininity looked like. While it moved sufficiently away from 1940s' styling to appear new and modern, it also inherited enough 1940s' characteristics to be seen not to break completely with tradition. A degree of continuity was important in helping the style to establish itself as market leader. By June 1951, the journal *Footwear* concluded that 'courts dominate the shoe market.'

In retrospect, we think of the stiletto as being of one type – a thin, tapering heel. In fact, this is the stiletto as it ultimately became rather than the one invented in the early 1950s. It was not a static design but a whole series of variations over a ten-year period. In these crucial ten years its design attempted to reconcile the demands of the dominant design philosophy, which emphasised simplicity above all, with the New Look femininity, which concentrated on styling. In order to answer the demands of fashion the heel changed in shape and construction from 1947, but by 1953 it had managed to establish a degree of resolution in its design . . . The court shoe shape, resolved prior to the heel, demonstrated the way in which femininity and modernity could be objectified. From 1953 the heel and toe took priority. The heel began as a two-inch thick but tapered shape which, by 1957, was gradually refined to the slender form we now recognise as a stiletto heel. The toe of the shoe underwent similar stylistic changes. The rounded toe of 1953 and before became sharper and eventually developed into an arrow-like point.

The choice of 'stiletto', the thin-bladed knife, to christen the heel is often thought to have originated from the invention of its metal core. The naming of a shoe from the style of heel was perhaps partly due to the fact that the shoe itself was very plain and the heel was therefore the focus of interest. When the *Daily Telegraph* published a photograph of a new heel called the 'Stiletto' on 10 September 1953, it was one of a number of terms denoting the *stylistic* characteristics and not an aspect of its manufacture.[15] The metal 'backbone' of the heel had not yet been invented! The heel of 1953 still used wood, the traditional material for heel construction. The 'spike', 'needle' and 'spindle' were all attempts to conjure up a name for a heel which was more tapered than ever before. Following the precedent set by the court shoe shape, the manufactures took elements of the 'Louis' heel, which was standard for a court shoe, but elongated and refined it.[16]

This produced a style of footwear which was impractical in a number of ways . . . The relative fineness of the heel meant that it would be difficult to walk on and that, with the pressure of walking, it could easily snap. Furthermore, the cut-away top of the shoe implied that it might not cling to the foot. But it was precisely this *appearance* of impracticality that made the 1940s' Utility styles look totally outdated.

As this shape of heel had never been seen before, a new name helped to identify it. Of all the names mentioned, some implied fragility, some implied strength and all suited the stylistic qualities. The stiletto seems to have prevailed at first because of its Italian association. 'Italian-ness' was a fashionable trend in the mid-fifties[17] and, along with the acknowledged traditional skill of Italian footwear manufacture in general, this helped to sell the product.

The problem for British manufacturers was how to make a commercially viable heel, one which would live up to its name and which looked like the fashion sketches. The initial experiments used wood as the reinforcement required to withstand prolonged pressure without breaking. By building a heel of interlocking pieces of wood, strength could be gained by a judicious use of the grain. Paradoxically, the heel which had consumer credibility in terms of wear was too heavy and clumsy to warrant the title of stiletto, while the one which did warrant the title by successfully reproducing the fashionable form did not stand up to wear. Pressure to produce the stiletto at this point seems to have come from the fashion industry, which continued to promote this airy, streamlined shoe. The demand was so great that in 1957, four years after the initial appearance of the stiletto in the *Daily Telegraph*, the perfect solution was still being sought.

> Without much doubt the biggest single constructional problem which the shoe trade has had to face in recent years has followed the trend in ladies' shoes towards even more slender heels.[18]

The motivation to continue with this seemingly impossible task was linked to the persistence of the *idea* of the stiletto. It was in the interest of the manufacturers to interpret the demands of fashion and the female consumer in a single, universal style which had the potential to dominate the market. In the 1950s a universal style was still possible, although the emerging youth commodity culture was beginning to break down such a dictatorial code of fashionable dressing. Perhaps the success of the stiletto was that its design allowed for variations. These variations were adopted by different consumer factions, but as a new product it was most popular with teenagers and women in their early twenties, anxious to ensure they looked modern and fashionable in a post-austerity era. It therefore became increasingly important to the shoe industry that a suitable method of production be found, which would be cost-effective and result in a heel which could endure protracted use and still look like a stiletto.

The pressure to create such a design caused shoe manufacturers to join forces and sponsor the Shoe and Allied Trades Retail Association (SATRA) to carry out research into the ergonomics of the stiletto heel. It had become clear that the wooden spindle heel would never be strong enough. A European solution pre-empted SATRA: in 1956 a plastic version with a metal strengthening core was shown at an Italian trade fair. Within a year a British heel component company puchased the UK rights and imported the machine process, which was based on the technique of injection moulding. From this point, the term 'stiletto' became the leader in the title stakes. The pointed shape that could now be achieved, together with the internal metal pin to sustain it, made the true meaning of the word directly pertinent.

In a sense, the plastic version can be seen as the second stage in the history of the stiletto, as it was only then that the concept for the design could be properly put into practice. It was four years since the shape had been created as the perfect solution to interpreting the feminine in shoe design, and ten years since the image had been drawn on paper. Now the manufacturing problem of combining style and form was finally solved. The new manufacturing process reinforced the newness of the product and gave the stiletto a permanent place in fashion vocabulary.

The plastic heel introduced a completely mechanised system of production in 1957 and ensured the stiletto's success by bringing it within reach of the lower end of the market. Ironically, this move created its own problem: how to produce a heel which could withstand any amount of wear. In high fashion the stiletto was a novelty item and, as such, worn only occasionally. The phenomenal retail success of the mass-produced version indicated that it was being worn far more, and in many situations not forecast by the manufacturers. What had previously been thought of as an evening shoe was now being subjected to much more rigorous use: women were wearing stilettos at work, when driving, running and catching a bus and for other everyday activities. The wide acceptability of the style did not mask the fact that the product still fell short of customers' expectations. While-you-wait heel repair kiosks appeared on every high street to service heels at a moment's notice. The volume of customer complaints encouraged SATRA to continue its research into what was then the relatively new field of plastics technology and chemical engineering.

It was not just the wearer who had cause for complaint: the minute heel-tip concentrated the wearer's weight so much that floors were often damaged beyond repair. The stiletto made news with stories like: 'The spike heels that English girls wear are ruining floors in factories, offices and dance halls . . .'[19] and 'Women's Stiletto heeled shoes are blamed for breaking up roads in Carshalton, Surrey . . .'[20] It was calculated that an eight-stone girl in stilettos exerted heel pressure of one ton per square inch.[21] This caused not only the banning of stiletto heels in various places from dance halls to aircraft, but also the redesign of floor surfaces. Bus platforms were altered: wooden boards were replaced with solid rubber matting in order to avoid the heels getting caught,[22] and aircraft designers had to find tougher materials for flooring.[23]

In 1959 the plastic heel was evolving into its most exaggerated form – up to six inches high with a tiny heel-tip. This development parallels the 'sharpening' of the round toe into a point. . . . The arrow-like form of both heel and toe reinforced the idea of harmony of style between the shoe and heel, giving further cause for the title of stiletto to be used for the whole shoe. However, its antisocial reputation increased as it became more pointed, and worsened when the medical profession, confronted by an enormous increase in foot and posture problems, pronounced against the wearing of such footwear on medical grounds. SATRA investigated the effect of the stiletto on the body and found that continued wearing of the extreme form over a period of time could cause a variety of medical problems. Any style of stiletto caused the protrusion of chest and bottom and the development of calf muscles. The higher the heel, the more exaggerated the effect on posture thus increasing back problems; the more pointed the toe, the more pressure was put on the foot to follow an unnatural shape. This inspired as much moral as medical denigration: the body shape imposed by the stiletto was associated with an obvious display of female sexuality. In the early 1950s when the stiletto shape was being established, it was not seen as representing anything other than conventional 'feminine' attributes. Once the aspired-to shape was a reality, the meaning had changed, though the ideology of form had remained the same. It was more aggressive and seemed to be *breaking* with those early ideas of femininity rather than *conforming* to them. It seems that the stiletto in its various forms was by now so firmly installed in women's culture that no diatribe could prove strong enough to dislodge it. Indeed, its very notoriety coincided with an increase in sales in 1958 until 1962. One can speculate whether the new meaning was mapped on to the form or whether the form was continuing to be a representation of social relations of that era.

This is not to suggest, however, that all women wore stilettos of the more extreme variety. These were mainly worn by the younger generation in an attempt to break away from the style popular with their mothers. The wearing of 'winklepickers' (as this extreme variety was known) was often a defiant gesture against the establishment. Female youth culture was partly redefining itself on its differences rather than its similarities. As Angela Carter recalls in *Nothing Sacred*:

> When I was eighteen, I went to visit her rigged out in all the atrocious sartorial splendour of the underground high style of the late fifties, black mesh stockings, spike-heeled shoes, bum-hugging skirt, jacket with a black fox collar.[24]

The implication is that the stiletto was used by some women to represent dissatisfaction with the conventional female image and to replace it with that of a 'modern' woman who was more active and economically independent than her predecessors. The paradox is that, in retrospect, it has been labelled a 'shackling' instrument which renders women immobile and passive. It has also been stressed that the heels gave added emphasis to breasts and bottoms, which were features of the 1950s' cinematic female stereotype. While this is undoubtedly true, I consider it a more important factor that the stiletto did *not* symbolise the housewife. From 1957 the stiletto was associated with glamour, with rebellion: it represented someone who was in some way 'modern' and 'up to date', and, above all, someone who inhabited a world outside the home – a go-getter! Therefore, it may be more accurate to suggest that this stiletto symbolised *liberation* rather than subordination, despite the fact that high heels of any form were part of a stereotyped framework of what women wore. I suggest that stiletto-wearing in the fifties was part of a broader discussion of how to express the 'new woman' – one who was not content with pre-war values and traditional roles. In this sense it could be seen as *progressive* rather than *retrogressive*. The stiletto did not break with all the traditions of what is female in footwear, but it certainly took those traditions to their furthest point, especiall when, in its most extreme form, it was used to symbolise a rejection of convention. It used what was acceptable to create non-acceptance.

The early stiletto could be said to represent traditional values. It was only as the shape changed that the meaning shifted and it therefore came to represent something other than its initial values. A crucial point to make is that the meaning became more radical at the same time as the style itself became more exaggerated. This reinforced its value as a commodity which represented women who were in the process of breaking with established female roles. The fashion industry of the fifties promoted the stiletto but the difficulties of production were such that the shoe industry would have welcomed a change in fashion dictates. However, consistent and increasing sales persuaded shoe manufacturers to continue. In this sense women were using consumer power to demand the production of the stiletto.

This exploration of an object which signified 'female' in the 1950s is not an attempt to prove that women were subordinate; it is rather a way of looking at how design works to objectify those characteristics which emphasised femaleness within the social context of that era. In a wider context, the objectification of gender traits of that decade seems to segregate the sexes rather than indicate the similarities. In later years, baggy clothes are an example of de-emphasis of the female form, disguising femaleness sometimes to the extent of making it look male. It has been said that this was a reaction against the fifties' stereotype which exaggerated those parts of the body which are female, and of course the stiletto played a part in this. Women have accepted too readily the notion that stilettos exploit women. By using male forms of clothing we are perpetuating the dominance of masculinity. Perhaps assertion of gender *difference* challenges the power relationship more effectively than any attempt to emulate what is seen as male. I am suggesting that power can be, and has been, represented in women's clothes if one explores ways in which 'femaleness' has been denoted.[25]

The exaggeration of gender attributes and an open display of gender difference has been labelled as exploitative when part of the female sartorial code. However, the physical changes imposed by the wearing of the stiletto need not be seen as an expression of submission. On the contrary, it exaggerated the existing physique by giving prominence to certain parts of the body and adding height. The body shape the stiletto creates depends on the shape and height of the heel. Again, the more extreme the stiletto, the more extreme physical prominence it gives. Given the suggestion that an overt representation of femaleness equals assertion, the most acute stiletto heel represents the most power. This is one example of the inter-dependence of form and meaning. The counter-argument, which says that the stiletto makes women less powerful by restricting their mobility, is secondary to the main issues concerning the stiletto in 1957. The stiletto put women on the edge of the dominance versus submission argument, but the fact that a fashion item could raise and explore those issues is significant and crucial to an understanding of women's role in the late fifties. I believe that from 1957 to 1962 the stiletto signified some liberation from traditional female values in object design. The sexual connotation was already established before the stiletto was invented, once high heels had come to symbolise the transition from adolescence to adulthood and had become the prerogative of women. The stiletto as the ultimate in high-heel styling served merely to crystallise what had already come to mean 'womanhood'. The purchase of a girl's first high-heels is often a signal of puberty and the onset of sexual maturity. The heel is used as a female rite of passage,[26] where the height of the heel indicates gradual progression towards maturity. The 'Kitten' stiletto of the early 1960s was devised for this purpose; the one-inch heel was the first step towards graduation. At the opposite end of the scale the stiletto could be so high that any pretence of function in terms of walking is lost. One symbolised sexual immaturity and a certain innocence, the other total maturity and sexual prowess. (Because the plastic construction of stilettos allowed for all these variations, the meaning became more strongly attached to the stiletto rather than any other type of high heel.) This is the point at which gender and sexuality become allied and the heel becomes an indicator of both 'female' and 'sex'. An example of this can be found in films of the fifties and sixties, where removal of stilettos was often used to imply a sexual encounter.

The stiletto is a 'grown-up' shoe in many senses of the word. By literally reaching new heights, combined with extreme thinness, it broke with the traditions of gender and form which initiated its production. That is, at first the stiletto was based on conventional interpretations of femininity. It was only later, when the basic form underwent certain stylistic changes, that a new set of assertive meanings was established. It seems, then, that in *one form* – the stiletto – there are *different meanings*, which originate from the polarities of the design. Therefore, at the point of design or production, not all meanings are set. In the case of the stiletto, some were 'in-built'. For example, the notion of femininity of the late 1940s was 'built' into the heel's design, but five years later both the meaning and the design had changed. I am unsure whether the object – the stiletto – came to represent particular ideologies or if representation created the need to change the object. In *Decoding Advertisements* Judith Williamson suggests the latter: 'Material things we need are made to represent other, non-material things we need . . . The point of exchange between the two is where "meaning" is created.'[27] Certainly, the stiletto in its more extreme manifestations went beyond the bounds of what was deemed 'acceptable' in that era – a crucial factor in the ability of the style to convey rebellion and dominance. This was based on the idea of the heel as a weapon to symbolise womanhood and its feminine attributes, and was put across in an aggressive, obvious manner rather than the subtle, passive way more commonly associated with femininity.

> I've been so mad at Johnny that I've gone for him with anything I could lay my hands on – a knife, a stiletto shoe, anything . . .[28]

The original motivation to produce a new type of attenuated heel survived the drawn-out development of the design and manufacture of the stiletto. The many methods devised all responded to a similar stylistic challenge, one which called for the invention of what could be termed a progressive product, a style which would announce its modernity and its affiliation to the feminine through a shape which could only be made possible through technical prowess. The stiletto mythology was completed in 1960 when the 'No Heel' stiletto appeared. The stiletto heel was so ingrained an image by this time that it no longer needed the very object that denoted it. The lightweight design of the heel had been ultimately achieved; it no longer existed! This novelty version, which appeared seven years after the stiletto's debut, served to make the point that both the technical and the stylistic challenge of the 'ideal' heel had been met.

The stiletto was devised and used to express femininity within the realms of what that meant in the 1950s. Therefore, it could be said that the ultimate form of the stiletto expressed extreme femininity in terms of its own traditions. It seems pertinent to raise the issue of whether we can criticise such overt expressions of the feminine in design as victimisation if we are basing our criticism on a male perspective. This negates the fact that expressions of femaleness can signify power and be objectified in ways other than masculine.

Notes

1   For example, Lisa Tickner writes that the stiletto 'isn't, and can't be, neutral; it is specifically female,' *Block*, No. 1, 1979.
2   This too has become a stereotype rather than an iconoclasm, as it was originally intended to be.

3   In an interview in *ID*, No. 45, March 1987, innovative fashion designer Vivienne Westward comments: 'I've never thought it powerful to be like a second-rate man'. See early 1987 advertisements for fashion designer Katherine Hamnett.

4   Wilson, Elizabeth, *Adorned in Dreams*, Virago, London, 1985; Swann, Jane, *Shoes*, Batsford, London, 1982.

5   Platform shoes of the 1970s are the one exception to this rule.

6   Another example is the Hoover.

7   The Utility scheme ended in 1952.

8   *Utility Furniture and Fashion*, Geffrye Museum catalogue, 1974.

9   *Footwear*, February 1947.

10 *Footwear*, February 1948.

11 This impression reinforced dominant beauty ideals for women when 'a good figure' was equated with a slender form.

12 Konig, René, *The Restless Image*, Allen and Unwin, London, 1973. One of the few theoretical texts on fashion which seeks to explain how fashions are created.

13 *Footwear*, February 1948.

14 In 1948 a last – the form on which a shoe is made – was devised which created a more slender product; this enabled the snug fit of the court shoe, which is necessary for it to cling to the foot, to be increased.

15 Information based on an interview with Edward Rayne, makers of the 'Telegraph' shoe.

16 In a similar way to the last-making of the 'new' court shoe.

17 *Block*, No. 5, 1981. Dick Hebdige discussed the introduction of Italian design to the UK in the 1950s via the scooter.

18 *High Heels*, SATRA, July 1957.

19 *Shoe and Leather News*, 1958 (month unknown).

20 *Shoe and Leather News*, 3 July 1958.

21 *Shoe and Leather News*, 2 April 1959.

22 *Daily Telegraph*, 21 November 1959.

23 *The Times*, 5 August 1958.

24 Carter, Angela, *Nothing Sacred*, Virago, London, 1982, p.11.

25 Spender, Dale, 'Re-inventing Rebellion', *Feminist Theorists*, The Women's Press, London, 1983. I disagree with Dale Spender's comment that 'power is still a concept about which women have codified very little'.

26 Just as long trousers are sometimes used in a male rite of passage from child to adult.

27 Williamson, Judith, *Decoding Advertisements*, Marion Boyars, London, 1979, p. 14.

28 Hamblett, Charles, and Deverson, Jane, *Generation X*, Tandem Books, London, 1964, p. 94.

Further Reading

Barthes, Roland, *The Fashion System*, Jonathan Cape, London, 1985.

Brownmiller, Susan, *Femininity*, Paladin, London, 1986.

French, Marilyn, *On Women, Men and Morals*, Summit Books, New York, 1985.

Goodall, Phil, 'Design and gender', *Block*, No. 9, 1983.

MacKenzie, Donald, and Wajaman, Judy, *The Social Shaping of Technology*, Open University Press, London, 1985.

Molloy, John, *Dress for Success*, Warner Books, New York, 1975.

Parker, Roszika, *The Subversive Stitch: Embroidery and the Making of the Feminine*, The Women's Press, London, 1984.

Chapter 18

Joanne Entwistle

'POWER DRESSING' AND THE CONSTRUCTION OF THE CAREER WOMAN

IN THE BRITISH EDITION of his dress manual, *Women: Dress for Success*, John T. Molloy proclaimed that most women 'dress for failure': either they let fashion dictate their choice of clothes, or they see themselves as sex objects, or they dress according to their socio-economic background. All three ways of dressing prevent women gaining access to positions of power in the business and corporate world. In order to succeed in a man's world of work, the business or executive woman's 'only alternative is to let science help them choose their clothes' (Molloy 1980: 18). The science of clothing management which he practised and called 'wardrobe engineering' helped introduce and establish the 'power dressing' phenomenon of the 1980s, defining a style of female professional garb which has now become something of a sartorial cliché; tailored skirt suit with shoulder pads, in grey, blue or navy, accessorised with 'token female garb such as bows and discreet jewellery' (Armstrong 1993: 278). Whilst Molloy might not have been the first, and indeed was far from the only self-proclaimed 'expert' to define a 'uniform' for the business or executive woman, his manual remains a classic explication of the rules of 'power dressing'. Molloy's manual, and his 'power suit' as it came to be known, provoked a good deal of discussion on both sides of the Atlantic and spawned an array of articles in newspapers and magazines, all of which served to establish a discourse on how the so-called career woman should dress for work.

'Power dressing' was effective in producing a particular construction of 'woman' new to the social stage; it was also in part responsible for the emergence of a new kind of 'technology of the self'. First, the discourse on the career woman and her dress offered a particular construction of 'woman' constituted across a range of different sites: within the fashion industry the notion of a career woman opened up new markets and become associated with particular designers such as Ralph Lauren and Donna Karan. This career woman was also constituted within a range of texts, from television, to advertising, to women's magazines, all of which produced a profusion of images of 'high powered' professional women. Some of the women in *Dallas* were to epitomise the style and she was to be found in the pages of magazines such as *Ms* and *Cosmopolitan*. Second, 'power dressing' can be seen as a 'technology of the self'. It was a discourse which was very effective at the embodied level of daily practice, rapidly gaining popularity with those women in professional career structures who were trying to break through the so-called 'glass ceiling' and providing them with a technique for self-presentation within this world of work. Photographs of the streets of Manhattan during the 1980s show women in the 'power-dressing' garb sprinting to work in their running shoes or sneakers. 'Power dressing' was to become embodied in the shape of such public figures as Margaret Thatcher, who according to *Vogue* was redesigned in the early 1980s in line with the principles of Molloy's 'dress for success' formula.

In this chapter, I want to outline the development of 'power dressing' and to suggest that it is significant for three not unrelated reasons. First, this sartorial discourse played an important part in bringing to public visibility the professional career woman who was, or sought to be, an executive or a business woman. Women have long held down professional jobs, but this woman was someone aiming to 'make it' to positions of power often in previously male-dominated career structures. The 'uniform' which the discourse on 'power dressing' served to establish was to play an important part in structuring the career woman's everyday experience of herself, serving as a mode of self-presentation that enabled her to *construct* herself and be *recognised* as an executive or business career woman. Indeed whilst the term 'power dressing' may have fallen out of use, the mode of dress associated with it, and perhaps more importantly the philosophy that underpinned it, have all become an established part of being a career woman in the 1990s. So prominent a part has this discourse on 'power dressing' played in the construction of the career woman that it would be hard for any professional or business woman today to escape its notice even if they chose not to wear the garb.

Second, I will attempt to show how this discourse on the career woman's dress fits into broader historical developments in the changing nature of work, especially the so-called 'enterprise culture' in the 1980s. In particular, 'power dressing' can be seen to fit with the neo-liberalism of the decade and the discourse on the so-called enterprising self. Finally, 'power dressing' is interesting because it marked the emergence of a new kind of consumption for women, who are traditionally associated with the 'frivolity' and aesthetics of fashion. What 'power dressing' served to inaugurate was a method for dressing which aimed to disavow fashion and which also necessitated the use of experts and expert knowledge for calculating what to buy.

Sartorial codes at work

How did a sartorial discourse mark out the career woman from previous generations of working women? For as long as women have been engaged in paid labour, dress has been a consideration at work. For example, the new department stores that developed in the nineteenth century were largely staffed by women, and their dress and overall appearance was under constant scrutiny from supervisors and managers. Gail Reekie in her history of the department store notes how female shop assistants were required to dress smartly on very modest incomes and this was a constant source of pressure and hardship for many women (Reekie 1993). The development of female white-collar work over the course of the nineteenth century also necessitated a wardrobe of suitable work clothes and may have likewise been subject to surveillance by managers and bosses. Over the course of the nineteenth century, as office work shifted from male clerks to female secretaries, there was an increasing proletarianisation and feminisation of clerical work. However, unlike the male clerk who preceded them, these new female workers had little hope of becoming the boss; indeed as Steele notes, 'their clothing – as workers and as women – set them apart from the upper-middle-class male employers' (Steele 1989: 83). This new breed of working woman could receive advice on how to dress from ladies' journals of the time. Steele notes how such journals at the turn of the century advised women to wear appropriate clothes that were smart but not provocative. There was, however, as yet no distinction between the dress of the female secretary and that of a female executive.

Many general fashion histories cite the war years as a significant moment in both the history of women's work and their dress. It is worth noting that during the Second World War we can find traces of the kind of female professional and business garb later advocated by Molloy: the tailored skirt suit with heavily accented shoulders. Joan Crawford in the classic film *Mildred Pierce* (1945) portrayed a tough, independent and career-minded business woman with a wardrobe of tailored suits to match; likewise in the same year Ingrid Bergman, as psychoanalyst Constance Peterson in Hitchcock's *Spellbound*, opts for attire which, like Mildred Pierce's, connotes toughness and masculinity. However, it is only over the last twenty years that representations of 'high powered', career-motivated women and their dress have gathered momentum. Discourse on 'power dressing' was a significant aspect in popular representations of career woman in the late 1970s and 1980s, serving to make her publicly visible. It is only at this time that we see a distinction being drawn between the female secretary and the female executive, largely through difference in the dress of each. The impetus behind Molloy's manual is precisely to make the female business or executive woman visible and distinguishable from her secretarial counterparts. Thus many of his rules include advice about avoiding clothes which are associated with secretaries and other female white-collar workers: fluffy jumpers and cardigans are to be avoided in the office, as are long hair, heavy make-up and too much jewellery.

Dress manuals and 'technologies of the self'

Important to the emergence of this phenomenon, then, was the dress manual where the rules of 'dress for success' were explicated. However, the dress manual is not a recent phenomenon and can be seen closely aligned with other kinds of self-help publications which have a longer history. We can find, in the eighteenth and nineteenth centuries, manuals on 'how to dress like a lady' and how to put together a lady's wardrobe on a moderate budget. The notion of successful dressing is in evidence in these, as in manuals on dress in the 1950s, for instance. What is different about the manuals on dress that emerged in the 1970s and 1980s was the *type* of woman they addressed (and thus the kind of success she sought) and the notion of *self* that they worked with. To take the first point, 'power dressing' marked a new development in the history of women and work; it addressed a new kind of female worker. It was a discourse that did not speak to all women; it did not address the cleaning lady or the manual worker or even the female white-collar worker, but a new breed of working woman who emerged in the 1970s, the university-educated, professional middle-class career woman entering into career structures previously the preserve of men: law, politics, the City and so on. The notion of success then was not about 'how to get a man and keep him', which was the implied success in many of the earlier manuals; it was about something previously the preserve of men, career success.

'Dress for success' 1980s style was also different in the notion of the self it conceived. A number of commentators have argued that a new type of self has emerged in the twentieth century which the dress manual can be seen to indicate (Sennett 1977; Featherstone 1991; Giddens 1991). Mike Featherstone calls this new self 'the performing self', which 'places greater emphasis upon appearance, display and the management of impressions' (Featherstone 1991: 187). He notes how a comparison of self-help manuals of the nineteenth and twentieth century provide an indication of the development of this new self. In the former self-help manual the self is discussed in terms of values and virtues, thrift, temperance, self discipline and so on. In the twentieth century we find the emphasis in the self-help manual is on how one appears, how to look and be 'magnetic' and charm others. The emphasis on how one looks as opposed to what one is, or should become, can be found in the 'dress for success' manuals of the 1970s and 1980s. This emphasis on the management of appearance is apparent in Molloy's earlier manual of dress for men, *Dress for Success* (1975) as well as in his later one for women.

Such a discourse on what the career woman should wear can be seen to open up a space for the construction of a new kind of feminine subject. The sartorial discourse of 'power dressing' constitutes a new 'technology' of the feminine self. 'Technologies of self', according to Foucault,

> permit individuals to effect by their own means or with the help of others a certain number of operations on their own bodies and souls, thoughts, conduct and way of being so as to transform themselves in order to attain a certain state of happiness, purity, wisdom, perfection or immortality.
>
> (Foucault 1988: 18)

Following Foucault, Nikolas Rose argues for the need to develop a 'genealogy of political technologies of individuality' (Rose 1991: 217). He goes on to say that

> the history of the self should be written at this 'technological' level in terms of the techniques and evaluations for developing, evaluating, perfecting, managing the self, the ways it is rendered into words, made visible, inspected, judge and reformed.
>
> (ibid.: 218)

The discourse of 'power dressing' did indeed render into words (and garb) this new 'careerist' woman, making her visible within the male public arena. It provided her with a means to *fashion* herself *as* a career woman. Molloy's manual offered women a *technical* means for articulating themselves as professional or business women committed to their work. The manual is full of detailed descriptions of the most effective dress for the professional and business work environment, and Malloy gives long lists of 'rules' as to what garments should combine with what. The detailed description is a formula for how to *appear*, and thus (if you are not already) *become* a female executive or a successful business woman. Hence his claim that:

> The results of wardrobe engineering can be remarkable. By making adjustments in a woman's wardrobe, we can make her look more successful and better educated. We can increase her chances of success in the business world; we can increase her chances of becoming a top executive; and we can make her more attractive to various types of men.
>
> (Molloy 1980: 18)

Whilst Molloy himself is careful to say 'can' and not 'will', the implications of his 'wardrobe engineering' are nothing less than the calculating construction of oneself as a committed career woman. As such they can be seen to constitute a 'technology of the (female, professional) self'.

Dressing for work

This 'technology of the self' can be seen to correlate with new work regimes developing from the 1970s onwards, a technology of the self commonly referred to as the 'enterprising self' because it is produced by a regime of work which emphasises internal self-management and relative autonomy on the part of the individual. We can contrast it with the technology of the self I am calling the 'managed-self', because it is produced within regimes of work characterised by a high degree of external constraint and management. It is important to point out here that I am using these two technologies of self as 'ideal types' which should be seen as two extremes on a continuum rather than discrete entities. Having said that, I want to outline what I see as ideal features of both, first looking at the technology of the managed self before moving on to consider the emergence of an enterprising self which forms the backdrop to a discourse on 'power dressing'.

The managed self

If we examine the managed self we find a high degree of management control and discipline, not simply over the labour process, but regarding the bodies, hearts and minds of the workers. Arlie Russell Hochschild's (1983) study of the world of the air steward, entitled *The Managed Heart*, gives us an example of the construction of a managed self. Her study of Delta Air found that all aspects of the recruitment, training, management, marketing and PR at Delta Air set out to produce a highly disciplined worker. The outcome of this intensive training and supervision of the steward is a highly disciplined self, or as Hochschild puts it, a managed heart, who is required to manage emotions, demeanour and appearance in order to project the principles defined by the corporation. The extent to which the stewards have to manage their emotions is summed up by the advertising slogan of one airline company, which goes, 'our smiles are not just painted on'; a request that does not call for a *performance* of happiness on the part of the steward, but the manufacture of genuine emotions. At Delta Air, the bodies and soul of the stewards are not simply a part of the service, they *are* the service and as such are subject to a high degree of corporate management. At least for the time that they are at work, the image and emotions of the stewards are not their own but part of the corporate image that Delta Air seeks to project.

What part does dress play in the construction of a managed self? Dress can be seen as an important aspect in the management and discipline of bodies within the workplace. Within many different spheres of work, strict enforcement of dress codes can be found. The high degree of corporate control within such spheres of work often involves the enforcement of a uniform which enables the image and identity of the corporation to be literally em*bodied*. Even where a strict uniform is not enforced, management exerts a significant influence over the dress of its workers. Many shop workers not required to wear a uniform are, however, often required to purchase clothes from the shop at a reduced cost in order to look appropriate.

Carla Freeman's (1993) study of women data-process workers in Barbados gives us one empirical example of how the enforcement of a dress code can be seen as part of a corporate technique of discipline. In her study she looked at corporate management in one American owned data-processing corporation, Data Air. Staffed predominantly by women, Data Air was marked by a high level of corporate discipline exerted over every aspect of the labour process: from how many airline tickets the women could process in an hour, to how long each woman took for lunch, to how many times they went to the loo, and how they dressed for work. Such discipline required a high degree of surveillance and this was made possible by the careful layout of the open-plan office. The design of the office enabled the panoptic gaze of supervisors and managers to monitor the performance, conduct and dress of the female workers. The enforcement of what Data, Air called a 'professional' dress code was so strict that it was not uncommon for women to be sent home by their supervisor for not looking smart enough. However, whilst the corporation demanded 'professional' dress and conduct, the work performed was anything but professional.

Freeman argues that the enforcement of a dress code enabled Data Air to discipline its female workers into projecting a positive image of the organisation, both to the women within and to those outside, one that belied the fact that the women were locked into a non-professional occupational structure which was low paid, boring and repetitive and offered very few opportunities for promotion. The women at Data Air carried an image of the corporation to the world outside which worked to create an illusion of glamour and sophistication so that even if they were paid no more than female manual workers in Barbados, and indeed less than many female agricultural workers, they were the envy of many women outside who longed for the opportunity to work in the sophisticated air-conditioned offices. Despite low wages, Data Air was never short of keen female labour. One of the things that is notable within this regime of work is the high degree to which workers' bodies and souls are subjected to corporate management. As with the air stewards at Delta Air, the bodies of the women at Data Air are disciplined into *embodying* the message of the corporation.

The enterprising self

It is at this point that we can begin to sketch out the features of the technology of self, referred to by a number of commentators as the enterprising self, which corresponds to a rather different regime of work. This 'enterprising' worker emerged out of historical developments commonly theorised in terms of post-Fordism and neo-liberalism and was to become the focus of New Right rhetoric in its proclamations about 'enterprise culture'. The term 'enterprise culture' is problematic, as indeed is the claim that Western capitalism has moved from a Fordist to a post-Fordist mode of production (see discussions of these problems in Cross and Payne 1991; Keat and Abercrombie 1991). However, the 1980s did see a significant growth in self-employment and, perhaps more importantly, the emergence of a powerful rhetoric of individualism and enterprise.

The restructuring of work which began in the 1970s served to sever the worker from traditional institutions and organisations (one element in the New Right's attack on 'dependency' culture; for more details see Keat 1991), so that by the 1980s individuals were called upon to think that they were not owed a living, but were embarked upon a career path of their own, and not the corporation's, making. From the 1970s onwards this new regime of work gathered momentum, replacing 'corporation man' [*sic*] and producing, in ever-increasing numbers, the worker who is a free-lancer, or an entrepreneur, or a 'self-made man' [*sic*]. However, as well as producing a shift in the organisation of work, the rhetoric of 'enterprise culture' aimed to stimulate a new attitude to work and as such gives considerable prominence to certain qualities and according to Rose

> designates an array of rules for the conduct of one's everyday existence: energy, initiative, ambition, calculation and personal responsibility. The enterprising self will make a venture of its life, project itself a future and seek to shape itself in order to become that which it wishes to be. The enterprising self is thus a calculating self, a self that calculates *about* itself and that works *upon* itself in order to better itself.
>
> (Rose 1992: 146)

Rose argues that one result of neo-liberal calls to make oneself into an enterprising self is the increasing incursion of 'experts' into private life to help one attain success and find fulfilment. The increasing pressure for self-fulfilment has necessitated the rise of new 'experts' to tell us how to live, how to achieve our full potential, how to be successful, how to manage our emotions, our appearances, our lives.

What is significant then about 'power dressing' as it develops in the 1980s is the degree of fit between this discourse on the presentation of self in the workplace and the emergence of an enterprising self. The rallying call to 'dress for success' or 'power dress' is a call to think about every aspect of one's self, including one's appearance, as part of a 'project of the self'. The mode of self advocated by the rallying phrase 'dress for success' is an enterprising one: the career woman is told she must be calculating and cunning in her self-presentation. Molloy's manual is one which seeks to encourage *responsibility* on the part of the female professional for her own success; one that demands the conscious *calculation* of her self-presentation; and calls on her to *work* upon herself in order to produce an image which makes visible her commitment to the life (and lifestyle) of an executive or business woman. Thus we can see that 'power dressing', with its rules, its manuals, its 'experts' or image consultants, in both philosophy and rhetoric, fits with that of 'enterprise culture'. 'Power dressing', then, can be thought of as a practice of dress which opened up a mode of sartorial presentation for the enterprising self of the 1980s.

Managed versus self-managed dress

If 'power dressing' did not abolish dress codes and sought the establishment of a 'uniform', how then does it differ from the dress codes enforced in the office and the department stores? What distinguishes these professional occupations from less 'high powered' occupations is the way in which dress codes are enforced: it is very unlikely a female executive will be told to go home and dress more appropriately by a supervisor. On the contrary, companies expect their professional female workers to have internalised the codes of dress required by the job. Rather than send her home, a company is more likely to suggest, or even purchase, the services of an image consultant to work with the woman. The difference then between the smart dress of a data processor in Barbados and a 'high powered' female executive is not that the first woman is exposed to a dress code and the latter not, it is a matter of different modes of enforcement: the career woman is expected to manage her dress to such an extent as to make external pressure unnecessary.

A further difference arises out of the issue of intent. What identifies the power dresser as different from her counterpart in the typing pool or office is a different attitude towards dress and self-presentation, an *intentionality* signalled by her attention to dress as much as by what she paid for her clothes and where she bought them. Once an individual has internalised the concept of a career as a project of the self, fewer external management constraints are required. As it became established as a uniform, the 'power suit' became a more or less reliable signal that a woman was taking her job seriously and was interested in going further. The woman who went out and bought the 'power suit' was already an enterprising self, if only that in order to think about one's career success in terms of personal presentation, one needed to be enterprising and subscribe to a notion of the individual as self-managing, responsible and autonomous. Closely related to the issue of intention is the issue of autonomy. Professional occupations can be characterised as granting greater autonomy to the worker. However, this is not freedom as such, rather the autonomy granted to the professional requires simply a different regime of management, in this instance not exerted by corporate surveillance and management, but shifted to the internal level of self-management.

'Power dressing' offered women a conception of power located at the level of the body and rooted in individualism. Unlike the secretary or the shop assistant, the career woman's dress does not simply transmit information about the company or corporation she works for: her appearance is important because it tells us something about *her*, about her professionalism, her confidence, her self-esteem, her ability to do her job. The role played by clothes in transmitting information about the woman is demonstrated in the film *Working Girl* which stars Melanie Griffith. In this 1980s film we witness the Griffith character effect a transformation from secretary to 'high powered' executive. In the beginning of the film Griffith is seen as a gauche, gaudily dressed but bright young secretary no one will take seriously and who is harassed by all her male employers as an object of sexual fun. It is only when she starts to work for a female boss, played by Sigourney Weaver, that she begins to see the importance of dress in her professional presentation and learns the codes of 'power dressing'. What might have been a nice feminist tale of female bonding quickly turns nasty when Griffith finds out that her boss has stolen a bright idea she has for a take-over bid, and the ensuing tale sees Griffith take on her boss whilst at the same time developing a very similar taste in dress. The moral of this story is a highly individual-istic one which emphasises that all a girl needs to succeed is self-motivation and good standards of dress and grooming. The message Griffith conveys is not a corpor-ate image but an image of her as an enterprising, autonomous and self-managing subject.

Working at dress

The great female renunciation?

'Power dressing' may be underpinned by an enterprising philosophy which fits with the individualism of neo-liberalism; however it was not about expressing individual-ity in dress. 'Power dressing' did not set out to rock any boats, its main aim was to enable women to steer a steady course through male-dominated professions, and it therefore sought to work with existing codes of dress. In this respect 'power dress-ing' was inherently conservative, recommending women to wear the female equiva-lent of the male suit, and to avoid trousers in the boardroom at all costs since these are supposedly threatening to male power. As I noted earlier, the aim of Molloy's manual was to establish a 'uniform' for the executive or business woman, one that would become a recognisable emblem. As such, it should be resistant to change in much the same way as the male suit. Fashion, with its logic of continual aesthetic innovation, is therefore deemed inappropriate for the business and corporate world and must be disavowed by the determined career woman.

Indeed, much of Molloy's book is given over to a condemnation of the fashion industry. Molloy's call for the disavowal of fashion on the part of the career woman can be heard echoing an earlier renunciation on the part of bourgeois men when entering the new public sphere opened up by the development of capitalism. The 'great masculine renunciation' noted by Flügel resulted in the rejection of elabor-ation and decoration, which had been as much a part of male dress as female dress prior to the end of the eighteenth century, and which, according to Flügel, had served to produce division and competition in terms of status (Flügel 1930). The sober dress of the bourgeois man aimed to diminish competition and bond him in new ways to his colleagues. In much the same way that bourgeois men donned themselves in sobriety, the executive and business woman is thus called upon to reject the divisive 'frivolity' of fashion. In doing so, these women will not only get on in the male world of work, but will likewise have a code of dress which will hopefully see them unite. Indeed Molloy suggests that 'this uniform issue will become a test to see which women are going to support other women in their executive ambitions' (Molloy 1980: 36).

'Wardrobe engineering': a 'science' of dress

Since women, rather than men, have traditionally been seen as the subjects of fashion, Molloy's manual heralded, at least in theory, a new era in the relationship between women and dress, which is perhaps something of an inversion of convention. He calls upon women to make their clothing decisions on the basis of 'science' and not aesthetics or emotion, which might have previously guided their decisions. Molloy's dress formula was the result of years of testing and monitoring of clothes. A strict positivist, the only validity he claims to be interested in is 'predictive validity' and only arrives at statements on what dress works for women if he can predict with accuracy the effects of clothes on the attitudes of others. The main 'effect' he is aiming for is 'authority'. This employment of technical means or 'wardrobe engineering' promised to reduce the problem of what an ambitious career woman should wear to work to a purely technical matter of knowledge and expertise.

We can note therefore that what distinguishes the discourse on 'power dressing' as it addressed the new career woman is the way it applies *technical rationality* to what is in effect a question of consumption: the appeal of Molloy's 'wardrobe engineering' is that it provided many women with a reliable shopping tool when purchasing a wardrobe for work. Problems of time and money are hopefully eliminated, as is the possibility of making mistakes and buying items of clothing that do not suit you, work for you, or fit in with the rest of your wardrobe. One of the rules he outlines in the manual is 'use this book when you go shopping', the aim being to make irrational or impulse buying a thing of the past.

'Power dressing' in the 1990s

'Power dressing' and 'dress for success' may sound rather dated today and therefore no longer of any import. However, the principles erected by this discourse on dress, and the subjectivity they helped to establish, have not disappeared. On the contrary the technique of 'dress for success' and the enterprising self it adorned have become institutionalised and integrated, not only into the personal career plans of individual women, but into the structure of corporate planning. From the publication of Molloy's manual in 1980 we have seen, in the 1990s, a steady rise of this new 'expert', the image consultant whose services are bought in by individuals who are either under-confident about their image or simply too busy to think about it; or by big businesses and organisations who are keen to up the profile of their female executives. From the 1970s onwards, Molloy's knowledge and expertise, along with the knowledge and expertise of a growing number of image consultants, was quickly bought by big organisations who were concerned about the small number of women reaching the upper echelons of management and wanted to be seen to be doing something about it.

Image consultancy is a generic word for a whole range of different services from manuals on dress, to consultants who advise on how to plan and budget for a career wardrobe, to specialist services which advise people on what to wear when going on television, to shopping services offered to the career woman with no time to lunch let alone shop. The combination of services that is offered by image consultancy marks a development in a new *method* of consumption; it also marks a new *attitude* to consumption. The career woman who buys in the services of a consultant to plan and purchase her wardrobe treats consumption as *work* and not as leisure (and therefore pleasure) as it is commonly experienced. This attitude to consumption requires the same application of instrumental rationality to consumption that is required by work. Molly not only advocates a formula of dress for the business and executive world of work, he advises career women to treat their dress as part of the work they must put in in order to increase their chances of career success. There may of course be pleasures associated with buying in a consultant, but these pleasures are themselves new and are distinct from the traditional pleasures normally associated with shopping.

To conclude, the development of a discourse on the career woman's dress throughout the 1980s and 1990s marks the emergence of a new 'technology of the self', a self who demonstrates that she is ambitious, autonomous and enterprising by taking responsibility for the management of her appearance. The fact that so many women buy in the services of a consultant is also testimony of the extent to which this modern woman is an enterprising self. In seeking out an expert to guide her in her self-presentation, the career woman demonstrates her own commitment, initiative and enterprise. It also marks the emergence of a new pattern of consumption: the use of clothes manuals, the buying in of expertise in the form of image consultants and the purchase of shopping services mark out a new attitude to consumption which sees it as serious labour requiring the application of technical rationality and knowledge to make decisions about what to consume.

References

Armstrong, L. (1993) 'Working girls', *Vogue*, October.

Cross, M. and Payne, G. (eds) (1991) *Work and Enterprise Culture*, London: Falmer Press.

Featherstone, M. (1991) 'The body in consumer society', in M. Featherstone, M. Hepworth and B. Turner (eds), *The Body: Social Process and Cultural Theory*, London: Sage.

Flügel, J.C. (1930) *The Psychology of Clothes*, London: The Hogarth Press.

Foucault, M. (1988) 'Technologies of the self', in L. Martin, H. Gutman and P. Hutton (eds) *Technologies of the Self: A Seminar with Michel Foucault*, Amherst MA: University of Massachusetts Press.

Freeman, C. (1993) 'Designing women: corporate discipline and Barbados' off-shore pink collar sector', *Cultural Anthropology* 8, (2).

Giddens, A. (1991) *Modernity and Self-Identity: Self and Society in the Late Modern Age*, Cambridge: Polity.

Hochschild, A. (1983) *The Managed Heart: Commercialisation of Human Feeling*, Berkeley CA: University of California Press.

Keat, R. (1991) 'Starship Enterprise or universal Britain?' in R. Keat, and N. Abercrombie (eds) (1991) *Enterprise Culture*, London: Routledge.

Keat, R. and Abercrombie, N. (eds) (1991) *Enterprise Culture*, London: Routledge.

Molloy, J.T. (1975) *Dress for Success*, New York: Peter H. Wyden.

Molloy, J.T. (1980) *Women: Dress for Success*, New York: Peter H. Wyden.

Reekie, G. (1993) *Temptations: Sex, Selling and the Department Store*, St Leonards, Australia: Allen and Unwin.

Rose, N. (1992) 'Governing the enterprising self', *The Values of the Enterprise Culture: The Moral Debate*, in P. and P. Morris (eds) London: Routledge.

Rose, N. (1991) *Governing the Soul: The Shaping of the Private Self*, London: Routledge.

Sennett, R. (1977) *The Fall of the Public Man*, New York: Alfred A. Knopf.

Steele, V. (ed.) (1989) *Men and Women: Dressing the Part*, Washington DC: Smithsonian Institute Press.

Chapter 19

Angela Partington

POPULAR FASHION AND WORKING-CLASS AFFLUENCE

[. . .]

Post-war histories

THE WORKING CLASS has been perceived as divided, in the period after the Second World War, between those on 'the margins' (who are thought to reject commodities or 'subvert' their values) and the mainstream (thought to consume passively). For instance, (masculinised) subcultural 'style' is distinguished from (feminised) mass cultural 'fashion'. While working-class women's activities have been associated with devalued cultural practices, male working-class culture has enjoyed the status of 'subversion', on the grounds that the commodity is either refused or creatively 'appropriated' – as in 'bricolage'.[1]

There are a number of links which have been made, between class domination and consumerism, which imply that feminity is a kind of weakness in working-class culture as a culture of resistance. It has often been assumed that in their role as consumers working-class women have helped to erode or disguise class differences. The 1950s, when working-class women were first actively pursued as consumers for many commodities, is often seen as a period in which contradiction and class conflict was absent. It is associated with a national consensus culture brought about by affluence, which was only interrupted by the emergence/identification of marginal groups in the 1960s (despite the fact that the 1960s were considerably *more* affluent and consumerist than the 1950s). It is this evocation of the 1950s against which I want to reconsider post-war femininity as a source of contradiction and conflict, by considering working-class women's adoption of New Look fashion.

The mechanism by which consumption is stimulated is often identified as 'fashion', or a similar conceptualisation such as 'built-in-obsolescence'. Definitions of post Second World War consumerism have emphasised the 'libidinisation' of consumption, the 'ideological manipulation' of the consumer, and the proliferation of 'needs'. But it can be argued that consumerism is an effect of the instability of capitalism as well as its expansion, and that fashion is a terrain on which new forms of class struggle have developed.[2] In the discussion of 1950s fashion which follows, I will show how the commodification of working-class culture involved contradictory attempts to regulate (i.e., discourage desires for certain kinds of commodities), as well as libidinise consumption, in order to try and create 'good consumers' who were predictable in their choices. In trying to impose certain standards of taste on consumers, the design profession and the marketing industries created the opportunity for the roles of 'good consumption' to be broken, inadvertently allowing consumers to produce unexpected meanings around fashion goods, as was the case with the New Look.

Rather than expressing dominant ideological values of the 1950s, such as those upholding traditional femininity and domesticity, the New Look can be seen as a site of conflicting meanings. Analysis of the adoption of the style reveals that relations between classes were actually negotiated through the exercise of specific tastes and preferences. It can be shown that the merchandising of fashion goods in the 1950s involved appealing to class-specific consumer skills and preferences, encouraging the consumer's active use of an increasingly complex 'language' of clothes to express differences. For the fashion product to be historically and culturally placed, it must be read interdependently with other design and media products which, for the first time, presented certain commodities for the 'desiring gaze' of working-class women. For working-class women in the 1950s, fashion signified in terms of the skills it demanded and the pleasures it offered, and these were specific to that market. Their investments in the style, and the meanings they produced with it, cannot therefore be reduced to the emulation of another consumer group.

Class distinction and fashion

There have been many explanations of fashion which acknowledge its role in the *expression* of class difference in capitalist society, but they tend to perceive it as working automatically in the interests of dominant or privileged groups. Middle-class affluence, and 'conspicuous consumption', are seen as means of exclusion – disidentification with other groups; whereas working-class affluence is seen as a means of emulation – identification with other groups.[3] It is assumed that mass-production threatens to erode, to absorb or to make meaningless class differences, making the preservation of 'distinction' the prerogative of privileged and elite groups. The implication is that those in subordinate groups, rather than having their own means of exclusion, supposedly covet those of the higher status groups.

Such explanations appear to be drawn from two influential theories of fashion, namely Veblen's 'conspicuous consumption' theory from the late nineteenth century, and the 'trickle down' model used by Georg Simmel to describe fashion adoption in 1904.[4] Veblen explained fashion as evidence of struggle for status in 'a new society where old rules disintegrated and all were free to copy their betters'.[5] The 'trickle down' model has become an almost common-sense explanation for the 'fashion cycle'. Briefly, it describes changes in taste as innovations made by the dominant class, as necessary in order to preserve the 'unity and segregation' of the class, given that modern social codes allow the immediately subordinate group to emulate the tastes and preferences of the one above. According to this model, the high status groups are forced to adopt new styles in order to maintain their superiority/difference, as these tastes filter down the social scale. This happens periodically so a cyclical process is created, generating the otherwise mysterious mutations we know as fashion.

These theories have informed more recent approaches, such as the analysis of affluence as an ideology which appears to create a 'classless' society by disguising class differences or making them less visible. The phenomena of 'affluence' and 'privatisation' (the increased consumption of 'non-essential' goods within the domestic sphere) have been used as key concepts with which to analyse post-Second World War commodified leisure, but it has been thought that 'beneath them lurks the image of a classless society . . . Differences are mobilised in the leisure market as a means of producing consumer identification – and produce what appear to be different groups of consumers . . . real divisions . . . are represented . . . as differences in taste'.[6]

Within all these frameworks, women's identification with the commodity is equated with the fetishism and spectacularisation which create the 'illusion' of changed conditions of existence. Women's acquisition of tastes and interests in fashion are identified as the means of social betterment, and the modern woman is understood as spectacle used for the display of wealth and distinction. But at the same time these are not recognised as indicators of 'real' social change, but only as the means by which socio-economic differences are disguised or denied, as in the use of the term 'embourgeoisification' in relation to working-class affluence.

In these frameworks conspicuous consumption, trickle-down, and affluence-as-ideology, are all notions which are based on an understanding of culture as a mere expression of socio-economic relations, rather than as a site of the active production of class-specific values and meanings by consumers. As a description of post-Second World War culture, the notion of affluence as ideology makes too many assumptions about, and disregards the historical specificity of, working-class markets for fashion goods. In such theorisations, it is simply assumed that working-class affluence is the *effect* of the *diffusion* of cultural practices, rather than the *condition* of *struggles* between classes. These established theories of fashion are incapable of explaining how class-specific consumer skills enable the reproduction of differences. They support the practice of 'reading off' goods instead of enabling a consideration of the relations between consumer groups and practices on which the meaningfulness of any commodity depends.

The developments to which the terms 'affluence' and 'privatisation' refer could more accurately be described as 'mass-markets' and 'gendered consumption', since they were objectives of the economic strategies which were deployed by the leisure industries, in the pursuit of profit, rather than the result of a philanthropic democratisation. The development of a mass-market fashion system enabled class-specific groups to be targeted as consumers, and relied increasingly on gender-specific consumer skills.

Consumerism did not create the illusion of a classless society then, but neither did it simply reinforce already established class relations. Rather it transformed the material relations between classes, and altered the conditions, means and processes through which, and the resources for which, class struggles were to be conducted. The introduction of mass-market systems for the production and distribution of goods (affluence), and the gendering of consumption (privatisation), while being necessary for capitalism's expansion of consumption, nevertheless enabled the production of new class-specific meanings for commodities by contributing to the development of a more complex 'language' of clothes which could be used by consumers in the articulation of class identity. My analysis of the marketing of 1950s fashion, and the popular adoption of the New Look, will exemplify this.

Mass-market fashion

In the post-Second World War period, it has been necessary for working-class markets to be found for commodities, in order for capitalism to expand or even survive. As with the marketing of other goods, it has been found necessary to develop a system for the production and distribution of fashion commodities, in which there is virtually no 'trickle down' in the ways in which styles are innovated or adopted by specific class groups. A 'trickle across' or 'mass-market' theory of fashion has been developed to describe this new system, which is based on several broad arguments about mass-market fashion. Firstly, that the fashion industry has reinvented the fashion 'season', and within this its manufacturing and merchandising strategies almost guarantee adoption by consumers across socio-economic groups simultaneously. Secondly, that there is always enough 'choice' between a range of equally fashionable styles to meet the demands of different tastes. Third, that discrete market segments within all social strata (not just privileged groups) are represented by 'innovators' who influence fashion adoption. And finally, that the mass media is also targeted at market segments, so the flow of information and influence is primarily within, rather than across, class groups.[7]

Within this system, the people who determine what becomes fashionable are professionals such as fashion editors in publishing, and fashion buyers in retailing. But these professionals act as agents of specific sections of the fashion-consuming public whose tastes and preferences it is their task to anticipate.[8] Styles in dress are either adopted and disseminated simultaneously by different class groups or remain contained within specific ones. So the roots of change in fashion design, manufacturing, and marketing 'are in response to the desire on the part of the large majority of consumers to innovate and to be fashionable in their styles of life.'[9] In a mass-market system, adoption of new styles is a process which depends on the flow of information *within* social strata rather than between them. Innovators are to be found amongst all classes and groups, not just amongst the privileged or elite, so there is no 'emulation' of privileged groups by subordinate groups in such a system. Difference exists in the *ways* in which fashions are adopted, rather than in any time lag, and many fashions receive wide acceptance within some class groups while being unsuccessful in others. Privileged groups can wear the same 'classic' styles and ignore the latest fashions in 'a concern for birth distinction and English heredity as against the distinction of occupational achievement'.[10] The upper-middle classes want clothes 'related to wealth and high living rather than to family connection'. Amongst the lower-middle classes 'there is a distaste for "high style", for what is "daring" or "unusual" '.[11] Women on very limited clothes budgets are keen to adopt the latest fashions, but often by making their own versions which are customised and individualised.

The traditional 'customer', who has an informal contract with the trader based on mutual expectations, is replaced by a 'consumer', whose 'expectations are altogether more specific: the maximisation of immediate satisfaction. If goods or services are not provided in the manner or at the price required, the consumer will go elsewhere'.[12] Exclusivity is not something confined to privileged groups, since all market segments can shop in retail outlets intended specifically for them. In a mass-market system women of all classes are responsible for the diffusion of fashion (preferences for innovative or restyled products), but class differences do not disappear in this system, on the contrary more complex and multiple differences are made possible through increasingly elaborate and complex manufacturing, media and retailing strategies.

For example, in the 1950s artificial fibres were being developed, especially in mass-produced and cheap clothing, but there was also a campaign to uphold the prestige of natural fibres, so they became associated with more expensive and exclusive ranges. Consequently the class connotations of fabrics changed, with cotton (previously associated with the labouring classes) and wool (the middle classes) both becoming more acceptable materials for high fashion products. Meanwhile the new synthetics became a sign of working-classness, because to working-class women quantity, disposability, colour, and 'easycare' became a priority while craftsmanship and 'naturalness' did not.

Christian Dior has been called the 'moderniser of the Haute Couture',[13] because he pioneered the system through which manufacturers and retailers could sell an 'Original-Christian-Dior-Copy' and clothes made from paper patterns licensed by Dior, and through which exact drawings and reproductions were allowed to appear only a month after the fashion show. In 1957 an estimated 30 per cent of Paris haute couture volume was accounted for by manufacturers and retail syndicates, and store buyers. The Fashion House Group of London, founded in 1958, produced 'the cream of British ready-to-wear'[14] for an upper-middle-class market. These goods were more expensive than chain store clothing but much cheaper than designer originals, and signalled the increased complexity of the system through which consumers could identify themselves according to much finer criteria. ' "Ready-mades", far from being the shoddily made confections that in pre-war days were regarded as beneath contempt, now began to compete with couture . . . Brand names started to appear on garments as a guarantee of quality.'[15] The higher levels of turnover in fashion retailing achieved by the multiples, and the emergence of self-service supermarket chains in food retailing, had an important influence on forms of garment display and shop interiors, making the goods much more accessible to the customer. Design had to become a substitute for the personal attention of a sales assistant, and retailers had to develop a 'house style' or corporate image which would enable the consumer to identify the companies whose products they preferred. This new relationship depended on a much greater level of consumer skills, and indicates one of the ways in which consumer choices became an integral part of identity-formation.

Alongside these developments in retailing, the new disciplines of market research grew:

> Investigations into consumer behaviour required a massive apparatus for the gathering and processing of data on consumer habits, preferences, tastes and whims . . . The unifying principle of diverse market research techniques was the regulation of information flows, which were to proceed in one direction only: from the consumer upwards to the institutions of the image production industries . . . In the first instance, it is capital which dictates the forms which commodity consumption takes; yet the market remains dependent on the development by the female consumer of specific sets of social competences and skills.[16]

All these developments are evidence of market segmentation rather than the diffusion, or democratisation, of leisure. The developments in the textiles and clothing industries, and the expansion of the retailing trades, have all been interpreted as the eradication of the differences between the classes, on the assumption that mass-production made fashion goods available to the working class and that it also brought an end to the elite ends of the market. Perhaps the first fashion to benefit from these changes was the New Look, and it has been said that therefore the real significance of the 'New Look' was 'that it ushered in a period when fashion was to be more important – and more available – to everyone'.[17] But these developments actually allowed differences to multiply, because they created finer distinctions and a more complex vocabulary in 'the language of clothes' for the articulation of class relations. These included 'make', retail 'brand', and fabric, as well as style and quality. Simultaneous adoption, therefore, does not mean identical adoption. Although the fashion industry may determine the range of styles from which choices have to be made, certain styles or 'looks' may become much more popular amongst some consumer-groups than others, and certain styles completely fail to be adopted by some, or even all groups. Many styles, including the New Look, become adopted in different ways, through a process of customisation in which certain elements become more important than others, and which the consumer controls.

The attempt to 'train' working-class affluence

In its self-promotion during the 1950s, the design profession assumed that the role of the designer was to 'open the eyes' of the consumer, claiming to open up new kinds of knowledge and relationships, because 'Untrained afffluence was a threat to the attainment of standards and stability in taste'.[18] Modernist design was clearly an expression of a commitment to rationalisation, and a belief in goods as measurable solutions to simple needs, rather than as bearers of meanings and unpredictable emotional values. The promotion of simplicity, functionalism, and the attempt to outlaw decoration and 'clutter' was a logical translation of this. The idea of the end of style, and the establishment of permanent design values, was echoed in the belief in a classless utopia. British fashion, as in other design fields, tended towards the encouragement of *in*conspicuous consumption, by promoting rather restrained and tasteful styles of dress, and tried to counter the threat of untrained affluence by imposing strict distinctions between glamour and utility, in the attempt to educate consumers in the rules of proper consumption. The British fashion industry, incredibly, attempted to eliminate seasonal fluctuations in fashion, for example by setting up a central information and design centre from which manufacturers could be instructed.[19]

This programme of regulation was managed by institutions such as the Council for Industrial Design, and involved campaigning to change the attitudes of both manufacturers and the consumer, and the production of propaganda 'aimed at familiarizing the public with that new concept "design".'[20] Looking at fashions in women's clothes in the 1950s however, it is apparent that this programme became limited and strained, since its prime target (working-class women) was fast acquiring consumer skills which ultimately enabled them to relate to goods in increasingly complex ways, which could not be reduced to simple needs or practical utility. As mass-market systems developed, working-class women were able to engage in forms of consumption to satisfy needs not anticipated or recognised by the professionals, and therefore 'improper'.

The New Look could only be tolerated within the perspective of the design establishment, if it was seen as a decorative but complementary contrast to utilitarian clothing. The utilitarian definition of the housewife (as an efficient machine for the reproduction of labour) co-existed with a notion of femininity drawn from the bourgeois ideal of womanhood as 'decorative'. Commentators have often noted the duality of 1950s femininity, in terms of the contrasting, but equally acceptable, images of womanhood which prevailed. Fashion historians have made two categories to accommodate these different identities:

> The ambiguities of the period's dress invested women with two very different personae: dutiful homemaker and tempting siren. The former wore the shirtwaist dress, apron and demure necklines – all proper symbols of domesticity. Yet at the same time an exaggerated image of sexuality prevailed. Woman-turned-temptress titillated her man with plunging necklines, veiled eyes and a come-hither walk. Fashion encouraged women to become chameleon-like characters, shifting effortlessly from wholesome homemaker to wanton lover with a change of clothes.[21]

Christian Dior's 'New Look', with its soft, rounded shoulders, nipped-in waist, and full, long skirts, contrasted sharply with the Utility styles of wartime, with their square shoulders and short, straight skirts. Previously, 'the silhouette was unadorned, a plain rectangle of clothing consisting of box-shaped jacket with padded shoulders and a narrow skirt. Even summer dresses and blouses had shoulder pads and conformed to the severity of outline demanded by wartime deprivation. Cecil Beaton said at the time that women's fashions were going through the Beau Brummel stage and were learning the restraint of men's taste.'[22] But a few years later: 'Paris clothes were conspicuously impractical for working women. Boned and strapless "self-supporting" bodices made it difficult to bend and corsets pinched the waist'.[23] However, fashion manufacturers were opposed to this change; on 17 March 1948, a delegation representing three hundred dress firms went to Harold Wilson (then head of the Board of Trade) and asked for a ban on long hemlines.[24] The new style was not in their interests because it meant less product for their investment of materials and labour.

Utility styles not only survived, but were translated and developed into the basis of a whole range of practical styles. The wartime shirtwaister, for example, flourished in the form of 1950s dresses which became almost symbolic of the housewife, and were invariably used to dress her in advertisements for household goods. Another example is the ubiquitous multi-purpose suit, often worn with sturdy shoes for women on their feet all day. Clothing, accessories and dress fabrics compatible with this aesthetic had been included in the Britain Can Make It exhibition in 1946, and due to the interest shown in the womenswear, a separate catalogue was produced to itemise the garments on display. Included in this was a 'typically British' sports outfit consisting of a beaver corduroy jacket and herringbone tweed skirt – the 'country look'. The hard-wearing materials and sensible accessories conveniently lent themselves to shopping as well as to rural walks. Variations on the Utility suit represented to the design establishment an image of 'modern' femininity, that is, the sensible and restrained attributes of the housewife. The look *signifies* restraint, rather than being necessarily functional (wartime clothing which *was* much more practical than the Utility suit, such as the siren suit and the turban, became fashion statements and were later translated into evening wear), but the utility image continued to represent an ideal to those professionals whose task it was to regulate and socialise consumption.

Fashion experts tended to preach the same virtues of rationality and aestheticism which were endorsed by the design establishment. The designs of couturiers such as Hardy Amies (known for reworking English classics rather than for the frivolous or ephemeral) were featured in women's weeklies, usually in the form of special patterns adapted from or inspired by them. These patterns were supplemented by articles on how to use line and colour in developing 'fashion sense'. In *Woman*, 9 September 1953, Amies draws parallels between dressing and cooking. So the promotions of the latest fashions were accompanied by advice and instruction which stressed the rules and regulations of 'good taste'. A certain amount of glamour was acceptable in its place, but only as a pleasing contrast to the rule of restraint.

As the consumers of fashion goods then, working-class women were being educated in the skills of 'good taste' (restraint, practicality, etc.) in much the same way as they were being trained as home-managers in order to consume domestic goods. But at the same time, feminine glamour was being promoted as a feature of high fashion. This glamour was not condemned unequivocally by all constituencies of the design profession (although the New Look was reviled by many as unpatriotic and irresponsible) but rather it was accepted as a separate but complementary look, which could exist alongside Utility styles as long as it was not adopted for 'inappropriate' situations. However, this attempt to construct clear distinctions between the utilitarian/practical and the decorative/glamorous and to impose codes of dress as a consequence, inadvertently encouraged consumers to acquire knowledges and competences which enabled them to be 'chameleon-like' in the production of these different femininities. I would argue that these competences make their 'improper' appropriation of fashion goods inevitable, and resulted in the sampling and mixing of different styles which ultimately characterised popular fashion of the 1950s.

Gendered consumption

Since it was working-class women who were the target of the consumption-regulation programme, it is necessary to consider how a specifically feminine relationship with goods may have enabled them to continue to use clothing in symbolic/emotional (rather than utilitarian/rational) ways, despite the best efforts of the design profession. Since designers discouraged identification with and emotional investment in objects, and encouraged 'objective' or 'disinterested' relationships with goods instead, traditionally 'feminine' ways of relating to goods were considered 'vulgar' or 'improper'. It can be argued, however, that the 'female gaze' enabled women to respond enthusiastically to modern design, without surrendering this ability to identify with objects.

I have argued elsewhere that to identify narcissistically with objects does not preclude the ability to fetishise or objectify them from a voyeuristic position.[25] Rather than seeing narcissism and exhibitionism as inevitably feminine, and fetishism and voyeurism as inevitably masculine, as many theorists have tended to do, it has to be recognised that these tendencies are interdependent, albeit differently for women and men. In order for women to become skilled in inviting the gaze, they have had to acquire knowledges and competences which enable them to discriminate between other objects, with which to adorn themselves and their surroundings. In order to express preferences, women have had to become subjects of the (female) gaze, while at the same time identifying with the objects of that gaze (goods), in order to fulfil a role as object of the male gaze. What has been referred to as 'masquerade' evokes very well this feminine fusion of voyeurism and exhibitionism. 'Masquerade' implies an acting out of the images of femininity, for which is required an active gaze to decode, utilise and identify with those images, while at the same time constructing a self-image which is dependent on the gaze of the other. In this sense, womanliness, or femininity, is a 'simulation', a demonstration of the representations of women – a 'masquerade', acted out by the female viewer. Although the design profession encouraged a pure and detached relationship with goods, the female gaze enabled objectification without sacrificing identification, therefore women were able to consume designed goods 'improperly', i.e. in ways not anticipated or understood by designers. The collective production of meanings takes place *within* consumer groups at specific moments; indeed, this is enabled and encouraged by a mass-market system. For example, 'masquerade' is a simulation of femininity, and as such confirms the existence of a feminine cultural code, or shared meanings for women as markets for fashion and beauty goods.

Popular fashion

The consumer's investment in a style may or may not involve a transformation of the fashion commodity's appearance, but any reworkings of the object are not simply a manipulation of a visual language. They are social acts in which the object only has meaning in relation to the circumstances surrounding them. A 'reproductive trans-formation' takes place, regardless of how much or how little the consumer alters the appearance of the object. The consumer determines the meaning of the fashion commodity through a redefinition of use-values which brings it within the circum-stances of a particular mode of life, and of a cultural code which is specific to a target market (e.g. working-class women).

. . . [I]f we approach fashion as a discursive articulation of class differences, a practice through which class relations, and therefore economic conditions, are actu-ally (re)produced, we can approach both the similarities and differences between high fashion and popular fashion quite differently. Both the changes and non-changes which take place in the series of mediations between production and consumption involve a number of investments in the style. The mass-market fashion system enables the consumer to appropriate fashionable style by altering and transforming them, in the process of 'copying' them. It is in the mixing together of copied elements with other 'incompatible' elements that the distinctions and oppositions, which the designers hold sacred, are broken down. In the consumption of fashion goods, working-class women collectively simulate class differences.

1950s fashions were 'improperly' consumed by working-class women, in the sense that they were used to satisfy needs other than those which had been assumed by the fashion industry and the design profession. For example, the two comple-mentary styles – 'Utility' and the 'New Look' – which 'express' the post-war ideologies of femininity so well, but which were clearly distinguished by designers as the 'functional' and the 'decorative', were sampled and mixed together by the consumer to create fashions which depended on class-specific consumer skills for their meaning.

A mass-market fashion system ensures that the diffusion of styles takes place *within* groups (rather than across class distinctions), so styles need not be adopted in the same way by different consumer groups. Indeed, the system itself encourages different forms of adoption. As I have already argued, differences in price, make, and retailer ensures this. But this does not mean that popular versions are merely cheaper or lower-quality copies of design-originals. If this were the case, popular fashion would resemble couture much more closely than it does. In the late 1940s and early 1950s, there were mass-produced copies of the New Look which were fairly 'accurate' . . . but it seems (from looking at my family album photographs) that these 'faithful' copies did not become widely popular among working-class women, while more 'hybrid' versions did. Working-class women did not keep away from the frivolous or the impractical, even at work; instead it was sampled and re-mixed with the comfortable and the serviceable, rather than kept separate and used on 'decorative' occasions only, as advised by fashion experts.

There were many professional designers who were outraged by the 'New Look', and who condemned it either as an antithesis to modernism and therefore regressive, or as a shameful indulgence in the face of economic restrictions. To an

extent then, its popularity amongst middle-class women, or amongst women generally, can be read as a 'rebellious' or 'subversive' use of fashion, not dissimilar to that
usually ascribed to youth subcultures. But there were those factions of the design
profession who regarded it as a distinct but complementary aspect of modern
femininity, which could exist alongside, and enhance, the dutiful housewife look. If
women used fashion to resist the dominant ideologies of femininity then, it was
through the 'improper' consumption, or appropriation, of the New Look. I will try
to show that working-class women did do this, not in an act of rebellion, but in an
investment of class-specific consumer skills.

If we take the cotton shirtwaist and the all-purpose suit as examples of 1950s
Utility (since these were routinely identified with the practical housewife image),
and the New Look cocktail dress . . . as an example of its complementary glamorous opposite, we can see that working-class women did not keep these styles
distinct and separate. They combined the practical and the glamorous in a range of
hybrid styles, completely 'ruining' the achievements of designers in their creation
of 'complementary' looks. Popular notions of the New Look . . . were quite different from both couture and 'accurate' (department store) mass-produced
versions. . . .

Popular fashion mixed the glamorous and the practical, fused function and
meaning (objectification and identification), by incorporating elements from styles
which designers assumed would take their meaning from the clear distinctions
between them. This can be read as a challenge to the dichotomy separating 'housewife' (functional woman) and sex object (decorative woman). But it can also be seen
as a complete redefinition of the values of the clothes, an insistence on the prerogative to use clothes in meaning-making practices which are dependent on class-
specific skills. Through fashion, as with homemaking, women invited the gaze of the
other, in that they identified with commodities, that is, that were not 'disinterested',
but conspicuously narcissistic, using goods to signify their economic and social
position rather than to fulfil needs presumed by designers.

'Good taste' versus design-led marketing

The tensions between attempts to 'train' affluence and regulate consumption (in
which the meaningfulness of goods is disavowed), and mass-marketing (which relies
precisely on the meaningfulness of commodities), creates an insoluble conflict
between design establishment and manufacturing/marketing industries. The
attempt to construct markets, through the use of design, provides consumers with
skills with which to counter the purism of the design establishment. The contradiction between design-led marketing and 'good taste' has been particularly marked in
Britain, where an aristocratic distaste for industrial culture has a long history.[26]
Attempts to renegotiate the relationships between designers, manufacturers, advertisers, and retailers, in the pursuit of a rational system of production and consumption, far from determining the meanings of goods, has actually ensured that the
struggles over meanings, and the constant reappropriation of goods by consumers,
has persisted.

As consumers, working-class women were able to articulate their own specific tastes and preferences, by using the cultural codes of the mass-market fashion system.

Notes and references

1 Dick Hebdige, *Subculture: The Meaning of Style*, London, 1979.
2 Mica Nava, 'Consumerism and its Contradictions', *Cultural Studies* vol. I, no. 2, 1987.
3 Georg Simmel, 'Fashion', (originally published in 1904) in Gordon Wills and David Midgley (eds), *Fashion Marketing*, London, 1973.
4 Charles King. 'A Rebuttal of the Trickle Down Theory', in Wills and Midgley, op. cit., p. 216.
5 Thorstein Veblen, '*The Theory of Conspicuous Consumption*', quoted in Elizabeth Wilson, *Adorned in Dreams*, London, 1985.
6 J. Clarke and C. Critcher, *The Devil Makes Work* – Leisure in Capitalist Britain, London, 1985, pp. 82, 189.
7 King, in Wills and Midgley, op. cit.
8 Herbert Blumer, 'Fashion: From Class Differentiation to Collective Selection', in Wills and Midgley, op. cit.
9 James Carman, 'The Fate of Fashion Cycles in our Modern Society', in Wills and Midgley, op. cit., p. 135.
10 Bernard Barber and Lyle Lobel, 'Fashion in Women's Clothes and the American Social System', in Wills and Midgley, op. cit., p. 362.
11 Ibid., p. 363.
12 Clarke and Critcher, op. cit., p. 96.
13 Ingrid Brenninkmeyer, 'The Diffusion of Fashion', in Wills and Midgley, op. cit., p. 271.
14 Prudence Glynn, *In Fashion*, London, 1978, p. 186.
15 Jane Dorner, *Fashion in the Forties and Fifties*, London, 1975, p. 53.
16 Erica Carter, 'Alice in Consumer Wonderland', in Angela McRobbie and Mica Nava (eds), *Gender and Generation*, London, 1984, pp. 200, 207.
17 Elizabeth Wilson and Lou Taylor, *Through the Looking Glass*, London, 1989.
18 Barry Curtis, 'One Long Continuous Story', *Block*, no. 11, Winter 1985/6, p. 51.
19 Glynn, op. cit., p. 187.
20 Penny Sparke, *An Introduction to Design and Culture*, London, 1986, p. 65.
21 Barbara Schreier, *Mystique and Identity: Women's Fashions of the 1950s*, Chrysler Museum, New York, 1984, p. 13.
22 Dorner, op. cit., p. 7.
23 Nicholas Drake, *The Fifties in Vogue*, London, 1987, p. 13.
24 Pearson Phillips, 'The New Look', in Sissons and French (eds), *The Age of Austerity*, Oxford, 1963.
25 Angela Partington, 'The Gendered Gaze', in Nancy Honey (ed.), *Woman To Woman*, 1990.
26 Dick Hebdige, 'Towards a Cartography of Taste', *Block*, no. 4, 1981.

Chapter 20

Herbert Blumer

FASHION
From class differentiation to collective selection

Deficiencies of fashion as a sociological concept

THIS PAPER IS AN INVITATION to sociologists to take seriously the topic of fashion. Only a handful of scholars, such as Simmel (1904), Sapir (1931), and the Langs (1961), have given more than casual concern to the topic. Their individual analyses of it, while illuminating in several respects, have been limited in scope, and within the chosen limits very sketchy. The treatment of the topic by sociologists in general, such as we find it in textbooks and in occasional pieces of scholarly writing, is even more lacking in substance. The major deficiencies in the conventional sociological treatment are easily noted – a failure to observe and appreciate the wide range of operation of fashion; a false assumption that fashion has only trivial or peripheral significance; a mistaken idea that fashion falls in the area of the abnormal and irrational and thus is out of the mainstream of human group life; and, finally, a misunderstanding of the nature of fashion.

Fashion restricted to adornment

Similar to scholars in general who have shown some concern with the topic, sociologists are disposed to identify fashion exclusively or primarily with the area of costume and adornment. While occasional references may be made to its play in other areas, such casual references do not give a proper picture of the extent of its operation. Yet, to a discerning eye fashion is readily seen to operate in many diverse areas of human group life, especially so in modern times. It is easily observable in the realm of the pure and applied arts, such as painting, sculpture, music, drama, architecture, dancing, and household decoration. Its presence is very obvious in the area of entertainment and amusement. There is plenty of evidence to show its play in the field of medicine. Many of us are familiar with its operation in fields of industry, especially that of business management. It even touches such a relative sacred area as that of mortuary practice. Many scholars have noted its operation in the field of literature. Its presence can be seen in the history of modern philosophy. It can be observed at work in the realm of political doctrine. And – perhaps to the surprise of many – it is unquestionably at work in the field of science. That this is true of the social and psychological sciences is perhaps more readily apparent. But we have also to note, as several reputable and qualified scholars have done, that fashion appears in such redoubtable areas as physical and biological science and mathematics. The domain in which fashion operates is very extensive, indeed. To limit it to, or to center it in, the field of costume and adornment is to have a very inadequate idea of the scope of its occurrence.

Fashion as socially inconsequential

This extensive range of fashion should, in itself, lead scholars to question their implicit belief that fashion is a peripheral and relatively inconsequential social happening. To the contrary, fashion may influence vitally the central content of any field in which it operates. For example, the styles in art, the themes and styles in literature, the forms and themes in entertainment, the perspectives in philosophy, the practices in business, and the preoccupations in science may be affected profoundly by fashion. These are not peripheral matters. In addition, the nature of the control wielded by fashion shows that its touch is not light. Where fashion operates it assumes an imperative position. It sets sanctions of what is to be done, it is conspicuously indifferent to criticism, it demands adherence, and it by-passes as oddities and misfits those who fail to abide by it. This grip which it exercises over its area of operation does not bespeak an inconsequential mechanism.

Fashion as aberrant and irrational

The third deficiency, as mentioned, is to view fashion as an aberrant and irrational social happening, akin to a craze or mania. Presumably, this ill-considered view of fashion has arisen from considerations which suggest that fashion is bizarre and frivolous, that it is fickle, that it arises in response to irrational status anxieties, and that people are swept into conforming to it despite their better judgment. It is easy to form such impressions. For one thing, past fashions usually seem odd and frequently ludicrous to the contemporary eye. Next, they rarely seem to make sense in terms of utility or rational purpose; they seem much more to express the play of fancy and caprice. Further, following the classic analysis made by Simmel, fashion seems to represent a kind of anxious effort of elite groups to set themselves apart by introducing trivial and ephemeral demarcating insignia, with a corresponding strained effort by non-elite classes to make a spurious identification of themselves with upper classes by adopting these insignia. Finally, since fashion despite its seeming frivolous content sweeps multitudes of people into its fold, it is regarded as a form of collective craziness.

Understanding the character of fashion

Nevertheless, to view fashion as an irrational, aberrant, and craze-like social happening is to grievously misunderstand it. On the *individual side*, the adoption of what is fashionable is by and large a very calculating act. The fashion conscious person is usually quite careful and discerning in his effort to identify the fashion in order to make sure that he is 'in style'; the fashion does not appear to him as frivolous. In turn, the person who is coerced into adopting the fashion contrary to his wishes does so deliberately and not irrationally. Finally, the person who unwittingly follows a fashion does so because of a limitation of choice rather than as an impulsive expression of aroused emotions or inner anxiety. The bulk of evidence gives no support to the contention that individuals who adopt fashion are caught up in the spirit of a craze. Their behavior is no more irrational or excited – and probably less so – than that of voters casting political ballots. On its *collective side*, fashion does not fit any better the pattern of a craze. The mechanisms of interaction are not those of circular transmission of aroused feelings, or of heightened suggestibility, or of fixed preoccupation with a gripping event. While people may become excited over a fashion they respond primarily to its character of propriety and social distinction; these are tempering guides. Fashion has respectability; it carries the stamp of approval of an elite – an elite that is recognized to be sophisticated and believed to be wise in the given area of endeavor. It is this endorsement which undergirds fashion – rather than the emotional interaction which is typical of crazes. Fashion has, to be true, an irrational, or better 'non-rational,' dimension which we shall consider later, but this dimension does not make it into a craze or mania.

The observations that fashion operates over wide areas of human endeavor, that it is not aberrant and craze-like, and that it is not peripheral and inconsequential merely correct false pictures of it. They do little to identify its nature and mode of operation. It is to this identification that I now wish to turn.

Simmel: fashion as class differentiation

Let me use as the starting point of the discussion the analysis of fashion made some sixty years ago by Georg Simmel. His analysis, without question, has set the character of what little solid sociological thought is to be found on the topic. His thesis was essentially simple. For him, fashion arose as a form of class differentiation in a relatively open class society. In such a society the elite class seeks to set itself apart by observable marks or insignia, such as distinctive forms of dress. However, members of immediately subjacent classes adopt these insignia as a means of satisfying their striving to identify with a superior status. They, in turn, are copied by members of classes beneath them. In this way, the distinguishing insignia of the elite class filter down through the class pyramid. In this process, however, the elite class loses these marks of separate identity. It is led, accordingly, to devise new distinguishing insignia which, again, are copied by the classes below, thus repeating the cycle. This, for Simmel, was the nature of fashion and the mechanism of its operation. Fashion was thought to arise in the form of styles which demarcate an elite group. These styles automatically acquire prestige in the eyes of those who wish to emulate the elite group and are copied by them, thus forcing the elite group to devise new distinctive marks of their superior status. Fashion is thus caught up in an incessant and recurrent process of innovation and emulation. A fashion, once started marches relentlessly to its doom; on its heels treads a new fashion destined to the same fate; and so on ad infinitum. This sets the fundamental character of the fashion process.

There are several features of Simmel's analysis which are admittedly of high merit. One of them was to point out that fashion requires a certain type of society in which to take place. Another was to highlight the importance of prestige in the operation of fashion. And another, of particular significance, was to stress that the essence of fashion lies in a process of change – a process that is natural and indigenous and not unusual and aberrant. Yet, despite the fact that his analysis still remains the best in the published literature, it failed to catch the character of fashion as a social happening. It is largely a parochial treatment, quite well suited to fashion in dress in the seventeenth, eighteenth, and nineteenth century Europe with its particular class structure. But it does not fit the operation of fashion in our contemporary epoch with its many diverse fields and its emphasis on modernity. Its shortcomings will be apparent, I think, in the light of the following analysis.

Modernity and the selection process

Some years ago I had the opportunity to study rather extensively and at first hand the women's fashion industry in Paris. There were three matters in particular which I observed which seem to me to provide the clues for an understanding of fashion in general. I wish to discuss each of them briefly and indicate their significance.

First, I was forcibly impressed by the fact that the setting or determination of fashion takes place actually through an intense process of selection. At a seasonal opening of a major Parisian fashion house there may be presented a hundred or more designs of women's evening wear before an audience of from one to two hundred buyers. The managerial corps of the fashion house is able to indicate a group of about thirty designs of the entire lot, inside of which will fall the small number, usually about six to eight designs, that are chosen by the buyers; but the managerial staff is typically unable to predict this small number on which the choices converge. Now, these choices are made by the buyers – a highly competitive and secretive lot – independently of each other and without knowledge of each other's selections. Why should their choices converge on a few designs as they do? When the buyers were asked why they chose one dress in preference to another – between which my inexperienced eye could see no appreciable difference – the typical, honest, yet largely uninformative answer was that the dress was 'stunning.'

Inquiry into the reasons for the similarity in the buyers' choices led me to a second observation, namely, that the buyers were immersed in and preoccupied with a remarkably common world of intense stimulation. It was a world of lively discussion of what was happening in women's fashion, of fervent reading of fashion publications, and of close observation of one another's lines of products. And, above all, it was a world of close concern with the women's dress market, with the prevailing tastes and prospective tastes of the consuming public in the area of dress. It became vividly clear to me that by virtue of their intense immersion in this world the buyers came to develop common sensitivities and similar appreciations. To use an old but valuable psychological term, they developed a common 'apperception mass' which sharpened and directed their feelings of discrimination, which guided and sensitized their perceptions, and which channeled their judgments and choices. This explains, I am convinced, why the buyers, independently of each other, made such amazingly identical choices at the fashion openings. This observation also underlines a point of the greatest importance, namely, that the buyers became the unwitting surrogates of the fashion public. Their success, indeed their vocational fate, depended on their ability to sense the direction of taste in this public.

The third observation which I made pertained to the dress designers – those who created the new styles. They devised the various designs between which the buyers were ultimately to make the choices, and their natural concern was to be successful in gaining adoption of their creations. There were three lines of pre-occupation from which they derived their ideas. One was to pour over old plates of former fashions and depictions of costumes of far-off peoples. A second was to brood and reflect over current and recent styles. The third, and most important, was to develop an intimate familiarity with the most recent expressions of modernity as these were to be seen in such areas as the fine arts, recent literature, political debates and happenings, and discourse in the sophisticated world. The dress designers were engaged in translating themes from these areas and media into dress designs. The designers were attuned to an impressive degree to modern developments and were seeking to capture and express in dress design the spirit of such development. I think that this explains why the dress designers – again a competitive and secretive group, working apart from each other in a large number of different fashion houses – create independently of each other such remarkably similar designs. They pick up ideas of the past, but always through the filter of the present; they are guided and constrained by the immediate styles in dress, particularly the direction of such styles over the recent span of a few years; but above all, they are seeking to catch the proximate future as it is revealed in modern developments.

Taken together, these three observations which I have sketched in a most minimal form outline what is significant in the case of fashion in the women's dress industry. They indicate that the fashion is set through a process of free selection from among a large number of competing models; that the creators of the models are seeking to catch and give expression to what we may call the direction of modernity; and that the buyers, who through their choices set the fashion, are acting as the unwitting agents of a fashion consuming public whose incipient tastes the buyers are seeking to anticipate. In this paper I shall not deal with what is probably the most interesting and certainly the most obscure aspect of the entire relationship, namely, the relation between, on one hand, the expressions of modernity to which the dress designers are so responsive and, on the other hand, the incipient and inarticulate tastes which are taking shape in the fashion consuming public. Certainly, the two come together in the styles which are chosen and, in so doing, lay down the lines along which modern life in this area moves. I regard this line of relationship as constituting one of the most significant mechanisms in the shaping of our modern world, but I shall not undertake analysis of it in this paper.

Fashion and the elite

The brief account which I have given of the setting of fashion in the women's wear industry permits one to return to Simmel's classic analysis and pinpoint more precisely its shortcomings. His scheme elevates the prestige of the elite to the position of major importance in the operation of fashion – styles come into fashion because of the stamp of distinction conferred on them by the elite. I think this view misses almost completely what is central to fashion, namely, *to be in fashion*. It is not the prestige of the elite which makes the design fashionable but, instead, it is the suitability or potential fashionableness of the design which allows the prestige of the elite to be attached to it. The design has to correspond to the direction of incipient taste of the fashion consuming public. The prestige of the elite affects but does not control the direction of this incipient taste. We have here a case of the fashion mechanism transcending and embracing the prestige of the elite group rather than stemming from that prestige.

There are a number of lines of evidence which I think clearly establish this to be the case. First, we should note that members of the elite – and I am still speaking of the elite in the realm of women's dress – are themselves as interested as anyone to be in fashion. Anyone familiar with them is acutely aware of their sensitivity in this regard, their wish not to be out of step with fashion, and indeed their wish to be in the vanguard of proper fashion. They are caught in the need of responding to the direction of fashion rather than of occupying the privileged position of setting that direction. Second, as explained, the fashion-adopting actions of the elite take place in a context of competing models, each with its own source of prestige. Not all prestigeful persons are innovators – and innovators are not necessarily persons with the highest prestige. The elite, itself, has to select between models proposed by innovators; and their choice is not determined by the relative prestige of the innovators. As history shows abundantly, in the competitive process fashion readily ignores persons with the highest prestige and, indeed, by-passes acknowledged 'leaders' time after time. A further line of evidence is just as telling, namely, the interesting instances of failure to control the direction of fashion despite effective marshalling of the sources of prestige. An outstanding example was the effort in 1922 to check and reverse the trend toward shorter skirts which had started in 1919 to the dismay of clothing manufacturers. These manufacturers enlisted the cooperation of the heads of fashion houses, fashion magazines, fashion commentators, actresses, and acknowledged fashion leaders in an extensive, well organized and amply financed campaign to reverse the trend. The important oracles of fashion declared that long dresses were returning, models of long dresses were presented in numbers at the seasonal openings, actresses wore them on the stage, and manikins paraded them at the fashionable meeting places. Yet, despite this effective marshalling of all significant sources of prestige, the campaign was a marked failure; the trend toward shorter skirts, after a slight interruption, continued until 1929 when a rather abrupt change to long dresses took place. Such instances – and there have been others – provide further indication that there is much more to the fashion mechanism than the exercise of prestige. Fashion appears much more as a collective groping for the proximate future than a channeled movement laid down by prestigeful figures.

Collective selection replaces class differentiation

These observations require us to put Simmel's treatment in a markedly different perspective, certainly as applied to fashion in our modern epoch. The efforts of an elite class to set itself apart in appearance takes place inside of the movement of fashion instead of being its cause. The prestige of elite groups, in place of setting the direction of the fashion movement is effective only to the extent to which they are recognized as representing and portraying the movement. The people in other classes who consciously follow the fashion do so because it is the fashion and not because of the separate prestige of the elite group. The fashion dies not because it has been discarded by the elite group but because it gives way to a new model more consonant with developing taste. *The fashion mechanism appears not in response to a need of class differentiation and class emulation but in response to a wish to be in fashion, to be abreast of what has good standing, to express new tastes which are emerging in a changing world.* These are the changes that seem to be called for in Simmel's formulation. They are fundamental changes. They shift fashion *from* the fields of *class differentiation* to the area of *collective selection* and center its mechanism in the process of such selection. This process of collective selection represents an effort to choose from among competing styles or models those which match developing tastes, those which 'click,' or those which – to revert to my friends, the buyers – 'are stunning.' The fact that this process of collective selection is mysterious – it is mysterious because we do not understand it – does not contradict in any way that it takes place.

Features of the fashion mechanism

To view the fashion mechanism as a continuing process of collective selection from among competing models yields a markedly different picture from that given by conventional sociological analysis of fashion. It calls attention to the fact that those implicated in fashion – innovators, 'leaders,' followers, and participants – are parts of a collective process that responds to changes in taste and sensitivity. In a legitimate sense, the movement of fashion represents a reaching out for new models which will answer to as yet indistinct and inarticulate newer tastes. The transformation of taste, of collective taste, results without question from the diversity of experience that occurs in social interaction in a complex moving world. It leads, in turn, to an unwitting groping for suitable forms of expression, in an effort to move in a direction which is consonant with the movement of modern life in general. It is perhaps unnecessary to add that we know very little indeed about this area of transformation of collective taste. Despite its unquestioned importance it has been scarcely noted, much less studied. Sociologists are conspicuously ignorant of it and indifferent to it.

Before leaving the discussion of fashion in the area of conspicuous appearance (such as dress, adornment, or mannerism), it is desirable to note and consider briefly several important features of the fashion mechanism, namely, its historical continuity, its modernity, the role of collective taste in its operation, and the psychological motives which are alleged to account for it.

Historical continuity

The history of fashion shows clearly that new fashions are related to, and grow out of, their immediate predecessors. This is one of the fundamental ways in which fashion differs from fads. Fads have no line of historical continuity; each springs up independently of a forerunner and gives rise to no successor. In the case of fashion, fashion innovators always have to consider the prevailing fashion, if for no other reason than to depart from it or to elaborate on it. The result is a line of continuity. Typically, although not universally, the line of continuity has the character of a cultural drift, expressing itself in what we customarily term a 'fashion trend.' Fashion trends are a highly important yet a much neglected object of study. They signify a convergence and marshalling of collective taste in a given direction and thus pertain to one of the most significant yet obscure features in group life. The terminal points of fashion trends are of special interest. Sometimes they are set by the nature of the medium (there is a point beyond which the skirt cannot be lengthened or shortened [see Richardson and Kroeber, 1947; Young, 1937]); sometimes they seem to represent an exhaustion of the logical possibilities of the medium; but frequently they signify a relatively abrupt shift in interests and taste. The terminal points are marked particularly by a much wider latitude of experimentation in the new fashion models that are advanced for adoption; at such points the fashion mechanism particularly reveals the groping character of collective choice to set itself on a new course. If it be true, as I propose to explain later, that the fashion mechanism is woven deeply into the texture of modern life, the study of fashion in its aspects of continuity, trends, and cycles would be highly important and rewarding.

Modernity

The feature of 'modernity' in fashion is especially significant. Fashion is always modern; it always seeks to keep abreast of the times. It is sensitive to the movement of current developments as they take place in its own field, in adjacent fields, and in the larger social world. Thus, in women's dress, fashion is responsive to its own trend, to developments in fabrics and ornamentation, to developments in the fine arts, to exciting events that catch public attention such as the discovery of the tomb of Tutankhamen, to political happenings, and to major social shifts such as the emancipation of women or the rise of the cult of youth. Fashion seems to sift out of these diverse sources of happenings a set of obscure guides which bring it into line with the general or over-all direction of modernity itself. This responsiveness in its more extended from seems to be the chief factor in formation of what we speak of as a 'spirit of the times' or a *zeitgeist*.

Collective taste

Since the idea of 'collective taste' is given such an important position in my analysis of the fashion mechanism, the idea warrants further clarification and explanation. I am taking the liberty of quoting my remarks as they appear in the article on 'Fashion' in the new *International Encyclopedia of the Social Sciences* V (1968: 341–5).

. . . It represents an organic sensitivity to objects of social experience, as when we say that 'vulgar comedy does not suit our taste' or that 'they have a taste for orderly procedure.' Taste has a tri-fold character – it is like an appetite in seeking positive satisfaction; it operates as a sensitive selector, giving a basis for acceptance or rejection; and it is a formative agent, guiding the development of lines of action and shaping objects to meet its demands. Thus, it appears as a subjective mechanism, giving orientation to individuals, structuring activity and moulding the world of experience. Tastes are themselves a product of experience; they usually develop from an initial state of vagueness to a state of refinement and stability, but once formed they may decay and disintegrate. They are formed in the context of social interaction, responding to the definitions and affirmations given by others. People thrown into areas of common interaction and having similar runs of experience develop common tastes. The fashion process involves both a formation and an expression of collective taste in the given area of fashion. Initially, the taste is a loose fusion of vague inclinations and dissatisfactions that are aroused by new experiences in the field of fashion and in the larger surrounding world. In this initial state, collective taste is amorphous, inarticulate, vaguely poised, and awaiting specific direction. Through models and proposals, fashion innovators sketch out possible lines along which the incipient taste may gain objective expression and take definite form. Collective taste is an active force in the ensuing process of selection, setting limits and providing guidance; yet, at the same time it undergoes refinement and organization through its attachment to, and embodiment in, specific social forms. The origin, formation, and careers of collective taste constitute the huge problematic area in fashion. Major advancement in our knowledge of the fashion mechanism depends on the charting of this area. . . .

Psychological motives

Now, a word with regard to psychological interpretations of fashion. Scholars, by and large, have sought to account for fashion in terms of psychological motives. A perusal of the literature will show an assortment of different feelings and impulses which have been picked out to explain the occurrence of fashion. Some students ascribe fashion to efforts to escape from boredom or ennui, especially among members of the leisure class. Some treat fashion as arising from playful and whimsical impulses to enliven the routines of life with zest. Some regard it as due to a spirit of adventure which impels individuals to rebel against the confinement of prevailing social forms. Some see fashion as a symbolic expression of hidden sexual interests. Most striking is the view expressed by Sapir in his article on 'Fashion' in the first edition of the *Encyclopedia of the Social Sciences* VI (1931: 139–141); Sapir held that fashion results from an effort to increase the attractiveness of the self, especially under conditions which impair the integrity of the ego; the sense of oneself is regained and heightened through novel yet socially sanctioned departures from prevailing social forms. Finally, some scholars trace fashion to desires for personal prestige or notoriety.

Such psychological explanations, either singly or collectively, fail to account for fashion; they do not explain why or how the various feelings or motives give rise to a fashion process. Such feelings are presumably present and in operation in all human societies; yet there are many societies in which fashion is not to be found. Further, such feelings may take various forms of expression which have no relation to a fashion process. We are given no explanation of why the feelings should lead to the formation of fashion in place of taking other channels of expression available to them. The psychological schemes fail to come to grips with the collective process which constitutes fashion – the emergence of new models in an area of changing experience, the differential attention given them, the interaction which leads to a focusing of collective choice on one of them, the social endorsement of it as proper, and the powerful control which this endorsement yields. Undoubtedly, the various feelings and impulses specified by psychologists operate within the fashion process – just as they operate within non-fashion areas of group life. But their operation within fashion does not account for fashion. Instead, their operation presupposes the existence of the fashion process as one of the media for their play.

The foregoing discussion indicates, I trust, the inadequacy of conventional sociological and psychological schemes to explain the nature of fashion. Both sets of schemes fail to perceive fashion as the process of collective selection that it is. The schemes do not identify the nature of the social setting in which fashion arises nor do they catch or treat the mechanism by which fashion operates. The result is that students fail to see the scope and manner of its operation and to appreciate the vital role which it plays in modern group life. In the interest of presenting a clearer picture of these matters, I wish to amplify the sketch of fashion as given above in order to show more clearly its broad generic character.

Generic character of fashion

It is necessary, first of all, to insist that fashion is not confined to those areas, such as women's apparel, in which fashion is institutionalized and professionally exploited under conditions of intense competition. As mentioned earlier, it is found in operation in a wide variety and increasing number of fields which shun deliberate or intentional concern with fashion. In such fields, fashion occurs almost always without awareness on the part of those who are caught in its operation. What may be primarily response to fashion is seen and interpreted in other ways – chiefly as doing what is believed to be superior practice. The prevalence of such unwitting deception can be considerable. The basic mechanism of fashion which comes to such a clear, almost pure, form in women's dress is clouded or concealed in other fields but is none the less operative. Let me approach a consideration of this matter by outlining the six essential conditions under which fashion presumably comes into play.

Essential conditions of its appearance

First, the area in which fashion operates must be one that is involved in a movement of change, with people ready to revise or discard old practices, beliefs, and attachments, and poised to adopt new social forms; there must be this thrust into the future. If the area is securely established, as in the domain of the sacred, there will be no fashion. Fashion presupposes that the area is in passage, responding to changes taking place in a surrounding world, and oriented to keeping abreast of new developments. The area is marked by a new psychological perspective which places a premium on being 'up to date' and which implies a readiness to denigrate given older forms of life as being outmoded. Above all, the changing character of the area must gain expression or reflection in changes in that subjective orientation which I have spoken of under the term, 'taste.'

A *second* condition is that the area must be open to the recurrent presentation of models or proposals of new social forms. These models, depending on the given areas of fashion, may cover such diverse things as points of view, doctrines, lines of preoccupation, themes, practices, and use of artifacts. In a given area of fashion, these models differ from each other and of course from the prevailing social forms. Each of them is metaphorically a claimant for adoption. Thus their presence introduces a competitive situation and sets the stage for selection between them.

Third, there must be a relatively free opportunity for choice between the models. This implies that the models must be open, so to speak, to observation and that facilities and means must be available for their adoption. If the presentation of new models is prevented the fashion process will not get under way. Further, a severe limitation in the wherewithal needed to adopt models (such as necessary wealth, intellectual sophistication, refined skill, or a esthetic sensitivity) curtails the initiation of the fashion process.

Fashion is not guided by utilitarian or rational considerations. This points to a *fourth* condition essential to its operation, namely, that the pretended merit or value of the competing models cannot be demonstrated through open and decisive test. Where choices can be made between rival models on the basis of objective and effective test, there is no place for fashion. It is for this reason that fashion does not take root in those areas of utility, technology, or science where asserted claims can be brought before the bar of demonstrable proof. In contrast, the absence of means for testing effectively the relative merit of competing models opens the door to other considerations in making choices between them. This kind of situation is essential to the play of fashion.

A *fifth* condition for fashion is the presence of prestige figures who espouse one or another of the competing models. The prestige of such persons must be such that they are acknowledged as qualified to pass judgment on the value or suitability of the rival models. If they are so regarded their choice carries weight as an assurance or endorsement of the superiority or propriety of a given model. A combination of such prestigeful figures, espousing the same model, enhances the likelihood of adoption of the model.

A *sixth* and final condition is that the area must be open to the emergence of new interests and dispositions in response to (a) the impact of outside events, (b) the introduction of new participants into the area, and (c) changes in inner social interaction. This condition is chiefly responsible for the shifting of taste and the redirection of collective choice which together constitute the lifeline of fashion.

If the above six conditions are met, I believe that one will always find fashion to be in play. People in the area will be found to be converging their choices on models and shifting this convergence over time. The convergence of choice occurs not because of the intrinsic merit or demonstrated validity of the selected models but because of the appearance of high standing which the chosen models carry. Unquestionably, such high standing is given in major measure by the endorsement and espousal of models of prestigeful persons. But it must be stressed again that it is not prestige, *per se*, which imparts this sanction; a prestigeful person, despite his eminence, may be easily felt to be 'out-of-date.' To carry weight, the person of prestige must be believed or sensed to be voicing the proper perspective that is called for by developments in the area. To recognize this is to take note of the importance of the disposition to keep abreast of what is collectively judged to be up-to-date practice. The formation of this collective judgment takes place through an interesting but ill-understood interaction between prestige and incipient taste, between eminent endorsement and congenial interest. Collective choice of models is forged in this process of interaction, leading to a focusing of selection at a given time on one model and at a different time on another model.

Fashion and contemporary society

If we view modern life in terms of the analytical scheme which I have sketched, there is no difficulty in seeing the play of fashion in many diverse areas. Close scrutiny of such areas will show the features which we have discussed – a turning away from old forms that are thought to be out-of-date; the introduction of new models which compete for adoption; a selection between them that is made not on the basis of demonstrated merit or utility but in response to an interplay of prestige-endorsement and incipient taste; and a course of development in which a given type of model becomes solidified, socially elevated, and imperative in its demands for acceptance for a period of time. While this process is revealed most vividly in the area of women's fashion it can be noted in play here and there across the board in modern life and may, indeed, be confidently expected to increase in scope under the conditions of modern life. These conditions – the pressure to change, the open doors to innovation, the inadequacy or the unavailability of decisive tests of the merit of proposed models, the effort of prestigeful figures to gain or maintain standing in the face of developments to which they must respond, and the groping of people for a satisfactory expression of new and vague tastes – entrench fashion as a basic and widespread process in modern life.

The expanding domain of fashion

This characterization may repel scholars who believe that fashion is an abnormal and irrational happening and that it gives way before enlightenment, sophistication, and increased knowledge. Such scholars would reject the thought that fashion is becoming increasingly embedded in a society which is presumably moving toward a higher level of intelligence and rational perspective. Yet, the facts are clear that fashion is an outstanding mark of modern civilization and that its domain is expanding rather than diminishing. As areas of life come to be caught in the vortex of movement and as proposed innovations multiply in them, a process of collective choice in the nature of fashion is naturally and inevitably brought into play. The absence or inadequacy of compelling tests of the merit of proposals opens the door to prestige-endorsement and taste as determinants of collective choice. The compelling role of these two factors as they interact easily escapes notice by those who participate in the process of collective choice; the model which emerges with a high sanction and approval is almost always believed by them as being intrinsically and demonstrably correct. This belief is fortified by the impressive arguments and arrays of specious facts that may frequently be marshalled on behalf of the model. Consequently, it is not surprising that participants may fail completely to recognize a fashion process in which they are sharing. The identification of the process as fashion occurs usually only after it is gone – when it can be viewed from the detached vantage point of later time. The fashions which we can now detect in the past history of philosophy, medicine, science, technological use and industrial practice did not appear as fashions to those who shared in them. The fashions merely appeared to them as up-to-date achievements! The fact that participants in fashion movements in different areas of contemporary life do not recognize such movements should not mislead perceptive scholars. The application of this observation to the domain of social science is particularly in order; contemporary social science is rife with the play of fashion.

The societal role of fashion

I turn finally to a series of concluding remarks on what seems to be the societal role of fashion. As I have sought to explain, the key to the understanding of fashion is given in the simple words, 'being in fashion.' These words signify an area of life which is caught in movement – movement from an outmoded past toward a dim, uncertain, but exploitable immediate future. In this passage, the need of the present is to be in march with the time. The fashion mechanism is the response to this need. These simple observations point to the social role of fashion – a role which I would state abstractly to be that of enabling and aiding collective adjustment to and in a moving world of divergent possibilities. In spelling out this abstract statement I wish to call attention to three matters.

The *first* is a matter which is rather obvious, namely, that fashion introduces a conspicuous measure of unanimity and uniformity in what would otherwise be a markedly fragmented arrangement. If all competing models enjoyed similar acceptance the situation would be one of disorder and disarray. In the field of dress, for example, if people were to freely adopt the hundreds of styles proposed professionally each year and the other thousands which the absence of competition would allow, there would be a veritable 'Tower of Babel' consequence. *Fashion introduces order in a potentially anarchic and moving present.* By establishing suitable models which carry the stamp of propriety and compel adherence, fashion narrowly limits the range of variability and so fosters uniformity and order, even though it be passing uniformity and order. In this respect fashion performs in a moving society a function which custom performs in a settled society.

Second, fashion serves to detach the grip of the past in a moving world. By placing a premium on being in the mode and derogating what developments have left behind, it frees actions for new movement. The significance of this release from the restraint of the past should not be minimized. To meet a moving and changing world requires freedom to move in new directions. Detachment from the hold of the past is no small contribution to the achievement of such freedom. In the areas of its operation fashion facilitates that contribution. In this sense there is virtue in applying the derogatory accusations of being 'old-fashioned,' 'outmoded,' 'backward,' and 'out-of-date.'

Third, fashion operates as an orderly preparation for the immediate future. By allowing the presentation of new models but by forcing them through the gauntlet of competition and collective selection the fashion mechanism offers a continuous means of adjusting to what is on the horizon.[1] On the one hand, it offers to innovators and creators the opportunity to present through their models their ideas of what the immediate future should be in the given area of fashion. On the other hand, the adoption of the models which survive the gauntlet of collective selection gives expression to nascent dispositions that represents an accommodation or orientation to the immediate future. Through this process, fashion nurtures and shapes a body of common sensitivity and taste, as is suggested by the congeniality and naturalness of present fashions in contrast to the oddness and incongruity of past fashions. This body of common sensitivity and taste is analogous on the subjective side to a 'universe of discourse.' Like the latter, it provides a basis for a common approach to a world and for handling and digesting the experiences which the world yields. The value of a pliable and re-forming body of common taste to meet a shifting and developing world should be apparent.

Conclusion

In these three ways, fashion is a very adept mechanism for enabling people to adjust in an orderly and unified way to a moving and changing world which is potentially full of anarchic possibilities. It is suited, *par excellence*, to the demands of life in such a moving world since it facilitates detachment from a receding past, opens the doors to proposals to to the future, but subjects such proposals to the test of collective selection, thus bringing them in line with the direction of awakened interest and disposition. In areas of life – and they are many – in which the merit of the proposals cannot be demonstrated, it permits orderly movement and development.

In closing, let me renew the invitation to sociologists to take fashion seriously and give it the attention and study which it deserves and which are so sorely lacking. Fashion should be recognized as a central mechanism in forming social order in a modern type of world, a mechanism whose operation will increase. It needs to be lifted out of the area of the bizarre, the irrational and the inconsequential in which sociologists have so misguidingly lodged it. When sociologists respond to the need of developing a scheme of analysis suited to a moving or modern world they will be required to assign the fashion process to a position of central importance.

Note

1   The recognition that fashion is continuously at work is, in my judgment, the major although unintended contribution of Simmel's analysis. However, his thesis that

the function of fashion is the oscillating differentiation and unification of social classes seems to me to miss what is most important.

References

Blumer, Herbert (1968) 'Fashion,' pp. 341–5 in *International Encyclopedia of the Social Sciences* V, New York: Macmillan.

Lang, Kurt and Gladys Lang (1961) *Collective Dynamics*, New York: Crowell.

Richardson, J. and A. L. Kroeber (1947) 'Three centuries of women's dress fashions: a quantitative analysis,' *Anthropological Records* 5: 111–53.

Sapir, Edward (1931) 'Fashion,' pp. 139–141 in [*International*] *Encyclopedia of the Social Sciences* VI, New York: Macmillan.

Simmel, G. (1904) 'Fashion,' *International Quarterly* 10.

—— (1957) 'Fashion,' *American Journal of Sociology* 62: 541–58 (reprint).

Young, A. B. (1937) *Recurring Cycles of Fashion: 1760–1937*, New York: Harper & Brothers.

Chapter 21

Emil Wilbekin

GREAT ASPIRATIONS
Hip hop, and fashion dress for excess and success

Calvin Klein's no friend of mine, don't want nobody's name on my behind.
— Run-D.M.C., "Rock Box," 1984

IN THE EARLY DAYS OF HIP HOP, Run-D.M.C.'s dismissal of the Calvin Klein brand name was a boast of neo-black power. Young black and Latino kids in the Big City didn't need to be down with a glitzy Seventh Avenue darling — rap music was the newest, edgiest pop phenomenon, and it was creating its own urban street style. From uptown to downtown, from Andy Warhol to Debbie Harry, everybody wanted to be a part of hip hop culture — but this ghetto-based movement based on boasting, playing the dozens, and living as a community didn't need all the rah-rah fashionistas or their champagne, diamonds, and cocaine.

Eventually, just like everybody else, hip hop got down with the big '80s — and urban culture's aspirations quickly turned into a yearning for *Lifestyles of the Rich and Famous*. From Wall Street to Harlem, love deluxe was the theme and makin' money was the scheme. Money, power, and respect became the posture of many rappers — like Slick Rick, who "put on my brand-new Gucci underwear" in "La Di Da Di," or Schoolly D "looking at my Gucci it's about that time."

Ironically, the hip hop nation, once so proudly self-sufficient, became obsessed with the finer things in life: designer clothing, imported champagne, Cuban cigars, luxury automobiles, and fine jewelry — all the things that prove how successful you are by American Dream standards. Now everybody in hip hop is donning gold or platinum pendants, watches, and rings encrusted with diamonds — "Name-brand niggers," as the late Notorious B.I.G. put it on his hit single "Hypnotize."

So while that quote from "Rock Box" is still one of the better-known rhymes in hip hop history today its sentiment couldn't be further from the truth. In the "gettin' jiggy with it," ghetto fabulous '90s, it's all about flexing the strength of hip hop's newfound pop status. Over the years, hip hop grew up, and while kids still like to "keep it real," today that often means having *other* people's names not only on their behinds, but also on their heads, chests, backs, wrists, and, of course, feet. Hip hop players like Russell Simmons, Sean "Puffy" Combs, and Master P have even gotten into the fashion game themselves with their own clothing lines.

An underground street sound/grassroots musical movement suddenly became an overwhelming force in the fabulous world of high fashion – Lil' Kim, Mary J. Blige, and Missy "Misdemeanor" Elliott share a group shot in *Vogue* illustrating an article entitled "Rapper's Deluxe," and Puff Daddy sits front row at the Versace couture show in Paris. This is a story about art imitating the new, changing face of America and its growing urban lifestyle; about music inspiring people to be creative and express themselves aristically, politically, and financially; and about the birth and development of a multicultural, modern youth-quake.

What is unique about the aesthetics of hip hop style is that the look changes as quickly as the sound does – which is to say, constantly. And while naysayers and cultural critics swore up and down back in the day that hip hop wouldn't last, that couldn't have been further from the truth. As rap started to grow at rapid speed, its image was changing and, like most pop culture movements, it started to splinter into various regional identifications and political ideologies.

By the mid-'80s, the b-boy wasn't just a black kid from the projects in the Bronx anymore. There was a burgeoning scene in Los Angeles (loosely related to gang culture) led by N.W.A, a Houston clique of rappers called the Geto Boys, and a sexed-out Miami mogul named Luke Skyywalker inventing bass music. New York, meanwhile, had broken down into its typical neighborhood crew mentality – from the Bronx's politicized KRS-One and Boogie Down Productions to Queens-bred pop-rappers Kid 'N Play.

While it wasn't uncommon to see a group of rappers still rocking Adidas track suits and Wallabees in the late '80s, there were also those, like Big Daddy Kane, who were embracing a more Afro-nouveau riche identity – opting for suits, fur coats, pointy dress shoes, and pimp-chic leather hats. There was also the Native Tongues movement, featuring De La Soul and A Tribe Called Quest, who were working a more suburban preppy stance (and helping blow up the big business of Polo by Ralph Lauren, Tommy Hilfiger, Nautica by David Chu, and even DKNY by Donna Karan) combined with a touch of Afrocentric kente cloth, plus some neo-boho twigs and potions for good measure.

As rap diversified, it was clear that for hip hop heads, clothes did define the man. And the more stylish hip hop became – introducing new ideas, styles, and clothing combinations – the more fashionistas started to pay attention. Soon, hip hop would start to change the sartorial landscape of Seventh Avenue, Paris, and Milan.

The first signs had already started bubbling up from downtown New York City, and the messenger, unlikely as it sounds, was Norma Kamali. A pioneer in making fashion functional and comfortable with her stretch-jersey tube-dressing, Kamali styled Chaka Khan's 1984 video for "I Feel for You," which featured models in her clothing (cool maxi-skirts, shoulder pads, and headwraps) while backup dancers spun and popped to a DJ's mixing and scratching. The energy of the music and the kids breaking wildly made it hip hop; the graffitied backdrops were the final touch.

A few years later, Isaac Mizrahi — a native New Yorker who fills his collection with references to pop culture (and who, as a teenager, appeared in the movie *Fame* for a few short moments) — made hip hop accessible to the mainstream. Mizrahi was inspired by the elevator operator at his SoHo showroom who wore a fat gold chain. Mizrahi's marriage of the hip hop look with high fashion was coined "Homeboy Chic" by *Women's Wear Daily*. Cindy Crawford, Christy Turlington, Linda Evangelista, Naomi Campbell, and Veronica Webb (cheered on by her then-boyfriend, Spike Lee) strolled down the runway wearing black cat suits adorned with gold chains, big gold nameplate-inspired belts, and bomber jackets with fur-trimmed hoods. At Todd Oldham's show in November 1991, female rapper turned TV and film actress Queen Latifah hit the catwalk in a high-style, bright, basket-weave kufi (an African crown that looks like a tube of fabric on your head).

At around the same time, Chanel's head designer Karl Lagerfeld showed women in leather jackets and piles of fat gold chains (complete with big double Cs) that simultaneously nodded to the label's habit of overaccessorizing with tons of jewelry and hip hop's current cool de force. Several seasons later, Lagerfeld (who uses hip hop and R&B in his shows and reportedly listens to the music in his Chanel workrooms) sent models down the runway in long black dresses complete with big silver chains with padlocks — which looked very similar to the metal chain-link and padlock that rapper Treach from Naughty By Nature was wearing at that time, in solidarity, he said, with "all the brothers who are locked down." In true fashion fancy, though, hip hop, like country-western, punk rock, glam rock, and grunge, enjoyed a few seasons of popularity and then seemed to fizzle; the buzz around Mizrahi, for instance, never translated into sufficient sales, and his company closed its doors in 1998.

Designer fashion wasn't the only avenue that profited from the growth of hip hop style. Black designers like Cross Colours and Karl Kani spearheaded the empowering moment when baggy jeans first came on the scene. Nor were African-American designers the only ones getting paid from hip hop's street chic: in 1992, Calvin Klein made Marky Mark his poster child. It was a way to use an image of rap more acceptable to middle America than, say, L.L. Cool J — the real thing.

Out of the blue in 1992 came three girls from Atlanta named TLC who pushed the bright-colored, baggy jeans look into fashionista focus. Suddenly, sweet-looking girls were walking down the streets of America sporting bras, men's underwear with the waistband showing, tennis shoes, and, of course, backward baseball caps and ski caps (also known as scullys). Even *Vogue* was featuring the homegirl look.

Cultural critics (the same ones who said that hip hop was a trend that would never live more than five years) and fashion editors (the same ones who once said, "A *Vogue* girl would never wear a ski cap") declared that the baggy pants look would be a passing phase. Fast forward to the present, and see how much bigger skate kids' pants have gotten, how all rappers and R&B artists (and their disciples nationwide) wear size 36 waist jeans, and how wide-legs have once again become the cool silhouette in high fashion. Like hip hop itself, wide-leg pants are now simply part of the style lexicon.

In 1994, Ralph Lauren — the king of established, well-bred, and high-class living — signed Tyson Beckford, a beautiful, buff, dark-skinned (Jamaican with Chinese roots) brother, to an exclusive modeling contract as the male face of Polo. With this deal, Lauren made it loud and clear that the world was changing. Tyson represented the Polo image (smart, clean, confident) and nodded to its urban market (street-smart, stylish, ambitious) without compromise. Tyson's strong African-American presence – wearing Purple Label suits and tennis whites – gave young black men in the United States a visible example of someone who was high-profile and successful, and not by playing sports, singing, or committing a crime.

At that same time, hip hop was really living up to the bravado that was so fundamental to its character and identity. Gangsta rap was building its foundation on the West Coast with lyrical leaders like Tupac Shakur, Ice Cube, Eazy-E, Dr. Dre, Snoop Doggy Dogg, and DJ Quik, who were all paying homage to the gangsters of the '30s and '40s with a combination of power, money, gunplay, and girls. With literal references, these rappers traded in their gang-inspired, dark denim prison gear and crew-related bandannas for expensive, double-breasted suits, silk shirts, and bowler hats which – with the growth of the Italian meanswear scene among designers like Giorgio Armani, Gianni Versace, Dolce & Gabbana, and Gianfranco Ferré – were becoming popular on the high-fashion circuit. Mike Tyson bouts in Las Vegas were packed with hip hop heads all sporting brightly printed silk shirts by Gianni Versace and puffing on Cuban cigars.

On the East Coast, a maverick by the name of Sean "Puffy" Combs was making noise with his 1994-established label, Bad Boy Entertainment. While the West Coast got its gangsta groove on, Combs and his crew (including the Notorious B.I.G. and his wife Faith Evans, 112, and Total) were – along with fellow music cronies Russell Simmons of Def Jam and Andre Harrell of Uptown and, later, Motown Records – coining the phrase "Ghetto Fabulous." The style was based on high-end designer clothing like Versace, Giorgio Armani, Prada, Fendi, and Dolce & Gabbana – but this was no runway look, baby. The suits were worn like the jeans, big and baggy. Italian designers make beautifully tailored suits and extravagant luxury items, and hip hop appropriated those labels, still wearing them with true ghetto grit. These rappers dictated a new urban uniform, shouting out the designers in song after song. Suddenly, it seemed like the *Dynasty* and *Dallas* dreams that hip hop grew up on had become a reality. Hip hop was now a big business, and the stars weren't afraid of flaunting their newfound wealth.

What did you wear when you weren't profilin'? Calvin Klein, Polo, Nautica by David Chu, and DKNY were all popular, but it was Tommy Hilfiger who became the sportswear designer of choice. Hilfiger's label was attractive because of its all-American, WASP-y, country club feeling – it was exclusive and aspirational. And Hilfiger actively embraced hip hop, unlike other designers – most notably Timberland, which was popular with hip hop kids but was perceived as being afraid of the hardcore urban attitude. Tommy used black models in his advertising campaigns and had Puffy, Coolio, and members of Jodeci walk down the runway modeling his Americana collection. He even enlisted Kidada Jones, daughter of Quincy Jones and former girlfriend of Tupac Shakur, to model and consult on his clothing and image.

And Tommy didn't stop there, either. He began to dress almost everyone in hip hop – like Q-Tip and Grand Puba, who rhymed "Tommy Hilfiger/top gear" on the "What's the 411?" remix with Mary J. Blige. When Snoop Doggy Dogg appeared on

Saturday Night Live in a Hilfiger sweatshirt, the item sold out of stores throughout New York the next day. And soon it seemed that Tommy Hilfiger had managed to costume not just urban America, but everyone who wanted to be traditional and established and cool all at the same time – Hilfiger dressed everyone from Aaliyah to Gwen Stefani of No Doubt, Treach from Naughty By Nature to Sheryl Crow.

The Hilfiger explosion gave a lot of Fashion Avenue garmentos an idea or two about both the power of celebrity product placement and the spending power of the new urban market. The urban sportswear market began to bulge at the seams with companies like FUBU (For Us By Us), Eckō Unlimited, Mecca USA, Lugz Walker Wear, Boss Jeans by IG Design, and Enyce. These companies took their cues from Hilfiger, making all-American style elements like sweatshirts, rugbys, and denim their own with huge logos blazing across the chest, back, and legs. FUBU became so popular that Samsung sank millions into their company to reap the benefits of the urban dollar. Even the National Basketball Association bought into FUBU, licensing them to make official NBA jerseys and sweatsuits.

Music and fashion make quite a good team – look at Jon Bon Jovi or Courtney Love and Gianni Versace, Madonna and Dolce & Gabbana, Jean Paul Gaultier, and Anna Molinari. The two communities influence each other artistically and philosophically. And so, predictably, soon the music industry itself started getting in on the act. Naughty By Nature launched Naughty Gear. Beastie Boy Mike D invested in a clothing line called X-Large. Def Jam's Russell Simmons started Phat Farm, a "new American design group" – on which he now spends more time than on any of his seemingly infinite other projects.

Members of the Wu-Tang Clan created a line called Wu-Wear. MC Serch, formerly a member of rap trio 3rd Bass, consulted for Eckō Unlimited for a spell. Pras from the Fugees launched Refugee Gear. And Tommy Boy Records made its own collection, Tommy Boy Gear. It seems that urban marketing doesn't just work for hip hop records – it's an attractive and lucrative opportunity to expand a brand name and buy into the hip hop lifestyle. Puffy (who debuted his Sean John line in 1998) and Master P (No Limit clothes) aren't stupid; they can see the success of FUBU and Phat Farm and smell the money.

And just as everyone wants to be a fashion designer, everyone also wants to be down with hip hop. Look at the various couplings that have turned up in ads, on stage, or on runways: Mary J. Blige and Stella McCartney (daughter of Paul), who designs for Chloe; TLC and Chanel's Karl Lagerfeld; Lil' Kim and Alexander McQueen; Tupac Shakur and Gianni Versace; the Fugees and Giorgio Armani; Usher and Tommy Hilfiger. As the *New York Times* reported on March 31, 1998, while it might have seemed odd for rapper Lil' Kim to be spotted in the front row at the Versus by Gianni Versace Fall '98 collection in New York, it was actually very appropriate; both she and Donatella Versace had lost their mentors the previous year – for Kim, her lover The Notorious B.I.G., and for Donatella, her brother Gianni Versace.

Beyond the blatant courting by both sides, fashion now takes aesthetic direction from hip hop culture more than ever. Many Fall '98 collections prominently featured hip hop gear – hoodies, cargo pants, bomber jackets, shearling coats, and sneakers. The difference is that Gucci, Versace, Calvin Klein, Armani, Cerruti, Louis Vuitton, and the like are creating these garments in luxe fabrics: cashmere, silk, mohair, and mink. And the more that high-end fashion designers are influenced by street style, the more the artists want to wear those familiar-looking clothes.

As we approach the millennium, what we're experiencing is a global remix of individual urban ideas combined with the marketing of big business. As Lil' Kim says on "No Time" from her platinum disc *Hard Core*, "I mama, Miss Ivana/Usually rock the Prada, sometimes Gabbana/Stick you for your cream and your riches/Zsa Zsa Gabor, Demi Moore, Princess Diana and all those rich bitches." It's a long way from considering designer jeans a sellout — but like they say, money changes everything. It's the American way.

Chapter 22

Elizabeth Wilson

OPPOSITIONAL DRESS

[. . .]

DICK HEBDIGE argues that the styles are neither arbitrary nor necessarily a substitute for politics or engagement with the 'real world'. Sub-cultural styles reinterpret conflicts of the wider society: in the case of punks and skinheads, it is racism. Punks really did aspire to be outsiders alongside blacks – 'we're niggers'; while the racism of the skinheads who wear their heads almost shaved, and caricature traditional working-class clothes in the shape of old-fashioned shirts, braces with shrunken trousers and heavy 'bovver boots', seemed 'to represent a conservative proletarian backlash to the radical "working class" posturings of the new wave'.

Blacks, and other ethnic minorities, have also developed their own oppositional styles, but these have usually had a conscious and deliberate message. With the expansion of Harlem in the early twentieth century came many, often exaggerated versions of fashionable wear. By the 1940s the young urban blacks had evolved a highly distinctive style: the zoot suit. This had exaggerated, padded shoulders and peg top trousers narrowing to the ankle, and both jacket and trousers were lavishly draped. The word 'zoot' came from the urban jazz culture of the 1930s, but the origins of the style itself are uncertain, and several explanations have been suggested, but it seems possible that the style was first developed by the second-generation children of migrant Mexican workers.

During the war, in 1943, zoot suits led to serious riots, for gangs of predominantly Mexican and black youths in suits that flouted rationing regulations outraged the servicemen stationed in Pacific ports. What were essentially race riots flared first in Los Angeles and then spread along the West Coast. According to one interpretation – unsurprisingly, the most popular explanation at the time – the zoot suiters came from the underworld of petty criminals, evading the draft (although many turned out to have medical exemption) and indulging in a traditional machismo.

Yet not all zoot suiters were men. At least two female gangs, the Slick Chicks and the Black Widows, were reported, the latter so named on account of their black uniforms of zoot suit jackets, short skirts and fishnet stockings. The active and aggressive role that these young women played suggests that the riots expressed something potentially more radical than juvenile deviance: social rebellion against poverty, against the alienation of American city life, especially for the ethnic minorities. They were also bred of the disruptions of wartime and women's rapidly changing role.

The zoot suit is an especially clear example of a symbolic counter-cultural style that caused a moral panic and led to actual violence in the streets. The zoot suit was defiance, a statement of ethnic pride and a refusal of subservience.[1]

Malcolm X, himself a zoot suiter in his youth, when he did live by petty crime, pimping and drugs, was later to reject any positive connotations of the style. His condemnation gestures to the ambivalence, perhaps, of any attempt to defy by stylistic means:

> I'd go through that Grand Central Station afternoon rush-hour crowd, and many white people simply stopped in their tracks to watch me pass. The drape and the cut of the zoot suit showed to the best advantage if you were tall — and I was over six feet. My conk was fire red. I was really a clown, but my ignorance made me think I was 'sharp'. My knob-toed, orange coloured 'kick up' shoes were nothing but Florsheim's, the ghetto's Cadillac of shoes in those days.

The 'conk' was hair straightened at home by a method of using lye, which burned the scalp:

> When Shorty let me stand up and see in the mirror, my hair hung down in limp, damp strings. My scalp still flamed . . . My first view in the mirror blotted out the hurting. I'd seen some pretty conks, but when it's the first time, on your *own* head, the transformation, after the lifetime of kinks, is staggering . . . on top of my head was this thick, smooth sheen of shining red hair — real red — as straight as any white man's . . .
> This was my first really big step towards self-degradation.[2]

Later, Malcolm X went to prison. There he became a Black Muslim, and, after his release, a black political leader until his assassination in 1965. Then, rebellion and a refusal of the dominant, white culture, took a more conscious and more explicit form. The natural, Afro hair and the slogan 'Black is Beautiful' were a much more openly ideological reassertion of the distinctive nature of the black experience. Before the 1960s, the majority of black women and men in the west had had only white models of beauty on which to base their own looks. Music stars such as the Supremes and Shirley Bassey had straightened hair, or wore wigs.

Yet although in the glass of fashion ethnic diversity was allowable, this was usually still — as in the 1920s — because it was 'exotic'. Indeed, Donyale Luna, who was the first internationally famous black fashion model, in the 1960s, was marketed not just as exotic, but even as freakish ('Is it a plane? No. Is it a bird? Yes . . . it's Donyale Luna') and she herself did not survive this objectification.[3]

Nevertheless, in the 1960s, 1970s and 1980s a variety of distinctively black styles developed, some wholly oppositional, some combining styles adapted, for example, from Africa, with western fashions. In Britain, Rastafarian men wear long, twisted dreadlocks beneath high crowned hats or knitted caps of red, gold and green. The style is an open and deliberate sign of affiliation and both friends and foes recognize it as such. It often leads to harassment on the streets and in prison, where dreadlocks may be forcibly cut off. Similarly Sikh men, who wear their hair long beneath a turban, are sometimes or have been until recently penalized, for example by being prosecuted for not wearing a safety helmet when riding a motorbike. (And of course white men with long hair have also been ritually punished: when two members of the editorial group of *Oz* were sent to prison in the early 1970s in London, their shorn hair made the national news headlines.)

The symbolic significance of long hair on men – in contemporary western culture at least – takes us beyond fashion and its use and subversion by black minority groups. In women's fashions, especially, fashion and dissidence may combine. The Afro-Caribbean fashion for beaded and plaited hairstyles originated in adaptations of African styles and asserted a pride in African descent; they may also reinterpret western styles, for example when a head of narrow plaits is then pinned into a 1940s sideswept roll, or recreated as a twenties bob.

Perhaps what is distinctive about counter-cultural, oppositional dressing as opposed to the direct statement of black identity made by the original Afro style, or the adoption of politically or religiously committed groups of what becomes virtually a uniform, is the ambiguity of the former. In the early days of the Harlem expansion, ghetto fashions seem to have expressed the desire of a particularly oppressed urban multitude for some joy and glamour in their lives, and counter-cultural dressing is usually most distinctive when it expressed hedonism and rebellion simultaneously.

[. . .]

Notes

1   Cosgrove, Stuart (1984) 'The Zoot Suit and Style Warfare', *History Workshop Journal*, Issue 18, Autumn.

2   Malcolm X (1965) *The Autobiography of Malcolm X*, Harmondsworth: Penguin, pp. 164, 137–8.

3   Keenan, Brigid (1977) *The Women We Wanted to Look Like*, New York: St Martins Press, p. 178.

Chapter 23

Dick Hebdige

STYLE

Style as intentional communication

> I speak through my clothes. (Eco, 1973)

THE CYCLE LEADING from opposition to defusion, from resistance to incorporation encloses each successive subculture. We have seen how the media and the market fit into this cycle. We must now turn to the subculture itself to consider exactly how and what subcultural style communicates. Two questions must be asked which together present us with something of a paradox: how does a subculture make sense to its members? How is it made to signify disorder? To answer these questions we must define the meaning of style more precisely.

In 'The Rhetoric of the Image', Roland Barthes contrasts the 'intentional' advertising image with the apparently 'innocent' news photograph. Both are complex articulations of specific codes and practices, but the news photo appears more 'natural' and transparent than the advertisement. He writes – 'the signification of the image is certainly intentional . . . the advertising image is clear, or at least emphatic'. Barthes' distinction can be used analogously to point up the difference between subcultural and 'normal' styles. The subcultural stylistic ensembles – those emphatic combinations of dress, dance, argot, music, etc. – bear approximately the same relation to the more conventional formulae ('normal' suits and ties, casual wear, twin-sets, etc.) that the advertising image bears to the less consciously constructed news photograph.

Of course, signification need not be intentional, as semioticians have repeatedly pointed out. Umberto Eco writes 'not only the expressly intended communicative object . . . but every object may be viewed . . . as a sign' (Eco, 1973). For instance, the conventional outfits worn by the average man and woman in the street are chosen within the constraints of finance, 'taste', preference, etc. and these choices are undoubtedly significant. Each ensemble has its place in an internal system of differences – the conventional modes of sartorial discourse – which fit a corresponding set of socially prescribed roles and options.[1] These choices contain a whole range of messages which are transmitted through the finely graded distinctions of a number of interlocking sets – class and status, self-image and attractiveness, etc. Ultimately, if nothing else, they are expressive of 'normality' as opposed to 'deviance' (i.e. they are distinguished by their relative invisibility, their appropriateness, their 'naturalness'). However, the intentional communication is of a different order. It stands apart – a visible construction, a loaded choice. It directs attention to itself; it gives itself to be read.

This is what distinguishes the visual ensembles of spectacular subcultures from those favoured in the surrounding culture(s). They are *obviously* fabricated (even the mods, precariously placed between the worlds of the straight and the deviant, finally declared themselves different when they gathered in groups outside dance halls and on sea fronts). They *display* their own codes (e.g. the punk's ripped T-shirt) or at least demonstrate that codes are there to be used and abused (e.g. they have been thought about rather than thrown together). In this they go against the grain of a mainstream culture whose principal defining characteristic, according to Barthes, is a tendency to masquerade as nature, to substitute 'normalized' for historical forms, to translate the reality of the world into an image of the world which in turn presents itself as if composed according to 'the evident laws of the natural order' (Barthes, 1972).

As we have seen, it is in this sense that subcultures can be said to transgress the laws of 'man's second nature'.[2] By repositioning and recontextualizing commodities, by subverting their conventional uses and inventing new ones, the subcultural stylist gives the lie to what Althusser has called the 'false obviousness of everyday practice' (Althusser and Balibar, 1968), and opens up the world of objects to new and covertly oppositional readings. The communication of a significant *difference*, then (and the parallel communication of a group *identity*), is the 'point' behind the style of all spectacular subcultures. It is the superordinate term under which all the other significations are marshalled, the message through which all the other messages speak. Once we have granted this initial difference a primary determination over the whole sequence of stylistic generation and diffusion, we can go back to examine the internal structure of individual subcultures. To return to our earlier analogy: if the spectacular subculture is an intentional communication, if it is to borrow a term from linguistics, 'motivated', what precisely is being communicated and advertised?

Style as *bricolage*

> It is conventional to call 'monster' any blending of dissonant elements.
> . . . I call 'monster' every original, inexhaustible beauty. (Alfred Jarry)

The subcultures with which we have been dealing share a common feature apart from the fact that they are all predominantly working class. They are, as we have seen, cultures of conspicuous consumption – even when, as with the skinheads and the punks, certain types of consumption are conspicuously refused – and it is through the distinctive rituals of consumption, through style, that the subculture at once reveals its 'secret' identity and communicates its forbidden meanings. It is basically the way in which commodities are *used* in subculture which mark the subculture off from more orthodox cultural formations.

Discoveries made in the field of anthropology are helpful here. In particular, the concept of *bricolage* can be used to explain how subcultural styles are constructed. In *The Savage Mind* Levi-Strauss shows how the magical modes utilized by primitive peoples (superstition, sorcery, myth) can be seen as implicitly coherent, though explicitly bewildering, systems of connection between things which perfectly equip their users to 'think' their own world. These magical systems of connection have a common feature: they are capable of infinite extension because basic elements can be used in a variety of improvised combinations to generate new meanings within them. *Bricolage* has thus been described as a 'science of the concrete' in a recent definition which clarifies the original anthropological meaning of the term:

> [Bricolage] refers to the means by which the non-literate, non-technical mind of so-called 'primitive' man responds to the world around him. The process involves a 'science of the concrete' (as opposed to our 'civilised' science of the 'abstract') which far from lacking logic, in fact carefully and precisely orders, classifies and arranges into structures the *minutiae* of the physical world in all their profusion by means of a 'logic' which is not our own. The structures, 'improvised' or made up (these are rough translations of the process of *bricoler*) as *ad hoc* responses to an environment, then serve to establish homologies and analogies between the ordering of nature and that of society, and so satisfactorily 'explain' the world and make it able to be lived in. (Hawkes, 1977)

The implications of the structured improvisations of *bricolage* for a theory of spectacular subculture as a system of communication have already been explored. For instance, John Clarke has stressed the way in which prominent forms of discourse (particularly fashion) are radically adapted, subverted and extended by the subcultural *bricoleur*:

> Together, object and meaning constitute a sign, and within any one culture, such signs are assembled, repeatedly, into characteristic forms of discourse. However, when the bricoleur re-locates the significant object in a different position within that discourse, using the same overall repertoire of signs, or when that object is placed within a different total ensemble, a new discourse is constituted, a different message conveyed. (Clarke, 1976)

In this way the teddy boy's theft and transformation of the Edwardian style revived in the early 1950s by Savile Row for wealthy young men about town can be construed as an act of *bricolage*. Similarly, the mods could be said to be functioning as *bricoleurs* when they appropriated another range of commodities by placing them in a

symbolic ensemble which served to erase or subvert their original straight meanings. Thus pills medically prescribed for the treatment of neuroses were used as
ends-in-themselves, and the motor scooter, originally an ultra-respectable means of
transport, was turned into a menacing symbol of group solidarity. In the same
improvisatory manner, metal combs, honed to a razor-like sharpness, turned narcissism into an offensive weapon. Union jacks were emblazoned on the backs of grubby
parka anoraks or cut up and converted into smartly tailored jackets. More subtly,
the conventional insignia of the business world – the suit, collar and tie, short hair,
etc. – were stripped of their original connotations – efficiency, ambition, compli-
ance with authority – and transformed into 'empty' fetishes, objects to be desired,
fondled and valued in their own right.

At the risk of sounding melodramatic, we could use Umberto Eco's phrase
'semiotic guerilla warfare' (Eco, 1973) to describe these subversive practices. The
war may be conducted at a level beneath the consciousness of the individual members of a spectacular subculture (though the subculture is still, at another level, an
intentional communication (see pp. 100–2)) but with the emergence of such a
group, 'war – and it is Surrealism's war – is declared on a world of surfaces'
(Annette Michelson, quoted Lippard, 1970).

[. . .]

Style in revolt: revolting style

> Nothing was holy to us. Our movement was neither mystical, com-
> munistic nor anarchistic. All of these movements had some sort of pro-
> gramme, but ours was completely nihilistic. We spat on everything,
> including ourselves. Our symbol was nothingness, a vacuum, a void.
> (George Grosz on Dada)

> We're so pretty, oh so pretty . . . vac-unt. (The Sex Pistols)

Although it was often directly offensive (T-shirts covered in swear words) and
threatening (terrorist/guerilla outfits) punk style was defined principally through
the violence of its 'cut ups'. Like Duchamp's 'ready mades' – manufactured objects
which qualified as art because he chose to call them such, the most unremarkable
and inappropriate items – a pin, a plastic clothes peg, a television component, a
razor blade, a tampon – could be brought within the province of punk (un)fashion.
Anything within or without reason could be turned into part of what Vivien
Westwood called 'confrontation dressing' so long as the rupture between 'natural'
and constructed context was clearly visible (i.e. the rule would seem to be: if the
cap doesn't fit, wear it).

Objects borrowed from the most sordid of contexts found a place in the punks'
ensembles: lavatory chains were draped in graceful arcs across chests encased in
plastic bin-liners. Safety pins were taken out of their domestic 'utility' context and
worn as gruesome ornaments through the cheek, ear or lip. 'Cheap' trashy fabrics
(PVC, plastic, lurex, etc.) in vulgar designs (e.g. mock leopard skin) and 'nasty'
colours, long discarded by the quality end of the fashion industry as obsolete kitsch,

were salvaged by the punks and turned into garments (fly boy drainpipes, 'common' mini-skirts) which offered self-conscious commentaries on the notions of modernity and taste. Conventional ideas of prettiness were jettisoned along with the traditional feminine lore of cosmetics. Contrary to the advice of every woman's magazine, make-up for both boys and girls was worn to be seen. Faces became abstract portraits: sharply observed and meticulously executed studies in alienation. Hair was obviously dyed (hay yellow, jet black, or bright orange with tufts of green or bleached in question marks), and T-shirts and trousers told the story of their own construction with multiple zips and outside seams clearly displayed. Similarly, fragments of school uniform (white bri-nylon shirts, school ties) were symbolically defiled (the shirts covered in graffiti, or fake blood; the ties left undone) and juxtaposed against leather drains or shocking pink mohair tops. The perverse and the abnormal were valued intrinsically. In particular, the illicit iconography of sexual fetishism was used to predictable effect. Rapist masks and rubber wear, leather bodices and fishnet stockings, implausibly pointed stiletto heeled shoes, the whole paraphernalia of bondage – the belts, straps and chains – were exhumed from the boudoir, closet and the pornographic film and placed on the street where they retained their forbidden connotations. Some young punks even donned the dirty raincoat – that most prosaic symbol of sexual 'kinkiness' – and hence expressed their deviance in suitably proletarian terms.

Of course, punk did more than upset the wardrobe. It undermined every relevant discourse. Thus dancing, usually an involving and expressive medium in British rock and mainstream pop cultures, was turned into a dumbshow of blank robotics. Punk dances bore absolutely no relation to the desultory frugs and clinches which Geoff Mungham describes as intrinsic to the respectable working-class ritual of Saturday night at the Top Rank or Mecca.[3] Indeed, overt displays of heterosexual interest were generally regarded with contempt and suspicion (who let the BOF/ wimp[4] in?) and conventional courtship patterns found no place on the floor in dances like the pogo, the pose and the robot. Though the pose did allow for a minimum sociability (i.e. it could involve two people) the 'couple' were generally of the same sex and physical contact was ruled out of court as the relationship depicted in the dance was a 'professional' one. One participant would strike a suitable cliché fashion pose while the other would fall into a classic 'Bailey' crouch to snap an imaginary picture. The pogo forebade even this much interaction, though admittedly there was always a good deal of masculine jostling in front of the stage. In fact the pogo was a caricature – a *reductio ad absurdum* of all the solo dance styles associated with rock music. It resembled the 'anti-dancing' of the 'Leapniks' which Melly describes in connection with the trad boom (Melly, 1972). The same abbreviated gestures – leaping into the air, hands clenched to the sides, to head an imaginary ball – were repeated without variation in time to the strict mechanical rhythms of the music. In contrast to the hippies' languid, free-form dancing, and the 'idiot dancing' of the heavy metal rockers . . ., the pogo made improvisation redundant: the only variations were imposed by changes in the tempo of the music – fast numbers being 'interpreted' with manic abandon in the form of frantic on-the-spots, while the slower ones were pogoed with a detachment bordering on the catatonic.

The robot, a refinement witnessed only at the most exclusive punk gatherings, was both more 'expressive' and less spontaneous' within the very narrow range such terms acquired in punk usage. It consisted of barely perceptible twitches of the head and hands or more extravagant lurches (Frankenstein's first steps?) which were abruptly halted at random points. The resulting pose was held for several moments, even minutes, and the whole sequence was as suddenly, as unaccountably, resumed and re-enacted. Some zealous punks carried things one step further and choreographed whole evenings, turning themselves for a matter of hours, like Gilbert and George,[5] into automata, living sculptures.

The music was similarly distinguished from mainstream rock and pop. It was uniformly basic and direct in its appeal, whether through intention or lack of expertise. If the latter, then the punks certainly made a virtue of necessity ('We want to be amateurs' – Johnny Rotten). Typically, a barrage of guitars with the volume and treble turned to maximum accompanied by the occasional saxophone would pursue relentless (un)melodic lines against a turbulent background of cacophonous drumming and screamed vocals. Johnny Rotten succinctly defined punk's position on harmonics: 'We're into chaos not music'.

The names of the groups (the Unwanted, the Rejects, the Sex Pistols, the Clash, the Worst, etc.) and the titles of the songs: 'Belsen was a Gas', 'If You Don't Want to Fuck Me, fuck off', 'I Wanna be Sick on You', reflected the tendency towards wilful desecration and the voluntary assumption of outcast status which characterized the whole punk movement. Such tactics were, to adapt Levi-Strauss's famous phrase, 'things to whiten mother's hair with'. In the early days at least, these 'garage bands' could dispense with musical pretensions and substitute, in the traditional romantic terminology, 'passion' for 'technique', the language of the common man for the arcane posturings of the existing élite, the now familiar armoury of frontal attacks for the bourgeois notion of entertainment or the classical concept of 'high art'.

It was in the performance arena that punk groups posed the clearest threat to law and order. Certainly, they succeeded in subverting the conventions of concert and night-club entertainment. Most significantly, they attempted both physically and in terms of lyrics and life-style to move closer to their audiences. This in itself is by no means unique: the boundary between artist and audience has often stood as a metaphor in revolutionary aesthetics (Brecht, the surrealists, Dada, Marcuse, etc.) for that larger and more intransigent barrier which separates art and the dream from reality and life under capitalism.[6] The stages of those venues secure enough to host 'new wave' acts were regularly invaded by hordes of punks, and if the management refused to tolerate such blatant disregard for ballroom etiquette, then the groups and their followers could be drawn closer together in a communion of spittle and mutual abuse. At the Rainbow Theatre in May 1977 as the Clash played 'White Riot', chairs were ripped out and thrown at the stage. Meanwhile, every performance, however apocalyptic, offered palpable evidence that things could change, indeed were changing: that performance itself was a possibility no authentic punk should discount. Examples abounded in the music press of 'ordinary fans' (Siouxsie of Siouxsie and the Banshees, Sid Vicious of the Sex Pistols, Mark P of *Sniffin Glue*, Jordan of the Ants) who had made the symbolic crossing from the dance floor to the stage. Even the humbler positions in the rock hierarchy could provide an attractive alternative to the drudgery of manual labour, office work or a youth on the dole. The Finchley Boys, for instance, were reputedly taken off the football terraces by the Stranglers and employed as roadies.

If these 'success stories' were, as we have seen, subject to a certain amount of 'skewed' interpretation in the press, then there were innovations in other areas which made opposition to dominant definitions possible. Most notably, there was an attempt, the first by a predominantly working-class youth culture, to provide an alternative critical space within the subculture itself to counteract the hostile or at least ideologically inflected coverage which punk was receiving in the media. The existence of an alternative punk press demonstrated that it was not only clothes or music that could be immediately and cheaply produced from the limited resources at hand. The fanzines (*Sniffin Glue, Ripped and Torn*, etc.) were journals edited by an individual or a group, consisting of reviews, editorials and interviews with prominent punks, produced on a small scale as cheaply as possible, stapled together and distributed through a small number of sympathetic retail outlets.

The language in which the various manifestos were framed was determinedly 'working class' (i.e. it was liberally peppered with swear words) and typing errors and grammatical mistakes, misspellings and jumbled pagination were left uncorrected in the final proof. Those corrections and crossings out that were made before publication were left to be deciphered by the reader. The overwhelming impression was one of urgency and immediacy, of a paper produced in indecent haste, of memos from the front line.

This inevitably made for a strident buttonholing type of prose which, like the music it described, was difficult to 'take in' in any quantity. Occasionally a wittier, more abstract item – what Harvey Garfinkel (the American ethnomethodologist) might call an 'aid to sluggish imaginations' – might creep in. For instance, *Sniffin Glue*, the first fanzine and the one which achieved the highest circulation, contained perhaps the single most inspired item of propaganda produced by the subculture – the definitive statement of punk's do-it-yourself philosophy – a diagram showing three finger positions on the neck of a guitar over the caption: 'Here's one chord, here's two more, now form your own band'.

Even the graphics and typography used on record covers and fanzines were homologous with punk's subterranean and anarchic style. The two typographic models were graffiti which was translated into a flowing 'spray can' script, and the ransom note in which individual letters cut up from a variety of sources (newspapers, etc.) in different type faces were pasted together to form an anonymous message. The Sex Pistols' 'God Save the Queen' sleeve (later turned into T-shirts, posters, etc.) for instance incorporated both styles: the roughly assembled legend was pasted across the Queen's eyes and mouth which were further disfigured by those black bars used in pulp detective magazines to conceal identity (i.e. they connote crime or scandal), Finally, the process of ironic self-abasement which characterized the subculture was extended to the name 'punk' itself which, with its derisory connotations of 'mean and petty villainy', 'rotten', 'worthless', etc. was generally preferred by hardcore members of the subculture to the more neutral 'new wave'.[7]

Style as homology

THE PUNK SUBCULTURE, then, signified chaos at every level, but this was only possible because the style itself was so thoroughly ordered. The chaos cohered as a meaningful whole. We can now attempt to solve this paradox by referring to another concept originally employed by Levi-Strauss: homology.

Paul Willis (1978) first applied the term 'homology' to subculture in his study of hippies and motor-bike boys using it to describe the symbolic fit between the values and lifestyles of a group, its subjective experience and the musical forms it uses to express or reinforce its focal concerns. In *Profane Culture*, Willis shows how, contrary to the popular myth which presents subcultures as lawless forms, the internal structure of any particular subculture is characterized by an extreme orderliness; each part is organically related to other parts and it is through the fit between them that the subcultural member makes sense of the world. For instance, it was the homology between an alternative value system ('Tune in, turn on, drop out'), hallucogenic drugs and acid rock which made the hippy culture cohere as a 'whole way of life' for individual hippies. In *Resistance Through Rituals*, Hall *et al.* crossed the concepts of homology and *bricolage* to provide a systematic explanation of why a particular subcultural style should appeal to a particular group of people. The authors asked the question: 'What specifically does a subcultural style signify to the members of the subculture themselves?'

The answer was that the appropriated objects reassembled in the distinctive subcultural ensembles were 'made to reflect, express and resonate . . . aspects of group life' (Hall *et al.*, 1976b). The objects chosen were, either intrinsically or in their adapted forms, homologous with the focal concerns, activities, group structure and collective self-image of the subculture. They were 'objects in which (the subcultural members) could see their central values held and reflected' (Hall *et al.*, 1976).

The skinheads were cited to exemplify this principle. The boots, braces and cropped hair were only considered appropriate and hence meaningful because they communicated the desired qualities: 'hardness, masculinity and working-classness'. In this way 'The symbolic objects – dress, appearance, language, ritual occasions, styles of interaction, music – were made to form a *unity* with the group's relations, situation, experience' (Hall *et al.*, 1976).

The punks would certainly seem to bear out this thesis. The subculture was nothing if not consistent. There was a homological relation between the trashy cut-up clothes and spiky hair, the pogo and amphetamines, the spitting, the vomiting, the format of the fanzines, the insurrectionary poses and the 'soulless', frantically driven music. The punks wore clothes which were the sartorial equivalent of swear words, and they swore as they dressed – with calculated effect, lacing obscenities into record notes and publicity releases, interviews and love songs. Clothed in chaos, they produced Noise in the calmly orchestrated Crisis of everyday life in the late 1970s – a noise which made (no)sense in exactly the same way and to exactly the same extent as a piece of *avant-garde* music. If we were to write an epitaph for the punk subculture, we could do no better than repeat Poly Styrene's famous dictum: 'Oh Bondage, Up Yours!', or somewhat more concisely: the forbidden is permitted, but by the same token, nothing, not even these forbidden signifiers (bondage, safety pins, chains, hair-dye, etc.) is sacred and fixed.

This absence of permanently sacred signifiers (icons) creates problems for the semiotician. How can we discern any positive values reflected in objects which were chosen only to be discarded? For instance, we can say that the early punk ensembles gestured towards the signified's 'modernity' and 'working-classness'. The safety pins and bin liners signified a relative material poverty which was either directly experienced and exaggerated or sympathetically assumed, and which in turn was made to stand for the spiritual paucity of everyday life. In other words, the safety pins, etc. 'enacted' that transition from real to symbolic scarcity which Paul Piccone (1969) has described as the movement from 'empty stomachs' to 'empty spirits – and therefore an empty life notwithstanding [the] chrome and the plastic . . . of the life style of bourgeois society'.

We could go further and say that even if the poverty was being parodied, the wit was undeniably barbed; that beneath the clownish make-up there lurked the unaccepted and disfigured face of capitalism; that beyond the horror circus antics a divided and unequal society was being eloquently condemned. However, if we were to go further still and describe punk music as the 'sound of the Westway', or the pogo as the 'high-rise leap', or to talk of bondage as reflecting the narrow options of working-class youth, we would be treading on less certain ground. Such readings are both too literal and too conjectural. They are extrapolations from the subculture's own prodigious rhetoric, and rhetoric is not self-explanatory: it may say what it means but it does not necessarily 'mean' what it 'says'. In other words, it is opaque: its categories are part of its publicity. To return once more to Mepham (1974), 'The true text is reconstructed not by a process of piecemeal decoding, but by the identification of the generative sets of ideological categories and its replacement by a different set.'

To reconstruct the true text of the punk subculture, to trace the source of its subversive practices, we must first isolate the 'generative set' responsible for the subculture's exotic displays. Certain semiotic facts are undeniable. The punk sub-culture, like every other youth culture, was constituted in a series of spectacular transformations of a whole range of commodities, values, common-sense attitudes, etc. It was through these adapted forms that certain sections of predominantly work-ing-class youth were able to restate their opposition to dominant values and institu-tions. However, when we attempt to close in on specific items, we immediately encounter problems. What, for instance, was the swastika being used to signify?

We can see how the symbol was made available to the punks (via Bowie and Lou Reed's 'Berlin' phase). Moreover, it clearly reflected the punks' interest in a deca-dent and evil Germany – a Germany which had 'no future'. It evoked a period redolent with a powerful mythology. Conventionally, as far as the British were concerned, the swastika signified 'enemy'. None the less, in punk usage, the symbol lost its 'natural' meaning – fascism. The punks were not generally sympathetic to the parties of the extreme right. On the contrary, as I have argued . . . the conflict with the resurrected teddy boys and the widespread support for the anti-fascist movement (e.g. the Rock against Racism campaign) seem to indicate that the punk subculture grew up partly as an antithetical response to the re-emergence of racism in the mid-70s. We must resort, then, to the most obvious of explanations – that the swastika was worn because it was guaranteed to shock. (A punk asked by *Time Out* (17–23 December 1977) why she wore a swastika, replied: 'Punks just like to be hated'.) This represented more than a simple inversion or inflection of the ordinary meanings attached to an object. The signifier (swastika) had been wilfully detached from the concept (Nazism) it conventionally signified, and although it had been re-positioned (as 'Berlin') within an alternative subcultural context, its primary value and appeal derived precisely from its lack of meaning: from its potential for deceit. It was exploited as an empty effect. We are forced to the conclusion that the central value 'held and reflected' in the swastika was the communicated absence of any such identifiable values. Ultimately, the symbol was as 'dumb' as the rage it provoked. The key to punk style remains elusive. Instead of arriving at the point where we can begin to make sense of the style, we have reached the very place where meaning itself evaporates.

[. . .]

Notes

1   Although structuralists would agree with John Mepham (1974) that 'social life is structured like a language', there is also a more mainstream tradition of research into social encounters, role-play, etc. which proves overwhelmingly that social interaction (at least in middle-class white America!) is quite firmly governed by a rigid set of rules, codes and conventions (see in particular Goffman, 1971 and 1972).

2   Hall (1977) states: '. . . culture is the accumulated growth of man's power over nature, materialised in the instruments and practice of labour and in the medium of signs, thought, knowledge and language through which it is passed on from generation to generation as man's "second nature" '.

3   In his P.O. account of the Saturday night dance in an industrial town, Mungham (1976) shows how the constricted quality of working-class life is carried over into the ballroom in the form of courtship rituals, masculine paranoia and an atmos-phere of sullenly repressed sexuality. He paints a gloomy picture of joyless even-ings spent in the desperate pursuit of 'booze and birds' (or 'blokes and a romantic bus-ride home') in a controlled setting where 'spontaneity is regarded by man-agers and their staff – principally the bouncers – as the potential hand-maiden of rebellion'.

4   BOF = Boring old Fart
Wimp = 'wet'.

5   Gilbert and George mounted their first exhibition in 1970 when, clad in identical conservative suits, with metallized hands and faces, a glove, a stick and a tape recorder, they won critical acclaim by performing a series of carefully controlled and endlessly repeated movements on a dais while miming to Flanagan and Allen's 'Underneath the Arches'. Other pieces with titles like 'Lost Day' and 'Normal Boredom' have since been performed at a variety of major art galleries through-out the world.

6   Of course, rock music had always threatened to dissolve these categories, and rock performances were popularly associated with all forms of riot and disorder – from the slashing of cinema seats by teddy boys through Beatlemania to the hippy happenings and festivals where freedom was expressed less aggressively in nudity,

drug taking and general 'spontaneity'. However punk represented a new departure.

7   The word 'punk', like the black American 'funk' and 'superbad' would seem to form part of that 'special language of fantasy and alienation' which Charles Winick describes (1959), 'in which values are reversed and in which "terrible" is a description of excellence'.

See also Wolfe (1969) where he describes the 'cruising' scene in Los Angeles in the mid-60s — a subculture of custom-built cars, sweatshirts and 'high-piled, perfect coiffure' where 'rank' was a term of approval:

> Rank! Rank is just the natural outgrowth of Rotten . . . Roth and Schorsch grew up in the Rotten Era of Los Angeles teenagers. The idea was to have a completely rotten attitude towards the adult world, meaning, in the long run, the whole established status structure, the whole system of people organising their lives around a job, fitting into the social structure embracing the whole community. The idea in Rotten was to drop out of conventional status competition into the smaller netherworld of Rotten Teenagers and start one's own league.

Bibliography

Althusser, L. and Balibar, E. (1968) *Reading Capital*, London: New Left Books.

Barthes, R. (1972) *Mythologies*, London: Paladin.

Clarke, J. (1976) 'Style', in S. Hall *et al.* (eds) *Resistance Through Rituals*, London: Hutchinson.

Eco, U. (1973) 'Social Life as a Sign System', in D. Robey (ed.) *Structuralism: The Wolfson College Lectures 1972*, Oxford: Clarendon.

Goffman, E. (1971) *The Presentation of Self in Everyday Life*, Harmondsworth: Penguin.

—— (1972) *Relations in Public*, Harmondsworth: Penguin.

Hall, S. (1977) 'Culture, the Media and the "Ideological Effect"', in J. Curron, M. Gurevitch and J. Woollacott (eds) *Mass Communication and Society*, London: Arnold.

Hall, S. *et al.* (eds) (1976)) *Resistance Through Rituals*, London: Hutchinson.

Hawkes, T. (1977) *Structuralism and Semiotics*, London: Methuen.

Lippard, L. (1970) *Surrealists on Art*, Englewood Cliffs. N.J.: Prentice-Hall.

Mepham, J. (1974) 'The Theory of Ideology in *Capital*', *W.P.C.S.*, No. 6, University of Birmingham.

Mungham, G. (1976) 'Youth in Pursuit of Itself', in G. Mungham and G. Pearson (eds) *Working Class Youth Culture*, London: Routledge and Kegan Paul.

Piccone, P. (1969) 'From Youth Culture to Political Praxis', *Radical America*, 15 November.

Willis, P. (1978) *Profane Culture*, London: Routledge and Kegan Paul.

Winich, C. (1959) 'The uses of Drugs by Jazz Musicians', *Social Problems* 7, 3 (Winter).

Wolfe, T. (1969) *The Pump House Gang*, New York: Bantam.

PART SEVEN

Fashion, clothes and the body

IT IS HARDLY SURPRISING that fashion theorists and commentators have recently paid much attention to the relation between fashion and the body: the relation is always present and operative, it is complex and it is full of ambivalences. The existence of this relation also seems utterly obvious: how could theorists overlook the fact that fashion and clothes are worn only on or by bodies, that they are embodied, or that people modify their bodies in the name of style and fashion? It is the case, however, that the body was indeed often neglected in early theorising, which once the matters of protecting it from extremes of heat or cold and covering those parts that were considered shameful or obscene had been dealt with, and once the matter of social emulation and display had been mentioned, demonstrated little interest in the body, *qua* body. As Joanne Entwistle and Elizabeth Wilson point out, 'fashion theorists have failed to give due recognition to the way in which dress is a fleshy practice involving the body' (Entwistle and Wilson 2001: 4). And in support of them, one might point out that Quentin Bell's ([1947] 1992) *On Human Finery*, whose publishers were pleased to call the 'classic study of fashion through the ages', for example, makes no mention of the body.

Analytically, there are two ways in which fashion may relate to the body. Firstly and most straightforwardly, the body may be covered or adorned by fashionable clothing; more or less stylish and fashionable clothes are worn on the body. Secondly and less straightforwardly, the body itself may become the object of fashionable attention: body parts, surfaces and features may be modified in various permanent or non-permanent ways in order to be perceived as fashionable. The list of such modifications includes a wide variety of practices, ranging from hair-styling, grooming and cosmetics, piercings, tattoos, cicatrisation and cosmetic dentistry and surgery, through to so-called 'body-art', as exemplified by Stelarc and Orlan, for example. This second relation is not straightforward because it does not preclude the possibility of permanent bodily modifications, and fashion is not obviously about permanent modifications. It is also complicated by the fact that some non-western and non-modern practices, which have been ruled out of the definitions of fashion in the Introduction, would appear to be fashionable. For instance, while modern western cosmetic dentistry and surgery, Chinese foot-binding and Congolese infant skull-bandaging are all ways of modifying the body, the non-western examples are not obviously examples of fashion, though a plausible case may be made for calling the modern western examples fashion. Having said that, even the most modern and western of us does not get our teeth 'corrected' or our nose modified every week, or every season; therefore there is a definite, if indistinct, limit to the sense in which such procedures can be called fashion.

This second and more complex relation also leads the topic of fashion and the body into other areas covered in this volume. The relations between fashion, clothes and the body relate to and overlap the sections on eroticism and fetishism (Part Twelve) and art (Part Three), for example. References to Trevor Sorbie or Andrew Collinge as 'hair artists' are not hard to find, and the performance artists Stelarc and Orlan are well known for radically modifying their bodies through the use of technological prosthetics and surgery respectively. The point to be made here is that various levels and types of bodily modification invite or require the questions, first, 'Is it fashion?' and second, 'Is it art?' The problem of fetishism may be described in similar terms. There is almost certainly nothing in the list of bodily modifications mentioned that is not an eroticised fetish and to that extent, therefore, there is probably nothing that can be done to the body that is not fashion and also erotic or fetishistic. The point to be made again, then, would be that any and all body modifications invite or require the questions: first 'Is it fashion?' and second 'Is it a fetish?' Thus does this second relation between fashion and the body, in which the body is itself the object of fashionable attentions, begin to (sometimes literally) bleed into or overlap with the questions of the erotic, the fetish and of what art is.

These overlaps are made quite explicit in the work of Rei Kawakubo. In their (1991) essay, Caroline Evans and Minna Thornton point out that in her Rose Rayon Dress of 1985, for example, the body is not simply or straightforwardly displayed or covered. The display/cover dichotomy is simply inadequate to describe what is going on with this dress. What the dress does is to reveal 'parts of the body through unexpected vents or holes' (1991: 65). The problem is that which parts are thus revealed are to some extent 'chosen' by the consumer, or wearer, of the garment. With this dress, and with much of Kawakubo's work in the early 1980s, the wearer decides how to wear the garments and therefore which body parts are revealed. Also, the parts of the body that are revealed are 'not presented as static, but as moving and hence constantly changing' (ibid.). Finally, the parts of the body that are revealed, by the 1985 dress at least, are those parts for which there is no obvious or well-known name: the back of the knee, the lower part of the ribcage, and so on. Kawakubo's work engages with many Derridean strategies here: the presence/absence of parts, the humorous display of body parts with no clear names, and the failure to engage with vulgar accounts of 'sexiness' in favour of what Thornton and Evans call an unconventional and complex account of femininity (ibid.). It also engages with the account of the erotic found in Part Twelve. Roland Barthes explains the erotic precisely in terms of gaps and gaping garments. It is the flashing of skin between bits of clothing (open-necked shirts and sleeves are mentioned), and the appearing and disappearing of skin and parts of the body, that Barthes identifies as erotic (1975: 9–10).

To return to the first of the two ways in which it was suggested that fashion and clothing relate to the body may seem initially to be something of a relief. However, while it is true to say that clothes literally cover and conceal the body, it is also the case that they reveal and display that same body. Anyone who has admired the gentle curve of a breast or the muscular chest beneath a t-shirt will appreciate that the covering/displaying dichotomy is hardly sufficient to the task of description. Does the t-shirt prevent you from seeing the breast or does it display it to you? It neither conceals the muscular chest (you are admiring it, after all) nor displays it to you directly (it is still under the shirt). 'Both', 'neither' and 'all of the above, all at the same time' would be equally appropriate answers to these questions. The simple inadequacy of the dichotomous terms of language to decide and then describe what is happening here is surely as disturbing as it is interesting.

And although men may feel a distinct sense of constriction whilst wearing a collar and tie, and women may feel similarly limited whilst wearing a pencil skirt, there is always the accompanying sense that some movements are encouraged, made possible or even forced upon one by these garments. A certain way of holding the head, or a certain kind of walk, is somehow both demanded and made possible by the garment. Yet again, the enabling/disabling dichotomy fails to help us explain what exactly is going on here. The failure of the dichotomous terms of our language adequately to describe our experience is a sure sign that what we are being asked to describe is ambivalent, or undecidable. As Rei Kawakubo of Commes des Garçons says, 'Body becomes dress becomes body becomes dress' (quoted in Loreck 2002: 260). These considerations are followed up with regard to the male anatomy in Umberto Eco's essay.

Similarly, while it is the case that clothes are literally lifeless and inanimate, they also suggest different forms or ways of being animate – ways of posing, holding ourselves or moving around. Even hanging on rails or cast to the floor, unworn (unoccupied, disembodied) clothes inevitably suggest the living, moving bodies that might once have inhabited or may yet inhabit them. They may also suggest certain very definite ways of being inanimate. As Elizabeth Wilson says:

> clothes are so much a part of our living moving selves that, frozen on display in the mausoleums of culture, they hint at something only half understood, sinister, threatening; the atrophy of the body and the evanescence of life.
>
> (Wilson 1985: 1)

Again, the animate/inanimate dichotomy is barely up to the task of describing our experience of fashion and clothing here. While clothes are not alive, they powerfully suggest the presence of live bodies, and, because they are such a part of our living selves, when we see them still and not moving they hint at the absence of our living selves. The oppositions between animate/inanimate and living/dead and present/absent seem to break down in the face of the inability to decide and describe what is happening with clothing here. Given the references to mausoleums and the evanescence of life, one is powerfully reminded of Derrida's account of what he calls 'hauntology', which begins with the notion of the 'specter' and continues until one is no longer sure whether the opposition between the thing and its simulacrum is one that 'holds up' (Derrida 1994: 10).

The extracts collected here deal with the body in a variety of ways: sociology, anthropology, gay studies, cultural studies and gender studies are the sometimes misleading names attached to some of the approaches that are represented in the collection. An extract from Joanne Entwistle's (2000) book *The Fashioned Body* introduces the topic. The notion of the body and its relation to dress is dealt with first, looking at how the body has been understood and presented in fashion theory. The contribution of cultural theory is covered next, before Michel Foucault's place in explaining fashion and the body is explored. The connections to modernity are foregrounded here, as are the relations between power, knowledge and fashion.

Paul Sweetman's (1999) essay 'Anchoring the (Postmodern) Self? Body Modification, Fashion and Identity' explicitly raises the question noted above of whether permanent body modifications and decorations are actually fashion. While tattoos or piercings may be fashionable, in the sense that fashionable people may be seen in the media wearing them for a while, there is a definite sense in which they are perhaps the very opposite of fashion. They may be considered to be anti-fashion in that they are permanent and cannot be easily changed. From a more anthropological perspective, Ted Polhemus considers tattoos to be 'as "anti-fashion" as it is possible to get' in that they render change almost impossible (Polhemus 1994: 13). Polhemus suggests that tattoos might be considered to be 'style' rather than fashion and says that '*style* isn't trendy. Quite the opposite. It's inherently conservative and traditional' (ibid.). Such examples of anti-fashion as tattoos and (to a lesser extent) piercings represent a desire for things not to change, for them to remain the same, and they are thus profoundly conservative in Polhemus's account.

Umberto Eco's essay on wearing jeans is less semiological and more humorous than one might be expecting, especially if one has just read the brief extract from him in Part Five. It does, however, continue the theme of discomfort and pain in pursuit of the fashionable that is raised by Sweetman's essay. Ruth Holliday's essay on what she calls the politics of comfort looks at some of these issues from a gender studies perspective. The notion that comfort, or in Eco's case the lack of it, might have a political dimension is one that repays serious attention and can be contrasted with Stoller's account of the divorced woman's experience of wearing Levi jeans in the selection from Gamman and Makinen in Part Twelve. Eco's account could also be read alongside Tim Dant's account of the same garment in the selection from his work in Part Eight.

Bibliography

Barthes, R. (1975) *The Pleasure of the Text*, New York: Hill and Wang.
Bell, Q. ([1947] 1992) *On Human Finery*, London: Allison and Busby.

Derrida, J. (1994) *Specters of Marx: The State of the Debt, the Work of Mourning and the New International*, London: Routledge.

Entwistle, J. (2000) *The Fashioned Body*, London: Polity.

Entwistle, J. and Wilson, E. (eds) (2001) *Body Dressing*, Oxford: Berg.

Evans, C. and Thornton, M. (1991) 'Fashion, Representation, Femininity', in *Feminist Theory* 38 (Summer): 48–66.

Loreck, H. (2002) 'De/constructing Fashion/Fashions of Deconstruction: Cindy Sherman's Fashion Photographs', *Fashion Theory* 6, 3 (September): 255–76.

MacKendrick, C. (1998) 'Technoflesh, or "Didn't That Hurt?" ', *Fashion Theory* 2, 1: 3–24.

Orlan (see www.orlan.net).

Polhemus, T. (1994) *Streetstyle: From Sidewalk to Catwalk*, London: Thames and Hudson.

Stelarc (1997) 'From Psycho to Cyber Strategies: Prosthetics, Robotics and Remote Existence', *Cultural Values*, 1, 2: 241–9.

—— (see http://www.stelarc.va.com.au/index2.html).

Wilson, E. (1985) *Adorned in Dreams*, London: Virago.

Chapter 24

Joanne Entwistle

ADDRESSING THE BODY

Dress and the body

'THERE IS AN OBVIOUS and prominent fact about human beings', notes Turner (1985: 1) at the start of *The Body and Society*, 'they have bodies and they are bodies'. In other words, the body constitutes the environment of the self, to be inseparable from the self. However, what Turner omits in his analysis is another obvious and prominent fact: that human bodies are *dressed* bodies. The social world is a world of dressed bodies. Nakedness is wholly inappropriate in almost all social situations and, even in situations where much naked flesh is exposed (on the beach, at the swimming-pool, even in the bedroom), the bodies that meet there are likely to be adorned, if only by jewellery, or indeed, even perfume: when asked what she wore to bed, Marilyn Monroe claimed that she wore only Chanel No. 5, illustrating how the body, even without garments, can still be adorned or embellished in some way. Dress is a basic fact of social life and this, according to anthropologists, is true of all known human cultures: all people 'dress' the body in some way, be it through clothing, tattooing, cosmetics or other forms of body painting. To put it another way, no culture leaves the body unadorned but adds to, embellishes, enhances or decorates the body. In almost all social situations we are required to appear dressed, although what constitutes 'dress' varies from culture to culture and also within a culture, since what is considered appropriate dress will depend on the situation or occasion. A bathing-suit, for example, would be inappropriate and shocking if worn to do the shopping, while swimming in one's coat and shoes would be absurd for the purpose of swimming, but perhaps apt as a fund-raising stunt. The cultural significance of dress extends to all situations, even those in which we can go naked: there are strict rules and codes governing when and with whom we can appear undressed. While bodies may go undressed in certain spaces, particularly in the private sphere of the home, the public arena almost always requires that a body be dressed appropriately, to the extent that the flaunting of flesh, or the inadvertent exposure of it in public, is disturbing, disruptive and potentially subversive. Bodies which do not conform, bodies which flout the conventions of their culture and go without the appropriate clothes are subversive of the most basic social codes and risk exclusion, scorn or ridicule. The 'streaker' who strips off and runs across a cricket pitch or soccer stadium draws attention to these conventions in the act of breaking them: indeed, female streaking is defined as a 'public order offence' while the 'flasher', by comparison, can be punished for 'indecent exposure' (Young, 1995: 7).

The ubiquitous nature of dress would seem to point to the fact that dress or adornment is one of the means by which bodies are made social and given meaning and identity. The individual and very personal act of getting dressed is an act of preparing the body for the social world, making it appropriate, acceptable, indeed respectable and possibly even desirable also. Getting dressed is an ongoing practice, requiring knowledge, techniques and skills, from learning how to tie our shoelaces and do up our buttons as children, to understanding about colours, textures and fabrics and how to weave them together to suit our bodies and our lives. Dress is the way in which individuals learn to live in their bodies and feel at home in them. Wearing the right clothes and looking our best, we feel at ease with our bodies, and the opposite is equally true: turning up for a situation inappropriately dressed, we feel awkward, out of place and vulnerable. In this respect, dress is both an intimate experience of the body and a public presentation of it. Operating on the boundary between self and other is the interface between the individual and the social world, the meeting place of the private and the public. This meeting between the intimate experience of the body and the public realm, through the experience of fashion and dress, is the subject of this chapter.

So potent is the naked body that when it is allowed to be seen, as in the case of art, it is governed by social conventions. Berger (1972) argues that within art and media representations there is a distinction between naked and nude, the latter referring to the way in which bodies, even without garments, are 'dressed' by social conventions and systems of representation. Perniola (1990) has also considered the way in which different cultures, in particular the classical Greek and Judaic, articulate and represent nakedness. According to Ann Hollander (1993) dress is crucial to our understanding of the body to the extent that our ways of seeing and representing the naked body are dominated by conventions of dress. As she argues, 'art proves that nakedness is not universally experienced and perceived any more than clothes are. At any time, the unadorned self has more kinship with its own usual *dressed* aspect than it has with any undressed human selves in other times and other places' (1993: xiii). Hollander points to the ways in which depictions of the nude in art and sculpture correspond to the dominant fashions of the day. Thus the nude is never naked but 'clothed' by contemporary conventions of dress.

Naked or semi-naked bodies that break with cultural conventions, especially conventions of gender, are potentially subversive and treated with horror or derision. Competitive female body builders, such as those documented in the semi-documentary film *Pumping Iron II: The Women* (1984), are frequently seen as 'monstrous', as their muscles challenge deeply held cultural assumptions and beg the questions: 'What is a woman's body? Is there a point at which a woman's body becomes something else? What is the relationship between a certain type of body and "femininity"?' (Kuhn 1988: 16; see also Schulze 1990, St Martin and Gavey 1996). In body building, muscles are like clothes, but unlike clothes they are supposedly 'natural'. However, according to Annette Kuhn,

> muscles are rather like drag, for female body builders especially: while muscles can be assumed, like clothing, women's assumption of muscles implies a transgression of the proper boundaries of sexual difference. (1988: 17)

It is apparent from these illustrations that bodies are potentially disruptive. Conventions of dress attempt to transform flesh into something recognizable and meaningful to a culture; a body that does not conform, that transgresses such cultural codes, is likely to cause offence and outrage and be met with scorn or incredulity. This is one of the reasons why dress is a matter of morality: dressed inappropriately we are uncomfortable; we feel ourselves open to social condemnation. According to Bell (1976), wearing the right clothes is so very important that even people not interested in their appearance will dress well enough to avoid social censure. In this sense, he argues, we enter into the realm of feelings 'prudential, ethical and aesthetic, and the workings of what one might call sartorial conscience' (1976: 18–19). He gives the example of a five-day-old beard which could not be worn to the theatre without censure and disapproval 'exactly comparable to that occasioned by dishonourable conduct'. Indeed, clothes are often spoken of in moral terms, using words like 'faultless, "good", "correct" (1976: 19). Few are immune to this social pressure and most people are embarrassed by certain mistakes of dress, such as finding one's flies undone or discovering a stain on a jacket. Thus, as Quentin Bell puts it, "our clothes are too much a part of us for most of us to be entirely indifferent to their condition: it is as though the fabric were indeed a natural extension of the body, or even of the soul" (1976: 19).

This basic fact of the body – that it must, in general, appear appropriately dressed – points to an important aspect of dress, namely its relation to social order, albeit micro-social order. This centrality of dress to social order would seem to make it a prime topic of sociological investigation. However, the classical tradition within sociology failed to acknowledge the significance of dress, largely because it neglected the body and the things that bodies do. More recently, sociology has begun to acknowledge dress, but this literature is still on the margins and is relatively small compared with other sociological areas. A sociology of the body has now emerged which would seem germane to a literature on dress and fashion. However, this literature, as with mainstream sociology, has also tended not to examine dress. While sociology has failed to acknowledge the significance of dress, the literature from history, cultural studies, psychology and so on, where it is often examined, does so almost entirely without acknowledging the significance of the body. Studies of fashion and dress tend to separate dress from the body: art history celebrates the garment as an object, analysing the development of clothing over history and considering the construction and detail of dress (Gorsline 1991, Laver 1969); cultural studies tend to understand dress semiotically, as a 'sign system' (Hebdige 1979, Wright 1992); or to analyse texts and not bodies (Barthes 1985, Brooks 1992, Nixon 1992, Triggs 1992); social psychology looks at the meanings and intentions of dress in social interaction (Cash 1985, Ericksen and Joseph 1985, Tseëlon 1992a, 1992b, 1997). All these studies tend to neglect the body and the meanings the body brings to dress. And yet, dress in everyday life cannot be separated from the living, breathing, moving body it adorns. The importance of the body to dress is such that encounters with dress divorced from the body are strangely alienating. Elizabeth Wilson (1985) grasps the importance of the body in terms of understanding dress and describes the unease one feels in the presence of mannequins in the costume museum. The eeriness of the encounter comes from the 'dusty silence' and stillness of the costumes and from a sense that the museum is 'haunted' by the spirits of the living, breathing humans whose bodies these gowns once adorned:

> The living observer moves with a sense of mounting panic, through a world of the dead . . . We experience a sense of the uncanny when we gaze at garments that had an intimate relationship with human beings long since gone to their graves. For clothes are so much part of our living, moving selves that, frozen on display in the mausoleums of culture, they hint at something only half understood, sinister, threatening, the atrophy of the body, and the evanescence of life. (Wilson 1985: 1)

Just as the discarded shell of any creature appears dead and empty, the gown or suit once cast off seems lifeless, inanimate and alienated from the wearer. The sense of alienation from the body is all the more profound when the garment or the shoes still bear the marks of the body, when the shape of the arms or the form of the feet are clearly visible. However, dress in everyday life is always more than a shell, it is an intimate aspect of the experience and presentation of the self and is so closely linked to the identity that these three – dress, the body and the self – are not perceived separately but simultaneously, as a totality. When dress is pulled apart from the body/self, as it is in the costume museum, we grasp only a fragment, a partial snapshot of dress, and our understanding of it is thus limited. The costume museum makes the garment into a fetish, it tells of how the garment was made, the techniques of stitching, embroidery and decoration used as well as the historical era in which it was once worn. What it cannot tell us is how the garment was worn, how the garment moved when on a body, what it sounded like when it moved and how it felt to the wearer. Without a body, dress lacks fullness and movement; it is incomplete (Entwistle and Wilson 1998).

A sociological perspective on dress requires moving away from the consideration of dress as object to looking instead at the way in which dress is an embodied activity and one that is embedded within social relations. Wright's analysis of clothing (1992) acknowledges the way in which dress operates on the body and how clothing worn deliberately small (such as leggings or trousers that do not meet the ankles) works to emphasize particular body parts. However, in general, studies of dress neglect the way in which it operates on the body and there remains a need to consider dress in everyday life as embodied practice: how dress operates on a phenomenal, moving body and how it is a practice that involves individual actions of attending *to* the body *with* the body. This chapter considers the theoretical resources for a sociology of dress that acknowledges the significance of the body. I propose the idea of dress as situated bodily practice as a theoretical and methodological framework for understanding the complex dynamic relationship between the body, dress and culture. Such a framework recognizes that bodies are socially constituted, always situated in culture and the outcome of individual practices directed towards the body: in other words, 'dress' is the result of 'dressing' or 'getting dressed'. Examining the structuring influences on the dressed body requires taking account of the historical and social constraints on the body, constraints which impact upon the act of 'dressing' at a given time. In addition, it requires that the physical body is constrained by the social situation and is thus the product of the social context as Douglas (1973, 1984) has argued.

Becoming a competent member involves acquiring knowledge of the cultural norms and expectations demanded of the body, something Mauss (1973) has examined in terms of 'techniques of the body'. Goffman (1971) has described forcefully the ways in which cultural norms and expectations impose upon the 'presentation of self in everyday life' to the extent that individuals perform 'face work' and seek to be defined by others as 'normal'. Dressing requires one to attend unconsciously or consciously to these norms and expectations when preparing the body for presentation in any particular social setting. The phrase 'getting dressed' captures this idea of dress as an activity. Dress is therefore the outcome of *practices* which are socially constituted but put into effect by the individual: individuals must attend to their bodies when they 'get dressed' and it is an experience that is as intimate as it is social. When we get dressed, we do so within the bounds of a culture and its particular norms, expectations about the body and about what constitutes a 'dressed' body.

Most of the theorists I discuss do not specifically relate their account of the body to dress, but I have aimed to draw out the implications of each theoretical perspective for the study of the dressed body. The main discussion focuses on the uses and limitations both of structuralist and post-structuralist approaches, since these have been influential in the sociological study of the body: in particular, the work of Mauss (1973), Douglas (1973, 1984) and the post-structuralist approach of Foucault (1977, 1980) are pertinent to any discussion of the body in culture. However, another tradition, that of phenomenology, particularly that of Merleau-Ponty (1976, 1981) has also become increasingly influential in terms of producing an account of embodiment. These two theoretical traditions have, according to Crossley (1996), been considered by some to be incommensurable but, as he argues, they can offer different and complementary insights into the body in society. Following both Csordas (1993, 1996) and Crossley (1995a, 1995b, 1996), I argue that an account of dress as situated practice requires drawing on the insights of these two different traditions, structuralism and phenomenology. Structuralism offers the potential to understand the body as a *socially constituted and situated object*, while phenomenology offers the potential to understand dress as an *embodied experience*. In terms of providing an account of the dressed body as a practical accomplishment, two further theorists are of particular importance, Bourdieu (1984, 1994) and Goffman (1971, 1979). Their insights are discussed at the end of this chapter to illustrate the ways in which a sociology of the dressed body might bridge the gap between the traditions of structuralism, post-structuralism and phenomenology.

Theoretical resources

The body as cultural object

All the theorists discussed in this chapter can broadly be described as 'social con-structivists', in that they take the body to be a thing of culture and not merely a biological entity. This is in contrast to approaches that assume what Chris Shilling (1993) refers to as the 'naturalistic body'. These approaches, for example, socio-biology, consider the body 'as a pre-social, biological basis on which the super-structures of the self and society are founded' (1993: 41). Since the body has an 'obvious' presence as a 'natural' phenomenon, such a 'naturalistic' approach is appealing and indeed it may seem odd to suggest that the body is a 'socialy con-structed' object. However, while it is the case that the body has a material presence, it is also true that the material of the body is always and everywhere culturally interpreted: biology does not stand outside culture but is located within it. That said, the 'taken-for-granted' assumption that biology stands outside culture was, for a long time, one of the reasons why the body was neglected as an object of study by social theorists. While this is now an object of investigation within anthropology, cultural studies, literary studies, film theory and feminist theory, it is worthwhile pointing out the ways in which classical social theory previously ignored or repressed the body, since this may account, at least in part, for why it has largely neglected dress.

Turner (1985) gives two reasons for this academic neglect of the body. First, social theory, particularly sociology, inherited the Cartesian dualism which priori-tized mind and its properties of consciousness and reason over the body and its properties of emotion and passion. Further, as part of its critiques of both behaviour-ism and essentialism, the classical sociological tradition tended to avoid explanations of the social world which took into account the human body, focusing instead on the human actor as a sign-maker and a maker of meaning. Similarly, sociology's concern with historicity and with social order in modern societies, as opposed to ontological questions, did not appear to involve the body. As Turner argues, instead of nature/culture, sociology has concerned itself with self/society or agency/structure. A further reason for the neglect of the body is that it treated the body as a natural and not a social phenomenon, and therefore not a legitimate object for sociological investigation.

However, there has been growing recognition that the body has a history and this has been influential in establishing the body as a prime object of social theory (Bakhtin 1984, Elias 1978, Feher et al. 1989, Laquer and Gallagher 1987, Laquer and Bourgois 1992, Sennett 1994). Norbert Elias (1978) points to the ways in which our modern understandings and experiences of the body are historically specific, arising out of processes, both social and psychological, which date back to the sixteenth century. He examines how historical developments such as the increasing centralization of power to fewer households with the emergence of aristocratic and royal courts served to reduce violence between individuals and groups and induce greater social control over the emotions. The medieval courts demanded increas-ingly elaborate codes of behaviour and instilled in individuals the need to monitor their bodies to produce themselves as 'well mannered' and 'civil'. As relatively social mobile arenas, the medieval courts promoted the idea that one's success or failure depended upon the demonstration of good manners, civility and wit and in this respect the body was the bearer of social status, a theme later explored in contemporary culture by Bourdieu (1984, 1994) in his account of 'cultural capital' and the 'habitus'. The impact of these developments was the promotion of new psychological structures which served to induce greater consciousness of oneself as an 'individual' in a self-contained body.

Along with histories of the body, anthropology has been particularly influential in terms of establishing the legitimacy of the body as an object of social study (Benthall 1976, Berthelot 1991, Featherstone 1991a, Featherstone and Turner 1995, Frank 1990, Polhemus 1988, Polhemus and Proctor 1978, Shilling 1993, Synnott 1993, Turner 1985, 1991). Turner (1991) gives four reasons for this. First, anthropology was initially concerned with questions of ontology and the nature/culture dichotomy; this led it to consider how the body, as an object of nature, is mediated by culture. A second feature of anthropology was its preoccupation with needs and how needs are met by culture, an interest which focuses in part on the body. Two further sets of concerns focus on the body as a symbolic entity: for example, the body in the work of Mary Douglas (1973, 1979, 1984) is considered as a primary classification system for cultures, the means by which notions of order and disorder are represented and managed; in the work of people like Blacking (1977) and Bourdieu (1984) the body is taken to be an important bearer of social status.

For the anthropologist Marcel Mauss the body is shaped by culture and he describes in detail what he calls the 'techniques of the body' which are 'the ways in which from society to society men [sic] know how to use their bodies' (1973: 70). These techniques of the body are an important means for the socialization of individuals into culture: indeed, the body is the means by which an individual comes to know and live in a culture. According to Mauss, the ways in which men and women come to use their bodies differ since techniques of the body are gendered. Men and women learn to walk, talk, run, fight differently. Furthermore, although he says little about dress, he does comment on the fact that women learn to walk in high heels, a feat which requires training to do successfully, and which, as a consequence of socialization, is not acquired by the majority of men.

Douglas (1973, 1979, 1984) has also acknowledged the body as a natural object shaped by social forces. She therefore suggests that there are 'two bodies': the physical body and the social body. She summarizes the relationship between them in *Natural Symbols*:

> the social body constrains the way the physical body is perceived. The physical experience of the body, always modified by the social categories through which it is known, sustains a particular view of society. There is a continual exchange of meanings between the two kinds of bodily experience so that each reinforces the categories of the other. (1973: 93)

According to Douglas, the physiological properties of the body are thus the starting-point for culture, which mediates and translates them into meaningful symbols. Indeed, she argues that there is a natural tendency for all societies to symbolize the body, for the body and its physiological properties, such as its waste products, furnish culture with a rich resource for symbolic work: 'the body is capable of furnishing a natural system of symbols' (1973: 12). This means that the body is a highly restricted medium of expression since it is heavily mediated by culture and expresses the social pressure brought to bear on it. The social situation thus imposes itself upon the body and constrains it to act in particular ways. Indeed, the body becomes a symbol of the situation. Douglas (1979) gives the example of laughing to illustrate this. Laughter is a physiological function: it starts in the face but can infuse the entire body. She asks, 'what is being communicated? The answer is: information from the social system' (1979: 87). The social situation determines the degree to which the body can laugh: the looser the constraints, the more free the body is to laugh out loud. In this way, the body and its functions and boundaries symbolically articulate the concerns of the particular group in which it is found and, indeed, become a symbol of the situation. Groups that are worried about threats to their cultural or national boundaries might articulate this fear through rituals around the body, particularly pollution rituals and ideas about purity (1984). Douglas's analysis (1973) of shaggy and smooth hair also illustrates this relationship between the body and the situation. Shaggy hair, once a symbol of rebellion, can be found among those professionals who are in a position to critique society, in particular, academics and artists. Smooth hair, however, is likely to be found among those who conform, such as lawyers and bankers. This focus on the body as a symbol has led Turner (1985) and Shilling (1993) to agree that Douglas's work is less an anthropology of the body and more 'an anthropology of the symbolism of risk and, we might add, of social location and stratification' (Shilling 1993: 73).

This analysis can of course be extended to dress and adornment. Dress in everyday life is the outcome of social pressures and the image the dressed body makes can be symbolic of the situation in which it is found. Formal situations such as weddings and funerals have more elaborate rules of dress than informal situations and tend to involve more 'rules', such as the black tie and evening dress stipulation. This dress in turn conveys information about that situation. In such formal situations one also finds conventional codes of gender more rigidly enforced than in informal settings. Formal situations, such as job interviews, business meetings and formal evening events tend to demand clear gender boundaries in dress. A situation demanding 'evening dress' will not only tend to be formal but the interpretation of evening dress will be gendered: generally this will be read as a gown for a woman and black tie and dinner jacket for a man. Men and women choosing to reverse this code and cross-dress risk being excluded from the situation. Other specific situations which demand clear codes of dress for men and women can be found within the professions, particularly the older professions such as law, insurance and City finance. Here again, the gender boundary is normally clearly marked by the enforcement, sometimes explicit, sometimes implicit, of a skirt for women. Colour is also gendered more clearly at work: the suit worn by men in the City is still likely to be black, blue or grey but women in the traditional professions are allowed to wear bright reds, oranges, turquoises and so on. Men's ties add a decorative element to the suits and can be bright, even garish, but this is generally offset by a dark and formal backdrop. The professional workplace, with its norms and expectations, reproduces conventional ideas of 'feminine' and 'masculine' through the imposition of particular codes of dress. In this way, codes of dress form part of the management of bodies in space, operating to discipline bodies to perform in particular ways. To follow Douglas's idea of the body as a symbol of the situation, the image of the body conveys information about that situation. Even within the professions there is some degree of variation as to the formality of bodily presentation: the more traditional the workplace, the more formal it will be and the greater the pressures on the body to dress according to particular codes which are rigidly gendered. I return to this theme in more detail below, when I examine the applications of Foucault's work to the analysis of power-dressing, which is a gendered discourse on dress operating in the professional workplace.

While anthropology has been influential in suggesting how the body has been shaped by culture, Turner (1985) suggests that it is the work of the historian and philosopher Michel Foucault that has effectively demonstrated the importance of the body to social theory, helping to inaugurate a sociology of the body. In contrast to classic social theorists who ignore or repress the body, Foucault's history of modernity (1976, 1977, 1979, 1980) puts the human body centre stage, considering the way in which the emergent disciplines of modernity were centrally concerned with the management of individual bodies and populations of bodies. His account of the body as an object shaped by culture has never been applied specifically to dress but is of considerable relevance for understanding fashion and dress as important sites for discourses on the body.

The influence of Foucault

Foucault's account of modernity focuses on the way in which power/knowledge are interdependent: there is no power without knowledge and no knowledge that is not implicated in the exercise of power. According to Foucault, the body is the object that modern knowledge/power seizes upon and invests with power since 'nothing is more material, physical, corporeal than the exercise of power' (1980: 57–8). Foucault's ideas about the relations between power/knowledge are embedded in his notion of a discourse. Discourses for Foucault are regimes of knowledge that lay down the conditions of possibility for thinking and speaking: at any particular time, only some statements come to be recognized as 'true'. These discourses have implications for the way in which people operate since discourses are not merely textual but put into practice at the micro-level of the body. Power invests in bodies, and in the eighteenth and nineteenth centuries this investment replaces rituals around the body of the monarch: 'in place of the rituals that served to restore the corporal integrity of the monarch, remedies and therapeutic devices are employed such as the segregation of the sick, the monitoring of contagions, the exclusion of delinquents' (Foucault, 1980: 55).

Turner (1985) suggests that Foucault's work enables us to see both how individual bodies are managed by the development of specific regimes, for example in diet and exercise, which call upon the individual to take responsibility for their own health and fitness (the discipline of the body), and how the bodies of populations are managed and co-ordinated (bio-politics). These two are intimately related, particularly with respect to the way in which control is achieved, namely through a system of surveillance or panopticism. This is forcefully illustrated in *Discipline and Punish*, in which Foucault describes how new discourses on criminality from the late eighteenth century onwards resulted in new ways of managing the 'criminal', namely the prison system. From the early nineteenth century new ways of thinking about criminality emerged: 'criminals' were said to be capable of 'reform' (rather than being inherently 'evil' or possessed by the devil) and new systems for stimulating this reform were imposed. In particular, the mechanism of surveillance encourages individual prisoners to relate to themselves and to their bodies and conduct in particular ways. This is reinforced by the organization of space in modern buildings around the principle of an 'all-seeing eye': an invisible but omnipresent observer such as that described in the 1780s by Jeremy Bentham (1843) in his design for the perfect prison, the 'Panopticon'. This structure allowed for maximum observation: cells bathed in light are arranged around a central watch tower which always remains dark, making the prisoners unaware of when they were watched and by whom. This structure is used by Foucault as a metaphor for modern society which he saw as 'carceral' since it was a society built upon institutional observation, in schools, hospitals, army barracks etc., with the ultimate aim to 'normalize' bodies and behaviour. Discipline, rather than being imposed on the 'fleshy' body through torture and physical punishment, operates through the establishment of the 'mindful' body which calls upon individuals to monitor their own behaviour. However, while from the eighteenth to the early twentieth century 'it was believed that the investment in the body by power had to be heavy, ponderous, meticulous and constant', Foucault suggests that by the mid-twentieth century this had given way to a 'looser' form of power over the body and new investments in sexuality (1980: 58). Power for Foucault is 'force relations'; it is not the property of anyone or any group of individuals but is invested everywhere and in everyone. Those whose bodies are invested in by power can therefore subvert that same power by resisting or subverting it. He therefore argues that where there is power there is resistance to power. Once power has invested in bodies, there 'inevitably emerge the responding claims and affirmations, those of one's own body against power, of health against the economic system, of pleasure against the moral norms of sexuality, marriage, decency . . . power, after investing itself in the body, finds itself exposed to a counter attack in the same' (1980: 56). This idea of 'reverse discourse' is a powerful one and can help to explain why discourses on sexuality from the nineteenth century onwards, used at first to label and pathologize bodies and desires, subsequently produced sexual types such as the 'homosexual'; such labels were adopted to name individual desires and produce an alternative identity.

Foucault's insights can be applied to contemporary society, which encourages individuals to take responsibility for themselves. As Shilling (1993) notes, potential dangers to health have reached global proportions, yet individuals in the west are told by governments that as good citizens they have a responsibility to take care of their own bodies. Contemporary discourses on health, appearance and the like tie the body and identity together and serve to promote particular practices of body care that are peculiar to modern society. The body in contemporary western societies is subject to social forces of a rather different nature to the ways in which the body is experienced in more traditional communities. Unlike traditional communities, the body is less bound up with inherited models of socially acceptable bodies which were central to the ritual life, the communal ceremonies of a traditional community, and tied more to modern notions of the 'individual' and personal identity. It has become, according to Shilling (1993) and others (Giddens 1991, Featherstone 1991b) 'a more reflexive process'. Our bodies are experienced as the 'envelope' of the self, conceived of as singular and unique.

Mike Featherstone (1991a) investigates the way in which the body is experienced in contemporary 'consumer culture'. He argues that since the early twentieth century there has been a dramatic increase in self-care regimes of the body. The body has become the focus for increasing 'work' (exercise, diet, make-up, cosmetic surgery etc.) and there is a general tendency to see the body as part of one's self that is open to revision, change, transformation. The growth of healthy lifestyle regimes is testament to this idea that our bodies are unfinished, open to change. Exercise manuals and videos promise transformation of our stomachs, our hips and thighs and so on. We are no longer content to see the body as finished, but actively intervene to change its shape, alter its weight and contours. The body has become part of a project to be worked at, a project increasingly linked to a person's identity of self. The care of the body is not simply about health, but about feeling good: increasingly, our happiness and personal fulfilment is pinned on the degree to which our bodies conform to contemporary standards of health and beauty. Health books and fitness videos compete with one another, offering a chance to feel better, happier as well as healthier. Giddens (1991) notes how self-help manuals have become something of a growth industry in late modernity, encouraging us to think about and act upon our selves and our bodies in particular ways. Dress fits into this overall 'reflexive project' as something we are increasingly called upon to think about: manuals on how to 'dress for success' (such as Molloy's classic *Women: Dress for Success, 1980*) image consultancy services (the US-based 'Color Me Beautiful' being the obvious example) and television programmes (such as the *Clothes Show* and *Style Challenge* in the UK) are increasingly popular, all encouraging the view that one can be 'transformed' through dress.

Featherstone (1991a) argues that the rise in products associated with dieting, health and fitness points not only to the increasing significance of our appearance but to the importance attached to bodily preservation within late capitalist society. Although dieting, exercising and other forms of body discipline are not entirely new to consumer culture, they operate to discipline the body in new ways. Throughout the centuries and in all traditions, different forms of bodily discipline have been recommended: Christianity, for example, has long advocated the disciplining of the body through diet, fasting, penance and so on. However, whereas discipline was employed to mortify the flesh, as a *defence* against pleasure which was considered sinful by Christianity, in contemporary culture such techniques as dieting are employed in order to *increase* pleasure. Asceticism has been replaced by hedonism, pleasure-seeking and gratification of the body's needs and desires. The discipline of the body and the pleasure of the flesh are no longer in opposition to one another: instead, discipline of the body through dieting and exercise has become one of the keys to *achieve* a sexy, desirable body which in turn will bring you pleasure.

Discourses of dress   Since Foucault said nothing about fashion or dress, his ideas about power/knowledge initially seem to have little application to the study of the dressed body. However, his approach to thinking about power and its grip on the body can be utilized to discuss the way in which discourses and practices of dress operate to discipline the body. As I argued at the beginning of this chapter, the dressed body is a product of culture, the outcome of social forces pressing upon the body. Foucault's account therefore offers one way of thinking about the structuring influence of social forces on the body as well as offering a way of questioning commonsense understandings about modern dress. It is common to think about dress in the twentieth century as more 'liberated' than previous centuries particularly the nineteenth. The style of clothes worn in the nineteenth century now seem rigid and constraining of the body. The corset seems a perfect example of nineteenth-century discipline of the body: it was obligatory for women, and an uncorseted woman was considered to be morally deplorable (or 'loose' which metaphorically refers to lax stays). As such it can be seen as something more than a garment of clothing, something linked to morality and the social oppression of women. In contrast, styles of dress today are said to be more relaxed, less rigid and physically constraining: casual clothes are commonly worn and gender codes seem less rigidly imposed. However, this conventional story of increasing bodily 'liberation' can be told differently if we apply a Foucauldian approach to fashion history: such a simple contrast between nineteenth- and twentieth-century styles is shown to be problematic. As Wilson argues (1992), in place of the whalebone corset of the nineteenth century we have the modern corset of muscle required by contemporary standards of beauty. Beauty now requires a new form of discipline rather than no discipline at all: in order to achieve the firm tummy required today, one must exercise and watch what one eats. While the stomach of the nineteenth-century corseted woman was disciplined from the outside, the twentieth-century exercising and dieting woman has a stomach disciplined by exercise and diet imposed by self-discipline (a transformation of discipline regimes something like Foucault's move from the 'fleshy' to the 'mindful' body). What has taken place has been a *qualitative* shift in the discipline rather than a quantitative one, although one could argue that the self-discipline required by the modern body is *more* powerful and more demanding than before, requiring great effort and commitment on the part of the individual which was not required by the corset wearer.

Foucault's notion of power can be applied to the study of dress in order to consider the ways in which the body acquires meaning and is acted upon by social and discursive forces and how these forces are implicated in the operation of power. Feminists such as McNay (1992) and Diamond and Quinby (1988) argue that Foucault ignores the issue of gender, a crucial feature of the social construction of the body. However, while he may have been 'gender blind', his theoretical concepts and his insights into the way the body is acted on by power can be applied to take account of gender. In this respect, one can use his ideas about power and discourse to examine how dress plays a crucial part in marking out the gender boundary which the fashion system constantly redefines each season. Gaines (1990: 1) argues that dress delivers 'gender as self-evident or natural' when in fact gender is a cultural construction that dress helps to reproduce. Dress codes reproduce gender: the association of women with long evening dresses or, in the case of the professional workplace, skirts, and men with dinner jackets and trousers is an arbitrary one but nonetheless comes to be regarded as 'natural' so that femininity is connoted in the gown, masculinity in the black tie and dinner jacket. Butler's work on performativity (1990, 1993), influenced by Foucault, looks at the way in which gender is the product of styles and techniques such as dress rather than any essential qualities of the body. She argues that the arbitrary nature of gender is most obviously revealed by drag when the techniques of one gender are exaggerated and made unnatural. Similarly Haug (1987), drawing heavily on Foucault, denaturalizes the common techniques and strategies employed to make oneself 'feminine': the 'feminine' body is an effect of styles of body posture, demeanour and dress. Despite the fact that Foucault ignores gender in his account of the body, his ideas about the way in which the body is constructed by discursive practices provides a theoretical framework within which to examine the reproduction of gender through particular technologies of the body.

A further illustration of how dress is closely linked to gender and indeed power is the way in which discourses on dress construct it as a 'feminine' thing. Tseëlon (1997) gives a number of examples of how women have historically been associated with the 'trivialities' of dress in contrast to men who have been seen to rise above such mundane concerns having renounced decorative dress (Flügel 1930). As Tseëlon (1997) suggests, women have historically been defined as trivial, superficial, vain, even evil because of their association with the vanities of dress by discourses ranging from theology to fashion. Furthermore, discourses on or about fashion have therefore constructed women as the object of fashion, even its victim (Veblen 1953, Roberts 1977). Dress was not considered a matter of equal male and female concern and, moreover, a woman's supposed 'natural' disposition to decorate and adorn herself served to construct her as 'weak' or 'silly' and open her to moral condemnation. A Foucauldian analysis could provide insight into the ways in which women are constructed as closer to fashion and 'vain', perhaps by examining, as Efrat Tseëlon (1997) does, particular treatises on women and dress such as those found in the Bible or the letters of St Paul.

These associations of women with dress and appearance continue even today and are demonstrated by the fact that what a woman wears is still a matter of greater moral concern than what a man wears. Evidence of this can be found in cases of sexual harassment at work as well as sexual assault and rape cases. Discourses on female sexuality and feminine appearance within institutions such as the law associate women more closely with the body and dress than men. Wolf (1991) notes that lawyers in rape cases in all American states except Florida can legally cite what a woman wore at the time of attack and whether or not the clothing was 'sexually provocative'. This is true in other countries as well. Lees (1999) demonstrates how judges in the UK often base their judgements in rape cases on what a woman was wearing at the time of her attack. A woman can be cross-examined and her dress shown in court as evidence of her culpability in the attack or as evidence of her consent to sex. In one case a woman's shoes (not leather but 'from the cheaper end of the market') were used to imply that she too was 'cheap' (1999: 6). In this way, dress is used discursively to construct the woman as 'asking for it'. Although neither Wolf nor Lees draws on Foucault, it is possible to imagine a discourse analysis of legal cases such as these which construct a notion of a culpable female 'victim' through a discourse on sexuality, morality and dress. In addition, greater demands are made upon a woman's appearance than a man's and the emphasis on women's appearance serves to add what Wolf (1991) calls a 'third shift' to the work and housework women do. Hence, the female body is a potential liability for women in the workplace. Women are more closely identified with the body, as Ortner (1974) and others have suggested; anthropological evidence would seem to confirm this (Moore 1994). Cultural association with the body results in women having to monitor their bodies and appearance more closely than men. Finally, codes of dress in particular situations impose more strenuous regimes upon the bodies of women than they do upon men. In these ways, discourses and regimes of dress are linked to power in various and complex ways and subject the bodies of the women to greater scrutiny than men.

Returning to the issue of dress at work, we can apply Foucault's insights to show how institutional and discursive practices of dress act upon the body and are employed in the workplace as part of institutional and corporate strategies of management. Carla Freeman (1993) draws on Foucault's notion of power, particularly his idea about the Panopticon, to consider how dress is used in one data-processing corporation, *Data Air*, as a strategy of corporate discipline and control over the female workforce. In this corporation a strict dress code insisted that the predominantly female workers dress 'smartly' in order to project a 'modern' and 'professional' image of the corporation. If their dress did not meet this standard they were subject to disciplinary techniques by their managers and could even be sent home to change their clothes. The enforcement of this dress code was facilitated by the open-plan office, which subjects the women to constant surveillance from the gaze of managers. Such practices are familiar to many offices, although the mechanisms for enforcing dress codes vary enormously. Particular discourses of dress categorizing 'smart' or 'professional' dress, for example, and particular strategies of dress, such as the imposition of uniforms and dress codes at work, are utilized by corporations to exercise control over the bodies of the workers within.

As I have demonstrated, Foucault's framework is quite useful for analysing the situated practice of dress. In particular, his notion of discourse is a good starting-point for analysing the relations between ideas on dress and gender and forms of discipline of the body. However, there are problems with Foucault's notion of discourse as well as problems stemming from his conceptualization of the body and of power, in particular his failure to acknowledge embodiment and agency. These problems stem from Foucault's post-structuralist philosophy and these I now want to summarize in order to suggest how his theoretical perspective, while useful in many respects, is also problematic for a study of dress as situated practice.

Problems with Foucault's theory and method   As a post-structuralist, Foucault does not tell us very much about how discourses are adopted by individuals and how they are translated by them. In other words, his is an account of the socially processed body and tells us how the body is talked about and acted on but it does not provide an account of practice. In terms of understanding fashion/dress, his framework cannot describe dress as it is lived and experienced by individuals. For example, the existence of the corset and its connection to moral discourses about female sexuality tell us little or nothing about how Victorian women experienced the corset, how they chose to lace it and how tightly, and what bodily sensations it produced. Ramazanoglu (1993) argues that the notion of reverse discourse is potentially very useful to feminists, but it is not developed fully in his analysis. It would seem that by investing importance in the body, dress opens up the potential for women to use it for their own purposes. So while the corset is seen by some feminists (Roberts 1977) as a garment setting out to discipline the female body and make her 'docile' and subservient, an 'exquisite slave', Kunzle (1982) has argued in relation to female tight-lacers that these women (and some men) were not passive or masochistic victims of partriarchy, but socially and sexually assertive. Kunzle's suggestion is that women more than men have used their sexuality to climb the social ladder and, if his analysis is accepted, could perhaps be seen as one example of the 'reverse discourse'. He illustrates (unwittingly since he does not discuss Foucault) that once power is invested in the female body as a sexual body, there is a potential for women to utilize this for their own advancement.

Foucault's particular form of post-structuralism is thus not sensitive to the issue of practice. Instead it *presumes* effects, at the level of individual practice, from the existence of discourse alone. He thus 'reads' texts *as if* they were practice rather than a possible structuring influence on practice that might or might not be implemented. In assuming that discourse automatically has social effects, Foucault's method 'reduce[s] the individual agent to a socialised parrot which must speak/perform in a determinate manner in accordance with the rules of language' (Turner 1985: 175). In failing to produce any account of how discourses get taken up in practices, Foucault also fails to give an adequate explanation of how resistance to discourse is possible. Rather, he produces an account of bodies as the surveilled objects of power/knowledge. This, as McNay (1992) argues, results in an account of 'passive bodies': bodies are assumed to be entirely without agency or power. This conception undermines Foucault's explicit contention that power, once invested in bodies, is enabling and productive of its own resistance.

Turner (1985) commends the work of Volosinov as an alternative to this version of structuralism. In Volosinov's work, language is a system of possibilities rather than invariant rules; it does not have uniform effects but is adapted and amended in the course of action by individuals. Bourdieu (1989) also provides a critique of structuralism that claims to know in advance, from the mere existence of rules, how human action will occur. He attempts a 'theory of practice' which considers how individuals orient themselves and their actions to structures but are not entirely pre-determined by them. His notion of practice is sensitive to the tempo of action; to how, in the course of action, individuals improvise rather than simply reproduce rules. . . .

This focus on structures (as opposed to practices) in Foucault's work is closely related to the second major problem with structuralism and post-structuralism, namely the lack of any account of agency. For Foucault, the body replaces both the liberal-humanist conception of the individual and the Marxist notion of human agency in history. However, the focus on 'passive bodies' does not explain how individuals may act in an autonomous fashion. If bodies are produced and manipulated by power, then this would seem to contradict Foucault's concern to see power as force relations which are never simply oppressive. The extreme anti-humanism of Foucault's work, most notably in *Discipline and Punish*, is questioned by Lois McNay (1992) because it does not allow for notions of subjectivity and experience. With this problem in mind, McNay is critical of the attention feminists have paid to this aspect of his work and turns instead to Foucault's later work on the 'ethics of the self'. She argues that in his later work Foucault develops an approach to questions of the self and how selves act upon themselves, thus counteracting some of the problems of his earlier work. He acknowledged the problems with his earlier work and addressed some of these criticisms by arguing that

> if one wants to analyse the genealogy of the subject in Western civilisation, one has to take into account not only technologies of domination but also technologies of self . . . When I was studying asylums, prisons and so on, I perhaps insisted too much on the technologies of domination . . . it is only one aspect of the art of governing people in our societies. (Foucault in McNay 1992: 49)

Hence, Foucault's later work began to examine techniques of subjectification – how humans relate to and construct the self – and he considered how, for example, sexuality emerges in the modern period as an important arena for the constitution of the self. In the second volume of *The History of Sexuality* Foucault (1985; also 1986, 1988) goes on to consider how the self comes to act upon itself in a conscious desire for improvement. These 'technologies of the self' do go some way to counteract the problems of Foucault's earlier work and are potentially useful for understanding the way in which individuals 'fashion' themselves. For example, discourses on dress at work operate less by imposing dress on the bodies of workers, and more by stimulating ways of thinking and acting on the self. Power-dressing can be analysed as a 'technology' of the self: in dress manuals and magazine articles the 'rules' of power-dressing were laid out in terms of techniques and strategies for acting on the self in order to 'dress for success'. Thus the discourse on power-dressing, which emerged in the 1980s to address the issue of how professional women should present themselves at work, invoked notions of the self as 'enterprising'. As I have argued elsewhere (Entwistle 1997, 2000) the woman who identified with power-dressing was someone who came to think of herself as an 'enterprising' subject, someone who was ambitious, self-managing, individualistic.

[. . .]

Bibliography

Bakhtin, M. (1984) *Rabelais and His World*, Bloomington: Indiana University Press.
Barthes, R. (1985) *The Fashion System*, London: Cape.
Bell, Q. (1976) *On Human Finery*, London: Hogarth Press.
Benthall, J. (1976) *The Body Electric: Patterns of Western Industrial Culture*, London: Thames and Hudson.
Berger, J. (1972) *Ways of Seeing*, Harmondsworth: Penguin.
Berthelot, J. M. (1991) 'Sociological Discourse and The Body', in M. Featherston, M. Hepworth and B. Turner (eds) *The Body: Social Process and Cultural Theory*, London: Sage.
Blacking, J. (1977) *The Anthropology of the Body*, London: Academic Press.
Bourdieu, P. (1984) *Distinction: A Social Critique of the Judgement of Taste*, Cambridge, Mass.: Harvard University Press.

—— (1989) *Outline of a Theory of Practice*, Cambridge: Cambridge University Press.

—— (1994) 'Structures, Habitus and Practices', in P. Press Staff (eds) *The Polity Reader in Social Theory*, Cambridge: Polity Press.

Brooks, R. (1992) 'Fashion Photography, the Double-Page Spread: Helmut Newton, Guy Bourdin and Deborah Turbeville', in J. Ash and E. Wilson (eds) *Chic Thrills*, London: Pandora.

Butler, J. (1990) *Gender Trouble: Feminism and the Subversion of Identity*, London: Routledge.

—— (1993) *Bodies That Matter*, London: Routledge.

Cash, T. F. (1985) 'The Impact of Grooming Style on the Evaluation of Women in Management', in M. R. Solomon (ed.) *The Psychology of Fashion*, New York: Lexington Books.

Crossley, N. (1995a) 'Body Techniques, Agency and Inter-Corporality: On Goffman's Relations in Public', *Sociology* 129, 1: 133–49.

—— (1995b) 'Merleau-Ponty, the Elusive Body and Carnal Sociology', *Body and Society* 1, 1: 43–63.

—— (1996) 'Body/Subject. Body/Power: Agency, Inscription and Control in Foucault and Merleau-Ponty', *Body and Society* 2, 2: 99–116.

Csordas, T. J. (1993) 'Somatic Modes of Attention', *Cultural Anthropology* 8, 2: 135–56.

—— (1996) 'Introduction: The Body as Representation and Being-in-the-World', in T. J. Csordas (ed.) *Embodiment and Experience: The Existential Ground of Culture and Self*, Cambridge: Cambridge University Press.

Diamond, I. and Quinby, L. (eds) (1988) *Feminism and Foucault: Reflections on Resistance*, Boston: Northwestern University Press.

Douglas, M. (1973) *Natural Symbols*, Harmondsworth: Penguin.

—— (1979) *Implicit Meanings: Essays in Anthropology*, London: Routledge.

—— (1984) *Purity and Danger: An Analysis of the Concepts of Pollution and Taboo*, London: Routledge and Kegan Paul.

Elias, N. (1978) *The History of Manners: The Civilising Process*, Vol. 1, New York: Pantheon.

Entwistle, J. (1997) ' "Power Dressing" and the Fashioning of the Career Woman', in M. Nava, A. Blake, I, MacRury and B. Richards (eds) *Buy This Book: Studies in Advertising and Consumption*, London: Routledge.

—— (2000) 'Fashioning the Career Woman: Power Dressing as a Strategy of Consumption', in M. Talbot and M. Andrews (eds) *All The World and Her Husband: Women and Consumption in the Twentieth Century*, London: Cassell.

Entwistle, J. and Wilson, E. (1998) 'The Body Clothed', in *100 Years of Art and Fashion*, London: Hayward Gallery.

Ericksen, M. K. and Joseph, S. M. (1985) 'Achievement, Motivation and Clothing Preferences of White Collar Working Women', in M. R. Solomon (ed.) *The Psychology of Fashion*, New York: Lexington Books.

Featherstone, M. (1991a) 'The Body in Consumer Society', in M. Featherstone *et al.* (eds) *The Body: Social Process and Cultural Theory*, London: Sage.

—— (1991b) *Consumer Culture and Postmodernism*, London: Sage.

Featherstone, M. and Turner, B. (1995) 'Introduction', *Body and Society* 1, 1.

Feher, M. *et al.* (1989) *Fragments for a History of the Human Body Part One*, New York: Zone.

Flügel, J. C. (1930) *The Psychology of Clothes*, London: Hogarth Press.

Foucault, M. (1976) *The Birth of The Clinic*, London: Tavistock.

—— (1977) *Discipline and Punish*, Harmondsworth: Penguin.

—— (1979) *The History of Sexuality*. Volume One 'Introduction', Harmondsworth: Penguin.

—— (1980) 'Body/Power', in C. Gordon (ed.) *Power/Knowledge: Selected Interviews and Other Writings*, New York: Pantheon.

—— (1985) *The History of Sexuality*. Volume Two: The Uses of Pleasure, New York: Vintage.

—— (1986) *The History of Sexuality. Volume Three: The Care of the Self*, Harmondsworth: Penguin.

—— (1988) 'Technologies of the Self' in L. Martin, H. Gutman and P. Hutton (eds) *Technologies of the Self: A Seminar with Michel Foucault*, Amherst: University of Massachusetts Press.

Frank, A. W. (1990) 'Bringing Bodies Back In', *Theory, Culture, Society*, 7, 1.

Freeman, C. (1993) 'Designing Women: Corporate Discipline and Barbados' Off Shore Pink Collar Sector', *Cultural Anthropology* 8, 2.

Gaines, J. (1990) 'Introduction: Fabricating the Female Body', in J. Gaines and C. Herzog (eds) *Fabrications: Costume and the Female Body*, London: Routledge.

Giddens, A. (1991) *Modernity and Self-Identity: Self and Society in the Late Modern Age*, Cambridge: Polity Press.

Goffman, E. (1971) *The Presentation of Self in Everyday Life*, London: Penguin Press.

—— (1979) *Stigma: Notes on the Management of Spoiled Identity*, Harmondsworth: Penguin.

Gorsline, D. ([1953] 1991) *A History of Fashion: A Visual Survey of Costume from Ancient Times*, London: Fitzhouse Books.

Haug, F. (1987) *Female Sexualisation*, London: Verso.

Hebdige, D. (1979) *Subculture: The Meaning of Style*, London: Routledge.

Hollander, A. (1993) *Seeing Through Clothes*, Berkeley: University of California Press.

Kuhn, A. (1988) 'The Body and Cinema: Some Problems for Feminism', in S. Sheridan (ed.) *Grafts: Feminist Cultural Criticism*, London: Verso.

Kunzle, D. (1982) *Fashion and Fetishism: A Social History of the Corset, Tight-Lacing and Other Forms of Body-Sculpture in the West*, Totowa, N.J.: Rowan and Littlefield.

Laquer, T. and Bourgois, L. (1992) *Corporal Politics*, Cambridge, Mass., MIT List, Visual Arts Centre.

Laquer, T. and Gallagher, C. (1987) *The Making of the Modern Body: Sexuality, Society and the Nineteenth Century*, London: University of California Press.

Laver, J. (1969) *Modesty in Dress*, Boston: Houghton Mifflin.

Lees, S. (1999) 'When in Rome', *Guardian*, 16 February.

McNay, L. (1992) *Foucault and Feminism: Power, Gender and the Self*, Cambridge: Polity.

Mauss, M. (1973) 'Techniques of the Body', *Economy and Society* 2, 1: 70–89.

Merleau-Ponty, M. (1976) *The Primacy of Perception*, Evanston, Ill.: University of Chicago Press.

—— (1981) *The Phenomenology of Perception*, London: Routledge and Kegan Paul.

Moore, H. L. (1994) *A Passion for Difference*, Cambridge: Polity.

Nixon, S. (1992) 'Have You Got The Look? Masculinities and Shopping Spectacle', in R. Sheilds (ed.) *Lifestyle Shopping: The Subject of Consumption*, London: Routledge.

Ortner, S. (1974) 'Is Female to Male as Nature is to Culture?', in M. Rosaldo and L. Lamphere (eds) *Women, Culture and Society*, Stanford, Calif.: Stanford University Press.

Perniola, M. (1990) 'Between Clothing and Nudity', in M. Feher (ed.) *Fragments of a History of the Human Body*, New York: MIT Press.

Polhemus, T. (1988) *Bodystyles*, Luton: Lennard.

Polhemus, T. and Procter, L. (1978) *Fashion and Anti-Fashion: An Anthropology of Clothing and Adornment*, London: Cox and Wyman.

Roberts, H. (1977) 'The Exquisite Slave: The Role of Clothes in the Making of the Victorian Woman', *Signs* 2, 3: 554–69.

Schulze, L. (1990) 'On the Muscle', in J. Gaines and C. Herzog (eds) *Fabrications: Costume and the Female Body*, London: Routledge.

Sennett, R. (1977) *The Fall of Public Man*, Cambridge: Cambridge University Press.

—— (1994) *Flesh and Stone: The Body and the City in Western Civilisation*, London: Faber and Faber.

Shilling, C. (1993) *The Body and Social Theory*, London: Sage.

St Martin, L. and Gavey, N. (1996) 'Women Body Building: Feminist Resistance and/or Femininity's Recuperation', *Body and Society* 2, 4: 45–57.

Synnott, A. (1993) *The Body Social: Symbolism, Self and Society*, London: Routledge.

Triggs, T. (1992) 'Framing Masculinity: Herb Ritts, Bruce Weber and the Body Perfect', in J. Ash and E. Wilson (eds) *Chic Thrills*, London: Pandora.

Tseëlon, E. (1992a) 'Fashion and the Significance of Social Order', *Semiotica* 91, 1–2: 1–14.

—— (1992b) 'Is the Presented Self Sincere? Goffman, Impression Management and the Post Modern Self', *Theory, Culture, Society* 9, 2.

—— (1997) *The Masque of Femininity*, London: Sage.

Turner, B. (1985) *The Body and Society: Explorations in Social Theory*, Oxford: Basil Blackwell.

—— (1991) 'Recent Developments in the Theory of the Body', in M. Featherstone, M. Hepworth and B. Turner (eds) *The Body: Social Process and Cultural Theory*, London: Sage.

Veblen, T. (1953) *The Theory of the Leisure Class*, New York: Mentor.

Wilson, E. (1985) *Adorned in Dreams: Fashion and Modernity*, London: Virago.

—— (1992) 'The Postmodern Body', in J. Ash and E. Wilson (eds) *Chic Thrills: A Fashon Reader*, London: Pandora.

Wolf, N. (1991) *The Beauty Myth*, London: Vintage.

Wright, L. (1992) 'Out-grown Clothes for Grown-up People', in J. Ash and E. Wilson (eds) *Chic Thrills*, London: Pandora.

Young, I. M. (1995) 'Women Recovering Our Clothes', in S. Benstock and S. Ferris (eds) *On Fashion*, New Brunswick: Rutgers University Press.

Chapter 25

Paul Sweetman

ANCHORING THE (POSTMODERN) SELF?
Body modification, fashion and identity

Introduction

THE LAST 20 TO 30 YEARS have seen a considerable resurgence in the popularity of tattooing and body piercing in the West, a process which has involved not only a remarkable growth in the numbers involved, but also their spread to an ever wider clientele (Armstrong, 1991; Armstrong and Gabriel, 1993; Armstrong et al., 1996; Blanchard, 1994; Curry, 1993; DeMello, 1995a, 1995b; Mercer and Davies, 1991; Myers, 1992; Rubin, 1988; Sanders, 1989). The popular image of the tattooee as young, male and working class is now increasingly outdated, as more and more men *and* women, of various age-groups and socio-economic backgrounds, choose to enter the tattoo studio. Piercing too, though once associated with particular marginal or subcultural groups, is now popular with an increasingly heterogeneous range of enthusiasts (Curry, 1993).[1]

These trends have accelerated since the mid- to late-1980s,[2] a period which has seen increasing numbers of tattooees and piercees become heavily involved with either one or both forms of body modification. Through their high profile in certain key publications, such 'hardcore' body modifiers – some of whom have been termed 'modern primitives' (Curry, 1993; Dery, 1996; Eubanks, 1996; Klesse, 1997; Myers, 1992; Pitts, 1998; Vale and Juno, 1989) – have done much to popularize the new styles of tattoo and piercing which have emerged in recent years. These include a variety of neo-tribal styles and techniques based more or less directly on the indigenous traditions of Polynesia and elsewhere (Curry, 1993: 76; Sanders, 1989: 20).

At the same time, the last ten years have also seen the partial incorporation of both forms of body modification into consumer culture. Numerous celebrities now sport tattoos and piercings, and related imagery is frequently featured in advertising copy, as well as in the work of designers such as Jean-Paul Gaultier (Alford, 1993;

Menkes, 1993). Together with their increased popularity, this has led some to dismiss contemporary tattooing and piercing as little more than a superficial trend, one instance among many of the incorporation of 'the exotic' into the fashion system (Craik, 1994: 25; Steele, 1996: 160–1).

Such a position is attractive, not only because of such practices' increasing visibility on the catwalk and in the media, but also because it accords with character-izations of postmodern fashion as an eclectic free-for-all, a 'carnival of signs' (Tseëlon, 1995: 124), where anything and everything is up for grabs in what some have described as the 'supermarket of style' (Polhemus, 1995). It is also, in one sense, largely irrefutable if one accepts the basic tautology that what is fashionable is what is popular, and anything that rapidly increases in popularity can thus be referred to in these terms.

There are, however, several difficulties with characterizing practices such as tattooing and piercing as fashionable per se, in part because of their status as permanent, or 'semi-permanent', modifications to the body (Curry, 1993: 79). Indeed, for writers such as Polhemus, 'any permanent body decoration . . . is as anti-fashion as it is possible to get' (Polhemus, 1995: 13), 'true fashion' being defined as 'a system of continual and perpetual . . . change' (Polhemus and Proctor, 1978: 25).

The following examines both sides of this debate, looking first at the extent to which the resurgence of tattooing and piercing might be seen not only as fashion-able, but also as a manifestation of the more or less superficial eclecticism that many argue is a key characteristic of the postmodern scene. Drawing – as throughout – from interviews with a variety of contemporary body modifiers,[3] this section will suggest that for some tattooees and piercees, there is indeed an extent to which their involvement can be described as little more than a fashionable trend. Even among these 'less committed' body modifiers, however, there is also evidence to suggest that their tattoos and piercings are perceived and experienced as more than mere accessories.

The article then goes on to explore these areas in more detail, focusing particu-larly on the permanence of tattooing and the pain associated with both forms of body modification, before considering whether such practices might instead be characterized as a form of anti-fashion. It is suggested that, for many contemporary body modifiers, an involvement in tattooing or piercing represents not so much an appropriation of the cultural detritus adrift within Baudrillard's 'carnival of signs', but rather a reaction to such superficiality: an attempt to lend corporeal solidity to expressions of individuality.

As corporeal expressions of *the self*, tattoos and piercings might thus be seen as instances of contemporary *body projects* (Shilling, 1993): as attempts to construct and maintain a coherent and viable sense of self-identity through attention to the body and, more particularly, the body's surface (Featherstone, 1991). This is explored in the final section of the article, where it is argued that contemporary tattooing and piercing can indeed be interpreted in these terms, as attempts to anchor or stabilize one's sense of self-identity, in part through the establishment of a coherent personal narrative.

A 'carnival of signs'?

As was noted above, certain commentators have dismissed the current popularity of tattooing and piercing as little more than a fashionable trend. Craik, for instance, argues that 'the popularity of tattooing has been revived in western fashion since the 1980s' before going on to suggest that, together, improved techniques of tattoo removal and the introduction of fake (transfer) tattoos, 'have alleviated some of the stigma attached to tattooing and enabled it to become a component of high fashion . . . that is desirable because of its exotic associations' (Craik, 1994: 25). Steele, similarly, points out that, '[t]oday tattoos and body piercing have become increasingly stylish; even fashion models get delicate piercing, and modern bohemians sport pierced lips, cheeks, nipples, tongues, and genitals' (Steele, 1996: 160).

For some, then, tattooing and piercing – as previously 'classed', 'raced' and gendered practices, associated strongly with specific marginal and subcultural groups – have now become so 'mainstream' as to almost be considered 'passé' (Steele, 1996: 161). This arguably accords well with characterizations of contemporary fashion as an eclectic and self-referential system, which freely quotes from any and every source, transforming the phenomena thus appropriated into more or less meaningless cultural ephemera: 'floating signifiers' that refer to nothing but themselves (Falk, 1995: 103).

As Tseëlon points out, for writers such as Baudrillard, postmodern fashion can be characterized as 'a carnival of signs with no meanings attached' (Tseëlon, 1995: 124), an eclectic mish-mash of once potent styles and devices, desperately appropriated from a variety of sources in a vain attempt to lend authenticity to that which is no longer imbued with meaning (Tseëlon, 1995: 132; see also Falk, 1995: 103). Postmodern fashion no longer refers to anything but itself, and this lack of external referentiality means that everything is up for grabs: we can all wear what we want, with the proviso that what we wear is no longer indexical of anything other than our participation in the fashion system.

There are a number of problems with this position: just because contemporary fashion has accelerated and fragmented, for instance, such increased complexity does not necessarily indicate the *absolute* self-referentiality that Baudrillard's position implies (Tseëlon, 1995: 134). Following Foster, however, Tseëlon distinguishes Baudrillard's 'postmodernism of resistance' from the 'postmodernism of reaction' associated with commentators such as Jameson (Tseëlon, 1995: 132). From the latter perspective, postmodern fashion – however, 'playful' and fragmented – retains a definite if tenuous link with an external social reality: it 'still alludes to a reality of signification' (Tseëlon, 1995: 132).

This is important for a number of reasons, not least that it helps to explain the current fascination with all things 'retro', the appropriation of 'bygone styles' representing a vain effort to lend 'historical depth to a world of surface signifiers' (Tseëlon, 1995: 132). Similar arguments apply to the appropriation of 'ethnic' and 'subcultural' styles, and as a system that freely quotes from any and every potential source, contemporary fashion can thus be described as 'a field of stylistic and discursive heterogeneity without a norm' (Jameson, quoted in Wilson, 1990: 223). Indeed, even if one rejects the more extreme theoretical position occupied by writers such as Baudrillard, it is generally accepted that – at the very least –

contemporary fashion is characterized by 'a blurring between mainstream and countercultural fashions: all fashion has become "stagey", self-conscious about its own status as discourse' (Wilson, 1990: 222).

Truly 'postmodern' or not, contemporary fashion thus problematizes the notion of sartorial strategies of resistance, as detailed, for instance, in the work of writers associated with the Birmingham Centre for Contemporary Cultural Studies during the 1970s and beyond (see, for example: Hall and Jefferson, 1976; Hebdige, 1988). Quite simply, if everything is 'quotable' and more or less divested of meaning, if there is no dominant dress code or hegemonic standard by which one's sartorial conduct might be judged, then it arguably makes little sense to speak of subcultural or counter-cultural styles of dress (Gamman and Makinen, 1994: 73; Wilson, 1990: 233).

Certain writers within fashion and 'subcultural' theory reject this position, however, suggesting that while contemporary fashion has indeed become increasingly diverse and fragmented, a 'mix & match' of any number of past stylistic devices, this does not necessarily negate the subversive potential of such counter-cultural or subcultural styles (Gottschalk, 1993; Polhemus, 1995). But while Gottschalk, for instance, argues that American counter-culturalists' appropriation and re-contextualization of 'various historical styles and ethnic traditions' (Gottschalk, 1993: 367) is both creative and expressive of the 'Freaks' 'social-psychological and ideological' dispositions (Gottschalk, 1993: 369), he also notes that his interviewees '*recognized that existing deviant styles were cliches that could no longer be adopted to express one's rebellious position*' (Gottschalk, 1993: 366–7, my emphasis; see also Lind and Roach-Higgins, 1985; Polhemus, 1995: 12).

To the extent that everything is now more or less up for grabs, it could thus be argued that Gottschalk's (1993) informants' 'mix & match' strategy represents a last-ditch attempt to retain a sense of subcultural style, a rearguard action which, through a process of *bricolage* (Hebdige, 1988: 102–6), attempts to squeeze the last drops of meaning from what are, in reality, increasingly empty signifiers. In this respect, though indicative of the current validity of subcultural or counter-cultural sartorial strategies, such studies could also be said to signal their impending demise.

To some extent, then, even the arguments put forward by writers such as Gottschalk (1993) and Polhemus (1995) are supportive of the notion that sartorial strategies of resistance are increasingly redundant: that even if one refutes the more extreme argument associated with writers such as Baudrillard, clothing, fashion and appearance are increasingly being absorbed into a *more or less* free-floating 'carnival of signs'. In relation to the increasing popularity of tattooing and piercing, one might then ask whether such forms of body modification should also be seen as all but empty signifiers, once marginal or subcultural devices that have now gone mainstream, thus joining the ranks of the other ephemeral products available in the 'supermarket of style'.

Mere accessories?

In support of this position, it should be noted that several of the lightly tattooed or pierced[4] informants interviewed for this study appeared – *in at least some respects* – to view their tattoos and piercings as little more than fashion accessories, on a par, for instance, with more standard forms of jewellery or other items intended to enhance a particular 'look'. Lightly tattooed and/or pierced interviewees, in particular, often regarded their own tattoos and piercings in primarily *decorative* terms: 'I thought it would look nice', or words to that effect, being a common response to enquiries regarding their motivation to acquire such forms of body modification.

When asked what she most liked about having her navel pierced, for example, one young interviewee noted the way in which 'we like to change our bodies', before adding, 'all girls like jewellery, don't they, and it's sort of an extension of that I think'. Although she felt that it was 'a bit more special' than necklaces or earrings, for example – thanks to its location 'in an unusual place' – the same interviewee reinforced this sense of treating her piercing as a fashionable accessory by noting her tendency to change the jewellery 'every couple of weeks or so . . . when I get bored with it', and, when asked if she deliberately wore clothes that would show off the piercing, replying: 'Erm, in the summer I do, but . . . I wore skirts that cut below my belly first, and then I had the piercing, to sort of fit with that, rather than the other way round.' The same woman also volunteered that having the piercing done was something of a 'treat': 'a bit like going into a really posh salon and having your hair done'.

More surprisingly, perhaps, certain lightly tattooed interviewees appeared to view their tattoos in similar terms, one young woman with two small designs – one on her back, the other on her ankle – noting: 'it's nice choosing your outfit depending on whether you want to show off your tattoo or whatever, and, I dunno . . . I just think it's kind of like an extra accessory kind of thing'.

At a number of points throughout the interview, the same woman also noted that becoming tattooed was 'not such a big deal', although at one stage she added, 'well I suppose it is kind of, 'cause it's there for the rest of your life, but . . .' Another young woman, also with two tattoos, noted that both these and her nostril piercing were mainly for show: 'recreating how I want to be on a certain evening or something, whether I've got my nose ring in or not, and whether I'm showing my tattoos or not'. When asked if her decision to become tattooed was a response to fashion, she replied, 'I suppose it is partly', though she subsequently added, '[b]ut I don't think it's something I'll ever think has gone out of fashion and I wish I hadn't got them'.

At the same time as describing their tattoos or piercings as decorative accessories, however, nearly all of the informants in this category *also* regarded tattooing and piercing as 'different', 'original' or 'out of the ordinary': when asked what they most valued about being tattooed or pierced, 'being different' was by far the most common response.

Often expressed rather vaguely, where 'difference' was specified in anything more than very general terms, being tattooed or pierced was seen to distinguish the interviewee either from the bulk of non-tattooed or pierced individuals, or from those within their more immediate peer group. One young male interviewee, for example, saw his nipple piercing as 'a distinction from people who don't have things like that', while a young female tattooee told me, 'it's just nice to be a bit different from my friends'.

Others were a little more cautious, recognizing a degree of tension between their perception of such forms of body modification as a mark of individuality – 'other people are just skin' – and their acknowledgement of tattooing and piercing's increased popularity: 'I do feel a bit different in some ways, but, you're surprised how many people have got tattoos'. Certain interviewees managed this apparent contradiction by referring to the timing of their tattoo(s) or piercing(s), and asserting that this preceded any current trend to which *others* may have been attracted.

In certain cases, such claims were rather questionable, but the extent to which the majority of lightly tattooed or pierced interviewees *perceived* their own tattoos and piercings as 'different' or 'out of the ordinary' arguably militates against a reading of such forms of body modification simply as 'free-floating' fashion accessories, *at least when viewed from the perspective of those involved*. So too does the seriousness with which many lightly tattooed or pierced interviewees appeared to take the decision to modify their bodies in this manner.

One lightly pierced interviewee, for instance, told me that he had 'toyed' with the idea of having his nipple pierced for some months before finally taking the plunge, or, as he put it, a 'massive step into an area I'm afraid of anyway . . . and I had no experience or knowledge of'. For him, the act of becoming pierced appears in itself to have been quite profound, his subsequent experience of a fractured shin described as 'nothing' in comparison to having 'a dirty great needle shoved through one of the most sensitive parts of my body'.

While not true of all, a number of the lightly tattooed interviewees similarly told me that they had spent some time building up to having a tattoo, either because they hadn't previously 'had the guts' to go ahead, or because they saw it as a serious step that demanded careful consideration. Thus one young tattooee told me that she had contemplated the decision for a 'couple of years', or long enough 'to really think seriously about it', a process that had also involved reading through several tattoo magazines to find out more about the process itself and the sorts of designs available. As she put it: 'I really wanted to look into it, 'cause its permanent, and I did think about it as a long-term sort of thing.' As will be discussed more fully below, such extensive 'background research' was also common among the more heavily tattooed and pierced interviewees, belying the popular perception of tattoo acquisition, for example, as a universally impulsive and ill-thought-out process (Foster Wallace, 1997: 206–11).

On the one hand, then, the tendency of certain of the more lightly tattooed and/or pierced interviewees to describe their tattoos or piercings as decorative accessories lends support to the notion that such forms of body modification are now just another product in the 'supermarket of style'. At the same time, however, a number of factors appear to contradict such an interpretation, not least the way in which most interviewees regarded their tattoos or piercings as 'different' or 'original', and the seriousness with which many approached the decision to modify their bodies in this manner. Among the tattooees, such caution was in large part thanks to the tattoo's permanence, though both tattooees and piercees also alluded to factors such as the pain involved in the acquisition of such forms of body modification.

Permanence, planning and pain

It was noted above that while certain less heavily tattooed or pierced interviewees appeared to regard their tattoos or piercings – to at least some degree – as decorative accessories, factors such as the permanence or 'semi-permanence' of such forms of body modification, and the pain involved in their acquisition, meant that they were also experienced as distinct from other, more ephemeral products in the 'supermarket of style'. Drawing now on interviews with both heavily *and* less heavily tattooed and pierced interviewees – but primarily the former – the following will expand upon these points before considering whether, rather than dismissing contemporary body modification as a superficial trend, it might instead be more appropriately viewed as a form of 'anti-fashion'.

To turn first to the more indelible of the two procedures, the bulk of those interviewed during the course of this study intimated that there was a 'fashionable element' to contemporary body modification, but several also pointed to the permanence of tattooing as problematic in this regard. When asked whether tattooing could be said to be fashionable, for example, one heavily tattooed and pierced female interviewee replied; 'I think it is going that way, but I don't think that's what it's about':

> Because . . . fashion is a passing thing isn't it? What's fashionable at the moment is not gonna be fashionable next year, or in a couple of years' time. So that's totally the wrong reason for having it done.

All of the body modifiers interviewed for this study regarded their tattoos as permanent modifications to the body, however, and while some had had designs re-worked or 'covered up' – and others intended to do so – none referred to the improved techniques of removal which Craik (1994: 25) suggests have contributed to tattooing's increasing popularity. Indeed, several interviewees saw the permanence of their tattoos as a 'very important' element in their overall appeal. A young, heavily tattooed and pierced male interviewee, for instance, argued that '[a] tattoo, whether it's good or bad, is very, very permanent, so it's making a statement of sorts', adding, '[t]hat's why I like them'. Another, lightly tattooed, interviewee distinguished between her tattoo and other modes of self-expression as follows: 'I don't know . . . before, I could express myself in clothes and things like that, but now it's actually something that's permanent and that's definitely me.'

At the same time as regarding the permanence of their tattoos as key to their overall appeal, however, a number of interviewees also noted that this was cause for a degree of caution. As had some of the more lightly tattooed interviewees, several of the more heavily tattooed informants indicated that they had thought for some time before acquiring a tattoo, with one now heavily tattooed and pierced female interviewee telling me:

> I wanted tattoos done ever since I was a kid, but I wanted to leave it until I was old enough to not make a mistake, because I think a lot of people have them done young and . . . regret it.

The same interviewee went on to tell me that in her opinion, the permanence of tattoos 'makes them really special, 'cause you've got be really sure of what you . . . put on yourself'. Another heavily tattooed and pierced interviewee told me that he had 'wanted tattoos' since he was 13 or 14, but though normally 'quite impulsive': 'with tattoos it was very permanent and I thought, "Well", you know, "I'm not gonna get it done unless I actually want the design." '

Like certain of the more lightly tattooed interviewees, several of the more heavily tattooed informants had undertaken a considerable amount of research before going ahead with their first tattoo. One younger male tattooee and piercee told me that he had 'found out' a good deal about the process before going ahead – a tactic which included investigating the various hygiene procedures employed by contemporary tattooists – while another, older interviewee described the way in which he chose his first tattooist as 'a really dull . . . mechanical process', which involved visiting 'fourteen studios within a certain radius of where [he] lived' and scoring them all according to the personality of the tattooist, the quality of the work and the apparent cleanliness of the studio: '[a]nd the one that came out on top in points terms, I went to'.

As one might expect, such 'background work' does not necessarily stop after the first tattoo. While certain tattooists continue to offer a 'walk-in' service, many now work by appointment only, and some are also selective about the sorts of design they will tattoo, the former point necessitating that sessions be booked in advance, and the latter demanding a certain amount of negotiation between tattooist and tattooee. Unless the tattooee prepares the design themselves, or is happy to give the tattooist free rein, *custom* work can also demand a good deal of collaboration between artist and client. Such background work need not be perceived negatively, however. One interviewee told me that he gets 'a lot of enjoyment out of' planning what to do next, and, indeed, out of 'the whole process of booking it, finding a design, going up there, [and] chatting to the artist'. He also noted that he enjoys the healing process, or 'looking after' his new tattoo, and that the procedure as a whole leaves him with a considerable sense of achievement, in part thanks to his necessary involvement at all stages of the creative process.

Planning, collaboration and after-care are not the only factors that can lead to a sense of achievement, however. When asked why she had felt 'proud of herself' after having her tattoos done, for instance, one lightly tattooed and pierced interviewee replied: ' 'Cause . . . it's quite painful . . . you know . . . it does hurt, and I was like, chuffed that I'd . . . sat there and done it.' To return to the process of being tattooed, then, a further factor which suggests that tattoos should not be viewed as free-floating products in the 'supermarket of style' – and which, in this case, applies to all tattoos, regardless of whether they are carefully planned custom designs, or a 'name' tattooist is employed – is the *pain* involved in their application. As one, heavily tattooed and ex-heavily pierced interviewee put it:

> [Y]ou can't, well you *can* buy it, but you can't like, go to the shop and try it on and say, 'I'll have one of them', and just walk out with it. You've gotta sit there for hours and put up with the pain. So even if you're really rich, if you can't stand the pain, you can't get tattooed.

In this sense, tattoos differ remarkably from other, sartorial modes of expression:

> [P]eople can buy an expensive outfit or, you know . . . a leather jacket, but, you *can* buy a tattoo, but you've still gotta put up with the pain and the process. . . . There's a lot more that goes into it.

As will be elaborated on below, the same could also be said of piercing, but in contrast to tattooing, most interviewees regarded the former as comparatively superficial. When questioned about the relative importance of her tattoos and piercings, for instance, one heavily tattooed but less heavily pierced female interviewee told me that she didn't 'really feel anything about piercing', adding, 'it's not permanent, so I really don't give it that much thought'. The same interviewee later described her septum piercing as 'just a fashion accessory'. Such responses were not confined to those with greater involvement in tattooing than piercing. One heavily tattooed *and* pierced interviewee, for instance, noted that his piercings were: 'kind of superfluous, 'cause I can take them out at any time . . . they're a lot less permanent, so they don't mean as much to me.'[5]

That is not to say that all piercings are regarded as equally superficial, however: certain interviewees distinguished between the more popular piercings – eyebrow and navel piercings, for instance – and those that were considered to be more 'extreme' or 'hardcore'. The 'extreme' category tended to include both genital piercing and various forms of 'stretch' piercing, with the former evaluated as distinctive thanks to their location, and the latter because of both the degree of commitment required to achieve the enlarged piercing and the relative permanence of the modification thus acquired. One heavily tattooed and pierced male interviewee, having described how he had stretched one of his genital piercings to thirteen millimetres in diameter, compared the process to becoming tattooed and argued that: 'there's as much validity, probably even more, in achieving that, because you have to do it yourself, you can't get there any other way'.

As a generic term, however, 'piercing' was considered by most to be more superficial than tattooing, thanks primarily to the ease with which most piercings can be discontinued. While the bulk of piercings *are* impermanent, however – and as such may not indicate the same level of commitment as implied by the decision to become tattooed – they still demand that the piercee experience a certain level of pain and/or discomfort while the piercing is applied, and that they indulge in the necessary after-care to ensure that the piercing heals successfully. Although the attendant preparations may take some time, the actual process of *being* pierced is generally over in a few seconds and, in contrast with tattooing, any pain is usually dulled by the use of local anaesthetic. The initial meeting of metal and flesh can still be painful, however, and while the pain associated with tattooing lasts only as long as the tattoo session itself, the pain, discomfort and attendant anxiety associated with piercing can extend well beyond the time one spends in the piercing studio.

One interviewee noted that while he was quite relaxed *prior to* his first genital piercing, things changed somewhat once he was actually in the studio: 'I wasn't too bothered, but . . . once you get in there [you see] all this like, . . . shiny, metal equipment, . . . and you think, "Shit, am I doing the right thing here?" ' However much you read up about things beforehand: 'you don't really appreciate it until you see it done; what's actually involved, and how thick the skin is, or how thick the tissue is. It does take a . . . lot of force to push it through sometimes.'

As well as being a more invasive process than tattooing, piercing is also more likely to lead to short- or long-term complications once one leaves the studio. Referring again to his first genital piercing, the interviewee quoted above also told me that:

> the Prince Albert[6] bled like mad the night I got it done. The anaesthetic wore off, and I woke up about three in the morning absolutely saturated in blood, like all over my boxer shorts, all over the bed, I thought I was dying, you know, it was gushing out. . . . And, that was like, 'Shit, what have I done?' [laughter], you know, 'Fucking outrageous, I've just stuck something through my knob, I'm either gonna get done or it's gonna fall off' [laughter].

Unlike tattoos, then, which generally offer little in the way of physical discomfort following the actual process of application, piercings can be painful – and bleed considerably – for some days after their acquisition. A further contrast lies in the fact that while one can be pretty sure about the time it will take a tattoo to heal – generally around two weeks – piercings can not only take far longer, but the healing time is also more variable, with certain piercings refusing to settle however long one lavishes them with care and attention. Several interviewees told me that they had reluctantly abandoned their navel piercings because, after a period of months, the piercings had refused to settle, and when asked if she had ever removed any of her piercings, one heavily tattooed and pierced interviewee replied: '[n]o . . . [but] the nipple piercings [are] still very sore, and I've had [them] done over a year now . . . I don't regret having them done, but, they do get quite sore.'

Anti-fashion?

As I hope to have indicated above, tattoos and piercings arguably differ from other 'free-floating' commodities, not only because of their status as permanent or 'semi-permanent' modifications to the body, but also because of the necessary physicality of their production. In respect of the former, several commentators have drawn a distinction between *fashion*, as characterized by continual and systematic change, and those more fixed modes of dress which are relatively static, conservative and resistant to change (Davis, 1985: 22).

Polhemus and Proctor (1978), for instance, distinguish between fashion and *anti-fashion*, nothing that the latter term 'refers to all styles of adornment which fall outside the organized system . . . of fashion change' (Polhemus and Proctor, 1978: 16). This definition encompasses 'traditional' forms of dress, as well as uniforms, subcultural styles and so on, all of which are united in their conservatism and opposition to change. While fashion suggests some degree of social mobility, however illusory, anti-fashion is characteristic of relatively 'fixed . . . social environments' (Polhemus and Proctor, 1978: 14), its adoption in a modern social context representing a deliberate attempt 'to symbolically defy . . . change' (Polhemus and Proctor, 1978: 22).

For Polhemus (1995) and Polhemus and Proctor (1978), tattooing, along with other permanent forms of body modification, can be described as 'the ultimate' in anti-fashion (Polhemus and Proctor, 1978: unnumbered), its irreversibility rendering 'change difficult if not impossible' (Polhemus, 1995: 13). As Falk has also noted (Falk, 1995: 102), such *irreversible* body-marking is 'antithetical to the mechanisms of fashion change' (Polhemus and Proctor, 1978: unnumbered), and, for Polhemus and Proctor, tattooing, scarification and the like are thus used to maintain the illusion, if not the reality, 'of social and cultural stability' (Polhemus and Proctor, 1978: 16). This helps to explain not only the widespread use of tattooing in 'traditional' or pre-modern contexts, but also the adoption of such techniques to indicate subcultural allegiances in the West. Tattooing and other forms of permanent body modification are typically employed:

> in situations where people feel . . . [the] need to preserve their individual and social identities and to advertise . . . the would-be permanence of their allegiances, values and beliefs. (Polhemus and Proctor, 1978: unnumbered)

There are, of course, considerable problems with the notion of 'anti-fashion' if one accepts Baudrillard's argument regarding the 'free-floating' nature of contemporary signifiers. In this context, however, it is equally important to note the potential difficulties associated with Polhemus and Proctor's (1978) designation of tattooing as the 'ultimate' in anti-fashion. While it is noted elsewhere that anti-fashions of various sorts are regularly co-opted by the fashion industry (Polhemus and Proctor, 1978: 17–19), the argument surrounding permanent body modification appears to suggest that such practices are so 'antithetical to the mechanisms of fashion change' that they would, or could not be so appropriated. This is certainly the position adopted by Curry (1993), who accepts Polhemus and Proctor's fashion/anti-fashion distinction, and argues that whatever its current popularity, tattooing 'can never be a true fashion . . . because tattoos cannot be put on and left off by the season', adding, '[t]he same is true for body piercing . . . with the proviso that piercings are semi-permanent rather than permanent' (Curry, 1993: 80).

The key difficulty with this argument – at least in relation to tattooing – is that while the permanence of the tattoo mark may disallow easy revisability in line with the dictates of fashion, this does not imply that the *meaning* of such forms of body modification is also fixed. In other words, Curry (1993) and Polhemus and Proctor (1978) arguably conflate the fixity of the signifier – ink under the skin – with the notion of a permanent signified, but while the tattoo mark *is* more or less irreversible, its external referents can and do change.

This does not mean that Curry's (1993) and Polhemus and Proctor's (1978) argument should be entirely discarded, what it does suggest is that tattoos might become more or less fashionable – signifying, at the connotative level, little more than one's participation in the fashion process – even though this would leave those so motivated to become tattooed in a difficult position once the wheels of fashion had turned. The permanence of tattooing, in other words, means that it is extremely *well-suited* to employment as an anti-fashion device, but it does not imply that its meaning is fixed in these terms.

At the same time, however, a number of other factors intrinsic to both tattooing *and* piercing arguably militate against their full incorporation into Baudrillard's 'carnival of signs'. Tattoos and piercings are not *only* permanent and/or 'semi-permanent' cultural products, they are also intrusive modifications to the body whose production involves pain, blood and the penetration of the skin in a non-medicalized setting, not to mention varying degrees of planning and 'after-care'.

In contrast to those free-floating signifiers that comprise the bulk of image-based products available in Baudrillard's 'carnival of signs', tattoos and piercings cannot be divorced from the manner of their production. One cannot simply purchase a finished tattoo or piercing in the same way that one might acquire a new sweater, the production and consumption of each form of body modification requiring the tattooee or piercee's active participation in the completion of what is, in effect, a combination of corporeal modification and cultural artefact.

As *corporeal artefacts* then, tattoos and piercings differ remarkably from sartorial accessories: part of the body rather than simply an adjunct to it, 'there is something in [both] which escapes the flow of commodification' (Blanchard, 1994: 292). Even in the case of standardized designs or piercings, 'the replication of the tattoo [or piercing, is] contingent upon its siting on the body of a specific subject' (Blanchard, 1994: 292), and the complete, or healed, tattoo or piercing is as much the work of the tattooee or piercee as it is of the tattoist or body piercer. In this sense, the modified body produces itself. A pair of jeans, or a new pair of training shoes, can be consumed and displayed as 'pure sign', in ignorance of the conditions under which the material product was fabricated. Tattoos and piercings, in contrast, *demand* one's presence as producer, consumer and living frame for the corporeal artefact thus acquired.

The invasive and painful nature of the modificatory process thus suggests that neither tattoos nor piercings can be consumed as 'pure signs'. Equally importantly, however, it also implies that however popular tattooing and piercing become, and however much tattooing and piercing *imagery* is appropriated by the fashion industry, real tattoos and piercings will continue to refer to the manner in which they are produced, and thus to resist full absorption into any free-floating 'carnival of signs'. While Curry (1993) and Polhemus and Proctor (1978) may be wrong to suggest that the permanence or 'semi-permanence' of tattooing and piercing *in and of itself* delimits their wider socio-cultural connotations, factors such as the pain involved in their application mean that, whatever their wider connotations, at the denotative level tattoos and piercings will continue to refer to the manner of their acquisition.

As Gell has pointed out, the underlying 'technical schema' of tattooing – as with body piercing – is 'external to culture as such' (Gell, 1993: 303), and while this may not entirely delimit the socio-cultural connotations, of such forms of body modification, it arguably ensures that such practices will retain a particular denotative impact whatever their wider significance. Tattooing's 'invariant processual contour' is such that it can always be broken down into three distinct stages: wounding, healing, and 'the subsequent acquisition of a permanent . . . mark' (Gell, 1993: 304). This is not to suggest a universal meaning for tattooing, but 'the integration of this technical schema into any given cultural matrix' (Gell, 1993: 303) acts to *invite* certain readings of the practice, with the dominant reading in any particular context dependent upon which of the three stages is most strongly 'focalized' (Gell, 1993: 304).

According to Gell, the dominant Western reading of tattooing contrasts strongly with the 'core Polynesian reading' (Gell, 1993: 307) in placing exclusive stress on the tattoo as completed artefact (Gell, 1993: 313). In traditional Polynesian settings, by comparison, '[t]he tattoo was significant, not so much as a thing in itself, than as a proof that the tattooing . . . had been done' (Gell, 1993: 305–6). As Gell *also* notes, however:

> the tattooing process . . . is always and everywhere submitted to in its entirety, not bit by bit. Hence differential focalization is always a relative matter; each distinct focalization carries all the others with it . . . It is a matter of emphasis, not a complete break. (Gell, 1993: 304)

In other words, while the core Western reading of tattooing may emphasize the tattoo as completed artefact, downgrading the importance of the tattoo process, this is only a matter of *relative* emphasis: the tattoo, as signifying mark, will always refer to the inevitably physical conditions of its production. It can thus be argued that Gell overstates his case when he suggests that the core Western reading represents 'the *complete* triumph of artefactualization' (Gell, 1993: 313, my emphasis): when compared with tattooing in many non-Western contexts, contemporary tattooing in the West may be *relatively* free-floating, but as *corporeal* artefacts even the most playful and ironic of contemporary tattoos retain an echo of the pain involved in their acquisition (Blanchard, 1994: 288). The same is true of body piercing, which also follows an 'invariant processual contour', the key distinction being that the completed body modification is semi-permanent rather than permanent.

That the process of becoming tattooed or pierced remains significant to those involved, however much emphasis is ultimately placed on 'the subsequent acquisition of a permanent [or semi-permanent] . . . mark' (Gell, 1993: 304), has already been illustrated above (see also: Sweetman, 1999a). That tattoos and piercings are denotative of the manner of their acquisition to the wider population of non-body modifiers, on the other hand, is evidenced by the standard response offered by those confronted with such forms of body modification. As several interviewees told me, and as has also been pointed out elsewhere (Miles, 1997: 4), one of the questions most frequently asked of contemporary body modifiers by those who have not so modified their bodies is as follows: '*Does [or Did] it hurt?*'

Body projects and expressive individualism

While Curry (1993) may be wrong to suggest that the permanence of tattooing and the 'semi-permanence' of piercing in and of themselves mean that such forms of body modification can never become 'a true fashion', the invasive and often painful manner by which such corporeal artefacts are produced adds weight to the argument that it would be misplaced to interpret tattoos and piercings simply as superficial accessories. The comments of several interviewees also suggest that while their meaning may not be entirely fixed in these terms, tattoos in particular are frequently perceived as distinct from other, more 'free-floating' fashion items, as, to a lesser degree, are piercings, thanks to the pain involved in their acquisition. Certain piercings are more permanent than others, but the ease with which most can be discontinued means that they are generally regarded as *relatively* superficial. As with tattoos, however, one cannot simply purchase a complete piercing: 'you've . . . gotta put up with the pain and the process'.

Such comments suggest that both forms of body modification, but tattoos in particular, may be employed by some as a form of 'anti-fashion': that even though their meaning is not fixed in these terms, they may be employed by certain body modifiers as a means of symbolically defying change, 'preserv[ing] their individual and social identities and . . . advertis[ing] . . . the would-be permanence of their . . . values and beliefs' (Polhemus and Proctor, 1978: unnumbered).

To the extent that this is the case, such forms of body modification might be argued to share certain affinities with the subcultural 'uniforms' adopted by skin-heads and others in the 1960s and 1970s (Clarke 1976; Cohen, 1997; Hebdige, 1987). In contrast to such subcultural styles, however, contemporary tattoos and piercings appear to act less as markers of group identification, and more as expressions of the self. Few interviewees linked their tattoos or piercings to 'membership' of *specific* subcultural groups, and those who did express an affiliative impact or intention behind their adoption of such forms of body modification tended to refer to this in loosely 'tribal' terms. This was not true of all interviewees, and it should also be noted that 'label-rejection' may have been adopted by some as a strategy to deflect suggestions of 'conformity to a group image' which, as Muggleton notes, 'invites accusations of conventionality by outsiders' (1995: 4; see also Muggleton, 1997: 9).

As discussed further below, however, several interviewees stressed the *personal* nature of their tattoos and piercings, and that both tattooing and piercing are popular among a range of 'subcultural' types, *and among many who appear not to identify with any particular subcultural group*, was confirmed by attendance at several tattoo conventions during the course of this research. Events such as Tattoo Expo and Bodyshow attract an extremely varied crowd, apparently united only by a shared interest in tattooing, piercing or related modificatory practices. Tattoo Expo, in particular – as the largest and longest running annual UK convention – is remark-able for the way in which Hells Angels rub shoulders with rubber-skirted SMers, glamorous fetishists, punks, goths, skinheads and clubbers, not to mention the rest of the international crowd of attendees, most of whom are heavily tattooed or pierced, but the majority of whom are not easily slotted into a particular subcultural group.

Observational data, then, lends tangential support to most interviewees' implicit rejection of specific affiliative intentions, while at the same time supporting arguments that we are witnessing a move 'towards affinity based on heterogeneity', or a form of 'neo-tribalism', which, as Muggleton notes, 'implies an alliance' of sorts, but one that 'can be contrasted with the more sharply defined and strongly collective connotations of "subculture"' (Muggleton, 1995: 8; see also Maffesoli, 1996). A further reason for accepting the majority of interviewees' rejection of any specific affiliative *intention* behind their tattoos or piercings lies with the strong emphasis that many placed on the personal nature of the modifications acquired. Several tattooees told me that they had chosen motifs that were expressive of personal interests or their own biographies, and many noted that they had gone for custom designs in order to ensure that 'no one else would ever have the same tattoos'. As one, lightly tattooed female interviewee put it: 'I saw various designs I liked, but I thought it would be more personal if I had something that was a design of my own.'

A number of interviewees also described their tattoos as 'a sign of [their] personality', but whether or not this was the case, both tattoos and piercings were frequently described as 'very personal' by virtue of their location on, or rather as part of, the body. Several interviewees also stressed that their tattoos or piercings were primarily for their own consumption, and were not intended to be widely displayed. One lightly tattooed and pierced interviewee, for instance, told me that she had chosen to locate her first and only tattoo on her back because she 'didn't particularly care about whether it was ever gonna be seen by anybody else, it was definitely just a personal thing for me'.

To the extent that contemporary tattooing and piercing act as expressions of self rather than as markers of group identification, they might thus be described as a form of 'expressive individualism' (Muggleton, 1997: 11) which, in attending to the body and its appearance, shares considerable affinities with other forms of contemporary 'body project' (Shilling, 1993). Writers such as Shilling (1993) and Giddens (1991) have recently emphasized the increasingly tight relationship between the body and self-identity, as manifest in a growing tendency to treat the body as a 'project' through which a sense of self-identity is constructed and maintained. While in traditional or pre-modern societies identity was relatively fixed, and the size, shape and appearance of the body accepted more or less as given, in late-, high- or postmodernity, identity is *increasingly* fluid, and the body is mobilized as a plastic resource on to which a reflexive sense of self is projected in an attempt to lend solidity to the narrative thus envisaged.

From this perspective, the rise of dieting, 'keep fit', and other corporeally oriented practices reflects the increasing tendency to treat the body as constitutive or expressive of the reflexively constructed self, and the growing popularity of 'non mainstream body modification' (Myers, 1992) might similarly be argued to reflect this trend. Like the forms of 'body project' considered by Shilling, for example, tattooing and piercing have the effect of transforming the exterior surfaces of the body 'in line with the designs of its owner', and can allow a 'wholesale transformation' of the body along these lines (Shilling, 1993: 3). Indeed, as well as regarding their tattoos and piercings as very personal, many interviewees also referred to such forms of body modification as marks of individuality; as 'a way of standing out [and] saying, "Look, I'm me, I'm an individual." ' Some also suggested that becoming tattooed or pierced could be seen as an act of 'self-creation'. As one heavily tattooed and ex-heavily pierced interviewee put it:

> [I]t makes you feel individual . . . you know like, everyone's born with roughly the same bodies, but you've created yours in your own image [in line with] what your imagination wants your body to look like. It's like

someone's given you something, and then you've made it your own, so you're not like everyone else any more.

Several interviewees also spoke of increased self-confidence as a result of having become tattooed or pierced, some because of the way in which they had endured the physical process itself, but others, because of the way in which it brought them closer in line with their own self-image. One heavily tattooed interviewee, for instance, told me that he felt 'a better, more rounded, and fuller person for being tattooed', more 'in tune with the person [he] really thought [he] was rather than the . . . shy, pleasant, reserved . . . kind of individual that [he had previously] portrayed'. Others simply noted that they felt 'more complete'.

On the one hand, then, becoming tattooed or pierced can be seen as an act of 'self-creation', that, through the modification of the body's surface, helps to construct a viable sense of self-identity. As the comments of several interviewees indicated, however, tattooing, in particular, can also assist in the construction of a coherent and *consistent* self-narrative.

Several interviewees told me that their tattoos acted as permanent reminders of particular periods or events, and as one heavily tattooed female interviewee pointed out, tattooing 'has . . . a lot to do with memory' because the tattoo itself 'will always remind you of the time . . . you had it done'. Certain interviewees noted that they had deliberately become tattooed to mark *specific* events such as weddings, while one young female informant, for example, told me that although she had wanted a tattoo for some time, she finally decided to get it done on her 21st birthday, both as a marker of adulthood and as a celebration of the event itself. Her eyebrow piercing was similarly intended to mark and celebrate a specific event, in this case the offer of her first full-time job.

Others noted that tattoos, in particular, served as an indelible connection with specific periods in their lives. As one young tattooee put it: 'It connects me with like, my . . . teenage years really.' Another lightly tattooed interviewee, told me that he regarded the two Native American designs on his upper-arms as 'a commitment to [him]self' and explained that:

> By marking myself I thought I could . . . keep . . . what I felt when I was 18, 19, for the rest of my life, 'cause I'd always remember the time. Because having a tattoo done is such a special thing, there's the pain to begin with, and then there's like the high you get afterwards when you first have it done . . . But, just looking at them reminds me of that time, and hopefully it will stop me from forgetting who I am, when life starts to get, you know, kick the door in a bit more. The older you get, mortgage, kids, whatever.

In this sense, becoming tattooed might be argued to commit the tattooee to a particular narrative, and at least one interviewee described his own tattoos as a permanent 'diary' that 'no one can take off you'. Others suggested that their tattoos could tell a story, with one heavily tattooed interviewee, for instance, suggesting that once he was completely tattooed, 'the realistic parts of [his] body suit [would] tell some kind of story about [his] view of the world'. The extent to which others would be able to read this text would depend on their ability to 'piece it all together', however, and as another heavily tattooed interviewee pointed out, while 'there's gonna be bits you can pick up', what can be gleaned from another person's tattoos is likely to be fairly limited. For the interviewee in question, tattoos *could* tell a story, but like other forms of diary, this was inherently personal:

> It's like the New Zealand *moko* is the story of the life, isn't it? That sort of thing. Kind of like that. But, I mean, it isn't an outward story of your life, you just remember it because you can see it on yourself, do you know what I mean?

Conclusion

Tattooing and piercing can be seen as postmodern practices in their eclectic appropriation of techniques and imagery from a global scrapbook of design sources and procedures, and it could be argued that their current popularity represents nothing more than the continued incorporation of 'the exotic' into the 'supermarket of style' (Craik, 1994: 25; Steele, 1996: 160–1). As was noted above, tattooing and piercing imagery is increasingly fashionable, and certain of the tattooees and piercees interviewed for this study did appear to regard their respective body modifications as little more than fashionable accessories. From this perspective, the contemporary popularity of tattooing and piercing could be seen not only as supportive of notions of a postmodern shift in a general sense, but also as evidence of the strength of such a shift, the incorporation of such once strongly connotative symbols into a more or less free-floating 'carnival of signs' indicative of the scope of the developments in question.

As was also indicated above, however, factors such as pain and permanence figure strongly in contemporary body modifiers' understandings and experiences of such corporeal artefacts. Despite the tendency of certain lightly tattooed or pierced body modifiers to describe them as accessories, among those involved, tattoos and piercings are not, generally, perceived simply as superficial products in the 'carnival of style'. Indeed, were tattoos and piercings regarded solely as fashionable accessories, then it would be difficult to see why anyone would become tattooed or pierced at all: in this context, stress would lie exclusively with the finished body decoration – as a purely visual signifier – and a tattoo-transfer, or clip-on piercing, would be as meaningful (if not as durable) as the real thing.[7]

To the extent that this is their intended argument, Polhemus and Proctor (1978) and Curry (1993) are arguably wrong to suggest that the permanence of tattooing – and in Curry's case the semi-permanence of piercing – guarantees the 'anti-fashion' status of such forms of body modification: a permanent or 'semi-permanent' signifier does not in and of itself imply a fixed signified. As *corporeal artefacts*, however, tattoos and piercings will arguably continue to refer to the manner of their production, and in this sense to resist full incorporation into Bauldrillard's 'carnival of signs', however popular related imagery becomes. The comments of tattooed and pierced interviewees also suggest that whether or not their meaning is fixed in these terms, tattoos, and to a lesser extent piercings, are often employed as a form of 'anti-fashion', or at least valued in terms of their contrast with more superficial, sartorial accessories.

In this sense, such forms of body modification can be argued to share certain affinities with the subcultural uniforms of the 1960s and 1970s, but in contrast with skinhead style, for instance, contemporary body modification appears to serve less as a marker of group identity, and more as an expression of the self. It might thus be argued that while the skinheads' adoption of an exaggeratedly macho style was as a class-specific response to a particular and 'localized' crisis, the growing popularity of tattooing and piercing among an increasingly diverse clientele can instead be seen as a similar, but more diffuse, response to a set of crises and insecurities that are now more felt by a far wider section of the population (Muggleton, 1997: 13; Rubin, 1988: 255). That this is expressed via the adoption of permanent or semi-permanent forms of body modification, rather than, say, a particular clothing style, might in turn be explained by pointing to the increasing redundancy of sartorial markers of identification.

This would accord with the characterization of contemporary tattooing and piercing as 'body projects', as practices dedicated to the construction of a coherent sense of self-identity, and it was noted above that certain interviewees did indeed regard their involvement with such forms of body modification as a form of 'self-creation'. It was also noted that the permanence of tattooing, in particular, meant that it was well-suited to the establishment of a consistent personal narrative.

In conclusion, however, it should be pointed out that while the permanence or 'semi-permanence' of tattoos and piercings, and the pain involved in their acquisition, lends itself well to such a project, it also renders problematic any subsequent attempts to reflexively *revise* one's sense of self through *re*-attention to the body's exterior. As one lightly tattooed interviewee put it: 'you cannot run away from them, you can't stop being a tattooed person'. In this sense, tattooing, and some types of piercing, can be argued to differ from other forms of contemporary body project, their lack of easy revisibility perhaps indicative of a rejection of the ideology of social mobility which practices such as 'keep fit' vigorously pursue. Postmodern practices in that they involve the 'refashioning of personal identities out of cultural materials' (Tseëlon, 1995: 123), tattooing and certain forms of piercing differ from other forms of 'identity project' in representing an attempt to fix, or anchor one's sense of self through the (relative) permanence of the modification thus acquired.[8]

In a recent article on 'body marking', Turner described contemporary tattooing and piercing as 'playful and ironic': 'empty signs' that fail to refer to one's wider social-status, and can instead be read as 'parodic messages to the self' (Turner, 1997 . . .). While it is undoubtedly correct to note that contemporary body modification no longer refers unambiguously to one's class, gender or sexuality, however, the above has indicated that such markings can – on at least two levels – be argued to be less 'empty' than Turner suggests. *Relatively* free-floating, when compared, for instance, with traditional 'marking' in non-Western contexts, contemporary body modification continues to signify at the denotative level, even if its connotative message is increasingly ambiguous. Taken together, factors such as the relative permanence of such forms of body modification, the pain involved in their acquisition, and the active role played by the tattooee or piercee in their completion, also suggest that it would be misleading to label contemporary tattooing and piercing simply as fashionable products in the 'supermarket of style'. As American tattooist Don Ed Hardy points out, while 'there *are* elements of fashion to it' (Hardy, in Vale and Juno, 1989: 58), '[i]t's on your body, it's permanent; you have to live with it; and it hurts' (Hardy, in Vale and Juno, 1989: 61).

Notes

I am grateful to Graham Allan, Kate Reed, Chris Shilling and an anonymous referee for their comments on an earlier version of this paper, and to the Department of Sociology and Social Policy at the University of Southampton for supporting the wider study of which it forms a part. Thanks are also due to the interviewees quoted above, and to the numerous others who have helped with my research in some way, shape or form. The usual disclaimers, of course, apply.

1   No accurate figures are available, but a number of authors have noted the increasing popularity of tattooing (Armstrong, 1991, Armstrong and Gabriel, 1993; Armstrong et al., 1996; Blanchard, 1994; Curry, 1993; DeMello, 1995a, 1995b; Rubin, 1988; Sanders, 1989) and piercing (Curry, 1993; Myers, 1992), as well as their spread to an increasingly heterogeneous clientele. Several writers have pointed to the growing numbers of middle-class and female tattooees (Armstrong, 1991: 215, 1993: 107–8; Armstrong et al., 1996: 412; Blanchard, 1994: 287; Curry, 1993: 70; DeMello, 1995a: 73, 79, 1995b: 48; Mercer & Davies, 1991; 380; Rubin, 1988: 235; Sanders, 1989: 28–9, 160), while Rubin (1988: 235) has also noted a rise in the number of older clients. Curry (1993: 75) notes that piercing is no longer 'confined to any class, age group or sexual proclivity'.

These points can be supported by a wealth of circumstantial evidence. During the course of this research, for example, several UK-based tattooists confirmed the increasing popularity of the practice since the late-1970s, as well as an increase in the number of middle-class, female and older clients (see also Dixon, in Bradberry, 1997: 21; 'K', 1995: 49; Knappett, 1997: 29; Papworth, 1998: 12; Potton, 1996: 34; 'Rabbit', 1997: 20–5; Treharne, 1996: 37; Venus, 1996: 45). A number of informants also pointed to an acceleration in these trends since the mid-to-late-1980s (see also 'Mark the Wanderer', 1998: 47; 'Annie', in Wainwright, 1996: 2). Similar confirmation was provided in respect of body piercing, with interviewees noting its growth in popularity since the early to mid-1980s, the acceleration of such trends since the late 1980s/early 1990s, and the increasingly diverse nature of the clientele: the practice is no longer confined primarily to those with an interest in the SM or fetish scene, and is popular among a range of age groups and occupational backgrounds (see also Grant, 1995: 15, 18; 'Barry', in Rowlands, 1998: 13).

The increased incidence of both tattooing and piercing is also indicated by reports of their popularity in the broadcast and print media (see, for example: Bayley, 1996; Bellos, 1996; Brooker, 1994; Garner, 1998; Grant, 1995; Millard, 1995; Moorhead, 1998; Mullen, 1997; Rowlands, 1998; Ryle, 1996; Wallace, 1997; Ward, 1998; Williams, 1996). Many of these articles have called for tighter regulation of body piercing, itself a further indication of the practice's recent rise in popularity: the Local Government (Miscellaneous Provisions) Act 1982 relates only to ear-piercing, reflecting the low incidence of other forms of piercing at the time the legislation was framed (Stokes, 1996). Following a recent Department of Health consulation exercise (Department of Health/Welsh Office, 1996), however, proposals have now been put forward to introduce relevant legislation, albeit alongside the deregulation of other forms of 'skin piercing' (Department of Health, 1998).

2   See note 1, above.

3   The article forms part of a wider study of contemporary body modification, for which in-depth, semi-structured interviews were conducted with 35 tattooed and/or pierced informants, as well as with several professional tattooists, body piercers and other key informants. The study also draws on observation conducted at a number of tattoo conventions and tattoo and/or piercing studios, as well as analysis of the popular literature devoted to the forms of body modification in question.

The 35 core interviewees were recruited in roughly equal numbers at tattoo conventions, through advertisements in a UK-based tattoo magazine and local student publications, and through introductions provided by existing informants, though there were already known to the author. A variety of methods was employed in order to allow contact with a range of contemporary body modifiers. The bulk of the interviews were conducted face-to-face, though seven took place by phone. Interviews were recorded, and ranged in duration from 20 minutes to approximately 3 hours.

Of the 35 tattooees and/or piercees interviewed, 15 were women, and ages ranged from 19 to 40 among the women, and 20 to 60 among the men. The mean ages for each group were 24 and 32 respectively. Occupations ranged from the unemployed and students to credit analysts, local government officers and company directors. Most of the interviewees were white, and while this was not an intentional outcome of the sampling methods employed, it does reflect a lack of ethnic diversity in the tattoo and piercing community. Around 40 percent of the women and 70 percent of the men were heavily tattooed and/or pierced, which generally implies that they had three or more of either form of body modification. This is a fairly loose definition, however: several standard ear-piercings, for example, would not place someone in the heavily pierced category, while someone with a full backpiece as their sole tattoo would certainly be counted as heavily tattooed.

·4   See note 3, above.

5   Certain lightly pierced, but non-tattooed informants also offered this as their rationale for choosing the former body modification rather than the latter. When asked if he had ever thought about getting a tattoo done, for instance, one male piercee replied: 'Err, no. Now that was another consideration for getting the piercing done over something like a tattoo, in that if I ever get fed up with it, it just comes out and heals over.'

6   A ring-piercing that enters through the urethra, and exits at the base of the glans. See Myers (1992: 300–1) for illustration and further description.

7   But however realistic their appearance, 'Stick on tattoos are not tattoos' (Curry, 1993: 70), and the very popularity of tattoo-transfers, while indicative of the popularity of tattoo-based *imagery*, also suggests that, for some, a *real* tattoo is simply not an option to be considered. A recent edition of *Tatler* carried an article extolling the merits of small, discrete and *tasteful* tattoos, before going on to suggest that 'temporary-tattoos' were perhaps a wiser option (Green, 1997: 55).

8   As I have suggested elsewhere, there is also an extent to which tattooing and
     piercing can be said to be resistant of gendered norms of appearance, in part
     because they move the tattooee or piercee further away from, rather than closer
     towards, the youthful, slim, and *unmarked* body that is the hegemonic Western
     ideal (Sweetman, 1999b; see also DeMello, 1995b).

References

Alford, L. (1993) 'Hard Look Story', *Observer Life Magazine* 7 November: 16–17.

Armstrong, M.L. (1991) 'Career-Oriented Women with Tattoos', *Image: Journal of Nursing Scholarship* 23(4): 215–20.

Armstrong, M.L. and D.G. Gabriel (1993) 'Tattoos on Women: Marks of Distinction or Abomination?', *Dermatology Nursing* 5(2): 107–13.

Armstrong, M.L., D.J. Stuppy and D.G. Gabriel (1996) 'Motivation for Tattoo Removal', *Archives of Dermatology* 132(4): 412–16.

Bayley, C. (1996) 'Straight for the Juggler', *Guardian section* 2 26 August: 10–11.

Bellos, A. (1996) 'As British as S&M', *Guardian section* 2 6 November: 7.

Blanchard, M. (1994) 'Post-Bourgeois Tattoo: Reflections on Skin Writing in Late Capitalist Societies', in Lucien Taylor (ed.) *Visualizing Theory: Selected Essays from V.A.R. 1990–1994*. New York and London: Routledge.

Bradberry, G. (1997) 'Branded for Life', *The Times* 20 November: 21.

Brooker, E. (1994) 'He Wears his Scars with Pride', *The Independent Section II'*, 11 May.

Clarke, J. (1976) 'The Skinheads and the Magical Recovery of Community', in S. Hall and T. Jefferson (eds) *Resistance through Rituals: Youth Subcultures in Post-War Britain*. London: Harper Collins.

Cohen, P. (1997) 'Subcultural Conflict and Working-Class Community', in K. Gelder and S. Thornton (eds) *The Subcultures Reader*. London: Routledge. (Orig. 1972.)

Craik, J. (1994) *The Face of Fashion: Cultural Studies in Fashion*. London: Routledge.

Curry, D. (1993) 'Decorating the Body Politic', *New Formations* 19: 69–82.

Davis, F.(1985) 'Clothing and Fashion as Communication', in M.R. Solomon (ed.) *The Psychology of Fashion*. Lexington, MA: Lexington Books.

DeMello, M. (1995a) ' "Not Just For Bikers Anymore": Popular Representations of American Tattooing', *Journal of Popular Culture* 19(3): 37–52.

DeMello, M. (1995b) 'The Carnivalesque Body: Women and Tattoos', in The Drawing Center, *Pierced Hearts and True Love: A Century of Drawings for Tattoos*. New York/Honolulu: The Drawing Centre/Hardy Marks Publications.

Department of Health/Welsh Office (1996) 'Regulation of Skin Piercing: A Consultation Paper', London: Department of Health/Welsh Office, 3 October.

Department of Health (1998) 'Regulation of Skin Piercing Businesses', London: Department of Health communique, 30 June.

Dery, M. (1996) *Escape Velocity: Cyberculture at the End of the Century*. London: Hodder and Stoughton.

Eubanks, V. (1996) 'Zones of Dither: Writing the Postmodern Body', *Body & Society* 2(3): 73–88.

Falk, P. (1995) 'Written in the Flesh', *Body & Society* 1(1): 95–105.

Featherstone, M. (1991) 'The Body in Consumer Culture', in M. Featherstone, M. Hepworth and B. Turner (eds) *The Body: Social Process and Cultural Theory*. London: Sage.

Foster Wallace, D. (1997) *Infinite Jest*. London: Abacus.

Gamman, L. and M. Makinen (1994) *Female Fetishism: A New Look*. London: Lawrence and Wishart.

Garner, C. (1998) 'There's a Hole in Dad's Argument', *The Independent Monday Review* 15 June: 10.

Gell, A. (1993) *Wrapping in Images: Tattooing in Polynesia*. Oxford: Clarendon Press.

Giddens, A. (1991) *Modernity and Self-Identity: Self and Society in the Late Modern Age*. Cambridge: Polity Press.

Gottschalk, S. (1993) 'Uncomfortably Numb: Countercultural Impulses in the Postmodern Era', *Symbolic Interaction* 16(4): 351–78.

Grant, L. (1995) 'Written on the Body', *Guardian Weekend* 1 April: 12–20.

Green, C. (1997) 'Ink on the Pink', *Tatler* 292(8): 55.

Hall, S. and T. Jefferson(eds) (1976) *Resistance through Rituals: Youth Subcultures in Post-War Britain*. London: Harper Collins.

Hebdige, D. (1988) *Subculture: The Meaning of Style*. London and New York: Routledge. (Orig. 1979.)

'K', B. (1995) 'Tattoo Crazy: Barry K' (interview by P. Callaby), *Skin Deep* 2(2): 44–51.

Klesse, C. (1997) 'The Representation of Primitivism in a Specialised Sexual Subculture', unpublished paper presented at 'Body Modification', a *TCS* conference, Nottingham Trent University, June. (A revised version of this paper appears in this issue.)

Knappett, J. (1997) 'John Knappett: Body Graphics' (interview by P. Callaby), *Skin Deep* 4(6): 28–35.

Lind, C. and M. Roach-Higgins (1985) 'Collective Adoption, Fashion, and the Social-Political Symbolism of Dress', in M. Solomon (ed.) *The Psychology of Fashion*. Lexington, MA: Lexington Books.

'Mark the Wanderer' (1998) 'Mark the Wanderer: A Happy Man' (interview by D. Smith), *Skin Deep* 5(1): 46–9.

Maffesoli, M. (1996) *The Time of the Tribes: The Decline of Individualism in Mass Society*. London: Sage.

Menkes, S. (1993) 'Fetish or Fashion?', *New York Times* 21 November: C1, 9.

Mercer, N. and D. Davies (1991) 'Tattoos: Marked for Life', *British Medical Journal* 303: 380.

Miles, C. (1997) 'Metalmorphosis', unpublished paper presented at 'Body Modification', a *TCS* Conference, Nottingham Trent University, June.

Millard, R. (1995) 'Your Body in the Firing Line for the Latest in Hot Fashion', *The Observer* 22 January: 8.

Moorhead, J. (1998) 'A Lesson in Needlework', *Guardian section* 2 14 January: 7.

Muggleton, D. (1995) 'From "Subculture" to "Neo-Tribe": Identity, Paradox and Postmodernism in "Alternative" Style', unpublished paper presented at 'Shouts from the Street: Culture, Creativity and Change', MIPC Conference on Popular Culture, Manchester Metropolitan University, September.

Muggleton, D. (1997) 'Resistance or Difference? Expressive Individualism, Alienation and Subcultural Disengagement', unpublished paper presented at 'Power/ Resistance', BSA Annual Conference, University of York, April.

Mullen, L. (1997) 'The Cutting Edge', *Time Out* 10–17 December: 20–31.

Myers, J. (1992) 'Nonmainstream Body Modification: Genital Piercing, Branding, Burning, and Cutting', *Journal of Contemporary Ethnography* 21(3): 267–306.

Papworth, J. (1998) 'Adventures in the Skin Trade', *Guardian Money* 28 February: 12.

Pitts, V. (1998) 'Provoking the Organic: Representations and Resistance in Extreme Body Marking', unpublished paper presented at 'Making Sense of the Body', BSA Annual Conference, University of Edinburgh, April.

Polhemus, T. (1995) *Streetstyle: From Sidewalk to Catwalk*. London: Thames and Hudson.

Polhemus, T. and L. Proctor (1978) *Fashion and Anti-Fashion*. London: Thames and Hudson.

Potton, S. (1996) 'Steve Potton' (interview by P. Callaby), *Skin Deep* 3(8): 30–7.

'Rabbit' (1997) 'Rabbit: Grin 'n' Wear It' (interview by P. Callaby), *Skin Deep* 4(2): 18–25.

Rowlands, B. (1998) 'There's a Hole in My Navel, My Nipple, My Nose', *The Independent* 1 September: 13.

Rubin, A. (1988) 'The Tattoo Renaissance', in A. Rubin (ed.) *Marks of Civilization: Artistic Transformations of the Human Body*. Los Angeles: Museum of Cultural History/University of California LA.

Ryle, J. (1996) 'Piercing Truths', *Guardian section 2* 15 March: 3.

Sanders, C. (1985) 'Tattoo Consumption: Risk and Regret in the Purchase of a Socially Marginal Service', *Advances in Consumer Research* 12: 17–22.

Sanders, C. (1989) *Customizing the Body: The Art and Culture of Tattooing*. Philadelphia, PA: Temple University Press.

Shilling, C. (1993) *The Body and Social Theory*. London: Sage.

Steele, V. (1996) *Fetish: Fashion, Sex and Power*. New York and Oxford: Oxford University Press.

Stokes, P. (1996) 'Mother Demands New Law on Body Piercing', *The Daily Telegraph* 8 June: 9.

Sweetman, P. (1999a) 'Only Skin Deep? Tattooing Piercing and the Transgressive Body', in M. Aaron (ed.) *The Body's Perilous Pleasures: Dangerous Desires and Contemporary Culture*. Edinburgh: Edinburgh University Press.

Sweetman, P. (1999b) 'Marked Bodies, Oppositional Identities? Tattooing, Piercing and the Ambiguity of Resistance', in S. Roseneil and J. Seymour (eds) *Practising Identities: Power and Resistance*. Basingstoke: Macmillan.

Treharne, J. (1996) 'John Treharne: Skin Creation' (interview by P. Callaby), *Skin Deep* 3(9): 30–7.

Tseëlon, E. (1995) *The Masque of Femininity: The Representation of Woman in Everyday Life*. London: Sage.

Turner, B. (1997) 'Body Marks: Neo-Tribalism in Cool Societies', unpublished paper presented at 'Body Modification', a *TCS* Conference, Nottingham Trent University, June. (A revised version of this paper appears in this issue.)

Vale, V. and A. Juno (1989) *Re/Search #12: Modern Primitives – An Investigation of Contemporary Adornment and Ritual*. San Francisco: Re/Search Publications.

Venus, J. (1996) 'Johnny Venus' (interview by B. Richmond), *Skin Deep* 3(9): 44–9.

Wainwright, M. (1996) 'Skin-Deep Beauty Treatment Makes a Point', *Guardian* 16 December: 2

Wallace, W. (1997) 'A Skin for Trouble', *Guardian section 2* 9 December: 16.

Ward, S. (1998) 'A Piercing Cry of Anger', *Guardian, Society* 25 February: 2.

Williams, S. (1996) 'Generation Gap', *The Independent Section II* 20 May: 7.

Wilson, E. (1990) 'These New Components of the Spectacle: Fashion and Postmodernism', in R. Boyne and A. Rattansi (eds) *Postmodernism and Society*. Basingstoke: Macmillan.

[. . .]

Chapter 26

Umberto Eco

LUMBAR THOUGHT

A FEW WEEKS AGO, Luca Goldoni wrote an amusing report from the Adriatic coast about the mishaps of those who wear blue jeans for reasons of fashion, and no longer know how to sit down or arrange the external reproductive apparatus. I believe the problem broached by Goldoni is rich in philosophical reflections, which I would like to pursue on my own and with the maximum seriousness, because no everyday experience is too base for the thinking man, and it is time to make philosophy proceed, not only on its own two feet, but also with its own loins.

I began wearing blue jeans in the days when very few people did, but always on vacation. I found – and still find – them very comfortable, especially when I travel, because there are no problems of creases, tearing, spots. Today they are worn also for looks, but primarily they are very utilitarian. It's only in the past few years that I've had to renounce this pleasure because I've put on weight. True, if you search thoroughly you can find an *extra large* (Macy's could fit even Oliver Hardy with blue jeans), but they are large not only around the waist, but also around the legs, and they are not a pretty sight.

Recently, cutting down on drink, I shed the number of pounds necessary for me to try again some *almost* normal jeans. I underwent the calvary described by Luca Goldoni, as the saleswoman said, 'Pull it tight, it'll stretch a bit'; and I emerged, not having to suck in my belly (I refuse to accept such compromises). And so, after a long time, I was enjoying the sensation of wearing pants that, instead of clutching the waist, held the hips, because it is a characteristic of jeans to grip the lumbar-sacral region and stay up thanks not to suspension but to adherence.

After such a long time, the sensation was new. The jeans didn't pinch, but they made their presence felt. Elastic though they were, I sensed a kind of sheath around the lower half of my body. Even if I had wished, I couldn't turn or wiggle my belly *inside* my pants; if anything, I had to turn it or wiggle it *together with* my pants. Which subdivides so to speak one's body into two independent zones, one free of clothing, above the belt, and the other organically identified with the clothing, from immediately below the belt to the anklebones. I discovered that my movements, my way of walking, turning, sitting, hurrying, were *different*. Not more difficult, or less difficult, but certainly different.

As a result, I lived in the knowledge that I had jeans on, whereas normally we live forgetting that we're wearing undershorts or trousers. I lived for my jeans, and as a result I assumed the exterior behavior of one who wears jeans. In any case, I assumed a *demeanor*. It's strange that the traditionally most informal and anti-etiquette garment should be the one that so strongly imposes an etiquette. As a rule I am boisterous, I sprawl in a chair, I slump wherever I please, with no claim to elegance: my blue jeans checked these actions, made me more polite and mature. I discussed it at length, especially with consultants of the opposite sex, from whom I learned what, for that matter, I had already suspected: that for women experiences of this kind are familiar because all their garments are conceived to impose a demeanor – high heels, girdles, brassieres, pantyhose, tight sweaters.

I thought then about how much, in the history of civilization, dress as armor has influenced behavior and, in consequence, exterior morality. The Victorian bourgeois was stiff and formal because of stiff collars; the nineteenth-century gentleman was constrained by his tight redingotes, boots, and top hats that didn't allow brusque movements of the head. If Vienna had been on the equator and its bourgeoisie had gone around in Bermuda shorts, would Freud have described the same neurotic symptoms, the same Oedipal triangles? And would he have described them in the same way if he, the doctor, had been a Scot, in a kilt (under which, as everyone knows, the rule is to wear nothing)?

A garment that squeezes the testicles makes a man think differently. Women during menstruation; people suffering from orchitis, victims of hemorrhoids, urethritis, prostate and similar ailments know to what extent pressures or obstacles in the sacroiliac area influence one's mood and mental agility. But the same can be said (perhaps to a lesser degree) of the neck, the back, the head, the feet. A human race that has learned to move about in shoes has oriented its thought differently from the way it would have done if the race had gone barefoot. It is sad, especially for philosophers in the idealistic tradition, to think that the Spirit originates from these conditions; yet not only is this true, but the great thing is that Hegel knew it also, and therefore studied the cranial bumps indicated by phrenologists, and in a book actually entitled *Phenomenology of Mind*. But the problem of my jeans led me to other observations. Not only did the garment impose a demeanor on me; by focusing my attention on demeanor, it obliged me to *live towards the exterior world*. It reduced, in other words, the exercise of my interior-ness. For people in my profession it is normal to walk along with your mind on other things: the article you have to write, the lecture you must give, the relationship between the One and the Many, the Andreotti government, how to deal with the problem of the Redemption, whether there is life on Mars, the latest song of Celentano, the paradox of Epimenides. In our line this is called "the interior life." Well, with my new jeans my life was entirely exterior: I thought about the relationship between me and my pants, and the relationship between my pants and me and the society we lived in. I had achieved heteroconsciousness, that is to say, an epidermic self-awareness.

I realized then that thinkers, over the centuries, have fought to free themselves of armor. Warriors lived an exterior life, all enclosed in cuirasses and tunics; but monks had invented a habit that, while fulfilling, *on its own*, the requirements of demeanor (majestic, flowing, all of a piece, so that it fell in statuesque folds), it left the body (inside, underneath) completely free and unaware of itself. Monks were rich in interior life and very dirty, because the body, protected by a habit that, ennobling it, released it, was free to think, and to forget about itself. The idea was not only ecclesiastic; you have to think only of the beautiful mantles Erasmus wore. And when even the intellectual must dress in lay armor (wigs, waistcoats, knee breeches) we see that when he retires to think, he swaggers in rich dressing-gowns, or in Balzac's loose, *drôlatique* blouses. Thought abhors tights.

But if armor obliges its wearer to live the exterior life, then the age-old female spell is due also to the fact that society has imposed armors on women, forcing them to neglect the exercise of thought. Woman has been enslaved by fashion not only because, in obliging her to be attractive, to maintain an ethereal demeanor, to be pretty and stimulating, it made her a sex object; she has been enslaved chiefly because the clothing counseled for her forced her psychologically to live for the exterior. And this makes us realize how intellectually gifted and heroic a girl had to be before she could become, in those clothes, Madame de Sévigné, Vittoria Colonna, Madame Curie, or Rosa Luxemburg. The reflection has some value because it leads us to discover that, apparent symbol of liberation and equality with men, the blue jeans that fashion today imposes on women are a trap of Domination; for they don't free the body, but subject it to another label and imprison it in other armors that don't seem to be armors because they apparently are not "feminine."

A final reflection – in imposing an exterior demeanor, clothes are semiotic devices, machines for communicating. This was known, but there had been no attempt to illustrate the parallel with the syntactic structures of language, which, in the opinion of many people, influence our view of the world. The syntactic structures of fashions also influence our view of the world, and in a far more physical way than the *consecutio temporum* or the existence of the subjunctive. You see how many mysterious paths the dialectic between oppression and liberation must follow, and the struggle to bring light.

Even via the groin.

Chapter 27

Ruth Holliday

THE COMFORT OF IDENTITY

IN THIS ARTICLE I examine material from video diaries which were undertaken by a number of people in 'queer communities'. I am interested in the ways in which identities are performed in different times and spaces – which I call work, rest and play – and also how these performances become mediated by academic, political and 'subcultural' discourses of sexuality. I do not propose these definitions as immutable, rather as organizing concepts with which to frame the empirical material. I aim to explore the similarities and differences in respondents' accounts, and want to chart their *experiences* of identity. In so doing I hope to illustrate some key aspects of theoretical debates around identity whilst also considering how far people's experiences of their own identities mirror the fractured selves currently described by academics (for example Hall, 1996) or the theoretical insights of notions of performativity in relation to identity (Butler, 1990): are identities outside the academy experienced as more or less fixed or more complex than these writings suggest? I would also like to examine how far academic discourses filter into and inform political discourses and what their relevance might be to 'subcultural' constructions of the self. In my analysis, then, there are three levels to theorize: the academic, and by this I really mean queer theory in this context; the political, usually conceived of as lesbian, gay, bisexual and transgender politics; and the everyday, which I call the subcultural (I define these terms in more detail later).

Performing identities for the camera

My research has involved giving respondents camcorders and asking them to make 'video diaries'. In the brief for these, respondents were asked to demonstrate (visually) and talk about the ways in which they managed or presented their identities in different settings in their everyday lives. The participants were asked to dress in the clothes they would wear in each situation, describing them in detail and explaining why they thought these self-presentation strategies were appropriate. This technique was designed to make sure that participants were as explicit as possible about the presentation of their identities in different spaces – at work, rest and play. Theoretical themes were then developed as they arose from the data, according to the significance that respondents afforded them and the frequency with which issues arose across all of the respondents' accounts.

I would like to stress the importance of the video diaries in capturing the *performativities* of identity in ways which are qualitatively different from other socio-logical research methods. In one sense, the self-representation is more 'complete' than the audiotaped interview, which only provides aural data. Ongoing debates around qualitative social research generally, and feminist research within that more specifically, have opened up space to consider modes of research which produce accounts of respondents' social worlds that are radically different from quantitative and survey-based studies, and my use of video diaries here reflects those debates (see for example Stanley, 1993). Moreover, the visual dimension of the construction and display of identity is obviously more easily gleaned through this method. The use of video as a *process* in the research is equally important (compared with, say, the use of still photography), not only in allowing a representation of the performativity of identity to show through, but also in running that alongside the narrativization of identity (through respondents' commentaries) and in reflecting the selection, edit-ing and refining that constitute identity and performativity as process in all our lives.

In many ways video diaries currently have a common currency, largely due to their recent extended television coverage (in the UK at least), which makes them a familiar form to respondents. In theory (if not necessarily in practice) video diaries afford respondents the potential for a greater degree of reflexivity than other methods, through the processes of watching, re-recording and editing their diaries before submission, and because each diarist has at least one month in which to create their diary. Regardless of the 'accuracy' or 'realism' of the diaries, then, they do at least afford the potential for the respondents to more fully represent themselves than other more traditional research methods. For example, Gill[1] says about the process:

> Why am I telling you all these things about myself? . . . um, because I think that it's important and I think I've got things to say . . . The least favourite bit of my body is this little bit in here, because I've got a fat bit there, and a front-on picture of my belly, although I let a bit of that be shown earlier and viewed that to see if I was going to let it stay in.

This implies that making a video diary can be a reflexive and even empowering process, since it offers the subject greater 'editorial control' over the material she chooses to disclose – and because she feels she has 'important' things to say that are here given a space to be said.

Perhaps the most interesting issue to emerge from this research process, how-ever, was precisely the *lack* of reflexivity that many participants displayed in examin-ing their self-presentations. This was slightly uneven depending on the context, as one might expect. For example, participants were very sensitive to the demands placed on them by uniforms and dress codes at work, and far less self-conscious when it came to their 'leisure wear'.

Uniforms

Dressing is intricately linked to queer employment patterns throughout contemporary history. There are many recent rediscoveries of women who cross-dressed or lived as men in the 19th century in order to pursue male careers which were not open to them as women (Garber, 1992). Moreover, during the first half of the 20th century, especially around the two world wars, the armed forces created opportunities and possibilities for queer men and women to earn money and leave home, to inhabit single-sex spaces, to engage in non-sex-specific occupations, and to dress in a particularly codified way – in uniform.

Uniforms can alleviate some of the problems of dressing. For example, one respondent in Rosa Ainley's (1995: 137) study explains:

> I didn't realize at the time, when I went into nursing, how much I would hide behind the uniform and how comfortable I felt in a traditional female role, where I could be totally hidden. Never mind that I used to walk with a bit of a sway or anything like that, I was in a dress with a little cap perched on my head. It wasn't really until I left the health service for another job that I realized I did not know how to dress, I did not know how I wanted to look. Or I did know how I wanted to look, but might well be accused of being lesbian and that bothered me.

Uniforms can thus be a mask (experienced either positively or negatively) or a marker of sexual identity. Even now uniforms (navy and police, for example) have a certain affectionate place in lesbian, gay and bisexual cultures, and lesbians continue to be attracted by careers in the army, police force, and prison service, for example (Ainley, 1995).

The freedom to be able to 'express' one's sexuality, or to 'be oneself' at work in terms of dress, is frequently cited as a motivation towards particular forms of employment. Take the examples of Seb and Jo. Seb, a bisexual psychiatric nurse in his early 30s, lives with his partner Gill (also in nursing) in a large communal house shared with six others in a city in the English Midlands. Both he and his partner are non-monogamous and have relationships with other men and women. Jo is a lesbian and a hospital technician who lives with her partner Sue (a trainee teacher) in an ex-council house in a small south Midlands town. Neither Seb nor Jo are 'out' at work, and both are obliged to wear uniforms in the workplace. They actually subvert these uniforms to a greater or lesser degree. In both cases they are required not to wear jeans, which they both *do* wear, although they only wear black and not blue ones. Jo is also required to wear a white tunic top which she does but always covers over with a jumper or sweat-shirt. Seb is not required to wear a tie but to wear 'a shirt which would facilitate the wearing of a tie'. To this he responds by wearing a collarless shirt. He is not required to wear 'sedate' colours, but all his workmates do so. He prefers to wear bright colours: green, red or orange shirts and brightly coloured trousers.

Steve is gay and the part-time manager of a clothing shop. He is in his early 20s and also studies law at a local university. He lives at home with his parents but has a partner, Patrick, at whose house he spends much of his time. At work Steve is obliged to wear suits from the store's range. He thus has separate wardrobes for work and for leisure, one comprising dark suits and the other with brighter and much more varied attire. As he explains:

> People who join the job don't necessarily know I'm gay. It is never necessarily spoken about. Everyone knows. Me and my close friends there go to clubs together and they all know Patrick, he comes in every week, it isn't a problem. But it does make you far more firm. The job itself requires that, but in terms of sexual identity, people don't necessarily associate that firmness with a gay man . . . I think you should dress appropriately for what the occasion is but hopefully the person has the good sense to apply their individualism to what they're wearing . . . it's part of the job and you have to accept it . . . I quite enjoy the whole feeling it gives to you of authority and control and feeling that you were dressed properly for the job.

Steve is less critical of his 'uniform' than Jo and Seb, as it is this which confers upon him the authority he fears will be presumed is lacking if his sexuality is equated with a weaker management style. Further, because the suits are not a uniform *per se*, and can be selected from a range, this allows an element of 'individual expression' through choice. For Jo, Seb and Steve, then, the tampering which they do with their uniforms is seen as a battle for queer individuality within a homogenized workplace. For example, Seb says:

> Although I don't think that the clothes I wear are an expression of my sexuality, as my confidence with my sexuality has increased my clothes have become brighter. I don't think my clothes say that I'm bisexual, but they do reflect my confidence in my identity.

This is interesting because, of course, it is not just sexuality which creates 'individuals' in the workplace. One has to look no further than the university to find examples of 'eccentric professors' who create a certain 'individual' style. However, in Seb's case his individuality is clearly tied to his sexual identity; thus, although he has not expressed it categorically, he feels individual within the (presumed) monolithic heterosexuality of his workplace. That this individuality is expressed through the wearing of colours is thus unsurprising given that heteromasculinity's uniform is grey, navy or black (McDowell, 1997).

Furthermore, Jo suggests that dress codes would certainly have an impact on what kind of job she might apply for. She says:

> I could never get a job where I would have to deal with the public. That would mean skirts and frocks and high heeled shoes and I'm not the kind of person that spends hours in front of the mirror in the morning.

Thus, her non-identification with the conventional patterns of femininity, combined with her recognition of the way in which this is exploited in the interactive service encounter, might prevent her from making certain career choices. This is an important point, since her comment is not about a definite choice from the position of sexual identification to work in the pink economy, but rather speaks of the incompatibility between subcultural dress codes and certain kinds of rigidly gendered employment practice.

A slightly different perspective on this issue is suggested by Carl, a gay nurse working in HIV and AIDS information and care, when he says:

> I get up at seven most days to get ready for work. This is what I wear, just the usual shirt and tie jobby [sic]; I prefer white shirts as they look smarter. I'd prefer to be wearing a suit, but I don't actually have the money to buy a decent suit, so I just wear a shirt and tie. I wear this because it's smarter. A lot of gay men doing my sort of work in the community – for example a friend of mine tends to wear Adidas T-shirts and a pair of jeans, and that's what he feels comfortable in, but I don't, I don't feel comfortable in that sort of stuff . . . except on a Friday when I tend to dress down a little bit as it's the start of the weekend.

Not everyone is able to 'power dress' in the way that Steve describes, even if this is what they desire. For Carl, the wearing of good suits to work is simply not an option given his access to economic capital. Thus we must not forget that the performance of identity is frequently far from the ideal one we might like to portray, and is often constrained by limited access to disposable income.

The politics of comfort

Clothing used to express identity in leisure time was viewed much more favourably and much less reflexively by respondents. Several of them, when dressing in their 'going out' or 'staying in' clothes, expressed as the primary motivation in their choice of these clothes the ideal of 'comfort' – that they had chosen the clothes that they were wearing because these were the most comfortable. In some cases participants were completely unable to add anything to this motive for buying and wearing these clothes, and here lies the key to the (limited) possibilities of identity performances I hope to explore.

Additionally, there was some attempt to pass over the question of 'labels' of clothing which clearly have social meanings in specific contexts at the time of writing. The clearest example of this is when Jo explains the purchase of an 'original' Adidas tracksuit top. She expresses the motive for this purchase as being about comfort and liking the look of the white stripes down the sleeves, but later in the diary provides a slightly different interpretation:

> I think I look at other clothes that other people wear and if they look nice and comfortable, then I choose to wear them. I mean I saw a woman in [a gay bar] that had an Adidas top on, and it really suited her, it looked

really nice . . . so that's probably why I choose to wear Adidas tops . . .
Plus she was damn sexy [laughs].

Thus what Jo initially describes as an acquisition for comfort we now discover to be
a highly inconvenient purchase (it had to be an original Adidas garment, only
available from particular second-hand shops) precipitated by a fleeting flirtation in a
highly specific location.

The *social* meaning of such purchases is perhaps reinforced through a quote from
Carl. He is about the same age as Jo and also frequents 'trendy' gay bars:

> I wear trainers now, rather than boots. Adidas trainers, very important,
> because they're quite fashionable at the moment and if you're going to
> be accepted on the scene, you've got to dress right.

On the scene – in queer social space – fashion enunciates identity, then, but this
carries a premium; the fact that 'you've *got to* dress right' reiterates the issue of
access to capital and credit as crucial determinants of who can wear what, and thus
who can *be* what.

The naturalizing discourse of comfort is, in fact, shot through with both political
and subcultural resonances. If we trace some of these resonances, we may be able to
build up a picture of what comfort means in different contexts. Although there are
many possible readings at this level, a brief consideration of two gives us a way into
considering how comfort works politically.

In a queer context, then, comfort might be read as embodying *resistance* to the
hegemonic discourses of 'proper' feminine behaviour and attire. This discourse
reproduces itself on the surface of the self as a return to the *natural* body, which,
ironically enough, is displayed by a rejection of unnatural (i.e. culturally produced
and enforced) femininity via feminism. For men, however, the rejection of accepted
patterns of masculinity may mean subjecting oneself to exactly those technologies of
the body from which feminists have struggled to emancipate women:

> I'm shaving my legs [on camera]. Because I get quite long hair on my legs
> and gay men don't like that. At least I don't anyway. And I don't feel
> comfortable with it . . . This is an important part, I s'pose, of me and my
> identity. In that, I don't feel comfortable being me if I've got quite long
> hair, because I do get quite long hair, all over really, on my arms and legs
> and chest. I don't know if you can see [pulls up arm hairs to demon-
> strate]. And the image at the moment is quite young and fit and smooth.
> So you feel quite out of it if you're not young and fit and smooth. And as
> I'm not young and fit, the closest I'm going to get is smooth. I cut my
> hair really, not shave it; if I ever get a body, as in muscles and stuff, I
> might get my chest waxed. But at the moment I can't see the point in
> spending all that money, because I don't show my body, and I'm not
> going to show my body until I feel comfortable with it. That's one of the
> problems of being gay I suppose. (Carl)

In this quote the dynamic of comfort is quite clearly contradictory, then; whilst

Carl does not feel 'comfortable' going out on the scene unless he attends to his body, he is quite clearly uncomfortable about having to do it.

Comfort also signifies the comfort one feels from the degree of fit between the outside of one's body and its inside (not blood, guts or organs, but the 'imagined' or 'true' self) – the way in which identity is mapped onto the body. Comfort means in this case expressing externally that which one feels inside. In other words, there is a wish to close the gap between performance (*acting*) and ontology (*being*), a desire to be self-present to both oneself and others. Comfort in this case derives from being 'recognizably' queer to both oneself and others.

Performing bodies

In the video diaries a number of respondents talked about a certain 'discomfort' when going out 'on the scene'. This tended to be expressed as a feeling of being watched or stared at; not being 'cruised' but being in some sense 'evaluated'. In fact Jo said that she sometimes felt more comfortable in 'straight' spaces than in queer ones, and Carl talked at length about wanting to wear clothes that he felt unable to on the scene because he did not have the necessary muscular body on which to wear 'skimpy' items of clothing:

> This is what I plan to wear. It's all black which makes me feel comfortable because it slims me down. I feel a bit chubby. Although I quite fancy the blue, which is very clingy and tends to show any lumps and as I've got them I don't think I'll wear that. This is what I want to wear one day. It's my favourite top ever. I've never worn this out yet. It's wonderful. I bought it in the gay part of New York – Greenwich Village. I think that it's really nice, I love this, but I don't actually wear it so far, basically because I don't think I've really got the body for it, so until I feel comfortable wearing that it'll be going back to the wardrobe. But hopefully by the end of this month I'll be able to wear it.

This gaze is not one of desire, then, but rather a disciplinary gaze, a policing of body shapes and styles of dress, which left several of the respondents feeling some kind of inadequacy in what they felt to be 'their own' queer spaces.

The diarists' accounts make clear the power at work within the so-called 'emancipatory' discourses of queer. This does not imply that the discourses of lesbian and gay culture are as destructive as homophobic ones (it is unlikely that one would get beaten up for poor fashion sense), but they are powerful and do constitute disciplinary technologies on the bodies of their subjects. These technologies in turn produce performativities of lesbian and gay identities which locate their performance exactly in the idea of the biological or psychological self. As Lauren Berlant (1997: 17) summarizes:

> [Poststructuralist theorists] . . . have shown how sexuality is the modern form of self-intelligibility: I am my identity; my identity is fundamentally

sexual; and my practices reflect that (and if they don't, they require submission to sexual science, self-help, or other kinds of laws).

She also notes that bisexuality has not made it fully into 'the sexual star system' because it is hard to *express* bisexuality. Similarly, Fraser argues that since bisexuality has been largely absent from queer discourse, then bisexuals may not be subject to the same disciplinary technologies of the self as lesbians and gays (Fraser, 1997). However, as one bisexual diarist who was becoming disillusioned with the 'bisexual scene' said:

> If I meet one more man with a beard, dressed in tie dye, who wants to hug me, I shall be sick.

Clearly, then, regulatory frameworks of dress, gesture, and even facial hair do exist in bisexual networks, implying that there may be much the same disciplinary technologies exerted on the body within bisexuality as elsewhere.

What this subcultural surveillance creates is a situation in which participants in queer culture have no language or concepts with which to express their discomfort at certain times. Instead of affording a recognition of the hierarchical power relations which exist within the culture, and thus a way to verbalize and transgress some of its more regulatory aspects or perhaps even lobby for change, people often resort to dismissing, for example, the 'bitchiness of the scene', or to setting up alternative gay groups such as gay conservatives and non-scene or anti-scene groups, a manoeuvre which individualizes sexual subjects and divides queer community.

Social identities, individual selves?

This brings me to another point about the empirical material presented here – that the link between the comfort of the outside of the body with the 'naturalness' of the inside ('self') prioritizes the individual over the social. Individuality is stressed in opposition to the uniform of work, but also in relation to the 'uniform of queer'. The misrecognition of oneself as an individual in opposition to uniform, fashion and subculture, denies the place of social interaction in the construction of identity positions. In Jo's case, for example, her choice of tracksuit top comes from a kind of queer aesthetic with which she identifies. Thus the desired object produces her physical and aesthetic comfort since it reflects her identity, and also allows her to 'express' it.

The scene may be 'uncomfortable' for certain people at certain times but it is not only here that the social operates. For many people, most discussion about their sexuality takes place in the 'comfort' of the home, rather than in the frenetic atmosphere of 'the scene'. At rest, as opposed to at play, performativities may be less intense – or at least deflected from the body onto the home itself. All of the lesbians, bisexuals and gay men in the diaries used signifiers of identity in their interior decor; for example, Jo uses posters of lesbian icons such as kd lang and Jodie Foster, and a naked woman with a large whip, as well as lesbian safer sex posters produced by the Terrence Higgins Trust. Carl says that his Patsy Cline, Bananarama,

Madonna, Janet Jackson and Eurovision CDs are indicative of his sexuality. Seb's house includes a cross-dressed mannequin as a central feature of his decor. Even Steve, who lives with his parents, has a tacit understanding with them that his bedroom is a private space which his father should not enter. His walls are adorned with posters of River Phoenix, Madonna and other gay icons, along with photographs of his boyfriend.

This is not to say that in the home the queer subject returns to a private 'backstage' self, or indeed to a place of privacy and security. Carl, for instance, found it necessary to turn up his music whilst talking on the video diary about non-monogamy in case he was overheard by his partner or his partner's friends. Similarly, as Johnston and Valentine (1995) show, lesbians living in the family home may be at best encouraged to perform heterosexuality, at worst may be physically harmed by family members for failing to do so. Furthermore, the lesbian home may come under the pressure of surveillance by neighbours (who may overhear through badly soundproofed walls or overlook from the garden fence or window) and visiting family members, for which 'de-dyking' strategies may be required – removing signifiers (and signifieds) from the home in preparation for such visits. The over-protected home risks the insularization of the lesbian relationship, creating additional pressures and feelings of confinement and social exclusion, and possibly domestic violence. Turning the home into a largely social space where visitors are frequent can also have its disadvantages, reinstating the pressures of lesbian performance through surveillance from other lesbians. As Johnston and Valentine state:

> 'Political correctness', which has come to haunt the lesbian feminist landscape, or other 'othodoxies', can be invoked by some women to regulate the performative aspects of others' lesbian identities within the domestic environment. (1995: 109)

However, in most cases for the diarists home was the place which they *experienced* as most comfortable, where they could 'slob out', wear comfortable clothes (not neutral clothes in terms of their identities, but perhaps less communicative ones). In one's home one most often has at least some control over who enters, who one spends time with, and how one's home is organized. Also, issues of sexual identity are here criss-crossed by the day-to-day things with which all householders must deal – paying bills, cooking and eating, and in some cases the care of children. Especially for middle-class respondents, there was some effort to find homes close to other lesbian, bisexual or gay households. In one case, some friends – a lesbian couple and a gay man – had moved in next door to one another. Also, for a lesbian respondent with children, living in a catchment area for a school that employed equal opportunities policies for the children of lesbian parents was an important factor in the choice of the location of her home. The choice of house, its interior decor, the way in which queer identities are expressed within the home, then, are not individualized, private decisions but rather highly social ones.

It is in the interplay of different discourses and social spaces, including the home, that people come to negotiate and formulate 'comfortable' identities. These comfortable identities might be equated with Foucault's ideas on the care of the self.

The Care of the Self (Foucault, 1986) offers an ethics which guides the subject in different spatial spheres or contexts. This work is done in the interplay of the 'soul' (that part of the self which lies beyond discourse, which one might access through private contemplation), the social, and the political. It is perhaps this process which occurs in Seb's earlier statement – that wearing bright colours as he becomes more confident with his sexuality marks his 'individuality' in his workplace. Through political discourses on sexuality Seb recognizes himself as an 'individual' in a workplace which he sees as hegemonically heterosexual. This is turn creates an ethics of the self which produces a bodily critique of that hegemonic norm. Bright clothes, as one aspect of his performative identity, help display his sexuality to those in the know, but are also a political statement and critique of the rigid dress codes enforced by hetero-normativity. The body is politicized in line with the social and political soul. Thus, though Seb clearly has the possibility of acknowledging his sexuality, whilst simultaneously conforming to conventional dress codes at work, he negotiates these oppositional discourses, creating an ethics of the self which aligns his body with his soul – ensuring that, rather than performing separate identities in different spaces, there is in fact a high degree of continuity of identity in moving between them.

Similarly, Jo clearly believes that she performs her lesbian identity at work without having to 'come out' in the political sense. Both Jo and Seb stress that they do nothing to hide their sexualities at work. For example, in the video diary the camera pans around Jo's workspace, focusing on two photographs of partially clad or naked 1920s style women pinned up on the wall next to her desk. She explains:

> Even with pictures like that on the wall, people still have no idea. You can be almost blatant and people still don't know. I never talk about men. I never talk about boyfriends. Whatever I do, that seems to be OK. Although I haven't told anybody here, there seems to be almost an understanding that I am [a lesbian]. I think they know, but nothing is ever said. But then again, sometimes they say some really homophobic things and I think they couldn't possibly know. But sometimes I say things to people here and I think I'm really surprised I get away with it. Sometimes it's really filthy, and I keep doing it. And I think sometime or other they're bound to get an idea, but they just don't.

In this way responsibility for being 'out' is shifted from herself (the author of her bodily text) to her colleagues (her readers). If they cannot recognize the signs of her identity then her failure to be out is in effect their fault, a product of their stupidity rather than her own lack of courage (as some more rigid political discourses might suggest).

The body as text

Identity is spread over the surface of the body, the outward text of the inner ethics of the self. As Elizabeth Grosz (1995: 20) explains, drawing on Derrida's notion of the signature:

> the paradoxical and divided position of the subject in and beyond the
> text, involves the necessary and irreducible trace of the one within the
> other, the implication of the text's outside with its inside, and of its
> inside with establishing its borders and thus the outside, in short, its
> fundamentally folded, 'invaginated' character.

Thus, the inscription on the body of the text of a subject's identity is an individual
inscription which also at once signs the subject as a product of other texts. In this
sense, then, the queer body is the signature of queer textuality. It is not static or
constant, but is shifting, like the signature, never manifesting itself twice in identical ways, yet at the same time carrying the mark of both its author and the texts
which produce it. Card's (1985) outline of Aristotle's notion of 'family resemblance' is useful here. The term resemblance can be applied to anything which is
called by the same name but does not 'possess any one characteristic in common'
(p. 213).

Elspeth Probyn sees this 'family resemblance' as an ensemble of images which
are written on the body, drawing on the Deleuzean notion of productive desire:

> The similarity of bodies, is a matter not of similar origins but rather is
> compelled by a similarity of desire to arrange one's body, to queer
> oneself through movement. As I see the configuration of my body as
> image on her body, I also can feel the configuration of hers on mine.
> However, this is not a constant or immediate fact; it has to be made, to
> be configured through the desire to conjoin images. (Probyn, 1995: 15).

This configuration is not total, however. Not all lesbians desire all lesbians (or look
like all lesbians), rather it is the social configuration in conjunction with the individual signature mapped onto the body, or parts of the body, which marks out
individual desires; something in the interplay, as Probyn puts it, between bodies and
representations. Thus, queer identities are constructed 'family resemblances',
mapped onto the body in different ways. They might be more or less subtle; they are
mediated by the physicality of bodies, by the interplay of other identities and by the
appropriateness of dress codes for particular spaces.

However, this is only part of the story – a story is created not only by writers,
but also by readers. A given bodily text can convey its intended meaning only if its
readers read it in the way the author requires. 'Family resemblances' can only be
spotted by those who 'know' the 'family', and therefore there are infinite
possibilities for the queer body to be misread. A short anecdote from one diarist
illustrates this point exactly. He was at college, arriving late one day:

> I walked in and this bunch of girls were going 'Martin's gay, Martin's
> gay' – Martin is this straight guy in our class. And Martin says, 'Yes, and
> for all you know Steve [the respondent] could be my lover'. And the girls
> said, 'Oh, don't be stupid, we *know* Steve isn't gay, you're the one who's
> gay because you're obsessed with your appearance, always looking in the
> mirror'. So I said '*Au contraire!*', and gave them my big 'I am gay' speech,
> because I've worked hard for this reputation and I'm not about to lose it.

And they said 'Oh Steve, you're so funny, you're such a wit and a wag,
I've told my parents all about you!' . . . They wouldn't believe me!

This causes Steve amusement, but also dismay. There is an extreme discomfort
in being read against one's signature (his reputation which he has worked hard for).
The misreading of cultural codes by his straight audience invokes a reaction where
Steve attempts to re-fix the meaning of his bodily text, supplementing it with the
intertextuality of gay political and subcultural discourses. When this too is misread,
the discomfort of the lack of homology between his self and his body leaves Steve
bemused.

Discomfort in this case, then, derives from the momentary dislocation of an
essentialist narrative: if I am gay, then I am comfortable dressing gay, and therefore
others will recognize that I am gay. Comfort follows from being a writerly rather
than readerly text, although what is written may be highly context-specific. The
disruption of this 'natural' flow of essentialistic discourse leads to a hyperperforma-
tivity of sexuality, the 'I am gay' speech – the momentary power of the confessional
which is subsequently reinterpreted or ignored.

Conclusion

Different spaces afford subjects more or less critical distance from the performances
of identity in which they engage. As suggested earlier, for example, work spaces may
provide a vantage point from which to examine the disciplinary technologies of the
self employed there. However, rejection of hegemonic discourses may be expressed
as individuality, rather than the 'other' social in which one is implicated. Subjects
are likely to be less critical of such technologies which operate on the 'scene',
reducing ontological contradictions and negative experiences of regulatory regimens
to individual faults such as 'bitchiness'. The space diarists are least critical of is the
home, the perceived safe haven in which one can truly be 'oneself'.

Comfort for the diarists is ultimately produced in the harmony of self-
explanations and self-presentations – the degree of fit between one's *explanation* of/
for oneself and one's *expression* of that self – matching the inside and outside of one's
body; becoming a writerly text. Where some disjuncture appears between these
discourses, discomfort is produced. Not having enough resemblance to one's 'family', for instance, is often disconcerting. Prevailing cultural and political discourses
only offer such harmonies through fixity and conformity, in the Foucauldian sense
'knowing thyself' – the alignment of the self with situated discourses (even if these
are subcultural rather than hegemonic). This fixity or definition, as Butler points
out, is always at the expense of an included but 'haunted' subjectivity (by the ghost
of the excluded 'other' or 'otherness').

Richard Sennett, in his book *Flesh and Stone* (1994), shows how comfort has
become linked with individualism. The development of comfortable chairs, car-
riages and trains in the 19th century, Sennett argues, effectively erased the everyday
sociability of public space. Tables placed outside cafes in 19th century Paris
'deprived political groups of their cover; the tables served customers watching
the passing scene, rather than conspiring with one another [for political reform]'

(p. 345). These outside customers ceased to become social actors or political con-
spirators, becoming instead passive voyeurs or flâneurs.

> On the terrace, the denizens of the cafe sat silently watching the crowd
> go by — they sat as individuals, each lost in his or her own thoughts . . .
> the people on the street now appearing as scenery, as spectacle. (p.
> 346)

Sennett's argument at this point has much in common with criticism of new queer
cultures, especially his discussion of cafes, which chimes with writings on queer
spaces of consumption. The argument here is that the tables which spill onto the
street prompt either a voyeuristic reaction from passing straights to which passive
queers are subject, or greater social acceptability through a loss of political dynamism produced through a toning down of queer behaviour in order to be palatable
to this voyeuristic public consumption (see Binnie, 1995).

In order to move away from these over-simplistic accounts I would like to
employ Freud's (1914) concept of narcissism, and especially the narcissistic gaze.
Unlike popular notions of narcissism (defined as self-love), Freud's position is not
about desire for one's own reflection but for what the self would like to be: an
idealized self. In another manoeuvre, one does not simply have desire for an object,
the idealized self, but also an identification *with* the object — a desire to be it and to
be desired by it. Thus, narcissistic desire is both desire *for* and desire *to be* one's
idealized self (Lewis and Rolley, 1997; Probyn, 1995). If one maps this framework
onto the social, then, queer subjects both desire the objects of their gaze (others
whom one identifies with an idealized version of oneself) and want to be their
desired object, to be objectified by them. This scenario explains how shared cultural
codes, of dress and adornment in particular, circulate in queer subcultures. That is
not to say that all lesbians desire all lesbians (Probyn, 1995), but that specific items
of clothing and jewellery, or haircuts or body modifications come to have currency
in specific queer subcultures. It explains very neatly Jo's motivation for the purchase
of her Adidas top.

Finally, an important point to note here is that dressing up to go out on the
scene is not simply a process of identifying oneself as a passive sexual object, but
rather a double movement of having and being, creating an idealized self in the gaze
of the other (object of one's desire). This explains one of the most fundamental and
pleasurable *activities* of the scene: to look and be looked at (Bech, 1997). As Lewis
and Rolley conclude (in relation to fashion magazines — but I feel the argument holds
in this context):

> The importance of dress as a signifier of sexual identity, and of looking as
> a social, identifying and *sexualized* activity . . . coalesce to provide a
> supplementary pleasure in the activity of consuming [queer culture]. . . .
> '[L]ooking like what you are' in terms of self-presentation is crucial for a
> recognisable [queer] identity and structurally central to the theorisation
> of marginal identities. (p. 299)

The comfort of identity is thus far from an individual or individualizing state within queer culture. Rather it is always social, though it may sometimes be produced through the rhetoric of individualism.

There is a second part to Sennett's argument, however. He implies that comfort provides a kind of social detachment, a kind of separation from real connections with others. Being comfortable – as in comfortably off – implies a lack of necessity to worry about the world or one's position in it. Comfort is an easy, unthinking state. Perhaps, then, comfort means social and personal atrophy. The comfort gained through many uncomfortable years of political struggle, the comfort of a revamped scene, the comfort of a more liberal state and some protection from discrimination in the workplace have all produced a more comfortable (lesbian and gay) identity and politics. But perhaps comfort is to be feared since it is discomfort, displacement, disruption which moves (queer) politics (and selves) forward into a more complex and less exclusive or complacent place. As Sennett (summarizing E. M. Forster) states:

> Displacement thus becomes something quite different . . . from sheer movement . . . Human displacements ought to jolt people into caring about one another, and where they are. (p. 353)

Acknowledgements

The support of the Economic and Social Research Council (ESRC) is gratefully acknowledged. The work was funded by ESRC award number R000236657. I would also like to thank David Bell, Jon Binnie, Jo Eadie, Azzedine Haddour, Clare Hemmings, Harriette Marshall, Rolland Munro, John O'Neill and Graham Thompson for their helpful discussions and comments on earlier drafts of this article.

Note

1   The names of the diarists have been changed for this article.

References

Ainley, Rosa (1995) *What is She Like: Lesbian Identities from the 1950s to the 1990s*. London: Cassell.

Bech, Henning (1997) *When Men Meet: Homosexuality and Modernity*. Cambridge: Polity.

Berlant, Lauren (1997) *The Queen of America Goes to Washington City: Essays on Sex and Citizenship*. Durham, NC: Duke University Press.

Binnie, Jon (1995) 'Trading Places: Consumption, Sexuality and the Production of Queer Space', in David Bell and Gill Valentine (eds) *Mapping Desire: Geographies of Sexualities*, pp. 182–99. London: Routledge.

Butler, Judith (1990) *Gender Trouble: Feminism and the Subversion of Identity*, New York: Routledge.

Foucault, Michel (1986) trans. by Robert Hurley, *The History of Sexuality. Vol. Three: The Care of the Self*. Harmondsworth: Penguin.

Fraser, Mariam (1997) 'Lose Your Face', in Bi Academic Intervention (eds) *The Bisexual Imaginary: Representation, Identity and Desire*, pp. 38–57. London: Cassell.

Freud, Sigmund (1914) 'On Narcissism: An Introduction', in *Standard Edition of the Complete Psychological Works of Sigmund Freud*, vol. 14, trans. and ed. James Strachey. London: Hogarth Press.

Garber, Marjorie (1992) *Vested Interests: Cross-Dressing and Cultural Anxiety*. New York: Routledge.

Grosz, Elizabeth (1995) *Space, Time and Perversion*. New York: Routledge.

Hall, Stuart (1996) 'Who Needs Identity?' in Stuart Hall and Paul du Gay (eds) *Questions of Cultural Identity*, pp. 1–17. London: Sage.

Johnston, Linda and Valentine, Gill (1995) 'Wherever I Lay My Girlfriend, That's My Home: The Performance and Surveillance of Lesbian Identities in Domestic Environments', in David Bell and Gill Valentine (eds) *Mapping Desire: Geographies of Sexualities*, pp. 99–113. London: Routledge.

Lewis, Reina and Rolly, Katrina (1997) '(Ad)ressing the Dyke: Lesbian Looks and Lesbians Looking', in Mica Nava, Andrew Blake, Iain MacRury and Barry Richards (eds) *Buy This Book: Studies in Advertising and Consumption*, pp. 291–308. London: Routledge.

McDowell, Linda (1997) *Capital Culture: Money, Sex and Power at Work*. Oxford: Blackwell.

Probyn, Elspeth (1995) 'Queer Belongings: The Politics of Departure', in Elizabeth Grosz and Elspeth Probyn (eds) *Sexy Bodies: The Strange Carnalities of Feminism*, pp. 1–18. London: Routledge.

Sennett, Richard (1994) *Flesh and Stone: The Body and the City in Western Civilization*. London: Faber and Faber.

Stanley, Liz (ed.) (1993) 'Auto/biography in Sociology', *Sociology* 27(1): 1–197.

[. . .]

PART EIGHT

Production and consumption

ARGUING AGAINST ALL FORMS OF REDUCTIONISM in
accounts of fashion, Elizabeth Wilson says that

> because the origins and rise of fashion were so closely linked with the
> development of mercantile capitalism, economic explanations of the
> fashion phenomenon have always been popular. It was easy to believe that
> the function of fashion stemmed from capitalism's need for perpetual
> expansion, which encouraged consumption.
>
> (Wilson 1985: 49)

While it is unwise to suggest that a complete explanation of fashion, or even only of
fashion's function, may be constructed in terms of economics, it would also be considered unwise to ignore the economic aspects of fashion and clothing completely. This
has not always been the case. Angela McRobbie quotes Stuart Hall as saying that
'[c]ulture has ceased . . . to be a decorative addendum to the "hard world" of production and things, the icing on the cake of material culture' (McRobbie 1998: 5). The
separation of cultural from economic concerns has been overcome and theorists now
see the work of culture in economics. Consequently, this section will concentrate on
production and consumption and it will present various ways in which a number
of disciplines, including economics, sociology and anthropology, have dealt with
production and consumption.

The word 'economy' comes from two Ancient Greek words, '*oikos*' (meaning
'house'), and '*nomos*' (meaning 'rule' or 'law'). Economics thus refers us to the management of the household; the regulation of family income and expenditure, for
example. These domestic origins have largely been forgotten and an economy is now
understood as the distinctive way in which the production, distribution, purchase and

consumption of goods and services are organised in a society. When we speak of 'feudal society' and 'capitalist society', for example, we are using the way that that society has arranged production and consumption to characterise the society itself. To simplify: in feudal society one either owns the land and the technology with which the land is worked, or one works the land with the technology; in capitalist society one either owns the factories or mines, and the plant and technology that accompanies them, or one works in the factories and mines with the plant and technology. In exchange for working the land for the landowner, one receives certain privileges – being allowed to produce one's own food from that land, for example. And in exchange for working in the factories and mines one receives money – a wage – which is in turn exchanged for goods and services. These are different economies, different ways of organising production and consumption, and it is with production and consumption that this section will be concerned. The most significant way in which fashion relates to economics is through production and consumption, and this section will concentrate on the nature of fashion and clothing as commodities and on the ways in which fashion and clothing are used by consumers to construct and communicate identity.

In its original reference to the 'regulation' of the household, economics already directs our attention to the role of politics – the role of power – in organising production and consumption. The Sumptuary Laws passed by King Edward III of England in 1327, for example, were an attempt on the part of a dominant social group (the aristocracy) to control and manage the expenditure of a subordinate social group (the people) by preventing them from buying and wearing 'outrageous and excessive apparel' that exceeded their 'state and degree' (Freudenberger 1973: 137). The consumption of fashion and clothing is an economic phenomenon and the king is exercising political power over people's consumption in order to maintain an existing and presumably beneficial social structure. This example also relates to the construction and communication of social identity insofar as those members of subordinate groups who wore such 'outrageous and excessive apparel' were emulating members of the class above them in the social structure. To that extent they were attempting to pass themselves off as being members of that class. It is partly the attempt at assuming an illegitimate identity, and partly the threat that such emulation represented, that the Sumptuary Laws were a response to. Although dominant social groups no longer resort to legislation (indeed Mary Douglas suggests that modern consumerism demands an absence of such laws [1996: 110], the recent 'banning' of people wearing hooded tops from malls and shopping centres in the UK may represent an attempt on behalf of those groups to control what people may and may not wear (see Hill 2005: 73–4 for more on this).

And the example of sumptuary laws introduces the question as to whether consumption is to be conceived and understood as passive or active consumption. Passive consumption may be understood as the sort of consumption described by Thorstein Veblen (and by Marx) in which commodities with already-existing meanings are consumed by individuals who are in turn conceived as having pre-existing needs and desires. It is this model of consumption that Wilson has in her sights in the quote on p. 333; she is objecting to the fact that in this account of consumption people are conceived as the passive victims of the fashion and advertising industries.

On Veblen's sociological account (1992), consumption is explicitly connected to social structure and politics via the notion of pecuniary strength or power. For Veblen, the lower classes emulate their social superiors, by consuming the same things as them (1992: 35). The higher-status social groups, those with most 'pecuniary power', those most able to pay, consume certain goods – furniture, clothes and household ornaments, for example. Consequently, the lower-status social groups strive to emulate them by consuming the same goods. These lower-status groups are trying to obtain some form of equality, a political matter, by buying and using the goods the higher groups buy and use. This is passive consumption – the desired goods are said to 'trickle down' to the lower social orders. It is 'passive' because the lower-status groups don't ascribe any meaning of their own to the things they consume: they consume them merely because the higher-status groups consume them.

Dress is the best example of conspicuous consumption and conspicuous waste in Veblen's account because what we wear is 'always in evidence and affords an indication of our pecuniary standing to all observers at the first glance' (1992: 119). Dress is the clearest way of demonstrating that the wearer can consume 'valuable goods in excess of what is required for physical comfort' (ibid.: 120). But it is also a way of demonstrating that not only can one consume freely and wastefully but also that one need not work at all – that one is not oneself productive (ibid.). Thus Veblen says that the main pleasures of 'neat and spotless' clothes derive from their suggestion that the wearer has no contact with 'industrial processes of any kind': similarly, the charm of items of clothing such as patent-leather shoes, stainless linen and top hats is a product of their disabling of the wearer from any form of productive employment. While many of these examples are worn by men, the corset is also introduced by Veblen at this point. And it is interesting to note that the corset, which is also discussed in Part Twelve in relation to the body and constructions of the erotic, is mentioned here by Veblen in an economic context. He says that, economically, the corset must be considered or theorised as a 'mutilation, undergone for the purpose of lowering the subject's vitality and rendering her obviously and permanently unfit for work' (1992: 121).

There are two aspects to active consumption. It is a process in which individuals or groups are actively engaged in constructing and communicating new identities for themselves through the purchase of goods. And it is a process in which groups and individuals attempt to change or even construct the meanings of the commodities by using (consuming) them in original ways. Angela Partington's essay (see Chapter 20) is an analysis of active consumption in that she shows how working-class women in the late 1940s and early 1950s adopted elements from the 'Official' version of the 'New Look' and adapted them to their own desires. In their (1991) essay 'Fashion, Representation, Femininity', Caroline Evans and Minna Thornton suggest that Rei Kawakubo's collections of the early 1980s were examples of fashion design in which active consumption was encouraged or actually forced on consumers. The garments of these collections were 'wrapped, torn, draped garments' and featured flaps and appendages that could be fastened in a number of ways (1991: 61). The person wearing (consuming) these items made the final decision as to how to construct and wear the garment, and for Kawakubo, 'clothes are not something we wear passively: they require our active collaboration' (ibid.).

As Karl Marx says, the thing that is produced and consumed, the commodity itself, 'appears at first sight an extremely obvious, trivial thing' (1976: 163). In and through their activity, people take cotton or wool and make shirts and cardigans out of them: cotton and wool are raw materials, and shirts and cardigans are products – things that may be bought and sold (exchanged for money) in a market. However, as soon as we start to analyse the commodity, it turns out to be 'a very strange thing' (ibid.). More accurately, as soon as the thing becomes a commodity, it turns out to be 'abounding in metaphysical niceties' (ibid.). For Marx, all commodities are fetish items insofar as their value is understood or experienced as exchange value and not as being generated by the amount of labour that went into their production. Once things start being exchanged for money, they become commodities and people behave as though their value is part of the things themselves, rather than the product of human labour. One consequence of this is that the commodity stands for or represents social differences: the Balenciaga coat referred to in the Introduction represents a higher social status, with attending distinctions of taste and refinement, than a Gap coat for example, and people buy it and wear it with this in mind. Marx's conception of commodity fetishism therefore bears a resemblance to the anthropological notion of fetishism (discussed in Part-Twelve) in which objects are imbued with divine powers. In both economics and anthropology inanimate and fashionable objects are credited with powers that are the products of human activity – powers that are subsequently concealed, or forgotten to be the products of human activity.

Anthropology is also interested in consumption. Mary Douglas's breathtaking essay 'On Not Being Seen Dead: Shopping as Protest' (1996) challenges all common accounts of consumption and reverses any number of priorities. In this essay consumption is not to be explained in terms of individual preferences or fashionable 'swings'; it is profoundly cultural: consumption is not to do with desires or wants but rather is the product of hatreds and dislikes. Nor is consumption a way of constructing and developing a personal identity ('too difficult', 1996: 104); it is cultural defiance and a way of asserting what one is not. This is in some contrast to her earlier work with Baron Isherwood in which, while goods are 'neutral', their social uses are not and are described as either 'fences' or 'bridges' (1979: 12). The use (consumption) of goods (commodities, including fashion and clothing) in this account is not innocent, and the metaphors of fences and bridges indicate the distancing/separating functions from the uniting/joining functions of those goods. The later essay eschews the bridge-building functions of goods and concentrates on the ways they articulate one's dislikes and hatreds of one's neighbours. It is also significant that in the later essay Douglas also distances her account from one given in terms of 'globalising', multinational, governmental and eco-disastrous policies in favour of an analysis that looks at how 'the household' is 'organised' (1996: 90).

In the *Grundrisse*, Marx famously insists that production is at least as significant as consumption (1973: 88ff.). Production is said to make consumption possible and consumption is actually said to be strictly not a part of economics at all, except insofar as it restarts the process and necessitates more production (ibid.: 89). 'Production mediates consumption', Marx says, meaning that production creates the objects (commodities) that people consume. And 'consumption also mediates production'; consumption creates the people (subjects) who consume commodities (ibid.: 91). Production and consumption are mutually conditioning then: each makes the other possible. Having said this, it is probably true to say that cultural studies, sociology and anthropology have been more interested in consumption than they have been in production (see Sweetman 2001: 135, for example), and this collection can only reflect that imbalance. However, Angela McRobbie's (1998) *British Fashion Design* provides a different perspective on the notion of 'production' in relation to fashion design. She quotes Robin Murray, who refers to the people working in design consultancies as 'the engineers of designer capitalism' and who thus effectively proposes the idea that fashion designers, those involved in fashion production, are essentially 'designing for capitalism' (1998: 1).

And Peter Braham's essay is intended to provide an insight into fashion production. It provides a sociological perspective on what has been called the political economy of cultural production. The essay begins to consider the relations between fashion and the political, social, economic and historical 'contexts' within which the consumption of fashion takes place. It may also be read as taking Marx's injunction seriously, to the effect that production is at least as significant as consumption, in that it looks at the various institutions, practices and personnel that make up the production of fashion. Consequently, where much of what cultural studies (and this Reader) has to say about fashion relates to creation, consumption and identity, the extract from Braham's essay concentrates on production, distribution and retailing.

Tim Dant's essay is also about consumption, providing an interesting sociological slant on consumption, accounts of which usually end 'at the checkout'. The extract from *Material Culture in the Social World* also bears interesting relations to the piece from Umberto Eco in Part Seven, and to Kurt Back's essay extracted in Part Nine.

Daniel Miller's essay on the Little Black Dress is included in the Bibliography because it raises an interesting and original question concerning the 'anxiety' that is caused by modern consumer practices. In particular, Miller is concerned to explain the 'leaching' of colour from fashion to the point where even 12-year-old girls will turn up to London birthday parties wearing 'very similar little black dresses'. He interrogates various suspects who might be expected to be responsible for this leaching – capitalism, history and modernism (all, you will notice, covered by headings in this volume) – and argues that the 'ethnography of consumption', including the aforementioned 'anxiety', forms the basis of an explanation.

Bibliography

Bourdieu, P. (1986) *Distinction: A Social Critique of the Judgement of Taste*, London: Routledge.

Douglas, M. (1996) 'On Not Being Seen Dead: Shopping as Protest' and 'The Consumer's Revolt', in *Thought Styles*, London: Sage.

Douglas, M. and Isherwood, B. (1979) *The World of Goods: Towards an Anthropology of Consumption*, London: Allen Lane.

Evans, C. and Thornton, M. (1991) 'Fashion, Representation, Femininity', *Feminist Review* No. 38 (Summer): 48–66.

Fine, B. and Leopold, E. (1993) *The World of Consumption*, London: Routledge.

Freudenberger, H. (1973) 'Fashion, Sumptuary Laws and Business', in G. Wills and D. Midgeley (eds) *Fashion Marketing*, London: Allen and Unwin.

Hill, A. (2005) 'People Dress So Badly Nowadays: Fashion and Late Modernity', in C. Breward and C. Evans (eds) *Fashion and Modernity*, Oxford: Berg.

McRobbie, A. (1998) *British Fashion Design*: *Rag Trade or Image Industry?*, London: Rutledge.

Marx, K. (1973) *Grundrisse*, Harmondsworth: Penguin/New Left Review.

—— (1976) *Capital, Volume One*, Harmondsworth: Penguin/New Left Review.

Miller, D. (2004) 'The Little Black Dress is the Solution, but What is the Problem?', in K. M. Ekström and H. Brembeck (eds) *Elusive Consumption*, Oxford: Berg.

Slater, D. (1996) *Consumer Culture and Modernity*, London: Sage.

Sweetman, P. (2001) 'Everything Starts with an E: Fashions in Theory, Fashion Theory and the Cultural Studies Debate', *Theory, Culture and Society*, 18, 4: 135–42.

Veblen, T. (1992) *The Theory of the Leisure Class*, New York: Transaction.

Wilson, E. (1985) *Adorned in Dreams: Fashion and Modernity*, London: Virago.

Chapter 28

Thorstein Veblen

DRESS AS AN EXPRESSION OF THE PECUNIARY CULTURE

[. . .]

IT WILL BE IN PLACE, by way of illustration, to show in some detail how the economic principles so far set forth apply to everyday facts in some one direction of the life process. For this purpose no line of consumption affords a more apt illustration than expenditure on dress. It is especially the rule of the conspicuous waste of goods that finds expression in dress, although the other, related principles of pecuniary repute are also exemplified in the same contrivances. Other methods of putting one's pecuniary standing in evidence serve their end effectually, and other methods are in vogue always and everywhere; but expenditure on dress has this advantage over most other methods, that our apparel is always in evidence and affords an indication of our pecuniary standing to all observers at the first glance. It is also true that admitted expenditure for display is more obviously present, and is, perhaps, more universally practiced in the matter of dress than in any other line of consumption. No one finds difficulty in assenting to the commonplace that the greater part of the expenditure incurred by all classes for apparel is incurred for the sake of a respectable appearance rather than for the protection of the person. And probably at no other point is the sense of shabbiness so keenly felt as it is if we fall short of the standard set by social usage in this matter of dress. It is true of dress in even a higher degree than of most other items of consumption, that people will undergo a very considerable degree of privation in the comforts or the necessaries of life in order to afford what is considered a decent amount of wasteful consumption; so that it is by no means an uncommon occurrence, in an inclement climate, for people to go ill clad in order to appear well dressed. And the commercial value of the goods used for clothing in any modern community is made up to a much larger extent of the fashionableness, the reputability of the goods than of the mechanical service which they render in clothing the person of the wearer. The need of dress is eminently a 'higher' or spiritual need.

This spiritual need of dress is not wholly, nor even chiefly, a naïve propensity for display of expenditure. The law of conspicuous waste guides consumption in apparel, as in other things, chiefly at the second remove, by shaping the canons of taste and decency. In the common run of cases the conscious motive of the wearer or purchaser of conspicuously wasteful apparel is the need of conforming to established usage, and of living up to the accredited standard of taste and reputability. It is not only that one must be guided by the code of proprieties in dress in order to avoid the mortification that comes of unfavorable notice and comment, though that motive in itself counts for a great deal; but besides that, the requirement of expensiveness is so ingrained into our habits of thought in matters of dress that any other than expensive apparel is instinctively odious to us. Without reflection or analysis, we feel that what is inexpensive is unworthy. 'A cheap coat makes a cheap man.' 'Cheap and nasty' is recognized to hold true in dress with even less mitigation than in other lines of consumption. On the ground both of taste and of serviceability, an inexpensive article of apparel is held to be inferior, under the maxim 'cheap and nasty.' We find things beautiful, as well as serviceable, somewhat in proportion as they are costly. With few and inconsequential exceptions, we all find a costly hand-wrought article of apparel much preferable, in point of beauty and of serviceability, to a less expensive imitation of it, however cleverly the spurious article may imitate the costly original; and what offends our sensibilities in the spurious article is not that it falls short in form or color, or, indeed, in visual effect in any way. The offensive object may be so close an imitation as to defy any but the closest scrutiny; and yet so soon as the counterfeit is detected, its æsthetic value, and its commercial value as well, declines precipitately. Not only that, but it may be asserted with but small risk of contradiction that the æsthetic value of a detected counterfeit in dress declines somewhat in the same proportion as the counterfeit is cheaper than its original. It loses caste æsthetically because it falls to a lower pecuniary grade.

But the function of dress as an evidence of ability to pay does not end with simply showing that the wearer consumes valuable goods in excess of what is required for physical comfort. Simple conspicuous waste of goods is effective and gratifying as far as it goes; it is good *prima facie* evidence of pecuniary success, and consequently *prima facie* evidence of social worth. But dress has subtler and more far-reaching possibilities than this crude, first-hand evidence of wasteful consumption only. If, in addition to showing that the wearer can afford to consume freely and uneconomically, it can also be shown in the same stroke that he or she is not under the necessity of earning a livelihood, the evidence of social worth is enhanced in a very considerable degree. Our dress, therefore, in order to serve its purpose effectually, should not only be expensive, but it should also make plain to all observers that the wearer is not engaged in any kind of productive labor. In the evolutionary process by which our system of dress has been elaborated into its present admirably perfect adaptation to its purpose, this subsidiary line of evidence has received due attention. A detailed examination of what passes in popular apprehension for elegant apparel will show that it is contrived at every point to convey the impression that the wearer does not habitually put forth any useful effort. It goes without saying that no apparel can be considered elegant, or even decent, if it shows the effect of manual labor on the part of the wearer, in the way of soil or wear. The pleasing effect of neat and spotless garments is chiefly, if not altogether, due to their carrying the suggestion of leisure — exemption from personal contact with industrial processes of any kind. Much of the charm that invests the patent-leather shoe, the stainless linen, the lustrous cylindrical hat, and the walking-stick, which so greatly enhance the native dignity of a gentleman, comes of their pointedly suggesting that the wearer cannot when so attired bear a hand in any employment that is directly and immediately of any human use. Elegant dress serves its purpose of elegance not only in that it is expensive, but also because it is the insignia of leisure. It not only shows that the wearer is able to consume a relatively large value, but it argues at the same time that he consumes without producing.

The dress of women goes even farther than that of men in the way of demonstrating the wearer's abstinence from productive employment. It needs no argument to enforce the generalization that the more elegant styles of feminine bonnets go even farther towards making work impossible than does the man's high hat. The woman's shoe adds the so-called French heel to the evidence of enforced leisure afforded by its polish; because this high heel obviously makes any, even the simplest and most necessary manual work extremely difficult. The like is true even in a higher degree of the skirt and the rest of the drapery which characterizes woman's dress. The substantial reason for our tenacious attachment to the skirt is just this: it is expensive and it hampers the wearer at every turn and incapacitates her for all useful exertion. The like is true of the feminine custom of wearing the hair excessively long.

But the woman's apparel not only goes beyond that of the modern man in the degree in which it argues exemption from labor; it also adds a peculiar and highly characteristic feature which differs in kind from anything habitually practiced by the men. This feature is the class of contrivances of which the corset is the typical example. The corset is, in economic theory, substantially a mutilation, undergone for the purpose of lowering the subject's vitality and rendering her permanently and obviously unfit for work. It is true, the corset impairs the personal attractions of the wearer, but the loss suffered on that score is offset by the gain in reputability which comes of her visibly increased expensiveness and infirmity. It may broadly be set down that the womanliness of woman's apparel resolves itself, in point of substantial fact, into the more effective hindrance to useful exertion offered by the garments peculiar to women. This difference between masculine and feminine apparel is here simply pointed out as a characteristic feature. The ground of its occurrence will be discussed presently.

So far, then, we have, as the great and dominant norm of dress, the broad principle of conspicuous waste. Subsidiary to this principle, and as a corollary under it, we get as a second norm the principle of conspicuous leisure. In dress construction this norm works out in the shape of divers contrivances going to show that the wearer does not and, as far as it may conveniently be shown, can not engage in productive labor. Beyond these two principles there is a third of scarcely less constraining force, which will occur to any one who reflects at all on the subject. Dress must not only be conspicuously expensive and inconvenient, it must at the same time be up to date. No explanation at all satisfactory has hitherto been offered of the phenomenon of changing fashions. The imperative requirement of dressing in the latest accredited manner, as well as the fact that this accredited fashion constantly changes from season to season, is sufficiently familiar to every one, but the theory of this flux and change has not been worked out. We may of course say, with perfect consistency and truthfulness, that this principle of novelty is another corollary under the law of conspicuous waste. Obviously, if each garment is permitted to serve for but a brief term, and if none of last season's apparel is carried over and made further use of during the present season, the wasteful expenditure on dress is greatly increased. This is good as far as it goes, but it is negative only. Pretty much all that this consideration warrants us in saying is that the norm of conspicuous waste exercises a controlling surveillance in all matters of dress, so that any change in the fashions must conform to the requirement of wastefulness; it leaves unanswered the question as to the motive for making and accepting a change in the prevailing styles, and it also fails to explain why conformity to a given style at a given time is so imperatively necessary as we know it to be.

For a creative principle, capable of serving as motive to invention and innovation in fashions, we shall have to go back to the primitive, non-economic motive with which apparel originated – the motive of adornment. Without going into an extended discussion of how and why this motive asserts itself under the guidance of the law of expensiveness, it may be stated broadly that each successive innovation in the fashions is an effort to reach some form of display which shall be more accept-able to our sense of form and color or of effectiveness, than that which it displaces. The changing styles are the expression of a restless search for something which shall commend itself to our æsthetic sense; but as each innovation is subject to the selective action of the norm of conspicuous waste, the range within which innov-ation can take place is somewhat restricted. The innovation must not only be more beautiful, or perhaps oftener less offensive, than that which it displaces, but it must also come up to the accepted standard of expensiveness.

It would seem at first sight that the result of such an unremitting struggle to attain the beautiful in dress should be a gradual approach to artistic perfection. We might naturally expect that the fashions should show a well-marked trend in the direction of some one or more types of apparel eminently becoming to the human form; and we might even feel that we have substantial ground for the hope that today, after all the ingenuity and effort which have been spent on dress these many years, the fashions should have achieved a relative perfection and a relative stability, closely approximating to a permanently tenable artistic ideal. But such is not the case. It would be very hazardous indeed to assert that the styles of today are intrinsically more becoming than those of ten years ago, or than those of twenty, or fifty, or one hundred years ago. On the other hand, the assertion freely goes uncontradicted that styles in vogue two thousand years ago are more becoming than the most elaborate and painstaking constructions of today.

The explanation of the fashions just offered, then, does not fully explain, and we shall have to look farther. It is well known that certain relatively stable styles and types of costume have been worked out in various parts of the world; as, for instance, among the Japanese, Chinese, and other Oriental nations; likewise among the Greeks, Romans, and other Eastern peoples of antiquity; so also, in later times, among the peasants of nearly every country of Europe. These national or popular costumes are in most cases adjudged by competent critics to be more becoming, more artistic, than the fluctuating styles of modern civilized apparel. At the same time they are also, at least usually, less obviously wasteful; that is to say, other elements than that of a display of expense are more readily detected in their structure.

These relatively stable costumes are, commonly, pretty strictly and narrowly localized, and they vary by slight and systematic gradations from place to place. They have in every case been worked out by peoples or classes which are poorer than we, and especially they belong in countries and localities and times where the population, or at least the class to which the costume in question belongs, is relatively homogeneous, stable, and immobile. That is to say, stable costumes which will bear the test of time and perspective are worked out under circumstances where the norm of conspicuous waste asserts itself less imperatively than it does in the large modern civilized cities, whose relatively mobile wealthy population today sets the pace in matters of fashion. The countries and classes which have in this way worked out stable and artistic costumes have been so placed that the pecuniary emulation among them has taken the direction of a competition in conspicuous leisure rather than in conspicuous consumption of goods. So that it will hold true in a general way that fashions are least stable and least becoming in those communities where the principle of a conspicuous waste of goods asserts itself most imperatively, as among ourselves. All this points to an antagonism between expensiveness and artistic apparel. In point of practical fact, the norm of conspicuous waste is incompatible with the requirement that dress should be beautiful or becoming. And this antagonism offers an explanation of that restless change in fashion which neither the canon of expensiveness nor that of beauty alone can account for.

The standard of reputability requires that dress should show wasteful expenditure; but all wastefulness is offensive to native taste. The psychological law has already been pointed out that all men — and women perhaps even in a higher degree — abhor futility, whether of effort or of expenditure — much as Nature was once said to abhor a vacuum. But the principle of conspicuous waste requires an obviously futile expenditure; and the resulting conspicuous expensiveness of dress is therefore intrinsically ugly. Hence we find that in all innovations in dress, each added or altered detail strives to avoid condemnation by showing some ostensible purpose, at the same time that the requirement of conspicuous waste prevents the purposefulness of these innovations from becoming anything more than a somewhat transparent pretense. Even in its freest flights, fashion rarely if ever gets away from a simulation of some ostensible use. The ostensible usefulness of the fashionable details of dress, however, is always so transparent a make-believe, and their substantial futility presently forces itself so baldly upon our attention as to become unbearable, and then we take refuge in a new style. But the new style must conform to the requirement of reputable wastefulness and futility. Its futility presently becomes as odious as that of its predecessor; and the only remedy which the law of waste allows us is to seek relief in some new construction, equally futile and equally untenable. Hence the essential ugliness and the unceasing change of fashionable attire.

Having so explained the phenomenon of shifting fashions, the next thing is to make the explanation tally with everyday facts. Among these everyday facts is the well-known liking which all men have for the styles that are in vogue at any given time. A new style comes into vogue and remains in favor for a season, and, at least so long as it is a novelty, people very generally find the new style attractive. The prevailing fashion is felt to be beautiful. This is due partly to the relief it affords in being different from what went before it, partly to its being reputable. As indicated in the last chapter, the canon of reputability to some extent shapes our tastes, so that under its guidance anything will be accepted as becoming until its novelty wears off, or until the warrant of reputability is transferred to a new and novel structure serving the same general purpose. That the alleged beauty, or 'loveliness,' of the styles in vogue at any given time is transient and spurious only is attested by the fact that none of the many shifting fashions will bear the test of time. When seen in the perspective of half-a-dozen years or more, the best of our fashions strike us as grotesque, if not unsightly. Our transient attachment to whatever happens to be the latest rests on other than æsthetic grounds, and lasts only until our abiding æsthetic sense has had time to assert itself and reject this latest indigestible contrivance.

The process of developing an æsthetic nausea takes more or less time; the length of time required in any given case being inversely as the degree of intrinsic odiousness of the style in question. This time relation between odiousness and instability in fashions affords ground for the inference that the more rapidly the styles succeed and displace one another, the more offensive they are to sound taste. The presumption, therefore, is that the farther the community, especially the wealthy classes of the community, develop in wealth and mobility and in the range of their human contact, the more imperatively will the law of conspicuous waste assert itself in matters of dress, the more will the sense of beauty tend to fall into abeyance or be overborne by the canon of pecuniary reputability, the more rapidly will fashions shift and change, and the more grotesque and intolerable will be the varying styles that successively come into vogue.

There remains at least one point in this theory of dress yet to be discussed. Most of what has been said applies to men's attire as well as to that of women; although in modern times it applies at nearly all points with greater force to that of women. But at one point the dress of women differs substantially from that of men. In woman's dress there is obviously greater insistence on such features as testify to the wearer's exemption from or incapacity for all vulgarly productive employment. This characteristic of woman's apparel is of interest, not only as completing the theory of dress, but also as confirming what has already been said of the economic status of women, both in the past and in the present.

As has been seen in the discussion of woman's status under the heads of Vicarious Leisure and Vicarious Consumption, it has in the course of economic development become the office of the woman to consume vicariously for the head of the household; and her apparel is contrived with this object in view. It has come about that obviously productive labor is in a peculiar degree derogatory to respectable women, and therefore special pains should be taken in the construction of women's dress, to impress upon the beholder the fact (often indeed a fiction) that the wearer does not and can not habitually engage in useful work. Propriety requires respectable women to abstain more consistently from useful effort and to make more of a show of leisure than the men of the same social classes. It grates painfully on our nerves to contemplate the necessity of any well-bred woman's earning a livelihood by useful work. It is not 'woman's sphere.' Her sphere is within the household, which she should 'beautify,' and of which she should be the 'chief ornament.' The male head of the household is not currently spoken of as its ornament. This feature taken in conjunction with the other fact that propriety requires more unremitting attention to expensive display in the dress and other paraphernalia of women, goes to enforce the view already implied in what has gone before. By virtue of its descent from a patriarchal past, our social system makes it the woman's function in an especial degree to put in evidence her household's ability to pay. According to the modern civilized scheme of life, the good name of the household to which she belongs should be the special care of the woman; and the system of honorific expenditure and conspicuous leisure by which this good name is chiefly sustained is therefore the woman's sphere. In the ideal scheme, as it tends to realize itself in the life of the higher pecuniary classes, this attention to conspicuous waste of substance and effort should normally be the sole economic function of the woman.

At the stage of economic development at which the women were still in the full sense the property of the men, the performance of conspicuous leisure and consumption came to be part of the services required of them. The women being not their own masters, obvious expenditure and leisure on their part would redound to the credit of their master rather than to their own credit; and therefore the more expensive and the more obviously unproductive the women of the household are, the more creditable and more effective for the purpose of reputability of the household or its head will their life be. So much so that the women have been required not only to afford evidence of a life of leisure, but even to disable themselves for useful activity.

It is at this point that the dress of men falls short of that of women, and for sufficient reason. Conspicuous waste and conspicuous leisure are reputable because they are evidence of pecuniary strength; pecuniary strength is reputable or honorific because, in the last analysis, it argues success and superior force; therefore the evidence of waste and leisure put forth by any individual in his own behalf cannot consistently take such a form or be carried to such a pitch as to argue incapacity or marked discomfort on his part; as the exhibition would in that case show not superior force, but inferiority, and so defeat its own purpose. So, then, wherever wasteful expenditure and the show of abstention from effort is normally, or on an average, carried to the extent of showing obvious discomfort or voluntarily induced physical disability, there the immediate inference is that the individual in question does not perform this wasteful expenditure and undergo this disability for her own personal gain in pecuniary repute, but in behalf of some one else to whom she stands in a relation of economic dependence; a relation which in the last analysis must, in economic theory, reduce itself to a relation of servitude.

To apply this generalization to women's dress, and put the matter in concrete terms: the high heel, the skirt, the impracticable bonnet, the corset, and the general disregard of the wearer's comfort which is an obvious feature of all civilized women's apparel, are so many items of evidence to the effect that in the modern civilized scheme of life the woman is still, in theory, the economic dependent of the man — that, perhaps in a highly idealized sense, she still is the man's chattel. The homely reason for all this conspicuous leisure and attire on the part of women lies in the fact that they are servants to whom, in the differentiation of economic functions, has been delegated the office of putting in evidence their master's ability to pay.

There is a marked similarity in these respects between the apparel of women and that of domestic servants, especially liveried servants. In both there is a very elaborate show of unnecessary expensiveness, and in both cases there is also a notable disregard of the physical comfort of the wearer. But the attire of the lady goes farther in its elaborate insistence on the idleness, if not on the physical infirmity of the wearer, than does that of the domestic. And this is as it should be; for in theory, according to the ideal scheme of the pecuniary culture, the lady of the house is the chief menial of the household.

[. . .]

Chapter 29

Karl Marx

THE FETISHISM OF THE COMMODITY AND ITS SECRET

[. . .]

A COMMODITY APPEARS AT FIRST SIGHT an extremely obvious, trivial thing. But its analysis brings out that it is a very strange thing, abounding in metaphysical subtleties and theological niceties. So far as it is a use-value, there is nothing mysterious about it, whether we consider it from the point of view that by its properties it satisfies human needs, or that it first takes on these properties as the product of human labour. It is absolutely clear that, by his activity, man changes the forms of the materials of nature in such a way as to make them useful to him. The form of wood, for instance, is altered if a table is made out of it. Nevertheless the table continues to be wood, an ordinary, sensuous thing. But as soon as it emerges as a commodity, it changes into a thing which transcends sensuousness. It not only stands with its feet on the ground, but, in relation to all other commodities, it stands on its head, and evolves out of its wooden brain grotesque ideas, far more wonderful than if it were to begin dancing of its own free will.[1]

The mystical character of the commodity does not therefore arise from its use-value. Just as little does it proceed from the nature of the determinants of value. For in the first place, however varied the useful kinds of labour, or productive activities, it is a physiological fact that they are functions of the human organism, and that each such function, whatever may be its nature or its form, is essentially the expenditure of human brain, nerves, muscles and sense organs. Secondly, with regard to the foundation of the quantitative determination of value, namely the duration of that expenditure or the quantity of labour, this is quite palpably different from its quality. In all situations, the labour-time it costs to produce the means of subsistence must necessarily concern mankind, although not to the same degree at different stages of development.[2] And finally, as soon as men start to work for each other in any way, their labour also assumes a social form.

Whence, then, arises the enigmatic character of the product of labour, as soon as it assumes the form of a commodity? Clearly, it arises from this form itself. The equality of the kinds of human labour takes on a physical form in the equal objectivity of the products of labour as values; the measure of the expenditure of human labour-power by its duration takes on the form of the magnitude of the value of the products of labour; and finally the relationships between the producers, within which the social characteristics of their labours are manifested, take on the form of a social relation between the products of labour.

The mysterious character of the commodity-form consists therefore simply in the fact that the commodity reflects the social characteristics of men's own labour as objective characteristics of the products of labour themselves, as the socio-natural properties of these things. Hence it also reflects the social relation of the producers to the sum total of labour as a social relation between objects, a relation which exists apart from and outside the producers. Through this substitution, the products of labour become commodities, sensuous things which are at the same time supra-sensible or social. In the same way, the impression made by a thing on the optic nerve is perceived not as a subjective excitation of that nerve but as the objective form of a thing outside the eye. In the act of seeing, of course, light is really transmitted from one thing, the external object, to another thing, the eye. It is a physical relation between physical things. As against this, the commodity-form, and the value-relation of the products of labour within which it appears, have absolutely no connection with the physical nature of the commodity and the material [*dinglich*] relations arising out of this. It is nothing but the definite social relation between men themselves which assumes here, for them, the fantastic form of a relation between things. In order, therefore, to find an analogy we must take flight into the misty realm of religion. There the products of the human brain appear as autonomous figures endowed with a life of their own, which enter into relations both with each other and with the human race. So it is in the world of commodities with the products of men's hands. I call this the fetishism which attaches itself to the products of labour as soon as they are produced as commodities, and is therefore inseparable from the production of commodities.

As the foregoing analysis has already demonstrated, this fetishism of the world of commodities arises from the peculiar social character of the labour which produces them.

Objects of utility become commodities only because they are the products of the labour of private individuals who work independently of each other. The sum total of the labour of all these private individuals forms the aggregate labour of society. Since the producers do not come into social contact until they exchange the products of their labour, the specific social characteristics of their private labours appear only within this exchange. In other words, the labour of the private individual manifests itself as an element of the total labour of society only through the relations which the act of exchange establishes between the products, and, through their mediation, between the producers. To the producers, therefore, the social relations between their private labours appear as what they are, i.e. they do not appear as direct social relations between persons in their work, but rather as material [*dinglich*] relations between persons and social relations between things.

It is only by being exchanged that the products of labour acquire a socially uniform objectivity as values, which is distinct from their sensuously varied object-ivity as articles of utility. This division of the product of labour into a useful thing and a thing possessing value appears in practice only when exchange has already acquired a sufficient extension and importance to allow useful things to be pro-duced for the purpose of being exchanged, so that their character as values has already to be taken into consideration during production. From this moment on, the labour of the individual producer acquires a twofold social character. On the one hand, it must, as a definite useful kind of labour, satisfy a definite social need, and thus maintain its position as an element of the total labour, as a branch of the social division of labour, which originally sprang up spontaneously. On the other hand, it can satisfy the manifold needs of the individual producer himself only in so far as every particular kind of useful private labour can be exchanged with, i.e. counts as the equal of, every other kind of useful private labour. Equality in the full sense between different kinds of labour can be arrived at only if we abstract from their real inequality, if we reduce them to the characteristic they have in common, that of being the expenditure of human labour-power, of human labour in the abstract. The private producer's brain reflects this twofold social character of his labour only in the forms which appear in practical intercourse, in the exchange of products. Hence the socially useful character of his private labour is reflected in the form that the product of labour has to be useful to others, and the social character of the equality of the various kinds of labour is reflected in the form of the common character, as values, possessed by these materially different things, the products of labour.

Men do not therefore bring the products of their labour into relation with each other as values because they see these objects merely as the material integu-ments of homogeneous human labour. The reverse is true: by equating their different products to each other in exchange as values, they equate their different kinds of labour as human labour. They do this without being aware of it.[3] Value, therefore, does not have its description branded on its forehead; it rather trans-forms every product of labour into a social hieroglyphic. Later on, men try to decipher the hieroglyphic, to get behind the secret of their own social product: for the characteristic which objects of utility have of being values is as much men's social product as is their language. The belated scientific discovery that the prod-ucts of labour, in so far as they are values, are merely the material expressions of the human labour expended to produce them, marks an epoch in the history of mankind's development, but by no means banishes the semblance of objectivity possessed by the social characteristics of labour. Something which is only valid for this particular form of production, the production of commodities, namely the fact that the specific social character of private labours carried on independently of each other consists in their equality as human labour, and, in the product, assumes the form of the existence of value, appears to those caught up in the relations of commodity production (and this is true both before and after the above-mentioned scientific discovery) to be just as ultimately valid as the fact that the scientific dissection of the air into its component parts left the atmosphere itself unaltered in its physical configuration.

[. . .]

Notes

1   One may recall that China and the tables began to dance when the rest of the world appeared to be standing still – *pour encourager les autres*. ('To encourage the others'. A reference to the simultaneous emergence in the 1850s of the Taiping revolt in China and the craze for spiritualism which swept over upper-class German society. The rest of the world was 'standing still' in the period of reaction immediately after the defeat of the 1848 Revolutions.)

2   Among the ancient Germans the size of a piece of land was measured according to the labour of a day; hence the acre was called *Tagwerk, Tagwanne* (*jurnale*, or *terra jurnalis*, or *diornalis*), *Mannwerk, Mannskraft, Mannsmaad, Mannshauet*, etc. See Georg Ludwig von Maurer, *Einleitung zur Geschichte der Mark-, Hof-, usw. Verfassung*, Munich, 1854, p. 129 ff.

3   Therefore, when Galiani said: Value is a relation between persons ('*La Ricchezza è una ragione tra due persone*') he ought to have added: a relation concealed beneath a material shell. (Galiani, *Della Moneta*, p. 221, Vol. 3 of Custodi's collection entitled *Scrittori classici italiani di economia politica, Parte moderna*, Milan, 1803.)

Chapter 30

Peter Braham

FASHION
Unpacking a cultural production

Introduction

[. . .]

IT IS PERHAPS only to be expected that in cultural studies fashion is treated as a cultural subject, in which most emphasis is on fashion as a badge or a means of identity. Yet fashion, as well as being a matter of creation, consumption and identity, is also a matter of production, distribution and retailing. It is therefore not just a cultural subject, but also a subject which has to do with apparently rather mundane matters of profit margins, response times, supply and demand, and so on. Accordingly, the assumption that fashion in clothes ought to be considered in terms of both its cultural aspects and its economic aspects is central to my approach, as is the contention that we must try to illuminate the connections between the production and consumption of fashion. It is the interplay between these different elements that will provide the main storyline of this chapter and it is this which allows us to raise 'external' as well as 'internal' questions about fashion by treating it as an illustration of the notion of a **cultural economy**. . . . In the case of fashion this means that the question of whether or not 'fashion' is homogeneous – in the sense that there is a single, prevailing style of dress – cannot be treated simply as a cultural or aesthetic matter of why or how quickly one fashion replaces or remains alongside another, it also has material implications for manufacturing, distribution, ordering and selling.

[. . .]

The consumption and production of fashion

The complex and uncertain relationship between the production and consumption of fashion may be illustrated by the following two stories. The first story concerns a major British retailer and the specifications they are said to have set for their suppliers of blue jeans. At the time, the prevailing fashion was for jeans to be faded: either they should be 'stone-washed' – resulting in a streaky pale blue colour – or they should be advertised to 'fade when washed'. The retailer was concerned about the implications of this for their reputation as a supplier of durable clothes of good quality. Should they maintain their preferred quality standards and risk losing out to their high street competitors in this lucrative market? They opted for insisting that their jeans should *not* fade. Later, this decision was criticized within the company for placing them outside the fashion market altogether – not just in relation to the sale of jeans.

The second story concerns a variant of a common nightmare that is said to haunt store buyers. It goes something like this: the buyer is in a hall which somehow combines elements of all the ready-to-wear collections held each year in Paris, Milan, New York and London. She is surrounded by jostling characters from the fashion circus who are holding out hundreds of dresses for her to inspect and, at the same time, waving order sheets in her face. Unable to resist such pressure she signs innumerable cheques and buys millions and millions of dollars worth of clothes. The scene then changes to the start of the next season: the buyer and the president of the store are standing just inside the store's main entrance. It is time for business. The doors are thrown open but no one comes in. An hour passes, then several hours, then a day, then a week – still the store is without customers. At the end of the week the president turns to the buyer and says, 'It is obvious that the public does not want your clothes. You have misread their taste. The best thing to do is pack all these strange garments and send them back' (adapted from Coleridge, 1988, p. 270).

[. . .]

Each of these stories offers a number of insights about fashion, though at first glance they seem to refer to very different worlds – indeed, while designer dresses are exclusive, produced on a small scale and appear to be the epitome of 'fashion', it seems more appropriate to see jeans, which are mass-produced for a market of millions, as mere 'clothes'. Yet there are good reasons for thinking that, perhaps, these differences are not so great after all.

Today, though jeans are no longer just the work clothes they once were, they still might be seen as a fairly standard item where style changes are limited and, as such, it may be thought that they would be far removed from considerations of fashion. Yet retailers have discovered, sometimes to their cost, that demand is far from predictable:

> [Retail buyers have] to guess four or five months down the road what a consumer who is fifteen years old is going to want in jeans. During that

time, a new movie can come out, and the trend goes from blue denim to black denim. And suddenly the inventory commitment is obsolete, causing costly mark-downs.

(Howard, 1990, p. 136)

In addition, certain brands of jeans have been heavily promoted precisely to distinguish them from the other brands that were piled high and sold cheaply: 'We needed people to value a pair of Levi's. They had . . . to become fashionable without becoming a fashion item, and to achieve a mystique' (Roy Edmondson, Managing Director, Levi Strauss UK, quoted in *The Sunday Times*, Culture Section, 26 November 1995).

The intriguing thing is that in order to become fashionable, jeans had not so much to overcome their firm identification with work, with the 'common man' and so on, as for it to become ambiguous as to whether what was now being emphasized was their original associations or their new-found hierarchical and distinctive aspects. We may see this particularly well in the case of faded jeans insofar as they make obvious reference to this original usage – the 'fashion' is that they must not look new, yet they do so in a way which reveals that *appearing* to be poor has really been a costly business for the wearer.

It took about one hundred years from the time that jeans had been devised by Levi Strauss in the American West as practical work clothes, to the moment that they became almost synonymous with youth – middle class, often rebellious youth especially. But what was most significant in transforming them into truly fashionable garments was the success of the fashion industry in extending the market for jeans far beyond both these old and new constituencies. This was achieved, above all, by the innovation of designer jeans, the first of which, by Calvin Klein, notched up 20,000 sales in their first week on the American market in 1978 – even though they were 50 per cent more expensive than Levi's – and by 1984 the sales of his jeans worldwide amounted to $400 million (Craik, 1994, p. 195). With Calvin Klein's success, other designers – not surprisingly – were quick to introduce their own variants and now we are quite familiar with jeans bearing none too discreet Calvin Klein, Donna Karen and Gloria Vanderbilt labels. And even though this practice of prominent labelling follows that of Levi Strauss, it seems to give a particular aura of conspicuous consumption to a garment of such humble origins, as well as suggesting to us that fashion does not just emanate from elite groups, but may also move 'upwards'. Yet perhaps the richest irony in this process of fashionability has been that, eventually, we find American consumers were prepared to pay much more for European designer jeans like Versace than for the original, quintessentially American garments that they imitated.

Our second story, centring on the store buyer's nightmare, also hinges on the impredictability of fashion, but it has other elements too. For example, it suggests that fashion in the shops has its origins in what we might think of as the 'high fashion' (haute couture) of the catwalks of Paris and elsewhere; that it is the creation of experts (designers); that it is brought to the department store (or high street) by other experts (buyers). It is, therefore, a relatively conventional view of the fashion industry, except insofar as it suggests that the public may decide to refrain from consuming the selections of these experts, giving credence, perhaps, to the notion that there may be a considerable gulf between 'the look' that appears on the catwalks and what works in everyday situations.

These stories raise – implicitly or explicitly – several of the issues that I wish to explore and which, though important, may be regarded as being 'internal' to this chapter. For example, is fashion predictable or unpredictable? How does something become a fashion item and what is fashionable about it? Who shapes and influences fashion? Is it those within the industry – perhaps it is haute couture designers who proclaim that this year skirts will be so many inches shorter than last year, or perhaps it is previously unknown designers – or is fashion now created at 'street level'? And if there are different fashion 'worlds', what is the relationship between them?

To a degree, questions like these form much of the stock-in-trade of the fashion pages in our newspapers and magazines, where attention is focused on the latest trends and the 'hottest' designer or most sensational collection. Here, as you will know, fashion is generally portrayed in breathless and exaggerated language: at one moment a simple leather skirt costing several hundred pounds might be described as 'basic' or 'essential', and at another moment a certain designer dress will be described as 'to die for' (or, for that matter, 'to kill for'). And, in particular, the world of high fashion inhabited by designers and store buyers alike that is conveyed in these pages seems extremely pressured, not to say frenzied – just as it does in the store buyer's nightmare.

Now, it is undeniable that what is, at least at first glance, especially striking about fashion – whether near the catwalk or on the street – is the capacity it has to excite people, which it does by offering them the means to express their identity or the prospect of transforming themselves, and so on. Indeed, in some cases, the desire or compulsion to be fashionable may give rise to still more extreme action that is implied by the proverbial advice 'shop till you drop'. For example, where it is not enough for fashion-conscious youth to wear *any* trainers because what they *must* have is a particular model of a costly, high-status brand, but the money to buy them is not available (and cannot be begged or borrowed from a parent), then the pressure to resort to crime in order to possess them may be difficult to resist. That this is indeed so, is demonstrated by the frequency with which high school students in the USA are being robbed of expensive fashion items – like trainers and Levi jackets – a phenomenon that has given fresh impetus to campaigns in favour of making school uniform compulsory.

If the extensive coverage of fashion in newspapers and magazines invariably makes fashion seem exciting, it is also likely to be fairly superficial. How then are we to achieve a more incisive theorization of the sort suggested by Roche (1994) when he speaks of the study of clothing and fashion being at the 'heart of social history'? First, if we are to do more than reiterate common-sense assumptions and myths about fashion, if we are – in terms of this chapter – to succeed in 'unpacking' fashion, rather than simply disturbing its packaging, we need to begin by thinking carefully about what is the appropriate context within which our analysis should be conducted. To do this it is important not only to address both so-called 'internal' and 'external' questions about fashion, some of which have just been mentioned, but also to understand how, by exploring internal questions, we might illuminate more general ones. For example, whether fashion is best seen as basically homogeneous, created centrally by and for an elite and then transmitted downwards to the mass and outwards to a periphery, or whether the sources of fashion are now more diverse and 'polycentric' is an important issue. . . . In order to discover if either of these perspectives is accurate, we need to focus on 'internal' matters – to examine, amongst other things, the power and influence of international fashion conglomerates and the intricate and long-standing relationship between haute couture designers and mass manufacturers of garments. But in so doing, we may be able to make a significant contribution to wider debates, such as those about the relationship between production and consumption and about globalization.

[. . .]

The consumption of fashion

The sources of fashion

Despite the considerable merits of Simmel's analysis of fashion, . . ., Blumer (1969) considers it to be deficient in certain important respects. His first criticism is that though Simmel's treatment is quite appropriate to fashion in dress in seventeenth-century, eighteenth-century and nineteenth-century Europe, it fails to measure up to the operation of contemporary fashion, characterized as it is said to be by an emphasis on **modernity**. In this context, 'modernity' refers in particular to:

1   the tremendous growth in complexity on the consumption side of fashion, and
2   the consequences that this complexity has had for the manufacture of clothes, particularly in terms of the arrangements of production and the organization of work.

In short, the variations in fashions and in styles have become much more complex whether viewed from the standpoint of consumption or from that production – where, until recently, the order of the day was for there to be long runs of standardized garments on a scale sufficient to justify the costs of installing the requisite machinery. . . .

Blumer was especially anxious to question one of Simmel's fundamental contentions: that a style comes into fashion because an elite gives its authority to that style. In Blumer's opinion, style comes into fashion only if it corresponds to what he terms 'the incipient taste of the fashion-consuming public'. Though the prestige of an elite may very well influence the direction of that taste, it does not control or determine it. In support of this argument, Blumer points out that there are plentiful examples of 'fashion' ignoring the taste of those of the highest prestige and so-called leaders of fashion: where fashion operates 'it assumes an imperative position'. By this he means that it sanctions what is to be done, that it is indifferent to criticism and that it bypasses those who do not accept it (Blumer, 1969, p. 276). For example, he mentions the failure of the well-financed campaign marshalled by clothing manufacturers in the period 1919–22, which enlisted the 'cooperation of the heads of fashion houses, fashion magazines, fashion commentators, actresses and acknowledged fashion leaders' to halt and reverse the trend towards shorter skirts. This campaign involved taking every opportunity that presented itself to declare that long dresses were returning – but these declarations were quite ineffective and the fashion for short skirts continued unabated (ibid., p. 281).

In Blumer's view, a fashion is born or dies not because a style is picked up or discarded by an elite, but because it is or is no longer in tune with developing taste. This, he contends, is a major departure from Simmel who depicted fashion as an outcome or process of class differentiation. Instead, fashion is treated by Blumer as an act of collective mood, taste and choice: 'the fact that this process of collective selection is mysterious – it is mysterious because we do not understand it – does not contradict in any way that it takes place' (ibid., p. 282). Nor does its mystery allow us to deny, Blumer argues, that the origin, formation and development of collective taste – for example, in the way fashion innovators may indicate the paths along which incipient taste may develop – constitutes 'the huge problematic area in fashion' and, moreover, constitutes the first aspect of modernity in fashion (ibid.).

Nevertheless, Blumer's study of the women's fashion industry in Paris helps us to begin to appreciate how this incipient taste emerges. What struck him included the following:

1   The setting of fashion involved an intense process of selection. For instance, of the hundred or more designs of women's evening wear presented by a major Parisian fashion house at its seasonal opening, the fashion house's management was able to indicate about thirty designs from among which the assemblage of between one and two hundred store buyers would then choose no more than six or eight. But for some unexplained reason they were generally unable to predict which these six or eight chosen designs would be.

2   He discovered that the similarity of the choices that the buyers made could be explained in relation to their immersion in and preoccupation with a strikingly common world consisting of, *inter alia*, the diligent study of fashion publications, close observation of the lines stocked in the 'competitor' stores which their fellow buyers represented and, above all, a constant examination of prevailing and emerging tastes in the women's dress market. Just as was suggested in my introduction (see the store buyer's nightmare), 'their success, indeed their vocational fate, depended on their ability to sense the direction of taste in (the fashion) public' (ibid., p. 279).

3   Blumer discovered that the dress designers created their new styles – it should go without saying that this was with the hope of securing their adoption by the store buyers – by

a)   scouring plates of former fashions and of costumes of 'far-off' people;
b)   examining both current and recent fashions; and most significantly by
c)   developing a deep familiarity with recent expressions of modernity – whether they be manifest in the arts, literature, politics or elsewhere – and translating the themes they uncovered thereby into dress designs (though this is not to say that fashion should be seen, as some see it, merely as a 'mirror' of a given moment or era).

From these observations, Blumer came to the conclusion that fashion was being set:

> through a process of free selection from among a large number of competing models; that the creators of the models are seeking to catch and give expression to what we may call the direction of modernity; and that the buyers, who through their choices set the fashion, are acting as the unwitting agents of a fashion-consuming public whose incipient tastes the buyers are seeking to anticipate.
>
> (ibid., p. 280)

It can be argued that of all these complex elements, closely interconnected as they clearly are, the most obvious is also the important, namely the way in which a new, would-be fashion relates to the fashion that is in mode. That is to say, the new fashion seeks – inevitably – to extend, qualify, comment on or contradict the existing fashion: in effect it stands in what Davis calls a sort of 'dialectical relationship' with the prevailing fashion (Davis, 1992, p. 130).

The diffusion of fashion

Broadly speaking, the first of the two aspects of modernity in fashion . . . can be equated with the consumption side of fashion, while the second aspect is more closely related to its production (though this demarcation should not be treated too rigidly). As I intend to show later on, this second aspect is complex enough, but the first aspect, which is examined next, is not only complex, it is also elusive.

As Blumer explains, because fashion is perennially modern it must keep up with developments not just in its own field – the appearance on the market of new fabrics would be an example – but also with those in related fields in the fine arts, and in the wider social world – the emancipation of women being an obvious example.

It should be quickly apparent to you that this portrait of modernity, to which designers are said to be trying to respond and to give expression in each season's collections, though it may be of great importance, is nevertheless bound to be extremely difficult to specify and pin down – a problem of which Blumer and others of like mind are acutely aware.

Thus we can speak of designers somehow sensing 'currents of identity instability pervading a people and seek[ing] through the artful manipulation of the conventional visual symbols of clothing presentation to lend expression to them, or alternatively to contain, deflect or sublimate them' (Davis, 1992, p. 17). But it is altogether more demanding to begin to delineate the precise contents of this communication or to trace its operation.

There is much less mystery, however, if for one moment we accept Simmel's analysis of the matter, in forming an appreciation of what happens once the designers have produced their designs and the buyers have made their choices from among these designs. . . . Here we have a straightforward scenario which commences with persons of social prestige taking up a new style, continues with a larger number following their example and ends with each individual (or at least with all but a small minority) feeling that she cannot afford to be different. This theory of **fashion diffusion**, which, as we have seen, is criticized by Blumer, is known technically as one of class differentiation, but it is known more popularly as the 'trickle-down' theory of fashion.

Suppose for a moment that we choose to distance ourselves from this view, which was, until recently, dominant, and opt instead for the view that fashion originates through designers identifying incipient collective tastes. What is far from clear is whether, if we do this, we must thereby abandon the idea that fashion – and here we are talking specifically about women's fashion – spreads from a 'creative centre' (usually thought of as a specific place – most often Paris – or places) to ever more remote fashion-consuming publics.

In other words, we may need to distinguish between the rather narrow concaption that fashion is determined solely by the prestige of a social elite and the apparently more sophisticated view that fashion is generally determined by a relatively small number of 'players' who really count: a small group of fashion designers, a larger group of fashion buyers, those publicists and editors who inform the 'fashion conscious' about the direction that fashion is taking, as well as a small minority of fashionable consumers (whether we term them 'fashion innovators', 'fashion leaders' or call them by some other name).

Amongst these several types of 'player', as we might expect, most attention has been devoted to the power and influence of the designers – especially those producing haute couture in Paris (and, to a lesser extent, those working in New York, though British- and Italian-based designers have not been ignored). In this respect, the scholarly focus has, until recently at least, resembled popular beliefs about fashion which are encapsulated very well in George Bernard Shaw's remark that 'a fashion is nothing but an induced epidemic, proving that epidemics can be induced by tradesmen' (Auden and Kronenberger, 1962, p. 126, quoted in Davis, 1992, p. 109). Of course, which designers really count will depend in large measure on other key players, notably certain fashion editors and store buyers, so there is an element of circularity here.

[. . .]

If we concentrate too much on who ought to be regarded as a key player or on which type of player has most influence on fashion, we may well neglect more important matters. We risk losing sight of the extent to which 'fashion' is these days an industry which not only employs millions of people, but also – and crucially – must *sell* to millions of people. In other words, our discussion of what is fashionable, and who it is that defines what is fashionable, might be thought to be incomplete if it did not take into account the size and nature of the market or markets for fashion and, by extension, the system of production for that market or markets.

In recent times the fashion industry has been transformed by a number of important developments. On the one hand we have the rise of mass production . . ., but on the other hand there has been a growth in the diversity of products and a growth both in the number of markets and types of selling.

Probably the key development in fashion has been the growth in ready-to-wear clothes – whether displayed and sold in department stores and other retail outlets or by mail order. The American innovation of purchase by mail order is especially interesting in this context, not just because it enabled consumers in the most remote of locations to keep up with trends in fashion, but because it helped to establish the importance of what may be described as non-elite fashion. The size of this mail order market may be gauged by the statistic that in the early years of the twentieth century more than ten million Americans shopped in this way and by the fact that the bulk of the often enormous catalogues (in 1921 the Sears catalogue ran to 1,064 pages) was devoted to women's wear. Yet, as Craik points out, there has been little academic research into the mail order industry in general, and still less into the influence that the mail order industry has had in the formation of taste in clothing or fashion (Craik, 1994, pp. 207–9). Despite these developments, even into the 1950s (and perhaps later still) many people would have accepted with little or no hesitation that 'fashion' had a distinct centre, namely Parisian haute couture. If this was indeed thought to be so, it was not, of course, meant in the sense that all who bought their clothes from, say, a Sears catalogue in America or a John Lewis department store in England, were buying one-off Parisian originals, but rather in the sense that it was Parisian couturiers who set the pace in the information landscape of fashion: in other words, it was they who decided whether an inch or two should come off skirts or whether shoulders should stay wide. As Wark puts it, it was 'they (who) dressed the fashion elites and sold each season's style to the mass manufacturers – or watched the latter simply steal the popular styles' (Wark, 1991, p. 62).

The taken for granted view of the diffusion of fashion was thus that it was created centrally and then transmitted towards the periphery. That is to say, the designs formulated by Parisian haute couturiers would move at varying pace not merely geographically outwards, but also socially downwards – probably losing a good deal in subtlety, quality and workmanship as they did so.

Davis aptly portrays this process as conveying a classic example of globalization, in that it contains 'the tacit assumption of a fashion-consuming public, international in scope, whose tastes and standards were located essentially within the vast shadow and penumbra of a Eurocentric culture' (Davis, 1992, p. 200).

In contrast to this picture, the increasingly heard contention is that in recent times – let us say from the 1960s or 1970s onwards – there has been an increase in what is variously termed 'polycentrism', 'polymorphism' and 'pluralism' in fashion. Thus, to use Wark's words once more, we now find ourselves confronted by 'new modes of fashionability in a far more widely dispersed information landscape' (1991, p. 62), by which he chiefly refers to increasing consumer affluence, the emergence of fashionable ready-to-wear clothes and, in particular, to the appearance of other sources and manifestations of fashion and style, notably those emanating from pop music and from youth culture. From this perspective, not only is it seen as pointless to turn to Paris or Milan to discover the direction of fashion – much less will there be a single fashion in play, such as, Dior's New Look – but in addition, it is said that fashion now originates from a diverse range of groups, sources *and* designers.

What this entails is that a whole series of cultural and sub-cultural groups may create their own fashions, or make something fashionable by adopting it and, as we have seen in the case of jeans, by adopting a fashion they may cause it to move outward and upward to other groups and social strata – even to the point of such an item eventually becoming high fashion itself.

Whereas in the classic 'trickle-down' model there are regular seasons, there are no such seasons with these new sources of fashion, notably 'street fashion', 'pop culture' and 'ethnic cultures'. The chief result of this is that the supposedly orderly dissemination of couture copies and derivatives on which mass production is assumed to depend is no longer possible (Wark, 1991, pp. 64–5). On the one hand, so-called 'street fashion' very often takes no notice of designer innovations or merely adopts certain of their elements (Craik, 1994, p. ix); and, on the other hand, the constant search for inspiration by high-fashion designers to which Blumer refers (see section 2.6) is nowadays just as likely to be directed at appropriating or adapting street fashions in their own creations as they are to be scouring more traditional sources for ideas.

On the basis of these and other developments it seems perfectly reasonable to conclude that what we have now are **multiple fashion systems** in which fashion moves up, down and along from a variety of starting positions and in several directions, rather than a single system in which fashion only moves in one direction, 'trickling down' from the elite to the majority. If this is so, we should be looking for new fashions in the street, from students in colleges of fashion, from 'pop' designers, among ethnic minorities and so on, and not simply – or perhaps not at all – in haute couture. In other words, what was global in origin has become, to a considerable degree, local.

To summarize, changing views about fashion in clothes – from Simmel onwards – seem to present us with a number of distinct epochs, each of which is characterized by different systems of production and contrasting types of consumption: thus at one moment fashion is determined by an elite before 'trickling down' to the mass and the dominant form of manufacture is craft production; at the next moment fashion is dominated by mass production and mass consumption; and at a third moment the emphasis is on 'flexible production' (see below) and consumption becomes more diverse and segmented in line with the increasingly 'polycentric' origins of fashion.

Re-evaluating haute couture

The role of Parisian haute couture (and that of haute couture in other countries as well) in setting the new fashions in women's clothes has clearly changed in certain important respects. Nonetheless, this is certainly not to concede that its role has been so sharply diminished that we should ignore haute couture altogether and simply look elsewhere to see who or what sets the fashion agenda. In the light of the developments that have been described (and with which you may be familiar from your own observations), this may seem to be an odd or even obstinate stance to take. Despite this, I hope to persuade you that my position is at least tenable.

Taking this position does not mean that we have to completely reject this more open view of the sources of new fashions – indeed, it would be rather foolish to do so. However, there are a number of important qualifications that need to be made to it. In the first instance, the growing emphasis on identifying other sources of fashion inspiration and influence, notably the growing fascination with pop designers, has often had more to do with the excitement and novelty of the actual designs than it has with the extent – if any – to which these designs are or will be in production.

Indeed in more than one case when an up-and-coming British designer has been telephoned by a fashion magazine and asked to send round one of their latest designs to be photographed for publication, it turns out that the design had never been produced at all – even as a prototype.

The question remains, however: should these developments cause us to desist from our traditional gaze on what is being worn on the catwalk and refocus our attention on the 'grassroots', on the 'street' itself? Or is it wiser to take account of these developments and use them as a reason for re-examining the relationship between high fashion and everyday fashion? Let me explain why the latter option has more to recommend it than the former.

First, it should be pointed out that because high fashion designers borrow from the 'street' this is, of itself, no reason to lose interest in high fashion; indeed, such borrowing does not necessarily diminish the ability of high-fashion designers to exploit their designs commercially and may actually enhance it by taking it in new directions.

Second, and more importantly, it is one thing to conclude that Paris is no longer the centre of fashion (in the sense that fashion should no longer be equated with haute couture), but it is quite another matter to overlook the extent to which the Parisian couturiers (and their counterparts elsewhere, notably in New York) have succeeded in becoming such major players that the designation 'pret-a-porter' may be not simply more pretentious sounding (which in Britain and the USA it is) than is the more down-to-earth phrase 'ready-to-wear', but is in fact somewhat more revealing about the sources of influence in fashion. Thus, the most compelling evidence of the continuing relevance of high fashion – and of the centre-to-periphery model – notwithstanding the developments that have been outlined, lies in the vast economic power and *global scope* of the international fashion conglomerates with their multi-billion dollar annual revenues: the St Laurents, Chanels, Armanis, Kleins, Laurens, Kawakubos etc.' (Davis, 1992, p. 203, emphasis added). These conglomerates, of course, encompass much more than just fashion in clothes, but deal as well in jewellery, cosmetics, accessories and, above all, in perfume.

Third, and equally important, rather than being replaced, the centre – periphery model of fashion has taken new and more complex forms – such that it is now profoundly changed. It is to some of these new forms that I now turn.

It is important to make clear that the relationship between high fashion and everyday fashion has in any case not been quite as straightforward as it might have seemed. For instance, this relationship had been significantly modified – long before any claims about growing polycentrism and the like were being made – in the late nineteenth and early twentieth centuries by the rapid rise of mass production. This allowed creditable facsimiles of clothes that for reasons of cost and complexity could previously only have been produced by the couturiers' own skilled workers (Davis, 1992, p. 139). Thereafter – despite the appearance of designs that the mass media are prone to highlight as demonstrating how far-removed high fashion is from everyday life – in practice, the artistic licence, creativity and fantasy of haute couture has been generally and seriously constrained by the presence of the mass manufacturers of garments and the vast orders that they may be prepared to place.

Davis provides a very interesting explanation of the effect that such constraints might have on the designers themselves and, more significantly, on their financial backers. What is said to happen is that the designers 'privilege' some of the offerings in their collections, namely those that are thought likely to prove popular with the fashion-buying public *and* which will not pose serious problems for the mass manufacturer, for example, in terms of the availability of fabric or because of threats to the integrity of the finished garment caused by too narrow cutting and joining tolerances:

> Thus, of the several dozen items of apparel presented on the (haute couture) runway, only a few are 'genuine entries'. The others are either sheer 'throwaways' meant to lend an aura of 'depth' to the show or, more strategically, purposefully exaggerated renditions of the more marketable items the design house hopes to cash in.
>
> (Davis, 1992, p. 152)

Not only are the 'privileged' items given favourable treatment when the collection is presented, but the fashion house is quite willing to provide toned-down versions of their designs that will be more suitable for the markets which the store buyers represent (ibid.). You might wish to compare this view with Blumer's findings on the same subject . . .

In other words, the apparent distinction between elite designer fashion and high street fashion has been nowhere near as great as it is often assumed to be. Perhaps the best illustration of this has been the exponential growth in licensing agreements by and on behalf of the major fashion houses – not just for ready-to-wear clothes, but also for various fashion accessories and a range of consumer products. For example, Pierre Cardin has licensed his name and logo to more than eight hundred products (Milbank, 1990, p. 64), though this is not to say that this process is always smooth, witness Geoffrey Beene's complaint that, 'Sometimes they [the licensees] want your name and what you stand for, and then they don't want any input . . . Sometimes I totally OK a collection and later I see in a store something with my name which I didn't even design. That gives me a cardiac arrest' (quoted in Coleridge, 1988, pp. 38–9).

This leaves open the possibility that even if we think we 'own' a designer label – after all, there it hangs in the wardrobe – our belief may be misplaced or at least open to question: leaving aside counterfeits (see below), is our prized garment really the creation of the designer whose name is on the label, did the designer merely approve a licensee's design, or did the designer even see it at all? And does this matter to us and if so, why? Is this comparable in some way to the differing reactions that we might have to possessing a work of art depending on whether it is an original (equivalent, perhaps, to haute couture), a limited edition, or simply an un-numbered print, and so on?

The cachet of the designer's name and logo is such that there has developed an extensive and sophisticated network to counterfeit designer items of all sorts. Indeed, as Craik says, counterfeiting amounts to an overt form of the practice of 'prestigious imitation' that constitutes the very foundation of the fashion industry, that is to say, the popularization of a style by means of modification and differentiation for different markets (Craik, 1994, p. 213). A good, and perhaps extreme, example of this is Katherine Hamnett's claim that thirty unlicensed manufacturers –

from South America to South-east Asia – had between them produced half a million copies of her slogan T-shirts. In general, by the 1970s and 1980s counterfeiting had become so efficiently managed that the overnight couriering of catwalk photographs to pirate manufacturers was common. (As I write it is probably all done on the Internet.) The most bizarre aspect of counterfeiting may be that, apparently, in some cases 'the vogue is not to wear the genuine item but the fashionable facsimile' (Stead, 1991, p. 41).

If haute couture was simply a matter of attending to its exclusive clientele, who number no more than a few thousand world-wide – that is, those personal customers who actually attend the collections, or who, even more impressively, have items from the collections sent *to them* – we might be able to make little sense of the alliances formed between haute couture houses, fabric and garment manufacturers, and financial backers. Yet it is these alliances that reveal one of the most significant connections that exist, linking the individual workmanship of haute couture and the huge edifice of the mass production of ready-to-wear clothes. One of the most important of such alliances was the so-called High Fashion-Industry Accord signed in Italy in 1971, by which Italian couturiers received a subsidy if their new season's lines conformed to prior guidelines that they had agreed with the major garment manufacturers (Wark, 1991, p. 64). Since this pioneering agreement, these alliances have developed in Italy to the point at which the decision to launch a new designer label is often taken jointly by the designer, the garment manufacturer and the fabric firm. Moreover, the costs of the first few collections will, like as not, be borne by the manufacturer and the fabric house until the stage is reached that the label is sufficiently profitable to allow the designer to repay whatever debt has built up.

What should we conclude from all this? In my view, the present day situation of haute couture is perfectly and succinctly expressed in the remark of George Jolles, president of the huge French manufacturer of designer clothes, Biderman: 'It's time to stop deifying our creativity and think about how we can sell' (quoted in Coleridge, 1988, p. 182), hardly the attitude that we might have once expected.

The manufacturing and retailing of fashion

The role of major retailers

If we try to assess the relative contributions to what is produced and what is consumed in fashion, there is a good case for saying that (major) fashion retailers (and the store buyers who act for them) are more significant than manufacturers, designers and even, the fashion-consuming public itself. However, the inter-relationships between these categories are complex and, in addition, some of these categories are not as distinct as they might seem at first – thus we find in one important instance a so-called 'manufacturer without factories' (Marks and Spencer), and in another what has been termed a 'producer with shops' (Benetton). These complications help to explain (in this section and the following sections) why the discussion of the role and character of the retailing of fashion is not, nor should it be, treated wholly separately from that of the manufacturing of fashion.

Many of the changes in the nature and terrain of fashion can, nevertheless, be grasped by examining the power of leading clothing retailers and, in particular, the relationship that they have with fabric producers and garment manufacturers and their involvement with production and design issues.

What is very striking is that in the advanced industrial countries (AICs) there has been a growing trend in the retail clothing sector for sales to become concentrated in major retailing chains and in large buying groups. This trend is especially pronounced in the UK where Marks and Spencer and the Burton Group together account for approximately 25 per cent of all clothes sold. Such a concentration of retailing power has led to these and other major retailers becoming more and more concerned with matters such as product specification and design: a development that may be contrasted with an era when such issues were habitually regarded as more the province of those higher up the 'textile chain' and manufacturers might have seen themselves as producing 'for stock' rather than for their (eventual) customers, the retailers.

It might be expected that in the UK this concentration of retailing power would have led to less competition between retailers, but this was not how it turned out. Perhaps because, since the 1950s, householders have allocated a diminishing proportion of their income to clothing and footwear, retailers have found themselves in an increasingly competitive market. One of the chief consequences of this is that they discovered slowly but surely that there was a limit to the sales and profits that could be secured by their long-standing reliance on the 'economies of scale' associated with large-scale production. Instead, they began to comprehend that there was significant advantage to be derived by encouraging the development of diverse markets in clothing and fashion, in so far as 'consumer pursuit of individuality offers firms a seemingly endless potential to extend the levels of market segmentation *and to generate product redundancy*' (Rhodes, 1993, p. 162; emphasis added).

This is hardly to be wondered at, for nowhere, of course, is product redundancy more of the essence than it is in fashion in clothes (think of the message of Alexander McKendrick's film, *The Man in the White Suit*, which shows how jobs and investment are threatened at all levels of the clothing industry when an 'indestructible' garment is invented). And so, in these circumstances, retailers have sought to extend the designation 'fashion' to more and more of their products. The degree to which they have succeeded in this endeavour may be gathered from an official survey carried out in America – but which may, nevertheless, also serve to suggest the general position in the UK. According to this survey, 80 per cent of apparel products had in-shop 'lives' of twenty weeks *or less* and 35 per cent had lives of ten weeks *or less* (Rhodes, 1992, p. 30).

In order to fulfil these twin goals of increasing both market segmentation and product redundancy, retailers have been obliged to go beyond their traditional areas of expertise in distribution, display and selling. It is now in their interest to keep in close contact with manufacturers in order not only to provide detailed feedback on patterns of sales, but, even more significantly, to become involved in the design of both individual products and ranges of products.

We can see these developments very clearly if we look at Marks and Spencer:

> In order that this technological approach to retailing could be realized
> in practical terms, it was not only essential that Marks and Spencer

technologists be consulted when a merchandiser detected a 'technical problem', but also that they should play an active part in the process of commercial decision taking.

(Braham, 1985, p. 130)

In the case of Marks and Spencer the close inter-connection between the commercial and the technological is evident in several ways: in its expertise in technical matters and production technologies Marks and Spencer came to outstrip many of its suppliers; this, together with Marks and Spencer's pre-eminence as a retailer, enabled them to set technical standards for much of the UK garment industry; and these advantages also left Marks and Spencer well placed to persuade their suppliers to invest in new equipment – a form of 'pull-through technology' – which helped garment manufacturers to respond effectively to shorter lead times and to the improved data collection by **electronic point-of-sale (EPOS) systems** (Braham, 1985, pp. 135 and 140).

The growth of segmented markets in fashion

For many years it had come to be assumed that the manufacture of clothes was increasingly a matter of the high-volume production of a slowly changing range of garments and that, therefore, 'fashion' was of relatively marginal importance. In these circumstances, it is to be expected that retailers – particularly those retailers capable of placing orders in bulk – would wish to take advantage of the economies of scale associated with mass production.

To the extent that this is true, the outlook for the AIC-based garment industries was bound to be gloomy. This is because it appeared that they would sooner or later be undercut by the transfer of technology to manufacturers in less developed and newly industrializing countries (LDCs and NICs) who would enjoy a number of vital advantages: not only would they be able to train workers in the simple and repetitive skills required, they would not be constrained by the burden of social and welfare costs as would manufacturers operating in AICs and, crucially, they would need to pay their workers very little. Indeed, this prognosis seems to find confirmation in what happened in the 1960s and 1970s, during which time the AICs commanded a declining share of world trade in clothing and, in addition, there was a continuing loss of jobs among AIC clothing workers.

Yet if the mass market for clothes becomes fragmented in the way that was described in the previous section, and if fashion comes to occupy a higher priority, the balance of advantage between manufacturers in AICs and those in LDCs and NICs might begin to shift back again: the differentiation of markets and products now favoured by retailers, and the likelihood that this, in turn, would contribute to (as well as express) frequent and volatile changes in consumer demand, may have several significant consequences for both retailers and manufacturers. It means, for example, that the practice of retailers keeping large reserves of limited and little-changing lines would have to end, or be applied with much more discrimination, and that the advantage to manufacturers of long production runs of garments would, therefore, be severely eroded. And by the same token, there is likely to be a bigger premium placed on the ability of manufacturers to operate with lower inventories of stock and to rely on being able to respond quickly and flexibly to orders from retailers – which are, in turn, going to be based closely on fluctuations in sales of different garments, styles and colours. (The evolving relationship between retailers and manufacturers is discussed in more detail in the next section.)

It is worth pausing for a moment, however, to consider whether it is sensible to modify this picture of there having been quite such a dramatic swing away from mass production to flexible, small batch, production as is often claimed, and as the preceding remarks might suggest. For example, Leopold contends that the degree of difference that is supposed to separate the craft-based system of individual produc-tion of high fashion from the mass production of everyday fashion has been much exaggerated. He believes that 'the rapidly changing proliferation of style in women's clothes' distinguishes their production not only from production in other industries, but also from other (more predictable) branches of the clothing industry. And he goes on to argue that this has meant that though the industry has adopted the rhetoric of mass production, it has never fully adopted its techniques, relying instead on hand-finishing and on the individual sewing machine (Leopold, 1992, pp. 102 and 105, cited in Craik, 1994, p. 211). In my view, not only is there a good deal of truth in this analysis, but it goes to what are, perhaps, the central issues in the manufacture and selling of fashion clothing, namely, those of unpredictability and the response to unpredictability, the very issues that were central to the store buyer's nightmare with which this chapter began. And to the extent that it *is* a valid analysis, it is especially relevant to some of the recent developments that have taken place in the production of designer clothes in Italy in particular . . .

In any event, retailers have come to accept that to gain competitive advantage they have to place more emphasis on non-price factors, such as quality and design and that they have to extend the degree of **market segmentation** that exists – a segmentation that seems to have become especially pronounced in that sector of the market aimed specifically at women in the age-range 25 to 44. As has been remarked, it is precisely this form of 'market niching' that has become the slogan of the high street – not just in clothing, but in respect of a whole range of commodities. Thus market researchers now break down the market by age, income, occupation and the like, and analyse 'lifestyles' by correlating the consumption of one type of product with another (Murray, 1988, p. 11) . . .

We can see this process particularly well in Burton's transformation from being a mass manufacturer of clothes with a large number of generalized retail outlets, to becoming, in the 1980s, 'a niche market retailer *with a team of anthropologists*, a group of segmented stores – Top Shop, Top Man, Dorothy Perkins, Principles and Burton's itself – with no manufacturing plants of its own' (Murray, 1988, p. 11; emphasis added).

[. . .]

Connections between the manufacturing and retailing of fashion

I have characterized the market for fashion in women's clothes as one in which styles change rapidly, in which product redundancy is high and shelf-life is low, and one in which market segmentation is well-established and growing. Not only are these factors intertwined, but they have become more pronounced in recent years. As has been suggested, this has important implications not just for retailers, but also for the relationship between retailers and their suppliers, a relationship which should be examined in the context of what is the most efficient form of production and where is the most desirable location for that production.

In this section these issues are further explored by outlining three models of garment production:

1　the relocation of production to LDCs or NICs where labour is both abundant and cheap;
2　subcontracting production within AICs to inner-city manufacturers who employ a mixture of cheap labour *in situ* and homeworkers who are cheaper still;
3　new forms of production and subcontracting (in particular, flexible specialization) that have been developed in some AICs, notably in parts of Italy.

As was suggested [above], it had come to be widely accepted in the 1960s and 1970s that manufacturers of garments in AICs would find it increasingly hard to fight off competition from LDCs and NICs. This belief found its most powerful expression in the idea which Frobel and his colleagues advanced: that a 'new international division of labour' had emerged (Frobel et al., 1980). Their thesis was that a number of developments had together permitted manufacturers to site their production facilities anywhere in the world depending on where the most profitable combination of capital and labour was to be found. These developments were that:

● the division and sub-division of manufacturing had gone so far that it now consisted largely of fragmented operations;
● advances in communications and transport meant that the location of production was much less constrained than it once was by technical, organizational and cost factors;
● these two factors enabled manufacturers to make use of the almost inexhaustible supplies of labour that were available in LDCs – thus operatives could be quickly trained in the minimal skills demanded by such fragmented operations and could be easily replaced by other suitable workers.

The chief consequence of these developments was the shutting down of certain types of manufacturing operations in AICs and the subsequent opening of these operations in LDCs or NICs – very often in the foreign subsidiaries of the same company. In Frobel et al's analysis, the garment and textile industries of the Federal Republic of Germany (as it still was at the time their work was published) provided one of the best exemplars of this process: 'Trousers for the Federal German market are no longer produced for example in Mönchengladbach, but in the Tunisian subsidiary of the same Federal company' (Frobel et al., 1980, p. 9).

Yet, as was explained earlier, the balance of advantage between manufacturing operations is not solely a matter of price, but may also be decided by factors such as flexibility and response time. Indeed, there has been a concerted attempt by manufacturers in AICs to counter the gains made by NICs and LDCs with a strategy that emphasizes their ability to provide variety in design, flexibility in production and, above all, 'quick response' – a slogan that is much heard in the garment industry today – to the changing orders from retailers and the fluctuations in consumer demand for different fashions, styles and designs (Mitter, 1991, p. 5).

In the second model, cost savings equivalent to those mentioned by Frobel et al., in certain cases and to some extent, are seen to have been obtained by sub-contracting production to inner-city firms. Thus, it might be emphasized that though the overall production of clothing in the UK has fallen consistently (replaced by increased imports), production in women's fashionwear – where demand for individual lines is most variable – has not declined to anything like the same degree. In consequence, most orders in this sector of the UK clothing market continue to be supplied by British producers.

From this perspective, the 'survival' of fashionwear production in the UK is attributed to two main factors. The first is the nearness of local producers to this unpredictable market. In other words, any competitive advantage that they have depends in large measure on the flexibility of their output, in which a vital element is that it 'is heavily dependent upon the casualization of labour, particularly an increased use of homeworkers' (Phizacklea, 1990, p. 11). This brings us to the second factor, that is the extent to which production is subcontracted to firms that are run by ethnic minority entrepreneurs, and, more particularly, the extent to which such firms depend on ethnic minority labour – which is prepared or com-pelled to work long hours at low wages, giving them the ability to produce 'at prices competitive with so-called Third World countries'. The casualization of employ-ment to which Phizacklea refers constitutes an important element in the way the UK clothing industry is depicted in this model. Thus a distinction can be drawn between (1) a stable sector of firms offering reasonably secure employment where firms can justify investment in new technology, perhaps because they have forged long-term relationships with major retailing chains, and (2) a multitude of precar-iously placed subcontractors which, given the abundance of cheap labour and the unpredictability of demand for their output, have little reason to invest in new capital equipment, and many of which are small independent producers employing less than ten workers (Phizacklea, 1990, p. 19). Thus we discover that the workers employed by 'local' manufacturers in the centre are sometimes indistinguishable from the workers in what we might think of as 'global' factories at the periphery.

The third model, usually referred to as **flexible specialization**, is the one I will discuss in the greatest detail. It must be conceded that the pattern that exists in the UK (outlined briefly in the second model, above) corresponds to *some* of the elements of flexible specialization, insofar as it relies on decentralizing production to small subcontractors who are capable of providing the diversity of output and the flexibility that the market demands. What is lacking in these instances, however, is the key aspect of extensive use being made of computer-controlled technology which, together with the flexible deployment and performance of the workforce, facilitates the establishment of close links between the point of production and the point of sale.

The essence of flexible specialization is to utilize new technology to permit both economic production in small batches and what is known as **just-in-time (JIT) production**. JIT enables the manufacturer to operate with minimal levels of inventory – with components arriving as near as possible to the moment at which they are required – as well as allowing production to be undertaken and completed, as far as is possible, only on the basis of firm orders from retailers, which themselves are based on actual sales of individual lines.

It is important to comprehend that in this key aspect, flexible specialization goes against the conventional opinion that it was precisely rapid fluctuations in fashion which precluded costly investment in capital equipment. In fact, this conventional view has been undermined by the development of microelectronically based technologies that can cope very well with short runs and frequent changes of style. In these circumstances, the need for a quick response to changing demand turns out to provide a compelling reason *for* investment in computer-aided design (CAD), computer-aided manufacturing (CAM) and the like, rather than a reason not to invest.

Perhaps the most interesting developments of flexible specialization are those that have taken place in what is often referred to as the 'Third Italy' – that is, the central and north-eastern regions of the country, which are thereby distinguished from the underdeveloped south and the more industrialized regions in and around Milan, for example, where what has been described as the most successful application of JIT on European soil has taken place (Mitter, 1991, p. 8). These developments should not be seen purely in technological terms however, important as these aspects have been. You may remember that in section 3.3, reference was made to the 1971 High Fashion-Industry Accord, the first of several such agreements that have been concluded in Italy. These agreements can be said to constitute a coherent policy for fashion, clothing and textiles, and one which 'combined both capital improvements and *cultural* capital development' (Wark, 1991, p. 71; original emphasis).

Possibly the ultimate expression of both these dimensions is provided by the creation and, much more to the point, the expansion of Benetton. All of those who have studied Benetton (e.g. Jones, 1987; Mahon, 1987; Mitter, 1991; Wark, 1991) seem to stress three inter-connected characteristics:

1   its awareness of trends in 'pop consumption' and its emphasis on quality and design;
2   its ability to respond to fluctuations in demand by producing in small batches, by utilizing state-of-the-art technology, for instance, to dye products at the last moment, and by developing a sophisticated computer network to integrate all stages of production, distribution and retailing;
3   its reliance on a plethora of small subcontractors, many of which have relatively few employees.

The system Benetton has developed offloads the less skilled and more variable parts of production onto these small subcontractors. This has the advantage of securing significant reductions in the cost of labour and minimizing the company's exposure to risk, while maintaining effective control of the entire process of production. But if this was all, though Benetton might well be judged to be more efficient than other subcontracting garment producers, it would not be radically dissimilar to them.

What *is* remarkable about Benetton is the way that it encompasses production, distribution, retailing and, in effect, consumption as well, and that it does so by combining a particular arrangement of production with a particular form of retailing. What is interesting about Benetton's production is that it relies on the utilization of advanced technology in its central operations while using more traditional methods of manufacture – including the employment of homeworkers – in its peripheral operations. What is interesting about the Benetton retailing format is that the majority of outlets are not owned by Benetton but run under what amounts to a form of franchising, and, although the franchise-holders pay no royalty to Benetton, they are obliged to sell only Benetton brand names and to conform strictly to Benetton's specifications on shop design and layout and the way the business is organized. And, again, what is distinctive about the enterprise as a whole is that:

> Benetton only produces goods in response to direct orders (that is from Benetton's retailers – both franchises and those that are directly owned) and both the pattern of sales and re-orders are continuously fed back to Ponzano headquarters by a private and exclusive information-technology network.
>
> (Phizacklea, 1990, p. 15)

Therefore, in assessing Benetton we might choose to stress, on the one hand, its character as a manufacturer and distributor of fashions – where cottage industry at the labour-intensive stage of production is linked to capital intensity in dyeing, packaging, warehousing and so on. On the other hand, we might emphasize the ingenuity with which Benetton has made available relatively cheap designer wear, the way it has developed the strong set of images and associations which mark its products and shops and which attract its consumers, and the success that it has had in selling its ranges, creating a global market. According to Luciano Benetton, co-founder of the Benetton company, 'If you are going to a country for the first time, you need to have a well-known brand, something that young people, even if they have not travelled, recognize' ('Profile of Luciano Benetton', *The Times*, 7 December 1996). To possess, as the company does, a name that is known throughout the world involves much more than the promotion of the clothes themselves in some 7,000 shop windows – important though that is. It is the result of advertising a brand and an image, and – more to the point, perhaps – of the publicity that this advertising regularly attracts because of its often controversial nature.

To neglect either of these dimensions – manufacturing/distribution and marketing/retailing -is unwise because what truly marks out the company is the manner in which both these dimensions have been developed deliberately and simultaneously.

[. . .]

Bibliography

Auden, W. and Kronenberger, L. (1962) *The Viking Book of Aphorisms*, New York: Dorset.
Barthes, R. (1983) *The Fashion System*, New York: Hill and Wang.

Belussi, F. (1987) 'Benetton: Information Technology in Production and Distribution: A Case Study of the Innovative Potential of Traditional Sectors', Occasional Papers No. 25, Science Policy Research Unit, University of Sussex.

—— (1991) 'Benetton Italy: Beyond Fordism and Flexible Specialization. The Evolution of the Network Firm Model' in S. Mitter (ed.) pp. 73–91.

Bigg, A. (1973) 'The Evils of "Fashion" ' in Wills and Midgley (eds) pp. 35–46. First published 1893 in Nineteenth Century, Vol. 3, No. 3.

Blumer, H. (1969) 'Fashion: From Class Differentiation to Collective Selection', Sociological Quarterly 10: 275–91.

Braham, P. (1985) 'Marks and Spencer: A Technological Approach to Retailing' in E. Rhodes and D. Wield (eds) Implementing New Technologies, Oxford: Blackwell.

Coleridge, N. (1988) The Fashion Conspiracy, Oxford: Heinemann.

Corrigan, P. (1993) 'The Clothes-horse Rodeo; or, How the Sociology of Clothing and Fashion Throws its (w)Reiters', Theory, Culture and Society 10, 4: 143–55.

Craik, J. (1994) The Face of Fashion, London: Routledge.

Culler, J. (1976) Ferdinand De Saussure, Glasgow: Collins.

Davis, F. (1992) Fashion', Culture and Identity, Chicago: University of Chicago Press.

Foley, C. (1973) 'Consumer Fashion', in Wills and Midgley (eds) pp. 157–70.

Forty, A. (1986) Objects and Desire: Design and Society, 1750–1980, London: Thames and Hudson.

Frobel, F., Heinrichs, J. and Drey, O. (1980) The New International Division of Labour, Cambridge: Cambridge University Press.

Hochswender, W. (1991) 'Patterns', New York Times, 1 January.

Howard, R. (1990) 'Values Make the Company: An Interview with Robert Haas' (Chairman of Levi Strauss), Harvard Business Review, September-October.

Jones, T. (1987) 'Mr Fiorucci: 20 Years of Global Pollination', i-D 51 (September).

Lurie, A. (1981) The Language of Clothes, Oxford: Heinemann.

Leopold E. (1992) 'The Manufacture of the Fashion System' in J. Ash and E. Wilson (eds) Chic Thrills, London: Pandora Press.

Mahon, R. (1987) 'From Fordism to?: New Technology, Labour Markets and Unions', Economic and Industrial Democracy 8, 1: 5–60.

Meyerson, R. and Katz, E. (1973) 'The Natural History of Fads', in Wills and Midgley (eds) pp. 391–400.

Milbank, C. (1990) 'When Your Own Initials Are Not Enough', Avenue, October.

Mitter, S. (ed.) (1991) Computer-Aided Manufacturing and Women's Employment: The Clothing Industry in Four European Countries, London: Springer-Verlag.

Murray, R. (1988) 'Life after Henry (Ford)', Marxism Today, October: 8–13.

Phizacklea, A. (1990) Unpacking the Fashion Industry: Gender, Racism and Class in Production, London: Routledge.

Rees, G. (1973) St Michael: A History of Marks and Spencer, London: Pan.

Rhodes, E. (1992) A Review of Design, Principles and Practice, T264, Milton Keynes: Open University.

—— (1993) 'The Interaction of Markets and Supply: A Case Study of Textiles', in R, McCormick et al. (eds) Technology for Technology Education, Workingham: Addison-Wesley.

Roche, D. (1994) The Culture of Clothing: Dress and Fashion in the 'Ancien Régime', Cambridge: Cambridge University Press.

Shilling, C. (1997) 'The Body and Difference', in K. Woodward (ed.) Identity and Difference, London: Sage/Open University.

Simmel, G. (1973) 'Fashion', in Wills and Midgley (eds) pp. 171–91. First published 1904 in *International Quarterly* 10 (October).

Stead, K. (1991) 'Heists of Fashion', *Australian Magazine*, 22 June.

Wark, M. (1991) 'Fashioning the Future: Fashion, Clothing, and the Manufacturing of Post-Fordist Culture', *Cultural Studies* 5, 1: 61–76.

Wills, G. and Midgley, D. (eds) (1973) *Fashion Marketing*, London: Allen and Unwin.

Chapter 31

Tim Dant

CONSUMING OR LIVING WITH THINGS?/WEARING IT OUT

[. . .]

Consumption as sublation

WITHIN THE FIELD OF SOCIOLOGY, Colin Campbell's (1987) compelling account of consumerism as a cultural force that emerges at the level of ideas as much as economics has given way recently to more general accounts of consumption. Material culture in these accounts remains tied to consumption as an economic process of exchange that is surrounded by ideas, advertisements and meanings which are oriented to leading the imagination towards making a purchasing choice. Bocock (1993) provides a broad introduction to the topic while Lury (1996) explores the place of consumption in defining various social locations and identities. Slater (1997) explores the relationship of social theory to the field of consumption and Corrigan (1997) articulates the field of consumption as including objects, advertising, magazines, food and drink, tourism and the settings for consumption as being the body, the home and the department store. These writers comment on material culture but they adopt a view of consumer culture as incorporating material culture; the way that people interact with objects is largely shaped by the discourse, the circulation of signs and values about consumption.

A similar position is reached by Daniel Miller (1987) although his interest in consumption develops from Hegel's concept of 'objectification', via Marx, Munn and Simmel, into a perspective that draws on a range of human sciences including anthropology, economics and cultural studies. His theory of consumption centres on the recovery of objects from the alienated process of production:

> The authenticity of artefacts as culture derives, not from their relation-

ship to some historical style or manufacturing process – in other words, there is no truth or falsity immanent in them – but rather from their active participation in a process of social self creation in which they are directly constitutive of our understanding of ourselves and others. The key [criterion] for judging the utility of contemporary objects is the degree to which they may or may not be appropriated from the forces which created them, which are mainly, of necessity, alienating. This appropriation consists of the transmutation of goods, through consumption activities, into potentially inalienable culture.

(Miller 1987: 215)

This is a sophisticated response to the emphasis that Marx places on the alienating effect of objectification through the labour of capitalist production. Miller begins to provide a way of responding to the 'quantitative advance in the material forms' (1987: 214) of modern societies by recovering the Hegelian concept of 'sublation' (reabsorption) (Miller 1987: 12, 28) as a strategy for self-creation in the face of alienation. Whereas for Hegel sublation was a philosophical practice of consciousness, for Miller it is a praxis based in the practical activities that he associates with consumption. These practices of everyday consumption achieve this transformation of alienated commodities into inalienable culture by means that are not visible to a traditional academic approach to design or aesthetics. Two of these practices he discusses briefly as 'play' (1987: 93) and 'framing' (1987: 100).

While there is much that I wish to adopt from Miller's theory of consumption [, . . .] one of [my] aims . . . is to unhook the link between material culture and consumption. Strangely, Miller has moved away from looking at material culture as a set of practices of sublation towards treating consumption as the 'vanguard of history', claiming a role for consumption in shaping the global as well as the local social order. He argues that it is the discipline of economics that has traditionally emphasized the centrality of production and of capital as the basic dynamic forces in modern history and politics. His anthropological perspective replaces production with consumption by studying the role of the supermarket, retailing, the market and shopping in modern culture. Miller challenges 'myths' that equate consumption with homogenization, loss of sociality and authenticity arguing that it is an 'attempt by people to extract their own humanity through the use of consumption' (1995: 31) from the alienating institutions of modern society. In late modernity the political importance of the 'male' productive worker is replaced by the 'housewife' as consumption worker acting on behalf of the moral economy of the household. Miller sees purchase as a form of 'voting', not only for goods but also for the social systems that deliver those goods. Consumption involves choice and the operation of imagination. Consumers express their will through exercising choice, within the constraints of the options of goods and services available for sale. They also have to imagine the consequences of goods – in terms of use, functionality, style, identity, status and so on – before these are purchased. For Miller, consumers, acting as a series of individuals in a 'relatively autonomous and plural process of cultural self-construction', shape the social worlds in which they live because purchase is 'the point at which economic institutions have direct implications for humanity' (Miller 1995: 41).

This approach claims a particular status for the actions of people as consumers but does not necessarily allow for the more complex interactions between people and objects that constitute material culture without direct economic consequences. To treat the consumer as an agent of political power is to re-emphasize the sphere of economics, of exchange mediated by money, as well as to emphasize the coherence of self and the location of agency within the individual, acting on the basis of will.

In laying such emphasis on consumption as shopping Miller is restating the social significance of material culture as being primarily economic. By taking the housewife as the archetypal consumer, he is emphasizing the role of the individual in the attempt to wrest the experience of modernity from the alienation of social institutions – a new form of *homo oeconomicus*. But what he overlooks is the complexity of the relationship between individuals with the objects that they acquire which extends far beyond the operation of choice and imagination prior to purchase. He also has little to say about the emergence of such relationships from social contexts – the learning of what Bourdieu and Featherstone treat as taste and lifestyles. There seems to be a drift from philosophical subtlety of his earlier writing (Miller 1987) and from the powerful evocation of material culture in constructing social lives in earlier empirical work (Miller 1988). In his most recent work, it is unequivocally shopping as a routine cultural activity that is centre stage rather than consumption as a developing relation between human beings and material objects (Miller, 1998).

Like Miller, Grant McCracken (1990) is an anthropologist who writes with an interdisciplinary audience in mind. He adopts a cultural studies orientation that leads to a view of consumption as a social process of distributing meaning – a much broader perspective than Miller's increasing focus on shopping. McCracken describes two stages in this process; advertising and fashion transfer meanings ('ideas and values': 1990: 76) from the world to goods, rituals transfer the meanings from goods to people. The rituals are those of exchange, possession, grooming and divestment (1990: 83–7). The work invested in these rituals is *producing* the thing in a living relationship with a person, after the choice and purchase of economic consumption that Miller focuses on. Divestment grooming for example is the work of cleaning and repairing and redecorating that is undertaken before the sale of an object such as a car, caravan or house or after its purchase from a previous owner.

The exchange of goods is central to economic process; goods that are produced must be bought but it does not matter what happens to the goods after purchase; they may be misused, unused or abandoned. Much of the social scientific analysis of consumption draws attention to consumption as buying in which the desire for goods is stimulated or managed through discursive processes that attribute social values and meanings. This economic model of consumption emphasizes the individual as using information and their imagination to make choices, which may affect their sense of identity and the perception of their social location. It is the success of selling ideas about things that are for sale that has led to the debate about consumption – the development of the department store, the shopping arcade and the shopping experience (Shields 1992; Miller 1998) as well as the impact of advertising (Leiss 1978; Haug 1986; Jhally 1987; McCracken 1990; Ewen and Ewen 1992; Corrigan 1997). These processes are of sociological importance and they are part of the context in which material culture emerges. But to focus too closely on them is to be pulled towards the economic relationship with objects and assume that the seller's ideas about objects are what constitutes their meaning or how human beings interact with them.

Social life beyond consumption

Many of those who discuss consumption emphasize that it does not end with purchase: 'What happens to material objects once they have left the retail outlet and reached the hands of the final purchasers is part of the consumption process' (Douglas and Isherwood 1979: 36). In his early work, Miller also makes an argument for the understanding of consumption as

> the start of a long and complex process, by which the consumer works upon the object purchased and recontextualizes it, until it is often no longer recognizable as having any relation to the world of the abstract and becomes its very negation, something which could be neither bought nor given.
>
> (Miller 1987: 190)

Some work on consumption has moved attention away from the act of purchase or acquisition as consumption to consider its consequences and the social contexts in which they might be felt. Alan Warde (1994) criticizes theorists of late modernity/ postmodernity (Beck, Giddens and Bauman) for treating the practices of consumption as the modal form of social action in the current epoch that affirm individual identity. He argues that the selection of an item for consumption can be careless and of no significance for identity. It might of course be chosen with care and consideration for its identity-forming consequences but then it will be chosen with reference to a social context of advice and help (peer example, consultation with family and friends, as well as advertisements and inducements to buy). Colin Campbell (1996) follows a similar line by pointing to the confusion between the meanings ascribed to objects and the meanings of actions of consuming those objects. He argues that clothing choices, for example, are more likely to be made to fit in with an existing lifestyle or sense of identity than to construct one. Silverstone et al. (1992) suggest that the consumption of information and communication technology into the home has to be understood in terms of the moral economy of the household. They theorize four processes (appropriation, objectification, incorporation and conversion) by which things such as video recorders and home computers are fitted into the value system of a household. Their argument moves the discussion of consumption on from considering commodities with sign (exchange) value and a functional (use) value to address the context of values and existing practices into which the object has to fit and the consequences that its acquisition and continuing use have for the maintenance or modification of that context.

These approaches attempt to explicate the non-economic features of consumption and avoid reductions to the point of sale and the identity of the individual consumer. They shift focus to the context in which an object is to be located and describe consumption in terms of the use of the thing in that context. Commodities do not have a predefined use-value, and even the sign value of an object is not determined by the discourse of advertising. Its use is variable and negotiable (for example in terms of ostentation, individual identity and leisure practices) and its precise form varies according to specific context. Michel de Certeau (1984: xii) has argued that consumption needs to be seen as a production in that as consumers appropriate goods, information or services there is a 'making' through their particular ways of using or making sense of them. He draws attention to the 'ways of using' objects, representations and rituals which adapt them from the intentions which might have been behind previous productions. He argues that everyday practices such as walking, cooking, dwelling and so on require an individual to construct a particular act from a set of possible actions, much as a speaker constructs an utterance from all the possibilities in a language. His perspective

> assumes that . . . users make (*bricolent*) innumerable and infinitesimal transformations of and within the dominant cultural economy in order to adapt it to their own interests and their own rules.
>
> (de Certeau 1984: xiii–xiv)

For de Certeau, far from being a given set of responses, consumption is an 'anti-discipline', a set of 'procedures and ruses' by which people appropriate culture, including material culture, to fit it into their own lives. While not a key feature of his analysis, Bourdieu (1984: 100) also writes of the 'labour of appropriation' and of the 'labour of identification and decoding' involved in consuming cultural products with an aesthetic dimension such as music, literature or a hairstyle. The work of learning what to consume by which 'the consumer helps to produce the product he consumes' is not for Bourdieu, however, a characteristic of consumption in general, or even especially of material objects.

Living with things

Theories of consumption put the emphasis on the exchange of goods and the media representations of them rather than on their uses and the ways that material objects are lived with. Consumption is about both goods and services being offered for purchase and then being purchased. The commodity is clean, new, often packaged, ready for use but not in use. It is amenable to discursive construction through advertisements, news items or sales pitch. The process of consumption as buying in late modernity occurs in what Leiss (1978) calls a 'high-intensity market' in which '[c]ommodities are not straightforward "objects" but are rather progressively more unstable, temporary collections of objective and imputed characteristics – that is, highly complex material-symbolic entities' (Leiss 1978: 92).

But living with objects extends much further than this 'high-intensity market' and in many ways continues much as it has done in earlier social forms. Material objects are appropriated into social lives with a variety of non-economic effects; they are used and lived with. Just think of the vast number of items in most of our homes that have considerable use-value to us but have no exchange-value – toothbrushes, fitted carpets, old magazines, crockery, out of fashion clothes, furniture, linen. All of these things have been personalized through use rather than through the discourse of advertisement. The age of these things and the very fact of their having been used may make them unattractive to others but does not mean that for us they are no longer useful. Some of these things are on the way to becoming rubbish when the next clearout comes. Some may have a residual value in an exchange circuit that is not part of the high intensity market – the jumble sale or car boot sale. Other household items that slip from the useful to the useless status will be thrown away, perhaps to be recycled (newspapers, bottles, cans). Some things will be 'recovered' from their status as rubbish to regain value and re-enter the cycle of exchange (Thompson 1979).

I have argued that consumption is a restricted way of understanding how material culture shapes and reflects social forms and processes. It has raised a number of interesting themes for the analysis of objects in material culture:

- as signs of status and identity (Veblen, Bourdieu)
- as vehicles of meaning and equivalence within and between different cultures (Appadurai, Sahlins, Douglas and Isherwood, Baudrillard)
- as bearers of aesthetic value (Simmel, Baudrillard, Featherstone)
- as components of ritual (Douglas and Isherwood, McCracken)
- as indicators of lifestyle and identity (Featherstone, Dittmar, Lunt and Livingstone)
- as knowledge and ideas (Appadurai, Campbell)
- as potentially inalienable (Miller)
- objects as the focus of discourse, both institutional and local, about their value (Leiss, McCracken, Jhally, Ewen and Ewen)

. . . I shall argue for an eclectic approach that brings material objects into the foreground of modern social life. One key element of this that will recur . . . is the idea that humans interact with objects, sometimes as if they are human, sometimes because through them we can interact with other humans and sometimes because they reflect back something of who we think we are. I shall argue that material culture involves taking on cultural practices in relation to material objects which define the uses and the values of those objects in everyday life. Their importance is not reducible to their political effects or to economic calculations but emerges through grasping the way that objects are fitted into ways of living.

[. . .]

Material surfaces

The discussions of clothes and fashion considered so far have been macro-social in that ideas of what is appropriate to wear derive from values that are sustained through cultural dissemination, through cultural groups, through the accepted meanings of clothes and through the fashion system including images. Peter Corrigan (1994) has looked at a more intimate economy of clothing – people's wardrobes. He found that between a quarter and a third of items were 'gifts' – some bought, others cast-offs, some had been borrowed without permission. This very small study reminds us that clothes are often acquired, chosen and worn through a variety of social processes that are on the margins of anything approaching a fashion system. Corrigan writes of a 'familial-sartorial world-view' (1994: 443) that refers to the non-cash, non-public, informal economy that determines what many of us actually wear. Within the family, in peer groups and among friends, ideas about what is appropriate clothing are passed on, criticized, refused and revised. These ideas moderate the influence of culture-wide forms of mediation – magazines, news-papers, television, film – and of style leaders – actors, singers, models, designers and so on. This informal approach to wearing clothes is not anti-fashion (as Baudril-lard points out, 'fashion makes the refusal of fashion into a fashion feature – blue-jeans are an historical example of this': 1993a: 98) and will take place within some established codes of appropriateness of different clothes for gender, occasion and activities. The everyday response to the clothes is oriented to what they look like rather than what they look like in a photograph, how they feel rather than how they are described, how others respond to them not as abstract indicators but as particu-lar clothes on a particular person's body and how the garment ages. In other words, how clothes are when they are being worn out.

Blue jeans are something of a conundrum because while they clearly are part of fashion in that they constitute a recognizable style of clothing, at the same time they express an ambivalence to fashion. They have remained a style of clothing that makes a fashion statement for 50 years but have never the less remained available for many different meanings to be attributed to them – as well as being regularly reintroduced as a 'classic' form of clothing. These features of jeans as fashion have often been commented on (Fiske 1989: 1–21; Davis 1992: 108; Fine and Leopold 1993: 140; R.R. Wilson 1995: 98) and some commentators have given direct attention to jeans as a fashion classic with a remarkable design history (Sudjic 1985; Cuomo 1989; Rica-Lévy 1989; Scheuring 1989; Finlayson 1990). But I wish to argue that there is something in the nature of the material form of the garment that makes jeans available for this particular fashion history and ambivalence of meaning.

Denim jeans threatened to break with the tranquil order of modern life when they moved from rural work clothes to become an emblem of urban youth reacting to authority.[1] These meanings became attached to the garment, according to the commentators, as they girded the loins of James Dean and Marlon Brando in films of the 1950s (Scheuring 1989: 227). Jeans went against the grain of the dominant clothes culture of western modernity and reversed many established clothing signi-fiers. They were made of cotton (vegetable) instead of wool (animal); fixed in shape instead of tailored; had visible seams but no pressed creases; revealed the form of the body rather than covering it. This can be summed up as a set of reversals of the material features of the tailored lounge suit (see Wright 1996). The tailored suit presents fineness of material, cloth which is smooth, consistent and restrained in colour but hangs from the body, seams which are invisibly stitched, buttons which blend in colour even when they are decorative. In contrast with the formality of the tailored suit, jeans are 'casual' or 'leisure' wear. But they are also 'workwear' in so far as that was how they originated – so the oft-repeated story of origins goes – and continue to be workwear for many people, both in paid work and private domestic work. Jeans are made from hardwearing cloth that is resistant to ripping when stressed through bending and stretching, many seams are double stitched and there are 'strengthening' rivets at key points. These are material indicators of the appropriateness of jeans for activities that will put the clothing under stress – using the body for lifting, pulling, carrying heavy objects, dealing with dirty or potentially damaging materials. They are of course no more appropriate for these tasks than overalls, work trousers and dungarees, all of which have become 'fashion' garments for periods of time. The difference is that jeans are made from denim and are cut in a distinctive way.

As leisure wear for men, jeans have replaced a range of trouser styles that retained a much closer affinity with the dark lounge suit:

- slacks – lighter in colour and material than the lounge suit but retaining the crease and the fineness of material and cut
- tweeds – a rougher, aristocratic form of the worsted suit, appropriate for the countryside, shooting, fishing, walking
- flannels – the soft light woollen version of suit trousers, used for sports like cricket and golf
- twills – the diagonal wool weave that tolerated the knee bending of horse riding.

The tweed 'sports' jacket or blue blazer together with slacks or flannels provided the ideal leisure wear for the white, western classes who could afford clothes purchased for leisure. Poorer classes traditionally wore third best clothes, originally bought to fit into a cycle of best, everyday work clothes and weekend clothes. In postwar USA the khaki cotton twill chinos, white T-shirts and leather 'bomber' jackets of ex-service personnel provided the model for leisure wear.

Perhaps the most powerful cultural feature of jeans as clothing objects is that they are worn by both sexes. The wearing of jeans by women signals their release from the gendered clothing of formal dress. Trousers became acceptable for women first of all in sporting and leisure situations (there is a long tradition of women wearing trousers or breeches for riding). Although designed for men (work trousers, front fly), jeans became an acceptable substitute for slacks and other leisure trousers (capri pants, pedal pushers) that women wore in the USA in the 1950s. These cotton, close fitting trousers often coded the gender of the appropriate wearer with a zip located at the side or the back with a minimal placket or overlap. Although masculinizing with their front flies, jeans became an acceptable substitute for other leisure trousers for women and they were possibly the first unisex garment. Jeans came from the same pattern, the same pile, in the same shop,[2] whereas suit jackets and riding breeches were structurally the same but tailored to distinguish the sex of the wearer. In the 1950s and early 1960s, jeans on women would have been regarded as a possible sign of lesbianism, along with short hair and no make-up.

In wearing jeans for leisure there is a parodic form of conspicuous consumption. For the office worker, wearing jeans to the cinema, the coffee bar, the pub or just for lounging, there is a display that the wearer is not working. There is a display of 'pecuniary strength', as Veblen (1953[1899]) puts it, in being able to purchase jeans just for leisure, but it is parodic of the display by the wealthy of their continuous leisure with the elite hallmarks of tailoring and quality cloth because jeans are workwear. Jeans are democratic rather than elite. Each pair is mass produced and cut the same, regardless of the shape of the body they cover, and all are made from the same, basic quality cloth in exactly the same colour – blue, the colour of the blue collared industrial worker, working with metals and machines.

Of course the fashion system has produced designer jeans with labels that signify degrees of pecuniary strength and the form of jeans has varied with fashion (flares, bell bottoms, hipsters, baggies etc.) as has the colour (black, white, stonewash etc.). But the 'authentic' or 'original' form and colour has remained dominant with its visible material features: dark blue colour; brass rivets; orange stitching; double seams on inside leg, back pockets, flies placket, crotch and back seam; through-stitched hem; belt loops; ticket pocket and the 'yoke seam' that gives the characteristic shape between hips and waist. This classic form also includes brand name indicators visible on the outside: stitching on the back pocket; 'leather' label on the outside of the waistband; tags inserted into seams. Jeans have always asserted their commodified, mass manufactured form by being self-advertising.

Distinctive and visible seams have been a constant features of jeans in all variants. With the exception of the outside leg seam, the interlocked joins of the main structural seams (inside leg, back, yoke) are strong but bulky, emphasized by the orange thread of double, parallel stitches. The visual effect of the seams is to dissect the form of the body, revealing it as made up of parts (legs) that are joined at the top (crotch, flies, back seam) and merge into a unity (the waistband). This material feature of jeans presents the body as a fetishized object, chopped up ready for consumption like the images of women in soft porn when clothing is used to divide parts of bodies – belt and garters, bra straps, shoe straps, stocking tops, half removed clothing. The cutting of the body by the seams of the jeans even presents the sexual parts. The buttocks are separated by the back seam, their cleavage is reflected in the yoke seam (and the Levi's pocket logo). The patch pockets, like a brassière, mark and emphasize the presence of buttock shapes. The flies, in true pornographic style, both hide and represent the sexual parts with a single seam on the opening edge and double seam parallel on the trouser front, both picked out with surface stitching in orange to create a six-inch long tube, running vertically from crotch towards the navel, which is both a flap and a gap in the material.

If the seams emphasize the form of the body underneath, this form is re-emphasized by the material of the denim. The cotton twill material does not 'hang' as woollen fabrics or thinner cotton weaves do. Unlike close fitting garments like tights, hose or stockings that fit with the form underneath, the cut and material of the jeans means they are stretched against the skin, moving against it, as the body moves.[3] The material takes up some of the shapes of the particular body that is wearing it. Knees, buttocks, testicles, labia, hips, thighs, all stretch the material, moulding it in a way that doesn't fall out when the pressure is released. The stiffness of the material gathers in creases which also become impressed in the material – beside and behind the knees, at the crotch, radiating from the top of the legs, under the buttocks. The twill weave, involving three directions (up, down and diagonal) retains distortions impressed upon it and even 'remembers' them after washing and ironing.

The regular process of washing actually reinforces this reflection of the body underneath on the surface of the denim. Denim is usually a mixture of white and blue dyed cotton yarns and when new, the outer surface is mainly dark blue, the inner surface white, but the colour is not smooth and continuous. As the jeans are worn and washed, their colour fades. The effect is variegated according to the thickness of the material and the creasing. Where the body pushes at the surface, knees and buttocks especially, it fades most. The bottoms of creases remain bluer and the tops fade most so that those features of the jeans that they take up as shape are re-emphasized as colour. The effect of fading is to re-emphasize the impact of the form of the body on the surface of the jeans like shading on a pencil drawing; the colour is darkest on those points furthest away from a viewer and bodily shape is picked out in a 'relief' effect in which the closer surface is lighter in colour. As the material wears out, the body may begin to represent itself, exposed through tears and damage to the fabric. As a unisex garment, jeans reflect the body and sex of the wearer while at the same time neutralizing gender distinction through form, material, colour or decoration.

The ambivalence of blue jeans is that they are all, more or less, the same cut and colour, but each pair becomes different when they are used. They take on their identity through being worn and washed and worn; it is the identity of the wearer, not of the designer or even the manufacturer. The form of the garment has very little to say for itself, which is precisely why manufacturers have such an aggressive branding and advertising strategy.[4] The form of jeans does not carry strong connotations of class, sex or even nationality.

Conclusions

Wearing clothes is social in that what people wear is treated by those around them as being some sort of indicator of who they are. The cultural system by which the values of clothing and people are connected is generally agreed to be 'fashion'. This is a system of relationships between ideas and values, material things (clothes) and people – who wear clothes out into society. The fashion system is in constant flux in modernity and it cannot be pinned down to one system; there are competing influences and ideas that have an influence but are not precisely represented in fashion. The fashion system does not represent in any direct way social relationships of status, gender, occupation or allegiance, but it does allow for these relationships to be reflected through the changing orientation to clothes. There are also competing fashion systems within the cultural field of clothing; second hand clothes, street styles, family and peer groups, that cut across the production/consumption system of mass manufactured clothing.

Following Barthes we found that the fashion system is not accessible as a linguistic code or as a material system but only through a combination of both. Material discourse is the term I have used to point to the connection between language, material and cultural values. Hollander (1993) is also persuasive (as are many books on clothing and fashion by their example) that images are as important as words and ideas in contributing to the material discourse of fashion.

What the discussion of fashion often avoids are the characteristics of clothes as they are worn. By discussing how the materiality of blue jeans works, I have tried to show how their status as clothes is not determined simply by the fashion system or any language of clothes but emerges from the interaction between the wearer and the garment. Wearing clothes is a material experience; they are available to be looked at on other people and to be worn by ourselves. Clothes are given meaning in the fashion system by the aesthetics of design, the mechanics of production and the inducements of consumption. But the engagement of the wearer with the garment such that they become part of each other, also gives clothes meaning. Jeans more than many garments have a rigid form as fashion but become a vehicle for individual identity through their material malleability.

Notes

1   The name 'jeans' derives from the material, 'jean fustian', the tough twill weave, cotton fabric used for workwear. Jean seems to be a transformation of Gene, for Genoa, indicating the original location of the material or its manufacture. Fustian is a hard wearing fabric in which cotton is mixed with flax or wool. The plural form, 'jeans', refers to the garment, which like the word 'trousers' is pluralized presumably to indicate its two legs. The word denim also derives from a place, 'serge de Nîmes'. Serge is a woollen fabric of twill weave; denim is a cotton variant.

2   Manufacturers have in recent years diversified the form of jeans so that different body shapes, including women's, can look similar when wearing jeans.

3   Umberto Eco writes entertainingly of the sensations of wearing jeans, of having 'a sheath around the lower half of my body' so that from waist to ankles his body was 'organically identified with the clothing' (Eco 1987: 192). The encasement within the clothing affects the way he moves; walking, turning, sitting, hurrying are all changed. In turn this affects his demeanour and the constraint on his body led to constraint in his behaviour. But the transformation did not stop there: 'A garment that squeezes the testicles makes a man think differently' (Eco 1987: 193).

4   In doing so, the sellers of jeans will reassert distinctions of taste, gender and sexuality. Stuart and Elizabeth Ewen are repulsed by a 1980s advertisement on a bus for Gloria Vanderbilt jeans that shows

> an assembly line of female backsides, pressed emphatically into their designer jeans. . . . These buttocks greet us from a rakish angle, a posture widely cultivated in women from time to time, in place to place. What was termed in nineteenth century America the *Grecian bend*. The bustle. Foot-bound women of China. Corsets. High heels. Hobble skirts. Here it is, women hobbled in the finery of freedom.
>
> (Ewen and Ewen 1992: 75)

Bibliography

Baudrillard, J. (1993) *Symbolic Exchange and Death*, London: Sage.

Bocock, R. (1993) *Consumption*, London: Routledge.

Bourdieu, P. (1984) *Distinction: A Social Critique of the Judgement of Taste*, London: Routledge.

Campbell, C. (1987) *The Romantic Ethic and the Spirit of Modern Consumerism*, Oxford: Blackwell.

—— (1996) 'The Meaning of Objects and The Meaning of Actions: A Critical Note on The Sociology of Consumption and Theories of Clothing', *Journal of Material Culture* 1, 1: 93–105.

Corrigan, P. (1994) 'Three Dimensions of the Clothing Object', in S. H. Riggins (ed.) *The Socialness of Things: Essays on the Socio-Semiotics of Objects*, New York: Mouton.

—— (1997) *The Sociology of Consumption: An Introduction*, London: Sage.

Cuomo, D. (1989) 'De l'Europe en Amerique et retour: le Voyage du Jeans', in *Blu Blue-Jeans: Il Blu Popolare*, Milan: Electa.

Davis, F. (1992) *Fashion, Culture and Identity*, Chicago: University of Chicago Press.

de Certeau, M. (1984) *The Practice of Everyday Life*, Berkeley: University of California Press.

Douglas, M. and Isherwood, B. (1979) *The World of Goods: Towards an Anthropology of Consumption*, London: Routledge.

Eco, U. (1987) 'Lumbar Thought', in *Travels in Hyperreality*, London: Picador.

Ewen, S. and Ewen, E. (1992) *Channels of Desire: Mass Images and the Shaping of American Consciousness*, Minneapolis: University of Minnesota Press.

Fine, B. and Leopold, E. (1993) *The World of Consumption*, London: Routledge.

Finlayson, I. (1990) *Denim: An American Legend*, Norwich: Park Sutton.

Fiske, J. (1989) *Understanding Popular Culture*, London: Unwin Hyman.

Haug, W. F. (1986) *Critique of Commodity Aesthetics: Appearance, Sexuality and Advertising in Capitalist Society*, Cambridge: Polity Press.

Hollander, A. (1993) *Seeing Through Clothes*, Berkeley: University of California Press.

Jhally, S. (1987) *The Codes of Advertising*, London: Routledge.

Leiss, W. (1978) *The Limits to Satisfaction*, London: Marion Boyars.

Lury, C. (1996) *Consumer Culture*, Cambridge: Polity.

McCracken, G. (1990) *Culture and Consumption: New Approaches to the Symbolic Character of Consumer Goods and Activities*, Bloomington: Indiana University Press.

Miller, D. (1987) *Material Culture and Mass Consumption*, Oxford: Blackwell.

—— (1988) 'Appropriating the State on the Council Estate', *Man* 23: 353–72.

—— (1995) 'Consumption as the Vanguard of History', in D. Miller (ed.) *Acknowledging Consumption: A Review of New Studies*, London: Routledge.

—— (1998) *A Theory of Shopping*, Cambridge: Polity Press.

Rica-Lévy, P. (1989) '1567–1967: du Bleu de Genes au bleu-jeans', in *Blu Blue-Jeans: il Blue Popolare*, Milan: Electa.

Scheuring, D. (1989) 'Heavy-Duty Denim: "Quality Never Dates" ' in A. McRobbie (ed.) *Zoot Suits and Second-Hand Dresses: An Anthology of Fashion and Music*, London: Routledge.

Shields, R. (ed.) (1992) *Lifestyle Shopping: The Subject of Consumption*, London: Routledge.

Silverstone, R. *et al.* (1992) 'Information and Communication Technologies and The Moral Economy of the Household', in R. Silverstone and E. Hirsch (eds) *Consuming Technologies: Media and Information in Domestic Spaces*, London: Routledge.

Slater, D. (1997) *Consumer Culture and Modernity*, Cambridge: Polity Press.

Sudjic, D. (1985) *Cult Objects: The Complete Guide to Having It All*, London: Paladin.

Thompson, M. (1979) *Rubbish Theory: The Creation and Destruction of Value*, Oxford: Oxford University Press.

Veblen, T. ([1953] 1899) *The Theory of the Leisure Class*, New York: Mentor.

Warde, A. (1994) 'Consumption, Identity-Formation and Uncertainty', *Sociology* 28, 4: 877–98.

Wilson, R. R. (1995) 'Cyber(body) Parts: Prosthetic Consciousness', in M. Featherstone and R. Burroughs, (eds) *Cyberspace/Cyberbodies/Cyberpunk: Cultures of Technological Embodiment*, London: Sage.

Wright, L. (1996) 'The Suit: A Common Bond or a Defeated Purpose?', in P. Kirkham, (ed.) *The Gendered Object*, Manchester: Manchester University Press.

PART NINE

Modern fashion

THERE IS A SENSE in which the phrase 'modern fashion' is true, or tau-
tologous – the simple and redundant repetition of meaning using different words.
This is the colloquial sense in which both 'modern' and 'fashion' mean 'of the present
moment' or 'up to date'. The tautology or repetition arises because, in these senses, if
something is fashion then it is also modern. However, there are other, more technical,
senses of the word 'modern' and these senses must be examined here in order to put
the following readings into context. 'Modern' may refer to either a period of time or to
a characteristic outlook or set of ideas. Consequently, following Boyne and Rattansi
(1990), 'modernity' will be used to refer to a period of time and 'modernism' will be
used to refer to a characteristic outlook or set of ideas. This introduction will briefly
explain modernity and modernism before pointing out two interesting problems that
the latter raises for fashion and fashion theory.

There is broad consensus as to when modernity was. Marshall Berman identifies the sixteenth century as the beginning of the first phase of modernity, when
Europeans are just starting to experience modern life and 'hardly know what has hit
them' (Berman 1983: 16–17). At this time, the social and economic structures that
made up feudalism are being replaced by early capitalist structures. Towns and
cities, along with transport and other communication systems and increasingly
industrialised modes of production and consumption, are beginning to develop; old
social classes (serfs and landowners) are being replaced by new social classes
(proletarians and factory owners) and entirely new personal, social and cultural
relations are being established. Berman's second phase begins with the 'revolutionary wave' of the 1790s, during which people in Europe are starting to understand
and make sense of their new personal, social and political lives but can still recall
pre-capitalist ways of existing (ibid.: 17). The third phase takes in the whole of
the twentieth century when modernisation spreads throughout the world and a

'developing world culture of modernism achieves spectacular triumphs in art and thought' (ibid.).

This account of when modernity began chimes with many accounts of when fashion began. Gail Faurschou explicitly identifies the beginnings of fashion with the rise of industrial capitalist economies:

> It is, of course, only with the rise of industrial capitalism and the market economy that fashion becomes a commodity produced for the realisation of economic exchange value in the division of labour and the separation of production and consumption.
>
> (Faurschou 1988: 80)

Faurschou is providing the links between modernity, fashion and production and consumption as they are organised under capitalist economic conditions, and the section should probably be read with Part Eight in mind. Similarly, in Chapter 1, Elizabeth Wilson also connects the beginning of fashion with the beginning of modern society. Fashion is first seen when European feudal economies begin to be replaced by a capitalist economy, and when European class structures develop from the old land-owner/serf hierarchies into capitalist/worker hierarchies. Wilson also suggests that the society of the Renaissance was modern in that it possessed both newly emerging middle classes and class competition between those middle classes and the existing feudal aristocratic landowning classes. Fashion was used by the middle classes to compete with the old landowning classes and to communicate their participation in the dynamism of the modern world (1985: 60).

There is also some consensus as to what modernism was. Lunn (1985) and Boyne and Rattansi (1990), for example, identify four key features that may be used to distinguish modern from pre-modern thinking. The first is 'aesthetic self-reflexiveness' (Boyne and Rattansi 1990: 6). This refers to the ways in which artists began to use the media they were working in to ask questions about those media, and Greenberg says that it is the defining characteristic of modernism (Greenberg 1982: 6). Giddens also identifies reflexivity as a central modernist idea when he says that the monitoring of the self is a project to be accomplished by modern people (1991: 75). The second feature is 'montage' (Boyne and Rattansi 1990: 7). Montage is a technique in which elements from often unrelated sources are combined to construct a piece of work. Breward and Evans suggest that the use of montage in early modernist cinema is a way of representing and communicating the 'fractured and dislocating experience of modernity' (2005: 3). The third feature consists in the use of 'paradox, ambiguity and uncertainty' (ibid.); either the absence of a clear meaning or the presence of contradictory meanings. Finally, the fourth feature involves the loss or absence of a single unified and integrated human subject; the presence in the individual of conflict or multiple personalities. These features are the aesthetic values, the set of ideas or 'rules', that have been held to characterise modernism.

However, it is possible to argue that there is less consensus on what modernism amounts to when it is 'embodied' in fashion. While Elizabeth Wilson is surely correct to say that '[m]odernity does seem useful as a way of indicating the restless desire for change characteristic of cultural life in industrial capitalism, the desire for the new that fashion expresses so well' (1985: 63), there are two aspects of modernism that would appear to limit that usefulness and cast doubt on the 'fit' between modernism and fashion. The first is to be found in Kurt Back's (1985) essay 'Modernism and Fashion'. Like Greenberg and Giddens, Back presents a version of aesthetic self-reflexivity as a defining characteristic of modernism and he suggests that the 'conscious display of the label or of the seam' is an example of such reflexivity because it is an example of the fashion item announcing itself as a fashion item. (Back's presentation of this point may be compared with Tim Dant's treatment of 'distinctive and visible seams' in the extract from his *Material Culture in the Social World* – see Chapter 32.) The conspicuously displayed label or seam 'are simply saying "This is clothing" ', in much the same way as visible brushstrokes and fingerprints in an oil painting say 'This is a painting'. Back's account limits the usefulness of these ideas as an account of modern fashion insofar as aesthetic self-reflexivity is also held to be a prominent feature of post-modern fashion. Various designers have been identified as essentially post-modern designers, and some of them are identified as such because their work involves the use of displayed seams. Ann Demeulemeester and Martin Margiela, for example, are regularly celebrated as post-modern designers and yet their work is known for the use of exposing the 'workings' of clothes through the conscious and deliberate exposure of seams.

And the second is to be found in Adolf Loos's ([1908] 1997) essay 'Ornament and Crime'. In this essay Loos argues, against the excesses of Art Nouveau, that ornament and decoration in art, design and everyday objects are to be avoided because they cause objects to go quickly out of style. The problem here is that Loos was a modernist architect and one of the leaders of the modernist movement: one of the leading theorists of modernism is advocating either the end, or the impossibility, of modern fashion. To advocate an end to unnecessary decoration and ornament in design is surely to advocate the end of much of what fashion is about. And to argue that an item's going out of style is to be avoided is effectively to argue that fashion itself is to be avoided. Loos's essay thus questions the 'fit' between the central ideas or 'rules' of modernism and fashion in such a way that one is obliged to doubt whether fashion is or can be fully modern.

Back's and Loos's essays may be taken as a warning against adopting or trying to construct too 'tidy' or too consistent a model of modernity and modernism. They may also remind us of the third and fourth features of modernism that have already been noted. These were the ideas that modernism involved paradox and uncertainty and that the single, unified subject has been lost or abandoned in modernity. It is certainly a paradox that fashion (as a series of stylistic and decorative changes, something that many have considered a profoundly modern phenomenon) may also be considered profoundly unmodern precisely because it *is* a series of stylistic and decorative changes. And it is paradoxical that the same formal feature (the display of seams, the 'workings' of the piece) is claimed by different theorists as both an essentially modern and an essentially post-modern characteristic. As such, therefore, the idea that modernism is a consistent, unified and stable entity must be questioned. And, appropriately enough, such questioning, in the form of self-criticism, is also one of the central features of modernism identified above. Fashion's place in modernity is thus both completely assured (because it exists as a series of stylistic changes and reflexive self-referencing, for example) and always questionable (for exactly the same reasons). There is probably no better indicator of modern/postmodern undecidability than the way in which the same reason supports entirely contradictory conclusions.

Ulrich Lehmann's (2000) account of modernism and fashion is complex and not an introductory text. The work is in fact a study of various modernist theorists' accounts of fashion, and Lehmann looks at Baudelaire, Mallarmé and Simmel while concentrating on Walter Benjamin's enormous and unfinished *Passagenwerk*, or Arcades Project, which was intended as an account of philosophy and fashion. In the extract that is included here, Lehmann provides a definition or account of modern fashion: fashion represents the totality of the historical process (2000: 201); it is that most elegant and ephemeral phenomenon that nevertheless indicates the most archaic and profound social and cultural rules (ibid.: 213). The central themes of the concept of the 'tiger's leap' are introduced in this extract, and Lehmann's account also refers to Marx's explanation of value and commodity fetishism and to Freud's explanation of the fetish object.

Richard Sennett presents a different aspect of modernity and fashion. He is interested in the ways in which modernity enables, or obliges, its inhabitants to take up new ways of appearing or being in public. The establishment and growth of towns and cities during the Industrial Revolution produced new spaces, different places to be, and they generated entirely new ways for people to relate to other people in those new and different places. It became possible for the individual to behave as an anonymous part of the crowd in the new cities that modernity generated, and fashion and clothing were part of these developments. And Elizabeth Wilson also notes the urban origins of fashion in capitalist modernity, pointing out that fashion articulates the unnaturalness of the new social arrangements that are made clear by and through everyday life in the city. In Wilson's account, fashion is especially modern; it is 'essential to the world of modernity' and fashion is the language that capitalism speaks.

Bibliography

Back, K. (1985) 'Modernism and Fashion: A Social Psychological Interpretation' in M. R. Solomon (ed.) *The Psychology of Fashion*, Lexington, Mass.: Lexington Books/D.C. Heath & Co.

Berman, M. (1983) *All That Is Solid Melts Into Air*, London: Verso.

Boyne, R. and Rattansi, A. (1990) *Postmodernism and Society*, London: Macmillan.

Breward, C. and Evans, C. (2005) *Fashion and Modernity*, Oxford: Berg.

Faurschou, G. (1988) 'Fashion and the Cultural Logic of Late Capitalism', in A Kroker and M. Kroker (eds) *Body Invaders: Sexuality and the Postmodern Condition*, Basingstoke: Macmillan.

Giddens, A. (1991) *Modernity and Self-Identity: Self and Society in the Late Modern Age*, Cambridge: Polity Press.

Greenberg, C. (1982) 'Modernist Painting', in F. Frascina and C. Harrison (eds) *Modern*

Art and Modernism: A Critical Anthology, London: Open University/Pane Chapman Publishing.

Lehmann, U. (2000) *Tigersprung: Fashion in Modernity,* Cambridge, Mass.: MIT Press.

Loos, A. (1997) *Ornament and Crime: Selected Essays,* Riverside, Calif.: Ariadne Press.

Lunn, E. (1985) *Marxism and Modernism,* London: Verso.

Sennett, R. (1988) *The Fall of Public Man,* London: Faber and Faber.

Wells, H. G. (1895) 'Of Conversation and the Anatomy of Fashion', in *Select Conversations With An Uncle Now Extinct,* London: John Lane.

Wilson, E. (1985) *Adorned in Dreams,* London: I. B. Tauris.

Wollen, P. (2003) 'The Concept of Fashion in The Arcades Project', *boundary 2,* 30, 1 (Spring): 131–42.

Chapter 32

Elizabeth Wilson

ADORNED IN DREAMS: INTRODUCTION

[. . .]

FASHION, IN FACT, ORIGINATES in the first crucible of this contradiction: in the early capitalist city. Fashion 'links beauty, success and the city'.[1] It was always urban (urbane), became metropolitan and is now cosmopolitan, boiling all national and regional difference down into the distilled moment of glassy sophistication. The urbanity of fashion masks all emotions, save that of triumph; the demeanour of the fashionable person must always be blasé – cool. Yet fashion does not negate emotion, it simply displaces it into the realm of aesthetics. It can be a way of intellectualizing visually about individual desires and social aspirations. It is in some sense inherently given to irony and paradox; a new fashion starts from rejection of the old and often an eager embracing of what was previously considered ugly; it therefore subtly undercuts its own assertion that the latest thing is somehow the final solution to the problem of how to look. But its relativism is not as senseless as at first appears; it is a statement of the unnaturalness of human social arrangements – which becomes very clear in the life of the city; it is a statement of the arbitrary nature of convention and even of morality; and in daring to be ugly it perhaps at the same time attempts to transcend the vulnerability of the body and its shame, a point punk Paris fashion designer Jean Paul Gaultier recognizes when he says, 'People who make mistakes or dress badly are the real stylists. 'My "You feel as though you've eaten too much" . . . collection is taken from exactly those moments when you are mistaken or embarrassed' (*Harpers and Queen*, September 1984).

In the modern city the new and different sounds the dissonance of reaction to what went before; that moment of dissonance is key to twentieth century style. The colliding dynamism, the thirst for change and the heightened sensation that characterize the city societies particularly of modern industrial capitalism go to make up this 'modernity', and the hysteria and exaggeration of fashion well express it. Whereas, however, in previous periods fashion is the field for the playing out of tensions between secular modernity and hedonism on the one hand, and repression and conformity on the other, in the contemporary 'post modernist' epoch rather than expressing an eroticism excluded from the dominant culture it may in its freakishness question the imperative to glamour, the sexual obviousness of dominant styles.

Fashion parodies itself. In elevating the ephemeral to cult status it ultimately mocks many of the moral pretensions of the dominant culture, which, in turn, has denounced it for its surface frivolity while perhaps secretly stung by the way in which fashion pricks the whole moral balloon. At the same time fashion *is* taken at face value and dismissed as trivial, in an attempt to deflect the sting of its true seriousness, its surreptitious unmasking of hypocrisy.

Writings on fashion, other than the purely descriptive, have found it hard to pin down the elusive double bluffs, the infinite regress in the mirror of the meanings of fashion. Sometimes fashion is explained in terms of an often over-simplified social history; sometimes it is explained in psychological terms; sometimes in terms of the economy. Reliance on one theoretical slant can easily lead to simplistic explanations that leave us still unsatisfied.

How then can we explain so double-edged a phenomenon as fashion? It may well be true that fashion is like all 'cultural phenomena, especially of a symbolic and mythic kind, [which] are curiously resistant to being imprisoned in one . . . "meaning". They constantly escape from the boxes into which rational analysis tries to pack them: they have a Protean quality which seems to evade definitive translation into non-symbolic — that is, cold unresonant, totally explicit, once-for-all-accurate — terms.'[2] This suggests that we need a variety of 'takes' on fashion if the reductive and normative moralism of the single sociological explanation is to be avoided while we yet seek to go beyond the pure description of the art historian. The attempt to view fashion through several different pairs of spectacles simultaneously — of aesthetics, of social theory, of politics — may result in an obliquity of view, even of astigmatism or blurred vision, but it seems that we must attempt it.

It would be possible to leave fashion as something that simply appears in a variety of distinct and separate 'discourses', or to say that it is itself merely one among the constellation of discourses of post-modernist culture. Such a pluralist position would be typical of post-modernist or post-structuralist theoretical discourse (today the dominant trend among the avant garde and formerly 'left' intelligentsia): a position that repudiates all 'over arching theories' and 'depth models' replacing these with a multiplicity of 'practices, discourses and textual play . . . or by multiple surfaces'.[3] Such a view is 'populist' and 'democratic' in the sense that no one practice or activity is valued above any other; moral and aesthetic judgments are replaced by hedonistic enjoyment of each molecular and disconnected artefact, performance or experience. Such extreme alienation 'derealizes' modern life, draining from it all notion of meaning. Everything then becomes play; nothing is serious. And fashion does appear to express such a fragmented sensibility particularly well — its obsession with surface, novelty and style for style's sake highly congruent with this sort of post-modernist aesthetic.

Yet fashion clearly does also tap the unconscious source of deep emotion, and at any rate is about more than surface. Fashion, in fact, is not unlike Freud's vision of the unconscious mind. This could contain mutually exclusive ideas with serenity; in it time was abolished, raging emotions were transformed into concrete images, and conflicts magically resolved by being metamorphosed into symbolic form.

From within a psychoanalytic perspective, moreover, we may view the fashionable dress of the western world as one means whereby an always fragmentary self is glued together into the semblance of a unified identity. Identity becomes a special kind of problem in 'modernity'. Fashion speaks a tension between the crowd and the individual at every stage in the development of the nineteenth and twentieth century metropolis. The industrial period is often, inaccurately, called the age of 'mass man'. Modernity creates fragmentation, dislocation. It creates the vision of 'totalitarian' societies peopled by identical zombies in uniform. The fear of depersonalization haunts our culture. 'Chic', from this perspective, is then merely the uniform of the rich, chilling, anti-human and rigid. Yet modernity has also created the individual in a new way – another paradox that fashion well expresses. Modern individualism is an exaggerated yet fragile sense of self – a raw, painful condition.

Our modern sense of our individuality as a kind of wound is also, paradoxically, what makes us all so fearful of not sustaining the autonomy of the self; this fear transforms the idea of 'mass man' into a threat of self-annihilation. The way in which we dress may assuage that fear by stabilizing our individual identity. It may bridge the loneliness of 'mass man' by connecting us with our social group.

Fashion, then, is essential to the world of modernity, the world of spectacle and mass-communication. It is a kind of connective tissue of our cultural organism. And, although many individuals experience fashion as a form of bondage, as a punitive, compulsory way of falsely expressing an individuality that by its very gesture (in copying others) cancels itself out, the final twist to the contradiction that is fashion is that it often does successfully express the individual.

It is modern, mass-produced fashion that has created this possibility. Originally, fashion was largely for the rich, but since the industrial period the mass-production of fashionably styled clothes has made possible the use of fashion as a means of self-enhancement and self-expression for the majority, although, by another and cruel paradox, the price of this has been world-wide exploitation of largely female labour. Fashion itself has become more democratic, at least so far as style is concerned – for differences in the quality of clothes and the materials in which they are made still strongly mark class difference.

Mass fashion, which becomes a form of popular aesthetics, can often be successful in helping individuals to express and define their individuality. The modernist aesthetic of fashion may also be used to express group and, especially in recent years, counter-cultural solidarity. Social and political dissidents have created special forms of dress to express revolt throughout the industrial period. Today, social rebels have made of their use of fashion a kind of avant gardist statement.

Fashionable dressing is commonly assumed to have been restrictive for women and to have confined them to the status of the ornamental or the sexual chattel. Yet it has also been one of the ways in which women have been able to achieve self expression, and feminism has been as simplistic – and as moralistic – as most other theories in its denigration of fashion.

Fashion has been a source of concern to feminists, both today and in an earlier period. Feminist theory is the theorization of gender, and in almost all known societies the gender division assigns to women a subordinate position. Within feminism, fashionable dress and the beautification of the self are conventionally perceived as expressions of subordination; fashion and cosmetics fixing women visibly in their oppression. However, not only is it important to recognize that men have been as much implicated in fashion, as much 'fashion victims' as women; we must also recognize that to discuss fashion as simply a feminist moral problem is to miss the richness of its cultural and political meanings. The political subordination of women is an inappropriate point of departure if, as I believe, the most important thing about fashion is *not* that it oppresses women.

Yet although fashion can be used in liberating ways, it remains ambiguous. For fashion, the child of capitalism, has, like capitalism, a double face.

The growth of fashion, of changing styles of dress, is associated with what has been termed 'the civilizing process' in Europe. The idea of civilization could not exist except by reference to a 'primitive' or 'barbaric' state, and:

> an essential phase of the civilizing process was concluded at exactly the time when the *consciousness* of civilisation, the consciousness of the superiority of their own behaviour and its embodments in science, technology or art began to spread over whole nations of the west.[4]

Fashion, as one manifestation of this 'civilizing process' could not escape this élitism. In more recent times capitalism has become global, imperialist and racist. At the economic level the fashion industry has been an important instrument of this exploitation . . .

Imperialism, however, is cultural as well as economic, and fashion, enmeshed as it is in mass-consumption, has been implicated in this as well. Western fashions have overrun large parts of the so-called third world. In some societies that used to have traditional, static styles of dress, the men, at least those in the public eye, wear western men's suits – although their national dress might be better adapted to climate and conditions. Women seem more likely to continue to wear traditional styles. In doing so they symbolize what is authentic, true to their own culture, in opposition to the cultural colonization of imperialism. Yet if men symbolically 'join' modernity by adopting western dress while women continue to follow tradition, there is an ambivalent message here of women's exclusion from a new world, however ugly, and thus of their exclusion from modernity itself.

On the other hand, in the socialist countries of the 'third' world, western fashion may represent both the lure and the threat of neo-colonialism. A young woman doing the tango in high heels and a tight skirt in a Shanghai tearoom symbolizes the decadence, the 'spiritual pollution' of capitalism (although in continued reaction against the Cultural Revolution, Chinese women and men have recently been encouraged to adopt and to manufacture western styles of dress).

Fashion may appear relativistic, a senseless production of style 'meanings'. Nevertheless, fashion *is* coherent in its ambiguity. Fashion *speaks* capitalism.

Capitalism maims, kills, appropriates, lays waste. It also creates great wealth and beauty, together with a yearning for lives and opportunities that remain just beyond our reach. It manufactures dreams and images as well as things, and fashion is as much a part of the dream world of capitalism as of its economy.

We therefore both love and hate fashion, just as we love and hate capitalism itself. Some react with anger or despair, and the unrepentant few with ruthless enjoyment. More typical responses, in the west at least, where most enjoy a few of the benefits of capitalism while having to suffer its frustrations and exploitation as well, are responses if not of downright cynicism, certainly of ambivalence and irony. We live as far as clothes are concerned a triple ambiguity: the ambiguity of capitalism itself with its great wealth and great squalor, its capacity to create and its dreadful wastefulness; the ambiguity of our identity, of the relation of self to body and self to the world; and the ambiguity of art, its purpose and meaning.

Fashion is one of the most accessible and one of the most flexible means by which we express these ambiguities. Fashion is modernist irony.

Notes

1   Moretti, Franco (1983), 'Homo Palpitans: Balzac's Novels and Urban Personality', *Signs Taken for Wonders*, London: Verso, p. 113.

2   Martin, Bernice (1981), *A Sociology of Contemporary Cultural Change*, Oxford: Basil Blackwell, p. 28.

3   Jameson, Fredric (1984), 'Postmodernism, or the Cultural Logic of Late Capitalism', *New Left Review*, no. 146, July/August.

4   Elias, Norbert (1978), *The Civilizing Process: The History of Manners*, Vol. I, translated by Edmund Jephcott, Oxford: Basil Blackwell, p. 50.

Chapter 33

Kurt W. Back

MODERNISM AND FASHION
A social psychological interpretation

Fashion and the social psychology of cultural products

CULTURAL ACTIVITIES such as arts, crafts, literature, and music are products of social norms, the state of technology, and the need for personal self-expression. They are also the products of individual creativity and of the structures in which this creativity can be translated into a recognized work. Thus cultural activities are partly determined by social and psychological factors and are partly free objects of creativity. For social scientists, psychologists, and social psychologists, this aspect of life is difficult to approach, just because of the great freedom and originality in creative cultural expression. The influence of society on cultural expression and vice versa is as difficult to tie down as the problematic determination of genius by individual personality traits.

Although fashion is almost synonymous with arbitrary, short-term changes, long-term trends can be discerned which are indications of cultural conditions. One-to-one relationships between cultural traits and fashion attributes are unlikely to be found, but the necessarily loose connection also has its advantages: the indicator may be complex and the cultural pattern indicated similarly difficult to isolate, but the whole indication may lead to a relatively deep level that cannot be readily expressed. Long-term trends in clothing are not "fashions" in the sense of fads, but expressions of historical trends.

Fashion is in many ways an extreme of cultural activity. It is concerned with a basic human need, clothing, but goes far beyond the simple biological necessity. Because it refers to a universal necessity, however, it becomes part of a large economic sector; individual creativity is often absorbed in a collective process. In addition, the lengthy path from producer to consumer is further continued by the intended audience. The consumer's arrangement of the final product, its composition, the occasion at which fashions are worn and displayed, become themselves creative occasions. Cultural creativity is continued in this way in the general public. This last step may be socially as important in the use and development of fashions as the original production link.

Fashion is therefore influenced strongly by all three factors: social norms, individual self-expression, and technology (Lurie 1981). The need of the whole society for clothes links fashion directly to the structure of society. At different periods, rules have been promulgated for appropriate clothing for different social groups, for the materials to be worn or outward signs to be displayed. Different kinds of clothes still define ethnic groups. Other rules prescribe clothing for different social occasions. In fact, the most strongly structured situations, army, diplomacy, and even the British universities (Venables and Clifford 1973 [1957]), are still best defined through clothing rules. Again, because of the universal use of fashion products, these norms are widely influential and clothes are of primary importance in social orientation in unfamiliar situations, serving as cues in impression formation and social perception.

Within the latitude given by these norms, fashion also gives a place for individual expression. Even within very rigidly defined situations, individuals have been able to introduce original variations. The second link in the production of fashions, from consumer to consumers' audience, depends on the ability and desire of individuals to express themselves, to give cues about themselves within the bounds of normative behavior. Fashion writing, which expresses individuality to a mass audience within the bounds of current rules of fashion, shows the interplay of norm and individuality in this field. Finally, fashion has been deeply influenced by changes in technology. Technical advances have influenced many forms of art. But this effect has usually been abrupt. For instance, mass reproduction of pictures and music has widened the audience immensely. In the industrial base of fashion, any small advance in material and production can bring about corresponding changes in design. Because industrial advances have gradually brought many types of clothing within the reach of ever-larger groups of people, the meaning of norms, of exclusivity and social cues, has to be changed. The complex position of fashion as an industry as well as a cultural activity has made it extremely sensitive to technical changes, more than similar aesthetic products (Blumer 1960; Horne 1967).

Dimensions in the communication of culture

Cultural products can be distinguished in many ways, as arts or crafts, as vanguard, mass, or folk culture, or in different branches such as literature, music, or fine arts; different time periods of cultural epochs can then be distinguished along all these lines, individually as well as in their interplay. Fashion as a cultural product has a mediating position between extremes; it partakes of art and of craft. It may be an esoteric art form, but its importance lies as well in mass production. It partakes of many special fields, in stage performances as well as in fine arts, besides being important for its own sake.

Three dimensions define culture as part of a communication process: the nature of the communication process, the relations between the communicator and the audience, and the distinction between the communicator and the message.

Information and redundancy

Any act of communication represents a compromise between providing a maximum of information and including redundancy. Redundancy detracts from the efficiency of the communication process, but its presence is necessary for several reasons. Within the process itself it contributes to fidelity of transmission; repetition or partial repetition makes it possible for the audience to receive the message without the strain of constant attention and therefore gives some relief and security to the audience. If one can predict up to a certain point what the next item of information is going to be, a sense of familiarity is established between the participants in the process. Tactics of introducing redundancy show great variety: any type of pattern— rules of language and design, rhythm, and formal rules of what goes together, to give just a few examples—can serve this purpose. However, the introduction of redundancy goes beyond the need for accuracy. The introduction of different devices into communication processes, such as flexibility and shading, result in additional effects on the receiver. Some patterns assert and produce group membership; some can arouse emotions; some have aesthetic qualities.

Fashion prescribes novelty and redundancy within and between individuals. Within individuals there are rules of combination of garments, of combinations of colors and forms, to give redundancy and certainty of perception and interpretation. Between individuals, social rules—such as sumptuary laws or uniform regulations—can increase redundancy. Thus, in general, social norms tend to increase redundancy, but some injunctions in fashion that encourage originality introduce social norms about providing information. The arrangement of costumes becomes a syntax of clothing (Barthes 1967).

Communicator and audience

The place of the participation of the audience or, conversely, the separation between communicator and recipient has varied in history. For instance, responses and visual participation by the audience are expected as long as art is a social ritual. In the nineteenth century an extreme position of separation was reached in almost all arts and crafts. Specialization and professionalization in many fields led to a break between the role of producer and consumer of cultural products. Clothes became parts of roles appropriate to certain scenes. This was true especially in the male, with business suits, evening dress, and uniform casual clothes (tweeds), but women followed a similar trend. Self-expression in this context was frowned upon in middle-class society. The revolt at the time, of the dandy, serves to underline the prevailing cultural standard (Moers 1960).

The communicator and the message

In some fields of culture the artists become the message themselves, whereas in others they are separated from the message. Here the division is frequently between forms of art, such as between performing arts and such fields as literature; but even here differences exist between periods. Fashion seems to lie closer to communicator as message. Sometimes the individual is mainly an object for the designer to send the message; however, this is true especially in the case of models and mannequins, but even the customer is sometimes used as a place for the display of the designer's message. At some periods the individuality of the wearer is the critical distinction of the message. Again the dominant characteristic of the nineteenth century was the separation of the originator and wearer of the message.

Self and style

The pattern of communication served more purposes than transmission of information. These additional functions become nowhere more apparent than in the transmission of art and other cultural experiences. These include aesthetic considerations, social factors, and personal expression. Enduring combinations of social norms, self-expression, and aesthetic values form the style of a person and a group or a period.

Style, in clothing as elsewhere, is thus a combination of personal expression and social norms, influenced by dominant values. Clothing occupies a special place, as the manner of communication which is closest, metaphorically and literally, to the self. It covers what is to be private and shows the world the presentation a person wants to make. It is in part determined by social and cultural norms: fashion is a function of society and period. In addition, it is frequently influenced by social standing, socioeconomic position, and stage in the life course, all circumstances that a person might want to assert in self-presentation. The obverse of the social influences is the expression of the individuality of the person. This may consist in variation of acceptance of social norms; it may also show itself in selection of certain admissible items to form an individual pattern, or it may go beyond the norms (Lurie 1981).

Style can be defined along the dimensions in which cultural products are described as communication, especially the distribution of information and redundancy. In addition, nonlinguistic aspects of style include the selection of modalities, whether color, shape, texture, or conventional signs are used as a code, the selection of alternative units within the codes, and the combination of these units. For each cultural expression, a practically infinite number of messages for the same information is available, but only a limited number are used. The pattern of these combinations forms the style of an epoch; the individual variations form the personal style patterns (Kroeber 1957). Thus, style is the form of communication, but it can be analyzed like communication itself. Unusual patterns of style reveal much about the person, while conforming patterns are redundant in the collectivity and do not transmit much about individuals. Certain aspects of style are common across different fields; they define the spirit of the times. Thus style in fashion can reflect or even anticipate the visual arts. Other styles are more peculiar to different arts, crafts, and intellectual endeavors.

Creators communicate their message, which may often restate cultural norms, with a certain style pattern. In some artistic productions, the style becomes more important than the content of the message itself. It can rightly be said then that the style is communicated. In some societies and in some social groups, the content of the messages is well known to the audience; that is, the content is redundant (Back

1972). In other cases the form may be prescribed and deviation is rarely tolerated; in this case form is redundant. The particular combination of redundancy of form and content reflects general social norms as well as particular social situations. Thus, in the military, uniforms (even by their name) are redundant in form, but give information about rank, organization, and special achievements. Similar rigorous form can be required at social affairs (again called *formal*). Relaxation of these social rules allows different styles for individuals: not only variabilities within formal dress, which give information on form and taste, but acceptance and rejection of the kind of dress at all, which give information on beliefs and standards of participants. The style of dress, including the kind of information transmitted, relates closely to the pattens of social interaction. A study among college students showed that political attitudes, along a liberal-conservative dimension, were regularly inferred from dress pattern and corresponded to the actual attitudes of students who wore these clothes. The social and historical situation—the University of California at Berkeley in the late 1960s—contributed to the ideological self-identification through style (Kelley and Starr 1971).

Modernism

The stylistic movement that dominated the early and middle part of this century can be summarized under the name *modernism*. It represents a conscious break with the past and a definite shift of cultural communication from the nineteenth-century styles. Modernism tried hard to change the communication patterns; different orientations within this larger perspective achieved it in different ways; but the total effort was a drive toward novelty (as shown by the name), and rejection of complacency that redundancy, including tradition and norms, can bring. Rejection of set roles and functions also produced a shift in the other two variables; creator and audience as well as creator and message were amalgamated as far as possible. In the rejection of past cultural traditions and creation of new ones, two features are important: the split between representation and communication, and the dissolution of the unity of self (Hodin 1972; Rosenberg 1972).

The first aspect has been analyzed by Foucault (1983). He distinguishes two principles in Western art from the Renaissance to the birth of modernism. One is the separation between visual representation and linguistic reference. Either a picture illustrates a text or a title represents a description of the painting. The second principle is the assumption of a close relation between representation and resemblance. If a picture is similar to an object, then it stands for this object. Both of these assumptions make the work of art a link between the audience and the meaning for the work of art stands: the communication goes *through* the art work.

The modernist movement arose by denying both assumptions. In the fine arts, words and letters became part of the picture: verbal meanings and puns could not be separated from pictorial representation. On the other hand, the title of an abstraction became an essential part of the whole work, not describing a painting, giving it shape or irony or contrast; visual production obtains meaning through verbal allusions. The illustrated novel vanishes, but literature includes visual effects such as Apollinaire's calligrams or E. E. Cummings's poems. Some writing has become a combination of visual and verbal presentation. Second, the transmission process has become an object in itself apart from function; in this way a work of art does not necessarily transmit meaning, but flaunts its other, nonsemantic aspects. Thus a picture of a woman does not depict a woman, but it is a picture of a woman. Many other art forms emphasize the interest in themselves, and not in anything beyond. They emphatically do not refer to any state of the world which the picture is trying to transmit. Even if the art object does look similar to another object, this similarity is not necessarily representation: the painting of a woman does not represent a woman. The Belgian painter Magritte emphasized this point by painting a pipe with the legend below: *Ceci n'est pas une pipe* ('This is not a pipe').

This aspect of modernism is related to scientific and technical advances, for instance, in sensory and cognitive psychology and in the epistemology of modern physics, all of which put the reality of the surrounding world in question and emphasize the problematic of the communication process. This development paralleled the insecurity of the individual in mass society, adding to it the insecurity in understanding the physical world. This questioning then justified the use of symbols and channels as objects in their own right. Modernism became an aid in this predicament by its playful emphasis on codes and channels for their own sake.

Another important aspect of modernism was a parallel dissolution in the unity of content, the splitting up of the self. Thus the unity of the subject as well as the relation to the object was questioned. Here scientific as well as social conditions were responsible. The variables that lead to a concept of self-unity are weakened or counteracted in mass society. Heterogeneity of life in metropolitan areas may lead to tolerance and enrichment of stimulation, but it also leads to ambivalence in norms, even in norms of perception.

Psychological research also questions the unity of the self. Inquiry into dissociated states in hypnosis and hysteria became important in medical psychology. From this concern into abnormal states rose depth psychology and psychoanalysis, which asserted equivalent processes in the normal person. Different layers of the person could be distinguished, such as superego, ego, id, and theory led to the hypothesis that the unity of what we call a person is only an arbitrary construct.

The fragmentation of the self is easily seen in literature, where a person can be analyzed into many heterogeneous units. The same result can be shown in painting; for instance, a person may be seen from several perspectives or appear several times in the same picture (Tomkins 1965). The nightmarish quality of surrealist and expressionist work derived from the loss of the familiar unity of objects. This is also designed to produce doubt about the existence or at least the unity of the perceiver, corresponding to the fragmentation of the self in modern society. The audience is called upon to accept the fragmentation of the objects in the artwork but in doing this, viewers also accept this process in themselves. Modern art as well as literature helps in a somewhat drastic way to adapt its public to contemporary conditions. Van Gogh and early expressionists are accepted today as quite realistic painters, just as Kafka can be looked at as an accurate reporter of self and society in the current scene. The dissolution of the self is in fact forced upon the audience, which then recognizes its own state.

The separation of the communication process as a content of artworks and the dissolution of the self of model and audience lead to the separation of a traditional division, that between art and audience. The audience becomes an active participant in the communication process; the reader or spectator has to work to ascribe meaning to the message; he is not a passive participant. The reaction of the recipient can be the most important part of the whole process. In the extreme, this development transformed drama into "happenings" or created earth sculptures—such as Robert Smithson's "Spiro Jetty" in Utah and Robert Morris's Park in Grand Rapids, Michigan—as part of the natural scene (Robinette 1976).

The role of the audience under these conditions becomes close to that of the consumer in fashion; conversely, this development in the culture strengthens the role of the consumer as part in the fashion-creating process. The distinction between creator and audience is almost overcome.

Modernism, style, and fashion

As in any other period, fashion in modernism depends on social norms, individual self-expression, technical opportunities, and the initiative of the fashion designer. The effort of modernism has been to break tradition, leading to claims of the priority of the individual over social norms. The isolation of the individual in modern society is reflected in variability of styles in modern dress: no clothes are "right" for a particular occasion, but consumers must make their own choices of self-presentation. How long has it been since department stores had college counselors from different schools to present the style at a particular place?

Fashion, even in its aspect as a craft, faces the same task as the artists who produced modernism, namely, to mediate a place for the individual in an increasingly complex mass society. The predominance of individual choice does not give complete range of freedom in clothes but produces a new set of arrangements. Just as the variation between occasions and according to social standing is diminishing, the variation between situations, asserting an individual style, is decreasing. The custom of wearing informal clothes to formal occasions, and sometimes vice versa (the "Teddy-Boy" style) is an indication of modernism's break with tradition. Conventional rules reflecting the formal organization of society are no more comforting guidelines for belongingness, but a certain self-assertion is. Norms, in addition to a permissible variability, make possible a conventional exposure of a unitary self in traditional society. One could be fashionable as well as original. The dissolution of the self makes the presentation of a unitary person questionable, but certain fragments may be asserted to an extreme degree. Thus, exaggerated clothes, which may look like parodies, assert a part of the self and make a person feel at home in a mass society.

In spite of the rejection of tradition and emphasis on individual diversity, culture and society still impose limits. Individual assertion becomes easily conventionalized; assertion of a part of the person, such as particular attitudes and values, easily becomes a group identity. Uniforms for subgroups of the society become standardized. Over and above these group identities, different fashion trends can be discerned throughout the periods of modernism. Spontaneous and anticonventional assertions of unconventional aspects of the self are eventually taken up as high fashion. The sans-culottes (rejection of knee breeches for trousers) of the French

Revolution became the elegant suits of the nineteenth-century middle class. In modern times the process goes quicker, and the proletarian self-presentation of overalls and jeans quickly becomes designer models.

A distinctive aspect of the recent period, adapting modernistic art to fashion, is the separation of style from social status; this status is not communicated through the channel of clothes. Older rules of fashion enjoined different styles for social groups and were even legally sanctioned in sumptuary and similar laws. In addition, the high differential expense for material accounted for great differences in the clothes of different social classes. Today rational rules still enjoin some working clothes, although the rationality is sometimes questionable. A study of nurses' uniforms has shown that the supposedly hygienic protection afforded by these uniforms is more symbolic than real. Nurses will go into tubercular patients' rooms in street clothes when they are off duty, apparently not in need of protective gear (Roth 1957). Other working clothes, such as overalls or hard hats, also have nonrational "reasons" for use.

But, in general, technical advances have decreased the difference in material and style according to wealth. Artificial fabrics and sophisticated methods of mass production have made possible replicas of high style so close to the original that it is difficult for the casual observer to determine the origin of the apparel or to derive the socioeconomic status of the wearer. The variety of types of clothes has become so pervasive that the prestige value of clothes has to be displayed by the designer label.

The use of labels for display is also an example of another aspect of modernism in fashion design, namely, the obliteration of the distinction between visual and verbal presentation. Clothing is more recognized for its own sake than for transmitting a message about the person, as the message has an independent value. The conscious display of the label or of seams, which used to be partially hidden as the mechanics of the message, are simply saying "This is clothing," as artwork asserts "This is a picture." Fashion has also discovered the use of the text as part of design. Verbal messages give the origin and manufacture of clothes; in addition, messages proliferate on the clothes themselves, giving readable texts about previous experiences, political views, social and commercial affiliations, and other currently important identities. They make feasible a self-presentation that has been made difficult through conventional, universally recognized symbols.

Social identity manifested in a wealth of messages corresponds better to the social conditions of modernism than the older sumptuary conditions based on social class. They allow the individual expression of some aspect of the self which is important currently but can be easily substituted when some other aspect of the self becomes prominent.

Fashion in the modernistic period had a role in the crisis of the individual in the transition from a tightly structured society to a mass society. It extended the ability of the individual for self-expression without social guidance, by making it possible to assert only some areas of the self and not the self as integrated into social matrix. Fashion also gave leeway to overassertion of certain peculiarities, especially by incorporating verbal messages into fashion design. As it could not transmit much socially recognized information, fashion, like other modernistic forms, gave prominence to the form of the message for its own sake.

Conclusion: fashion and social indicators

Modernism has been a factor in our culture in many decades; its influence has helped the understanding of individuals caught up in a rapidly changing society. The stated intention of many leaders in the modernist movement has been acceptance of technology and the conditions of city life. The fashion trends during this time have kept pace with these aims. Creation of fashions that could accentuate the individual without the mediation of traditional community groups, use of new technical advances in fabric and design, and even flaunting the details of construction–all these features conform to and reinforce the modernist influence. Even direct influence of modernist artists can be seen; patterns show traces of such painters as Picasso, Matisse, and Mondrian, and in turn these artists look more familiar because of this exposure.

Fashion, because of its widespread visibility, can be a good indicator of the kind of stabilization which might occur. One may watch for indicators in this area: homogeneity of clothing by occasion becomes important with less assertion of personality; role becomes important in the presentation of self (a president should not wear jeans). Thus redundancy is shown across persons: one person in a gathering can show the traits of everybody's clothes, but a one-time sample of a person does not show the clothes for all times. Consequently, there would be less emphasis on showing clothing as clothing, less exposing techniques of fashion design and clothing manufacture in the end product. Fashion will be able to carry communication about the self and its social position, not relying on text to carry the message. All these changes would be indicators of a separation from modernism and of change from the social conditions which gave rise to this movement.

This change does not mean retrogression and retreat into the pre-modern age. The events that led to the change have had their effects and the experiences of the intervening years have left their mark. The rapid technological and social changes have been disruptive and a new level of adjustment had to be found. One of the important new conditions has been the importance of communication technology, which makes communication itself the stabilizing force. Thus new communication patterns will determine the distribution of population and to modes of social inter-action and self-presentation. New fashions may be indicators as well as precursors of new types of adjustment; learning to read the structure of clothing according to the principles indicated here may help the fashion designer as well as the social scientist.

References

Back, K. W. 1972. "Power, Influence and Pattern of Communication." In S. Moscovici, ed., *The Psychology of Language*. Chicago: Markham.

Barthes, R. 1967. *Systeme de la Mode*. Paris: Edition de Seuil.

Blumer, H. 1960. "Fashion." In *Encyclopedia of the Social Sciences* New York: Macmillan, vol. 5, 341–45.

Foucault, M. 1983. *This Is Not a Pipe*, Berkeley: University of California Press.

Hodin, J. P. 1972. *Modern Art and Modern Man*. Cleveland: Press of Case Western University.

Horne, M. J. 1967. *The Second Skin: An Interdisciplinary Study of Clothing*, Boston: Houghton-Mifflin.

Kelley, J., and S. A. Starr. 1971. "Dress and Ideology: The Non-verbal Communication of Political Attitudes." Presented at meetings of the American Sociological Association.

Kroeber, A. L. 1957. *Style and Civilization*. Ithaca, N.Y.: Cornell University Press.

Lifton, R. J. 1976. *The Life of the Self*. New York: Simon and Schuster.

Lurie, A. 1981. *The Language of Clothes*. New York: Random House.

Moers, E. 1960. *The Dandy: Brummell to Beerbohm*. London: Secker and Warburg.

Robinette, Margaret A. 1976. *Outdoor Sculpture*, New York: Whitney Library of Design.

Rosenberg, H. 1972. *The De-definition of Art*. New York: Horizon.

Roth, J. 1957. "Ritual and Magic in the Control of Contagion." *American Sociological Review* 23:310–14.

Tomkins, C. 1965. *The Bride and the Bachelors*. New York: Viking.

Venables, D. R., and R. E. Clifford. 1973. "Academic Dress." In M. Douglas, ed., *Rules and Meanings*. Hammondsworth, England: Penguin. (Originally published in 1957.)

Chapter 34

Richard Sennett

PUBLIC ROLES/PERSONALITY IN PUBLIC

[. . .]

The body is a mannequin

A MODERN CITY DWELLER suddenly transported back to Paris or London in the 1750s would find crowds whose appearance was at once simpler and more puzzling than the crowds of our time. A man in the street now can distinguish the poor from the middle class by sight and, with a little less precision, the rich from the middle class. Appearances on the streets of London and Paris two centuries ago were manipulated so as to be more precise indicators of social standing. Servants were easily distinguishable from laborers. The kind of labor performed could be read from the peculiar clothes adopted by each trade, as could the status of a laborer in his craft by glancing at certain ribbons and buttons he wore. In the middle ranks of society, barristers, accountants, and merchants each wore distinctive decorations, wigs, or ribbons. The upper ranks of society appeared on the street in costumes which not merely set them apart from the lower orders but dominated the street.

The costumes of the elite and of the wealthier bourgeoisie would puzzle a modern eye. There were patches of red pigment smeared on nose or forehead or around the chin. Wigs were enormous and elaborate. So were the headdresses of women, containing in addition highly detailed model ships woven into the hair, or baskets of fruit, or even historical scenes represented by miniature figures. The skins of both men and women were painted either apoplexy-red or dull white. Masks would be worn, but only for the fun of frequently taking them off. The body seemed to have become an amusing toy to play with.

During his first moments on the street, the modern interloper would be tempted to conclude that there was no problem of order in this society, everybody being so clearly labeled. And if this modern observer had some historical knowledge, he would give a simple explanation for this order: people were just observing the law. For there existed on the statute books in both France and England sumptuary laws which assigned to each station in the social hierarchy a set of "appropriate" clothes, and forbade people of any one station from wearing the clothes of people in another rank. Sumptuary laws were especially complicated in France. For instance, women of the 1750s whose husbands were laborers were not permitted to dress like the wives of masters of a craft, and the wives of "traders" were forbidden certain of the adornments allowed women of quality.

Laws on the statute books, however, do not indicate laws observed or enforced. By the opening of the 18th Century, very few arrests were made for violation of the sumptuary laws. Theoretically, you could go to jail for imitating another person's bodily appearance; practically, you need have had no fear by 1700 of doing so. People in very large cities had little means of telling whether the dress of a stranger on the street was an accurate reflection of his or her standing in the society, for all the reasons elaborated in the last chapter; most of the migrants to the cosmopolitan centers came from relatively far away, following new occupations once in town. Was what the observer saw on the street then an illusion?

According to the logic of an egalitarian-minded society, when people do not have to display their social differences, they will not do so. If both law and strangerhood allow you to "get away" with being any person you choose to be, then you will try not to define who you are. But this egalitarian logic breaks down when applied to the *ancien régime* city. Despite the fact that sumptuary laws were seldom enforced throughout western Europe, despite the fact that in the great cities it would be difficult to know much about the origins of those one saw in the street, there was a desire to observe the codes of dressing to station. In doing so, people hoped to bring order to the mixture of strangers in the street.

The clothing of most urban middle- and upper-class Frenchmen and Englishmen showed a remarkable stability in cut and general form from the late 17th Century to the middle of the 18th Century, certainly more stability than in the previous eighty years. With the exception of the female's pannier (a flattened-out skirt) and the gradual change in the ideal male build—from corpulent to thin and narrow-waisted— there was a clinging in the 18th Century to the basic shapes of the late 17th. However, the use of these forms was changing.

Clothing which in the late 17th Century was worn on all occasions was by the middle of the 18th Century conceived of as appropriate only on stage and in the street. In the 18th Century home, loose-fitting and simple garments were the growing preference of all classes. There appears here the first of the terms of the divide between the public and the private realm: the private realm being more natural, the body appeared as expressive in itself. Squire remarks that, during the Régence,

> Paris saw the complete adoption of a negligé appearance. The costume of the boudoir had descended to the drawing-room. The "private" quality of dress was emphasized by the general use of forms distinctly "undress" in origin.[1]

On the street, by contrast, clothes were worn which recognizably marked one's place—and the clothes had to be known, familiar bodily images if the markings were to be successful. The conservation of the late 17th Century gross forms of bodily appearance cannot thus be viewed as a simple continuity with the past. The attempt was to use proven images of where one belonged in the society in order to define a social order on the street.

Given the changes in urban life, this attempt was bound to encounter difficulties. For one thing, many of the new mercantile occupations had no 17th Century precedent, so that those who worked in the accounts-receivable section of a shipping firm had no appropriate clothing to wear. For another, with the collapse of the guilds in the great cities, much of the repertoire of familiar clothing based on guild markings was useless, because few people were entitled to it. One way people solved these difficulties was by taking as street wear costumes which clearly labeled a particular trade or profession but had little relation to the trade or profession of the wearer. These people were not necessarily dressing above themselves. In fact, the records indicate that lower-middle-class people seem to have been only sporadic counter jumpers in the matter of clothes. Nor, if these old clothes were donned by someone of a different but equivalent trade or profession, was there much thought given to altering the garments to suit or to symbolize their own particular station. That would have been idiosyncratic; the clothes would not have meant much to a person on the street who did not know their wearer, much less the reason why he might have altered a familiar form. Whether people were in fact what they wore was less important than their desire to wear something recognizable in order to be someone on the street.

We would say of a shipping clerk in a poultry firm who dressed like a butcher or falconer when he went out for a walk that he was wearing a costume; that notion of costume would help us comprehend his behavior as having something to do with the dress of an actor in the theater, and we could easily understand that such a mode of dressing could be called observing a convention.

What makes 18th Century street wear fascinating is that even in less extreme cases, where the disparity between traditional clothes and new material conditions had not forced someone into an act of impersonation, where instead he wore clothes which reasonably accurately reflected who he was, the same sense of costume and convention was present. At home, one's clothes suited one's body and its needs; on the street, one stepped into clothes whose purpose was to make it possible for other people to act as if they knew who you were. One became a figure in a contrived landscape; the purpose of the clothes was not to be sure of whom you were dealing with, but to be able to behave as if you were sure. Do not inquire too deeply into the truth of other people's appearances, Chesterfield counseled his son; life is more sociable if one takes people as they are and not as they probably are. In this sense, then, clothes had a meaning independent of the wearer and the wearer's body. Unlike as in the home, the body was a form to be draped.

In articulating this rule, we should specify "men" in place of "people." For women were rather more carefully scrutinized for a relationship between their rank and their clothing: within a general rank, like men, they might adopt one street face or another, but they could incur hostility for jumping the line between ranks. The problem was most acute in the shades of ranking, none too clear themselves, between middle-middle levels and upper-middle levels, and the reason for this lay in the means by which fashion was disseminated at the time among the female population.

France was the model for feminine London's taste in both the middle and upper ranks of society. In this decade, middle-rank English women usually wore what upper-rank Frenchwomen had been wearing ten or fifteen years before. French clothes were disseminated by means of dolls; the dolls were dressed in exact replicas of current fashion, and then salesmen, their cases packed with fifteen or twenty perfect mannequins in miniature, would travel to London or Vienna. In Paris itself something of a similar time lag existed between classes, though, of course, the dolls were unnecessary.

The cast-off system would have created a tremendous blurring of class lines if the dolls were brought back to human size exactly, or, rather, the differences between middle and upper classes would have been that the former were exact echoes of what the fashionable ladies wore when they were much younger. In fact, when the dolls were brought back to life-size proportions, the dresses were system-atically simplified. In Paris, where the dolls were not needed, the same simplifying pattern also occurred. The result was that middle-class women were faint echoes of their aristocratic contemporaries when they were younger, but also simplified versions of them.

Codes of dress as a means of regulating the street worked by clearly if arbitrarily identifying who people were. The cast-off pattern could threaten this clarity. The following is the reaction of one middle-class husband, an oil merchant, to his wife's dressing above herself, reported in the *Lady's Magazine* of a slightly later period, 1784:

> When down dances my rib in white, but so bepukered and plaited, I could not tell what to make of her; so turning about, I cried, "Hey, Sally, my dear, what new frolic is this: It is like none of the gowns you used to wear." "No, my dear," crieth she, "it is no gown, it is the *chemise de la reine*." "My dear," replied I, hurt at this gibberish . . . "let us have the name of your new dress in downright English." "Why then" said she, "if you must have it, it is the queen's shift." Mercy on me, thought I, *what will the world come to, when an oilman's wife comes down to serve in the shop, not only in her own shift, but in that of a queen.*

If the oil merchant's wife or anyone else could wear a *chemise de la reine*, if imitation was exact, how would people know whom they were dealing with? Again, the issue was, not being sure of a rank, but being able to act with assurance.

Thus when one saw that a woman was dressing above her station, it was considered only good manners to hold her up to ridicule, even to point out to other strangers that she was an impostor. This shaming however, was behavior which, like the clothes themselves, had a specific geography: if you found out someone dressing above station in a social gathering in your home, it would be the height of bad taste to subject her to the treatment you felt entitled to inflict on the street.

The clothing of the aristocracy and the higher bourgeois classes can now assume its place in relation to that of the lower orders. The principle of dressing the body as a mannequin, as a vehicle for marking by well-established conventions, drew the upper and lower realms of society closer together than a casual visitor might first surmise from the actual costumes, or more precisely, the upper classes drew this principle to its logical conclusion; they literally disembodied bodily imagery. If that casual visitor were to stop for a moment, indeed, and consider in what the playfulness and fantasy of the upper-class clothing lay, he would be struck by the fact that the wig, the hat, the vest-coat, while attracting attention to the wearer, did so by the qualities of these adornments as objects in themselves, and not as aids to setting off the peculiarities of his face or figure. Let us move from tip to toe to see how the upper orders arrived at this objectification of the body.

Headdresses consisted of wigs and hats for men, and tied and waved hair, often with artificial figurines inserted, for the women. In commenting on the evolution of wigs by the middle of the 18th Century, Huizinga writes:

> [T]he wig is swept up into a regular panache of high combed hair in front with rows of tight little curls over the ears and tied at the back with laces. Every pretence of imitating nature is abandoned; the wig has become the complete ornament.

The wigs were powdered, and the powder held in place with pomade. There were many styles, although the one Huizinga describes was the most popular; the wigs themselves required great care to maintain.[2]

Women's approach to dressing their hair is best illustrated by *La Belle Poule*. A ship of that name defeated an English frigate and inspired a hairdo in which hair represented the sea and nestled in the hair was an exact replica of *La Belle Poule*. Headdresses like the *pouf au sentiment* were so tall that women often had to kneel to go through doorways. Lester writes that

> the *pouf au sentiment* was the favorite court style, and consisted of various ornaments fastened in the hair—branches of trees representing a garden, birds, butterflies, cardboard cupids flying about, and even vegetables.

The shape of the head was thus totally obscured, as was much of the forehead. The head was support for the real focus of interest, the wig or hairdo.[3]

Nowhere was the attempt to blot out the individual character of a person more evident than in the treatment of the face. Both men and women used face paint, either red or white, to conceal the natural color of the skin and any blemishes it might have. Masks came back into fashion, worn by both men and women.

Marking the face with little patches of paint was the final step in obliterating the face. The practice was begun in the 17th Century, but only by the 1750s had it become widespread. In London patches were placed on the right or left side of the face, depending on whether one were Whig or Tory. During the reign of Louis XV, patches were placed to indicate the character of the Parisian: at the corner of the eye stood for passion; center of the cheek, gay; nose, saucy. A murderess was supposed to wear patches on her breasts. The face itself had become a background only, the paper on which these ideograms of abstract character were mounted.

The surfaces of the body followed the same principles. In the 1740s women began displaying more of their breasts, but only as a ground on which to place jewels or, in only a few cases, let us hope, patches. The male at the same time used lace at the edges of sleeves, and other sewn-on adornments, more and more delicate. With the slimming of the body, the body frame became simpler, so that it permitted more plasticity and variety in adornment.

Women's skirts largely hid their legs and feet. Men's breeches did not hide the feet. On the contrary, during this period, leggings divided the limb in half visually, and attention was focused on the shoe rather than, as in the early 1700s and again at the end of the century, on the leg as a whole. The bottom extremity of the body was, as were the face and upper torso, an object on which were placed decorations.

The body as an object to be decorated bridged stage and street. The bridge between the two had an obvious and a not so obvious form. The obvious bridge was in the replication of clothes in the two realms; the not so obvious bridge was the way in which stage designers still conceived of allegorical or fantastic characters through the principle of the body as mannequin. In addition, it is important to note one area in which the clothing already described, which was street clothing, was forbidden to be replicated upon the stage.

Above the level of degrading poverty, the street clothing of all ranks was usable almost intact as stage costume. But its use in the mid-18th Century theater produced certain anomalies, at least to a modern observer. In plays with relatively contemporary settings, like Molière's comedies, mid-18th Century audiences saw characters dressed for the street even when the scene was a boudoir. Intimate dress for intimate scenes was out. In plays with historical settings, the clothing of the street was the clothing of the stage, no matter whether the play performed was set in ancient Greece, medieval Denmark, or China. Othello was played by David Garrick dressed in a fashionable, elaborate wig; by Spranger Barry in a gentleman's cocked hat. Hamlet as played by John Kemble, appeared in gentleman's attire and a powdered wig. The idea of historical presentation, of what a Dane or a Moor looked like in a certain place at a certain time, was largely absent from theatrical imagination. A critic wrote in 1755 that "historical exactitude is impossible and fatal to dramatic art."[4]

The bridge between stage costume and street clothing cannot thus be thought of as part of a general desire for art to mirror life. The bridge in images of the body distorted a mirror, of setting or of time. In addition, similarity between stage and street in the clothing itself was limited by one fact of social position.

The theater audiences of this decade demanded a sharp discontinuity between the two realms when stage characters were those of the lower orders of society; these wretches people turned a blind eye toward in the city; they wanted to be equally blind in the theater. Occasionally, some respectable manual occupations were also prettied up—especially servants. The servants dressed by the designer Martin in Paris "were all silks and satins with ribbons everywhere: the type has been preserved for us in the porcelain figures of the period." In 1753 Madame Favart appeared once on the stage in the sandals, rough cloth, and bare legs of a real working woman of the provinces; the audience was disgusted.

Within these class limits, and within the generally conservative lines of dress, stage costume was often the proving ground of new wig styles, new face patches, new jewelry. Just as in the Renaissance designers would often try out new architectural forms first as stage backdrops, couturiers in the middle of the 18th Century would often experiment with new styles on the stage before they attempted to make them into everyday street clothing.

If one moves from specific costumes to the principles of costuming employed by the great costume designers of the time, Martin and Boquet in Paris, there appears a less obvious way the theater bridged the rule of appearance which governed the street.

Martin gave theater costumes a lightness and delicacy unknown in the days of Louis XIV; his costumes for Roman characters began to show an exaggeration which is whimsical. This element of fantasy was picked up by Boquet, his successor in the mid-18th Century. Allegorical figures ceased to be creatures; they became an assemblage of decorative elements draped on the body but wholly unrelated to its movements or form. The actress Mlle Lacy would appear in the role of Amour dans l'Eglé with exposed breasts, but the breasts were not exposed by intent. The costumer simply had no drapery he wanted to put under the lace garlands which were to be draped across the chest. The bare upper torso was like a background for the real focus of interest—the lace frills. The actor Paul would appear as Zéphire with drapery tied at an awkward point on his chest—no matter, it is not the chest the costumer is dressing, he is rather presenting a beautiful and delicate arrangement of cloth.

It is the rule of appearance in the everyday world—the body as mannequin—that this theater costuming elaborated. Allegorical figures were "fantastications of contemporary dress," street dress which itself expressed freedom and social dominance in terms of fantasy.

Costume's "fundamental lines changed with the fluctuations of fashion," Laver writes. That is true as well in terms of actual clothes; the bridge between the street and the stage also existed when a woman would think of showing herself on the street as Amour dans l'Eglé. The rules of bodily appearance in London and Paris in the 1750's show an almost pure type of a structural continuity between the street and the stage.[5]

[. . .]

Personality in public: new images of the body

The decades of the middle of the 19th Century bore most historians of clothing and costume, as indeed they should. Squire's judgment is short and damning: "The dullest decade in the history of feminine dress began in 1840. An insipid mediocrity characterized an entirely middle-class epoch." Seldom had the female body appeared in more ungainly form, seldom had male dress been so drab. But these decades are all-important. In them, personality entered the public realm in a structured way. It did so by meshing with the forces of industrial production, in the medium of clothes. People took each other's appearances in the street immensely seriously; they believed they could fathom the character of those they saw, but what they saw were people dressed in clothes increasingly more homogeneous and monochromatic. Finding out about a person from how he or she looked became, therefore, a matter of looking for clues in the details of his costume. This decoding of the body on the street in turn affected the bridge between stage and street. The codes of belief about street appearances began to be fundamentally different from the belief in appearances on the stage. In these ways, the cosmopolitan bourgeoisie were trying to see in terms comparable to Balzac's, but their vision led to a divorce between art and society.

Terms like "homogeneous," "uniform," or "drab" must be used with caution. Compared with the garb of modern-day Peking, with its single military costume for all ages and both sexes, the clothing of the 1840's would hardly appear uniform or drab. Compared with the 1950s in the United States, it would be a celebration of style. But compared with what came before it, either in the *ancien régime* or in the Romantic era, it was homogeneous, it was drab. As numerous writers comment, it was the beginning of a *style* of dressing in which neutrality—that is, not standing out from others—was the immediate statement.

The epoch's clothes pose two problems. The first is how and why clothing became more neutral. The second is the insistence on reading personality from neutral appearances. The first problem involved a new relationship between clothing and the machine.

The sewing machine made its appearance in 1825, was worked on by various American and European firms, and was finally patented by Singer in 1851. In the 1840s, watches became a mass-production item. In 1820, hats became the same when an American developed a machine for producing felt. By the middle of the 19th Century, almost all shoes sold in cities were made by machine.

The impact of these production changes on the clothes of Paris and London cannot be understood apart from a new means of disseminating fashion in the city. One hundred years before, there were two ways in which a Parisian fashion was broadcast: within the city, the most effective was direct contact on the streets or in public gardens; and dolls were used, dressed in exact replica of what Countess so-and-so was wearing at the moment. By 1857, this had all changed. Through "fashion plates" the pages of the newspaper disseminated fashion instantly, fashion depicted in its exact original form. The 1840s were the first great age of the mass-circulation newspaper; the sheer size of the newspapers' circulation meant that most buyers, indeed, no longer needed to make contact with a living salesman in order to know what to buy. Fashion dolls were still being made in the 19th Century, but had lost their purpose; they were treated as archaic objects, interesting to collect, but were no longer used by salesmen of clothes. What happened within the department store was thus echoed within the world of clothes; active interchange between buyer and seller was transformed into a more passive and one-sided relationship.

By 1857, these changes in mass production and dissemination of clothes had penetrated the world of high fashion. In that year L. Worth opened up his fashion salon in Paris. He was the first high-fashion designer to use machine-made, mass-reproducible clothes. Today the technical quality of the Worth clothes, rather than their beauty, holds the eye. One hundred and twenty years ago, they made an impact because his "good taste" and "beautiful design" were realized in patterns which could easily be copied by the new clothing machines, just as Worth used these machines on a limited scale to prepare costumes for his royal and aristocratic patrons. As a result, there died out the simplifying process that operated in the 18th Century, as clothes passed from elite originators to middle-class imitators. After Worth, such simplification was rendered mechanically obsolete. Differences between upper- and middle-class appearance moved to a new and more subtle terrain.

In the 1830s and 1840s the feminine silhouette came to be defined by the wasp waist and the leg-of-mutton sleeve. The extremely thin waist was achieved only by straitjacketing the body in a corset. The appeal of this imprisonment was, to bourgeois ladies, that it smacked of the dignity of bygone court years when royalty wore tight corsets and full dresses. By 1840, almost all of the female body below the collarbone was covered with clothing of some kind, for by this time the skirt had gradually descended to cover up the feet once again.

In the 1830s the male costume began to subside from the flowing and exaggerated lines of Romantic dress. By 1840 the cravat lost its flamboyance and lay close to the neck. Masculine lines became simpler in these two decades, and the color of clothing more drab. Above all, broadcloth of a black color became the basic material for the streetwear of middle- and upper-class men and the "Sunday clothes" of the working class when they went to church.

Now all these garments were cut by machine from patterns; if a gentleman or a lady could afford a tailor or seamstress, the patterns for hand-sewn clothes followed those of the machine-made patterns, unless the client was very rich or very eccentric. And eccentricity in dress was itself frowned upon increasingly in these decades.

We come here to a "puzzle of taste," in François Boucher's words, which was in fact a sign of a deep-seated and complex belief. In public, people did not want to stand out in any way; they did not want to be conspicuous. Why?

Historians of fashion have ascribed this fear of standing out to rather trivial causes. They speak, for instance, of the influence of Beau Brummell. While Romantics like the Comte d'Orsay dressed flamboyantly, Brummell presented himself as clean, neat, and immaculately controlled. Just as bourgeois ladies deformed their bodies in pursuit of a vanished royal *bon ton*, gentlemen thirty to forty years after Brummell's fall from fashion in 1812 could imagine that in being prim and drab they were showing good taste.

But that is not enough as an explanation. Consider, for instance, a painting in the Royal Museum of Fine Arts in Copenhagen of a street crowd in that city, done by the painter A. M. Hounoeus in the middle of the century. The children's garb is purely Danish, the adults are dressed "Parisian fashion." It is a bad painting but an extraordinary document. Here is a crowd of people, all rather somberly dressed, a large crowd. Who are they? How could we divine their work, their specific status, their backgrounds? By sight it is impossible. They are shielded.

Differences between cosmopolitan and provincial life were involved in this taste for anonymity. It became in the 1840s a sign of middle-class cosmopolitan breeding, or the desire for urbanity among provincials. During the decade on the Continent, people outside the great cities, conversely and in another mood, began to place emphasis on conserving their "native" dress, as opposed to dressing "Paris style." The growing ideas of a folk and a folk spirit, which gave nations their rationale and rights, produced in part this consciously delineated line between Paris and "native" fashion. The idea of the folk began in Herder's generation, and survived as Herder's romantic contemporaries passed from the scene—the folk being always rural or village, the cosmopolitan city being anti-folk.

This new nativism produced extraordinary contrasts in the realm of fashion. If one looks at male fashion plates in Lyons and Birmingham newspapers, one finds in both countries that provincial ideas of good taste were far more colorful, more various, and, to put it finely, more interesting than cosmopolitan ideas. To dress up in a sophisticated way, a cosmopolitan way, meant to learn how to tone down one's appearance, to become unremarkable.

One can make then an easy connection. Given all the material upheaval in the city, people wanted to protect themselves by blending into the crowd. The mass-produced clothes gave them the means to blend. If the story were left here, one could sensibly conclude that now machine society controlled the expressive tools of the culture of the city. And if this were true, then all our familiar friends—dissociation, alienation, and the like—come into the picture: people must have felt dissociated from their bodies because their bodies were expressions of the machine, there was alienation because man no longer expressed his individuality through his appearance, and so on. These descriptions have become so familiar that they are almost comforting; they tell so easily what went wrong.

Yet dissociation is exactly what people so dressed did not do. As the images became more monochromatic, people began to take them more seriously, as signs of the personality of the wearer. The expectation that even blank or trivial appearances had great importance as clues to personality, an expectation which Balzac seized on in his work, his audience also maintained in their own lives. Cosmopolitans, more drab in appearance, tended to use clothes more than their provincial opposites as psychological symbols. The contradiction of their lives in public was that they wanted to shield themselves from individual attention, and the machines provided them the means to do so, yet they scrutinized the appearances of others so shielded for revealing clues about states of personal feeling. How does a black broadcloth suit come to seem a "social hieroglyphic," to use Marx's phrase? The answer lies in seeing the new ideas of immanent personality mesh with the mass production of appearances in public.

The two phenomena which bourgeois people personalized in public appearances were class and sex. Through reading details of appearance strangers tried to determine whether someone had metamorphosed economic position into the more personal one of being a "gentleman." Sexual status became personalized in public as strangers tried to determine whether someone, for all her seeming propriety, gave out little clues in her appearance which marked her as a "loose" woman. Both the "gentleman" and the "loose" woman lurking behind the respectable lady were visually meaningful only as public phenomena. The gentleman and the loose woman out of the public light, at home, had wholly different connotations. A gentleman at home was an attentive person, especially to the needs of his wife. His appearance was not the issue. The perception of a woman's looseness within the family was a perception of her behavior, not of giveaway clues in how she looked or dressed.

How do you recognize a gentleman when you meet a stranger? In *La Diorama*, a popular story set in Paris in the 1840s, a young man suddenly comes into an inheritance. He immediately resolves to buy some good clothes. When he has finished outfitting himself, he encounters a friend on the streets who is a republican, scornful of privileged wealth. And this friend does not by looking at him recognize that he has suddenly acquired wealth, because the clothes do not obviously proclaim the facts. But here there is a second step. He is hurt because, as a young man initiated, he can tell whether the clothes are those of a gentleman or not. Since the friend doesn't know the rules, he can notice nothing. This works in reverse too. When the young man goes to a factory he cannot read the rank of the various workers, although his friend can instantly. That is to say, this clothing does speak socially; it has a code which can be broken.

In 1750, the use of color, emblems, hats, trousers, breeches were instant signs of social place that everyone on the street could know; they may not have been an accurate index, but they were clear if arbitrary signs. These young people of the 1840s inhabit a world where the laws are accessible only to initiates. The clues the initiate reads are created through a process of miniaturization.

Details of workmanship now show how "gentle" a man or woman is. The fastening of buttons on a coat, the quality of fabric counts, when the fabric itself is subdued in color or hue. Boot leather becomes another sign. The tying of cravats becomes an intricate business; how they are tied reveals whether a man has "stuffing" or not, what is tied is nondescript material. As watches become simpler in appearance, the materials used in their making are the mark of the owner's social standing. It was, in all these details, a matter of subtly marking yourself; anyone who proclaims himself a gent obviously isn't.

A Russian visitor to the Jockey Club asked his hosts to define a gentleman: was this an inherited title, a caste, or a question of cash? The answer he received was that a gentleman disclosed his quality only to those who had the knowledge to perceive it without being told. The Russian, a rather abrupt soul, demanded to know what form these disclosures would take, and one member replied to him, as though breaking a confidence, that one could always recognize gentlemanly dress because the buttons on the sleeves of a gentleman's coat actually buttoned and unbuttoned, while one recognized gentlemanly behavior in his keeping the buttons scrupulously fastened, so that his sleeves never called attention to this fact.

Miniaturization extended down into the ranks of the petite bourgeoisie and upper working classes. The use of lace frills becomes in the 1840s a mark of social standing, a mark gentlemen could not pick up. The sheer cleanliness of small articles of clothing like the neckband may be enough for a shopkeeper, inspecting someone to whom he is introduced, to decide whether he is one of us or not.

The characters of loose and respectable women were read through the same combination of inflation and miniaturization. In his study of Victorian sexuality, *The Other Victorians*, Steven Marcus has shown how the medical and social picture of the mid-19th Century prostitute laid great stress on her resemblance to the ordinary respectable woman. Here is Acton, a physician, on the physical similarities:

> If we compare the prostitute at thirty-five with her sister, who perhaps is the married mother of a family, or has been a toiling slave for years in the over-heated laboratories of fashion, we shall seldom find that the constitutional ravages thought to be necessary consequences of prostitution exceed those attributable to the cares of a family.

Nor in street behavior do loose women show themselves specially. They give off small clues only, a glance held too long, a gesture of languor, which a man who knows how to read will understand.[6]

This similarity worked from the other side as well. How was a respectable woman to set herself off from a loose one, let alone a fallen woman, if the resemblance was so close? How could she, presumably innocent and pure, pick up the knowledge to guide her? There arose out of this dilemma a need to pay great attention to details of appearance and to hold oneself in, for fear of being read wrong or maliciously; indeed, who knew, perhaps if one gave off miniature signals of being loose, one really was.

Miniaturization operated, in the perception of "looseness," in terms of the body itself. Since the major limbs of the body were covered, and since the shape of the female body dressed bore no relationship to the body undressed, little things like the slight discoloration of the teeth or the shape of the fingernails became signs of sexuality. Furthermore, inanimate objects which surrounded the person could in their details be suggestive in such a way that the human being using or seeing them felt personally compromised. Some readers may remember the piano-leg covers in their grandfather's homes, or the dining-room table-leg covers; it was considered improper for the legs of anything to show. The idiocy of such prudery can so cloud the mind that its source is forgotten. All appearances have personal meanings: if you believe that little gestures with the eyes may involuntarily betray feelings of sexual license, it becomes equally rational to feel that the exposed legs of a piano are provocative. The root of this indiscriminate fear is as much cultural as sexual, or, better, it was the change in culture which permitted the Victorian bourgeoisie to become more prudish than their 18th Century forebears. And that cultural change, leading to the covering of piano legs, has its roots in the very notion that all appearances speak, that human meanings are immanent in all phenomena.

One's only defense against such a culture was in fact to cover up, and from this came the stony feminine fear of being seen in public. To be shielded from light, from the streets, from exposure of the limbs, was the rule for bodily appearance. Here is how one writer describes it:

> Few Victorians were seen closely in strong light once they had passed their youth. At night they were aureoled by oil lamps and gaslights; during the day they lay in semi-darkness. They undressed in the dark; the rich woman would breakfast in bed and come down to the main part of the house when her husband had left for his office, his club, or his estate.

The 1840s were an age in which the hooded bonnet reappeared as an article of genteel dress; later the thick veil appeared as a feature of middle-class garb, one which shielded the face almost completely.

As people's personalities came to be seen in their appearances, facts of class and sex thus became matters of real anxiety. The world of immanent truths is so much more intense and yet so much more problematical than the public world of the *ancien régime* in which appearances were put at a distance from self. In the coffeehouse, in the theater, in one's clothing, the facts of social standing were so suspended or so stated, even if false, that they needn't of necessity raise questions in a social situation. A man might or might not be what his clothes proclaimed, but the proclamation was clear. Through convention, the anxiety about whom you were talking to was less than in the Victorian situation, where a process of decoding had become necessary. Investigative logic is necessary as a means of making contact with the individual who might or might not flourish behind the façade of appearance. If, however, one did not know the rules that governed particular appearances, did not know how to "read" a cravat tied, or the existence of a kerchief worn over the chignon, you could never be sure of your deductions about whom you were meeting on the street. The compulsive attention to detail, the anxiety for facts which has since come to obsess us in so many ways, was born out of this anxiety about what appearances symbolize.

Closely tied to a code of personality immanent in public appearances was a desire to control these appearances through increasing one's consciousness of one-self. Behavior and consciousness stand, however, in a peculiar relationship; behavior comes before consciousness. It is involuntarily revealed, difficult to control in advance, precisely because there are no clear rules for reading the miniature details; they are clear only to initiates, and neither in acting as a gentleman nor in appearing as a woman of absolute respectability is there ever a stable code to use. In sexuality as in fashion, once "anyone" could pass on a certain set of terms, those terms became meaningless. A new set of clues, a new code to penetrate arises; the mystification of personality is as continued as the mystification of new goods in stores. Consciousness becomes therefore retrospective activity, control of what has been lived—in the words of G. M. S. Young, the work of "unraveling" rather than "preparing." If character is involuntarily disclosed in the present, it can be controlled only through seeing it in the past tense.

A history of nostalgia has yet to be written, yet surely this past-tense rela-tionship of consciousness to behavior explains a crucial difference between 18th and 19th Century autobiography. In 18th Century memoirs like Lord Hervey's, the past is nostalgically recalled as a time of innocence and modest feeling. In the 19th Century memoir, two new elements are added. In the past one was "really alive," and if one could make sense of the past, the confusion of one's present life might be lessened. This is truth via retrospection. Psychoanalytic therapy comes out of this Victorian sense of nostalgia, as does the modern cult of youthfulness.

In a more happy light, it thus arose that during the 19th Century in both Paris and London the detective and the mystery novel became a popular genre. Detectives are what every man and woman must be when they want to make sense of the street. Take, for example although the example comes from later in the century), passages from Conan Doyle's Sherlock Holmes stories—like the following—which so delighted us as children. In "A Case of Identity," a young woman walks into Holmes's Baker Street flat; he takes one glance at her.

> "Do you not find," he said, "that with your short sight it is a little trying
> to do so much typewriting?"

The girl and, as always, Watson are amazed that Holmes could deduce this. After she has left, Watson remarks:

"You appeared to read a good deal upon her which was quite invisible to me."

To which Holmes makes the famous reply:

"Not invisible but unnoticed, Watson. You did not know where to look, and so you missed all that was important. I can never bring you to realize the importance of sleeves, the suggestiveness of thumbnails, or the great issues that may hang from a boot-lace."[7]

That sentence could easily have served Balzac as a motto; his methods of characterization, too, were based on decoding isolated details of appearance, magnifying the detail into an emblem of the whole man. Indeed, that magnification he practiced upon himself, as with his famous canes, writing to Madame Hanska one day, for instance:

You cannot exaggerate the success my latest cane has had in Paris. It threatens to create a European fashion. People are talking about it in Naples and Rome. All the dandies are jealous.

Remarks like this were, unfortunately, innocent of any irony.[8]

[. . .]

Notes

1 Geoffrey Squire, *Dress and Society, 1560–1970* (New York: Viking, 1974), p. 110.
2 Quotation from Johan Huizinga, *Homo Ludens* (Boston: Beacon Press, 1955), p. 211; Elizabeth Burris-Meyer, *This Is Fashion* (New York: Harper, 1943), p. 328; R. Turner Wilcox, *The Mode in Hats and Headdress* (New York: Scribner's, 1959), pp. 145–46.
3 Lester and Kerr, *Historic Costume* (Peoria, Ill.: Chas. A. Bennett, 1967), pp. 147–48; quotation from *ibid.*, pp. 148–49.
4 Wilcox, *The Mode in Hats and Headdress*, p. 145; quotation in Iris Brooke, *Western European Costumes, 17th to Mid-19th Centuries, and Its Relation to the Theatre* (London: George Harrap & Co. Ltd., 1940), p. 76.
5 Quotation from James Laver, *Drama, Its Costume and Decor* (London: The Studio Ltd., 1951), p. 154.
6 Quoted in Steven Marcus, *The Other Victorians* (New York: Random House, 1964), pp. 5–6.
7 Quotations from A. Conan Doyle, *The Complete Sherlock Holmes* (Garden City, N.Y.: Doubleday, 1930), p. 96.
8 Quotation from Balzac in Pritchett, *op. cit.*, p. 166.

Chapter 35

Ulrich Lehmann

BENJAMIN AND THE REVOLUTION OF FASHION IN MODERNITY

Die Mode ist die ewige Wiederkehr des Neuen.
–Gibt es trotzdem gerade in der Mode Motive der Rettung?
Walter Benjamin, "Zentralpark" (1939/1940)[1]

THE VARIOUS INTERPRETATIONS of fashion follow an immanent logic. First, Baudelaire, Gautier, and others established *la mode* at the birth of *la modernité*. Mallarmé brought this concept to its most fugitive and sophisticated conclusion: *La Dernière Mode*, the la(te)st fashion—a sartorial *Gesamtkunstwerk* conceived in the age of commodities. These original conceptualizations of fashion in modernity, both pictorial and literal, had to generate an analytical interest in its tendencies. Simmel was the first, some two decades after Mallarmé's magazine was published, to inquire into the possible rationale behind sartorial intricacies. In this chapter we will see how Walter Benjamin went one step beyond Simmel. Once fashion's rationale had been explained, its political potential had to be explored. In the tiger's leap, Benjamin applied that rationale, taking it in the obvious direction.

The object

The hallmark of modernity is the ever-growing objectification of society. Marx interpreted particular aspects of this tendency as *Entfremdung* (alienation), Simmel characterized it more neutrally as *Verdinglichung* (reification), and Weber as *Rationalizierung* (rationalization).

In order to explain the new sociocultural parameters in society, these theoreticians thus perceived the *object* as representative of the grander social structure, the cultural fragment as representative of the totality of the historical process. A Hegelian heritage leads scholars, especially German ones, to focus on the subject–object relation, now seen not as "man-nature" but as "man (subjective perception–object (inorganic commodity)." One object in particular, because of its spatial and metaphysical proximity to the subject itself, came to express the intricate and varied aspects of modernity—that is, sartorial fashion, adorning and enveloping the human body and comprising a faceted multitude of garments and accessories.

Most significant for fashion is its ephemeral, transient, and futile character, which changes with every season. This insubstantiality with regard to linear historical progress, as well as fashion's marginal position in the cultural spectrum, appealed especially to those who considered the fragment particularly expressive for modern culture, representing *in nuce* (as well as *in novità*) the shape of modernity. Not least because of Simmel's influential view of the fragment, a number of men who had listened to his lectures as students continued to explore the inherent metaphysical value in the marginal and popular expressions of culture.

Walter Benjamin (1892–1940) closely followed Simmel in defining fashion as the ultimate metaphor for the varied views on modern life concentrating on its fragmentation and diversity. Based on his reading of Baudelaire and Proust, whose works he translated and analyzed, Benjamin looked back on the nineteenth century both as the birthplace and the childhood of modernity and as a "prehistory" that would influence contemporary historicism and a materialist/messianic interpretation of society.

From 1927 up to his premature death in 1940, Benjamin assembled material for a study of the nineteenth century that was to decipher modernity's political, poetical, and philosophical potential from the visual and literary fragments he found in the streets and libraries of Paris, a city he proclaimed as the "capitale du XIXe siècle."[2] The assemblage of this material he provisionally titled *Passagenarbeit* (*Arcades Project*) after what he considered to be the architectural cradle of modern society. For him, the glass-roofed links between Parisian streets and boulevards maintained, in their often-dilapidated condition, the mystique of nineteenth-century life and the remembrance of the first age of consumerism.

In the tradition of Baudelaire, Mallarmé, Proust, and Simmel, Benjamin focused on sartorial fashion as the single metaphor capable of evoking the time he was trying to recapture for his work. The simple number of references to the word *Mode*, as well as the multiple connections and far-reaching conclusions drawn from them, renders fashion the central issue, somewhat obfuscated by epistemological excerpts, for his incomplete *chef d'œuvre*. Within the project, a great number of topoi are raised and elaborated on. Yet fashion is rarely mentioned, let alone interpreted.[3] One of the aims of this chapter is to assess fashion's significance for the *Arcades Project*. Benjamin's view of the relation *mode et modernité* is described in the context of studies of the subject both literary (Baudelaire and Proust) and theoretical (Marx and Simmel)—studies he quoted directly for his project or that coincide with his own approach to the sartorial.

The idea of fashion

Reading through the French and German sources up to 1928 in order to trace out a philosophical tradition concerned with the sartorial, Benjamin remained frustrated by his search. In a letter to the poet Hugo von Hofmannsthal he bemoaned "the sparse material that thus far constitutes all efforts to describe and fathom fashion philosophically."[4]

Implicitly, Benjamin's task would be to come up with a more penetrating and inspirational study of the subject. Yet within an academic or "intellectual" context, the question always arises whether fashion is, in its "frivolity," not just one marginal element in the much larger fabric of life. Isn't it a phenomenon that merely manifests instead of occupying a cultural (let alone metaphysical) sphere and thus meriting philosophical speculation? Does Benjamin merely show the interest of someone who takes pleasure in reading between the lines (or folds) of a text, but not of a theorist who aims at a final assessment of culture or modernity as such?

The presumptions behind such questions, partly founded on a biased view of fashion's inherent insubstantiality and transitoriness, which accordingly appears to mark Benjamin's interest in fashion as nothing but indulgence, were refuted by an altogether unexpected source. In his last work, titled *Aesthetic Theory*, Theodor Adorno, much more inclined to follow the prosaic and substantial in his philosophical discourse, acknowledged his debt to Benjamin in battling for a perception of fashion as fundamental to aesthetics and politics alike.

> The usual tirades against fashion that equate the fugitive with the futile are not only allied with the ideology of inwardness and interiority, which has long since been exposed politically and aesthetically as an inability to externalize something and as a narrow-minded concern with the thusness of the individual. Despite its commercial manipulation fashion reaches deep into the works of art, not simply exploiting them. Inventions like Picasso's painting with light appear as transpositions of experiments in haute couture where the cloth for dresses is merely draped around the body and pinned together with needles for one night, instead of tailoring it in the usual sense. Fashion is one of the ways in which historical change affects the sensory apparatus and through it works of art—in minimal traits, often hidden from themselves.[5]

Here, Adorno moved directly from the sartorial surface to sensual perception and historical progress. He thus followed both Simmel and Benjamin toward the same goal, fashion's metaphysics. Benjamin had postulated some forty years earlier that it was integral to modernity that contemporary fashion (i.e., a fashion aware of its heritage and tradition) came to play the counterpoint to apolitical and restricted forms of sensualism—precisely because it appeared to have originated from such an apolitical stance. Significantly, Adorno deduced a material insubstantiality from the fact that any haute couture creation is unique and remains singular (even if the same dress is at times measured for up to three clients) until the next collection. The pride that both those in ancillary industries (weavers, embroiderers, etc.) and the seamstresses take in producing, often right up to the *défilé*, perfect examples of their craftsmanship is negated because of the facile appearance of the design. The dialectical structure that lies in the perfect creation of sartorial fashion, namely that it was designed to last forever by those aware that it will "die" within six months (cf.

Simmel), remained unrecognized by Adorno, since he does not consider the topic capable of carrying such profound meaning.

More apparent for Adorno is the Benjaminian notion that *die Mode* possesses the power to fashion a new look for history. It does so on a large scale, by reshaping the silhouette of historical structures, by altering the way one perceives the succession of past epochs and the relation of the present to them—thus time itself. On a smaller scale it also focuses on the sociohistorical accessories, on the nuances within the appearance of the past, that reveal and determine more than mere historicism ever would.

After having considered a possible structure for his project, Benjamin in 1928 felt confident about coming to terms with the amount of literature and research that would provide him with the foundation for his work on Paris in the nineteenth century. However, up to that point he had focused merely on topical interpretations and did not foresee the multitude of possible approaches. "I continue to think about the things you said to me concerning the *Paris Arcades* project when you were here," wrote Benjamin to Hofmannsthal, a poet and dramatist whom he greatly respected, not least because of his role in Berlin's cultural life (in conjunction with Count Kessler, Simmel, etc.). "What you said drew on your own plans and was supportive and lent precision to my thinking, while making what I should most emphasize ever clearer to me. I am currently looking into the sparse material that thus far constitutes all efforts to describe and fathom fashion philosophically: into the question of what this natural and totally irrational, temporal measure of the historical process is all about."[6]

The "irrational" aspect was later given a more complete analysis in Benjamin's "Central Park" fragments and in the equally fragmentary "Theses on the Philosophy of History" (both ca. 1938–1940), written in close conjunction with his study on Baudelaire, whose essay on the painter of modern life first sparked Benjamin's awareness of the paradigmatic value of fashion within modernity. Yet did he continue to regard fashion and its relation to historiography as the main topic of the *Arcades Project* after his first studies on the Parisian arcades were undertaken (1927–1929)?

The answer can be found in a conversation that would take place in 1939: Georges Bataille, part of the troika that led the Collège de Sociologie, had earlier that year approached Benjamin to give a talk on the ambitious project that was known to be consuming most of his time and energy. In autumn he finally caught up with the German immigrant and inquired what the topic of the promised lecture would be. Benjamin's reply was terse: "Fashion." The German philosopher Hans Mayer, who witnessed the exchange, maintains that this was a "coded" answer.[7] In fact, what Benjamin intended to talk about was the *Arcades Project* as a whole. His reply had been just one of the "understatements and mystifications he favoured so much."[8] Indeed, the choice of subject must have been hard to appreciate. To those aware of existing on the brink of a catastrophe and having an at least partial knowledge of the atrocities being committed in Mayer and Benjamin's native country,[9] as well as knowledge of their own precarious existence in the French capital, the idea of anyone presenting (to a largely politicized and progressive audience) a paper on a topic as "marginal" as fashion must have seemed impudent. For Benjamin, however, that was the subject foremost in his thoughts. It had guided him first through a labyrinth of visual and textual sources and subsequently directed him toward a materialist concept of history. By 1939, fashion had already changed from being just one element of nineteenth-century cultural history to the essence of the *Arcades Project*.

Mode and metaphor

Skirting the memory

From the outset Benjamin was concerned with what his project could evoke in the reader's mind. One highly symbolic passage is retained throughout the years that lay between his earliest notes of 1927/1928, containing observations and quotes for his first exposition on the "Pariser Passagen," and the later manuscript sheafs, assembled in his Parisian exile, which constitute the base from which the project would have grown: "What the child (and in much weaker recollection the man) discovers in the folds of an old fabric, into which he pressed himself while holding on to the mother's skirt—this has to be part of these pages."[10] We see here some of the connotations that fashion is able to carry, and that Benjamin's writing explores: the tactile and olfactory qualities of the fabric as well as the warmth and the intimate scent of the skirt, evoking not only the wearer but also her surroundings, as the much-worn textile takes on the odor of the room she moves in. These qualities universalize the metaphor, as the sensation has a collective, archetypal air about it—something every person has experienced at some point in his or her childhood. In designating the sex of the child in the phrase added in parentheses, Benjamin's adds a psychological dimension to the metaphor. Pressing one's face deep into the folds (and not just on the plain surface of the fabric) of a textile that clothes the female lower body has strong fetishistic connotations. Thus this act would determine to some degree the boy's sexual rite of passage.[11]

But above all, the passage is about remembrance—about "the remembrance of things past" to be precise, since Benjamin's project on the Parisian passages had also followed on his preoccupation with Proust's evocation of *le temps perdu*, the observation of nineteenth-century Paris that would also, despite their different premises, become Benjamin's subject matter. "When the Romans described a text as a fabric," as we have read already in Benjamin . . ., "then none is finer and more densely woven than Marcel Proust's." And he adds:

> There is yet another sense in which remembrance issues a strict weaver's notation [diagram to plot weaving patterns]. Only the actus purus of remembering itself, not the character of the author, let alone the narrative, constitutes the unity of the text. Indeed, one could say that this intermittence is merely the reverse side of remembrance's continuum, the back pattern of a tapestry. This is what Proust meant, and this is how he must be understood, when he said that he would prefer to see his entire work printed in one volume in two columns, without any paragraphs at all.[12]

Text becomes textile; the collected works of remembrance are ideally woven like a tapestry or fabric, similar both in epistemological structure and in textual appearance. Benjamin described the appearance this fabric was meant to lend to life: "*À la recherche du temps perdu* is the continuous attempt to charge an entire existence with the utmost presence of mind. Proust's method consists of realization [*Vergegenwärtigung*], not reflection." This *Vergegenwärtigung*, which in German stands for both realization and the act of bringing something into the present, was read as the dialectical image, a tiger's leap into historical awareness: "This dialectical penetration and realization [*Vergegenwärtigung*] of past correlations puts the truth in present action to the test. This means: it causes the explosive that is contained in the past (and whose symbol proper is *fashion*) to ignite. To approach the past in such a way means not to deal with it, as previously, in a historical but rather in a political manner, within political categories."[13]

The sartorial brings in its train the political, and an intricate pattern begins to take shape. Benjamin's analysis of nineteenth-century Paris and its arcades has to constitute an act of remembrance. For this notion, this textum, Proust's *Recherche* offers a complex notion for the weaver. Moreover, it represents in itself the aspiration to render text into a fabric, designing the pattern for a narrative silhouette defined by openly visible seams: *temps perdu* becomes *temps retrouvé*. However, the fabric forms an infinite number of pleats and folds in which the child's memory is embedded, and the meanings of the work remain hidden.[14] Benjamin used this model as more than a mere reference. He also developed from it, as becomes clear in the close relation between metaphors, a structure for a new approach to the philosophy of history. He finds in Proust's textum the constant realization of the past within the present, leading him to the concept of the "dialectical image" in which the explosive within history is ignited and subsequently blasts the very foundations of historicism.[15] As this explosive is fashion, it becomes apparent that fashion is the indispensable catalyst for both remembrance and a new political—that is, materialist—concept of history. Yet this model is not simply a structural abstract, it is also deeply and sensually woven into Proust's literary style, as Benjamin observed in his essay "The Image of Proust." Throughout his work on the *Passagenarbeit* Benjamin would move between the analytical and materialist approach to fashion taking it as an indicator of social relations, and the poetic one that regards fashion as a simulacrum for the human figure and his or her emotions.

Like his work on Baudelaire,[16] Benjamin's study on Proust developed initially from efforts to render the author into German. Parts of the *Recherche* had been translated by Benjamin, working closely with the Berlin author Franz Hessel, between November 1925 and December 1926.[17] The project began with *Sodome et Gomorrhe*, which Benjamin translated on his own (the manuscript has apparently been lost); then followed *A l'ombre des jeunes filles en fleurs* and *Le Côté de Guermantes*, which were published in 1927 and 1930, respectively. During that period Benjamin made frequent allusions to an essay he envisaged bearing the title "En traduisant Marcel Proust" ("To Translate Marcel Proust").[18] Early "arabesques" for this project were "spun" by Benjamin in February 1929[19] at a time when he reached also the first conclusions for his project on the Parisian arcades. One of the notes for the Proust essay, which was published some four months later, read: "The hallmark of his creation which is hidden in the folds of his text (textum = fabric) is remembrance.

To put it differently: before Proust no one had been able to prize open the secret drawer of "atmosphere" and make what had been inside truly his own (so far only a scent had been pouring out from it)."[20] Benjamin's metaphor of the fold, which at first appeared to generate and determine the child's memory, and later that of the grown man, thus is revealed to have originated in his engagement with Proust's literary method. In "Neoclassicism in France," an essay published earlier that year, Benjamin altered and amended this metaphor to establish the connection between the Proustian use of fabric and gowns to evoke memories and the metaphysical value of the actual object—that is, the significance that fashion and elegance carry for the perception of past and present time. Musing about the gods in Jean Cocteau's version of *Orphée*, which had been staged in Berlin during the winter of 1928/1929, Benjamin concludes: "Perhaps these gods are very good at understanding the threshold between times. In Proust they thus trouble a scent with a whiff of their presence or break from a fold (and it is always the most recent vial, the cut of the latest fashion; it is always the most elegant, most ephemeral medium of these archaic workings)."[21]

Why the fascination with the metaphor of the fold? On the one hand it is obvious that Benjamin ascribed great stylistic value to metaphor—both for literary and, following Simmel's method, philosophical reasons. In a letter to Hofmannsthal he wrote: "I am currently paying close attention to Proust's use of metaphor. In an interesting controversy with Thibaudet about Flaubert's style, Proust declares metaphor to be the essence of style itself. I admire the way in which he updates the perhaps generalized tradition of the great poets to extract a metaphor from the nearest and most banal element, adapts it to today's situation, and as it were mobilizes a whole complex of worn-out circumstances in order to employ them for a more fundamental expression."[22] Within this context, and in a vein perhaps instrumental for understanding his *Arcades Project*, Benjamin continues to lament the "difficulty of finding a place for the publication for my ephemeral, although perhaps not at all superficial, considerations."[23] Here he sides clearly with the French author's sentiment. Benjamin employed the metaphor of the fold, especially in conjunction with Proust's writing, because it appears mundane and banal—and, more important, because the fold determines the object that is closest to the human body and can be metaphorically transposed into writing.

Back in the fold

The skirt, or any other piece of clothing, for that matter, in which the child buries his face is inseparably tied to its wearer, even when it seems to have been discarded . . . As Théophile Gautier observed in *De la mode*: "The garment of the modern age has become for man of a sort of skin, which he is not prepared to forsake under any pretext and which clings to him like an animal's hide, nowadays to the point that the real shape of the body has been quite forgotten."[24] The drapes, pleats, and folds move with man, but they are not an actual part of his body. They are capable of forming their own microcosm of meanings, psychological as well as sociological. The intriguing task for the writer is to take this microcosm and develop out of it, or transpose it into, the macrocosm of human material existence. From this relation between micro- and macrocosm stems the potency of the sartorial metaphor. It is perfectly tailored to express in itself the position individuals assume toward their contemporaries as well as to history; but the metaphor is far from being direct, as it still carries with it the notion of replacement or estrangement. Although clothing is *worn*, it *does not belong to* the wearer. In representative fashion like formal attire, it even remains essentially alien to its possessor. In determining the wearer's every move, granting self-confidence or hindering his or her physical or social progress, fashion inflicts its own system of legality. Such power is especially evident in the dress code of the nineteenth century, since it had been to the utmost degree subject to social rules and customs. Suits and dresses were meant essentially to denote membership to a certain social caste and were not intended to make the wearer feel protected, warm, or comfortable. With the growth of a prosperous bourgeois class it became more difficult to establish class distinctions, as money could now buy access to what had formerly been exclusive in the code. Thus fashion changed its degree of formal rigidity and estrangement for those men and women who were already well versed (by birthright and upbringing) in its expressions and could play the rules of garb to their own taste. To be truly fashionable meant to possess a barely detectable (at least to the outsider) yet nevertheless expressive sign of sartorial individuality, within the confines of a vesture determined by the socially de rigueur.

Through representation and displacement, fashion comes to symbolize a human being. Thus the nineteenth-century poet, or the writer looking retrospectively at that period, sees fashion as the ultimate metaphor. When modernity led to a changing of the social and economic parameters, it also changed the cultural outlook. Artists who were progressive and contemporary enough to accept this challenge started looking for a way to engage with these changes that would at the same time reflect rationality—thus mirroring the positivism that was dominant in the nineteenth century due to the widespread belief in scientific and technological progress. Fashion, occupying the position of the eternally new, the constant pacesetter within rapidly progressing modernity, seemed from a positivist viewpoint a perfect agent. What fascinated the truly modern artist was fashion's mystique, its understanding of historical, even archaic expression, and—what Benjamin came to emphasize—its sense of the mythic, which offered a counterpoint to the threat of modern reification and rationalization, as well as providing a vehicle for aesthetic experience. The notion of the mythic became in turn the "other" in the ambiguity of modern existence, as observed by Bataille, Lacan, and others who regarded the subject as no longer in conflict with the object but in ambiguous rivalry with itself.[25]

More mundanely speaking, fashion is also an integral part of daily life—more so than any other form of applied art, let alone the "sublime" expressions of the fine arts. The great majority of us, at least of those who are not required wear a specific uniform, deeply contemplate dressing almost every morning of our life, whereas thoughts that concern art or artifacts come to us much less frequently.

What had been considered as artistically marginal, sociologically banal, and metaphysically ephemeral became—not within a season, but within the formative period of modernity—valuable and virtuous for the painters of modern life, that is, for those who attempted to artistically probe the myths of modern society. The spirit of elegance and contemporariness in fashion provided its original appeal for many artists, yet those who were able to see through the upper layer of clothing, beyond the outer pleats, realized, as Benjamin observed in Proust, that "it is always the most elegant, most ephemeral" that serves to indicate the archaic rules and perceptions that influence society and culture alike.

Much as happened in the debate between *modernité* and *antiquité*, the diametric opposition of up-to-date elegance and archaic spirit would prove to be fashion's greatest challenge to both philosophical and historical thought. Encompassing every-thing that was at the height of its time, yet in the same moment leading us back into antiquity, fashion became for Walter Benjamin the one dialectical image, the "tiger's leap in the open air of history"; and ultimately, as he would observed in Marx, it also became a symbol of modernity's potential for not merely stylistic but fundamental change.[26]

It was not for this reason alone that Benjamin intended to analyze and discuss fashion at length in his unfinished work on nineteenth-century Paris. The sheer volume of notes and excerpts he assembled concerning the topic speaks for itself. First there is the manuscript sheaf composed of almost a hundred notes and quota-tions on *Mode*. Next to it, the references to clothes or fashion in general—but like Simmel, Benjamin is almost exclusively concerned with sartorial fashion—are more than just numerous. They can be singled out among the notes he used for his first exposition, as the very foundations of the project; they thus become both the chalk marks for the outline and the seams on the fabric from which Benjamin would design his project.[27]

[. . .]

Within the historical continuum, a scientific or artistic product is appreciated only if considered stable and complete. Anything in a transient state has the suspect label of insubstantiality attached to it. Yet the changed modes of perception cham-pioned by modernity deliberately challenged this perception. The *Recherche* is of course "complete" insofar as the author was able to conclude the narrative (in *Le Temps retrouvé*); yet one can imagine how different the various proofs would have looked if Proust had lived to subject them to the same technique of constant addition that he had employed on all his manuscripts before 1922, when part 2 of *Sodome et Gomorrhe* appeared. Proust's remembrance was never to be completed, since every detail spurred a whole string of subsequent memories. The narrator's final reflection on his remembrance of things past meant that the whole process had to become almost infinite and self-perpetuating. Proust's position within the French narrative tradition makes it impossible to call the *Recherche* (unlike that other modernist mainstay *Finnegans Wake*) a "work in progress." Yet the idea that some writing, even when published, derives part of its meaning and appeal, from remaining essentially incomplete and transient would become a feature of modernity.

After a Proustian fashion, although owing partly to different reasons, Benjamin's *Arcades Project* was meant to appear like a fabric—a fabric constantly in the making, woven from notes, materials, excerpts, and theoretical patterns, from which sub-sequent pieces on Baudelaire, fashion, revolution, history, and so forth were tail-lored. It was meant to remain a progressing assemblage of texts, and its fragmentary and ambiguous character, its discontinuity, was an inherent part of its potential. These *Passagen* are no "buildings"; this architectural metaphor merely establishes the surface. These *Passagen* are "passages" in the original French sense of *passer*, both "sujet nom d'être animé ou d'objet en mouvement" and "partie, fragment d'un texte."[28] Their significance appears complex and transient, shifting as the reader becomes a flâneur who saunters through them. Their transitoriness, the way in which an archaic, mythic quality becomes fused into the modern, is important for Benjamin's perception of the past, of *antiquité*: "*Rites de passage*. . . . These periods of transition have become increasingly hard to recognize and are experienced less and less. We have become lacking in threshold experience. Perhaps the only one that is left to us is the sensation of going to sleep. (But with it also the sensation of waking.)"[29] The rites of passage in modernity are not elaborated rituals in the anthropological sense, aimed, for example, at initiating an adolescent into the society of adults. They occur in a much more subtle, less recognizable way. One of the most significant *rites de passage vestimentaire* in the nineteenth century took place on the first special occasion on which a boy was allowed to discard his short pants or knee breeches in favor of the long trousers worn by grown men. This change of attire was the primary outer expression for the actual rite of passage in society, the boy's leaving home to go to a boarding school or *école*.

The emphasis Benjamin put on the sensation of going to sleep and subsequently awakening, as the only "threshold of experience" left to modern men and women, again refers to Proust's act of remembrance: "In the same way in which Proust begins his life story with waking, each representation of history has to start with waking; in fact, it should not be concerned with anything else. So this one [the *Arcades Project*] is about waking from the nineteenth century."[30] The historian has to be able not only to read a dream psychoanalytically but also to understand its literary transposition. In dreams as in fashion, the truth lies in the folds, not merely in appearance. He notes, "the exploitation of dream elements in waking is the canon for dialectics. It is exemplary for the thinker and imperative for the historian."[31] Dialectical historiography evolves from the transition between dream and waking, and the history, in this instance that of the nineteenth century, is one of collective memory (perhaps part of the collective unconscious) into which we sink while sleeping, only to travel forward through time to wake up and find ourselves confronted with the remembrance of these dream fragments. This is indeed what the young Marcel experiences at the very beginning of *La Recherche*. Waking in the middle of the night, still half asleep, he feels at first like a prehistoric man, equipped only with archaic sensations. Yet memories quickly "would come like a rope let down from heaven to draw me up out of the abyss of not-being, from which I could never have escaped myself: in a flash I would traverse centuries of civilization, and out of a blurred glimpse of oil-lamps, then of shirts with turned-down collars, would gradually piece together the original components of my ego."[32] The vague image of turned-down collars is an ambiguous memory. It could refer back to a period before the nineteenth century (throughout which high collars had been de rigueur or to the time when the protagonist had been a little child, too young to wear anything but soft shirts with *cols rabattus*. Yet the memory helps Marcel find himself and, as he remembers an ephemeral element from the past, helps establish his own presence within the course of history.[33]

Barthes would some decades later also evoke the symbolic dimension of clothes within a mythical dream and connect it with the transitory that we find expressed both in Benjamin's project and in fashion itself: "On the one hand, we could say that in its profane way the garment reflects the old mystical dream of the "seamless" ["*sans couture*"]: since the garment envelops the body, is not the miracle precisely that the body can enter it without leaving behind any trace of this passage?"[34] Clothing has an essence that is unrelated to the body it adorns. Clothes and accessories take on a symbolic value that requires abstract perception, omitting the human element. The sartorial is seen thus as object influencing the physical subject and not vice versa. Yet a conflicting tendency rose throughout the nineteenth century: words that had been essentially metaphorical and flexible in their possible connotations became to some extent victims of the rationalizing tendencies in materialist society. Despite the "heroic" efforts of the decadent poets and symbolists, they began to appear almost one-dimensional, reconstructed, and immobile. For example, the evocative symbolic meaning of the *passage* was lost with the iron construction of the new arcades; and the "threshold," which had acted previously as the demarcation line of a metaphysical crossing into mythic territories, became exclusively used to describe the boundary of a private bourgeois *intérieur*.[35]

Siding with surrealist perception, Benjamin attempts to overcome this limitation by evoking a past multitude of meanings and by returning to the metaphysics of the *passage*. After having established a dialectical image for the more than century-old arcade by incorporating its past rational appearance, its archaic symbolism, and its mythic qualities (present and in retrospect), Benjamin uses arcades as a setting for numerous phenomena in his "prehistory of the nineteenth century," as Adorno fittingly characterized it. Fashion, because of its marginal and ephemeral character, could more easily escape the existing rigidity of attribution. Its varied, ever-changing appearance made it best suited to become the most frequent and most complex of metaphors in the *Passagenarbeit*. Its having been left theoretically unexplored—except by Simmel—further accounts for its significance.

With the emergence of a modern bourgeois society, the importance of history as a philosophical foundation for the present declined, while modernity created a history for itself. Substituting for knowledge handed down through earlier generations was a less examined hope and a positivist expectation in the future. This was partly due, as Tarde and subsequently Simmel argued, to the ever-growing dominance of "l'époque extériorisée" over "la vie intérieure," and to the modernist belief that technology could create an utopian construct. On a metaphysical level, the change was rooted in the dominance of anticipation over experience.

Apart from an "Iconoclastic" attitude toward a past that came to be perceived almost as ballast, this teleological understanding of history had to neglect the revolutionary potential that lay within things to come. "Where progress coagulates into historical norm, the quality of novelty and the emphasis upon unpredictable beginnings are eliminated from the present's relationship with the future," observes Habermas in discussing Benjamin's work.[36] Past experiences are merely additions to the mass of facts with which historicism—that is, a continuous, apparently logical progression of historical facts—fills "the homogeneous and empty time."[37]

While the future is robbed of its ability to exert force, the past becomes without relevance to present time. Also, and even more drastically, the present itself becomes a mere transitional period without any significant value of its own. Early in 1937, in an essay on Eduard Fuchs, a Viennese cultural historian, Benjamin wrote down a number of reflections that would later become part of his fragmented "Theses." His solution to the shortcomings in historicism was to create a new concept of historiography, "whose object is not a ball of mere facticities, but [which] creates it [historiography] out of the counted group of threads which represent the weft of the past fed into the fabric [*Textur*] of the present. (It would be a mistake to equate this weft with a mere causal nexus. Rather, it is a thoroughly dialectical mode. For centuries threads can become lost and are picked up by the actual course of history in a disjointed and inconspicuous manner.)"[38] Here again Benjamin returned to the equation text = textum (a root of which *Textur* is but an inflection). He describes weft yarn from the past inconspicuously woven into present fabric . . . a construct that again underlines the paradigmatic value that Benjamin attached to fashion in the *Arcades Project*.

To some extent, Benjamin equates the "dialectical" reasoning mentioned in this context with his reading of historical materialism. In the later stages of the *Arcades Project* a number of references to "fetish character" and "accumulation of value" emerged. They focus on Marx's famous evocation of twenty yards of fabric and the one garment that is made from it.[39] In "Walter Benjamin's Historicism," H. D. Kittsteiner describes the "true myth of modernity" as "the myth of complete heteronomy, one in which no gods, heroes, or men appear—only things. It has been told by Karl Marx: it is the story of the birth of money from the mutual reflection of twenty yards of linen and one coat."[40]

At first Marx's example seems arbitrary; one would think that any number of commodities could assume the character of a fetish. Yet in light of Freud's adoption of the term from its anthropological source, it becomes obvious that the aptness of the psychoanalytical coinage of "fetish" arises from its reference, via Marx's earlier use, to a particular aspect of substitution: the sartorial one. The organic product of linen is not only represented by the "equivalent form" of the coat, it is also a raw material that, through the labor process, would become an artificial, inorganic commodity for which it originally constituted a "relative form of value."[41] The sartorial product itself is extremely close to its wearer—a second skin—but as a commodity, not to mention an artificial status symbol, essentially estranged from him or her. It maintains a distinct meaning and value of its own. Therefore it has an additional potential to become a fetish.

As the original point of reference for Marx's dialectics, as well as for his notion of subject and object,[42] Hegel had anticipated the "objective" position of clothing in his *Aesthetics*: fashion has to follow its very own principle, "for the body is one thing, the clothing another, and the latter must come into its own independently and appear in its freedom."[43] Fashion's independence is expressed positively as freedom: a freedom exemplified in creative designs to clothe the human body as well as a freedom to exist without it, as an object that is altered depending on the subject who slips on the clothes. Yet this independence alienates the object, as a commodity, as a fetish, from the body it is originally meant to warm, protect, or cover in modesty. And although not a product of modern times as such, the estrangement of the sartorial commodity from its wearer first became significant in nineteenth-century capitalism with its broadened consumer base.

A fetish in fashion

Benjamin begins by including an analytical assessment of the fetish character in the world of commodities found in a 1928 analysis of Marx.[44] In the fashion manuscripts of the *Arcades Project*, he then progresses to a much more revealing evocation that floats between psychoanalysis and a surrealist dreamworld.

> In fetishism, the sexus puts down barriers separating the organic and the inorganic world. Clothing and jewelry are its allies. It is as much at home with what is dead as it is with living flesh. And the latter directs the accommodation of the sexus in the former. The hair is a confined region between both realms of the sexus. Another realm reveals itself in the raptures of passion: the landscapes of the body. These have ceased already to be animated, yet are still accessible to the eye, which, of course, as it ventures further, relinquishes its lead through this realm of death more and more to the sensations of touch and smell. Within a dream breasts often begin to swell, dressed like the earth in woods and rocks, and glances have sunk their lives far below the water surfaces that slumber in the valleys. These landscapes are crossed by paths that escort the sexus to the world of the inorganic. Fashion itself is only another medium that lures it even deeper into the material world [Stoffwelt].[45]

Unfettered by materialism, the character of the fetish is taken here from its historical, political confines and brought into a dream state, where death and *sexus* meet. This "chance encounter" (partly in a surrealist spirit)[46] is initiated by fashion—we will see how for Benjamin eros and thanatos coexist within it—and the waking from this dream is defined by the last two sentences, where fashion's allure guides *sexus* into the *Stoffwelt*: a world made of fabrics, as well as materially fabricated.

Although the fetish is an integral part of Marx's socioeconomic analysis, it did not relate originally to dialectics. Nor does it relate, as Benjamin recognized in his postulates, to a new concept of history. However, modernity makes it possible for the sartorial fetish to adopt even this most complex of roles. To explain the connection, one has to go back to Benjamin's "initiation" into modernity: his translation of the *Tableaux parisiens* by Charles Baudelaire.

In "A une passante" the woman in her black robe passing the flâneur in the street epitomizes modernity, directing the poet's attention to the ephemeral nuance. In gathering and swinging the hem of her dress, specified by Baudelaire's scrutiny as being embroidered as if with festoons, she reveals her leg and thus provokes the erotic and subsequently sublimated thoughts of the beholder. The character of the fetish alludes in the poem both to the commodity, that is, the fashionable detail on the garment, and to the eroticism of the leg, which in itself can be seen only in its sartorial representation: adorned by stocking and shoe—in turn the most common objects of fetishism, as Freud would come to observe.[47]

After 1848 the length of the skirt fell and the *volants* became more numerous. Thus at the time of Baudelaire's poetic observation, the leg could no longer be seen beneath what his contemporary Gautier called the "mass of rich fabrics." The male gaze was forced to console itself with the shoe as a substitution for the original erotic focus on the female upper thigh and pelvis. Freud writes that fetishism originates in the boy's desire to peer at the woman's genitalia from below, that is, from the foot or shoe upward.[48] But it originates equally in the visually impenetrable crinoline fashion of the early 1860s and its subsequent transformation into the long bustled skirts of the 1880s. These forms of womenswear had provided the men, who came into Freud's practice at the turn of the century and after, with their childhood fascination for the shoe as the only visible lead to the female lower body. This remembrance then develops as a neurosis into adult fetishistic tendencies. Thus one can view the symptoms of fetishism, which were prefigured in the psyche, as having been initiated through the sartorial or its visual representation (e.g., in Guys's drawings).

The confluence of *mode et modernité*

The second paradigmatic value with which Benjamin credited fashion is explained by the sisterhood of *mode* and *modernité*. The sublime ideal within modernity—that is, the true nature of beauty, as Baudelaire defined it through the eyes of the painter of modern life—is found in clothing. It marks the starting point for his modern aesthetics because it possesses a distinct ambiguity, a dual attraction. Drawing on Guys's quest "de dégager de la mode ce qu'elle peut contenir de poétique dans l'historique, de tirer l'éternel du transitoire,"[49] Hans Robert Jauß stresses that fashion

> contains a twofold attraction. It embodies the poetical in the historical, the eternal within transitoriness. Beauty steps forth in fashion, not as a well-worn, timeless ideal but as the idea that man forms for himself of beauty, an idea that reveals the mores and aesthetics of his time and that allows man to get closer to what he aspires to be. Fashion demonstrates what Baudelaire calls the "double nature of beauty," which he conceptually equates with modernity: "La modernité, c'est le transitoire, le fugitif, le contingent, la moitié de l'art, dont l'autre moitié est l'éternel et l'immuable."[50]

Modernity defines beauty's double nature as incorporating both aspects of *la vie moderne*, that of historical presence and that of political actuality. And both are linked inseparably in Baudelaire's famous postulate on fashion, and of course in his own sensuality as well.

Benjamin took up the poet's notion some sixty years later and put particular emphasis on the historiopolitical side by ascribing to it an immanent—perhaps revolutionary, perhaps messianic—potential for historical change. For this potential to be realized, he had to find in modernity the time nexus [*Zeitkern*] in which the transitory element of aesthetics coincides with the standstill of the historical present. What Baudelaire established as the ideal of beauty, Benjamin thus transfers to a novel concept of history: "The historical materialist cannot deny himself the concept of a present which is not understood as a transition, but in which time stands still and has come to a stop. For this notion defines *the* present in which he himself is writing history. While historicism presents an "eternal" image of the past, the historical materialist describes a unique experience in it," he wrote in his reflections of 1940.[51] Between the ideas developed three years before in the essay on Fuchs and the late epistemological fragment above lies a note that defines the time nexus and ties it in with the *Tableaux* poem that Benjamin had translated and analyzed some fifteen years earlier. In one of the manuscripts of sheaf N (on epistemology and his theory of progress), he notes: "An emphatic refusal of the concept of 'timeless truth' is in order. Yet truth is not simply, as Marxism claims, a temporal form of cognition, but is bound to a time nexus [*Zeitkern*] which is contained in both the known and the knower [*Erkannten und Erkennenden*]. This holds so much truth, as the eternal is rather a ruche on a dress than an idea."[52]

In the encounter on the Parisian boulevard, the flâneur becomes captivated by the image of the woman "balançant le feston et l'ourlet." The transitory movement passing in front of him transfixes the poet. The woman's leg becomes statue-like, not merely in its sublime and "classical" beauty but because time is perceived as standing still, and he finds himself unable to move, "crispé comme un extravagant." The festoon or, for Benjamin, the ruche on the dress becomes eternal; her fashion is immortalized in a momentary time nexus, although it will change so very quickly and its wearer's "beauté fugitive" has already passed from his view. Here one finds the poetic in the historical, since the writer recounts the situation to a reader, and the eternal within the transitory. Constellations like the above were defined by Benjamin, in an aestheticization of Marx's theorem, as "dialectical images." The image of the eternal ruche was singled out and repeated in the fashion manuscript of the *Passagenarbeit*, which directly preceded the surreal description of the fetish.[53]

On the surface it appears as if sexual attraction prompted the poet-flâneur to pause and glance at the woman, and initially of course this is the case. But the desire was a specific one, that of the fetishist: the man whose eroticism is objectified, distanced from any interpersonal relationship. Analyzing Baudelaire's persona in the poem, Benjamin writes: 'The "jamais" is the climax of the encounter, when the poet's passion seems to be frustrated at first but in reality only now bursts out of him like a flame. . . . What makes body twitch spasmodically is not the excitement of a man in whom images has taken possession of every fibre of his being; it partakes more of the shock [*Chock*] with which the imperious desire suddenly overcomes a lonely man.'[54] The *Chock*, a Benjaminian term in its idiosyncratic spelling, is the sudden realization or materialization of the metaphysical element in the world. It generates the time nexus in which man, whether flâneur, poet, historian, or philosopher, finds the eternal within a transient passage.

> Where the thought stops short in a configuration that is saturated with tensions, it gives the latter a Chock, by which it crystallizes into a monad. The historical materialist approaches the historical object only where he encounters it as a monad. Within such a structure he recognizes the sign of a messianic cessation of the event, or, to put it differently, a revolutionary chance in the fight for the oppressed past. He takes cognizance of it in order to blast a specific epoch from the homogeneous course of history; thus he blasts a specific life from the epoch, thus a specific work from the lifework.[55]

As we have seen, Benjamin states in the fashion manuscripts that the "explosive agent" for the historical materialist is to be fashion. Its preference for quotation from the past allows for a clear separation from the continuum of history. The constant citation of clothing styles from the past within the present style liberates Benjamin from the prevalent concept of the *Wirkungsgeschichte*—the history of effects. In this structure, the anticipation of the future by the present directs its understanding of the past. Anticipation wins out over reflected experience . . . Friedrich Nietzsche called this concept a "critical view of history," Marx had employed it in historical materialism, and Heidegger ontologized it in *Sein und Zeit*.[56] Benjamin himself looks for "crystallization" and a *Chock* that would enable him to focus on each monad in the past century. Concurrently drawing on historical materialist thought, he aims at isolating the action which he ambiguously saw as both a messianic standstill that grants deliverance and a revolutionary act that could spark a violent conflict. The materialist experience in history can be subsumed under recurrent motifs that illustrate (for example) class conflicts or the relation between base and super-structure. But Benjamin frowns on adhering too closely to such orthodox notions. His concern is rather with the aesthetic experience, a singular idea of beauty or of life within an epoch. Following again the lead of the Baudelairean flâneur, he prefers the aesthetic reality of an epoch, as embodied in the newest cut, in the latest fashion, to flash momentarily before the eyes of the historian or philosopher.

Acquiring past experience in a way that is solely oriented toward the future renders the present an indistinct place for both the continuation of tradition and unqualified positivism alike; they combine in an objectivity that is essentially *wirkungsgeschichtlich*. Although there are different ways of reading this history of effects—stressing either the continuity within it or its discontinuous character—it is essentially influenced by the anticipation of the future and always regards the past as a "prehistory" of the present.[57] Only when the historian overcomes the tendency "to have the series of occurrences pass through his fingers like the beads of a rosary" is he able to understand the singular constellation that makes up an earlier epoch and, more important, his own. "He thus establishes a conception of the present as 'now-time' which is shot through with splinters of a messianic time."[58] Or, to quote Simmel's earlier metaphor, he recognizes the parts where weft yarn is shot into past's fabric. The hallmark of fashion, to constantly cite from the past in order to propagate the latest "revolution" in style, helps Benjamin reverse the relation between anticipation and experience and dispel the false sense of hope contained in exclusively positivist materialism. And the unashamedly open fetishistic character of the sartorial commodity, in both its materialist and psychoanalytic connotation, encourages a cynical view of society, as it recycles the old in order to generate new commerce. Being supremely realistic about its own limited life span, fashion continually proclaims the rift—through immanent death and rebirth—in the historical continuum, which can only be bridged by a great (tiger's) leap.

Benjamin ascribes to all former epochs a multitude of expectations that had been left unfulfilled: "The past carries with it a secret index, by which it is referred to redemption."[59] The present that eagerly awaits the future is left now with the task of remembering the past and accomplishing what had been expected. For Benjamin there exists no *querelle* between the ancient and the modern but a fusion of the archaic and modernity in the object, positively realized in fashion's potential and negatively expressed in the "hell of commodities" that was part of nineteenth-century Paris. Thus in his dialectical image, above all in the tiger's leap, one conflicting element folds into another. In these images the archaic coalesces with modern aesthetic expression; it contains both the threat of a repetition of past errors and a generic force that counter balances the destructive potential of modernity. The latter is the "redemption" Benjamin describes, which gives the remnants of commodities from a past century a mythic quality. When fashion makes its own use of these remnants by quoting past attire for new clothing styles, it visualizes and materializes the demand that was raised by Benjamin's dialectical image on a metaphysical level.

In a letter to Benjamin, dating from 1935, Adorno questioned this dialectical image, expressing doubts about both the redemptive and the mythic character of the commodity to which it was to apply: "To understand the commodity as a dialectical image simply means to understand it also as the motif of its own demise and its 'abolition' ['Aufhebung'], instead of regarding it as pure regression to the old. On the one hand, the commodity is the alienated object and thus its utility value has withered away; on the other hand it is a surviving object that, having become alien, outlives its immediacy."[60] In discussing the perception of the dated dress either as a quote or as merely of "historic" interest, one has to look at its role in each use as a commodity. The bustled dress from the 1880s, for example, is the commodity whose utility value has died, since no one could wear such a dress expecting anything but to be seen as in disguise or costume. On the other hand, if someone puts on a bustled dress that is a sartorial quote (e.g., a design by Christian Lacroix from the late 1980s), she sports a commodity that, according to Adorno, has "outlived its immediacy" because it has been alienated from its origin and activated for the present. Obviously, a truly fashionable design can never hope to be anything *but* in the present; it will not be capable of overcoming the present, because the design then would cease to exist as fashion and would become an object with another function, perhaps that of the eternal artwork. What the fashion commodity can achieve, however, is to escape its demise by ironically advancing its death and perpetually renewing itself. When the design has been accepted into the sartorial mainstream, the actual innovation dies and the process of inventing and promoting a new style or look begins anew. The "rewriting" of (costume) history thus continues in frequent installments, and by constantly prompting its own "abolition" fashion ideally avoids any regressive tendency. Therefore, the one commodity that is tailor-made as a dialectical image must be clothing, and Benjamin accordingly captures it in the tiger's leap. Adorno concurs with Benjamin in seeing the pressure of future problems demanding a present ready to act with a responsibility toward the past and at the same time aware of the implications its actions carry for the future. In extending this awareness retrospectively to the past, Benjamin created an intricate patterns of a future open to alternatives, a "mobilized" past (visualized by sartorial fashion), and, in their midst, a transient present.

[. . .]

Notes

1   "Fashion is the eternal recurrence of the new. Are there nevertheless motifs of redemption precisely in fashion?" Walter Benjamin, "Zentralpark," in Benjamin, *Gesammelte Schriften*, 7 vols. (Frankfurt a.M.: Suhrkamp, 1974–1989), 1.2:677; trans. L. Spencer (with M. Harrington) as "Central Park," *New German Critique*, no. 34 (winter 1985), 46.

2   The title of Benjamin's second précis, written in March 1939 by request of the Institute for Social Research in New York so that he might secure founding for his ongoing project.

3   The bibliography that aims to list all publications on Benjamin up to 1986 has fashion as a topic of only two essays—and both mention the subject merely in passing. Few critics—to my knowledge—have ventured to explain Benjamin's relationship with fashion. Anne, Margaret, and Patrice Higonnet, in "Façades: Walter Benjamin's Paris," *Critical Inquiry* 10, no. 3 (spring 1984), 391–419, touch very briefly on fashion (405–406); Susan Buck-Morss, in *Dialectics of Seeing: Walter Benjamin and the Arcades Project* (Cambridge, Mass.: MIT Press, 1989), presents fashion as one aspect among many in the *Arcades Project* (see 99–101); while the elaborately titled contribution by Doris Kolesch, "Mode, Moderne und Kultur-theorie—eine schwierige Beziehung. Überlegungen zu Baudelaire, Simmel, Benjamin und Adorno" (Fashion, Modernity, and Cultural Theory—Difficult Relations: Reflections on Baudelaire, Simmel, Benjamin, and Adorno), in *Mode Weiblichkeit und Modernität* (Fashion, Femininity, and Modernity], ed. Gertrud Lehnert (Dortmund: Ebersbach, 1998), 20–46, formulates a relationship between fashion and modernity, but simply lists the various contributors to that relation-ship without exploring further the intricate connections among them. Other authors, like Hans Robert Jauß in his essay "Tradition, Innovation, and Aesthetic Experience," *Journal of Aesthetics and Art Criticism* 46, no. 3 (spring 1988), 375–388, arrive, through a reading of *la querelle* and Baudelaire, at the paradigmatic value of fashion for Benjamin (cf. 383), but then leave the subject unexplored.

4   Walter Benjamin, letter dated Berlin-Grunewald, 17 March 1928, in Walter Ben-jamin, *Briefe*, ed. Gershom Scholem and Theodor W. Adorno, 2 vols. (Frankfurt a.M.: Suhrkamp, 1978), 1:464; trans. M. R. and E. M. Jacobson as *The Correspond-ence of Walter Benjamin, 1910–1940* (Chicago: University of Chicago Press, 1994), 329. Benjamin's letters were edited by his friends Scholem and Adorno for publication in 1975; the complete edition is currently being published in Germany (the years 1910 to 1937 have already been covered in five separate volumes).

5   Theodor W. Adorno, *Asthetische Theorie* (Frankfurt a.M.: Suhrkamp, 1973), 265–266; trans. C. Lenhardt as *Aesthetic Theory* (London: Routledge & Kegan Paul, 1984), 255 (translation slightly modified).

    The example of Picasso's *Lichtmalerei* is perhaps too singular and not very fortunate. Adorno wrote this passage around 1967/1968, at a time when Henri Clouzot's film, which included the famous footage of the artist drawing with a candle, marked a peak in the postwar reverence for Picasso in Germany. Adorno was himself of course never free from fashionable influences in the cultural sphere. A more "avant-garde" German critic would probably have referred to the use of light in paintings by "Zero" artists such as Otto Piene and Günter Mack (from ca. 1963), rather than to Picasso's work.

6   Walter Benjamin, letter dated Berlin-Grunewald, 17 March 1928, in Benjamin, *Briefe*, 1:464; trans. in *The Correspondence of Walter Benjamin*, 329.

7   Hans Mayer, *Der Zeitgenosse Walter Benjamin* (Frankfurt a.M.: Jüdischer Verlag, 1992), 66; see also Denis Hollier, in his biographical note for Mayer, in *Le Collège de Sociologie*, ed. Hollier (Paris: Gallimard, 1979), 447–448; trans. B. Wing as the foreword to *The College of Sociology (1937–39)*, ed. Hollier (Minneapolis: University of Minnesota Press, 1988), 21.

8   Professor Mayer, letter to the author, 12 October 1993.

9   Benjamin had known, for example, of the imprisonment of his brother Georg since 1938.

10 Walter Benjamin, *Das Passagen-Werk*, ed. Rolf Tiedemann, in Benjamin, *Gesammelte Schriften*, 5.1:494, and 5.2:1015.

11 Baudelaire had reminisced (as an adult) about the scent of a skirt in his poem "Le Léthé," the mythical river that prompts humans to forget their earthly past: "Dans tes jupons remplis de ton parfum/Ensevelir ma tête endolorie,/Et respirer, comme une fleur flétrie, / Le doux relent de mon amour défunt" (Swathe my head in thy skirts swirling/Perfumes that one never borrows, /Perfumes of some flower unfurling/Leaves like loves that hate their morrows). Charles Baudelaire, "Le Léthé" (second stanza; part of the collection "Les Épaves"), in Baudelaire, *Œuvres complètes*, 2 vols. (Paris: Gallimard, 1975–1976), 1:155; trans. J. M. Bernstein in *Baudelaire, Rimbaud, Verlaine: Selected Verse and Prose Poems* (New York: Citadel, 1947), 33.

12 Walter Benjamin, "Zum Bilde Prousts," in Benjamin, *Gesammelte Schriften*, 2.1:312; trans. Harry Zohn as "The Image of Proust," in Benjamin, *Illuminations* (London: Pimlico, 1999), 198–199 (translation modified).

13 Benjamin, *Das Passagen-Werk*, 495.

14 See Baudelaire's exclamation: "Mais le génie n'est que l'enfance retrouvée à volonté" (But genius is nothing more nor less than *childhood recovered* at will). Charles Baudelaire, "Le Peintre de la vie moderne III: L'Artiste, homme du monde, hommes des foules et enfant," in Baudelaire, *Œuvres complètes*, 2:690; trans. J. Mayne in Baudelaire, *The Painter of Modern Life and Other Essays* (London: Phaidon, 1995), 8.

15 The martial metaphors may appear peculiar here, but we will come to see how fashion and the notion of revolution interact closely in both Benjamin's concept of remembrance and his "Theses on the Concept of History."

16 See Charles Baudelaire, *Tableaux Parisiens* (Heidelberg: Weißbach, 1923). The volume was published as a bilingual edition; preceding the German translation is a text by Benjamin titled "Die Aufgabe des Übersetzers" (trans. Harry Zohn as. "The Task of the Translator," in Benjamin, *Illuminations*, 70–82). His original manuscript for the *Tableaux* translation was written between 1920 and 1921.

17 Benjamin and Hessel were approached by the publisher after the previous attempt to bring *A côté de chez Swann* into German had ended in a "great editorial and critical fiasco." See Benjamin, *Briefe*, 1:431; trans. in *The Correspondence of Walter Benjamin, 1910–1940*, 304.

18 See Benjamin, *Briefe*, 1:412, 432; trans. in *The Correspondence of Walter Benjamin, 1910–1940*, 289, 305.

19 Benjamin, *Briefe*, 1:492; trans. in *The Correspondence of Walter Benjamin, 1910–1940*, 349 (the translators use the unevocative "hatching" for the German *spinnen*). See

also notes to the essay "Zum Bilde Prousts," in Benjamin, *Gesammelte Schriften*, 2.3:1044–1047.

20 Benjamin, notes for "Zum Bilde Prousts," 1057.

21 Walter Benjamin, "Neoklassizismus in Frankreich," in Benjamin, *Gesammelte Schriften*, 2.2:627.

22 Walter Benjamin, letter dated 28 December 1925, in Benjamin, *Briefe*, 1:406–407; trans. in *The Correspondence of Walter Benjamin, 1910–1940*, 286 (translation not used). For Proust's disagreement with Thibaudet, see Marcel Proust, "A propos du 'style' de Flaubert." *Nouvelle Revue Française* 7, vol. 14, no. 76 (1 January 1920), 72–90; see also his *Contre Sainte-Beuve* (Paris: Gallimard, 1971), 586–600.

23 Benjamin, *Briefe*, 1:407; trans. in *The Correspondence of Walter Benjamin, 1910–1940*, 286 (translation slightly amended).

24 Théophile Gautier, *De la mode* (Paris: Poulet-Malassis & de Broise, 1858), 5–6.

25 See, e.g., Samuel Weber, *Return to Freud: Jacques Lacan's Dislocation of Psychoanalysis* (Cambridge: Cambridge University Press, 1991).

26 See once again Walter Benjamin, "Über den Begriff der Geschichte," in Benjamin, *Gesammelte Schriften*, 1.2:701.

27 See Walter Benjamin, notes on "Paris, die Haupstadt des XIX. Jahrhunderts," in Benjamin, *Das Passagen-Werk*, 1206–1254.

28 *Dictionnaire de la langue française* (Paris: Larousse, 1992), s.v. "passer."

29 Benjamin, *Das Passagen-Werk*, 617.

30 Ibid., 580.

31 Ibid.

32 Marcel Proust, *Du côté de chez Swann*, part 1 of *À la recherche du temps perdu* (Paris: Gallimard, 1987), 5–6; trans. C. K. Scott Moncrieff and T. Kilmartin as "Overture" to *Swann's Way*, part 1 of *Remembrance of Things Past* (London: Chatto & Windus, 1981), 5–6. See also Benjamin on "the child's side of the dream" in *Das Passagen-Werk*, 1006.

   For the relationship between Proust's and Benjamin's epistemologies, see, e.g., Henning Goldbæk, "Prousts *Recherche* und Benjamins *Passagen-Werk*: Eine Darstellung ihrer Erkenntnistheorie," *ORBIS Litterarum*, no. 48 (1993), 83–95.

33 In 1965 Adorno referred back to Benjamin and, through him, to Proust and surrealism when he wrote: "What Surrealism adds to illustration of the world of objects is the element of childhood that we have lost; when we were children, those illustrated papers, already obsolete by then, must have leaped out at us the way Surrealist images do now." Theodor W. Adorno, "Rückblickend auf den Surrealismus," in *Noten zur Literatur*, vol. 1 (Frankfurt a.M.: Suhrkamp, 1958), 157; trans. Shierry Weber Nicholsen as "Looking Back on Surrealism" in Adorno, *Notes to Literature*, vol. 1 (New York: Columbia University Press, 1991), 88.

34 Roland Barthes, *Système de la mode* (Paris: Seuil, 1967), 144; trans. M. Ward and R. Howard as Barthes, *The Fashion System* (London: Cape, 1985), 136–137.

35 See also Benjamin's reflection on etymology in *Das Passagen-Werk*, 617–618.

36 Jürgen Habermas, *Der philosophische Diskurs der Moderne: Zwölf Vorlesungen* (Frankfurt a.M.: Suhrkamp, 1985), 22; trans. F. Lawrence as *The Philosophical Discourse of Modernity* (Cambridge: Polity, 1987), 12 (translation slightly modified). (The English rendition had to be changed because the translator read *des unvorhersehbaren Anfangs* as "predictable beginnings" instead of "*un*predictable beginnings," which

obviously changes the phrase's relation to novelty.)

37   Benjamin, "Über den Begriff der Geschichte," 702; trans. Harry Zohn as "Theses in the Philosophy of History," in Benjamin, *Illuminations*, 254.

38   Walter Benjamin, "Eduard Fuchs, der Sammler und der Historiker," *Zeitschrift für Sozialforschung*, no. 6 (1937); in Benjamin, *Gesammelte Schriften*, 2.2:479; trans. K. Tarnowski as Benjamin, "Eduard Fuchs: Collector and Historian," *New German Critique*, no. 5 (spring 1975), 37 (translation slightly modified).

   Benjamin might have adopted the metaphor from Simmel, who in 1907 had warned in his preface to the third edition of *Die Probleme der Geschichtsphilosophie* (Problems in the Philosophy of History) that one of the "violations of modern man" is a particular understanding of history: "It renders the soul as a simple connection of social threads that have been spun throughout history, and dilutes its productivity to merely administrating the legacies of our species." Georg Simmel, "Die Probleme der Geschichtsphilosophie," in Simmel, *Das Individuelle Gesetz* (Frankfurt a.M.: Suhrkamp, 1987), 31.

39   See, e.g., Benjamin, *Das Passagen-Werk*, 808–810; on the character of the fetish, see also 806.

   The example of the linen and the coat can be found in Karl Marx, *The Capital*, trans. S. Moore and E. Aveling, vol. 1, in Karl Marx and Friedrich Engels, *Collected Works*, vol. 35 (London: Lawrence & Wishart, 1996), 59–69 and passim. Marx makes a distinction between the weaving of the linen as "concrete work" and the tailoring of the coat as "abstract work" (68–69), he also hints at the fashionable connotation and the sociocultural implication of the "braided" coat (61–62).

   Helmut Salzinger, *Swinging Benjamin*, rev. ed. (Hamburg: Kellner, 1990), 111, writes: "Benjamin read in Lukács's work that all social life in capitalism is but an exchange of commodities Which means that in capitalism each and every manifestation of life takes on the shape of a commodity. This thought, which in Lukács remains abstract, has been applied by Benjamin to the artwork and thus rendered concrete. In portraying Baudelaire as a producer among producers, he showed that there is no difference in the nature of products. As commodities, the *Fleurs du Mal* and Marx's coat are the same thing."

40   H. D. Kittsteiner, "Walter Benjamins Historismus," in *Passagen: Walter Benjamin's Urgeschichte des XIX. Jahrhunderts*, ed. Nobert Bolz and Bernd Witte (Munich: Fink, 1984), 196; trans. J. Monroe and I. Wohlfarth as Kittsteiner, "Walter Benjamin's Historicism," *New German Critique*, no. 39 (fall 1986), 214 (translation not used).

   The English language version of this article wrongly translates *Rock* (= "coat" in nineteenth-century German usage) as "skirt" (the contemporary meaning of the word). Thus to avoid altering the meaning of the metaphor discussed, I have preferred to use my own translation.

41   Obviously, as linen itself is woven from plant fibers, it is itself manufactured and to some extent an artificial product. But as a basic material it remains unfinished, while the tailored coat is not—it can only be altered or cut up.

42   Marx clearly criticizes the "mythic" side of Hegelian dialectics, however; see the 1873 afterword to the second edition of Marx, *Das Kapital*, in Karl Marx and Friedrich Engels, *Werke*, vol. 23 (Berlin: Dietz, 1993), 27; trans. as *The Capital*, 1:19–20. Benjamin in his reading of Marx would repossess the mythic or "messianic" qualities without mentioning Hegel.

43   Georg Wilhelm Friedrich Hegel, *Vorlesungen über die Ästhetik*, in *Werke*, vol. 14

(Frankfurt a.M.: Suhrkamp, 1986), 408; trans. T. M. Knox as *Aesthetics: Lectures on Fine Art*, 2 vols. (Oxford: Clarendon, 1975), 2:747.

44 The quotation in Benjamin, *Das Passagen-Werk*, 245, comes from Otto Rühle, *Karl Marx: Leben und Werk* (Hellerau: Avalun, 1928), 384–385; for a discussion of the commodity fetish as phantasmagoria in Benjamin, see Henrik Stampe Lund, "The Concept of Phantasmagoria in the *Passagen-Werk*," *ORBIS Litterarum*, no. 48 (1993), 96–108, esp. 98.

45 Benjamin, *Das Passagen-Werk*, 118. The term *Stoffwelt* can also be translated literally as "world of fabric"—surely an intentional ambiguity, given Benjamin's metaphorical style.

46 The "surrealist" fetish—that is, the adoption of a signifier from "tribal" cultures into Western modernism—essentially takes second place to Benjamin's exploration of the Freudian and Marxist notions of the fetish character.

47 See Sigmund Freud's "Fetishism" (1925), trans. James Strachey in *The Standard Edition of the Complete Psychological Works of Sigmund Freud*, vol. 21 (London: Hogarth, 1961), 152–154.

48 Ibid., 155.

49 Charles Baudelaire, "Le Peintre de la vie moderne IV: La Modernité," in Baudelaire, *Œuvres complètes*, 2:694.

50 Hans Robert Jauß, *Literaturgeschichte als Provokation* (Frankfurt a.M.: Suhrkamp, 1970), 54–55. Baudelaire's quote can be found in "Le Peintre de la vie moderne IV: La Modernité," in Baudelaire, *Œuvres complètes*, 2:695; trans. in Baudelaire, *The Painter of Modern Life and Other Essays*, 12. See also Jauß's comment on Baudelaire's "fashion's paradigm," in "Tradition, Innovation, and Aesthetic Experience," 383.

51 Benjamin, "Über den Begriff der Geschichte," 702; trans. as "Theses on the Philosophy of History," 254 (translation slightly modified).

52 Benjamin, *Das Passagen-Werk*, 578; trans. L. Hafrey and R. Sieburth as "N [Re the Theory of Knowledge, Theory of Progress]," in *Benjamin: Philosophy, History, Aesthetics*, ed. Gary Smith (Chicago: University of Chicago Press, 1989), 51 (translation modified).

53 Benjamin, *Das Passagen-Werk*, 118; see Barbara Vinken, "Eternity: A Frill on the Dress," *Fashion Theory* 1, no. 1 (March 1997), 59–67.

54 Walter Benjamin, "Das Paris des Second Empire bei Baudelaire," in Benjamin, *Gesammelte Schriften*, 1.2:548; trans. Harry Zohn in Benjamin, *Charles Baudelaire: A Lyric Poet in the Era of High Capitalism* (London: NLB, 1973), 45–46.

55 Benjamin, "Über den Begriff der Geschichte," 702–703; trans. as "Theses on the Philosophy of History," 254 (translation slightly modified).

56 See Habermas, *The Philosophical Discourse of Modernity*, 13.

57 Adorno's description of the *Arcades Project* in a letter from Oxford, 20 May 1935; reprinted in Theodor W. Adorno, *Über Walter Benjamin*, rev. ed. (Frankfurt a.M.: Suhrkamp, 1990), 118; trans. N. Walker in Theodor W. Adorno and Walter Benjamin, *The Complete Correspondence, 1928–1940* (Cambridge: Polity, 1999), 84.

58 Benjamin, "Über den Begriff der Geschichte," 704; trans. as "Theses on the Philosophy of History," 255 (translation modified).

59 Ibid., 693; trans., 245 (translation modified).

60 Theodor Adorno, letter dated "Hornberg i. Schwarzwald, 2 August 1935," in Benjamin, *Briefe* 2:675; trans. in *The Correspondence of Walter Benjamin, 1910–1940*, 497–498 (translation modified).

PART TEN

Post-modern fashion

THERE IS A SENSE in which the phrase 'post-modern' is false, or self-contradictory – the attempt to combine conflicting meanings in a single statement. This is the sense in which 'post' means 'after' or 'later than' (as in 'post meridian' or p.m.) and 'modern' means 'the latest'. The self-contradiction arises because nothing can be both 'later than' and 'the latest' at the same time. When one adds 'fashion' (in the sense of 'the latest style') to the phrase, to make 'post-modern fashion', the contradictions are only multiplied. However, as with 'modern' in Part Nine, there are other senses of the term 'post-modern' and this introduction will examine them in order to contextualise the following readings. Post-modern may refer to either a period of time or to a characteristic outlook or set of ideas. Following Boyne and Rattansi (1990) again, 'post-modernity' will be used in this introduction to refer to a period of time and to the experience of living in that period of time. 'Post-modernism' will be used to refer to a characteristic outlook or set of aesthetic rules or ideas.

Helen Thomas and Dave Walsh provide a useful summary of some of the main features of post-modernity, saying that

> [p]ostmodernity is a globalising, post-industrial world of media, communication and information systems. It is organised on the basis of a market-orientated world of consumption rather than work and production . . . it is a world of culture in which tradition, consensual values . . . universal beliefs and standards have been challenged, undermined and rejected for heterogeneity, differentiation and difference.
>
> (Thomas and Walsh 1998: 364)

These main features include consumption, the challenge to traditional cultural values and, most importantly, differentiation and difference. There is some doubt as to when post-modernity was, and as to whether, and if so how, it differs from modernity. Post-modernity is often assumed to refer to a period that started in the 1960s or 1970s, but Boyne and Rattansi have found references to the post-modern in the 1930s and claim that the term 'gained currency' in the 1950s and 1960s. Giddens complicates the matter considerably by suggesting that globalisation, which Thomas and Walsh identify as post-modern in the extract quoted, is in fact an 'inherent' part of modernity (1990: 63). Indeed, and in the Communist Manifesto, written in 1848, Marx and Engels already refer to capitalists chasing markets and products all over the surface of the globe (Marx and Engels 1985: 83–4). This complication indicates that the relation between modernity and post-modernity is not straightforward and counsels against conceiving it as a simple or clean 'break' or discontinuity, for example.

Post-modernism, as a set of aesthetic 'rules' or ideas, is slightly less problematical in that a fundamental or founding 'crisis of representation' may be identified and its consequences explored (Boyne and Rattansi 1990: 12), but it is not without its twists and turns. 'Representation' is the name for the way in which one thing stands for, or represents, another thing. In semiology, for example, the signifier stands for the signified: the Balenciaga dress (signifier) represents 'fashion' (signified) and jeans (signifier) stand for 'youth and freedom' (signified). Representation is therefore (central to) the way in which meaning is generated or produced and, indeed, (to) the way in which thinking works. The 'crisis' concerns the relation between signifier and signified: where it once was stable, predictable and reliable (modernism), it is now unstable, unpredictable and unreliable (post-modernism).

What this means is that when, for example, in 1850s England exposed female flesh would have simply signified that one was improperly dressed, now it can signify leisure, seductiveness, fetishism, empowered display and playfulness, as well as that one is improperly dressed. As Andrew Hill points out, 'clothing is no longer associated with the type of social hierarchies it once was' (2005: 73), and those hierarchies are no longer sufficient to generate and guarantee a definite meaning. The potential guarantors of meaning, in the form of a social class's moral, political or aesthetic code, for example, have been lost and there are now any number of 'games' or codes within each of which the meaning of the exposed flesh is subtly and unpredictably different. The signifier that is exposed flesh now has no secure and fixed signified (or meaning) and all previous rules are at best unreliable guides to post-modern meaning.

The result of this 'crisis' – that meaning, the relation between signifier and signified is no longer guaranteed by a moral code or a fixed set of aesthetic rules – is that meaning is now recognised as being the product of shifting and unstable relations of difference. And it is significant in this respect that Thomas and Walsh mention difference three times, as 'heterogeneity, differentiation and difference' (Thomas and Walsh 1998: 364). For example, denim jeans exist in many forms and styles and they exist alongside every other trouser-like garment, and for post-modernism it is only these differences that generate the meaning of jeans. Boot-cut, flared or straight-leg jeans are not meaningful on their own but because they are different from each other and because those wearing them recognise those differences as meaningful differences.

Jeans signify 'youth and freedom' only because they are different from twills or flannels, which signify 'middle aged', or 'conservative', for example.

Baudrillard's conception of the role of difference in the production of meaning in fashion includes the idea that even the experience of beauty is differentially generated in postmodernism. He says that neither long skirts nor short skirts have any value or meaning in themselves: it is only the difference between them that produces their meanings (1981: 79). Having become accustomed to long skirts on women, the effect of seeing short skirts is novel and, Baudrillard says, 'precipitates' both a new, different meaning and the 'effect of "beauty" ' (ibid.). As he points out, exactly the opposite move, the move from short to long skirts, has the same effect – new meaning and the experience of beauty. This account of the beautiful in fashion and dress is slightly different from that provided by Thorstein Veblen in 1899. In *The Theory of the Leisure Class*, Veblen explains beauty in dress as a 'feeling' ([1899] 1992: 125), which is generated by two things. The first is the current item's difference from what went before it; the second is the sense of 'reputability' that the item possesses. It is the 'novelty' and difference of an item of dress that is at least partly responsible for the effect of the beautiful. Clearly, the difference that Veblen sees between the item of dress and those items that preceded it is the same difference that Baudrillard sees; for both of these very different theorists beauty is predominantly a product of difference.

The way in which certain features of fashion could be identified as both modern and post-modern was noted in Part Nine. Kurt Back's explanation of unfinished seams was that the seams were especially modern because they were a way of drawing attention to the construction of the piece and (following Greenberg) self-reflexivity was a key feature of modernist aesthetics. However, it was also pointed out in Part Nine that this feature of clothing could also be identified as a post-modern characteristic because post-modern designers such as Martin Margiela and Ann Demeulemeester regularly used it. One response to this situation, in which the same fashion technique is explained as two different things, would be to suggest that this undecidability is itself a product of post-modernist thought (see Barnard [1996] 2002: 196ff., for example). Derrida's account of undecidability (in Derrida 1978: 99, 103–5, and 1981: 42–3), in which the value or meaning of words, for example, is seen to be both produced and destroyed by those words' relations to all other words in a shifting and non-stable network of differences and relations, could be used to explain how fashion 'is' undecidable in terms of modern/post-modern. A different response is provided by Alison Gill in her (1998) essay 'Deconstruction Fashion'. She, too, starts from the work of Margiela, Demeulemeester, Dries van Noten and others whose work has been described as 'unfinished' or 'coming apart' (ibid.: 25). The Derridean term she uses to pursue the connections between fashion and philosophy with in this essay is 'deconstruction'. Deconstruction is Derrida's attempt to describe any critical strategy that finds itself in a situation where any and all critical strategies must inevitably use the terms of the thing they are attempting to critique (Derrida 1981: 35–6). This essay also provides an interesting perspective on the relation between fashion and theory, pointing out that the introduction of a theory to a practice can often appear awkward or as though it is an attempt to provide some spurious credibility to that practice.

Deconstruction, she says, can also be used to seek a 'serious relation' between theory and fashion and to show its debt to philosophy (Gill 1998: 29).

As a different way of thinking about fashion (as a different theorising of fashion), Gill suggests that both Derrida and Margiela are asking (Kantian) questions about the conditions for the possibility of something: the something is philosophy in Derrida's case and fashion in Margiela's case. Following the eighteenth-century philosopher Kant, who asked 'How is knowledge possible?', Derrida is understood as asking 'How is philosophy possible?' and Margiela is asking 'How is fashion possible?' The latter's display of darts, seams, tacking and facings (which would usually be hidden) is 'like Derrida's "critique" of philosophy' in which what philosophy performs is displayed, rather than brought to a logical or satisfactory end, or closure (1998: 42–3). On the simplest level, Margiela's darts, seams, tacking and facings are the conditions for the possibility of fashion along with the fabric they are 'literally' what make garments possible. On a rather more complex level, Derrida's undecidable 'concepts' and non-strategic strategies are the conditions for the possibility of philosophy. In both cases, however, what is commonly understood and experienced as fashion and philosophy depends on effacing or hiding those conditions and appearing as 'seamless' and logic-ally perfect. Gill therefore feels comfortable in calling Margiela's fashion design 'deconstruction fashion'.

Kim Sawchuk's essay refers to and comments upon the work of Walter Benjamin and Jean Baudrillard. The notion of 'allegory' is one that Benjamin uses to explain modern fashion and it is one that Sawchuk also takes up in her account of post-modern fashion. The idea that fashion items are not and cannot be 'symbolic' in post-modernity, and that they are therefore 'allegorical' (as on Benjamin's account) or 'simulacra' (on Baudrillard's), is explored in Sawchuk's essay.

Bibliography

Barnard, M. ([1996] 2002) *Fashion as Communication*, London: Routledge.

Baudrillard, J. (1981) *For a Critique of the Political Economy of the Sign*, St. Louis, Mo.: Telos Press.

Baudrillard, J. (1993) 'Fashion, or The Enchanting Spectacle of the Code', in *Symbolic Exchange and Death*, translated by Iain Hamilton Grant, with an Introduction by Mike Gane, London: Sage.

Boyne, R. and Rattansi, A. (1990) *Postmodernism and Society*, London: Macmillan.

Derrida, J. (1978) *Spurs/Eperons*, Chicago: University of Chicago Press.

—— (1981) *Positions*, London: Athlone Press.

Emberley, J. (1988) 'The Fashion Apparatus and the Deconstruction of Postmodern Subjectivity', in A. Kroker and M. Kroker (eds) *Body Invaders: Sexuality and The Postmodern Condition*, London: Macmillan.

Faurschou, G. (1988) 'Fashion and the Cultural Logic of Postmodernity', in A. Kroker and M. Kroker (eds) *Body Invaders: Sexuality and the Postmodern Condition*, London: Macmillan.

Giddens, A. (1990) *The Consequences of Modernity*, Cambridge: Polity Press.

Gill, A. (1998) 'Deconstruction Fashion', *Fashion Theory* 2, 1: 25–50.

Hill, A. (2005) 'People Dress So Badly Nowadays: Fashion and Late Modernity', in C. Breward and C. Evans (eds) *Fashion and Modernity*, Oxford: Berg.

Marx, K. and Engles, F. (1985) *The Communist Manifesto*, Harmondsworth: Penguin Classics.

Sawchuk, K. (1988) 'A Tale of Inscription/Fashion Statements', in A. Kroker and M. Kroker (eds) *Body Invaders: Sexuality and the Postmodern Condition*, London: Macmillan.

Thomas, H. and Walsh, D. (1998) 'Modernity/Postmodernity', in C. Jenks (ed.) *Core Sociological Dichotomies*, London: Sage.

Veblen, T. ([1899] 1992) *The Theory of the Leisure Class*, New York: Transaction Books.

Chapter 36

Jean Baudrillard

THE IDEOLOGICAL GENESIS OF NEEDS/ FETISHISM AND IDEOLOGY

[. . .]

A logic of signification

SO IT IS NECESSARY to distinguish the logic of consumption, which is a logic of the sign and of difference, from several other logics that habitually get entangled with it in the welter of evidential considerations. (This confusion is echoed by all the naive and authorized literature on the question.) Four logics would be concerned here:

1   A functional logic of use value;
2   An economic logic of exchange value;
3   A logic of symbolic exchange;
4   A logic of sign value.

The first is a logic of practical operations, the second one of equivalence, the third, ambivalence, and the fourth, difference.

Or again: a logic of utility, a logic of the market, a logic of the gift, and a logic of status. Organized in accordance with one of the above groupings, the object assumes respectively the status of an *instrument*, a *commodity*, a *symbol*, or a *sign*.

Only the last of these defines the specific field of consumption. Let us compare two examples;

The wedding ring: This is a unique object, symbol of the relationship of the couple. One would neither think of changing it (barring mishap) nor of wearing several. The symbolic object is made to last and to witness in its duration the permanence of the relationship. Fashion plays as negligible a role at the strictly symbolic level as at the level of pure instrumentality.

The ordinary ring is quite different: it does not symbolize a relationship. It is a non-singular object, a personal gratification, a sign in the eyes of others. I can wear several of them. I can substitute them. The ordinary ring takes part in the play of my accessories and the constellation of fashion. It is an object of consumption.

Living accommodations: The house, your lodgings, your apartment: these terms involve semantic nuances that are no doubt linked to the advent of industrial production or to social standing. But, whatever one's social level in France today, one's domicile is not necessarily perceived as a "consumption" good. The question of residence is still very closely associated with patrimonial goods in general, and its symbolic scheme remains largely that of the body. Now, for the logic of consumption to penetrate here, the exteriority of the sign is required. The residence must cease to be hereditary, or interiorized as an organic family space. One must avoid the appearance of filiation and identification if one's debut in the world of fashion is to be successful.

In other words, domestic practice is still largely a function of determinations, namely: symbolic (profound emotional investment, etc.), and economic (scarcity).

Moreover, the two are linked: only a certain "discretionary income" permits one to play with objects as status signs – a stage of fashion and the "game" where the symbolic and the utilitarian are both exhausted. Now, as to the question of residence – in France at least – the margin of free play for the mobile combinatory of prestige or for the game of substitution is limited. In the United States, by contrast, one sees living arrangements indexed to social mobility, to trajectories of careers and status. Inserted into the global constellation of status, and subjugated to the same accelerated obsolescence of any other object of luxury, the house truly becomes an object of consumption.

This example has a further interest: it demonstrates the futility of any attempt to define the object empirically. Pencils, books, fabrics, food, the car, curios – are these objects? Is a house an object? Some would contest this. The decisive point is to establish whether the symbolism of the house (sustained by the shortage of housing) is irreducible, or if even this can succumb to the differential and reified connotations of fashion logic: for if this is so, then the home becomes an object of consumption – as any other object will, if it only answers to the same definition: being, cultural trait, ideal, gestural pattern, language, etc. – anything can be made to fit the bill. The definition of an object of consumption is entirely independent of objects themselves and *exclusively a function of the logic of significations.*

An object is not an object of consumption unless it is released from its psychic determinations as *symbol*; from its functional determinations as *instrument*; from its commercial determinations as *product*; and is thus *liberated as a sign* to be recaptured by the formal logic of fashion, i.e., by the logic of differentiation.

[. . .]

Fashion

This deep-seated logic is akin to that of fashion. Fashion is one of the more inexplicable phenomena, so far as these matters go: its compulsion to innovate signs, its apparently arbitrary and perpetual production of meaning – a kind of meaning drive – and the logical mystery of its cycle are all in fact of the essence of what is sociological. The logical processes of fashion might be extrapolated to the dimension of "culture" in general – to all social production of signs, values and relations.

To take a recent example: neither the long skirt nor the mini-skirt has an absolute value in itself – only their differential relation acts as a criterion of meaning. The mini-skirt has nothing whatsoever to do with sexual liberation; it has no (fashion) value except in opposition to the long skirt. This value is, of course, reversible: the voyage from the mini- to the maxi-skirt will have the same distinctive and selective fashion value as the reverse; and it will precipitate the same effect of "beauty."

But it is obvious that this "beauty" (or any other interpretation in terms of chic, taste, elegance, or even distinctiveness) is nothing but the exponential function – the rationalization – of the fundamental processes of production and reproduction of distinctive material. Beauty ("in itself") has nothing to do with the fashion cycle.[1] In fact, it is inadmissible. Truly beautiful, definitively beautiful clothing would put an end to fashion. The latter can do nothing but deny, repress and efface it – *while conserving, with each new outing, the alibi of beauty.*

Thus fashion continually fabricates the "beautiful" on the basis of a radical denial of beauty, by reducing beauty to the logical equivalent of ugliness. It can impose the most eccentric, dysfunctional, ridiculous traits as eminently distinctive. This is where it triumphs – imposing and legitimizing the irrational according to a logic deeper than that of rationality.

[. . .]

[Fetishism and ideology]

The concepts of commodity fetishism and money fetishism sketched, for Marx, the lived ideology of capitalist society – the mode of sanctification, fascination and psychological subjection by which individuals internalize the generalized system of exchange value. These concepts outline the whole process whereby the concrete social values of labor and exchange, which the capitalist system denies, abstracts and "alienates," are erected into transcendent ideological values – into a moral agency that regulates all alienated behavior. What is being described here is the successor to a more archaic fetishism and religious mystification ("the opium of the people"). And this theory of a new fetishism has become the icing on the cake of contemporary analysis. While Marx still attached it (though very ambiguously) to a *form* (the commodity, money), and thus located it at a theoretically comprehensive level, today the concept of fetishism is exploited in a summary and empirical fashion: object fetishism, automobile fetishism, sex fetishism, vacation fetishism, etc. The whole exercise is precipitated by nothing more sophisticated than a diffuse, exploded and idolatrous vision of the consumption environment; it is the conceptual fetish of vulgar social thought, working assiduously towards the expanded reproduction of ideology in the guise of a disturbing attack on the system. The term fetishism is dangerous not only because it short-circuits analysis, but because since the 18th century it has conducted the whole repertoire of occidental Christian and humanist ideology, as orchestrated by colonists, ethnologists and missionaries. The Christian connotation has been present from the beginning in the condemnation of primitive cults by a religion that claimed to be abstract and spiritual; "the worship of certain earthly and material objects called fetishes . . . for which reason I will call it fetishism."[2] Never having really shed this moral and rationalistic connotation, the great *fetishist metaphor* has since been the recurrent leitmotiv of the analysis of "magical thinking," whether that of the Bantu tribes or that of modern metropolitan hordes submerged in their objects and their signs.

As an eclecticism derived from various primitive representations, the fetishist metaphor consists of analyzing myths, rites and practices in terms of *energy*, a magical transcendent power, a *mana* (whose latest avatar would possibly be the libido). As a power that is transferred to beings, objects and agencies, it is universal and diffuse, but it crystallizes at strategic points so that its flux can be regulated and diverted by certain groups or individuals for their own benefit. In the light of the "theory," this would be the major objective of all primitive practices, even eating. Thus, in the animist vision, everything happens between the hypostasis of a force, its dangerous transcendence and the capture of this force, which then becomes beneficent. Aborigines apparently rationalized their experience of the group and of the world in these terms. But anthropologists themselves have rationalized their experience of the aborigines in these same terms, thus exorcising the crucial interrogation that these societies inevitably brought to bear on their own civilization.[3]

Here we are interested in the extension of this *fetishist metaphor* in modern industrial society, insofar as it enmeshes critical analysis (liberal or Marxist) within the subtle trap of a rationalistic anthropology. What else is intended by the concept of "commodity fetishism" if not the notion of a false consciousness devoted to the worship of exchange value (or, more recently, the fetishism of gadgets or objects, in which individuals are supposed to worship artificial libidinal or prestige values incorporated in the object)? All of this presupposes the existence, somewhere, of a non-alienated consciousness of an object in some "true," objective state: its use value?

The metaphor of fetishism, wherever it appears, involves a fetishization of the conscious subject or of a human essence, a rationalist metaphysic that is at the root of the whole system of occidental Christian values. Where Marxist theory seems to prop itself up with this same anthropology, it ideologically countersigns the very system of values that it otherwise dislocates via objective historical analysis. By referring all the problems of "fetishism" back to superstructural mechanisms of false consciousness, Marxism eliminates any real chance it has of analyzing the *actual process of ideological labor*. By refusing to analyze the structures and the mode of ideological production inherent in its own logic, Marxism is condemned (behind the façade of "dialectical" discourse in terms of class struggle) to expanding the reproduction of ideology, and thus of the capitalist system itself.

Thus, the problem of the generalized "fetishization" of real life forces us to reconsider the problem of the reproduction of ideology. The *fetishistic* theory of infrastructure and superstructure must be exploded, and replaced by a more comprehensive theory of productive forces, since these are *all structurally* implicated in the capitalist system – and not only in some cases (i.e., material production), while merely superstructurally in others (i.e., ideological production).

The term "fetishism" almost has a life of its own. Instead of functioning as a metalanguage for the magical thinking of others, it turns against those who use it, and surreptitiously exposes their own magical thinking. Apparently only psycho-analysis has escaped this vicious circle, by returning fetishism to its context within a perverse *structure* that perhaps underlies all desire. Thus circumscribed by its struc-tural definition (articulated through the clinical reality of the fetish object and its manipulation) as a refusal of sex differences, the term no longer shores up magical thinking; it becomes an analytic concept for a theory of perversion. But if in the social sciences, we cannot find the equivalent – and not merely an analogical one – of this strict use of the term, *the equivalent of the psychoanalytic process of perverse structure at the level of the process of ideological production* – that is, if it proves impos-sible to articulate the celebrated formula of "commodity fetishism" as anything other than a mere neologism (where "fetishism" refers to this alleged magical thinking, and "commodity" to a structural analysis of capital), then it would be preferable to drop the term entirely (including its cognate and derivative ideas). For in order to reconstitute the *process of fetishization* in terms of structure, we would have to abandon the fetishist metaphor of the worship of the golden calf – even as it has been reworded by Marxists in the phrase "the opium of the people" – and develop instead an articulation that avoids any projection of magical or transcendental animism, and thus the rationalist position of positing a false consciousness and a transcendental subject. After Lévi-Strauss' analysis, the "totem" was overthrown, so that only the analysis of the totemic system and its dynamic integration retained any meaning. This was a radical breakthrough that should be developed, theoretically and clinic-ally, and extended to social analysis in general. So, we started by meddling with received ideas about fetishism, only to discover that the whole theory of ideology may be in doubt.

If objects are not these reified agencies, endowed with force and *mana* in which the subject projects himself and is alienated – if fetishism designates something other than this metaphysic of alienated essence – what is its real process?

We would not make a habit of this, but here an appeal to etymology may help us sort through the confusion. The term "fetish" has undergone a curious semantic distortion. Today it refers to a force, a supernatural property of the object and hence to a similar magical potential in the subject, through schemas of projection and capture, alienation and reappropriation. But originally it signified exactly the oppos-ite: a *fabrication*, an artifact, a labor of appearances and signs. It appeared in France in the 17th century, coming from the Portuguese *feitiço*, meaning "artificial," which itself derives from the Latin *factitius*. The primary sense is "to do (to make," *faire*), the sense of "to imitate by signs" ("act as a devotee," etc.; this sense is also found in "makeup" [*maquillage*], which comes from *maken*, related to *machen* and to make). From the same root (*facio, facticius*) as *feitiço* comes the Spanish *afeitar*: "to paint, to adorn, to embellish," and *afeite*: "preparation, ornamentation, cosmetics," as well as the French *feint* and the Spanish *hechar*, "to do, to make" (whence *hechizo*: "artificial, feigned, dummy").

What quickly becomes apparent is the aspect of faking, of artificial registering – in short, of a cultural sign labor – and that this is at the origin of the status of fetish object, and thus also plays some part in the fascination it exercises. This aspect is increasingly repressed by the inverse representation (the two still exist in the Portuguese *feitiço*, which as an adjective means artificial and as a noun an enchanted object, or sorcery), which *substitutes a manipulation of forces for a manipulation of signs* and a magical economy of transfer of signifieds for a regulated play of signifiers.

The "talisman" also is lived and represented in the animist mode as a receptacle of forces: one forgets that it is first an object marked by signs – signs of the hand, of the face, or characters of the cabal, or the figure of some celestial body that, registered in the object, makes it a talisman. Thus, in the "fetishist" theory of consumption, in the view of marketing strategists as well as of consumers, objects are given and received everywhere as force dispensers (happiness, health, security, prestige, etc.). This magical substance having been spread about so liberally, one forgets that what we are dealing with first is signs: a generalized code of signs, a totally arbitrary code of differences, *and that it is on this basis, and not at all on account of their use values or their innate "virtues," that objects exercise their fascination.*

If fetishism exists it is thus not a fetishism of the signified, a fetishism of substances and values (called ideological), which the fetish object would incarnate for the alienated subject. Behind this reinterpretation (which is truly ideological) it is a *fetishism of the signifier.* That is to say that the subject is trapped in the factitious, differential, encoded, systematized aspect of the object. It is not the passion (whether of objects or subjects) for substances that speaks in fetishism, it is the *passion for the code*, which, by governing both objects and subjects, and by subordinating them to itself, delivers them up to abstract manipulation. This is the fundamental articulation of the ideological process: not in the projection of alienated consciousness into various superstructures, but in the generalization at all levels of a structural code.

So it appears that "commodity fetishism" may no longer fruitfully be interpreted according to the paleo-Marxist dramaturgy of the instance, in such and such an object, of a force that returns to haunt the individual severed from the product of his labor, and from all the marvels of his misappropriated investment (labor and effectiveness). It is rather the (ambivalent) fascination for a form (logic of the commodity or system of exchange value), a state of absorption, for better or for worse, in the restrictive logic of a system of abstraction. Something like a desire, a perverse desire, the desire of the code is brought to light here: it is a desire that is related to the systematic nature of signs, drawn towards it, precisely through what this system-like nature negates and bars, by exorcising the contradictions spawned by the process of real labor – just as the perverse psychological structure of the fetishist is organized, in the fetish object, around a mark, around the abstraction of a mark that negates, bars and exorcises the difference of the sexes.

In this sense, fetishism is not the sanctification of a certain object, or value (in which case one might hope to see it disappear in our age, when the liberalization of values and the abundance of objects would "normally" tend to desanctify them). It is the sanctification of the system as such, of the commodity as system: it is thus contemporaneous with the generalization of exchange value and is propagated with it. The more the system is systematized, the more the fetishist fascination is reinforced; and if it is always invading new territories, further and further removed from the domain of economic exchange value strictly understood (i.e., the areas of sexuality, recreation, etc.), this is not owing to an obsession with pleasure, or a substantial desire for pleasure or free time, but to a progressive (and even quite brutal) systematization of these sectors, that is to say their reduction to commutable sign values within the framework of a system of exchange value that is now almost total.[4]

Thus the fetishization of the commodity is the fetishization of a product emptied of its concrete substance of labor[5] and subjected to another type of labor, a labor of signification, that is, of coded abstraction (the production of differences and of sign values). It is an active, collective process of production and reproduction of a code, a system, invested with all the diverted, unbound desire separated out from the process of real labor and transferred onto precisely that which denies the process of real labor. Thus, fetishism is actually attached to the sign object, the object eviscerated of its substance and history, and reduced to the state of marking a difference, epitomizing a whole system of differences.

That the fascination, worship, and cathexis (*investissement*) of desire and, finally, even pleasure (perverse) devolve upon the system and not upon a substance (or *mana*) is clarified in the phenomenon, no less celebrated, of "money fetishism." What is fascinating about money is neither its materiality, nor even that it might be the intercepted equivalent of a certain force (e.g., of labor) or of a certain potential power: it is its *systematic nature*, the potential enclosed in the material for total commutability of all values, thanks to their definitive abstraction. It is the abstraction, the total artificiality of the sign that one "adores" in money. What is fetishized is the closed perfection of a system, not the "golden calf," or the treasure. This specifies the difference between the pathology of the miser who is attached to the fecal materiality of gold, and the fetishism we are attempting to define here as an ideological process. Elsewhere we have seen[6] how, in the *collection*, it is neither the nature of objects nor even their symbolic value that is important; but precisely the sense in which they negate all this, and deny the reality of castration for the subject through the systematic nature of the collective cycle, whose continual shifting from one term to another helps the subject to weave around himself a closed and invulnerable world that dissolves all obstacles to the realization of desire (perverse, of course).

Today there is an area where this fetishist logic of the commodity can be illustrated very clearly, permitting us to indicate more precisely what we call the process of ideological labor: the body and beauty. We do not speak of either as an absolute value (speaking of which, what is an absolute value?), but of the current obsession with "liberating the body" and with beauty.

This fetish-beauty has nothing (any longer) to do with an effect of the soul (the spiritualist vision), a natural grace of movement or countenance; with the transparency of truth (the idealist vision); or with an "inspired genius" of the body, which can be communicated as effectively by expressive ugliness (the romantic vision). What we are talking about is a kind of anti-nature incarnate, bound up in a general stereotype of *models of beauty*, in a perfectionist vertigo and controlled narcissism. This is the absolute rule with respect to the face and the body, the generalization of sign exchange value to facial and bodily effects. It is the final disqualification of the body, its subjection to a discipline, the total circulation of signs. The body's wildness is veiled by makeup, the drives are assigned to a cycle of fashion. Behind this *moral* perfection, which stresses a valorization of exteriority (and no longer, as in trad-itional morality, a labor of interior sublimation), it is insurance taken out against the instincts. However, this anti-nature does not exclude desire; we know that this kind of beauty is fascinating precisely because it is trapped in models, because it is closed, systematic, ritualized in the ephemeral, without symbolic value. It is the sign in this beauty, the mark (makeup, symmetry, or calculated asymmetry, etc.), which fascin-ates; *it is the artifact that is the object of desire*. The signs are there to make the body into a perfect object, a feat that has been accomplished through a long and specific labor of sophistication. Signs perfect the body into an object in which none of its real work (the work of the unconscious or psychic and social labor) can show through. The fascination of this fetishized beauty is the result of this extended process of abstraction, and derives from what it negates and censors through its own character as a system.

Tattoos, stretched lips, the bound feet of Chinese women, eyeshadow, rouge, hair removal, mascara, or bracelets, collars, objects, jewelry, accessories: anything will serve to rewrite the cultural order on the body; and it is this that takes on the effect of beauty. The erotic is thus the reinscription of the erogenous in a homo-geneous system of signs (gestures, movements, emblems, body heraldry) whose goal is closure and logical perfection – to be sufficient unto itself. Neither the genital order (placing an external finality in question) nor the symbolic order (putting in question the division of the subject) have this coherence: neither the functional nor the symbolic can weave a body from signs like this – abstract, impeccable, clothed with marks, and thus invulnerable; "made up" (*faict* and *fainct*) in the profound sense of the expression; cut off from external determinations and from the internal reality of its desire, yet offered up in the same turn as an idol, as the *perfect phallus for perverse desire*: that of others, and its own.[7]

Lévi-Strauss has already spoken of this erotic bodily attraction among the Caduvéo and the Maori, of those bodies "completely covered by arabesques of a perverse subtlety," and of "something deliciously provocative."[8] It suffices to think of Baudelaire to know how much sophistication alone conveys charm (in the strong sense), and how much it is always attached to the *mark* (ornamentation, jewelry, perfume) – or to the "cutting up" of the body into partial objects (feet, hair, breasts, buttocks, etc.), which is a profoundly similar exercise. It is always a question of substituting – for an erogenous body, divided in castration, source of an ever-perilous desire – a montage, an artifact of phantasmagorical fragments, an arsenal or a panoply of accessories, or of parts of the body (but the whole body can be reduced by fetishized nudity to the role of a partial object as well). These fetish objects are always caught in a system of assemblage and separation, in a code. Circumscribed in this way, they become the possible objects of a security-giving worship. This is to substitute the line of demarcation between elements-signs for the great dividing line of castration. It substitutes the significant difference, the formal division between signs, for the irreducible ambivalence, for the symbolic split (*écart*).

It would be interesting to compare this perverse fascination to that which, according to Freud, is exercised by the child or the animal, or even by those women "who suffice to themselves, who properly speaking love only themselves" and who for that reason "exercise the greatest charm over men not only for aesthetic reasons . . . but also on account of interesting psychological constellations." "The charm of a child," he says again, "lies to a great extent in his narcissism, his self-sufficiency and inaccessibility, just as does the charm of certain animals which seem not to concern themselves about us, such as cats and the large beasts of prey."[9] One would have to distinguish between the seduction associated, in the child, the animal or the women-child, with *polymorphous perversity* (and with the kind of "freedom," of libidinal autonomy that accompanies it), and that linked to the contemporary commercialized erotic system, which precipitates a "fetishistic" perversion that is restricted, static and encompassed by models. Nevertheless, what is sought for and recognized in both types of seduction is another side or "beyond" of castration, which always takes on the aspect either of a harmonious natural state of unity (child, animal) or of a summation and perfect closure effected by signs. What fascinates us is always that which radically excludes us in the name of its internal logic or perfection: a math-ematical formula, a paranoic system, a concrete jungle, a useless object, or, again, a smooth body, without orifices, doubled and redoubled by a mirror, devoted to perverse autosatisfaction. It is by caressing herself, by the autoerotic maneuver, that the striptease artist best evokes desire.[10]

What is especially important for us here is to demonstrate the general ideo-logical process by which beauty, as a constellation of signs and work upon signs, functions in the present system simultaneously as the negation of castration (per-verse psychic structure) and as the negation of the body that is segmented in its social practice and in the division of labor (ideological social structure). The modern rediscovery of the body and its illusions (*prestiges*) is not innocently contemporary with monopoly capitalism and the discoveries of psychoanalysis:

1. It is because psychoanalysis has brought the fundamental division of the subject to light through the body (but not the same "body"), that it has become so important to ward off this menace (of castration), to restore the individual (the undivided subject of consciousness). This is no longer achieved, however, by endow-ing the individual with a soul or a mind, but a body properly all his own, from which all negativity of desire is eliminated and which functions only as the exhibitor of beauty and happiness. In this sense, the current myth of the body appears as a process of *phantasmagorical rationalization*, which is close to fetishism in its strict analytical definition. Paradoxically, then, this "discovery of the body," which alleges itself to be simultaneous and in sympathy with psychoanalytic discoveries, is in fact an attempt to conjure away its revolutionary implications. The body is introduced in order to liquidate the unconscious and its work, to strengthen the one and homogeneous subject, keystone of the system of values and order.

2. Simultaneously, monopoly capitalism, which is not content to exploit the body as labor power, manages to fragment it, to divide the very expressiveness of the body in labor, in exchange, and in play, recuperating all this as individual needs, hence as productive (*consummative*) forces under its control. This mobilization of cathexes at all levels as productive forces creates, over the long-term, profound contradictions. These contradictions are still political in nature, if we accept a radical redefinition of politics that would take into account this totalitarian socialization of all sectors of real life. It is for these reasons that the body, beauty and sexuality are imposed as new universals in the name of the rights of the new man, emancipated by abundance and the cybernetic revolution. The deprivation, manipulation and con-trolled recycling of the subjective and collective values by the unlimited extension of

exchange value and the unlimited rival speculation over sign values renders necessary the sanctification of a glorious agency called the body that will become for each individual an ideological sanctuary, the sanctuary of his own alienation. Around this body, which is entirely positivized as the capital of divine right, the subject of private property is about to be restored.

So ideology goes, always playing upon the two levels according to the same process of labor and desire attached to the organization of signs (process of signification and fetishization). Let us consider this articulation of the semiological and ideological a little more closely.

Take the example of nudity as it is presented in advertising, in the proliferation of erotica, in the mass media's rediscovery of the body and sex. This nudity claims to be rational, progressive: it claims to rediscover the truth of the body, its natural reason, beyond clothing, taboos and fashion. In fact, it is too rationalistic, and bypasses the body, whose symbolic and sexual truth is not in the naive conspicuousness of nudity, but in the *uncovering* of itself (*mise à nu*), insofar as it is the symbolic equivalent of putting to death (*mise à mort*), and thus of the true path of desire, *which is always ambivalent*, love and death simultaneously.[11] Functional modern nudity does not involve this ambivalence at all, nor thus any profound symbolic function, because such nudity reveals a body *entirely positivized by sex* – as a cultural value, as a model of fulfillment, as an emblem, as a morality (or ludic immorality, which is the same thing) – and *not a body divided and split by sex*. The sexualized body, in this case, no longer functions, save on its positive side, which is that of:

– need (and not of desire);
– satisfaction (lack, negativity, death, castration are no longer registered in it);
– the *right* to the body and sex (the subversiveness, the social negativity of the body and sex are frozen there in a formal "democratic" lobby: the "right to the body").[12]

Once ambivalence and the symbolic function have been liquidated, nudity again becomes one sign among others, entering into a distinctive opposition to clothing. Despite its "liberationist" velleities, it no longer radically opposes clothing, it is only a variant that can coexist with all the others in the systematic process of fashion: and today one sees it everywhere acting "in alternation." It is this nudity, caught up in the differential play of signs (and not in that of eros and death) that is the object of fetishism: the absolute condition for its ideological functioning is the loss of the symbolic and the passing over to the semiological.

Strictly speaking, it is not even because (as has just been said) "once the symbolic function has been liquidated there is a passage to the semiological." In fact, it is the semiological organization itself, the entrenchment in a system of signs, that has the goal of reducing the symbolic function. *This semiological reduction of the symbolic properly constitutes the ideological process.*

[. . .]

Notes

1   Any more than originality, the specific value, the objective merit is belonging to the aristocratic or bourgeois class. This is defined by signs, to the exclusion of "authentic" values. See Goblot, *La Barrière et le Niveau* (Presse Universitaire de France, 1967).

2   De Brosses, *Du Culte des dieux fetiches* (1760).

3   Being *de facto* rationalists, they have often gone so far as to saturate with logical and mythological rationalizations a system of representations that the aborigines knew how to reconcile with more supple objective practices.

4   In this system, use value becomes obscure and almost unintelligible, though not as an original value which has been lost, but more precisely as a *function derived from exchange value.* Henceforth, it is exchange value that induces use value (i.e., needs and satisfactions) to work in common with it (ideologically), within the framework of political economy.

5   In this way labor power as a commodity is itself "fetishized."

6   In my *Le Système des objects* (Paris: Gallimard, 1968), pp. 103ff.

7   Now this is how the body, re-elaborated by the perverse structure as phallic idol, manages to function simultaneously as the ideological model of socialization and of fulfillment. Perverse desire and the ideological process are articulated on the same "sophisticated" body. We will return to this later.

8   Claude Lévi-Strauss, *Tristes Tropiques*, trans. John and Doreen Weightman (New York: Atheneum, 1975), p. 188.

9   Sigmund Freud, "On Narcissism: An Introduction" (1914), in *Collected Papers* (New York: Basic Books, 1959), Vol. IV, p. 46.

10 Ideological discourse is also built up out of a redundancy of signs, and in extreme cases, forms a tautology. It is through this specularity, this "mirage within itself," that it conjures away conflicts and exercises its power.

11 These terms are drawn from Georges Bataille, *L'Erotisme* (Paris: Les Editions de Minuit, 1957).

12 The whole illusion of the *Sexual Revolution* is here: society could not be split, divided and subverted in the name of a sex and a body whose current presentation has the ideological function of veiling the subject's division and subversion. As usual, everything holds together: the reductive function that this mythical nudity fulfills in relation to the subject divided by sex and castration is performed simultaneously on the macroscopic level of society divided by historical class conflicts. Thus the sexual revolution is a subsidiary of the industrial revolution or of the revolution of abundance (and of so many others): all are decoys and ideological metamorphoses of an unchanged order.

Chapter 37

Jean Baudrillard

FASHION, OR THE ENCHANTING SPECTACLE OF THE CODE

The frivolity of the *déjà vu*

THE ASTONISHING PRIVILEGE accorded to fashion is due to a unanimous and definitive resolve. The acceleration of the simple play of signifiers in fashion becomes striking, to the point of enchanting us – the enchantment and vertigo of the loss of every system of reference. In this sense, it is the completed form of political economy, the cycle wherein the linearity of the commodity comes to be abolished.

There is no longer any determinacy internal to the signs of fashion, hence they become free to commute and permutate without limit. At the term of this unprecedented enfranchisement, they obey, as if logically, a mad and meticulous recurrence. This applies to fashion as regards clothes, the body and objects – the sphere of 'light' signs. In the sphere of 'heavy' signs – politics, morals, economics, science, culture, sexuality – the principle of commutation nowhere plays with the same abandon. We could classify these diverse domains according to a decreasing order of 'simulation', but it remains the case that every sphere tends, unequally but simultaneously, to merge with models of simulation, of differential and indifferent play, the structural play of value. In this sense, we could say that they are all haunted by fashion, since this can be understood as both the most superficial play and as the most profound social form – the inexorable investment of every domain by the code.

In fashion, as in the code, signifieds come unthreaded [*se défiler*], and the parades of the signifier [*les défilés du signifiant*] no longer lead anywhere. The signifier/signified distinction is erased, as in sexual difference (H.-P. Jeudy, 'Le signifiant est hermaphrodite' [in *La mort du sens: l'idéologie des mots*, Tours/Paris: Mame, 1973]), where gender becomes so many distinctive oppositions, and something like an immense fetishism, bound up with an intense pleasure [*jouissance*][1] and an exceptional desolation, takes hold — a pure and fascinating manipulation coupled with the despair of radical indeterminacy. Fundamentally, fashion imposes upon us the rupture of an imaginary order: that of referential Reason in all its guises, and if we are able to enjoy [*jouir*] the dismantling or stripping of reason [*démantèlement de la raison*], enjoy the *liquidation* of meaning (particularly at the level of our body — hence the affinity of clothing and fashion), enjoy this endless finality of fashion, we also suffer profoundly from the corruption of rationality it implies, as reason crumbles under the blow of the pure and simple alternation of signs.

There is vehement resistance in the face of the collapse of all sectors into the sphere of commodities, and a still more vehement resistance concerning their collapse into the sphere of fashion. This is because it is in this latter sphere that the liquidation of values is at its most radical. Under the sign of the commodity, all labour is exchanged and loses its specificity — under the sign of fashion, the signs of leisure and labour are exchanged. Under the sign of the commodity, culture is bought and sold — under the sign of fashion, all cultures play like simulacra in total promiscuity. Under the sign of the commodity, love becomes prostitution — under the sign of fashion it is the object-relation itself that disappears, blown to pieces by a cool and unconstrained sexuality. Under the sign of the commodity, time is accumulated like money — under the sign of fashion it is exhausted and discontinued in entangled cycles.

Today, every principle of identity is affected by fashion, precisely because of its potential to revert all forms to non-origin and recurrence. Fashion is always *rétro*, but always on the basis of the abolition of the *passé* (the past): the spectral death and resurrection of forms. Its proper *actuality* (its 'up-to-dateness', its 'relevance') is not a reference to the present, but an immediate and total recycling. Paradoxically, fashion is the *inactual* (the 'out-of-date', the 'irrelevant'). It always presupposes a dead time of forms, a kind of abstraction whereby they become, as if safe from time, effective signs which, as if by a twist of time, will return to haunt the present of their inactuality with all the charm of 'returning' as opposed to 'becoming' structures. The aesthetic of renewal: fashion draws triviality from the death and modernity of the *déjà vu*. This is the despair that nothing lasts, and the complementary enjoyment of knowing that, beyond this death, every form has always the chance of a second existence, which is never innocent since fashion consumes the world and the real in advance: *it is the weight of all the dead labour of signs bearing on living signification* — within a magnificent forgetting, a fantastic ignorance [*méconnaissance*]. But let's not forget that the fascination exerted by industrial machinery and technics is also due to its being dead labour watching over living labour, all the while devouring it. Our bedazzled misconstrual [*méconnaissance*] is proportionate to the progressive hold of the dead over the living. Dead labour alone is as strange and as perfect as the *déjà vu*. The enjoyment of fashion is therefore the enjoyment of a spectral and cyclical world of bygone forms endlessly revived as effective signs. As König says, it is as though fashion were eaten away by a suicidal desire which is fulfilled at the moment when fashion attains its apogee. This is true, but it is a question of a *contemplative* desire for death, bound to the spectacle of the incessant abolition of forms. What I mean is that the desire for death is itself recycled within fashion, emptying it of every subversive phantasm and involving it, along with everything else, in fashion's innocuous revolutions.

Having purged these phantasms which, in the depths of the imaginary, add the bewitchment and charm of a previous life to repetition, fashion dances vertiginously over the surface, on pure actuality. Does fashion recover the innocence that Nietzsche noted in the Greeks: 'They knew how to live . . . to stop . . . at the surface, the fold, the skin, to believe in forms, tones, words. . . . Those Greeks were superficial – out of *profundity*' (*The Gay Science*, Preface, 2nd edition, 1886 [tr. Walter Kaufmann, New York: Random House, 1974], p. 38)? Fashion is only a simulation of the innocence of becoming, the cycle of appearances is just its recycling. That the development of fashion is contemporary with that of the museum proves this. Paradoxically, the museum's demand for an eternal inscription of forms and for a pure actuality function simultaneously in our culture. This is because in modernity both are governed by the status of the sign.

Whereas styles mutually exclude each other, the museum is defined by the virtual co-existence of all styles, by their promiscuity within a single cultural super-institution, or, in other words, the commensurability of their values under the sign of the great gold-standard of culture. Fashion does the same thing in accordance with its cycle: it commutes all signs and causes an absolute play amongst them. The temporality of works in the museum is 'perfect', it is perfection and the past: it is the highly specific state of what has been and is never actual. But neither is fashion ever actual: it speculates on the recurrence of forms on the basis of their death and their stockpiling, like signs, in an a-temporal reserve. Fashion cobbles together, from one year to the next, what 'has been', exercising an enormous combinatory free-dom. Hence its effect of 'instantaneous' perfection, just like the museum's perfec-tion, but the forms of fashion are ephemeral. Conversely, there is a contemporary look to the museum, which causes the works to play amongst themselves like values in a set. Fashion and the museum are contemporary, complicitous. Together they are the opposite of all previous cultures, made of inequivalent signs and incompatible styles.

The 'structure' of fashion

Fashion exists only within the framework of modernity, that is to say, in a schema of rupture, progress and innovation. In any cultural context at all, the ancient and the 'modern' alternate in terms of their signification. For us however, since the Enlightenment and the Industrial Revolution, there exists only an historical and polemical structure of change and crisis. It seems that modernity sets up a linear time of technical progress, production and history, and, simultaneously, a cyclical time of fashion. This only *seems* to be a contradiction, since in fact modernity is never a radical rupture. Tradition is no longer the pre-eminence of the old over the new: it is unaware of either – modernity itself invents them both at once, at a single stroke, it is always and at the same time 'neo-' and '*rétro-*', modern and anachronistic. The dialectic of rupture very quickly becomes the dynamics of the amalgam and recycling. In politics, in technics, in art and in culture it is defined by the exchange rate that the system can tolerate without alteration to its fundamental order. Con-sequently fashion doesn't contradict any of this: it very clearly and simultaneously announces the *myth* of change, maintaining it as the supreme value in the most everyday aspects, and as the structural law of change: since it is produced through the play of models and distinctive oppositions, and is therefore an order which gives no precedence to the code of the tradition. For binary logic is the essence of modernity, and it impels infinite differentiation and the 'dialectical' effects of rupture. Modernity is not the transmutation but the commutation of all values, their combination and their ambiguity. Modernity is a code, and fashion is its emblem.

This perspective allows us to trace only the limits of fashion, in order to conquer the two simultaneous prejudices which consist:

1   in extending its field up to the limits of anthropology, indeed of animal behaviour;
2   in restricting, on the other hand, its actual sphere to dress and external signs.

Fashion has nothing to do with the ritual order (nor *a fortiori* with animal finery), for the good reason that it knows neither the equivalence/alternation of the old and the new, nor the systems of distinctive oppositions, nor the models with their serial and combinatory diffraction. On the other hand, fashion is at the core of modernity, extending even into science and revolution, because the entire order of modernity, from sex to the media, from art to politics, is infiltrated by this logic. The very appearance of fashion bears the closest resemblance to ritual – fashion as spectacle, as festival, as squandering – it doesn't even affirm their differences: since it is precisely the *aesthetic* perspective that allows us to assimilate fashion to the ceremonial (just as it is precisely the concept of festival that allows us to assimilate certain contemporary processes to primitive structures). The aesthetic perspective is itself a concern of modernity (of a play of distinctive oppositions – utility/gratuity, etc.), one which we project onto archaic structures so as to be better able to annex them under our analogies. Spectacle is our fashion, an intensified and reduplicated sociality enjoying itself *aesthetically*, the drama of change in place of change. In the primitive order, the ostentation of signs never has this 'aesthetic' effect. In the same way, our festival is an *'aesthetics' of transgression*, which is not the primitive exchange in which it pleases us to find the reflection or the model of our festivals – to rewrite the 'aesthetics' of potlach is an ethnocentric rewriting.

It is as necessary to distinguish fashion from the ritual order as it is to radicalise the analysis of fashion within our own system. The minimal, superficial definition of fashion restricts itself to saying: 'Within language, the element subject to fashion is not the signification of discourse, but its mimetic support, that is, its rhythm, its tonality, its articulation . . . in gesture . . . This is equally true of intellectual fashions: existentialism or structuralism – it is the vocabulary and not the inquiry that is taken on' (Edmond Radar, *Diogène* [50, Summer, 1965]). Thus a deep structure, invulnerable to fashion, is preserved. Consequently it is in the very production of meaning [*sens*], in the most 'objective' structures, that it must be sought, in the sense that these latter also comply with the play of simulation and combinatory innovation. Even dress and the body grow deeper: now it is the body itself, its identity, its sex, its status, which has become the material of fashion – dress is only a particular case of this. Certainly scientific and cultural popularisations provide fertile soil for the 'effects' of fashion. However, along with the 'originality' of their procedures, science and culture themselves must be interrogated, to see if they are subject to the 'structure' of fashion. If indeed popularisation is possible — which is not the case in any other culture (the facsimile, the digest, the counterfeit, the simulation, the increased circulation of simplified material, is unthinkable at the level of ritual speech, of the sacred text or gesture) — it is because there is, at the very source of innovation in these matters, a manipulation of analytic models, of simple elements and stable oppositions which renders both levels, the 'original' and the 'popularisation', fundamentally homogeneous, and the distinction between the two purely tactical and moral. Hence Radar does not see that, beyond discourse's 'gestures', the very meaning [*sens*] of discourse falls beneath the blow of fashion as soon as in an entirely self-referential cultural field, concepts are engendered and made to correspond to each other through pure specularity. It may be the same for scientific hypotheses. Nor does psychoanalysis avoid the fate of fashion in the very core of its theoretical and clinical practice. It too goes through the stage of institutional reproduction, developing whatever simulation models it had in its basic concepts. If formerly there was a *work* of the unconscious, and therefore a determination of psychoanalysis by means of its object, today this has quietly become the determination of the *unconscious by means of psychoanalysis itself*. Henceforth psychoanalysis reproduces the unconscious, while simultaneously taking itself as its reference (signifying itself as *fashion*, as the *mode*). So the unconscious returns to its old habits, as it is generally required to do, and psychoanalysis takes on social force, just as the code does, and is followed by an extraordinary complexification of theories of the unconscious, all commutable and basically indifferent.

Fashion has its society: dreams, phantasms, fashionable psychoses, scientific theories, fashionable schools of linguistics, not to mention art and politics — but this is only small change. Fashion haunts the *model* disciplines more profoundly, indeed to the extent that they have successfully made their axioms autonomous for their greater glory, and have moved into an *aesthetic*, almost a play-acting stage where, as in certain mathematical formulae, only the perfect specularity of the analytic models counts for anything.

The flotation of signs

Contemporary with political economy and like the market, fashion is a universal form. In fashion, all signs are exchanged just as, on the market, all products come into play as equivalents. It is the only universalisable sign system, which therefore takes possession of all the others, just as the market eliminates all other modes of exchange. So if in the sphere of fashion no general equivalent can be located, it is because from the outset fashion is situated in an even more formal abstraction than political economy, at a stage when there is not even any need for a perceptible general equivalent (gold or money) because there remains only the *form of general equivalence*, and that is fashion itself. Or even: a general equivalent is necessary for the *quantitative* exchange of value, whereas models are required for the exchange of differences. Models are this kind of general equivalent diffracted throughout the matrices which govern the differentiated fields of fashion. They are shifters, effectors, dispatchers, the media of fashion, and through them fashion is indefinitely reproduced. There is fashion from the moment that a form is no longer produced according to its own determinations, but *from the model itself* – that is to say, that it is never produced, but always and immediately *reproduced*. The model itself has become the only system of reference.

Fashion is not a *drifting* of signs – it is their *flotation*, in the sense in which monetary signs are floated today. This flotation in the economic order is recent: it requires that 'primitive accumulation' be everywhere finished, that an entire cycle of dead labour be completed (behind money, the whole economic order will enter into this general relativity). Now this process has been managed for a long time within the order of signs where primitive accumulation is indeed anterior, if not always already given, and fashion expresses the already achieved stage of an accelerated and limitless circulation of a fluid and recurrent combinatory of signs, which is equivalent to the instantaneous and mobile equilibrium of floating monies. All cultures, all sign systems, are exchanged and combined in fashion, they contaminate each other, bind ephemeral equilibria, where the machinery breaks down, where there is nowhere any meaning [*sens*]. Fashion is the pure speculative stage in the order of signs. There is no more constraint of either coherence or reference than there is permanent equality in the conversion of gold into floating monies – this indeterminacy implies the characteristic dimension of the cycle and recurrence in fashion (and no doubt soon in economy), whereas determinacy (of signs or of production) implies a linear and continuous order. Hence the fate of the economic begins to emerge in the form of fashion, which is further down the route of general commutations than money and the economy.

The 'pulsion'[2] of fashion

Were the attempt made to explain fashion by saying that it serves as a vehicle for the unconscious and desire, it would mean nothing if desire itself was 'in fashion'. In fact there is a 'pulsion' of fashion which hasn't got a great deal to do with the individual unconscious – something so violent that no prohibition has ever exhausted it, a desire to have done with meaning [*sens*] and to be submerged in pure signs, moving towards a raw, immediate sociality. In relation to mediated, economic, etc., social processes, fashion retains something of a radical sociality, not at the level of the psychical exchange of contents, but at the immediate level of the distribution of signs. As La Bruyère has already said:

> Curiosity is not a taste for the good or the beautiful, but for the rare, for what one has and others have not. It is not an affection for the perfect, but for what is current, for the fashionable. It is not an amusement, but a passion, sometimes so violent that it only yields to love and ambition through the modesty of its object. ('De la Mode 2' [in J. Benda (ed.), *Oeuvres Complètes*, Paris: Gallimard, 1951], p. 386)

For La Bruyère, the passion for fashion connects the passion for collecting with the object-passion: tulips, birds, engravings by Callot. In fact fashion draws nearer to the collection (in those terms) by means of subtle detours, 'each of which', for Oscar Wilde, 'gives man a security which not even religion has given him'.

Paying tribute to it, he finds salvation in fashion [*faire son salut dans la mode*]. A passion for collecting, passion for signs, passion for the cycle (the collection is also a cycle); one line of fashion put into circulation and distributed at dizzying speeds across the entire social body, sealing its integration and taking in all identifications (as the line in collection unifies the subject in one and the same infinitely repeated cyclic process).

This force, this enjoyment, takes root in the sign of fashion itself. The semiurgy of fashion rebels against the functionalism of the economic-sphere. Against the ethics of production[3] stands the aesthetics of manipulation, of the reduplication and convergence of the single mirror of the model: 'Without content, it [fashion] then becomes the spectacle human beings grant themselves of their power to make the insignificant signify' (Barthes, *The Fashion System* [tr. Mathew Ward and Richard Howard, Berkeley: University of California Press, 1983], p. 288). The charm and fascination of fashion derives from this: the decree it proclaims with no other justification but itself. The arbitrary is enjoyed like an election, like class solidarity holding fast to the discrimination of the sign. It is in this way that it diverges radically from the economic while also being its crowning achievement. In relation to the pitiless finality of production and the market, which, however, it also stages, fashion is a festival. It epitomises everything that the regime of economic abstraction censures. It inverts every categorical imperative.

In this sense, it is spontaneously contagious, whereas economic calculation isolates people from one another. Disinvesting signs of all value, it becomes passion again – passion for the artificial. It is the utter absurdity, the formal futility of the sign of fashion, the perfection of a system where nothing is any longer exchanged against the real, it is the arbitrariness of this sign at the same time as its absolute coherence, constrained to a total relativity with other signs, that makes for its contagious virulence and, at the same time, its collective enjoyment. Beyond the rational and the irrational, beyond the beautiful and the ugly, the useful and the useless, it is this immorality in relation to all criteria, the frivolity which at times gives fashion its subversive force (in totalitarian, puritan or archaic contexts), which always, in contradistinction to the economic, makes it a *total social fact* – for which reason we are obliged to revive, as Mauss did for exchange, a total approach.

Fashion, like language, is aimed from the outset at the social (the dandy, in his provocative solitude, is the *a contrario* proof of this). But, as opposed to language, which aims for meaning [*sens*] and effaces itself before it, fashion aims for a theatrical sociality, and delights in itself. At a stroke, it becomes an intense site from which no-one is excluded – the mirror of a certain desire for its own image. In contradistinction to language, which *aims* at communication, fashion *plays* at it, turning it into the goal-less stake of a signification without a message. Hence its aesthetic pleasure, which has nothing to do with beauty or ugliness. Is it then a sort of festival, an increasing excess of communication?

It is especially fashion in dress, playing over the signs of the body, that appears 'festive', through its aspect of 'wasteful consumption', of 'potlach'. Again this is especially true of *haute couture*. This is what allows *Vogue* to make this tasty profession of faith:

What is more anachronistic, more dream-laden than a sailing ship? *Haute couture*. It discourages the economist, takes up a stance contrary to productivity techniques, it is an affront to democratisation. With superb languor, a maximum number of highly qualified people produce a minimum number of models of complex cut, which will be repeated, again with the same languor, twenty times in the best of cases, or not at all in the worst. . . . Perhaps two million dresses. 'But why this debauchery of effort?' you say. 'Why not?' answer the creators, the craftsmen, the workers and the four thousand clients, all possessed by the same passion for seeking perfection. Couturiers are the last adventurers of the modern world. They cultivate the *acte gratuit* . . . 'Why *haute couture?*' a few detractors may think. 'Why champagne?' Again: 'Neither practice nor logic can justify the extravagant adventure of clothes. Superfluous and therefore necessary, the world is once more the province of religion.'

Potlach, religion, indeed the ritual enchantment of expression, like that of costume and animal dances: everything is good for exalting fashion against the economic, like a transgression into a play-act sociality.

We know, however, that advertising too wants a 'feast of consumption', the media a 'feast of information', the markets a 'feast of production', etc. The art market and horse races can also be taken for potlach – 'Why not?' asks *Vogue*. We would like to see a functional squandering everywhere so as to bring about symbolic destruction. Because of the extent to which the economic, shackled to the functional, has imposed its principle of utility, anything which exceeds it quickly takes on the air of play and futility. It is hard to acknowledge that the law of value extends well beyond the economic, and that its true task today is the jurisdiction of all models. Wherever there are models, there is an imposition of the law of value, repression by signs and the repression of signs by themselves. This is why there is a radical difference between the symbolic ritual and the signs of fashion. In primitive cultures signs openly circulate over the entire range of 'things', there has not yet been any 'precipitation' of a signified, nor therefore of a reason or a truth of the sign. The real – the most beautiful of our connotations – does not exist. The sign has no 'underworld', it has no *unconscious* (which is both the last and the most subtle of connotations and rationalisations). Signs are exchanged without phantasms, with no hallucination of reality.

Hence they have nothing in common with the modern sign whose paradox Barthes has defined: 'The overwhelming tendency is to convert the perceptible into a signifier, towards ever more organised, closed systems. Simultaneously and in equal proportion, the sign and its systematic nature is disguised as such, it is rationalised, referred to a reason, to an agency in the world, to a substance, to a function' (cf. *The Fashion System*, p. 285). With simulation, signs merely disguise the real and the system of reference as a sartorial supersign. The real is dead, long live the realistic sign! This paradox of the modern sign induces a radical split between it and the magical or ritual sign, the same one as is exchanged in the mask, the tattoo or the feast.

Even if fashion is an enchantment, it remains the enchantment of the commodity, and, still further, the enchantment of simulation, the code and the law.

Sex refashioned

There is nothing less certain than that sexuality invests dress, make-up, etc. – or rather it is a *modified* sexuality that comes into play at the level of fashion. If the condemnation of fashion takes on this puritan violence, it is not aimed at sex. The taboo bears on futility, on the passion for futility and the artificial which is perhaps more fundamental than the sexual drives. In our culture, tethered as it is to the principle of utility, futility plays the role of transgression and violence, and fashion is condemned for having within it the force of the pure sign which signifies nothing. Its sexual provocation is secondary with regard to this principle which denies the grounds of our culture.

Of course, the same taboo is also brought to bear on 'futile' and non-reproductive sexuality, but there is a danger in crystallising on sex, a danger that puritan tactics, which aim to change the stakes to sexuality, may be prolonged – whereas it is at the level of the *reality principle* itself, of the referential principle in which the unconscious and sexuality still participate, that fashion confrontationally sets up its pure play of differences. To place sexuality at the forefront of this history is once again to *neutralise the symbolic by means of sex and the unconscious*. It is according to this same logic that the analysis of fashion has traditionally been reduced to that of dress, since it allows the sexual metaphor the greatest play. Consequences of this diversion: the game is reduced to a perspective of sexual 'liberation', which is quite simply achieved in a 'liberation' of dress. And a new cycle of fashion begins again.

Fashion is certainly the most efficient neutraliser of sexuality (one never touches a woman in make-up – see 'The Body, or The Mass Grave of Signs' below) – precisely because it is a passion which is not complicitous, but in competition with sex (and, as La Bruyère has already noted, fashion is victorious over sex). Therefore the passion for fashion, in all its ambiguity, will come to play on the body confused with sex.

Fashion grows deeper as it 'stages' the body, as the body becomes the medium of fashion.[4] Formerly the repressed sanctuary, the repression rendering it undecodable, from now on it too is invested. The play of dress is effaced before the play of the body, which itself is effaced before the play of models.[5] All at once dress loses the ceremonial character (which it still had up until the eighteenth century) bound up with the usage of signs *qua* signs. Eaten away by the body's signifieds, by this 'transpearence' of the body as sexuality and nature, dress loses the fantastic exuberance it has had since the primitive societies. It loses its force as pure disguise, it is neutralised by the necessity that it must signify the body, it becomes a reason.

The body too is neutralised in this operation however. It too loses the power of disguise that it used to have in tattooing and costume. It no longer plays with anything save its proper truth, which is also its borderline: its nudity. In costumery, the signs of the body, mixed openly with the signs of the not-body, play. Thereafter, costume becomes dress, and the body becomes nature. Another game is set up – the opposition of dress and the body – designation and censure (the same fracture as between the signifier and the signified, the same play of displacement and allusion). Fashion strictly speaking begins with this partition of the body, repressed and signified in an allusive way – it also puts an end to all this in the simulation of nudity, in *nudity as the model of the simulation of the body*. For the Indian, the whole body is a face, that is, a promise and a symbolic act, as opposed to nudity, which is only sexual instrumentality.

This new reality of the body as hidden sex is from the outset merged with woman's body. The concealed body is feminine (not biologically of course; rather mythologically). The conjunction of fashion and woman, since the bourgeois, puritan era, reveals therefore a double indexation: that of fashion on a hidden body, that of woman on a repressed sex. This conjunction did not exist (or not so much) until the eighteenth century (and not at all, of course, in ceremonial societies) – and for us today it is beginning to disappear. As for us, when the destiny of a hidden sex and the forbidden truth of the body arises, when fashion itself neutralises the opposition between the body and dress, then the affinity of woman and fashion progressively diminishes[6] – fashion is generalised and becomes less and less the exclusive property of one sex or of one age. Be wary, for it is a matter neither of progress nor of liberation. The same logic still applies, and if fashion is generalised and leaves the privileged medium of woman so as to be open to all, the prohibition placed on the body is also generalised in a more subtle form than puritan repression: in the form of general desexualisation. For it was only under repression that the body had strong sexual potential: it then appeared as a captivating demand. Abandoned to the signs of fashion, the body is sexually disenchanted, it becomes a *mannequin*, a term whose lack of sexual discrimination suits its meaning well.[7] The mannequin is sex in its entirety, but sex without qualities. Fashion is its sex. Or rather, it is in fashion that sex is lost as difference but is generalised as reference (as simulation). Nothing is sexed any longer, everything is sexualised. The masculine and the feminine themselves rediscover, having once lost their particularity, the chance of an unlimited second existence. Hence, in our culture alone, sexuality impregnates all signification, and this is because signs have, for their part, invested the entire sexual sphere.

In this way the current paradox becomes clear: we simultaneously witness the 'emancipation' of woman and a fresh upsurge of fashion. This is because fashion has only to do with the feminine, and not with women. Society in its entirety is becoming feminine to the extent that discrimination against women is coming to an end (as it is for madmen, children, etc., being the normal consequence of the logic of exclusion). Hence *prendre son pied*, at once 'to find one's feet', and a familiar French expression of the female orgasm [*jouissance*], has now become generalised, while simultaneously, of course, destabilising its signification. We must also note however, that woman can only be 'liberated' and 'emancipated' as 'force of pleasure' and 'force of fashion', exactly as the proletariat is only ever liberated as the 'labour force'. The above illusion is radical. The historical definition of the feminine is formed on the basis of the destiny of the body and sex bound up with fashion. The historical liberation of the feminine can only be the realisation of this destiny writ large (which immediately becomes the liberation of the whole world, without however losing its discriminatory character). At the same moment that woman accesses a universal labour modelled on the proletariat, the whole world also accesses the emancipation of sex and fashion, modelled on women. We can immediately, and clearly, see that fashion is a labour, to which it becomes necessary to accord equal historical importance to 'material' labour. It is also of capital

importance (which by the same token becomes part of capital!) to produce commodities in accordance with the market, and to produce the body in accordance
with the rules of sex and fashion. The division of labour won't settle where we
think, or rather there is no division of labour at all: the production of the body, the
production of death, the production of signs and the production of commodities –
these are only modalities of one and the same system. Doubtless it is even worse in
fashion: for if the worker is divided from himself under the signs of exploitation and
of the reality principle, woman is divided from herself and her body under the signs
of beauty and the pleasure principle!

The insubvertible

History says, or so the story goes, that the critique of fashion (O. Burgelin) was a
product of conservative thinking in the nineteenth century, but that today, with the
advent of socialism, this critique has been revived by the left. The one went with
religion and the other with revolution. Fashion corrupts morals, fashion abolishes
the class struggle. Although this critique of fashion may have passed over to the left,
it does not necessarily signify an historical reversal: perhaps it signifies that with
regard to morality and morals, the left has quite simply taken over from the right,
and that, in the name of the revolution, it has adopted the moral order and its classic
prejudices. Ever since the principle of revolution entered into morals, quite a
categorical imperative, the whole political order, even the left, has become a moral
order.

   Fashion is immoral, this is what's in question, and all power (or all those who
dream of it) necessarily hates it. There was a time when immorality was recognised,
from Machiavelli to Stendhal, and when somebody like Mandeville could show, in
the eighteenth century, that a society could only be revolutionized through its vices,
that it is its immorality that gives it its dynamism. Fashion still holds to this immorality: it knows nothing of value-systems, nor of criteria of judgement: good and evil,
beauty and ugliness, the rational/irrational – it plays within and beyond these, it acts
therefore as the subversion of all order, including revolutionary rationality. It is
power's hell, the hell of the relativity of all signs which all power is forced to crush
in order to maintain its own signs. Thus fashion is taken on by contemporary youth,
as a resistance to every imperative, a resistance without an ideology, without
objectives.

   On the other hand, there is no possible subversion of fashion since it has no
system of reference to contradict (it is its own system of reference). We cannot
escape fashion (since fashion itself makes the refusal of fashion into a fashion feature
– blue-jeans are an historical example of this). While it is true that one can always
escape the reality principle of the content, one can never escape the reality principle
of the code. Even while rebelling against the content, one more and more closely
obeys the logic of the code. Why so? It is the diktat of 'modernity'. Fashion leaves no
room for revolution except to go back over the very genesis of the sign that
constitutes it. Furthermore, the alternative to fashion does not lie in a 'liberty' or in
some kind of step beyond towards a truth of the world and systems of reference. It
lies in a deconstruction of both the form of the sign of fashion and the principle of

signification itself, just as the alternative to political economy can only lie in the deconstruction of the commodity/form and the principle of production itself.

Notes

1   [I have translated the French noun *jouissance* and the verb *jouir*, whose admixture of libidinal and political economy is well known in contemporary French theory, variously according to context. In the main I have translated it as 'enjoyment'; sometimes as 'intense pleasure', with the French following in brackets. – tr.]

2   [*Pulsion* is the French translation of Freud's *Trieb*, which the *Standard Edition* translates as 'instinct', a move which for many reasons has been found inadequate. The current translation is 'drive', which I have sometimes used for reasons of euphony. The French *pulsion*, however, seems preferable since it confers a less mechanistically dominated energetics than does 'drive'. These are the only options used throughout the present text. – tr.]

3   But we have seen that the economic today conforms with the same indeterminacy, ethics drops out in aid of a 'finality without end' of production whereby it rejoins the vertiginous futility of fashion. We may say then of production what Barthes says of fashion: 'The system then abandons the meaning yet does so without giving up any of the *spectacle of signification*' [*The Fashion System*, p. 288, J.B's emphasis].

4   The three modalities of the 'body of fashion' cited by Barthes (cf. *The Fashion System*, pp. 258–9):

   1   It is a pure form, with no attributes of its own, tautologically defined by dress.

   2   Or: every year we decree that a certain body (a certain type of body) is in fashion. This is another way of making the two coincide.

   3   We develop dress in such a way that it transforms the real body and makes it signify the ideal body of fashion.

These modalities more or less correspond to the historical evolution of the status of the model: from the initial, but non-professional model (the high-society woman) to the professional mannequin whose body also plays the role of a sexual model up until the latest (current) phase where everybody has become a mannequin – each is called, summoned to invest their bodies with the rules of the game of fashion – the whole world is an 'agent' of fashion, just as the whole world becomes a productive agent. General effusion of fashion to all and sundry and at every level of signification.

It is also possible to tie these phases of fashion in with the phases of the successive concentration of capital, with the structuration of the economic sphere of fashion (variation of fixed capital, of the organic composition of capital, the speed of the rotation of commodities, of finance capital and industrial capital – cf. *Utopie*, Oct. 1971, no. 4). However, the analytic principle of this interaction of the economic and signs is never clear. More than in the direct relation with the economic, it is in a sort of movement homologous to the extension of the market that the historical extension of the sphere of fashion can be seen:

   1   In the beginning fashion is concerned only with scattered details, minimal

variations, supported by marginal categories, in a system which remains essentially homogeneous and traditional (just as in the first phase of political economy only the surplus of a yield is exchanged, which in other circumstances is largely exhausted in consumption within the group – a very weak section of the free labour force and the salariat). Fashion then is what is outside culture, outside the group, the foreigner, it is the city-dweller to the country-dweller, etc.

2   Fashion progressively and virtually integrates all the signs of culture, and regulates the exchange of signs, just as in a second phase all material production is virtually integrated by political economy. Both systems anterior to production and exchange are effaced in the universal dimension of the market. All cultures come to play within fashion's universality. In this phase fashion's reference is the dominant cultural class, which administers the distinctive values of fashion.

3   Fashion is diffused everywhere and quite simply becomes *the way of life* [*le mode de vie*]. It invests every sphere which had so far escaped it. The whole world supports and reproduces it. It recuperates its own negativity (the fact of not being in fashion), it becomes its own signified (like production at the stage of reproduction). In a certain way, however, it is also its end.

5   For it is not true that a dress or a supple body stocking which lets the body 'play' 'frees' something or other: in the order of signs, this is a supplementary adulteration. To denude structures is not to return to the zero degree of truth, it is to wrap them in a new signification which gets added to all the others. So it will be the beginning of a new cycle of forms. So much for the cycle of formal innovation, so much for the logic of fashion, and no-one can do anything about it. To 'liberate' structures (of the body, the unconscious, the functional truth of the object in design, etc.) still amounts to clearing the way for the *universalisation of the system of fashion* (it is the only universalisable system, the only one that can control the circulation of every sign, including contradictory ones). A *bourgeois* revolution in the system of forms, with the appearance of a bourgeois political revolution; this too clears the way for the *universalisation of the system of the market*.

6   There are of course other, social and historical, reasons for this affinity: woman's (or youths') marginality or her social relegation. But this is no different: social repression and a malefic sexual aura are always brought together under the same categories.

7   [The French *mannequin* signifies a masculine, a feminine and a neuter; a man with no strength of character who is easily led, a woman employed by a large couturier to present models wearing its new collection, and an imitation human. Its gender is masculine (*le mannequin*). – tr.]

Chapter 38

Kim Sawchuk

A TALE OF INSCRIPTION/FASHION STATEMENTS

> ". . . so many political institutions of cryptography."]
> Jacques Derrida
> *Scribble (writing-power)*

Still life

LET ME BEGIN with two allegories, two dreams, for it is precisely the question of allegory and representation in relationship to the social sciences, particularly cultural studies and feminism, which is at issue in this paper. The first is taken from literature, the second from experience.

In Franz Kafka's short story, "In the Penal Colony", an explorer is invited to the colony to observe and report on its system and method of punishment. At the colony, the explorer is introduced to a machine, a fantastic machine upon which the condemned are placed and their punishment meted. However, prior to their placement on this machine the condemned have been told neither their sentence nor their punishment; knowledge of their transgression and the lesson they are are to learn from it will be inscribed on their bodies by vibrating needles as the inviolable dictums of the community such as "Honour thy Superiors" or "Be just" are written into their flesh in a beautiful and decorative script.[1]

Meanwhile, it is November in Toronto, and my mother visits me. We travel to Harbourfront which is packed with holiday shoppers. The crowds circulate throughout the complex amongst the glittering gold and silver decorations in a frenzy of buying and selling. Mannequins have been strategically placed throughout the mall to draw attention to and create desire for the fashions that are for sale.

As we approach these dolls our sensibilities are startled. What we have taken to be plastic models are, in fact, flesh and blood women imitating replicas of real women; representations of representations, women who cannot move, cannot respond to the excited gestures of this mob of consumers. Having exchanged their mobility for a wage, they are compelled to stand in awkward poses for extremely long durations of time while curiosity seekers gaze at them, poke fingers in their direction to force a smile, a movement, and photograph this spectacle of female beauty.

The object of fashion

Fashion: what, or whom, are the objects of its discourse? It is a subject without the institutional support or legitimacy granted to other academic subjects, save a few obscure accounts of changes in dress and costume, fleeting references to fashion in the history of European commerce and trade, and the occasional semiotic analysis.[2] What is most conspicuous is the lack of material on the subject, a subject which raises both metaphysical and political questions.

Perhaps this is because, as a topic, we do not know how to frame it how to address the questions it asks of us. Films, books, photographs, paintings, are all bound by a border that renders them analysable. However, the question of what constitutes the field of fashion is far more ambiguous. As I will argue, it is a phenomenon which threatens the very stability of segregated zones: man/woman, subject/object, the personal/political, reality/illusion. The body, lying in both the realm of the public and private, is a metaphor for the essential instability of objects in their relationship to each other. Like a fence, or the bar between signified and signifier, it is bound to both, but the property of neither.

As Kafka's allegory reminds us, when we are interested in fashion, we are concerned with relations of power and their articulation at the level of the body, a body intimately connected to society, but which is neither prior to it, nor totally determined by it. For example, in the 1950s Frantz Fanon commented on the French colonial government's attempt to destroy Algerian society by outlawing the veil under the guise of liberating Algerian women.

> The way people clothe themselves, together with the traditions of dress and finery the custom implies, constitutes the most distinctive form of a society's uniqueness, that is to say, the one that is most immediately perceptible.[3]

Whether naked or clothed, the body bears the scatalogical marks, the historical scars of power. Fashionable behaviour is never simply a question of creativity or self-expression; it is also a mark of colonization, the "anchoring" of our bodies, particularly the bodies of women, into specific positions, and parts of the body in the line of the gaze.

In this respect, it is ironic that the French Fashion conglomerate Christian Dior's summer make-up line was titled "Les Coloniales". "Les Coloniales" with an 'e' on the end to signify woman as the colonized subject at the same time as she is elevated to the level of the exotic. European woman, whose unveiled white skin, blue eyes exuding "the coolness of water and shade", peers from behind a cluster of bright red flowers. From a distance, these flowers seem to be a traditional headscarf. On closer inspection it is clear that they are anthuriums, whose phallic resemblance cannot be coincidental. The bloody history of French colonialism and the Algerian war is magically transformed, re-written with the stroke of eyebrow pencils and lipgloss. The white light of the camera attempts to erase the lines and creases of this history which might be sedimented on the face of this woman; "White mythology," a cool and distant look has displaced the face of the desert. "Les Coloniales" is an appropriate third metaphor in our triumverate of allegories.

Theoretically, it is tempting to interpret Kafka's allegory, Harbourfront and "Les Coloniales", as relatively clear examples of how ideology functions; patriarchal ideology to repress women, white mythology to distort the reality of colonialism. However, these images are more paradoxical than is obvious at first sight. "Fashion", like "woman" is not an undifferentiated object in-it-self which suddenly appears on the stage of history; nor should it be easily reduced to a mere reflection of social and economic developments, to what Freud called a "master key" which seems to account for the manifestation of the object. Within both Marxism and feminism there is the tendency to treat the object as simply a reflection of social movements, or as an index of the horrific effects of capitalism. It is this analysis which currently dominates the feminist and Marxist interpretation of fashion and popular culture.

For example, Anne Oakley, in her section on fashion and cosmetics in *Subject Women*, says that certain styles of dress reflect specific ideologies. In periods of feminist rebellion, women have called for changes in dress towards "a plainer, more masculine style of dress."[4] In the modern era, types of dress, such as work boots or spike heels indicate either the radical or conservative nature of female subjects in a relatively transparant manner.

Furthermore, women's relationship to fashion and the fashion industry is said to reflect the positioning of women within patriarchal capitalism. Women in European cultures have been socialised to be passive objects: they "appear," while men "act." Many feminists draw upon John Berger's *Ways of Seeing*,[5] in which he argues that the history of European painting shows that the looks of women are merely displays for men to watch, while women watch themselves being looked at. This determines relationships between men and women, women's relationship to other women, and women's relationship to themselves.[6] Whenever women look at themselves, they are acting like men. Laura Mulvey's seminal article "Visual Pleasure and Narrative Cinema", develops this concept of the gaze in its three manifestations, objectification, narcissism, and fetishism, as predominantly gender-determined and male, in relationship to film.[7] Like the women at Harbourfront, whether through economic necessity or their internalization of patriarchal values, they turn themselves into objects for this gaze and further reinforce this phallic economy of desire.

Women's love of clothes, cosmetics, jewellery, their obsession with style and fashion, reinforces the myth that we are narcissitic and materialistic. In turn this reinforces capitalism, which depends upon this obsession with our bodies for the marketing of new products. Griselda Pollack's work expands on this thesis by showing how the solidification of the identity between a woman's body and the notion "for sale" is an extension of the tradition of European high art within popular culture.[8]

There is an element of truth to these arguments, given the historical development of the advertising and clothing industry. But they tend to fall within the trap of decoding all social relations within patriarchy and capitalism as essentially repressive and homogeneous in its effects. As Teresa de Lauretis explains, the visual world is treated as a series of static representations. It is assumed that images are literally absorbed by the viewer, that each image is immediately readable and meaningful in and of itself, regardless of the context, the circumstances of its production, circulation and reception. The viewer, except of course for the educated critic who has learned to see beyond this level of deception, is assumed to be immediately susceptible to these images.[9]

However, fashion, like social being, is constituted through the effects of language, through the circulation and vagaries of discourses which affect the very nature of its images and its objects. Derrida writes:

> Whether in the order of spoken or written discourse, no element can function as a sign without referring to another element which itself is not simply present. This interweaving results in each "element" – phoneme or grapheme – being constituted on the basis of the trace within it of the other elements of the chain or system. This interweaving, this textile, is the *text* produced only in the transformation of another text. Nothing, neither among the elements nor within the system, is anywhere ever simply present or absent. There are only, everywhere, differences and traces of traces.[10]

It for this reason that I emphasize that these inscriptions of the social take place *at* the level of the body, not *upon* it. We must take care in our own theoretical discourse not to position the body or the social in a relationship of radical alterity to one another. Neither fashion nor woman can be seen as objects determined simply by two variables, such as sex and class, for they are constructed in this fabric of intertextual relations.

At any specific historical juncture, fashion is located in a discourse on health (corsets, suntanning, fitness), beauty (ideal shapes of breasts, buttocks or lips), morality and sexuality (dress as sign of one's moral fibre), the nation and the economy (the question of the veil in Algeria), and location (climate geography, seasonal variations), to name only a few possibilities. These discourses involve the body, produce the body as a textured object with multi-dimensional layers, touched by the rich weave of history and culture.

The intertextual constitution of subjectivity and objects has repercussions for what has been the standard Marxist and feminist interpretation of fashion; fashion as a reflection of the social onto the body, fashion as the repression of the natural body; fashion simply as a commodity to be resisted; fashion as substitute for the missing phallus. Derrida's description of intertextuality is, I believe, theoretically related to the concept of allegory developed by Walter Benjamin, and to Freud's critique of previous methods of dream analysis. Both writers challenge the relative transparency of the object as simple sign, symbol or icon.[11]

In *The Interpretation of Dreams*, Freud noted that the difference between his theory and past methods of dream analysis was that for him, ". . . memory is not present at once, but several times over, that is, laid down (*neiderlegt*) in various species of indications [*Zeichen*, lit. signs] . . ."[12] He emphasized that dream interpretation must begin its analysis "en detail," not "en masse," as dreams are of a composite character, and as such, are often confusing.[13] He suggested that there were three understandings of this relationship, and three techniques of dream analysis: the symbolic, which "seems to be a relic and a mark of a former identity;"[14] decoding, which "treats events as a kind of cryptography in which each sign can be translated into another sign having a known meaning in accordance with a fixed key"[15] and a third method which is one of interpretation, of deciphering.

> My procedure is not so convenient as the popular decoding method which translates any given piece of a dream's content by a fixed key. I on the contrary am prepared to find that the piece of content may conceal a different meaning when it occurs in different people or in various contexts.[16]

The memory of events, and of history, is never completely transparent; it is constantly rewritten or overdetermined by present cultural practices. For this reason, language and culture should not be understood as symbolic, for this implies that they are fixed within the chain of signification or in relationship to the "signified." It is this critique of culture as symbolic (i.e., expressive) that is at play in Benjamin's cultural analysis.

Benjamin's study of baroque drama and its allegorical nature critiques the concept of the symbol from the perspective of its ahistoricity. "The measure of time for the experience of the symbol is the mystical instant in which the symbol assumes the meaning in its hidden, and if one might say so, wooded interior."[17] Instead, allegory treats each object as a cultural ruin in which the temporality of all life is encapsulated. Quoting Dante, Benjamin noted that the basic characteristic of allegory is its absolute fluidity, where "any person, any object, any relationship can mean absolutely anything else".[18]

> The basic characteristic of allegory, however, is ambiguity, multiplicity of meaning; allegory and the baroque, glory in richness and meaning. But the richness of this ambiguity is the richness of extravagance; nature, however, according to the old rule of metaphysics, and indeed, also of mechanics, is bound by the law of economy. Ambiguity is therefore always the opposite of clarity and unity of meaning.[19]

A shop window, a photograph, or the line of a song, these fragments or ruins are the most significant aspect of any dream or culture. It is this potential richness of objects, their infinite number of associations, and their possible reconstellation in another field which makes dream analysis, and all interpretation, tentative rather than subject to rational decoding.

The "meaning" of cultural phenomena is neither expressive of one or two primary social relations, nor is it "symbolic". One cannot assume that a crucifix worn by Madonna is an expression of her essentially Christian nature, or that the wearing of high heels reflects a woman's identification with a patriarchal sexual economy.[20] Part of the challenge of alternative fashion adherents has been to dislodge and re-appropriate the traditional significance of fetishised objects. Spike heels, fishnet stockings and crucifixes juxtaposed with black leathers and exaggeratedly teased hairdos were all adopted as costumes by punk women. Not only did this condense different and often disparate styles, but it pushed the most common indices of femininity to their extreme limits, in order to draw attention to its artificiality and construction. Of course, as in the case of Madonna, these trends were re-appropriated by capitalism and the fashion industry as quickly as they appeared, necessitating yet another transformation in style for those interested in establishing an alternative to the industry.

Feminist criticism must regard events, objects, images, as cultural signs or allegories which do not have one fixed or stable meaning, but which derive their significance both from their place in a chain of signifiers, a chain which is itself unstable because of the constant intervention of historical change. Allegories are like the fragments of a dream in which remembrances of the past leave their historical traces, at the same time overdetermining future interpretations of events by an individual subject.

This makes the question of political or aesthetic judgment more complex than the discourses of Marxism and feminism which have only allowed the dichtomization of the world into polarities; man/woman, capital/labour, bourgeoisie/proletariat. Judgments have to be made within the context of discursive situations making a fixed position on any one issue problematic. For example, as Fanon notes in the case of Algeria, the veil was assigned a significance by the colonist that it had not had. "To the colonist offense against the veil, the colonised opposes the cult of the veil."[21] In other words, it was the highly charged atmosphere of the national liberation struggle, as well as the attempt by the French to "Westernise" Algerian women which lead to the polarization of positions.

Likewise, within the history of the dress reform movement, judgments about 'fashion' itself must be understood in the context of our predominantly Christian heritage. Contrary to the assumption of Anne Oakley, an anti-fashion discourse cannot be assumed to be inherently feminist, for it has often been tied to a discourse which is intent on repressing women's potentially subversive sexuality and returning them to the proper sphere of the home. In many writings from the late 19th and 20th centuries, fashion was anthropomorphized into a tyrant, who was said to deprive all, and women in particular, of their freedom and money, block them from more fulfilling pursuits, jeopardize their health, and drop them into the stagnant waters of immorality. As Pope Pius said in 1940, women who were bowing to the tyranny of fashion were "like insane persons who unwittingly threw themselves into fires and rivers."[22] In fact the dress reform movements of the early 20th century were often less concerned with making women more comfortable than with returning them to the proper sphere of the home; they were part of the movement for social purity. Just as improper dress indicated a woman's lack of reason and her immorality a proper form of dress was said to enhance her "natural" beauty, emphasizing her health and freshness, and promising her fecundity.[23]

A woman's concern for the aestheticization of her body was seen as a sign of her unreasonableness, her potential weakness in contrast to the rationality of men. The argument for austerity in dress and the return to more neutral forms not only valorizes what is seen as characteristic of men (their rationality), but there is the possibility that an anti-fashion sentiment feeds into an already existing discourse of woman's superficiality, duplicity, and the threat that her sexuality poses to men.

Not only does this discourse falsely believe that there is a natural beauty, a core of being beyond socialization, but this position can be accused of a typically 'masculinist' belief that one can be transcendent to one's body; to one's culture, and immune to the seductions of the material world. Although one should not invest one's identity in crass consumer behaviour, it is neverthless true that you are what you eat, wear, and consume; as Spinoza said, there is no separation between the formation of mind and its ability to recollect, to remember, and the impingement of the senses onto our subjectivities. To believe otherwise is to engage in a Cartesian opposition between the 'in-itself' and the 'for-itself'.

The problem in all of these cases is not that we respond in a sensual manner to the world, but the fixing or territorialization of desire into a restricted economy: the closure on erotic pleasure that the culture industry can create by reinforcing and fixing very specific notions of what is desirable in women, in men, in sexuality, in clothing, and its hegemonic control over the "imaginary" through its domination of cultural mediums. While promising Nirvana to all, the restricted economy limits the flow of goods and services to those with access to capital thus reproducing the forms of class domination; it creates desires while denying them and making them dependent on the flow of capital. In phrasing the necessary critique of capitalism, one must be careful not to lapse into a discourse of economy and restraint, which opposes the ethics of thrift, hard work, and self-discipline to the 'immorality' and 'decadence' of capitalism. As Nietzsche says in *The Will to Power*, "residues of Christian value judgments are found everywhere in socialistic and positivistic systems. A critique of Christian morality is still lacking."[24] Perhaps capitalism's only saving grace is the decadence that it produces, its excesses and surpluses, that allow the person who delights in its cast-offs to live a parasitical existence on its margins.

To assume that all clothing is reducible to the fashion industry in this restrictive sense, and that all looking, and aestheticization of the body is an objectifying form of commodification is simplistic. As Marx himself noted, objectification is part of the process that allows human beings to create themselves, their social relations, and their history.[25]

As Laura Mulvey has argued the film industry has capitalised on scopophilic pleasure. However, one must be careful in transferring paradigms from film theory, which tends to concentrate solely on the notion of the look, and on the eye as the primary organ of experience. Clothing, the act of wearing fabric, is intimately linked to the skin, and the body, to our tactile senses. As author Jean Rhys reflects, women have been sensitized to the relationship between their personal and cultural history as it is inscribed in their clothing. "It is as though we could measure the degree of happiness of particular events in her life through the clothing she was wearing and the rooms she inhabited."[26] Fashion and clothing – being stylish – can also be a poetic experience, intimately connected to the history and remembrance of the lived body. Again it was Freud who suggested the importance of material objects, of memories of clothing, jewellery, in triggering memory and overdetermining thought and action in both the waking and dream states. Because the fashion industry is constantly resurrecting histories and cultures, placing us all in a perpetual schizophrenic present, the experience of fashion and clothing is contradictory for women. It is, perhaps, this longing for a world of fantasy, this desire for the return, and the smell and touch of the body which the fashion industry (in fact all of our sentimental culture) capitalizes on. The acts of shopping, of wearing an article of clothing, of receiving clothing as a gift, can be expressions of recognition and love between women, or between women and men, which should not be ignored, though they may fail to transcend the dominant phallic economy of desire.

Simulation and representation: the object in postmodern culture

The foregoing analysis is not intended to suggest that we totally reject a Marxist analysis of the commodity or the feminist analysis of patriarchy; but the metaphysical assumptions in place within these discourses must be rethought, rearticulated, reinscribed, for they have produced a history of theoretical closure regarding fashion.

The latter, I believe, has come about for two reasons. First, it seems as if the idea of fashion has been articulated so closely with women, the body and the personal, and therefore with doxa, unreason, and the inessential, that it has been ignored by academic institutions dominated by a sort of antiseptic Platonism. Secondly, and concomitantly, the study of fashion has required a methodological shift in the social sciences: not just a shift from the idea of cultural phenomenon as symbolic or expressive of some fundamental social relation, but away from a metaphysics of presence which favours denotation over connotation, as in semiotics, and use-value over exchange value, as in Marxism. This critique of the metaphysics of presence links the work of Benjamin and Derrida to that of Baudrillard. Some aspects of feminist thought, which criticize fashion on the basis of its 'misrepresentation' of women, and advocate a return to the 'natural" body, and 'natural' beauty have also had to be abandoned. Moving beyond these polarizations makes possible a more in-depth reading and understanding of fashion.

A discourse of representation, which is connected to the concept of the symbol, is inappropriate for an analysis of fashion; yet as we have seen, this is the basis of the majority of writings on fashion. What the phenomenon of women imitating models brings into play is the question of the real, of the referent, as in any sense originary in (post-) modern culture. The live mannequins mentioned in my second allegory do not startle us simply because these women have been reified into a stationary position; they shock us precisely because we are living in an age which anticipates an image. The present era, the age of the postmodern, marks a collapsing of the space of these borders. Reality, the referent, is called into question at that juncture where artificial signs are intertextually mixed with 'real elements.'

In this sense, Kafka's allegory, "In the Penal Colony," does not signify a modern form of repressive, administrative power; what it seems to signal is the end of a mapping of a predetermined code of the social onto the body. The latter was a judicial form of power based on the notion of the pre-existing authority of the norm, or the rules of a cohesive community over the individual body. It is the system of justice and control of the explorer, rather than the keeper of the machine, who will triumph in the postmodern era, the age of late capitalism. Gone is the archaic writing machine which treats the body as a *tabula rasa* upon which a predetermined message is scrawled. In the present age, forms of self-discipline anticipate the self-colonization of the body and its enslavement in an intertextual web.

Baudrillard's writings explore the demise of any transcendental posture that one may be tempted to adopt in cultural critique. He states:

> The first implies a theology of truth and secrecy (to which the notion of
> ideology still belongs), the second inaugurates an age of simulacra . . . in

which there is no longer any God to recognize His own, nor any judgement to separate the true from the false, the Real from Artificial resurrection, since everything is already dead and risen in advance.[27]

The power of late capitalism is in the imaginary, where subjects are maintained
in a circuit of desire and anxiety. Baudrillard's work echoes Kafka's sentiments, and
is seminal for further discussions of the implications of the fashion industry within
the present economy. "Abstraction today is no longer that of the map, the double,
the mirror, or the concept. Simulation is no longer that of a territory, a referential
being or substance. It is the generation by models of a real without origin or reality;
hyper-reality."[28]

Fashion, with its lack of commitment to this world, with its attempt to create
clothes, figures, looks that are irreverent, towards any form of natural beauty, is
emblematic of this "precession of simulacra", and the dis-simulation of the logic of
the symbol and representation. Baudrillard terms this collapse and instability of
border an implosion – "an absorption of the radiating model of causality, of the
differential mode of determination with its positive and negative electricity – an
implosion of meaning. This is where simulation begins."[29] Where simulation begins,
the notion of representation ends. The failure of the distinction between poles
marks the age of the politics of simulation, embodying both the potentially liberating collapse of old borders, while at the same time making possible hegemonic
manipulation through control of capital flow and the production of new
technologies.

However, the history of this implosion, this circuitry, is not simply a modern
phenomenon. Baudrillard's radical deconstruction of these poles is both epistemological and historical. In fact, the archeology of this tendency for the implosion of
the space between the imaginary and the real can be seen in the relationship between
the naked body and the development of clothing styles. As Anne Hollander shows in
her book, *Seeing Through Clothes*, styles of the female body have changed; indeed, the
figures admired and hence idealized within the tradition of nude art are themselves
shaped by current clothing styles. For example, in Europe, the upper body, i.e. the
breasts, was strictly corsetted to emphasize the sweeping outward curve of the belly.
Nude paintings which were thought to reflect the natural shape of the body, in fact
retain the shape of these clothes; what is depicted by the artist as a "natural body", a
representation of a woman's figure, is itself overdetermined by these fashions.[30]
Thus, a neat causal relationship between an object and its transcription in some form
of "writing" is problematic. It implies that there is an objective reality outside of the
critic or artist – a natural body as the originary site – depicted or distorted by mass
culture; but images are not mimetic of a natural world prior to representation. As
Barthes says, "your body, the thing that seems the most real to you is doubtless the
most phantasmic."[31] Not only does a feminist politics based on a notion of representation, on a return to the natural body, or neutral forms of dress, ignore the
pleasures involved in the possession of an article of clothing, but the impossibility of
this return to the represented.

This process is exacerbated in the era of postmodernism, where technologies
make possible the doubling of life, giving a new force to the powers of the imaginary
and the memory trace to dominate and completely substitute the real. Baudrillard's

social theory, like Derrida's philosophy and Freud's psychoanalysis, signals the continual collapsing of the scene and "the mirror," the prerequisite for any notion of representation as reflection or imitation:

> . . . instead there is the scene and the network. In place of the reflexive transcendence of mirror and scene, there is a smooth, non-reflecting surface, an immanent surface where operations unfold — the smooth operational surface of communication.[32]

This smooth operational surface which ruptures the depth model implicit in classical Marxist humanism inaugurates a different notion of causality: neither 'expressive,' nor simple structural, it questions the possibility of isolating all determinations of a given phenomenon, object, or event.

All of the social sciences have been predicated on a notion of system, either as a relatively stable set of signifiers, as in semiotics, or upon the isolation of a community, as in Marxism, in which human activity is localizable in space and time, generalizable because common meanings are shared amongst its members. Baudrillard's analysis of postmodernity, or late capitalism, throws these assumptions into question. As Philip Hayward notes in "Implosive Critiques," Baudrillard problematizes the notion of a cohesive social upon which the disciplines are based.[33] In a world of fluidity and fragmentation in which the stable boundaries of traditional communities such as the family, the church and the nation are in constant disruption, relocation, and solidification into exaggerated forms, we need a new methodology to complement these transformations.

One way to approach the fragmentation of the social is to study cultural signs as allegorical objects which have a multiplicity of possible meanings rather than any one fixed interpretation. This is not simply an idle, idealistic or nihilistic pursuit. As Elizabeth Cowie explains, meaning is never absolutely arbitrary in any text.

> Rather, the endless possible signification of the image is always, and only a theoretical possibility. In practice, the image is always held, constrained in its production of meaning or else becomes meaningless, unreadable. At this point the concept of anchorage is important; there are developed in every society decisive technologies intended to fix the floating chains of signifieds so as to control the terror of uncertain signs.[34]

The contradiction within any analysis is that in order to communicate, one is faced with having to "modify" a text; that is, to classify and identify the regime of codes which govern its production, while being vigilant to their inevitable mutation. Benjamin's concept of allegory, like Derrida's notion of intertextuality, is a strategy of reading which opens up the possibility of deciphering, rather than decoding, the fashion object and other cultural texts. Decoding, as Freud explicated, implies that there is a master system to which all signs can be returned; deciphering, on the other hand, implies that we are cognizant of the instability of all meaning.

This method, or anti-method — *allegoresis* — takes cultural sign objects as emblematic. As Benjamin said "Allegories are, in the realm of thoughts, what ruins are in the realm of things."[35] Like all forms of cultural production, fashion cannot be considered a mere expression of the current *Zeitgeist*, for it is a constituent relational element in the fabric of the social.

Conclusion

Capitalism and the colonization of the imaginary

I began this excursion into a discussion of fashion with two dreams, supplemented by a third; a dream of inscription of the social, the mapping of a typically modern form of power onto the body, and its eclipse in the era of postmodernism with its dependence on an abstract disembodied form of self-discipline; secondly a dream of a woman caught, trapped, embedded within a circuitry of power, of competing discourses which not only position her, affect her, but name her "Woman" as distinct in nature and temperament from "Man", thus naming her as both subject and object; thirdly, a dream of a resurrected past, capitalism's cannibalization of the other, its treatment of them as already dead museum pieces, and its resurrection of them as fashion – the colonialism of advanced capitalism powered by the energy of seduction and desires.

The use of allegory in relationship to fashion and postmodernism is appropriate, given postmodernism's use of allegory as a form of artistic practice and criticism, and given the breakdown of stable communities, upon which the social sciences base their use of representation as a concept for giving meaning to behaviours. In the place of 'real communities' and the 'social', a simulated community is born; tribes of consumers who buy Tide, T.V. families on shows such as Family Feud, the world in Harmony as in the Coke commercials, a world that we may not feel compelled to conform to but which offers itself to us as a type of hyper-reality. Capitalism operates in full knowledge of the power of the imaginary, of our desire to join into these masquerades, and re-creates the social as a series of dream-works, much like the landscapes analysed by Freud in *The Interpretation of Dreams*.

The imaginary, as Freud, Lacan, and Althusser knew, must be taken seriously because it has very real effects; any rigid separation between the two realms is impossible. In fact, both zones, if indeed there are only two, are always over-determining, collapsing in on each other. It is the imaginary which informs what is to be our experience of both past and future. Hence, the colonization that capitalism achieves is also an imperialism of the imagination – not just domination over such physical spaces as the third world.

Indeed, as postmodernist forms of architecture such as the Eaton's Centre in Toronto, the new Air Canada Building in Winnipeg, and the West Edmonton Mall indicate, this resurrection of defunct fictions can either be a pleasurable fantasy or a nightmare. In these architectural dreamscapes one can experience life in a Paris café, on a beach in Miami or in a submarine, without ever having to leave one's province or suburb. On the other hand, many other pieces of postmodern architecture are a direct reaction to the monumentalism of modernist style, which reduced every city to the megalopolis, and flattened every indigenous horizon to "the Same".

Postmodernism fluctuates between the poles of kitsch and a return to the local. It is both a form of populism, and a totally artificial rendering of history and space.

Pee Wee Herman's America is the best example of this hyper-reality: it results in more livable spaces at the same time that it degenerates into a celebration of consumer culture.

Likewise, postmodern thought does not merely extoll naively what Frederic Jameson describes as the superficial and artificial surface. It is pragmatic in its realization that the modernist valorization of the real and of authenticity was insensitive to the superficial. Modernism tended to be a romantic discourse, it longed for a return to some prehistoric origin, and positioned itself, as educated critic outside and above the culture it criticised – in the place of God. While modernism valued what it took to be the essential, the real, the substantial over the ephemeral, the imaginary the formal, postmodernism has been engaged in questioning these divisions, and this transcendental position. As I have argued, this was a most dangerous abdication of power. Postmodern thought realises the full ability of capital to capitalize on every alternative discourse, every act of charity, every emotion and sentiment. Therefore it forces one to adopt the strategy of guerilla warfare, of insurgency, interference and destabilization, rather than the archaic model of revolution that is a part of the language of classical Marxism.

Most importantly, postmodernism enjoins us in the necessity for engaging in a cultural politics, politics that exploits the media, that is based on a language of celebration and ecstasy, as in the most recent efforts of the Toronto Arts Community in bringing attention to the need for sanctions against South Africa. It is not surprising that the most interesting theoretical works and reflections on the state of contemporary culture and politics have come out of art and literary magazines such as *ZG, October, Impulse, Borderlines*, and the French "fashion magazine" *Pole Position*; and that significant interventions in photography and art have come from women such as Mary Kelly, Cindy Sherman, Martha Rosler, Lynne Fernie and Christine Davis, who have attempted to grapple with these issues, particularly the issue of the representation of women. They do not necessarily offer positive images of women, but they do question the notion of "Woman" as a natural construct. They do not offer solutions, but instead force the readers of their works to develop skills in interpreting and reading. It is important to transmit skills that will allow consumers of capitalism to understand the power of images in general and to question the notion of the immutability of that which we take to be real. It is at this juncture that aesthetic judgment and politics meet.

Notes

1   Franz Kafka, "In The Penal Colony", *The Penal Colony: Stories and Short Pieces*, trans. Willa and Edwin Muir (New York: Schoken Books, 1961), pp. 191–230.

2   The most interesting recent work on fashion is by Valerie Steele, *Fashion and Eroticism* (New York: Oxford University Press, 1985). Roland Barthes, *The Fashion System* (New York: Hill and Wang, 1983), is another seminal piece, although it is rife with difficulties for the reader because of its extremely technical semiotic approach to the topic. Barthes' own critique of this work can be found in *The Grain of the Voice: Interviews 1962–1980*, trans. Linda Coverdale (New York: Hillard and Wang, 1985). As well, I recommend Kathy Meyers, "Fashion N' Passion",

Screen, vol. 23 # 3 (October, 1983), pp. 89–97. and Rosetta Brooks, "Fashion: Double Page Spread," *Cameraworks*, #17 (Jan./Feb., 1980), pp. 1–20.

3   Frantz Fanon, "Algeria Unveiled", *A Dying Colonialism*, trans. Haaken Chevalier (New York: Grove Press, 1965), p. 35. Read Fanon's piece in conjunction with the essay by Jacques Derrida, "White Mythologies", *Margins of Philosophy*, trans. Alan Bass (Chicago: University of Chicago Press, 1982). This "white mythology" contained in the most trivial of objects, the fashion photo for a cosmetic company, is integrally connected to another "white mythology", the history of metaphysics. It is the metaphysical position which privileges the notion of Reason over the emotional and the sensual which I will argue has relegated the topic of fashion to the inessential. Derrida, p. 213.

4   Anne Oakley, *Subject Women* (New York: Pantheon Books, 1981), p. 82.

5   John Berger, *Ways of Seeing* (Harmondsworth: Pelican, 1972).

6   Oakley, pp. 45–47. See also, E. Ann Kaplan, *Women and Film: Both Sides of the Camera* (New York: Methuen, 1983). She says: "The construction of woman as spectacle, internalized, leads women to offer their bodies in professions like modelling and advertising, and film acting, and to be generally susceptible to demands to be made a spectacle." (p. 73).

7   Laura Mulvey, "Visual Pleasure and Narrative Cinema," *Women and the Cinema: A Critical Anthology*, eds. Karyn Kay and Gerald Pearcy (New York: E.P. Dutton, 1977), p.p. 412–428.

8   Griselda Pollack, "What's Wrong With Images of Women?" *Screen Education*, 3 24 (Autumn, 1977).

9   Teresa de Lauretis, *Alice Doesn't: Feminism, Semiotics, Cinema* (Bloomington: Indiana University Press, 1984), p. 38. De Lauretis' work provides a clear and cogent summary of many of the theoretical debates within both Marxist-feminist and semiotic analysis as they pertain to the question of the representation of women in film images.

10 Jacques Derrida, *Positions*, trans. Alan Bass (Chicago: University of Chicago Press, 1981), p. 26.

11 Walter Benjamin, *The Origins of German Tragic Drama*, trans. John Osborne (London: New Left Books, 1977). Given Benjamin's very clear sympathy with the concept of allegory over and against the classical notion of the symbol, it is unfathomable how Lukacs could so misread Benjamin's work. Lukacs, pp. 40–44. Paul de Man's work on allegory and symbol should be read in conjunction with Benjamin. As de Man notes in relation to European literature ". . . in the latter half of the eighteenth century . . . the word symbol tends to supplant other denominations for figural language including that of allegory." Paul de Man, "The Rhetoric of Temporality", *op. cit.*, p. 188. For examples of how deeply the concept of the symbol permeates Marxism's understanding of culture as symbolic, see William Leiss, Stephen Kline and Sut Jhally's excellent study, *Social Communication in Advertising: Persons, Products and Well-Being* (Toronto: Methuen, 1986), pp. 55, 66.

12 As quoted in Jacques Derrida, "Freud and the Scene of Writing", *Writing and Difference*, trans. Alan Bass (Chicago: University of Chicago Press, 1978), p. 206.

13 Sigmund Freud, *The Interpretation of Dreams*, trans. James Strachey (Harmondsworth: Pelican, 1976), p. 178.

14 *Ibid*, p. 468.

15 *Ibid*, p. 171.

16 *Ibid*, p. 179. This distinction originally was brought to my attention in a footnote

in a friend's Masters Thesis. Forest Barnett Pyle, "Walter Benjamin: The Constellation of a Cultural Criticism", University of Texas at Austin 1983, p. 51. Pyle attributes this distinction to Gayatri Spivak, but does not reference a source. I have traced the distinction to Freud.

17   Benjamin, p. 165.

18   *Ibid*, p. 175.

19   *Ibid*, p. 177.

20   The work of Louis Althusser still provides the most important critique of this notion of causality, relating it to the philosophical legacy of Hegel within Marxism. Louis Althusser, *Reading Capital*, trans. Ben Brewster (London: New Left Books, 1970).

21   Fanon, pp. 47–48.

22   Jeanete C. Lauer and Robert Lauer, *Fashion Power: The Meaning of Fashion in American Society* (New Jersey: Prentice-Hall Inc., 1981), pp. 73–101.

23   *Ibid*, p. 80.

24   Friedrich Nietzsche, *The Will to Power*, trans. Walter Kaufmann and R.J. Hollingdale (New York: Random House, 1968), p. 17.

25   I owe this reading of Marx to another friend, Lori Turner. Lori Turner, "Marx and Nature," unpublished manuscript, York University, 1986, p. 8.

26   Jean Rhys, *Good Morning Midnight* (New York: Harper and Row, 1930), p. 113. See the anthology, *The Female Body in Western Culture: Contemporary Perspectives*, Susan Rubin Suleiman, ed. (Cambridge: Harvard University Press, 1983).

27   Jean Baudrillard, *Simulations*, trans. Paul Foss, Paul Patton and Philip Beitchman (New York: Semiotext(e), 1983), pp. 12–13.

28   *Ibid*, p. 2.

29   *Ibid*, p. 57.

30   Anne Hollander, *Seeing Through Clothes* (New York: The Viking Press, 1978), pp. 97–104.

31   Barthes, *Grain of the Voice*, p. 365.

32   Jean Baudrillard, "The Ecstasy of Communication", *The Anti-Aesthetic: Essays on Postmodern Culture*", Hal Foster, ed. (Washington: Bay Press, 1983), p. 127.

33   Philip Hayward, "Implosive Critiques", *Screen*, vol. 28, 3–4–5– (July–Oct., 1984), p. 128.

34   Elizabeth Cowie, "Women, Representation and the Image", *Screen Education*, # 2–3 (Summer, 1977), pp. 15–23.

35   Benjamin, p. 178.

Chapter 39

Alison Gill

DECONSTRUCTION FASHION
The making of unfinished, decomposing and re-assembled clothes

Introduction: deconstruction "in fashion"

THE TERM DECONSTRUCTION has entered the vocabulary of inter-national fashion magazines, a label associated specifically with the work of Rei Kawakubo for Comme des Garçons, Karl Lagerfeld, Martin Margiela, Ann Demeulemeester and Dries Van Noten amongst others, and more loosely used to describe garments on a runway that are "unfinished," "coming apart," "recycled," "transparent" or "grunge." The same characteristics are referred to by the French as the style "Le Destroy" ("La mode Destroy" 1992; O'Shea 1991: 234), confirming for many who read the forms appearing on Paris runways as a literal *dismantling* of clothes and embodiment of aestheticized *non-functionality*, that deconstruction "in fashion" amounts to an anti-fashion statement (a willful avant-garde desire to destroy "Fashion") or an expression of nihilism (i.e., absence of belief). It would be worth-while to consider the parallels this style has with the influential French style of philosophical thought, deconstruction, associated with the writings of Jacques Derrida, and in doing so to re-visit its announcement in fashion and other design fields where the term deconstruction circulates.[1]

The name "Deconstruction" has been quite self-consciously embraced as a form of criticism by philosophers and literature specialists across the world as it repre-sents for them a method of reading and writing to "uncover" the instabilities of meaning in texts (see Norris 1991 on literature). In addition, architects, graphic designers, film-makers, multi-media designers, and media theorists have embraced deconstruction as a mode of theoretical practice (see Brunette and Wills 1989, 1994; Byrne and Witte 1990; Wigley and Johnson 1988; Wigley 1993). For instance, a group of high-profile international architects have received quite exten-sive coverage, in a series of Academy Editions publications, of their various projects initiated in the 1980s as examples of deconstructive thinking in architecture. Also, it was in the late 1980s that deconstruction was discussed in graphic design circles by designers hoping to release their pages from the invisible laws, security, and tradition of the Modernist grid and its accompanying type-fonts (see Byrne and Witte 1990). Yet the name "deconstruction" has come into vogue, and is increasingly invoked by critics and commentators who use it quite loosely to mean analysis and/ or critique (i.e., locating and undoing the essence of an argument), using it as a legitimated late twentieth-century emblem for change and risky transformation, specifically with reference to the undoing of Modernist cultural forms. It is in this sense that the American fashion commentator Amy Spindler (1993: 1) announced "deconstructionism" as a rebellion against the 1980s, the undoing of fashion as we have known it, or the "coming apart" of fashion's heritage, as it moved into the last decade of the twentieth century.

Richard Martin and Harold Koda (1993) insightfully trace deconstructionist tendencies in 1980s couture and ready-to-wear fashion, in the catalog essays of *Infra-Apparel*, tendencies which consolidated in a proclaimed "trend" in the early 1990s.[2] Mary McLeod (1994: 92) has suggested that the label "deconstruction fashion" was coined by fashion writers following the Deconstructivist Architecture exhibition in 1988 at MOMA. This might imply that the exhibition at MOMA helped to raise the profile of deconstruction, enabling and legitimating its cultural dissemination, and, more specifically, that fashion itself was enabled, even encouraged, by the experiments in architectural design. As an architect, McLeod is aware that architecture and fashion share a lexicon of concepts like structure, form, fabric, construction, fabrication, and she can see clear points in the history of Modernism where a shared language has made a conversation between these practices possible (see McLeod 1994). In fact, the garments of designer Martin Margiela, a graduate of the Antwerp Royal Academy of Arts, and identified by Spindler (1993) and Cunningham (1990) as a leading proponent of "deconstructionism," appear to share with deconstructivist architecture a point of connection around the analytics of construction. Margiela sells linings extracted from recovered "vintage" dresses, giving these linings a chance of a new-old life "on the outside," that is, as lining-dresses in their own right (see *Infra-Apparel* for example). His dresses are made from mis-matched fabrics, lining-silks with jerseys, and one can see the inside mechanics of the dress structure—darts, facings, and zippers. Or old jackets have been re-cut, tacked, sewn and re-detailed, their seams and darts reversed and exposed to the outside. Accepting that a seamstress or tailor performs a certain labor of "outfitting" bodies and giving them an enclothed form, a labor stitched inside as the secrets of a finished garment, a secret that is kept by the garment itself as it performs "seamlessly," Margiela literally brings these secrets to its surface.[3] For Margiela, the garment is an architecture that "fits out" the body, and thus he shares an architectural inquiry into the process and mechanics of construction. Martin and Koda (1993: 94) very simply state the paradox of these clothes when they write "destruction becomes a process of analytical creation."

A designer like Margiela appears to have something to say about the operations of clothing as a frame for bodies and, potentially, the influences of fashion, as a mechanism, structure or discourse, that is, as (invoking Roland Barthes) a "fashion system" with vast cultural, economic and ontological effects. By fashion system, I mean the industry and its supporting infrastructure (media, education, economics, cosmetic and pharmaceutical industries, politics, technology, sports sciences) that bring regular changes to men's and women's clothes and bodies. Like Anne Hollander, I observe that these changes arrive by way of the name of "Fashion" in the media and designers' collections, worn first by "star" bodies on runways, in a continuing flow of new commodifiable themes, gestures and styles; fashion "is now the general modern condition of all Western clothing" (Hollander 1994: 11). Yet we must also acknowledge the immaterial domain that has arrived with the material forms of fashion and extends its effects beyond clothing; fashion both designs and is designed by an empire of signs that propel and commutate at an ever-increasing speed, a domain into which we are all interpellated as "fashioned people" whether we like it or not. The empire of signs that fashion plays amidst is a kind of vertical world of unending perceptual expansion. Within this empire, a world that eludes measurement and the language of systems, our bodies come to (trans-)form and are repetitively styled and styling across lived domains both spectacular and mundane.

Deconstruction in fashion is something like an auto-critique of the fashion system: It displays an almost X-ray capability to reveal the enabling conditions of fashion's bewitching charms (i.e., charms conveyed in the concepts ornament, glamor, spectable, illusion, fantasy, creativity, innovation, exclusivity, luxury repeatedly associated with fashion) and the principles of its practice (i.e., form, material, construction, fabrication, pattern, stitching, finish).[4] At one level, the word "deconstruction" suggests a simple reversal of construction and therefore, at this common-sense level, a reading of clothes that look unfinished, undone, destroyed as "deconstructed" fits. With this view, the many who know the work of the garment-maker—cutting, constructing, altering—that is, a uni-directional making toward a goal of a "finished" garment, will not find deconstruction fashion startlingly original or more than a reversal of this practice of the garment-maker. Yet, what is marked about the practices of these designers and represents a "new thinking" in fashion is an explicit care for the "structur-*ing* ontology" of the garment. By "structur-*ing* ontology" I mean that visibility is given to the simultaneous bidirectionality of the labor that the garment-maker and clothes perform—i.e., the garment-maker is simultaneously forming and deforming, constructing and destroying, making and undoing clothes. This bidirectional labor continues in dressing and wearing clothes, as clothes figure and disfigure the body, compose and decompose. In the garments of a handful of designers, some concerns shared with deconstructionist philosophy can be observed. In this article these observations have been gathered around examples loosely compiled from Martin Margiela's ready-to-wear collections from 1989 onwards, examples that appear in conversation with deconstructive thinking; these garments suspend in paradox the formation/wear/decay of clothing, a paradox imbued in Jacques Derrida's inserted and privative "*de*" of *de*construction.

In the disciplines and practices where deconstruction has been embraced and appears to constitute a new "movement" or direction for practice, this direction has been to investigate the underlying principles and conditions of operation of these disciplines, bringing challenging questions about the nature of disciplinarity and modes of practice to these inquiries. Often the introduction of "theory" to a discipline or practice can appear an awkward application, say, a theory latched on or applied to a field in order to award it value or credibility based on a predetermined absence of value. Or worse, a critique whose single goal is to "destroy" the pre-existing field by exposing the non-viability of its thinking or practice. Deconstructionist movements, however, are characterized by a dialogue of mutual effect, a two-way exchange between philosophy and these disciplines; an exchange that has in practice brought a soliciting eye to disciplinary differences and boundaries, and moreover, brought boundary dissolutions and new formations. In "deconstruction fashion," one can find an interesting type of encounter between philosophy and fashion, less disciplinary in orientation, that works, in a sense, from the inside of a garment and through the practice that has always been fashion's domain—"dressing the body." In this article I wish to outline the complexities of using the name "deconstruction" to describe a style of clothing fashion, while at the same time enabling its association with fashion. In doing so, I am using the very terms of a glib or facile nomenclature—"deconstruction fashion"—to seek a serious relation of fashion and its debt to philosophy. The article will remain obedient to the topic under consideration, in that any form that I introduce like "deconstruction fashion" and "deconstruction philosophy" can only end in an unravelling and decomposition peculiar to deconstructive thinking.

The complexities of nomenclature are, on the one hand, symptomatic of a general problem of theoretical dissemination and, on the other, specific to what a deconstructive thinking makes visible, both generally and in regard to fashion in particular. When gesturing to the traces of this term in the cultural and public ethos it is difficult to map, like many enigmatic influences or forces, definitive moments of emergence, intersection, cross-fertilization, and their effects. The appearance of deconstruction is characteristic, speaking now at a general level, of the dissemination and commodification of other intellectual trends that have come before it like structuralism, psychoanalysis, and semiotics, together with the obvious problems of application, importation, translation, derivation, stylization, and diffusion that go hand-in-hand with the reception of theoretical models. Philosophy has been thought to "own" its passing trends, like fashion its passing styles and fancies, the discipline of philosophy being home to a powerful hierarchy that deciphers authentic thought from the artful style that one might find in literature and fashion. In addition, frequently the movement of a new theory *into* mainstream discourses, *into fashion*, or its appearance in a discourse other than its "origin," is considered a second-rate application and marks, for some, the dispossesion of its 'true' innovation and radicality, if you like, the "taming" or loss of a (fashionable) high ground. However, such an understanding adheres to this hierarchical structure that proffers a reductive rendering of the problems of theoretical diffusion and might itself dispossess "deconstruction fashion" of any innovation or difference at all. Also, "deconstruction fashion" might be doubly dismissed for moving *into fashion*: firstly, in becoming a disseminated theoretical "motif" and secondly, in moving, more literally, into the domain of "Fashion" frequently thought to be a domain of play, in distinction from the seriousness of philosophy, a domain where things are aestheticized, trivialized, hyperbolized, commodified, and robbed of significance. That is, "deconstruction fashion" has emerged as a symptom of this general problem of theoretical dissemination and a casualty of perpetuating hierarchies, and confirms, for many, the materialization of deconstruction as another superficial trend rather than significant thought.

It is somewhat difficult to judge the response to deconstruction fashion and its profile as a "mainstream" fashion, a term I use with little confidence as a measure anyway. Yet there is, I will suggest later, evidence of an interest in trying to wear transparent and layered clothing that is an effect of this style. Significantly, deconstruction fashion is part of a general climate where the aura of couture is being devolved onto ready-to-wear collections. There are certainly well-documented signs that old hierarchies dividing designer clothes from "everyday" clothes, the runway from the street as mutually exclusive spheres, are being eroded. Today, in the terms of a highly publicized fashion industry, the temporal and spatial measures that mark the difference between "true" innovation and its disseminated popular forms, between new and prior historical forms, between a fashionable high ground and a middle ground of being *in fashion*, are constantly being eroded by rapid media circulation, the widespread practices of reinventing historical styles, mass production and international distribution (manufacturers of mass-produced clothes constantly watch the runway, reproducing styles with small changes and cheaper fabrics for mass market audiences). Despite this, however, some hierarchies are unsuppressable, for the institutional, economic, and libidinal investments in fashion, like the investments in philosophy's institutionalization, as I have suggested, locate a certain power or authority in being a point of origin for "innovation" and a source of a kind of systemic momentum of dissemination. We use the word "fashion" in different ways, yet the continuous seasonal rituals of the industry remind us of a "Fashion" domain of aesthetic experimentation and "revolutions," with its "new heights" of innovation, that constantly rebuilds a hierarchical structure in order to "stay on top" of *clothes* in the secular levels "below."[5] In this manner of dialectical progression, "Fashion" sustains a sense of itself as a rational modernist system made up of "new looks" as its basic economic, aesthetic, and idealized units. For instance, in a perpetual hunt for the new, subcultural clothing gestures have been remarketed by designers such as Vivienne Westwood and Jean-Paul Gaultier as "styles" from the "Street," hyperbolically accessorized and montaged for the runway as a new direction called "anti-fashion" designer fashion—"Fashion" reappropriates and sublates its other. While this article will return later to consider anti-fashion, this simple rendition might serve here as an example of the exaggeration, the illusion of difference, that "Fashion" must indulge to distinguish itself from clothes, even while these are of the same world.

Although an expanded description of Derridean deconstruction will follow below, suffice it to say here that Derrida does not claim to present a critique of Western metaphysics, or an original philosophy. He is the first to say that a critique of metaphysics can only ever rely on the very principles that it puts into question. Yet, critics of deconstructionist philosophy have argued its inherent nihilism, its anarchy, its irrationality or disregard for philosophical tradition, misunderstanding the root of Derrida's word in Martin Heidegger's "*destruktion*." To argue thus is to ignore the two terms rolled into one—de(con)struction—and Derrida's implicit respect for philosophical writing and its complex fabric. The garments that appeared on runways in the early 1990s—images of decay, poverty, and disaffection— appeared to mock fashion from its site of privilege.[6] Yet, Margiela's garments indicate an implicit care for the material object and sartorial techniques, and therefore they would suggest the impossibility of a simple destruction or anarchy; for instance, the look of distressed or unfinished tacking around an arm hole is executed by the tailor's hand with, paradoxically, a quality "finish." In Margiela's guiding of the tailor's hand one can see a desire to leave a "trace" in an, albeit reconceived, fashion tradition of techniques, patterns, and details. His "trace" will always carry with it past eras of fashion that cannot simply be eradicated just as for Derrida Western philosophy cannot be discarded.[7] So Margiela's work could perhaps be seen as both a critique of fashion's impossibility, against its own rhetoric, to be "innovative," while at the same time showing its dependence on the history of fashion. That "trace" could perhaps be that which allows fashion to be innovative, at the same time as being that which ensures that it can never be innovative. Thus Margiela deconstructs the aura of the designer garment, and by extension the industry that upholds the myth of innovation, by messing with its integrity and innovation, by stitching a dialogue with the past into its future. When his recycled garments are literally turned inside out, apart from ravaging the finish of the garment, the frame that holds them together is also revealed like a clothing skeleton. The revelation of this skeleton affirms the ties of this garment to a history of fashion, and its own history as everyday garment, but at the same time it enables the making of a new-old and fashionable garment. By extension, Margiela also deconstructs the hierarchical relation that persists between the exclusivity of designer fashion and everyday clothes.

I suggest that the appearance of various guides about how to wear decayed style in the 1990s, that is, "decomposing" and "transparent" clothes (see Johnson 1997: 6–7), how to make these "difficult" clothes inhabitable, reveals a social desire to explore deconstruction dressing as a "new thinking" and "practice." While much of the advice of these guides—for instance, a guide to layering transparent garments so that one feels comfortable rather than exposed—are reinscriptions of the familiar languages of social etiquette and moralism about nudity, exposure, deportment, and beauty, there is something quite significant about the way they frame the problem of *wearing* these clothes. The principle of layered transparency dressing gives visible form to the experience of being late twentieth-century embodied subjects, "works-in-progress," dispersed across layered, multiple and incorporated domains through clothes. Outside the terms of this article a more detailed study of the wearing of transparent clothes would, I suggest, deliver an interesting thinking of body styling and, more, a thinking relevant to clothes in general. However, by the end of this article I hope to have given a preliminary sense of the manner in which clothes and fashion style bodies habitually and repetitively, (trans-)forming and (dis-)figuring the living parameters of embodied existence and activity—that is, material and immaterial existences.

Interpreting "Le Destroy": anti-fashion, recession zeitgeist, eco-fashion or theoretical dress?

Olivier Zahm (1995: 74) summarizes the platitudes of fashion commentary in reference to Margiela's designs: "Recycled style? Anti-fashion provocation? High fashion's answer to a grungy zeitgeist? Add to them the promiscuous moniker *deconstruction* and it is plain that not only have Margiela's clothing designs disconcerted and shocked, they have also been misunderstood." Margiela, Dries Van Noten and Ann Demeulemeester, three 1981 graduates of the Antwerp Academy, have been described as a united "movement" intent on dismantling fashion (Spindler

1993: 1, 9). With the exception of Martin and Koda (1993) and Zahm (1995), the responses to this movement have presumed that it is another example of a vanguard-ism and/or anti-fashion. That is, the specificities of this phenomenon have been confounded by platitudes of "revolution" within, destruction or negative critique of, the fashion system, interpretations fueled by the "negativity" of world recession and/or environmental and industrial crisis. Or interpretations have been fueled by a presumption that "deconstruction fashion" is a representation of a philosophical method intent on destructive critique—i.e., it exemplifies a philosophical position which is itself a negative reaction. In this article I would prefer to suggest that there is more to the association of dress and deconstruction than a wish to destroy functionality, and will proceed to outline, briefly, four possible interpretations of this movement—*anti-fashion, recession zeitgeist, eco-fashion,* or *theoretical dress*—and, while no less valid or fruitful as interpretations, their shortcomings in addressing the new stakes introduced by this association. In fact it is characteristic of a decon-structive thinking to think again about common-sense associations, platitudes, and tried/tested explanations.

The style could easily take its place in a history of *anti-fashion* statements brought to bear on "high fashion" by designers who have introduced counter-cultural or alternative influences, implying that couture is disconnected with the "street," the "night club" or the dynamics of counter-cultural sign bricolage. Vivienne Westwood, Jean-Paul Gaultier, Gianni Versace, John Galliano, and Katharine Hamnett are fre-quently referred to as innovators attuned to these spaces that have become fully invested with the language of political, sexual, and class *resistance.* Counter-cultural fashion has been marked by its ability to uncover taboo practices and mess with normative gender or class coding, in a sense bringing taboo practices like sado-masochism and explicit nudity, or the infusion of working-class signs, to the surface of clothing. The "affinity" these designers show for counter-cultural styles has oper-ated as a licence for a postmodern two-way practice of appropriation, parody, and sign entropy, that is in keeping with a broader postmodern strategy of "raiding" fashion history and popular culture as an eclectic resource for reinvention.[8] Mar-giela, as the "son of Gaultier," his assistant for six years, could be positioned easily in a post-punk lineage (Spindler 1993: 1). About "Le Destroy" it could be said that there are explicit references to a punk sensibility of ripping, slashing and piercing clothing as well as an artificially enhanced "grungy" or "crusty" dress, thus setting up a fantasy dialogue with urban zones of the dispossessed and disaffected. Here sign entropy would refer to the destruction of clothing's "functionality" and "exclusivity" as the clothes are literally remade as unusable, distasteful, and/or aged. The main point, however, is that anti-fashion statements are painted in the oppositional terms of a negative critique, as the term *anti*-fashion clearly signifies, with the additional tones of playfulness, provocation, and parody frequently used. To take a negative or oppositional position is to assume a symmetrical posture in relation to the term one seeks to oppose, thus depending on it, in this case fashion, to provide the "ground" and principle of resistance, with little leverage actually to question or reconstitute its ground. Here, a deconstructive thinking can be differentiated, to be explained shortly, as it refuses the path of negative critique.

A by now very familiar interpretation of fashion, one that can be repeated at any time or place, is that it serves as a cultural reflection of the times, or more specifically, an expression of the **zeitgeist** (spirit of the times). It is very easy to find in this style "reflections" of a whole host of ideas and issues of our time, a time of economic, political, environmental, and aesthetic crises. In "Le Destroy" one can see, if one wishes to put it in these terms, a mirror image in these decaying garments of social stress and degradation brought by economic recession in the early 1990s. More particularly, Bill Cunningham (1990) has suggested that Margiela's choice of site and his ravaged clothes, launched in October 1989 in a vacant block in a Paris "ghetto," echoed "the collapse of political and social order in Eastern Europe."[9] Cunningham's interpretation hinges on the power of the image of crumbling walls to prophesize the symbolic end of the Berlin Wall in November and the dismantling of the European "divide," for he suggests that the image of the models parading along half-demolished walls, worked as a prophetic image of "jubilant Berliner's dancing on the crumbling wall in November." On the environment, the aesthetic of "patching," combining mismatched fabrics or reworking "salvaged" jackets, might reflect what it is to live with an "ensuing" environmental crisis that may well bring dramatic reductions in resources. This aesthetic of reuse and recyclability provides an image that correlates with a popular notion of the environmental imperative, the 4R's imperative (reduce, reuse, recycle, recover) to resist obsolescence, to recycle materials, and use resources efficiently. Correspondingly, it could be argued that the reassembled and decomposing forms reflect an aesthetic crisis, following in the wake of the formalist project that sought to locate the origins of pure expression in the delights of abstract formations. While there is some truth to all of the above as forces informing this time in fashion, a *zeitgeist* reading does very little to examine the relations between fashion and its historical moment, rather accepting the role of fashion as a passive reflection and measure of agencies found elsewhere in (deeper) social concerns. A *zeitgeist* reading entertains a belief in a singular essence or force that has produced a parallelism between cultural form and historical moment; the concepts of resemblance, similarity, or, in fashion terms, "fit" between cause and effect are the foundations of parallelism.

Stephen O'Shea (1991: 238) has called the designs of Margiela "Recycled Style." He writes of Margiela's practice:

> According to the Belgian bomber, the word of the moment is *récupera-tion*, the recovery and re-use of any material that comes to hand. Con-sider it fashion's version of *object trouvé*. (If Picasso used bicycle seats and car parts for sculpture, Margiela can use socks for sweaters.) Maybe it's more like the contemporary Italian school of *arte povera*, which also loots industrial sites for art's sake. Some utopians might consider it a form of eco-fashion.

A novel example of what Margiela calls *récupération* is his turtleneck sweater made from a patchwork knit of cotton-and-wool socks (O'Shea 1991). It does seem premature to call this *eco-fashion*, for which there are better precedents to turn to that meet the demands, based on material life-cycle analyses, for efficiency through-out a product's manufacture, use, and recovery (for instance, fleeces and ski jackets made out of PET bottles). The image or aesthetic of recyclability provided in Margiela's garments is based on a fairly limited practice of eco-design; while they may look the part, Margiela only partially reuses secondhand garments. That is, Margiela gives recovered garments a new life, making use of a practice fairly well established by secondhand clothing stores, stores that now call themselves, in the language of ecology, "recycling outlets." On the other hand, I would not like to diminish the significance of the appearance of this practice on international runways. A question that warrants further consideration and detail than this article can provide is whether such an aesthetic reinforces, or contributes to the deflection of, a desire to bring transformations to consumer society and its practices of obsolescence and disposability. Like a hole in a faithful sweater, Comme des Garçon's "lace" sweater of fall/winter 1982–3 (where lace refers to the distressed "crafting" of gaping holes), could operate as a potent image of decomposition and material limitations, rather than careless or indulgent technology, and perhaps a reminder to produce either longer-lasting or biodegradable substances.[10] Yet, as an aesthetic representation of biodegradable forms, neither materially substantiated nor tied to any sort of practice that delivers sustainable solutions, such an image may simply operate as a "dead-end" for any such concern. As the example of ski jackets suggests, there is a complex issue to contend with in the fact that the term eco-fashion embodies the incompatible agendas of sustainability and consumerism: eco-fashion as oxymoron. Therefore, eco-fashion has to involve a radical rethinking of the "grounds" of fashion and ecology in order to deliver sustainable solutions that can only ever partially arrive with recycling.

The term deconstruction arrived in fashion magazines and style pages with a pre-packaged reputation, as a risky and extremely complex, if not deliberately obfuscating and elitist, style of theoretical critique. Yet, precîsely as a consequence of this packaging, it "arrived" as both an agent of transformative critique (i.e., bringing theory to dress) and something of a philosophical "trend." Amy Spindler (1993) of *The New York Times* attributes the label "deconstructionism" in fashion to Bill Cunningham in a 1989 [sic] *Details* magazine. She defines "deconstructionism" in the following manner: "ORIGINS: The term first described a movement in literary analysis in the mid-20th century, founded by the French philosopher Jacques Derrida. It was a *backlash* against staid literary analysis, arguing that no work can have a fixed meaning, based on the complexity of language and usage" (*my emphasis*, Spindler 1993: 1). Note, here, that deconstructionism is described as a reactive form of analysis. Significantly, she paints the relationship between deconstruction and fashion in terms of an enabling and even liberating application of a theory. Under the question "So what does that have to do with fashion?" she continues her exposition: "The Oxford English Dictionary defines deconstruction as 'the action of undoing the construction of a thing.' So not only does that mean that jacket linings, for example, can be on the outside or sleeves detached, but the function of the piece is re-imagined" (Spindler 1993: 1). In that deconstruction has been defined *very* generally, as a practice of "undoing," deconstructionist fashion *liberates* the garment from functionality, by literally *undoing* it. Importantly here, through this association *dress becomes theoretical*, only by *exemplifying* a theoretical position developed in philosophical thought and brought to fashion in order to transform it. Yet, clothes are not liberated or released from functionality because of deconstruction (as causal force coming from somewhere outside fashion), for the liberation of clothes from functionality is something realized as a complex interaction between bodies, clothing, and the various settings in which they are worn. Significantly, clothes do not have, and never have had, a singular origin meaning, or function. There are two points here: one is that deconstruction is, in a certain sense, "dressed up" (or "dressed down") for its application to the field of fashion, and secondly, in proposing that fashion is a *representation* of deconstructive thinking it might be presupposed that fashion has a prescribed function, or worse, as if fashion were not already on a philosophical ground, that it is unphilosophical and unthought. This latter presupposition entertains a thinking that a theory has been inappropriately, awkwardly, or insensitively applied to an (untheoretical) subject; that is, it is thought an inappropriate mixing of "light" with "heavy." This criticism appears to resent fashion being thought of as philosophical and constitutes a refusal to think a "ground" of fashion where new stakes can be introduced.

(Un-)dressing deconstruction

In a *Letter to a Japanese Friend* Jacques Derrida (1983) attempts to convey to his friend and translator his intentions and some of the problems he has encountered in giving the name "deconstruction" to what it is he does:

> When I chose this word, or when it imposed itself upon me—I think it was in *Of Grammatology*—I little thought it would be credited with such a central role in the discourse that interested me at the time. Among other things I wished to translate and adapt to my own ends the Heideggerian word *Destruktion* or *Abbau*. Each signified in this context an operation bearing on the structure or traditional architecture of the fundamental concepts of ontology or of Western metaphysics. But in French "destruction" too obviously implied an annihilation or a negative reduction much closer perhaps to Nietzschean "demolition" than to the Heideggerian interpretation or to the type of reading that I proposed. So I ruled that out. I remember having looked to see if the word "deconstruction" (which came to me it seemed quite spontaneously) was good French. I found it in the *Littré*. The grammatical, linguistic, or rhetorical senses [*portées*] were found bound up with a "mechanical" sense [*portée "machinique"*]. This association appeared very fortunate, and fortunately adapted to what I wanted to at least suggest (Derrida 1983: 1–2).

He continues to explain the multiple meanings this term has in French, giving support to his frequently cited claim that deconstruction can never be said to be only *one thing*. Later in the letter Derrida is clear on why this is, as he outlines the stakes of any attempt to name what is essentially a multiplicity:

> To be very schematic I would say that the difficulty of *defining* and therefore also of *translating* the word "deconstruction" stems from the fact that all the predicates, all the defining concepts, all the lexical significations, and even the syntactic articulations, which seem at one moment to lend themselves to this definition or to that translation, are

also deconstructed or deconstructible, directly or otherwise, etc. And that goes for the *word*, the very unity of the *word* deconstruction, as for every word. *Of Grammatology* questioned the unity of "word" and all the privileges with which it was credited, especially in its *nominal* form. It is therefore only a discourse or rather a writing that can make up for the incapacity of the word to be equal to a "thought." All sentences of the type "deconstruction is X" or "deconstruction is not X" a priori miss the point, which is to say that they are at least false (Derrida 1983: 4).

Fairly obviously, Derrida's refusal to say what deconstruction *is*, has consequently led to certain blocks or resistances to understanding his writings. However, his refusal is an indication of Derrida's reading of the history of philosophy, its language, its defining concepts and approach to naming (Benjamin 1988: 34): to define deconstruction in the terms of "it is X" would be to repeat the tradition that has dominated the history of philosophy, a history of presence, a tradition beginning with the Platonic dialogues and mode of questioning where a name seeks to represent the *essence (ousia)* of the subject under discussion. In short and schematic terms, for Derrida Western metaphysics repeats a logocentric practice of essence fabrication where a word (*logos*) names the essential *being* of a thing, consequently equated with full-presence, meaning, and universal truth. Such a practice has given rise to the distinction between an outer surface level of polysemy and an inner, unified original meaning, and the work of the philosopher has been to identify through the name that inner content, its identity, by which the *proper* passage to knowledge has been formularized (Benjamin 1988: 34). The distinction between singular essence and polysemics thus becomes oppositional, the latter devalued for inhibiting the naming of the first. A logocentric tradition of thought tries to ensure the impossibility of thinking at once terms positioned oppositionally, instead valuing one term above another; philosophy has repeatedly privileged being over becoming, presence over presencing, unity over difference, origin over dissemination. Thus, for Derrida, who refuses this tradition, no answer that attempts to say in essence what deconstruction *is*, or, for that matter, any other word that claims to represent thought, can ever be exhaustive.

Many have interpreted Derrida's position as "against" reason, truth and presence, that is, *anti*-essentialist, an invitation to delight in the resonances, the traces and the violence of the word, to revel in an unrestricted free play of surface polysemics and/or irrationality. To argue such is to suggest that Derrida has only inverted the hierarchy imbued in the Platonic heritage, in order to revalue indeterminacy and instability, against certainty and truth. However, Derrida does more than this for his writing uncovers the dangers of a thinking centered around hierarchical oppositions, a thinking which would leave their underlying presuppositions "unthought." In retracing philosophical texts he seeks to destroy neither the power of the word nor the history of philosophy but rather he examines the enabling conditions by which defining terms and concepts operate but also delimit philosophy at the same time; relations emerge in argument that make it necessary to exclude alternative paths of thought, relations that come to constitute hierarchical oppositions that enable the argument to operate effectively, delineating at the same time a carefully regulated boundary between an inside and outside of its "structure." In retracing the hierarchical relations between such terms as speech/writing, being/becoming, physis (nature)/techne (culture), Derrida's writing analyzes and hopes to displace the traditional operations that have constituted an inside and outside of philosophy, by exposing its inside to unseen aspects of its outside. In the process this boundary is illuminated as less than stable. The force of Derrida's writings is to highlight the manner in which the operations of logocentrism are founded on instabilities and slippages; indeterminacies and slippages of meaning are an enabling condition of the arrival of philosophical thought.

In his statements about the term deconstruction in the first quote above, Derrida conveys a sense of the tradition, an extensive "architecture" of Western metaphysics, in relation to which his philosophical readings must negotiate and position themselves, as his comments on the Heideggerian heritage *Destruktion* and *Abbau* also reveal. Philosophical speculation has strived to locate an origin of Being, a pre-ontological moment, where Being could be identified in an ideal form, uninscribed in the palimpsest of subsequent philosophy. The pursuit of this originary moment necessitates the forgetting of metaphysics, the history of thought, the history of Being, the very history that creates a desire for this ideal. For Derrida a thinking of this pre-ontological moment will always elude philosophy, for a thinking outside of the Greek philosophical position since Plato is ultimately impossible. Thus, for Derrida, there is no safe meta-position outside philosophy from which objectively to examine this tradition; for "outside" is always a product of that which excluded it and named itself "inside," thus opening on to an understanding that has become the "by now well-worn postmodern catchphrase 'there is no outside' (of discourse, patriarchy, history, power)" (Grosz 1995: 131). In addition, any writing about deconstruction as a "current thinking" necessitates a reflection on "its" place in the history of philosophy (Benjamin 1988: 34), a reflection that puts current thinking in dialogue with a tradition of thought and with its limits. Significantly, this would include a reflection on the relations that philosophy has established with discourses like art and literature which are frequently positioned as philosophy's "others."[11] Derrida's writing has been characterized by the dialogues it establishes with other discourses—interdisciplinary dialogues of mutual effect.[12] It is the effects of these dialogues that are being explored by various disciplines—literary criticism, art history, cultural and media studies, architecture, philosophy—which have received Derrida's writings as an opportunity to reconsider the nature of dialogue in the past, and the disciplinary boundaries and hierarchical relations that have underpinned these dialogues. The discipline of fashion studies, too, might force a reflection on fashion's "ground," its relation to philosophy, and the characteristics that remain invisible and unthought in the fabric of scholarship.

In a sense, Derrida observes philosophy and its others in a mobilizing exchange, and embarks on a twisting path of thinking that is always a rethinking of their relationality.[13] Or more precisely, a process of negotiating the exchanges that both elide and separate a boundary of philosophy, a line that marks a discourse from its heritage and the chance of a new beginning, and marks an inside from an outside. Above all, his thinking arrives in the form of an imperative to (re-)write; to repeat Derrida's paradoxical positioning of the philosopher: "It is therefore only a discourse or rather a writing that can make up for the incapacity of the word to be equal to a 'thought' " (Derrida 1983: 4).

From here, it will only be a short step to understand Derrida's resistance to painting deconstruction in the terms of a method or system of critique or analysis, where analysis strives to isolate the *pure* and *singular* underlying essence of some-*thing*. For if deconstruction is to be called a method, it is to promote it—i.e., *Deconstruction*—as a repeatable formula, as a united project and entity in itself, something that is at odds with a practice of reading and writing which only comes to presence *in* and *though* a process of interaction with the operational terms of the texts at hand. Nor is deconstruction a single act that involves an intentional subject who performs the application. In Derrida's (1983: 4) words again,

> Deconstruction takes place, it is an event, that does not await the delib-eration, consciousness, or organization of a subject, or even of modern-ity. *It deconstructs it-self. It can be deconstructed.* [*Ça se déconstruit.*] The "it" [*ça*] is not here an impersonal thing that is opposed to some egological subjectivity. *It is in deconstruction* (the *Littré* says "to deconstruct it-self [*se déconstruire*] . . . to lose its construction").

In Derrida's terms, deconstruction is not a unified method applied across his diverse inquiries into the history of philosophy—Saussure, Rousseau, Heidegger, Nietzsche, Hegel, Husserl, etc. In a sense, deconstruction comes from nowhere in particular; it *goes on, takes place* between philosophy and it other, between the author and a specific text.

Yet we cannot ignore the fact that "deconstruction" has become a word, a motif and sign of transformation with certain privileged terms/themes and advocating a "mobile" strategy. For one, deconstruction cannot itself avoid the problems of nam-ing, translation (naming and translation are always linked for Derrida), and method-ological "styling" through dissemination and application; *it* exists within and as discourse, has come to wear the label of -*ism*, and is subject to being reinscribed into logocentric forms and discussions themselves deconstructible. On the other hand, the word itself, as it resounds with mechanical and technical significations, Derrida indicates (1983: 2–3), encourages a thinking of deconstruction as a neat formula for dismantling and disassembling, in the style of a method and critique. The mechanical significations of the name have served to explain the appeal deconstruction might have for disciplines and cultural practices already imbued with a sense of technical and skill-based methods of construction like architecture, graphic design, film and fashion. It is important to observe that the forms subjected to deconstruction and the conditions under which a deconstructive thinking of these forms has become possible are also responsible for the "designing" of deconstruction as a technique of disassembly and a method to be applied. The reception of Derrida's writings, especially in US universities, has been surrounded by fierce debate about its status as a method for reading and interpretation, its validity as a philosophical practice, and its translation and "domestication" from the French situation into an American one.[14] Brunette and Wills (1989: 5) have outlined Derrida's response to this debate, a response that will always place him in a double bind:

> he has refused to arbitrate between authorized and unauthorized ver-sions or uses of his work, in spite of the reproach to which his refusal has

laid him open, preferring instead to make the questions of "ownership," "inheritance," "seal," and "signature" major topics of address in his writing. Obviously, the problem with insisting upon a distinction between Derrida and deconstruction, in spite of the loose and often ill-informed use of the latter term, is that an appeal is inevitably, if unconsciously, being made to a "correct" or "true" Derrida or deconstruction, as opposed to a cheap or not-so-cheap imitation of it. Such a gesture remains firmly within the logocentric will to truth that Derrida has been at pains to identify and critique.

However, Derrida's position is neither prone to silence nor that of the apologist, for he has unrelentingly defended his writing in debates, like the one with John Searle published in *Limited Inc.* Derrida would be the first to say that the full force of deconstructive thinking, its potential, can only be realized through the conditions of its dissemination, conditions that will both enrich and confound his words on the subject. For all my insistence on Derrida's position and words on this matter of the name "deconstruction," I do not wish to present them here as the word of the master, but as a part of a close reading of the features and reception of deconstruction that will, all the same, resound unfortunately with the tone of correction and take its place amongst the many (derived) readings on this matter. In the process, it will become exemplary of many of the problems outlined, especially the problem of presenting deconstruction as a unified project.

Partly due to the various cultural sites where deconstructive thinking is being explored, there is a tendency to think of this time as an "era" or "epoch of Deconstruction" (Derrida 1983: 4). It is seductive to give way to this relativist mode of thinking, of an era of being-in-deconstruction, in the way that some writers mistakenly celebrated postmodernism as a "new era" bringing an absolute end to modernity. To assert an epoch of deconstruction is to proclaim a unified time and mode of being, a "we" *of* "deconstruction," and suggests that there are clear temporal markers that are going to deliver the fate of obsolescence to a deconstruction considered appropriate for the contemporary moment, yet a style that will at one point reach an expiry date (and from which "we" will move away).

A dialogue of mutual effect

Now we can begin to draw out the implications of the fashion media's announcement of deconstruction fashion. Both Spindler (1993) and Cunningham (1990) imply that an ontology exists prior to the manifestation of deconstruction fashion, suggesting that the style plays no role in the construction of such an ontology. To repeat, firstly, Cunningham suggests that European social and political conditions exist and deconstruction fashion is a cultural response to, and expression of, these conditions. Cunningham, against his own position as a fashion writer, would seem to deny the importance of fashion as constitutive of a Western ontology, an evolving social fabric of interrelating cultural, political and economic forces. Secondly, Spindler proposes that deconstruction is a phenomenon particular to the discipline of philosophy which is then merely applied to fashion, whereby deconstruction fashion is presented as an expression of ideas originating in philosophy. As in Cunningham, Spindler would seem to suggest that fashion is always a secondary effect of an originary position. In Spindler's case, this originary position is the position of the philosophical, reflective subject, in this instance Derrida as the "founder" of deconstruction, who *produces* a deconstructive mode of thinking. For Spindler, then, a split is introduced and sustained between fashion as a domain of expression and the field of philosophy, simply implying that fashion is unphilosophical. Here deconstruction suggests itself as a form in fashion with little agency or effect in an ontological realm where deconstruction circulates and is being explored. In both cases the identification of this style prescribes a separation between fashion and this ontology, where fashion can only ever be figured as a *product* hopefully attempting to realize itself as an expression, a measure of a prior constitutive subject.

Can the meeting of these two terms—deconstruction and fashion—constitute a different relation between fashion and philosophy? Is it possible that deconstruction fashion might enable an alternative relation to emerge, one that doesn't position fashion as dependent on a prior ontology or philosophy in order to constitute itself as a legitimate cultural form? I would propose that deconstruction fashion indicates an engagement of fashion and philosophy in a dialogue of mutual effect.[15] Deconstruction fashion is an encounter neither purely *about* philosophy nor purely *about* fashion, neither simply owned by a philosophy posited as prior to its fashioned expression, nor owned by fashion as its latest innovation. It is not my intention to judge this fashion as a good or bad application of deconstruction, but rather to illuminate it as a different thinking of fashion.[16] I would also suggest that a dialogue has always existed within clothing and that the lived relations of making and wearing clothes—involving technical skills, habits, movement, thinking, desire, memory, imagination, sensation, etc.—have always had to account for a dialogue between the different modes of Being contained by these positions. Finally, then, it might be interesting to consider deconstruction fashion's capacity to reflect on the nexus of making, wearing, thinking, and dwelling that happens in fashion and people's relations with all clothing; making and wearing clothes are processes by which presence, thought, meaning, and form are transported *through* garments and into the spaces in which we dwell.

Margiela explicates this concern by realizing a deconstructive thinking in the process of making clothing. By producing tailored garments *through* the tailor's patterns Margiela converts the disintegrating material forms and structures of fashion, the instabilities in fashion's *modus operandi*—fashion fighting to be both historical and innovative—into garments.[17] Analogous to Derrida's capacity to summon the defining terms of philosophical debate, Margiela's deconstruction fashion brings forth the question "What are the conditions under which Fashion continues to make forms as seamless presence?" Like Derrida's "critique" of philosophy that brings an imperative to rethink what philosophy performs rather than bringing its closure, Margiela returns our attention from the question of fashion's future to the garment and what it does.[18] Ultimately, Margiela reproduces the seamlessness of fashion, the idealized form, by the literal production of seams: seamlessness through seams. In doing so he admits that to be formed through garments involves a *process* of being formed or an analytics of construction. As such, these seams, by being the "traces" of both history and innovation, are the condition of the impossibility of seamlessness as a fixed objectified ideal. This making of seamlessness as always seamed must be considered as an embodied phenomenon, because clothes are "figured," literally animated, as a presencing of body. One need only think of the shop-window mannequin whose often abstract presentation of bodies does little to hinder the clothes animating themselves; the clothes in this instance bring the mannequin to life.[19] Implicit in Margiela's making and its logistics of patterns, darts, facings and seams, is a making always presenced as wearing.

Fashion is an ontological domain; in and through an interaction with fashion subjectivities are literally *made* and worldly relations established between clothes and bodies. In everyday speech, informed as it is by a pervasive metaphysical opposition between subject and object, we speak of the "body" that is *subject* to the clothes that literally enclothe it with a significance. It would also follow that the "fashionable body" is a body-product, an object, of the modern system of fashion. These static bodies seem far removed from the living body as a configuring subjectivity. Instead, the enclothed body is a body in process, a configuring subjectivity; it is at once styling clothes and styled by them, both styling the world and styled by it. In a similar sense, wearing clothing is a gradual process by which the body is at once fitted into a sartorial structure whilst itself accommodating this structure. A notion of the living body as a configuring subjectivity informs the use of the word "wearing" in this article; wearing as a process of accommodation, interaction, and exchange through which bodies come into form as beings.

Wearing clothing can also involve repetition that constructs an experience of the familiar and the habitual, an experience captured in the frequently cited but apt metaphor for clothing, "like a second skin." An experience of the familiar in clothing can be thought of as a "habitus," as clothing becomes a space of everyday inhabitance, dwelling and self-configuration.[20] Margiela articulates this notion of clothing as habitus in his practice of repeating favorite designs over the period of several collections with slight variations in color or detail (Zahm 1995: 119). In doing so he refuses simply to adhere to the demand for the "new" and the "now." Margiela's "new look" is a return to the ground of clothing, literally the knowing foregrounded through repetitiously wearing the familiarity of a garment's structur-*ing*. In Margiela's garments, motifs like darts, facings, and tacking that are repeated throughout a history of making clothing are isolated and exposed as features. He then repeats these features as explicit design motifs across his lines of clothing, the clothes changing and becoming new with each reappearance of a motif across jackets, dresses and shirts. The garments continue to repeat themselves in one another, each time with a significant difference. That is, the repetition of the motif changes both the former garment and its newest manifestation. In doing so, he is articulating a process of revisiting a garment and its motifs, of revisiting the experience of inhabiting clothing as a differential, a reconfiguring of self and transfiguration of body over time and place.[21]

It should be apparent that with each new line of clothing, with each repetition, Margiela is reconfiguring fashion and its drive to be innovative. He illuminates that the innovative form is always produced through fashion's history, that its innovations always rely on the sartorial tradition that it seems to want to leave behind. Thus he reveals that the push toward an ideal form is at the expense of the very history that creates a desire for that ideal. Instead, for Margiela each innovation is a reflection on its place in the history of fashion. In this way, his practice parallels a thinking in deconstruction that is able to reflect on the fundamental ambivalence toward philosophical heritage and innovation—the reproduction of idealized truths in spite of the truths maintained by this heritage—that is incorporated into the ground of philosophy. Similarly, deconstruction fashion is an "*un-doing*" of fashion, where this "un-" tarries with the impetus merely to make anew by inflecting this making through a history of its pursuit.

Notes

I would like to thank Anthea Fawcett, Freida Riggs, and Abby Mellick for reading this article and providing both insightful comments and encouragement.

1   A later section of the article will address Derridean deconstruction in more expansive terms, for in this introduction I hope to describe the object "deconstruction fashion," its popular characterization, as well as the features of the dissemination of a deconstructive thinking in fashion.

2   The essays of Martin and Koda (1993) and Zahm (1995), while short, have been formative in the thinking presented in this article. I would recommend the final essay "Analytical Apparel: Deconstruction and Discovery in Contemporary Costume" in *Infra-Apparel* as a clear history of the proto-deconstructionist tendencies of the 1980s, a history I cannot revisit here, as we turn, instead, to consider the nature and consequences of fashion's association with deconstruction.

3   I use the word *garment* with a rhetorical force to suggest the mechanical significations and verb function implicit in its etymology. OED refers to its French origins in *garnir* "to furnish, to fit out, equip." Or in English "to dress, to clothe."

4   It will become clear that economy might be a more useful word to substitute for "system," as a consequence of points made later in the article. Economy can connote the continuous, repetitive, and regulated exchanges of a structure or system, implicit in the systemic momentum or systematicity necessary to sustain itself. These exchanges will always undermine any attempt to define fashion as a coherent system.

5   Fashion has always produced its momentum literally through the "ideal," which means its disposition is always toward the "new," the "of the moment," in a manner that dissolves its past. Quite simply, fashion announces what it is to be "in fashion," in a manner that is always dialectically opposed to what came before it, now "out of fashion." Later in this article it will be observed that the discourse of philosophy equally follows this structure of production.

6   Garments and features of Martin Margiela's October 1989 Paris collection included a recovered jacket showing darts and facings on its "outside"; a dismembered jacket with sleeves that tie onto the arm with bias ribbon (including tacking around the arm holes and industrial snaps instead of buttons); a clear plastic "suit" worn over layered pants and top. The seams of other plastic suits in the collection were outlined in white tailor's tape to accentuate the "architecture" of the garment.

7   Derrida refers to the "trace" in various writings, notably *Of Grammatology* (1976).

The trace may be thought of as the mark left by writing, where writing figures as the former presence of a writer suggesting the writer's presence through the mark of a literal absence. The trace names that which designates the possibility of systematicity, the movement by which any system of reference—language, culture—in general is constituted. This movement marks an irreconcilable difference. Hence, within the system of fashion, we must already presuppose the trace in order to account for the use of the terms innovation and history.

8   Sign entropy refers to the forced destruction of signs.

9   The site of Martin Margiela's October 1989 show held in a vacant block in Paris included signs of urban "crisis" and both cultural intermixing and schisms: graffitied and half-demolished walls, rap and dub music, and local residents who sat on surrounding walls to have a peek at this unlikely event in their neighborhood (a lot of these were kids who later took to the runway themselves, erasing any idea of foreignness, by imitating the walk of models).

10   The "lace" effect is created by randomly loosening the tension on the knitting machine (Kawakubo cited in Koda 1985: 8). See Martin and Koda 1993 for a photograph of this sweater.

11   Frequently philosophy has called on art and literature as an example or representation of a philosophical claim, in a way that re-expresses both art and literature in, and overshadows them with, the language of philosophy. The harm here is less in making an example of art, and more in the authority awarded to philosophy to *explain* these practices, an authority embodied, for instance, in the philosophical discourse of aesthetics. Andrew Benjamin (1988: 35) outlines some of the consequences of this hierarchical relation:

> Art, from within this perspective, is taken to be outside of philosophy and therefore its relationship to philosophy includes, if not ensnares it within, philosophical discourse . . . It is not difficult to see that this way of construing the relationship between philosophy and that which is other than philosophy (here art and literature) is articulated in terms of the opposition between the inside and outside; an opposition to be deconstructed.

12   For examples of Derrida's writing on art and literature see Derrida 1987 and 1986. For an exposition of Derrida's involvement and reception in the 'spatial arts' see Brunette and Wills 1994. What becomes evident from the analogy of a dialogue or economy of exchange is that these writings cease to be simply either about philosophy or about visual arts but about both: that is, there would be no pure theory, pure art or pure literature as a priori terms constituting an origin or end point of the exchange. Yet, neither would this exchange have to drain each discipline of its differences of language, concepts, and practices. See Norris 1991 for an exposition on the reception of Derrida into literary criticism circles. He argues that it is only on the basis of a longstanding hierarchy and prejudice that Derrida can be criticized for trying to reverse this hierarchy and elevate literature, rhetoric, and artful style above philosophical reasoning and serious argument (thought to be incompatible with rhetoric). This criticism, still prevalent among Derrida's detractors who argue he is not a philosopher but a literary critic, largely chooses to miss the point of re-examining this hierarchy.

13   The operations of metaphysics have been described by Derrida as an economy,

from the Greek (*oikos*), for house. Giving further resonance to the notion of a structure or architecture of Western metaphysics, its operations are those of a domestic economy that ensures and regulates continuous exchange. In sum, Derrida wants to open up this economy to a thinking of the uncanny and alterity, that is, the bizarre homeless guest never allowed to settle in the house of metaphysics.

14 See Weber 1987: 42–5. Weber has proposed that the arrival of Derrida's philosophy in America has been mediated by the liberal "universalist ethos," a tradition ingrained in the American university and institutional intellectualism, making it profoundly different to the French positioning of the university and intellectualism. Weber argues, deconstructing the features of deconstruction's reception, that the tradition of the American university institution has strongly regulated its inside as a safe place of pluralist debate. The disciplines and their theoretical modes of operation "inside" the university have excluded and delegitimized conflict (meaning radical disruption), marking the "inside" as a pluralist environment that can tolerate multiple styles of interpretation. Further, the price of admission to the American academy, Weber argues, is the "universalization" of the work of a philosopher as it is removed from its political and social specificity, and presented conflict-free and reproducible. In this process the work is "individualized" as the work of one man and labelled as a self-standing methodology that counteracts the disruption to master narratives and authorial power that the texts speak of.

15 The relation of mutual effect that I describe is not a classical dialogue, but more accurately a hermeneutic, as it means a process of interpretation and understanding. For Martin Heidegger (1988: 195) a hermeneutic is circular where no point of beginning emerges from another. One should not think that the circle as a contained entity represents the totality of understanding, rather the circular structure delineates a pathway of interpretation, encounter, and a relation of mutual understanding and effect.

16 Here, the reader might like to think about the manner in which deconstruction in fashion could generate, supplement, and enrich other deconstructive inquiries.

17 We are left to puzzle over two potential interpretations of the phenomenon of Margiela's clothing; as a designer is Margiela performing a deconstruction of clothing, or are the clothes effecting their own deconstruction? Neither position can be in itself true, for it could be said that both are possible.

18 Zahm rightly observes that Margiela's use of a blank white label stitched inside the garment has the effect of bringing one's attention back to the clothes, after its blankness has refused the excesses of the designer label and demystified its aura (Zahm 1995: 119). Of course, this label still *is* a designer signature. Margiela is frequently characterized by his silence, invisibility, and his refusal of fashion hype (Spindler 1993; Blanchard 1997). In his rare interviews with the press he has distanced his garments from the label deconstruction and resists explaining what the clothes mean, leaving the clothes to "do the talking" through their use and wear (O'Shea 1991).

19 Margiela's practice, in his spring 1996 show, of masking his models with a black stocking, reducing their subjectivity in favor of a blank object-like status, similarly allows the clothes to reanimate their wearers.

20 Habitus, defined by Bourdieu (1977), refers to those ingrained dispositions of taste, experience, perceptions, preferences and appreciations that inscribe

themselves into the body and organize an individual's capacity to act socially. Habitus can represent a set of "clothing" habits and a space inhabited.

21   In Margiela's spring collection of 1996/7, he extends his earlier idea of the tie-on sleeve (i.e., clothes as prosthetic limb) to explore a full-torso strap-on body piece in different contours (Blanchard 1997: 24). Clothes and lingerie have always contoured and shaped bodies to varying degrees, yet, here, the clothes mimic temporary and permanent body-alteration technologies like toning-programmes, breast enhancement/reductions, liposuction, and tummy lifts, and they indulge a popular fantasy of choosing a "new body" (a fantasy that finds frequent expression in advertising for anything from gym classes to plastic surgery to bottled water). Margiela deconstructs the binary relation of clothing and bodies, a dissolution that occurs in wearing clothing, as clothes become bodies and bodies become clothes.

References

Benjamin, Andrew. 1988. "Deconstruction and Art/The Art of Deconstruction." In *What is Deconstruction?*, edited by Christopher Norris and Andrew Benjamin, London and New York: Academy Editions/St. Martin's Press.

Betts, Katherine. 1992. "La Nouvelle Vague." *Vogue* (New York). September.

Blanchard, Tamsin. 1997. "A Cut Above: Will Margiela Deconstruct Hermes?" *Vogue* (Australia). August.

Bourdieu, Pierre. 1977. *Outline of a Theory of Practice*. Translated by Richard Nice. Cambridge and New York: Cambridge University Press.

Brunette, Peter, and David Wills. 1989. *Screen/Play: Derrida and Film Theory*. Princeton: Princeton University Press.

— eds. *Deconstruction and the Visual Arts: Art, Media, Architecture*. Cambridge: Cambridge University Press, 1994.

Byrne, Chuck, and Marthe Witte. 1990. "A Brave New World: Understanding Deconstruction.' *Print* 44, no. 6: 80–87, 203.

Cunningham, Bill. 1990. "Fashion du Siecle." *Details* 8, no. 8: 177–300.

Davis, Fred. 1992. *Fashion, Culture, and Identity*. Chicago: University of Chicago Press.

Derrida, Jacques. 1976. *Of Grammatology*. Translated by Gayatri Chakravorty Spivak. Baltimore: Johns Hopkins University Press.

— 1983. "Letter to a Japanese Friend," In *Derrida and Différance*, edited by David Wood and Robert Bernasconi, Evanston: Northwestern University Press, 1988.

— 1986. *Glas*. Translated by John P. Leavey and Richard Rand. Lincoln: University of Nebraska Press.

— 1987. *The Truth in Painting*. Translated by Geoff Bennington and Ian McLeod. Chicago: University of Chicago Press.

Finkelstein, Joanne. 1996. "Speaking of Fashion." In *After a Fashion*. Melbourne: Melbourne University Press.

Grosz, Elizabeth. 1995. "Architecture from the Outside." *Space, Time, and Perversion*. London and New York: Routledge.

Heidegger, Martin. 1988. *Being and Time*. Translated by John Macquarie and Edward Robinson. Oxford: Basil Blackwell; first published in German in 1927.

Hollander, Anne. 1994. *Sex and Suits: The Evolution of Modern Dress*. New York: Kodansha.

Johnson, Judy. 1997. "Grin and Bare It." *Sun-Herald* (Sydney). 6 April, Tempo section, pp. 6–7.

Koda, Harold. 1985. "Rei Kawakubo and the Aesthetic of Poverty." *Costume: Journal of Costume Society of America* 11: 5–10.

"La mode Destroy." 1992. *Vogue* (Paris), May.

Martin, Richard. 1992. "Destitution and Deconstruction: The Riches of Poverty in the Fashion of the 1990s." *Textile & Text* 15, no. 2: 3–12.

Martin, Richard, and Harold Koda. 1993. *Infra-Apparel*. New York: Metropolitan Museum of Art/Harry Abrams Inc.

McLeod, Mary. 1994. "Undressing Architecture: Fashion, Gender, and Modernity." In *Architecture: In Fashion*, edited by Deborah Fausch et al., Princeton: Princeton Architectural Press.

Norris, Christopher. 1991. *Deconstruction: Theory and Practice*. Rev. ed. London and New York: Routledge.

O'Shea, Stephen. 1991. "Recycling: An All-New Fabrication of Style." *Elle* 7, no. 2: 234–9.

Spindler, Amy M. 1993. "Coming Apart." *New York Times*. 25 July, Styles section, pp. 1, 9.

Weber, Samuel. 1987. *Institution and Interpretation*. Theory and History of Literature, Vol. 31. Minneapolis: University of Minnesota Press.

Wigley, Mark, and Phillip Johnson. 1988. *Deconstructivist Architecture*. New York/Boston: Museum of Modern Art/Little Brown & Co.

Wigley, Mark. 1993. *The Architecture of Deconstruction*. Cambridge, MA: MIT Press.

Zahm, Olivier. 1995. "Before and After Fashion." *Artforum* 33, no. 7: 74–77, 119.

PART ELEVEN

Fashion and (the) image

THIS SECTION will be concerned with fashion theory as it is articulated via or through graphic design and photography. It will also be concerned with the two senses of 'image', as indicated by the use of parentheses in the title, and with how fashion relates to those senses.

'Image' in one sense is synonymous with 'likeness' or 'picture', and photography and drawing are two techniques or media in which likenesses and pictures may be produced and reproduced. The reference to technique here may explain what some will understand as the 'technical' bent of the material written by the photographer Erica Lennard, for example. As a photographer, Lennard is profoundly interested in the technical details of the images she produces, and she writes in the extract here of lenses, film speeds, different types of paper, and so on. The idea of the image has a long philosophical history and, as Lipovetsky argued in Chapter 2, it is not always an attractive one. It will be recalled that Lipovetsky (1994) traced theorists' universal mistrust of fashion as superficial and deceptive back to the Platonic story of the Cave. In this story, or metaphor, human knowledge is likened to being able to see the shadows playing on the cave walls but being unable to see either the things themselves or the source of the light that casts the shadows (see *The Republic* Book VII 514ff, in Hamilton and Cairns 1961: 747ff.). Fashion as an image, or a series of images, therefore, already trails negative connotations in much western theorising.

In another sense, 'image' means something like 'identity', as in the phrases 'personal identity' and 'brand-identity', where personal identity is the unique character of someone and brand identity is the perceptible (visible) image or essence of a product or service. We talk, for example, of someone's image or of our own self-image, meaning the sense of identity one perceives in others or that one constructs for oneself. Clearly fashion and clothing are central to both of these projects. It may be indicative of our self-commodification that we use these words as easily of ourselves as we do of the things (objects) that we buy. Regarding the latter, Naomi Klein (2000) notes in her *No Logo* that in the mid-1980s companies began to recognise that what they were producing and selling were not products, but brands. More precisely, what companies such as Tommy Hilfiger, Nike and Calvin Klein realised was that they were producing and selling 'images of brands' (Klein 2000: 4). They began to understand that they were selling brand identities or images. This recognition is consistent with Baudrillard's claim that what is consumed in post-modernity is not the commodity but the sign, or rather the commodity 'produced as a sign': the image or sign is what is consumed, not the commodity *qua* commodity (1981: 147). The post-modern commodity is consumed as an image, a constructed sign, and not as the functional thing or object as object.

Images or identities in this sense may be constructed and communicated by wearing fashion; they may also be constructed and communicated in photography, graphic design or illustration. Significantly, Klein goes on to explain the brand, or brand image, in terms of a meaning; she says that we should think of the brand as the 'core meaning' of the company. Advertising, in turn, is the 'vehicle used to convey that meaning to the world' (Klein 2000: 5). Image here, then, is akin to meaning: a brand's image is the unique meaning it communicates within a culture or market. In this sense it is linked to marketing and advertising, and images are inevitably constructed in fashion photography with a view to selling clothes.

Explaining the role of fashion photography, the *Vogue* photographer Chris Von Wangenheim said that '[f]ashion photography is a way to sell clothes. The way to sell clothes or anything else connected with it, is through seduction' (Di Grappa 1981: 152). It is worth noting that the seduction through imagery that Von Wangenheim presents here in a positive light is not unconnected to the untrustworthy and deceptive play of images that Plato condemns in *The Republic*. Fashion photography is used to create a likeness or picture, which is in turn used to construct an image (in the sense of a brand identity or meaning). That image is then used to sell fashion/clothes. In order to do this it must be attractive and persuasive, if not downright deceptive; it must be seductive. This is what Barthes refers to when he writes of fashion photography as a 'rhetoric' (Barthes 1990: 302): it is meaningful and it is persuasive.

These two senses of image may be summarised as sense (a), in which image means likeness or picture, and sense (b), in which image means identity or meaning. Various disciplines are represented by the readings in this section: photography itself, semiology, and graphic design. And they each deal with senses (a) and/or (b) in their own ways. Photography provides likenesses and pictures and also contributes to the identity or brand meaning of fashion designers and companies. Graphic design will use photography to provide illustrations of fashion items, but it also has a more significant function in producing and communicating identities and meanings. This function is accomplished through the construction of logos, labels, typefaces, and so on, for use on shop fronts, carrier bags, garment labels and till receipts. Semiology can deal with senses (a) and (b). It may be worth noting here that another level of the debate as to whether fashion is art or not (see Part Three) is revealed by Abigail Solomon-Godeau, when she says that

[d]etached from its surrounding glossy or newsprint environment and even its original size in halftone or four-colour reproduction, any fashion photograph that departs from conventions that might otherwise anchor its meaning (whether glamorous professional models or certain protocols of lighting and composition) becomes indistinguishable from an art photograph of similar style.

(Solomon-Godeau 2004: 195)

Where it can be argued that fashion turns into art once it is put into an art gallery, it can also be argued that fashion photography turns into art photography once it is taken out of context and freed from certain 'giveaway' protocols.

The suspicion may arise, reading this section, that much of the material that is written about and around graphic design and photography bears little relation to theory as it has been explained in this book so far. Such writing may appear to be entirely anecdotal, to be made up of interesting stories or to be mere description. Such writing may also appear to be entirely technical, concerned solely with f-stops, film speed and the grain of the paper. It is neither entirely anecdotal nor entirely technical; the theory in such writing is occluded, or, more accurately, it is simply not recognised as theory by the people writing the words. What appears and is experienced as pure or innocent description is always already informed by theory. I argued in the Introduction to this book that theory was 'inevitable': I am now obliged to argue that if theory is inevitable or inescapable then it must be present, in some way and at some level, in the material that relates to graphic design and photography. Consequently, I am now obliged to demonstrate where the theory is and what its nature is.

In her Introduction to *Fashion and Graphics*, for example, which can usefully be compared with Hebdige's treatment of graphics in the extract from his *Subculture* (see Chapter 24), Tamsin Blanchard openly admits that the book will be anecdotal. She says that it is 'dedicated to . . . telling the stories behind some of fashion's most famous labels' (2004: 11). This sounds as though it is an outright rejection of the analytical and the theoretical. However, she also makes use of a theory of communication and of what fashion is in this same introduction and in the chapters that follow it. While her theory of communication is unacknowledged and unexamined, it is not unsophisticated. So, although she refers to 'expression' and a 'visual language' (ibid.: 8), which might make one think of transmitting something from one place to another and which might remind one of Lurie's account of fashion, there is little sense of the sender/receiver model that was presented and critiqued in Part Five. Indeed, there is a sign that the theory of communication presupposed here would involve cultures and values. Blanchard says that a brand's graphic identity 'shows what it wants to belong to and talks to its customer with its chosen visual language' by finding 'an expression that suits its values' (ibid.). What it is that the graphic identity wants to 'belong to' is not clear, but 'belong' suggests that it might be a cultural group and the implicit suggestion that the brand's graphic identity constructs cultural membership is not unwelcome. Similarly, the implication that communication depends on a sharing of values – that one needs to find an expression that 'suits' one's own cultural values and those of the person or people one is communicating with – is far from the sender/

receiver model. Having said this, the suggestion that the brand 'talks to' the customer with 'its chosen visual language' sounds less like a conversation with someone than an imposition on someone. Thus, while the crudities of the sender/receiver model have largely been avoided here, and while there are suggestions of a more sophisticated theory of communication, there are still hints of communication as sending a message present and unexamined in Blanchard's text.

While there is no explicit definition of fashion provided in the Introduction, there is an implicit theory of fashion and fashion is understood to be a certain sort of thing. Fashion is 'not about cut and cloth, but about graphic design, packaging and communication' (Blanchard 2004: 7). Fashion, the 'product itself', takes a back seat in the account of fashion that is presented here and graphic design does all the driving. So, for example, a plain white T-shirt may sell for £5.99 or £59.99, depending on the label that is appended to it. And a white shirt from Comme des Garçons will be much the same as a white shirt from Hugo Boss; the design of each may be 'similar' or they may be indistinguishable. What makes the difference here is the message that is being communicated. A Comme des Garçons shirt will be attractive to an architect because of the 'message it is communicating', and a businessman will buy a Hugo Boss shirt because it 'speaks to him' (ibid.). The fit or homology between the architect and the CDG shirt and between the businessman and the Boss shirt are constructed and communicated by the graphic design, despite the facts that the shirts are 'similar' and the customers live in 'different worlds' (ibid.). Crucially, it is the graphic design, the label, the packaging and the advertising that enable the shirt to communicate something that these members of cultural groups will be interested in, thus overcoming the problems represented by the facts that the shirts may be very similar and that the cultural groups may be very different.

Erica Lennard's interest in the 'technical' details of the images she produces has already been noted. She writes:

> I was using my Leica and a 50mm lens. I always work in 35mm. I exposed for her face and overexposed because I wanted it bleached out. I diffuse black and white prints in the enlarger.
>
> (in Di Grappa (ed) 1981: 92)

Compared to Arthur Elgort, however, she has relatively little to say about the 'technical'. Elgort writes:

> For Balanchine, I used Ektachrome in a Nikon, and for myself, Tri-X in the Graflex. All the Graflex pictures that day were f/4 at 1/60th, shot hand-held. I overexpose and overdevelop in Ilford Microfin . . . Microfin is mixed 1:1 . . . I like a dense negative printed with an Arista cold head.
>
> (in Di Grappa (ed) 1981: 49)

Now, even supposing that one knows that Ektachrome is film and that Microfin 1:1 refers to mixing powdered developer, there is a lot of photographic 'jargon' and technical detail here. However, what seems to be happening here is that the photographers are using the technical to stand as shorthand for the cultural and what Barthes would call the connotational. Lennard gives a clue to this when she says that she exposes for the face and then overexposes, 'because I wanted it bleached out'. The 'bleached out' is an effect that will have a meaning within the culture or to the audience that the pictures are intended to be seen by. The technical instruction for this is to 'overexpose'. Similarly, the 'diffused' is an effect that will have certain predictable connotations to magazine editors and viewers: many editors don't like it because it obscures detail and many viewers do like it because it creates a romantic 'Wuthering Heights' effect, or connotation. Elgort's use of the Arista cold head refers to the fluorescent or 'cold' light and the resulting range of contrasts that are generated when using a particular Arista enlarger. Clearly, whether light is 'cold' or not is culturally dependent and thus the meaning will change from culture to culture. In this way what is apparently a purely technical concern with the paraphernalia of photography actually masks a wealth of cultural variables, and thus a range of ways in which meanings can be created and manipulated. There is in fact a cultural theory and a theory of meaning (Barthes' connotation) hidden in or behind the technical language used by these photographers: whether it is 'jargon' or not depends on whether the reader knows how to translate the technical into the cultural.

Bibliography

Barthes, R. (1990) *The Fashion System*, Berkeley: University of California Press.

Baudrillard, Jean (1981) *For a Critique of the Political Economy of the Sign*, St. Louis, Mo.: Telos Press.

Blandard, T. (2004) *Fashion and Graphics*, London: Laurence King.

Di Grappa, C. (ed.) (1981) *Fashion: Theory*, New York: Lustrum Press.

Falk, Pasi (1997) 'The Benetton–Toscani Effect: Testing the Limits of Conventional Advertising', in M. Nava, A. Blake, I. MacRury and B. Richards (eds) *Buy This Book: Studies in Advertising and Consumption*, London: Routledge.

Fashion Theory (2002) Vol. 6, Issue 1, Special Issue on Fashion and Photography.

Hamilton, E. and Cairns, H. (1961) *The Collected Dialogues of Plato*, Princeton: Princeton University Press.

Klein, Naomi (2000) *No Logo*, London: Flamingo.

Koenig, R. (1973) *The Restless Image: A Sociology of Fashion*, London: George Allen and Unwin Ltd.

Lipovetsky, G. (1994) *The Empire of Fashion: Dressing Modern Democracy*, Princeton: Princeton University Press.

Solomon-Godeau, A. (2004) 'Dressing Down', in *Artforum* (May): 193–5.

Taylor, John (1981) Review of Carol Di Grappa (ed) *Fashion: Theory*, New York: Lustrum Press, in *Ten-8*, 5/6 (Spring): 58.

Von Wangenheim, Chris (1981) Essay in Carol Di Grappa (ed.) *Fashion: Theory*, New York: Lustrum Press.

Chapter 40

Roland Barthes

FASHION PHOTOGRAPHY

[. . .]

PHOTOGRAPHING THE FASHION SIGNIFIER (i.e., the garment) poses problems of method which were set aside at the outset of the
analysis. Yet Fashion (and this is increasingly the case) photographs not only its
signifiers, but its signifieds as well, at least insofar as they are drawn from the "world"
(*A* ensembles). Here we shall say a word about photographing Fashion's worldly
signifieds, in order to complete the observations relating to the rhetoric of the
signified.

In Fashion photography, the world is usually photographed as a decor, a background or a scene, in short, as a theater. The theater of Fashion is always thematic: an
idea (or, more precisely, a word) is varied through a series of examples or analogies.
For example, using *Ivanhoe* as theme, the decor develops Scottish, romantic, and
medieval variations: the branches of naked shrubs, the wall of an ancient, a ruined
castle, a postern gate and a moat; this is the tartan skirt. The travel cloak for
countries where the cold is misty and damp? The Gare du Nord, the Flèche d'Or,
the docks, slag heaps, a ferryboat. Recourse to these signifying ensembles is a very
rudimentary process: the association of ideas. *The sun* evokes *cactuses, dark night*
evokes *bronze statues, mohair* evokes *sheep, fur* evokes *wild beasts* and *wild beasts* evoke *a
cage:* we'll show a woman in fur behind heavy bars. And what about *reversible* clothes?
Playing cards, etc.

The theater of meaning can assume two different tones here: it can aim at the
"poetic," insofar as the "poetic" is an association of ideas; Fashion thus tries to
present associations of substances, to establish plastic or coenesthetic equivalences:
for example, it will associate knitwear, autumn, flocks of sheep, and the wood of a
farm cart; in these poetic chains, the signified is always present (autumn, the country

weekend), but it is diffused through a homogeneous substance, consisting of wool, wood, and chilliness—concepts and materials mixed together; it could be said that Fashion aims at recapturing a certain homochrony of objects and ideas, that wool is made into wood, and wood into comfort, just as the Sunda Islands kallima hanging from a stem takes on the form and color of a dried leaf. At other times (and perhaps increasingly often), the associative tone becomes humorous, the association of ideas turns into simple wordplay: for the "Trapeze" line, models are put on trapezes, etc. Once again, within this style, we find the main opposition in Fashion between the serious (winter, autumn) and the gay (spring, summer).[1]

Within this signifying decor, a woman seems to live: the wearer of the garment. Increasingly, the magazine substitutes a garment-in-action for the inert presentation of the signifier:[2] the subject is provided with a certain transitive attitude; at least the subject displays the more spectacular signs of a certain transitivity: this is the "scene." Here Fashion has three styles at its disposal. One is objective, literal; travel is a woman bending over a road map; to visit France is to rest your elbows on an old stone wall in front of the gardens of Albi; motherhood is picking up a little girl and hugging her. The second style is romantic, it turns the scene into a painted tableau; the "festival of white" is a woman in white in front of a lake bordered by green lawns, on which float two white swans ("*Poetic apparition*"); night is a woman in a white evening gown clasping a bronze statue in her arms. Here life receives the guarantee of Art, of a noble art sufficiently rhetorical to let it be understood that it is acting out beauty or dreams. The third style of the experienced scene is mockery; the woman is caught in an amusing attitude, or better still, a comic one; her pose, her expression are excessive, caricatural; she spreads her legs exaggeratedly, miming astonishment to the point of childishness, plays with outmoded accessories (an old car), hoisting herself up onto a pedestal like a statute, six hats stacked on her head, etc.: in short, she makes herself unreal by dint of mockery; this is the "mad," the "outrageous."[3]

What is the point of these protocols (poetic, romantic, or "outrageous")? Probably, and by a paradox which is merely apparent, to make Fashion's signifieds unreal. The province of these styles is always, in fact, a certain rhetoric: by putting its signifieds in quotation marks, so to speak, Fashion keeps its distance with regard to its own lexicon;[4] and thereby, by making its signified unreal, Fashion makes all the more real its signifier, i.e., the garment; through this compensatory economy, Fashion shifts the accommodation of its reader from an excessively but uselessly signifying background to the reality of the model, without, however, paralyzing that model in the rhetoric which it freezes on the margins of the scene. Here are two young women sharing a confidence; Fashion *signs* this signified (the sentimental, romantic young girl), by endowing one of the girls with a huge daisy; but thereby the signified, the world, *everything which is not the garment*, is exorcised, rid of all naturalism: nothing plausible remains but the garment. This exorcism is particularly active in the case of the "outrageous" style: here Fashion ultimately achieves that *disappointment* of meaning which we have seen defined in the world of *B* ensembles; the rhetoric is a distance, almost as much as denial is; Fashion effects that sort of shock to consciousness which suddenly gives the reader of signs the feeling of the mystery it deciphers; Fashion dissolves the myth of innocent signifieds, at the very moment it produces them; it attempts to substitute its artifice, i.e., its culture, for the false nature of things; it does not suppress meaning; it points to it with its finger.

Notes

1   What must be recovered (but who will teach it to us?) is the moment when winter became an ambiguous value, converted at times into a euphoric myth of home, of sweetness, and of comfort.

2   Actually, and this is what is strangest about Fashion photography, it is the woman who is "in action," not the garment; by a curious, entirely unreal distortion, the woman is caught at the climax of a movement, but the garment she wears remains motionless.

3   We were not able, within the framework of this study, to date the appearance of the "outrageous" in Fashion (which perhaps owes a good deal to a certain cinema). But it is certain that there is something revolutionary about it, insofar as it upsets the traditional Fashion taboos: Art and Woman (Woman is not a comic object).

4   This deliberate rhetoric is served by certain techniques: the excessive vagueness of a decor (as opposed to the clarity of the garment), enlarged like a photogenic dream; the improbable character of a movement (a leap frozen at its climax); the frontality of the model, who, in contempt of the conventions of the photographic pose, looks right in your eyes.

Chapter 41

Rosetta Brookes

FASHION PHOTOGRAPHY

The double-page spread: Helmut Newton, Guy Bourdin & Deborah Turbeville[1]

FASHION PHOTOGRAPHY has traditionally been regarded as the lightweight end of photographic practice. Its close relationship to an industry dependent on fast turnover makes the fashion photograph the transitory image par excellence. For historians and critics concerned with isolating 'great' photographic images and according them enduring significance, the commercial sphere of photography – the domain of the everyday image – represents the debasement of a conventional history of photography. Fashion advertising, in particular, is seen as negating the purity of the photographic image. We see the typical instead of the unique moment or event.

Given this prevalent critical and historical attitude, photographers are inclined to regard the 'captured' moment, as opposed to the contrived, stylised fashion shoot, as the most powerful point in the photographic process, the point at which the 'real' world reproduces itself. It is considered more creative than the mass-production processes which are seen as stamping the image with the uniformity and monotony of a commodity. This has prevented a serious investigation of those features of photography which have been produced by the combination of these processes. Although photography has its origins in the reproduction of nature by the machine, fashion and advertising photography must be studied, as Walter Benjamin recognised in the 1940s, as a process of the mechanical reproduction of the *contrived* image.

Throughout the 1980s and as the 1990s progress, fashion photography reflects more and more the segmentation of the fashion market-place – between mass production at one end and couture at the top. The blurred photographic image which rejects both the garment and the human body relies on the viewer's familiarity only with the designer's logo. This type of imagery is apparent in the promotional material of Yohji Yamomoto, Issey Miyake and Comme des Garçons and represents the upper end of the market, the 'creativity' of innovative couture design, which has potential for inclusion in a retrospective of 1980s and 1990s fashion photography in an art gallery. Whereas the proliferation of fashion advertising imagery, particularly in mail order catalogues, represents the mass-production end of the market-place and is most visible in the United States and Britain. American fashion photography has been little affected by more 'impressionistic' couture promotional material and has tended towards a 'lifestyle' imagery at both ends of the market. Here the viewer is required to identify with the purchasing of the garments rather than with the 'mood' or imagined potential of a Yamomoto collection. In mass-produced fashion advertising the image is not simply something we see; it is also something we 'wear'. The mass circulation of photographic images emphasises our awareness of self-image, and establishes a relationship between the particular and the typical.

Historians of photography have yet to do justice to this 'other' side of photography, possibly because it is too familiar. How does one look at photographic history and do justice to the processes which make the imagery typical and transitory, without selecting certain great images for their uniqueness? Changes in the nature of advertising and fashion photography necessitate an analysis, as well as a reappraisal of the caricatures of commercial photography. In the late 1970s and early 1980s there were dramatic changes in street photography; one of these aspects was the advent of the intimacy of the double-page spread.

Helmut Newton: manipulating stereotypes

Many see the 1970s representation of women in advertisements and especially in fashion photographs as a sort of masculine counter-offensive against the feminist consciousness of sexual stereotyping. That some of the significant individual contributions to this change happened to come from women in no way contradicts the claim that we saw then the development of the most perniciously sexist imagery yet encountered in the very core of sexual stereotyping, fashion photography.

Fashion photography in the 1970s in one sense produced nothing particularly new, no recognisable ideal like Jean Shrimpton or Twiggy in the 1960s. No particular look or appearance dominated the decade. Models seemed to come straight off an assembly line, representing a well-established physical norm. Most conspicuous was the repression of the model's distinctive individuality. She was wholly identified with her type, and seen not as an individual but as a model.

Stereotyping appeared to occur through suppression of the awareness of stereotype and by identification with the unique. The dynamics of fashion are embodied in the dualism of the world itself: fashion is what is general and typical, and yet it is also restricted and individual. Another peculiarity of the fashion photograph is that it is positioned on a threshold between two worlds: the consumer public and a mythic elite created in the utopia of the photograph as well as in the reality of a social group maintained by the fashion industry. One distinctive feature of fashion photography in the 1970s was that it converted utopias into dystopias.

The Helmut Newton model is one of a type, presented with the cold distance of a fleshy automaton, an extension of the technology which manipulates her and converts her into an object. Her veneer, which is at one with the gloss of the image, is to be flicked past and consumed in a moment. When the models strike up stereotyped poses, it is their deadness and frozen quality that strikes the viewer most strongly. The suggestion that they are frozen from a narrative continuum emphasises their strangeness and their discontinuous, fragmented nature, like film stills isolated from the cinematic flow.

Some have interpreted the strange, unusual settings in the work of Guy Bourdin and Helmut Newton (accidents and suicides) as the intrusion of a 'real world' into fashion photography. I think the reverse is true: it is because scenes of rape and death are commonplace in film and television that they can be treated with such distance in fashion photography. The aura of a particular kind of image, not the aura of the streets, is utilised. The artificiality of the image is emphasised. It is the deathly aura of mediation which encases everything in gloss. Newton's harsh colours, particularly his use of red and blue, make an association with poor quality reproduction, and thus invoke the limitations of the medium.

The emphasis upon the alien and artificial qualities of the picture makes a straightforward accusation of sexism problematic. All fashion photography, as the dominant currency of female images, could be seen as inherently sexist, manipulating exchanges between self and self-image. Yet this exchange is conventionally suppressed in the image of the moment, as it binds us to a model of femininity beyond existing norms, converting them into stereotypes. To recognise an image as a constraint, as a violation or repression of femininity, is to glimpse the demise of a stereotype going out of circulation. Each ascendant, newer image promises to escape those constraints. Accordingly, fashion photography seeks to suppress any sense of the strangeness of sexual typification, the conversion of femininity into a static type or commodity. The sense of stereotype must be reserved for hindsight in the succession of female images.

Newton manipulates existing stereotypes; their alienness is accentuated, and yet they are almost archetypes in their sexual dramas. The passive reclining woman offers no threat; she is completely malleable, a dummy made of flesh. The object of gratuitous sexual violence and violation, she offers no resistance, but because of this she becomes unreal, like de Sade's libertines. As the threat of personality diminishes, her image-like quality transports her beyond the eroticism of the living to the fetishism of the inanimate object. She fits into dominant stereotypes so completely that she ceases to connote any reality apart from the images which constitute her.

For example, by mixing dummies with live models in the French *Vogue* of June 1977 Newton makes impossible an unambiguous erotic response (from either sex). Instead, the picture sequence directs voyeuristic attention to the conversion point between object and flesh, and to their deathly reciprocity in the photographic act. While the photographs are erotic, the eroticism is a part of the process of mediation itself.

Many of Newton's more successful photographs hold a distanced engagement with the manipulative devices of fashion photography and with the process of mediation. Those alien features present in suppressed form in fashion photography and current images of women are exposed and made explicit. The image is presented as alien, as a threat rather than an invitation. Stereotypes are presented as falsity.

Guy Bourdin: 'a trap for the gaze'

In the post-war period the growth of mass production and reproduction was greeted in some circles as a threat to individuality and to the uniqueness of human activity. The horrific spectre of the totality of industrial culture was the familiar expression of a fear of what seemed inevitable as a result of consumer culture: the false universalisation and homogenisation of human experience. Theodor Adorno saw the stamp of the machine everywhere, reducing everything to a 'sameness', reflecting and reinforcing a sense of alienation in all aspects of private life and experience. As mass entertainment and advertising became more dominant, they increasingly levelled experience down to the 'lowest common denominator'. The threat of the culture industry was the production and reproduction of sameness in all spheres of cultural life. Adorno saw the media as part of a great machine serving to encompass, assimilate and absorb all opposition and all individual variation by acceding to the sameness of machine production.

Current cultural trends could be interpreted as posing quite the opposite threat: the loss of common cultural experience. The decentralisation of fringe cultures and the increase of minority opinions cannot be accounted for in the view which foresees the media industry triumphing in a uniformity of cultural experience. For Marcuse, writing in the same period as Adorno, avant-garde art as oppositional culture was depleted by absorption and assimilation into mainstream 'affirmative culture'. While this may seem prophetic in view of the current state of art, indifference to oppositional art is the result not of a depletion or assimilation of its meanings, but of its isolation. It appears as one cultural ghetto among many, with its own diminishing media stake. It is not that the values of a minority culture are distorted and absorbed into the mainstream, but that, on the contrary, they pose no threat at all.

The principle of negation itself, which avant-garde culture once represented, is now built into all spheres of cultural activity. Even disco music, a human expression – dance – aligned with the rhythm of the machine, is negated in groups like Kraftwerk, for whom the machine pulse which 'animates' disco dance is the object of morbid contemplation. It is not merely a 'progressive' extension of popular culture. What is incorporated is negation, which guarantees a sort of all-round authenticity. We can enjoy it either for itself, or alternatively for its parody of itself. Irony mediates our experience, our alienation. It is, however, no escape from it.

Tolerance of mechanised cultural products has risen to a higher level: an acceptance of the limitations of the medium in an engagement with the process of mediation. As Adorno and Horkheimer said: 'The triumph of advertising in the culture industry is that consumers feel compelled to buy and use its products though they see through them.'[2]

They could not, however, have predicted the peculiar route to this triumph. From the vantage point of the 1940s and 1950s when they were writing, it was difficult to imagine that a fashion photographer would ever have occasion to complain that his work was being censored by the machinery that Adorno predicted would incorporate cultural producers like Helmut Newton. Yet Newton's complaints about English *Vogue* are echoed by fashion photographers who have begun to talk about being 'given free rein' by magazines. When Guy Bourdin claims to be an artist, he is laying claim to a specific type of formal problem encountered with a particular kind of image in circulation. It is not so much that 'the double page is his canvas', but that the double page is *not* canvas that is the basis of the claim.

Canvas stands in antithesis to his material, to the texture of mechanical reproduction. In Bourdin's work, the double page is not the vehicle for communicating the image, but is a structure characteristic of a particular kind of encounter. He organises his images around the form of mechanical reproduction, around the divide of the double page and the turn of the page. In a fashion photograph in French *Vogue* of May 1978 the female voyeur/spectator figure is divided by the centrefold as she watches the almost symmetrical division of her reclining self-images. To turn the page is not only to open and close the spectacle of the fashion spread, but is also to cut up the figure with which we are spatially identified – to open and close her legs. The model is completely engulfed in the vertical divide as though by a mistake in binding, leaving the two legs isolated on facing pages.

At other times the double page becomes its own mirror. In a March 1976 French *Vogue* spread, a colour reproduction faces a black and white reproduction of almost the identical scene, as though frozen from successive moments. The process of reproduction itself is being reproduced. With these more dramatic formal devices, spatial relationships are set up within the picture which rebound upon the strangeness of our ordinary encounter with the double page, with the photograph and with the advertisement itself. In a photograph in French *Vogue*, May 1978, we are re-directed from the object (the product) to the spatial ambiguities of its setting, which jar with the expectations built into encounters with photographs and advertisements. Bourdin enhances the spatial strangeness of the conventional spread, to accentuate the alien quality of what is unfolded in that horizontal continuum and around the vertical division in the process of unfolding. This spread best exemplifies the division and alternation of shallow and deep spaces, which is used to juxtapose façade and depth, the frontality of the image with the three-dimensionality of the setting. Bourdin plays upon a hesitation in the spatial and temporal expectations of the double page, emphasising the alien manner in which both product and advertisement are positioned. Brechtian distancing techniques and the formalist 'exposure of the device' have become mainstream.

Bourdin's shoe advertisements provide a case in point. Without the manufacturer's name as caption, some would be unrecognisable either as advertisements or as having shoes as their subject. In a passing encounter with the image that the fashion magazine produces, it is profitable to exert the negative principle as a subversion of the neutrality of 'flicking through'. An arrest of vision is required at all costs – even at the expense of accentuating the alien quality of clothing itself. Our sense of puzzlement seeks double confirmation which is provided by the product name.

A 'trap for the gaze'[3] may be the solution to the immediate pressures of the market, but the implications of an increasing dependence upon an enlarging and increasingly autonomous advertising industry are less easy to estimate. The autonomy and independence from the product achieved by the product-image seems to promise a fulfilment of the totalitarian ideal of propaganda for its own sake. In 'The Work of Art in the Age of Mechanical Reproduction', Walter Benjamin saw fascism as the 'political consummation of [art for art's sake]', in an elevation of propaganda to a new level of aesthetic self-justification.[4] The emancipation of the image from its caption, and of the product-image from the product, means that the advertising image has become the pure imperative, not divisible into form and content, the pure veneer, the absolute facade for and of itself.

Deborah Turbeville

This new autonomy of the product-image has created another market sector. The collecting of ephemera, the practice of surrounding oneself with old and sometimes not so old advertisements, is now almost a cliché of middle-class lifestyles. A large business has established itself, selling not so much old as 'fixed' brand images. Mass production exploits the borderline between consuming and collecting, between connoisseurial attention to qualities, and the sheer neutrality of the product-image in the context of the cash exchange. Obsolete product-images have been revived as nostalgia for the mythical past of the product itself. There is an obsession with the conversion point between the currency and redundance of the image.

In the same way, fashion trends in the 1970s were predominantly nostalgic. Even more recent sci-fi and high-tech fashions came over as a nostalgia for older stereotypes of 'futurism', as a taming of images of technology which once were threatening. But recent forms of revivalism are not specific attachments to a specific bygone age; they are more romantic nostalgias for some 'essence' – peasant life or primitivism in the late 1960s, or some vague idea of Hollywood 1930s' glamour in the early 1970s. This nostalgic undercurrent has come to dominate and has almost caught up with itself: in 1989 the French haute-couture designer Martine Sitbon was showing pastiche 1970s' garments, the originals of which had themselves been pastiche recreations of 1940s' fashion.

Nostalgic attachment to the immediate past becomes an attachment to the process of turnover, a narcissistic identification with the alien qualities of one's own past. That point of self-awareness at the juncture of the up-to-the-minute and the out-of-date becomes an identification with the very process of mediation that fashion represents.

The photography of Helmut Newton and Guy Bourdin radiates a knowing self-awareness of fashion photography and its falsities. These photographers convey the sense of an impenetrable veneer, resistant to the very movement of stereotypes. In the work of one of the best women fashion photographers, Deborah Turbeville, a different sense of the alien nature of the image is represented as a sort of hesitation between self-images. In many ways her photographs are at variance with character-istics of the work of her male counterparts. For example, her models are not chosen for their identity with a stereotype, but usually for their divergence from the type or image which they appear to represent. At its best her work involves this hesitation between the image presented by the model and the image presented by the picture, although finally the meaning is always communicated by the latter. Conveying this uncomfortable relationship with the model's self-presented image pushes her towards portraiture, or her models towards acting. However, she is clearly not satisfied with communicating the strangeness of the female image through the illustrative neutrality of the photograph. In her book, *Wallflower*, her photographs are presented scratched, violated and montaged together.

In the foreword to this book she describes her photographs as:

> . . . like the women you see in them. A little out of balance with their surroundings, waiting anxiously for the right person to find them, and thinking perhaps that they are out of their time. They move forward clutching their past about them, as if the ground of the present may fall away.[5]

Perhaps they accede a little too easily to the automatic overlay of nostalgia resulting from the association of limited colour range with the faded photograph, or with the technical qualities of early photography. Her work seems unresolved, as she herself says: 'My pictures walk a tight rope . . . I am not a fashion photographer, I am not a photo-journalist, I am not a portraitist'.[6]

Whatever the viewer's opinion of the 'success' of her pictures, it is interesting that a photographer preoccupied with the kinds of self-image mass circulation produces should find the fashion spread the most accommodating site for her exploration, however provisional she may feel this to be.

Whether the recent dominance of the 'alien' fashion image is an extreme expression of the autonomy of fashion photography, whether this implies a distancing from the form of coercion which the fashion spread represents, whether it constitutes the elevation of the advertisement to a higher power and greater autonomy, or whether it is the beginning of a break up of that structure of representation, these questions have implications far beyond fashion alone.

Notes and references

1   This article (now revised) first appeared in *Camerawork*. I should like to acknowledge the writings of John Stezaker, especially his idea on stereotyping. I refer to 'Archetype and Stereotype', a paper delivered to the Photography Convention organised by the Department of Psychology at Southampton University, and to *Fragments*, published by the Photographers' Gallery, London.

2   Max Horkheimer and Theodor Adorno, 'The Culture Industry: Enlightenment as Mass Deception', in *The Dialectic of Enlightenment*, trans. John Cumming, London, 1973.

3   Jacques Lacan characterises all pictures as 'traps for the gaze', but the phrase is used in the context of a discussion of the use of distorted images to 'catch' the eye and maintain the engagement of the gaze.

4   Walter Benjamin, 'The Work of Art in the Age of Mechanical Reproduction', in *Illuminations*, trans. Harry Zohn, London, 1973, p. 244.

5   Deborah Turbeville, *Wallflower*, London, 1979, p. 1.

6   Ibid., p. 1.

Chapter 42

Erica Lennard

'DOING FASHION PHOTOGRAPHS'

WHAT I FIND INTRIGUING about doing fashion photographs is the idea that I am photographing a person, often a beautiful woman (even if the point now has become more and more reduced to the element of selling the clothes, perfume, etc.), and that I am still trying to make a photograph with the same aesthetic concerns that I bring to my own work.

The models I photograph are human beings with doubts about their beauty and who they are. In most fashion magazines, women look synthetic, unreal and unattainable. I try to work with girls who seem to have something beyond the perfect face and it is perhaps the rapport I have with them when I am shooting that helps to bring out that personal quality I look for. I am often very quiet, which surprises everyone since the classic idea of a shooting has always been loud music and lots of "Oh you look gorgeous, etc.," but I figure that they know they look good and I only try to direct their movements and make them relaxed enough to be natural. Still they sometimes ask "Do I look okay?" and that feeling of vulnerability is what I look for.

I like the hair and makeup to be as simple or unartificial as possible. There is always a team of people I feel best working with. I get ideas on how to pose models from looking at paintings, films and real life. It's difficult when you work with girls who have spent their time studying the pages of *Vogue* to see how to stand. I often have to ask them not to hunch their shoulders over and not to put one hip out. Those kinds of movements have nothing to do with the way people really stand. I am constantly saying to the models, "Why don't you fold your hands in front of you, or keep your feet together." Sometimes during a shooting I may look around the room and notice the way one of the editors is sitting and that will give me an idea about how the model can be.

I consider my fashion photography an extension of my own work as an artist. I started five years ago to do fashion, and for five years before that, I'd been photographing women for myself. I made books and exhibitions (which I continue to do). The reason I wanted to do fashion was that with the particular vision of women I have I thought it would be interesting to reach an audience outside of the traditional photo world habitues.

A picture in the *New York Times* for Bloomingdale's or in *Mademoiselle* influences a different kind of woman, perhaps to re-think an attitude about themselves, feelings they can relate to instead of the frozen hard sex-symbols habitually seen.

When I was growing up in California, we never looked at fashion or thought about style in the traditional sense. Since then I have lived in Paris and New York where women are conditioned to believe in the images presented to them in the magazines; fashion now is, of course, much more relaxed than it was in the fifties and sixties, and many magazines and designers I work with also agree with the idea of a more realistic and wearable, comfortable fashion and "look."

Everyone knows fashion is a business, but when I started, I was totally naive and romantic. I didn't really know anything about the procedure for getting jobs since I had never worked as an assistant. I used to go around to art directors with portraits of my friends. Even though I knew that these girls could be replaced by models, the magazines thought it would be great to give me a job if I could use my friends and were wary of having me do a real shooting. I had a hard time making a living in the beginning, as everyone does, I suppose, and for a while thought about being an assistant. But after seeing the first real fashion photographer who told me he preferred Japanese assistants because they worked the hardest and never complained, I decided I should just keep doing my own work.

About six months later, I went with my portfolio to *Elle* Magazine. At the time, in 1975, it was one of the most innovative magazines in Europe. The art director, Peter Knapp said, "You shouldn't be an assistant. You already have a style. Don't put together a fashion portfolio. Just keep doing what you're doing, because it's strong and even if you're not going to work, you shouldn't compromise."

It took about a year until I got my first assignment at *Elle*. One of the editors of *Elle* had been to China; it was a very important experience for her. It's a country where everybody dresses more or less the same way, the hair and makeup are simple and essential. Yet all the women seem to be beautiful and happy. She wanted to convey that idea without using Chinese clothes—just comfortable Western clothes. Originally they wanted me to use my friends as models but it didn't work out, so they found a young girl who later became a very well-known model. I shot these photographs at Versailles behind the gardens.

It was February and the sky was dark with clouds. It had been raining and the sun came out for a few moments. I had them look into the sun because I liked direct sunlight in my photographs. Maybe the magic of photography for me is how light can, at moments, transform reality. I don't want to lose that magic and be in a studio and say, okay, all these photographs will be controlled with artificial lights. I'd rather make a document of what happens in a room or a landscape at a point when light is falling a certain way and a model moves into it, or away from it. Technically I'm sure it is possible to re-create the quality of natural light but for me the element of mystery would be gone. I do all my pictures in available light. If it happens to be overcast, then I shoot in a soft, even light. If the sun happens to come out, then I shoot in contrasty sunlight. Late afternoon light is ideal. However, when I'm doing 8 photographs a day, it's impossible to wait until the end of the day to do everything.

I had wanted to photograph Dominique Sanda for a long time. In 1977, I was at the Cannes film festival on assignment for a magazine and she was there for her film "1900." She was extremely busy but through mutual friends she heard my photographs were good, so she agreed. I arrived at the hotel early so that I would have time to choose a location as I knew I would have very little time for the shooting. I walked around the lobby and decided to shoot on a stairway because the light was best for the kind of picture I wanted. When I went up to her room she said we could do it in the room, but I said I'd rather she came downstairs. She was wearing a dress designed for her by a friend in Paris, and the first thing she said to me when we got downstairs was, "You know, I'm really not photogenic."

I couldn't believe it. I had always thought how magnificent she was in films, and in person she had the same presence. I said that I was sure we could do a good photograph. She told me that when she's in front of a moving camera, it's completely different. She has her voice and her movement, and she can go through an action thinking about a part she's playing.

Throughout the whole session, she was insecure in front of the camera. At first she was standing and she seemed uncomfortable. She didn't know what to do with her hands. I had asked her to move into the area of the direct sunlight, then I asked her to sit down and lean against the bannister. Later, when I gave her the photograph, she asked me to come and photograph her again.

I was using my Leica and a 50mm lens. I always work in 35mm. I exposed for her face, and overexposed because I wanted it bleached out. I diffuse black and white prints in the enlarger, with a diffusion disc attached to the lens.

'The Nude' was the first job I did for *Italian Vogue*. The editor called me from Milan and asked for a beautiful nude. I chose the model and the hairdresser. We went to a friend's house and spent the afternoon doing the photograph. It was shot on a bed, with the afternoon light. The exposure was made for the highlights.

In many fashion photographs, you don't see the girl's face because she's looking away or the exposure is made for the dress. I burned in the sky and background, and dodged the face of 'The Girl on the Pier in Santa Margarita, Italy'. For this advertising shot, things were rather disorganized but that's normal in Italy. The dress was too big and the shoes were a pair she just happened to bring along, but the photograph worked well in the end. It has a kind of timeless quality that I like very much to evoke.

I went to Italy to do some photographs for Luciano Soprani for *Italian Vogue*. We drove to a seaside resort, 3½ hours from Milano, in an uncomfortable van and when we arrived, there was a terrible storm. We'd called before we left and, maybe being Italians they said, "Oh, the weather's beautiful, come down, it's wonderful." It was obvious that there had been storms there for weeks because the entire beach was devastated. I wanted to photograph on a clean, white, sandy beach with the ocean behind, but there were piles of wood and junk all over the place.

Everybody was upset and the editor said, "Let's go back to Milano," but I don't like to give up. I've never reshot a job and I've never been rained out or unable to shoot because of weather. You would think somebody who uses available light would have problems, but even in London in the rainy season, I always managed to do my jobs. So I said, "Let's stay."

The sky was gray, the clouds were dark, it was cold, but I said, "Let's just drive along and try to find a place where we can shoot." I found these little beach houses, and then all of a sudden the sun broke through low, heavy clouds and it was an extraordinary moment. Everybody got dressed quickly and I shot the whole series in 45 minutes, the time the sun stayed out.

The last photograph was taken after the clouds came back. The light was low and it was freezing but I wanted to finish. I found a place that was sheltered behind the beach cabanas and my brave models went back there. The wind was blowing hard and it gave the photograph an animate quality—the hair and clothes and everything was moving. I told one girl to look away and the other one to put her head down.

I shot it with a Leica and a 50mm lens. The print is diffused. The client was enthusiastic about the photographs, perhaps because the photographs gave the clothes the kind of personality and atmosphere they needed.

I used to diffuse all my photographs, but unfortunately reproduction in magazines is very bad. When there are details on a black dress, they melt away because the ink isn't controlled in the printing. I like the blending effect but editors sometimes worry about seeing detail on clothes.

I used to develop all my film and print all my photographs myself. But now, when I shoot 50 rolls of film on a job and need to have the film the next day, I'm too exhausted to go into the darkroom all night. Actually, the labs know the way I want my negatives. I think the problem is more in the printing than developing the negative. Sometimes I end up making the prints to retain certain qualities in the sky and skin tones.

In Europe, magazines seem to give you complete freedom. They let you choose your models, locations, etc. The editor's job is essentially to choose the clothes, then to oversee the shooting and make sure the girl's clothes and hair will suit their audience.

In America, the editors are more concerned about maintaining a certain kind of look. Models are chosen from a small group of girls who are seen all the time in their magazines. Sometimes when I arrive for a job the editors and models are shocked. The fact that I'm a woman, look young and often work without an assistant and lots of equipment, doesn't inspire a tremendous amount of confidence.

For the last two years, I've been working with Perry Ellis, a New York designer whose clothes have an original and timeless quality. We seem to have a similar sensibility about beauty and how it feels to wear clothes. His clothes do inspire me and I re-interpret the moods that they seem to express. He knows very well what he wants but he always gives me complete freedom when I do his ads. Perry gives me the clothes and sketches of the way the outfits are put together and says, "Come back with a beautiful photograph." The kind of natural quality in the light and attitude of the girl in my pictures seems to be an ideal marriage with his designs. They are the kind of clothes I like to wear.

The photograph from his collection of 1979 has a Wuthering Heights kind of feeling for me. But when I went to do the shooting I did not have a specific image in mind. I knew that I wanted to shoot it in a forest or a garden so I went to Fort Tryon Park, being in New York at the time. It was one of the first warm days of spring and I went with Audrey Matson, a model I work with often. We chose this one because of the feeling of movement, going forward and looking back which seemed to reflect the idea of the collection.

Figure 42.1 The Girl on the Pier, Santa Margarita, Italy, 1979

Figure 42.2 Audrey, Deauville, 1980

Figure 42.3 Untitled

Chapter 43

Tamsin Blanchard

INTRODUCTION/ABOUD SODANO AND PAUL SMITH

IT IS JUST A TINY RECTANGLE of fabric, sewn into the back of a jacket. But what power it holds. Tied up in that little label is money, aspiration, sex appeal and status. Unpick it, and the jacket might as well be worthless. The label has become its own form of currency. It is the maker's mark: the reason the garment was sold in the first place. In the fashion industry, it is all about labels, branding and identity. A simple label can mean the difference between a plain, white T-shirt selling for £5.99 or £59.99.

Increasingly, fashion brands rely on packaging and presentation rather than the product itself. The brand image defines a particular aspiration or set of references that attract the consumer to choose one polo shirt, one pair of jeans or a particular pair of trainers over another. There comes a point when designer clothing is not about cut and cloth, but about graphic design, packaging and communication, whether it is a rubber band sewn into collar and stamped with John Galliano in Gothic script, or a catalogue for Yohji Yamamoto, photographed by Inez van Lamsweerde and Vinoodh Matadin and art directed by M/M (Paris), a collector's item in its own right, but seen only by a chosen few within the fashion industry. Not surprisingly, the graphic designer responsible for the look of a label or the art direction of the ad campaign has taken on a status and power within the fashion industry that was unheard of in the early 1980s.

Fashion companies have become mini publishing empires, often employing their own graphic-design teams, and producing not just invitations to fashion shows, but 'look books', catalogues, press mail-outs, magazines, advertising and even Christmas cards. But this is all a relatively new phenomenon. And much of the material, although highly sophisticated, expensive to produce, exquisitely designed and highly influential, is totally ephemeral, and thrown away without another thought.

British maverick Peter Saville was one of the pioneers who paved the way for the current generation of fashion graphics. 'Be careful what you wish for' is his motto; he intends to blow it up large in neon, and hang it on his Clerkenwell studio wall. As a young graduate in post-punk, bombed-out Manchester, he wished for a time when the world would be a better place because of the way it was designed. It would look better; it would work better. Twenty-five years later, the landscape not just of Manchester, but of the whole consumer universe has changed beyond recognition. It has been designed. In Saville's opinion, it has gone too far. It has been over-designed, given a lick of gloss just for the sake of it. Things don't necessarily look better. They certainly don't necessarily work any better. But one thing is for sure: they have been designed.

In the mid-1980s, when Saville began collaborating with photographer Nick Knight and creative director Marc Ascoli on the advertising and imagery for Yohji Yamamoto, the concept of a graphic designer working on a fashion brand – creating layouts of images for brochures to be sent to press and buyers, deciding on the size and position of a logo, or simply editing a set of pictures – was something quite new. When Nick Knight requested that Saville work on the Yamamoto project with him, the idea was met with some degree of mystification. Nobody was quite sure what exactly a graphic designer would do. But the collaboration between Knight and Saville was to prove groundbreaking. 'When the Yohji catalogues appeared on the scene in autumn/winter 1986, they had a really profound effect,' remembers Saville. 'They became collected immediately because they were different. When you look back at them now, they are actually a little bit naive by contemporary graphic standards.'

The fashion industry is one of the most overcrowded and competitive industries. What makes one designer's white shirt stand out from another's is not necessarily the design. An architect might be attracted to a shirt by Comme des Garçons because of the message it is communicating to him or her. The way that message is communicated is carefully coded in language he will understand, through the advertising, the label, the packaging, the store design – it's a matter of presentation rather than fashion. Likewise, a businessman might buy his shirt from Hugo Boss because the logo speaks to him. It is confident, direct and has a very clear, corporate message. However similar the shirts may be, their customers live in totally different worlds.

Graphics have become an integral part of any fashion house; in some cases, the graphic designer or art director is also the fashion designer. For Giorgio Armani, he is the all-seeing eye: both art director and fashion director. 'A designer label is his or her business card,' he says. 'It not only reflects the spirit and integrity of each collection; it also expresses the philosophy and character of the line to the customer. The final product is the most important part of the package, but a label and logo secures a recognizable identity. The graphic identity is a natural extension to what my products are trying to express and reflect.'

In many cases, the graphic designer takes on a role as important – if not more important – than the fashion designer. As creative director of Burberry, Fabien Baron was closely involved in many aspects of the British brand's relaunch at the end of the 1990s. Working alongside managing director Rose Marie Bravo, he signalled the new direction of the brand by not only modernizing the logo (losing the confusing apostrophe in the process), but by creating an advertising campaign before there was any new product to advertise. His first ads for the brand, working with the photographer Mario Testino and promoting a certain English eccentricity and humour, were to set the tone for the rest of the highly successful turnaround from purveyor of old-fashioned raincoats to dynamic, high-fashion, luxury label.

The Belgian designer Walter Van Beirendonck has always incorporated graphics into his fashion, both for his own labels and for the streetwear brand, W&LT, with the help of Paul Boudens, the Antwerp-based graphic artist who has worked with many of the new wave of Belgian designers since the late 1980s. Van Beirendonck sees graphics and fashion as so inseparable as to include graphics as part of the fashion degree for students at the prestigious Antwerp Academy of Fine Art. 'It is an important "first presentation" to the real world,' he says. 'A graphic communication identity is important because it is the impression and language between designer and public.'

When Stella McCartney launched her own label under the Gucci umbrella in 2002, she worked with Wink Media – the multi-disciplinary creative agency set up in London by Tyler Brulé in 1998 – to define her identity as a graphic logo. Her debut show was held in March 2002, at the Ecole des Beaux Arts in Paris. It was as though she were starting with a blank canvas; the catwalk was bright white and her new logo, her name apparently punched out as a series of dots, was emblazoned across it in silver. Although the assembled press and buyers were very familiar with Stella McCartney's name, this was the first time they would see a fully-fledged collection bearing it.

Erik Torstensson is one of a team of art directors at Wink Media. Wink offers a wide range of creative services, including advertising, brand development and corporate identity. But Stella McCartney was a unique project. 'We were creating a new brand for a very well-known designer, so it was already loaded with values and perceptions, which made it very interesting but also much more demanding, as the expectations on Stella launching her own label were very high.' His job was to create a brand image for a designer who already had a very strong brand image of her own. Everybody knew who Stella McCartney was, but nobody knew what her fashion label looked like. The process was a collaboration between Torstensson, McCartney and typeface designer Richard Hart. 'We worked very closely with Stella to explore different directions based on her personal style and professional requirements,' says Torstensson. 'We would often visit Stello's studio to study the fabrics and the designs so we could get a very clear idea of the collection – and of course the designer behind it.' The initial brief was to create a logotype for the launch of her own-name brand. 'The logo had not only to convey a sense of luxury but also the freshness, quality, charm and edge that are embodied in the spirit of Stella McCartney's designs.' It was also important that the logo would have longevity, versatility and accessibility to different markets.' McCartney might be based in London, but Gucci is an international luxury-goods group and the new label had to have the same appeal in Dubai as New York, Sydney or Tokyo.

A brand's graphic identity is how it expresses itself, shows what it wants to belong to and talks to its customer with its chosen visual language. The graphic identity will be applied to everything that the brand uses so it is vital to find an expression that suits its values. If your brand has a well-produced and managed graphic identity or design strategy, it will pay off tenfold. A badly managed and implemented corporate identity can prove to be very expensive and damaging. The responsibility, therefore, is on the designer to get it right. An identity for a brand like Stella McCartney must be as confident and sure of itself as the woman herself.

For any fashion house, a well-designed, universally recognized logo is the key to commercial success. The logo becomes its own currency, whether printed on a T-shirt, embossed on a wallet, packaged around a face cream or, of course, sewn into an item of clothing. No one has proved this better than Yves Saint Laurent, who has one of the most famous and enduring logos in fashion history. He was one of the first to turn to a graphic artist for help in translating the abstract idea of a new fashion house into a logo. Yves Saint Laurent had met A.M. Cassandre through his previous employer, Christian Dior, and he approached the old master (who was already well known for his stylish, graphic posters for Dubonnet and the *Normandie* ocean liner) in the late 1950s to create his own logo. It is said to have taken just a few minutes for Cassandre to sketch the three letters Y, S and L into their elegant, interlocking shape. Those three letters, beautifully and timelessly drawn, were to form the basis of one of the most prestigious and lucrative fashion houses ever. Even people who have never owned a Saint Laurent handkerchief, let alone a piece of *haute couture*, could draw the logo from memory.

Alice Rawsthorn, director of the Design Museum in London and author of *Yves Saint Laurent – A Biography*, says the YSL logo is successful because it is a beautiful piece of lettering. 'It is exquisitely drawn in an instantly recognizable but distinctive style. Also, its central characteristics – elegance and a sleek sensuality – fuse perfectly with those of the brand and it has been reproduced more or less consistently over the years. Those are the generic characteristics of any classic logo and the YSL symbol encapsulates them perfectly.' The logo is so strong, that when the Gucci Group took control of the brand in 2000, it was one of the few things that was not updated. 'Even a visual obsessive like Tom Ford has restrained himself to making just a few tiny tweaks since the Gucci Group took control of YSL,' says Rawsthorn. 'Everything else about the company has changed – but not the logo.'

Fabien Baron is not surprised that Tom Ford didn't change the logo: 'I would not have changed it either. Cassandre was one of the best graphic designers in the world. He was an artist. That logo can stay forever. It's beautiful. It's the lettering, the intricacy of the logo, the way the letters are stacked up. It's very elegant and very French with a sense of history. Why change it if it works? It would be like going to Egypt and changing the pyramids.'

It was in the 1980s, however, that fashion houses began to take graphic design and art direction seriously. Yohji Yamamoto's creative director, Marc Ascoli, was persuaded into hiring Peter Saville by Nick Knight, a photographer who had come to his attention after a series of 100 portraits of the 1980s for *i-D* magazine. Saville's work with the Manchester band Joy Division impressed Ascoli. 'Marc had the confidence in the mid-1980s to break new ground and break new photographers,' says Saville. 'Nick had never shot fashion before, his portraits for *i-D* were as close as he'd come to the style magazine world. But Marc would take a sports photographer if he wanted to because he knows he could put the clothes in front of the photographer and say just take the picture. That's how he started with Nick – he did a men's shoot. As I understand it, during the shoot, Nick asked who would be doing the graphics. Apparently Marc said, 'I don't know. What is the graphics?' He didn't really know what Nick meant. There was not a close relationship of any sort between graphic designer and fashion.'

The graphic designer was, however, already well-established in the music business. Stephanie Nash and Anthony Michael, who formed the design agency Michael Nash after they graduated from St martins in the early 1980s, had made a name for themselves in the music industry long before they began their work with designers such as John Galliano, Alexander McQueen and Marc Jacobs. 'I think we started off doing music – including work for Neneh Cherry and Massive Attack – because in the early Eighties, there wasn't any fashion to be done,' says Nash. 'If somebody makes music and they have made a record then you have a respect for that music. You have got to be their graphic designer in the same way that if you've made a frock, you've got to graphically represent that brand and that frock. You have got to do the same for the musician.

I suppose we were doing it in a fashion, corporate identity kind of way and I think music sits in the middle and you do all these photo sessions and get heavily involved with the hairstyling and makeup. Despite the fact that they were at St Martin's School of Art around the same time as John Galliano, and remember him playing with Letraset for his logo in the college library, fashion and graphics students were not encouraged to work together. Nowadays it seems impossible to have one without the other. 'It would have been a great experience doing the final show material for one of the students' shows.' It was not until almost twenty years later that their paths crossed once more and Michael Nash Associates was commissioned to work on a new brand identity and packaging for Galliano, to coincide with the opening of the designer's first store.

Michàel Amzalag and Mathias Augustyniak, the French designers who formed the creative partnership M/M (Paris) in 1991, also work with both music and fashion. It is possible to trace the evolution between their 2001 cover for Björk's 'Hidden Place' single and their two short but impactful seasons worth of advertising images for Calvin Klein. The two clients could not be further apart – one is fairly specialist, artistic and independent and the other mass – market and corporate – but their markets are surprisingly similar. Fashion houses, no matter how mainstream, need to keep a step ahead if they are to maintain their credibility. M/M (Paris), with their playful, hands-on techniques, including drawing over images and scratching into photographs, have been incredibly influential in the late 1990s and into the new millennium. Their approach is the antithesis to that of Baron & Baron, who has had a long-standing, close, working relationship with Calvin Klein. Baron's work for the company has always been clean, slick and utterly consistent. But M/M (Paris) had a completely different approach.

'The whole set-up needed a shake-up,' says Amzalag. They like to work in bold statements rather than subtle nuances. Their way of making people sit up and take notice of the brand again – of injecting it with some credibility and freshness – was to take the Calvin Klein logo, the very core of the fashion empire, and rip it up and start again. They re-drew it, as a schoolkid might make a doodle in his exercise book. They felt the Calvin Klein brand had become schizophrenic and needed to have a single stamp to bring all the strands back together again. 'The character of Calvin Klein had become like a ghost,' they say. They wanted the logo to look as though someone had redrawn it from memory. The ads were no longer about the clothes. They were about rebranding a brand that had become so familiar it was almost invisible.

Previously, M/M (Paris) had worked for Yohji Yamamoto. In 1994 they were asked to design ads for the Y's diffusion range for which Peter Saville had drawn the logo. They were, of course, aware of Saville's previous work for the label, and their own work became an evolution of that. 'Peter Saville was one of the first modern art directors,' they say. 'He understood that graphic design is about ideas. He is fed by different fields of creativity.'

At their best, graphic designers have brought to the fashion industry another set of eyes, a fresh perspective and an uncompromising vision. At worst, they are simply another marketing tool, a way for the designer to create a visual peg on which to hang sales of perfumes, face creams, scarves and T-shirts. In the early 1990s, when Saville's contract with Yohji Yamamoto came to an end, he thought there was nowhere else to go in the fashion industry, that it had become a dead end. 'As we got to the end of the Eighties it all seemed really stupid and unnecessary, and there was a recession and it was nonsense really,' says Saville. 'At the time, I said, fashion clients are never going to pay a grand a day. I wrote the fashion business off as a new business area for graphic design. I just couldn't see it happening.' But of course, the domino effect had only just begun. A whole new generation of graphic designers – and fashion designers – had been studiously collecting those Yohji Yamamoto catalogues, as well as *Six*, the ground-breaking magazine published by Comme des Garçons which was one of the defining moments of the fusion between fashion and graphics. 'By the time we got to the mid-1990s, I looked back and reconvened with fashion to see that, oh!, they've embraced the graphic element big time,' says Saville. Fashion designers themselves – the ones who were just starting out and still couldn't afford to pay a graphic designer – were even having a go. 'I looked at the scene in the mid-1990s and fashion had really embraced graphics,' he says. But perhaps it has gone too far. The design has overtaken the content. Although he says it is what he wished for, Saville confesses that he didn't really want it to turn out like this. 'Design is the new advertising. It's the insidious influence. It was better when it was a form of rebellion, when you had to fight with business. Now it's the other way round. It's entirely superficial. The result of it all is that design loses its credibility, its truth. Rather than design communicating a certain integrity, it begins to be the opposite. If it looks good, don't trust it.'

The whole process has certainly speeded up, and graphic designers are treated much the same as photographers are: with a certain awe and reverence, but also often with the same short shelf-life of a few seasons only. As the fashion industry grows and grows, each company fighting for its slice of the action, what they are saying becomes less important than how they are saying it. There is a conflict of power between fashion and graphics designer. 'What is more powerful,' asks Mathias Augustyniak of M/M (Paris), 'the image or the object?' Presentation is in danger of becoming everything.

Nevertheless, what is remarkable is that fashion graphics have become a genre all their own, often existing in their own private universe occupied by the fashion industry and rarely seeing the light of a day beyond that. 'Many times, there are images that could have several lives,' agrees Michael Amzaiag. 'In fashion, once you've seen it, it's dead, which I think is stupid because it's not dead. If you are a fashion addict, the idea is to have several cupboards and then you store your old clothing, and then do some kind of rotation – you wait ten years or five years, and pull it out again. It's just a matter of shifting things. Of course you don't wear it with the same shoes.'

So in the spirit of the true fashion addict, this book is dedicated to airing some of the fashion graphics that deserve a life longer than a single season, and telling the stories behind some of fashion's most famous labels.

[. . .]

Alan Aboud began his relationship with Paul Smith in 1989, when he was still a student at Saint Martins School of Art in London's Covent Garden, next door to Paul Smith's offices. 'They were looking for a freelancer at the time. The head buyer came to the show and shortlisted about ten of us', he remembers. Aboud got the job. The same year, he and his college friend. Sandro Sodano, went into business together and formed Aboud Sodano. Paul Smith was their first client, and he has remained a client ever since. At the time, there was just the main line collection and the jeans line. Aboud started working two to three days a week. 'I've grown with them, he says. It's quite a unique partnership. In a way I'm part of the furniture. I'm the art director, but I'm also the client.'

'We only used real people – i.e. "non models" – for the first two to three years', he says. 'It was quite a daring thing to do at the time. We instigated it. One of our failings is that we've moved on from good ideas too quickly.' Strategic ad placement gives the illusion that the ad spend is more than it is. The relationship between Aboud and Smith is key to the longevity of their partnership. It took him several years before he gained Smith's trust completely, but over the years he has grown to understand both Smith himself and the way he runs the company. Paul Smith is still independently owned and the designer has resisted pressure to sell to bigger conglomerates. He is very hands-on. It is typical that he chooses to remain working with Aboud rather than with a big agency. 'He'll choose absolutely the wrong person to work with', says Aboud who never intended to work in fashion. But somehow it works.

At college Aboud was always more interested in typography. Sandro Sodano concentrated on photography and has shot many of the campaigns with Aboud over the years. 'Sandro and I have a very loose business partnership,' says Aboud, 'whereby we both do individual projects with respective photographers and art directors, and then come together on other projects.' He will use Sodano if he is right for the job, but will equally use another photographer if he is better equipped for a particular shoot.

'You really need to know how the company works. People think Paul is like a child and that he likes a laugh. But he's more childlike than childish. People can get it so wrong with him. In reality he's very knowledgeable about photography, design and art. He's a very complex character. I'm lucky that I've grown to know him well.' They meet every couple of weeks to discuss everything from the carrier bags to the advertising – anything to do with the image of the company. The meetings between Smith, Aboud, the creative director, Häkan Rosenius, and womenswear designer, Sandra Hill, are informal. It is very different to the way Aboud works with other companies like H&M and Levis, which is more structured and purely business.

Figure 43.1 Paul Smith labels (art direction Alan Aboud)

Figure 43.2 Paul Smith bag campaign, 1997 (design and art direction Alan Aboud, photography Sandro Sodano)

'He holds off from cashing in', says Aboud of Smith. And in return, Aboud – as an idealist more than a capitalist – has relative creative freedom within the Paul Smith universe that he has helped define. 'You have to be more resourceful with a limited budget. One single H&M campaign (which changes every three weeks) would be the equivalent of a whole season at Paul Smith. These days, his job involves finding ways to integrate the many strands of the Paul Smith empire – the main line, PS, watches, bags, shoes, jeans and fragrance. 'We do stuff on a whim and a hunch', says Aboud. And it works: it is not design by committee or led by market research.

When Aboud began working at Paul Smith, the signature logo was already in place. 'We redrew the logo, and refined it slightly', says Aboud. Before that, it was simply a photocopy that was faxed around. It was not properly defined. Surprisingly enough, it is not the designer's actual signature. 'It was a friend of his in Nottingham in the 1970s who drew Paul Smith for him – probably on the back of a cigarette packet or something', says Aboud. Over the years it has become Smith's own signature. His logo has become his hand-writing rather than the other way round. 'In the beginning we wanted to change it just for the sake of it. But if you've got a recognizable signature and it ain't broken, don't fix it. It's quite a tricky logo. It can look dreadful in terms of scale. It looks good small but on a large scale it is difficult to control.'

Perhaps the single most memorable thing that Aboud has done with the Paul Smith branding has been to introduce the signature multicoloured stripes. They first appeared on show invites for 1996 and then on bags in 1998. He wanted to change the carrier bag design because he felt that it was dull and not reflective of the vibrant Paul Smith collections. So he transformed it from grey with a black logo to a carnival of stripes. 'We took inspiration from a textile print in the archive', he says.

Figure 43.3 Paul Smith Fragrance 2000 (design Sophie Hicks, Alan Aboud, Maxine Law)

'It was based on a Bridget Riley style painting. I loved it. Everything we had before was grey, which was a bizarre anomaly for a designer who was so known for his use of colour. Since then, everyone's got them. It's incredible. They're everywhere.'

The original straight stripe pattern, and its sister swirly stripe for women, has not only been used on the clothing itself, but by other fashion houses, department stores. Channel 4 and Swatch. 'The final straw is the Euro flag,' says Aboud. The Dutch architect, Rem Koolhaas, has produced a stripy flag that *Creative Review* magazine connected to Aboud's bag for Paul Smith rather than the united colours of

Europe. 'Its great that it's recognizable as ours, but not so great that it's copied and you don't make anything out of what you've done', says Aboud. The company decided to stick with it and weather the storm.

Figure 43.4 Paul Smith women's stripe bag, 1999 (art direction Alan Aboud, design Maxine Law)

Figure 43.5 Paul Smith Eau Extreme fragrance bottles, 2002 (art direction Alan Aboud, design Maxine Law)

PART TWELVE

Fashion, fetish and the erotic

THE CONCEPTUAL RELATIONS between fashion, the erotic and the fetish have become so complex and so confused that they are often used as though they were synonyms of each other. Both the erotic and the fetish are commonly understood to be that which tends to arouse sexual desire and fashion is routinely described as though its only function is to arouse sexual desire. It is believed to do this predominantly via the senses of sight and touch, although smell (see Freud 1953: 155) and sometimes hearing and taste are also appealed to.

This complexity and confusion is perhaps not surprising, given that the words 'fashion' and 'fetish' share the same Latin etymological root. Both words come to us via the Latin 'facticium' (meaning 'artificial'), from the original 'facere', which means 'to make'. The term 'fetish' is used in both economics and anthropology in senses that are not so different from the original Latin sense. In anthropology, for example, it refers to a made or constructed item that is believed to be imbued with divine or other powers. In economics, as was seen in Part Eight, fetishisation is what happens to a product or commodity, a made item, under capitalist economic conditions. And in psychoanalysis, fetishism is also something that happens to objects; people fetishise objects or parts of objects. It seems worth while to try to separate two aspects of the fetish here. First, there is the sense of fetish as 'made object' or 'something made'. This is common to the Latin root, economics, anthropology and psychoanalysis. In economics, the thing that is made is the commodity; in anthropology, it is the fetish object; and in psychoanalysis it is an object or item that is associated with a particular psychological episode. Second, there is the sense of 'special' powers accruing or being ascribed to that made object. This is not found in the Latin root, but phenomena that could be called 'special powers' are discernible in economic, psychoanalytic and anthropological versions of fetishism. In economics the special power is that the commodity stands for or represents social relations; in anthropology the special power is the power of a god or gods, and in psychoanalysis the special power enables the subject to establish satisfactory sexual relations.

The word 'erotic' derives from 'eros', an Ancient Greek noun meaning sexual desire, and 'Eros', the name of the Ancient Greek god of love and sexual desire. In Freudian psychoanalysis, eros is a productive, creative and universally animating force (contrasted in his later work with thanatos, the death drive or desire for oblivion). Indeed, Freud suggests that the 'enlarged' notion of sexuality with which psychoanalysis deals closely resembles the notion of Eros that is found in the works of Plato (Preface to the 4th edition of the 'Three Essays on Sexuality': Freud 1953: 134). Platonic eros was a spiritual/philosophical, aesthetic and bodily energy that, handled correctly, could facilitate the pursuit of the good, the beautiful and the true through the human world of the City and on to Heaven. It may be thought of as a generalised, eroticised motive force.

Writing in 1905, Freud suggests that a fetish is one of the 'deviations in respect of the sexual aim' (1953: 149) in which an 'unsuitable' substitute for the sexual object is made (ibid.: 153). The 'normal sexual aim' is understood to be copulation (ibid.: 149). Deviations from this aim include perversions, and there are two forms of perversion. The first form consists in sexual activities that 'extend in an anatomical sense' beyond those bodily parts designed for sexual union; the second form consists in sexual activities that 'linger over' any intermediate stages on the way to sexual union (ibid.: 150). He also says that a degree of fetishism is present in 'normal love', especially if the course of that love runs less than smoothly (ibid.: 154). These unsuitable substitutes for the sexual object may be parts of the body (metonyms) or inanimate objects that bear some relation to the person they replace (synechdoches), such as pieces of clothing for example. At this point, Freud says that 'such substitutes are with some justice likened to the fetishes in which savages believe that their gods are embodied' (ibid.). There are also cases of fetishism in which the sexual object must 'fulfil a fetishistic condition', such as a particular hair-colouring or item of clothing, if the sexual aim is to be attained (ibid.: 153). Later, in the 1927 essay 'Fetishism', (Chapter 45 in this volume), the analysis is more complicated and Freud suggests that a fetish is now explicitly 'a substitute for the woman's (the mother's) penis that the little boy once believed in and . . . does not want to give up' (1953: 352). The fetish now becomes a way of negotiating the experience of that realisation and enabling sexual activity to continue.

James Laver (1969) provides us with another definition of the fetish and with an account of the so-called 'shifting erogenous zone'. Following Binet (and Lombroso, Krafft-Ebing and Havelock Ellis), Laver suggests that erotic fetishism is 'the tendency whereby sexual attraction is unduly exerted by some special part or peculiarity of the body or by some inanimate object which has become associated with it' (1969: 112). It will be noted that this definition is closer to Freud's 1905 account and slightly different from that proposed by Freud in 1927, and the difference is enlarged by Laver when he emphasises Havelock Ellis's account of the fetish as some object that is on the periphery or even outside of a 'normal' and 'healthy' love (1969: 112). In the essay in this section, Freud suggests that fetishism is a necessary part of the process in which women become 'tolerable as sexual objects' (1953: 154) to non-homosexual men. To this extent all heterosexual men must be fetishists, and following Laver, what we might want to call normal heterosexual sexuality is dependent on this fetishisation of women. That is, the fetish is central to Freudian male heterosexual sexuality but on the periphery of Laver's account of that same sexuality.

As Laver points out, the idea of the fetish is closely related to John Flügel's account of the shifting erogenous zone. Strictly, 'erogenous' means 'generative of erotic excitement' but in popular understanding it has also come to mean 'sensitive to sexual stimulation'; in fashion theory it indicates items of clothing and fashion that generate erotic desire or sexual interest. Flügel's theory of this phenomenon as it applies to fashion and clothing reads as though it were a development of Rudovsky's almost biological account of human attraction. Rudovsky notes that it is commonly male animals and birds that use their brighter colours or striking plumage to impress female mates, whereas in human society it is women who have to keep men permanently excited and interested by the use of colourful clothing and attractive accessories (quoted in Rouse 1989: 11). In order to do this, he says, women change their shapes and colours by every means, including fashion and clothing. Although possibly misnamed, Flügel's idea of shifting erogenous zones is a development of Rudovsky's theory. He thinks that the sequential emphasis on different parts of women's bodies using fashion is a similar response to the problem of establishing and maintaining sexual interest. When interest in the legs wanes, fashion and clothing draw attention to the hips, and when the hips become tiresome and uninspiring fashion emphasises the bust, and so on.

Although he is usually presented as a sociologist, René Koenig takes a slightly different, not to say psychoanalytic, approach to the erotic in his (1973) *The Restless Image*. Pages 81 to 83 are entitled 'To See and to be Seen', and he is interested in how the erotic manifests itself in scopophilia and exhibitionism – the desires to see and be seen respectively. Explaining the origins and development of exhibitionist tendencies, Koenig says that 'the exhibitionist urge is originally auto-erotic, that is, refers to the subject's own body' (1973: 81). Here the pleasure is gained from looking at one's own body. At a later stage, one desires to see and to get pleasure from seeing the bodies of other people: 'Only afterwards is the urge to see directed towards another body for comparison' (ibid.: 82). Finally, Koenig says that scopophilia is abandoned in favour of exhibitionism: 'In the end, this object too is abandoned and . . . the activity of looking is transformed into passivity and the establishment of a new goal, that of being seen' (ibid.). The desire to see and the desire to be seen therefore grow 'from the same erotic root' (ibid.); the root here is the subject's own body.

Jean Baudrillard's (1981) account of commodity fetishism begins from the same place as Marx's account (see Chapter 30), but quickly takes a semiological turn. The fetishisation of the commodity, he says, 'is the fetishization of a product emptied of its concrete substance of labor and subjected to . . . a labor of signification' (1981: 93). The commodity becomes a sign, or 'sign-object', and a marker of difference in an entire system of objects whose only meaning is the product of their differences from other objects. The fetishised commodity is therefore an object divested of its 'substance and history' and made a marker of social difference. Consequently, on Baudrillard's account the erotic is the rewriting of the 'erogenous' – as that which generates erotic or sexual desire – as a 'system of signs', and anything can serve as an erotic sign – 'tattoos . . . bound feet . . . eyeshadow, rouge, hair removal, mascara, or bracelets, collars, objects, jewelry, accessories' (1981: 94). The body is now 'disqualified' and its drives are 'assigned to a cycle of fashion' (ibid.).

Barthes explains the erotic in terms of photography in *Camera Lucida* (1981). He argues here that the erotic photograph is a pornographic photograph that has been 'disturbed' or 'fissured'. The pornographic photograph is what he calls a 'unary' photograph; it is banal and displays a 'unity of composition'. Therefore the erotic photograph is a unary photograph that has been fissured. The erotic photograph, then, is full of duality, delay, distraction and disturbance. Barthes says that while a pornographic photograph is always naive and homogeneous, 'like a shop window which shows only one illuminated piece of jewellery', an erotic photograph contains something that distracts and introduces an element of 'indirection'. The example he uses to illustrate the difference here is that of Robert Mapplethorpe: 'Mapplethorpe shifts his close-ups of genitalia from the pornographic to the erotic by photographing the fabric of underwear at very close range: the photograph is no longer unary, since I am interested in the texture of the material' (1981: 40–2). Where, presumably, a close-up of genitalia in a pornographic photograph would be like the shop window with only one item illuminated, Mapplethorpe's photograph of genitalia is erotic because Mapplethorpe also shows the texture of the underwear in some detail, thus providing distraction and some form of 'disturbance'.

What all the accounts of the erotic and the fetish thus far have had in common is a gender bias. With the possible exception of some parts of Freudian psychoanalysis, all assume a masculine point of view. Apart from one or two tantalising comments to the effect that 'all women are clothing fetishists' (reported in Gamman and Makinen 1994: 60), Freud's essays that deal with fetishism assume and imply that only men are fetishists. Consequently, it is not by accident that Lorraine Gamman and Merja Makinen's (1994) *Female Fetishism* is subtitled 'A New Look'. They are making the point that examining fetishism from a female perspective represents a new and alternative 'look'. Consequently, the selections from their book have been chosen to try to reconstruct their argument as it applies to fashion and fetishism. What Gamman and Makinen are trying to do in the book is to rethink traditional psychoanalytic male-centred (or 'phallocentric') accounts of fetishism and to construct a theory of fetishism that will explain women's experience of fetishism. So where, for example, Freud stresses the Oedipal and post-Oedipal dramas experienced by male children, Gamman and Makinen want to examine pre-Oedipal elements in the development of women that can enable them to explain women as sexual fetishists. They say that this new account of fetishism must recognise 'an underlying anxiety about separation from the mother . . . an oral component . . . [and] the need for a new theoretical representation of female desire' (Gamman and Makinen 1994: 7). Their discussion of David Kunzle's *Fashion and Fetishism* also makes the point that fetishism and eroticism are often conflated in accounts of fashion.

Finally, it is worth pointing out that in his essay 'On the Threshold: Psychoanalysis and Cultural Studies', James Donald reminds us of Freud's warning against using psychoanalysis in the pathology of culture (looking for and interpreting the signs of disease); he says that psychoanalysis is to be used as an analytic tool and not as a therapy or a remedy (Donald 1991: 3). As a theory, or set of theories about the unconscious, psychoanalytic theory is understood here as a tool for analysing and explaining what culture does, not as a set of cures, talking or otherwise.

Bibliography

Barthes, R. (1975) *The Pleasure of the Text*, New York: Hill and Wang.
—— (1981) *Camera Lucida*, London: Fontana.
Baudrillard, J. (1981) *For a Critique of the Political Economy of the Sign*, St. Louis, Mo: Telos Press.
Donald, J. (1991) 'On the Threshold: Psychoanalysis and Cultural Studies', in J. Donald (ed.) *Psychoanalysis and Cultural Theory*, Basingstoke: Macmillan.
Fashion Theory (1999) Vol. 3, Issue 4, Special Issue on Fashion and Eroticism.
Freud, S. (1953) *The Standard Edition of the Complete Psychological Works of Sigmund Freud*, Volume VII, London: Vintage, Hogarth Press and the Institute of Psycho-Analysis.
Gallop, J. (1982) *Feminism and Psychoanalysis: The Daughter's Seduction*, Basingstoke: Macmillan.
Gamman, L. and Makinen, M. (1994) *Female Fetishism: A New Look*, London: Lawrence and Wishart.
Koenig, R. (1973) *The Restless Image*, London: George Allen & Unwin.
Kunzle, D. (1982) *Fashion and Fetishism*, New York: Rowman and Littlefield.
Laver, J. (1969) *Modesty in Dress: An Inquiry into the Fundamentals of Fashion*, Boston: Houghton Mifflin Co.
Rouse, E. (1989) *Understanding Fashion*, Oxford: Blackwell.
Steele, V. (1985) *Fashion and Eroticism: Ideals of Feminine Beauty from the Victorian Era to the Jazz Age*, Oxford: Oxford University Press.
—— (1996) *Fetish: Fashion, Sex and Power*, Oxford: Oxford University Press.

Chapter 44

Sigmund Freud

FETISHISM

IN THE LAST FEW YEARS I have had an opportunity of studying analytic-ally a number of men whose object-choice was dominated by a fetish. There is no need to expect that these people came to analysis on account of their fetish. For though no doubt a fetish is recognized by its adherents as an abnormality, it is seldom felt by them as the symptom of an ailment accompanied by suffering. Usually they are quite satisfied with it, or even praise the way in which it eases their erotic life. As a rule, therefore, the fetish made its appearance in analysis as a subsidiary finding.

For obvious reasons the details of these cases must be withheld from publica-tion; I cannot, therefore, show in what way accidental circumstances have contrib-uted to the choice of a fetish. The most extraordinary case seemed to me to be one in which a young man had exalted a certain sort of 'shine on the nose' into a fetishistic precondition. The surprising explanation of this was that the patient had been brought up in an English nursery but had later come to Germany, where he forgot his mother-tongue almost completely. The fetish, which originated from his earliest childhood, had to be understood in English, not German. The 'shine on the nose' [in German '*Glanz auf der Nase*']—was in reality a '*glance* at the nose'. The nose was thus the fetish, which, incidentally, he endowed at will with the luminous shine which was not perceptible to others.

In every instance, the meaning and the purpose of the fetish turned out, in analysis, to be the same. It revealed itself so naturally and seemed to me so compel-ling that I am prepared to expect the same solution in all cases of fetishism. When now I announce that the fetish is a substitute for the penis, I shall certainly create disappointment; so I hasten to add that it is not a substitute for any chance penis, but for a particular and quite special penis that had been extremely important in early childhood but had later been lost. That is to say, it should normally have been given up, but the fetish is precisely designed to preserve it from extinction. To put it more plainly: the fetish is a substitute for the woman's (the mother's) penis that the little boy once believed in and—for reasons familiar to us—does not want to give up.[1]

What happened, therefore, was that the boy refused to take cognizance of the fact of his having perceived that a woman does not posses a penis. No, that could not be true: for if a woman had been castrated, then his own possession of a penis was in danger; and against that there rose in rebellion the portion of his narcissism which Nature has, as a precaution, attached to that particular organ. In later life a grown man may perhaps experience a similar panic when the cry goes up that Throne and Altar are in danger, and similar illogical consequences will ensue. If I am not mistaken, Laforgue would say in this case that the boy 'scotomizes' his perception of the woman's lack of a penis.[2] A new technical term is justified when it describes a new fact or emphasizes it. This is not so here. The oldest word in our psycho-analytic terminology, 'repression', already relates to this pathological process. If we wanted to differentiate more sharply between the vicissitude of the *idea* as distinct from that of the *affect*,[3] and reserve the word '*Verdrängung*' ['repression'] for the affect, then the correct German word for the vicissitude of the idea would be '*Verleugnung*' ['disavowal'].[4] 'Scotomization' seems to me particularly unsuitable, for it suggests that the perception is entirely wiped out, so that the result is the same as when a visual impression falls on the blind spot in the retina. In the situation we are considering, on the contrary, we see that the perception has persisted, and that a very energetic action has been undertaken to maintain the disavowal. It is not true that, after the child has made his observation of the woman, he has preserved unaltered his belief that women have a phallus. He has retained that belief, but he has also given it up. In the conflict between the weight of the unwelcome perception and the force of his counter-wish, a compromise has been reached, as is only possible under the dominance of the unconscious laws of thought—the primary processes. Yes, in his mind the woman *has* got a penis, in spite of everything; but this penis is no longer the same as it was before. Something else has taken its place, has been appointed its substitute, as it were, and now inherits the interest which was formerly directed to its predecessor. But this interest suffers an extraordinary increase as well, because the horror of castration has set up a memorial to itself in the creation of this substitute. Furthermore, an aversion, which is never absent in any fetishist, to the real female genitals remains a *stigma indelebile* of the repression that has taken place. We can now see what the fetish achieves and what it is that maintains it. It remains a token of triumph over the threat of castration and a protection against it. It also saves the fetishist from becoming a homosexual, by endowing women with the character-istic which makes them tolerable as sexual objects. In later life, the fetishist feels that he enjoys yet another advantage from his substitute for a genital. The meaning of the fetish is not known to other people, so the fetish is not withheld from him: it is easily accessible and he can readily obtain the sexual satisfaction attached to it. What other men have to woo and make exertions for can be had by the fetishist with no trouble at all.

Probably no male human being is spared the fright of castration at the sight of a female genital. Why some people become homosexual as a consequence of that impression, while others fend it off by creating a fetish, and the great majority surmount it, we are frankly not able to explain. It is possible that, among all the factors at work, we do not yet know those which are decisive for the rare pathological results. We must be content if we can explain what has happened, and may for the present leave on one side the task of explaining why something has *not* happened.

One would expect that the organs or objects chosen as substitutes for the absent female phallus would be such as appear as symbols of the penis in other connections as well. This may happen often enough, but is certainly not a deciding factor. It seems rather that when the fetish is instituted some process occurs which reminds one of the stopping of memory in traumatic amnesia. As in this latter case, the subject's interest comes to a halt half-way, as it were; it is as though the last impression before the uncanny and traumatic one is retained as a fetish. Thus the foot or shoe owes its preference as a fetish—or a part of it—to the circumstance that the inquisitive boy peered at the woman's genitals from below, from her legs up; fur and velvet—as has long been suspected—are a fixation of the sight of the public hair, which should have been followed by the longed-for sight of the female member; pieces of underclothing, which are so often chosen as a fetish, crystallize the moment of undressing, the last moment in which the woman could still be regarded as phallic. But I do not maintain that it is invariably possible to discover with certainty how the fetish was determined.

An investigation of fetishism is strongly recommended to anyone who still doubts the existence of the castration complex or who can still believe that fright at the sight of the female genital has some other ground—for instance, that it is derived from a supposed recollection of the trauma of birth.[5]

For me, the explanation of fetishism had another point of theoretical interest as well. Recently, along quite speculative lines, I arrived at the proposition that the essential difference between neurosis and psychosis was that in the former the ego, in the service of reality, suppresses a piece of the id, whereas in a psychosis it lets itself be induced by the id to detach itself from a piece of reality. I returned to this theme once again later on.[6] But soon after this I had reason to regret that I had ventured so far. In the analysis of two young men I learned that each—one when he was two years old and the other when he was ten—had failed to take cognizance of the death of his beloved father—had 'scotomized' it—and yet neither of them had developed a psychosis. Thus a piece of reality which was undoubtedly important had been disavowed by the ego, just as the unwelcome fact of women's castration is disavowed in fetishists. I also began to suspect that similar occurrences in childhood are by no means rare, and I believed that I had been guilty of an error in my characterization of neurosis and psychosis. It is true that there was one way out of the difficulty. My formula needed only to hold good where there was a higher degree of differentiation in the psychical apparatus; things might be permissible to a child which would entail severe injury to an adult.

But further research led to another solution of the contradiction. It turned out that the two young men had no more 'scotomized' their father's death than a fetishist does the castration of women. It was only one current in their mental life that had not recognized their father's death; there was another current which took full account of that fact. The attitude which fitted in with the wish and the attitude which fitted in with reality existed side by side. In one of my two cases this split had formed the basis of a moderately severe obsessional neurosis. The patient oscillated in every situation in life between two assumptions: the one, that his father was still alive and was hindering his activities; the other, opposite one, that he was entitled to regard himself as his father's successor. I may thus keep to the expectation that in a psychosis the one current—that which fitted in with reality—would have in fact been absent.

Returning to my description of fetishism, I may say that there are many and weighty additional proofs of the divided attitude of fetishists to the question of the castration of women. In very subtle instances both the disavowal and the affirmation of the castration have found their way into the construction of the fetish itself. This was so in the case of a man whose fetish was an athletic support-belt which could also be worn as bathing drawers. This piece of clothing covered up the genitals entirely and concealed the distinction between them. Analysis showed that it signi-fied that women were castrated and that they were not castrated; and it also allowed of the hypothesis that men were castrated, for all these possibilities could equally well be concealed under the belt—the earliest rudiment of which in his childhood had been the fig-leaf on a statue. A fetish of this sort, doubly derived from contrary ideas, is of course especially durable. In other instances the divided attitude shows itself in what the fetishist does with his fetish, whether in reality or in his imagin-ation. To point out that he reveres his fetish is not the whole story; in many cases he treats it in a way which is obviously equivalent to a representation of castration. This happens particularly if he has developed a strong identification with his father and plays the part of the latter; for it is to him that as a child he ascribed the woman's castration. Affection and hostility in the treatment of the fetish—which run parallel with the disavowal and the acknowledgment of castration—are mixed in unequal proportions in different cases, so that the one or the other is more clearly recogniz-able. We seem here to approach an understanding, even if a distant one, of the behaviour of the 'coupeur de nattes'.[7] In him the need to carry out the castration which he disavows has come to the front. His action contains in itself the two mutually incompatible assertions: 'the woman has still got a penis' and 'my father has castrated the woman'. Another variant, which is also a parallel to fetishism in social psychology, might be seen in the Chinese custom of mutilating the female foot and then revering it like a fetish after it has been mutilated. It seems as though the Chinese male wants to thank the woman for having submitted to being castrated.

In conclusion we may say that the normal prototype of fetishes is a man's penis, just as the normal prototype of inferior organs is a woman's real small penis, the clitoris.[8]

Notes

1   This interpretation was made as early as 1910, in my study on Leonardo da Vinci, without any reasons being given for it. [Standard Ed., 11, 96. Cf. Editor's Note above, p. 150.]

2   I correct myself, however, by adding that I have the best reasons for supposing that Laforgue would not say anything of the sort. It is clear from his own remarks [Laforgue, 1926] that 'scotomization' is a term which derives from descriptions of dementia praecox, which does not arise from a carrying-over of psycho-analytic concepts to the psychoses and which has no application to developmental

processes or to the formation of neuroses. In his exposition in the text of his paper, the author has been at pains to make this incompatibility clear.

3   [Cf. 'Repression' (1915*d*), *Standard Ed.*, **14**, 152f. and the Appendix to the first paper on the neuro-psychoses of defence (1894*a*).]

4   Some discussion of Freud's use of this term and of the English rendering of it appears in an Editor's footnote to the paper on 'The Infantile Genital Organization' (1923*e*), *Standard Ed.*, **19**, 143. It may be remarked that in Chapter VIII of the *Outline of Psycho-Analysis* (1940*a* [1938]) Freud makes a different distinction between the uses of the two words: 'repression' applies to defence against internal instinctual demands and 'disavowal' to defence against the claims of external reality.]

5   Cf. Rank, 1924, 22–4.

6   'Neurosis and Psychosis' (1924*b*) and 'The Loss of Reality in Neurosis and Psychosis' (1924*e*).

7   [A pervert who enjoys cutting off the hair of females. Part of the present explanation was given by Freud in his study of Leonardo (1910*c*), *Standard Ed.*, **11**, 96.]

8   [This is an allusion to Adler's insistence on 'organ-inferiority' as the basis of all neuroses. Cf. a footnote to the paper on 'Some Psychical Consequences of the Anatomical Distinction between the Sexes' (1925*j*), *Standard Ed.*, **19**, 253–4, and a longer discussion in Lecture XXXI of the *New Introductory Lectures* (1933*a*).]

Chapter 45

David Kunzle

THE SPECIAL HISTORIC AND PSYCHOLOGICAL ROLE OF TIGHT-LACING

FASHION IS THE CULTURALLY dominant mode of dress expressing, as a rule, the dominance of a social class. But fashion can also express, in ways that we do not yet fully comprehend, the finer nuances of shifting relationships between the sexes, as well as between segments of dominant, rival, or upwardly mobile classes.

Fetishism may be defined as the individual displacement of private erotic feeling onto a non-genital part of the body, or onto a particular article of clothing by association with a part of the body, or onto an article of clothing in conjunction with its effect on the body. As such it serves to express a special socio-sexual attitude or relationship within the normal functioning of fashion as outlined above; manifested publicly, it may be an attention-getting device used by a socially repressed or aspirant individual or minority. If it is manifested by people in sufficient numbers, or of sufficient social standing, it can acquire a certain limited or temporary status as custom or fashion. In modern times certain 'fetishistic fashions' (corsets, high heels) were deemed dangerous and were sharply censured, and there is a very real sense in which fashion and fetishism must always be regarded as potentially antagonistic, even or especially when the fetishism is an exaggeration of what is fashionably acceptable (the tight-laced as opposed to the moderately slim look).

Never, not even during the 1870s, arguably the most fetishistic decade in the history of Western costume, can one speak of fashion and fetishism as one. When fashion (group cultural expression) and fetishism (exaggerated, individual sexual expression) are perfectly harmonised, we may speak of a 'cultural' or 'national' fetish. Such a term is, I believe, best applied to non-Western, non-individualistic cultures such as China, where foot-binding was a universally accepted and, for much of its history, a relatively uncontested component of social and sexual life. But the compressed waist and foot in the West come at times close to being a true cultural fetish.

The capitalist West has been under constant and often acute tension between assertions of individualism and the demands of conformism. The 'kaleidoscope of fashion' represents one of the most spectacular arenas of this struggle. The fashion established by the élite has, in the modern age, permitted a high degree of variation according to individual taste, as well as the particular needs of essentially labile economic, professional and other social groups. Fashion at court or among ruling aristocratic circles may, for obvious reasons, be characterised by extreme luxury of economic display; but it also permitted a luxury of sexual display (in décolletage, for instance) prohibited to a lower social group that saw both economic advantage and cultural identity in the exercise of sexual self-restraint (puritanism). The 'immoral' luxury (economic *and* sexual) of the aristocracy has been a topos of middle-class morality ever since the emergence of the commercial middle classes as a social force – for our purposes, with the 'birth' of tight-lacing, in the mid-fourteenth century. Those individual members of a lower but ascendant social order who engaged in erotic display were condemned, mostly from within their own class, for exploiting their sexuality in order to win attentions that might propel them upwards. As we shall see, the law sometimes tried to prevent this ('sumptuary laws'). All this is true of the dress of both sexes, but more so of women's than men's. Women used their sexuality, and sexualised forms of dress, as women always have, to rise out of a socio-sexually subject position. And they got morally scapegoated for their pains.

Our assumption here is that female sexuality is a very special, socially manipulable, psychologically separable, and subversive force. As such, it has been severely repressed by male authority. The history of tight-lacing is part of the history of the struggle for sexual self-expression, male and female. This may not be immediately apparent, because the corset has often been regarded in a light essentially no different from other accessories of clothing, and its extreme use, in tight-lacing, has not been recognised as essentially different from the 'small waist of fashion', and as involving forces and motivations essentially different from those that underlie other extreme or eccentric sartorial effects. Whatever the erotic intention concealed in other articles or styles of dress, that inherent in tight-lacing remains unique and overt, and thus subject to a unique and overt level of moral repression. Its appeal to hand and eye is strident.

The crusade against tight-lacing and other erotic forms of dress is part of the crusade against sexuality, which is as old as Christianity. The socio-sexual symbolism of tight-lacing and its ritual components reveal its essentially ambivalent purpose – to enforce the sexual taboo by objectively oppressing the body, and simultaneously to break that taboo by subjectively enhancing the body.

Apart from its overt sexualisation, its sheer longevity sets tight-lacing apart from other fashions and tends to elevate it from a mere (changeable) style in dress to the status of a continuing social practice. Its capacity for survival, which so astonished and vexed the nineteenth century, represents an element of continuity in the perpetual flux of taste. Tight-lacing is not worn, cast on or off like, say, an outrageous hat, but practised as a continuous ritual. It tends to permanence, when fashion generally thrives on change.

The taste for novelty for its own sake, the commercial pressures towards constant change in style, and the small, year-to-year political and economic 'accidents' to which clothing styles tend to make symbolic reference are all factors which may determine the flow of fashion in general, but appear to have had relatively little influence upon the evolution of tight-lacing. Here the causes are more radical, striking deep into the roots of our sexual culture, which changes but slowly.

Anthropologists use the term 'body-sculpture' to cover various forms of mutilation, compression, distortion, piercing, scarification and relief tattooing of the flesh, customs which have been termed 'the most enduring as well as the most intimate of the cosmetic arts . . . the permanent reminders of a new and irreversible identity'. Body-sculpture in the West, limited as it is in scope, shares some of this purpose, and partakes, all along the range from strictly private to fully public, of some of the symbolic and ritual functions normally associated with primitive custom.

The arts of costume work by optical illusion. A small (clothed) waist can also be a matter of illusion. Historians, like fashion advertisers, accept that the waist can be small without being compressed, and that it can *appear* tight without actually being so. They tend to describe it as becoming objectively smaller and tighter, larger and looser, without specifying whether this is a physical reality, a visual illusion, or a combination of both. Enter the mania for exact measurement, which should solve the problem, but doesn't.

The manner in which a skirt, a sleeve or a hat grows or shrinks over the years can be objectively measured by means of surviving costumes and (to a degree) pictures. But what is meant by a 'small' waist? Small in comparison to the skirt or sleeve, smaller than the 'natural' waist, or simply smaller than that of the preceding fashion? We are concerned here, not with the degree to which fashion may be perceived, as the popularisers put it, to 'decree a small waist', but with deliberate acts of constriction, the making of 'conspicuous waist' (to pun on Veblen) as a social provocation, and for private gratification. The only workable definition of tight-lacing as opposed to 'normal' lacing is as the *conscious and visible* process of artificial constriction of the waist, whereby the very artifice becomes an attraction (or repellent).

In the nineteenth century comparisons were always being drawn between European tight-lacing and Chinese foot-binding. Horrible as the latter seemed, the comparison was usually made to its advantage, such was the hyperbolic revulsion provoked by the habit of a small European minority. The differences between the truly cultural fashion of the Chinese and the controversial minority fashion-fetish of the West are revealing. Today, foot-binding is morally doubly repugnant to us, because it was inflicted universally on small children of all but the poorest classes, and only female children. Tight-lacing was never universal, although corseting in one form or another was usual. Corsets were, as a general rule, imposed on children only in a relatively mild form when even small children were dressed like adults; in the course of the nineteenth century corsets on children tended to disappear. Their purpose was to protect the body, rather than restrict it, to keep it growing straight rather than confine it in the middle.

The chronological coincidence in the life span of tight-lacing and foot-binding is close; at the beginning less so, but at the end quite remarkably and not fortuitously so. The Chinese custom arose probably in the twelfth century AD, the European one in the fourteenth. The fact that both customs expired simultaneously during the early years of this century is not a matter of chance, for there was a direct interaction in the campaigns against them.

Chinese foot-binding gives us an important analogical context which the body-sculpture of primitive peoples cannot provide, not only for Western waist-constriction, but also for the immediate anatomical counterpart of the Chinese custom and the second major fetish of Western fashion, constrictive footwear. This has been an essential concomitant of tight-lacing over the more important half of the latter's history. We who still take a degree of impracticality in footwear for granted may regard as far-fetched the Victorians' comparison between the (to us) mild constriction of Western fashion and the severe deformation of the Chinese. But the constriction of fashionable footwear in the eighteenth and nineteenth centuries was viewed by contemporaries as very severe indeed; the 'average' high heel of fashion was considered by some as positively crippling to the internal organs, as well as the feet. Yet this historic heel was much lower, broader and altogether more stable than that of the mid-twentieth century. The 'stiletto' fashion shoe of our own age would have staggered the Victorian imagination as much as Victorian tight-lacing does ours, and it is evident that vis-à-vis Victorian footwear, postwar styles have grown more, not less, 'Chinese' – this at the very time, ironically, when foot-binding disappeared completely from China, and the People's Republic gained a reputation for a looseness, bagginess, work-practicality and classless uniformity – anti-fashion.

Tight-lacing and high heels appear, for a good two centuries, as a kind of inseparable Siamese twins, sustained by the same historical, psychological and per-haps complementary physiological circumstances, and following each other into the same decline. But the high heel, the dramatically sculptured foot, revived concretely in the mid-twentieth century, whereas tight-lacing returned only vestigially at that time. The meteoric career of the stiletto heel (returning dramatically in recent decades) is a phenomenon in itself, which is here no more than sketched.

This brings us to our second major 'fashionable fetish'. The shoe and boot clearly sculpt in a sense very different from, and less permanent than, the corset. The traditional compression of the toes, rendering them pointed in their alignment where nature made them broad and square, is very real, and certainly significant; but even more significant (and more akin to the Chinese custom) is the way the high heel has radically modified the range of action in the foot, and thereby the stance and walk of the wearer. This heel has altered not so much a form as a relationship of forms in movement, transforming body posture and body action; it is kinetic sculpture, as indeed is tight-lacing, with its variety of kinetic side effects.

After the essentially female corset and high heel, the third most prominent target under intermittent attack was primarily a male fashion. Constrictive neck-wear, like shoe and corset, compresses a vulnerable and sensitive part of the body; like the high heel, it rigidly restricts movement over adjacent areas. A fourth poten-tially constrictive article of dress, the glove, was the object of relatively slight and rare criticism, presumably because although it can readily incapacitate for basic manual tasks, it cannot subject the hand to the basic visual transformations of which footwear and corset are capable; the reign of the tight glove was relatively short and shadowy, and its explicit enemies few and faint.

The long, exquisitely manicured fingernail is another fetish with which, although technically body-sculptural (as is head-hair), we cannot deal here, despite its obvious more-than-symbolic hostility to physical (here manual, clerical) labour that it shares with restriction of thorax and foot.

We now turn to a fetishism in many ways inseparable, and yet also distinct, from that for small waists. Breast fetishism has become a major cultural phenomenon of the postwar era. The postwar admiration for largeness of bust, arguably, replaced that for smallness of waist and extremities per se; and the big bust was until very recently regarded (as it still is in some sectors) as a virtue in itself, irrespective of other proportions.

Tight-lacing has traditionally presupposed a degree of breast sculpture. Mammary tissue, even more than that of the waist, is a malleable substance, which responds to pressures both subtle and extreme. Normally, the breast has been both raised and reshaped (the upper half being made to rise and swell by pushing from below). Breast flattening, obviously the 'pure' form of reductive breast sculpture, is always associated in the popular imagination with the waistless, corsetless twenties, but it is also characteristic, to a degree, of the sixteenth and seventeenth centuries, when the whole thorax was sometimes rigidly encased.

Breast reshaping and exposure attracted a censure that, in the violence of its tone and the sexual disgust which it discloses, can only be compared with that engendered by tight-lacing in the nineteenth century. Any form of décolletage was already offensive; to use artificial means to thrust the breasts even more prominently into view was doubly damnable.

What of the commoner contemporary fetishes which are discernibly linked with developments in fashion but which will not otherwise concern us? Lingerie fetishism has been with us since the late nineteenth century, and is, like the voyeurism upon which it thrives, relatively uncontroversial, customarily acceptable and commercially profitable. When corset fetishism survives as an aspect of lingerie fetishism, it does so independently of and ancillary to its sculptural function. Lingerie is essentially body-extensive and body-additive, when it is not merely a means of simultaneously concealing and revealing. It is decorative and passive, or externally active, rather than sculptural and internally active; the psychology is quite different.

Since around 1960 there has thrived a fetish for total envelopment of the naked body in a 'second skin' of rubber and leather, analogous to that of the diver's wetsuit, but generally of a much finer-gauge material. These pass commercially as slimming garments, and being occlusive, cause sudden loss of body moisture, which many people find erotic. Insofar as they are designed to exert a light, even pressure over the whole body, they may be defined as sculptural. In terms of contour the change caused by a rubber suit is minimal, that of a smoothing out or unifying, although the visual transformation can be striking, like that of a dancer's all-black leotard. Rubber- or leather-suit fetishism is often combined with truly constrictive fetishes (bondage, corsetry), when of course the body-contour *is* radically altered. The paramount psychological factor in rubber-suit fetishism is, however, that of a physical sensation of change in shape via a rise in body temperature, local cutaneous sensations, and small, local muscular restraints; these may combine to create the sense of having acquired a second skin, which is so overwhelming as to offer the experience of a total change of identity. In one important respect rubber-suit fetishism is diametrically opposed to truly sculptural fetishism: in its 'pure' form it provides a total and relatively benign enclosure, which is very far from the object of the latter.

Rubber and leather, like velvet and fur, are basically fetishes of material or texture, which induce or enhance certain tactile or cutaneous sensations. Rubber and leather fetishisms are often combined with body-sculpture fetishism. A leather corset, with its soft, shiny surface of black skin stretched taut over the hard boning, is held by many fetishists to be the superior kind. Having been made in recent years supple and workable like a textile, and retaining its strength at the same time, leather is able to supplant older corsetry materials like coutil. Bondage devices in leather unite pleasures on two levels – the associative atavistic one of the animal skin, and the immediate sculptural one.

Leather is considered a 'masculine' fetish, and is certainly characteristic, perhaps the commonest form, of homosexual fetishism. Silk and satin are considered 'feminine' fetishes; for a long time the only clinical studies of female fetishism concerned satin and silk kleptomaniacs.

Sculptural tattooing, or scarification, that is the creation of relief patterns over the skin, is little practised in the West. Surface tattooing has been common since the nineteenth century, and has in recent years spread from its traditional locus, military and seafaring men, to civilians and women. Both tattooing and sculptural fetishes involve a degree of discomfort or pain in the initiation, and both involve or at least invite, to very different degrees, the concept of irreversibility and permanence. Temporary relief-tattoo or scarification effects, as a by-product of tight-lacing, are prized by some who admire the visual impression and tactile invitation of the striation and criss-cross pressure-marks left by the boning and laces of a corset after its removal. Such pressure-marks apparently increase epidermal sensitivity for erotic purposes, as do tattooing and scarification.

Piercing is the only real mutilation common in the West. Technically, although very mildly sculptural, it has been customarily confined in a non-sculptural and inconspicuous way to the ear-lobe. Fetishists, however, including many who also tight-lace, pierce elsewhere (ear-rim, nostrils, nipples, navel, male and female genitals, etc.) and sometimes enlarge the holes, like primitive peoples. While piercing has lost much of its ancient magical and status-conferring purpose in the West, its psychological significance may be on the increase today, as ear-lobe piercing among girls becomes a commonplace minor puberty or sexual initiation ritual, and acceptable among heterosexual as well as homosexual men (usually one ear only is pierced); while studs and rings in the nostril, once seen in the West only on East Indian ladies, have metastasised all over the body, visible and invisible. Here again fashion has caught up with fetishism.

The resistance to mutilation beyond piercing, in the West, is so great that it is never for a moment considered even as an adjunct to traditional forms of body-sculpture. The relevant mutilations would be, admittedly, very severe indeed: the surgical removal of lower ribs to facilitate extreme tight-lacing, and the amputation of toes to enable smaller, tighter shoes to be worn. While rumours and allegations circulated in public papers that certain women in the late Victorian and Edwardian ages, and since then certain actresses today (Jane Fonda, Cher), willingly subjected themselves to rib removal, I have never found confirmation of them; and it is surely significant that the festishists seldom, if ever, fantasise about them.

A peculiar form of 'zöofetishism', that relating to the horse, belongs here for its evident relationship to human fetishism. The horse and its trappings in the nineteenth century were eminently a matter of fashion. Styles changed and were highly connotive of social status and artistic taste. The automobile has, of course, today superseded the horse (and carriage) as the basic fashionable sex-power symbol: and, comically, even its overall shape has been deemed subject to a fashionable 'waist reduction'. The horse, like the car, served as a vehicle of transportation and (sexual) 'transport', but being a living thing, was a more natural and responsive embodiment of fantasy and symbology, with correspondences between human body-sculpture and equine disciplines. The connection survives most starkly today, when few people ride, in the sado-masochistic games where the human mount substitutes for the horse.

Fetishism and metaphor: fetishistic discipline and Christian asceticism

The historical origins of fetishist psychology are not to be limited to the sexual domain in any narrow sense. The idea of an object being endowed with powers properly attributable only to a person (or to nature) is rooted in the most ancient magical thinking. In medieval Europe a literary tradition developed, in conjunction with the cult of religious relics, which elevated this kind of magical process by investing an object associated with the beloved with her amorous power. An article of clothing is treated as sacred because it has touched a body which is ultimately untouchable; it incorporates and reconciles the paradox of desire to possess that which is essentially unattainable. In possessing the glove or handkerchief, the lover in a symbolic sense possesses the beloved whom he cannot possess in reality. This mode of thinking survives in literature through the baroque age down to our own day.

The 'fetish-object' in the tradition of courtly love is a surrogate, and decreases in value as the loved one is present or appears more attainable. Similarly, the true tight-lacing fetishist does not wish to possess (or masturbate with) the corset in itself, but to apply it possessively upon the beloved, so that it, his desire and her body become one. The male corseting the female symbolically enacts possession of her, even as she, physically possessed only (or initially) by the corset, is preserved from real violation. The fetish-object serves both as a symbol of union and as symbolic obstacle. It separates the lovers, and yet incorporates emotions of conquest and surrender, resistance and yielding. To the female, it is the armour of virtue (like the chastity belt, without functioning as such), to the male it is a symbol of his dominance and desire. The committed female tight-lacer is 'married', in the first place, to the corset, if worn permanently, day and night; the rest is, in a way, ancillary. The night-corset is the prior bed-partner, the chaste one.

Another aspect of the metaphorical fusion of object and person can be derived from Christianity. It is from within the Christian tradition that had absorbed and revived primitive belief in sympathetic magic in the form of the doctrine of transubstantiation that fetishism as a form of sexual transubstantiation emerges.

The word 'fetish' derives from the Portuguese *feitiço*, meaning fated, charmed, bewitched, and entered the English language with reference to primitive belief in magic. Our own sexual form of fetishism retains primitive associations of erotic, magical and religious power, through which a semblance of supernatural control is achieved, and states of transcendence and ecstasy may be entered. The fetishist act becomes a means of acceding to grace and power, and of uniting the participants in a religious-erotic ritual, which (unlike Christian sacramental ritual) is based upon a real and visible/physical transformation – real and visible, but also comparable to the internal physical transformation experienced by Christian and other mystics. The sexual motive of this transformation is effectively purified through elevation to the moral realm.

Spirituality and asceticism have often been represented by thin and emaciated bodies; north European late Gothic art (fourteenth–sixteenth centuries) especially has used extreme narrowness of waist to convey the purity of spirit and suffering in figures of Christ and the saints, while on contemporaneous clothed figures of court-iers, the wasp-waist expressed aristocratic elegance. In anatomically detailed Ger-man statuary of the Reformation era the extreme contraction of the lower ribs and the sucking in of the belly appear as the primary physiological indicators, after the expression of the face, of sacrificial agony.

Modern fetishist-masochist practices may be regarded as a late flowering of monastic penitential disciplines. (See *Klara* insert for fetishist fiction raising tight-lacing to the realm of religious asceficism.) Once suffered in Christian humility and penance, where the sexuality was only latent, corporal disciplines were turned by women into an expression of sexual pride, and were condemned as such by the clerical and medical descendants of the ascetics who had invented them. Most clerics and physicians saw only the sexual exhibitionism, not the penitential or self-disciplinary component of masochistic fashion. Alone, in the sixteenth century, Montaigne honoured both.

In the late seventeenth century, when (as Molière's *Tartuffe* reminds us) physic-ally painful forms of penitence were losing their spiritual sanction, the Viennese Augustinian monk and Imperial preacher Abraham à Sancta Clara tried to reconcile the paradox of physical asceticism and sexual display, by reminding his flock that not only the seeking of pleasure, but also the self-infliction of pain could minister to pride and the devil. In a sermon all the more impressive for its breathless, dialectal, spontaneous style (very close, one imagines, to its original pulpit delivery), the preacher tells how he chanced upon a corset lying on a table, and asked a chamber-maid what it was. 'A corset (Mieder)? Almighty God! But it is so tight that a marten (Mader=Marder) could not slip into it; it is rightly called Mieder, for it is no small torture (Marter). Oh, if only the body could speak, how it would moan, that it must live all the time in such agony, and suffer more than a Carthusian monk, who always wears a rough hair-shirt.' Sancta Clara goes on, ingenuously, to ask the chamber-maid why the corset is cut so low at the top, and wonder 'that the tender skin does not complain at suffering such cold in winter'. He then passes, with a powerful oath, to fashionable footwear, which causes the toes to be squeezed together 'like herrings in a box' and 'like the damned in hell'. 'Ach, such suffering, such suffering? And suffering only for the sake of the devil . . . so little suffering for God . . . but for hell the proud suffer gladly.'

The nineteenth century set the paradox of masochism aside altogether, until the very end, when psychology and physiology began very hesitantly to throw light upon it. A cartoonist as early as 1878 shows the witty doctor feeling obliged morally to

***Klara*, by Stephen** (Internet, via LISA)

The theme of this story (posted 1998) is lifelong corset discipline approached as a kind of religious vocation involving the sacrifices and privations of a rigidly ruled, cloistered life. The momentous idea is first broached when Klara is 10, the age of sexual discovery. The magic of her mother, Lady Ilse's 16in waist is revealed to her, hitherto a secret both sexual and spiritual, and she is minutely catechised first by the mother (a high aristocrat at the Schliessen court), then by the corsetière, acting as it were in the role of a Mother Confessor or Superior of the Order she is about to enter. The careful examination, quite properly, is designed to make sure that this is Klara's very own, mature decision, to be made and acted on from 12 years (but is this still too young?). The commitment will be to an arduous life in which the gradual reduction over the years of her waist, from her natural 24 to 15, is posited as a gradual spiritual refinement. The figure 15 is set by Klara herself in order to outdo her mother, and to be achieved by the time of her marriage (i.e. final vows). She is warned, as zealous neophytes often were in religious practice, not to go too fast and too far in her self-denials. Klara welcomes the discomforts of lost sleep, confined movement and scarce eating, and the pleasures of occasional fainting – and even accepts what is perhaps the ultimate denial for the time being, the prohibition on showing her figure in public.

When, revealed in all her glory at her first public ball, she is kissed and embraced by the young heir and Duke, and her corset breaks, it is as the breaking of her hymen. The Duke finds himself committed to marry her – to celebrate which Klara promises to work her waist down a further inch, to 14, the exact span of his hands, and, moreover, at the wedding, 'never to loosen the staylace ever more' (i.e. till death do us part). They live happily ever after, in this fetishist fairy tale, but there is no mention, rather a tacit denial, of progeny, as irrelevant or improper as they would be for a real nun.

condone the excessively tight cuirasse style, 'for in so narrow a space no mortal body can exist, only the soul has room'. But the dress reformer takes refuge in the 'typically female spirit of contradiction' as she invents a pseudo-historical origin for an object that can have no historical, that is rational, origin: women in the 'Dark Ages' obstinately 'refusing to yield under pressure of a barbarous punishment [that of the thoracic vice, allegedly inflicted by the husband for adultery] and in a spirit of contradiction turning their prison into an attractive article of fashion'. In 1910, the pioneer sexologist Havelock Ellis struck half the truth when he said that 'the corset arose to gratify an ideal of asceticism rather than sexual allurement'. Ellis should have written 'as well as' for 'rather than'. The concomitance of the asceticism or pain and the sexual allurement is accurately sensed by the popular versifier, who projects the amorous pain back onto himself, the lover: 'How dex't'rously she'll waste the lace/And lace the pretty waist . . . Till the whole effect is stunning and immaculately chaste . . . The sterner sex they torture, caring nothing how it hurts.'

In an Austrian poem of 1890, the pain of a girl's love is equated with the pain of the corset, with the heart bursting like and with the tight-laced body; and when the lover becomes bride, at last, she summons the 'ironclad corset, as befits the chaste woman . . . pull and heave on the laces, that the bridally enhanced body be truly *ethereal*' (my stress).

Given the view that corporal disciplines by their very severity could minister to personal pride and dangerous forms of ecstasy, it is surely no accident that fetishistic disciplines were domesticated and moralised primarily in a Protestant country. For Protestantism discouraged the showier forms of religious self-denial, and refused women the right to set themselves apart in nunneries in order to practise them. Penitential pain and discipline were transferred to everyday life and ordinary things: education, household, work and even dress. The religious-ascetic and the erotic stand overtly in a psychological contradiction that mystics and fetishists in their very different ways attempt to reconcile.

The German reformer Troll–Borostnani in 1897 spoke, as much in amazement as anger, of the 'fanaticism' and 'intoxication' of woman's 'lust for self-torment', expressed in clothing whose constriction induced states of consciousness she likened to those of flagellants and Asiatic dervishes. There is a sense here that tight-lacing sought to circumvent specifically modern and European strictures against 'irrational' and 'immoral' forms of mysticism.

Social and sexual symbolism

Sexology and repression of fetishism

Psychoanalysis originated at a time when sexual repression had reached an intolerable level, and new avenues of sexual expression were forged, one of which took the form of fetishism. Scientific recognition of the sexual origins of certain forms of aberrant behaviour did not, however, induce sympathy, nor did research into sexual deviance increase tolerance; indeed, the very opposite happened.

Medical science has rendered even innocent forms of fetishism pathological, or potentially so. 'Scientific' study, as well as the law, has focused on the pathological and criminological manifestations of fetishism, impaired social tolerance of private and harmless fetishist behaviour, and sought to repress or erase it.

Krafft-Ebing's grim, pioneering *Psychopathia Sexualis* of 1886 placed heavy, criminological emphasis on sado-masochistic foot and shoe fetishism and the kleptomaniac collector syndrome. The latter, involving gloves and handkerchiefs, hair-despoliation, and even the improper touching of hair, was treated with great severity. In Germany, the censor banned innocent, strictly non-pornographic books catering to fetishism, such as the short story collections of Delorme and Dolorosa, which contain sentimental, poetic and moral (not to say didactic and therapeutic) tales applauding the transference of Eros from fetish-object to person.

Judges have enacted the repressive and ignorant theory that it is 'fear of punishment that keeps many criminal fetishists from capitulating to their impulses', and that gaol is the proper place for men who like to sit in shoe shops watching women try on shoes. Aversion therapy represents the ultimate cruelty in contemporary treatment of fetishists. In the 1970s privately masturbating could land a California boy with a twelve-year gaol sentence.

Given that Wilhelm Stekel in 1924 plunged the whole phenomenon of sexual symbolism in relation to clothing into a miasma of psychosis, it is not surprising that costume theorists, who are concerned with the 'cultural norm', were wary of applying psychoanalytic method, phallic symbolism, etc., to their material. The reduction by psychoanalysis of human personality to intrapsychic traits, and its elimination of the social factor, has rendered it useless, if not actually harmful, when dealing with fetishism.

Sexualisation of form and action: shoe, corset, collar, horse

'I have gloved my language as you gloved my hands because they were vulgar . . . my feet are encased in boots made by the shoemakers of the Parisian Cinderellas; my torso has been inured to the torture of the corset, and my waist has become so slender, that if I lost my belt, I could just about replace it with my bracelet!' Thus was the simple nineteenth-century country girl transformed into a Parisian mistress.

In the taste for small extremities and a small middle, sexual and hierarchical or social principles are mutually supportive. Feet, hands, neck and torso, when used for labouring tasks, grow thick and muscular. The physically idle upper classes can afford to keep them small and confined, preserving them as symbols of sexual refinement and social leisure. It was Thorstein Veblen, in his famous *Theory of the Leisure Class* (1899), who first enunciated the theory that women tight-laced in order to show distance from labour, and dedication to conspicuous leisure. This idea was taken up by Flügel as the 'hierarchical principle'. It was, as I show, principally lower-class or lower-middle-class women, certainly the tight-lacing majority, who sought to acquire the physical insignia of leisured status that they lacked in reality. The hierarchical principle governs not only predilection for smallness of foot, but also the desire literally and symbolically to lift it out of the mud, via high heels raising the woman visually above the common herd and at the same time suggesting that walking is a special and difficult, rather than commonplace, activity for her.

Take first the foot and shoe, which have been imbued by the most ancient folklore with a broad symbolic range and powerful magical properties. A rich proverb lore relates the shoe with female sexuality, the fitting of foot into shoe with sexual union and (in the Cinderella myths, for instance – treated below) the small female foot with aristocracy, purity and virtue.

Uniquely sensitive to touch, despite the fact that they have constantly to bear the full weight of the body, often played with and cosseted in infancy, and phallic in shape, the feet have naturally become a special erotic centre and sexual symbol. The foot is moreover a special mark of human superiority to the animal. 'The voluptuous architecture of the body owes much of its sensuous character to the foot, which was responsible for the upright posture and gait that altered the entire anatomy . . . [and this] also made possible frontal human copulation, a coital position unique in all nature.'

East and West, the foot has traditionally played an essential role in erotic preliminaries, and is sometimes used in the sexual act itself. The use of the foot as a phallic stimulant, and in some sense as a phallic substitute as well, was customary in

China, and is by no means uncommon in the West. The Chinese believed, in addition, that compression of her foot by the male hand was erotically stimulating to the female; binding increased its responsiveness and sensitivity. This was also experienced as true of the bound Western torso. Permanent compression of the foot was also believed by the Chinese to induce a kind of walk which enlarged the hips, which in turn increased the capacity and constrictive power of the vagina. A similar idea presented itself on a less conscious level also to the Western imagination, for which the restriction of high heels and tight shoes (as also waist compression) was a means of enlarging the thighs, and enhancing the hips and hip action, as we shall see. The expressed Chinese ideal of a foot small enough to fit inside a man's mouth probably reflects an oral-genital fantasy (or replicates an oral-genital act), which in the West takes the milder form of a foot small enough to fit into the hand, and fit to be raised to the lips for a kiss; or else, in the ceremonially sanctioned form of the shoe serving as champagne glass. In the Western tradition a woman's foot, believed to be proportionately smaller than a man's, is viewed as ideally to be encompassed in the grasp of a male hand, and thus lends itself to possession symbolism. Similarly, the phrase 'handspan waist' connotes manual possessibility . . . The small foot = small vagina is best sought in pornography.

Apart from the compression of the whole foot in a boot too small for it, there are two other major ways in which the foot has been sculpted: the forcible raising of the instep arch, and the formation of a slender pointed shape at the toes. All three methods are of course interdependent.

The raising and arching of the instep is achieved in the West principally by means of a high heel, and is sometimes reinforced by means of arched inner soles; a boot shorter than the foot can also serve this purpose. An extreme instep arch was procured in China by permanently binding the toes towards the heel; this radically shortened and reduced the foot in size. The raised wedge beneath the heel (equivalent to the Western high heel) also contributed illusionistically. The high heel and/or arched insole shortens the foot, in reality and optically; and, by a visual incorporation of the permanently stretched ankle, lends it a kind of phallic extension, which is also present in the artificial heel. The narrow, finely arched foot was supposedly aristocratic and high on the evolutionary scale, whereas the lower classes and races, as well as many quadrupeds, supposedly had flatter and broader feet. Paradoxically, today we see such a foot, although historically imbued with hierarchical symbolism, as functional, in that the high arch is generally regarded as facilitating nimble movement.

Freud did not identify the high shoe heel specifically as a phallic symbol, but it is generally accepted as such by the laity today. The peculiar visual emphasis on the high shoe heel in postwar advertising, coupled with the tendency in fashion at certain periods (notably the 1870s, and even more in the 1950s) to equate sheer height with chic (in fetishism, height equals difficulty equals chic) is strongly suggestive of phallic-erectile symbolism. Slenderness of heel, which has often accompanied height as an absolute aesthetic criterion, has weapon-related sado-masochistic associations ('stiletto' heel) heightened by sharpness of toe.

Now to our third factor in foot-sculpture. Unlike Chinese footwear, the precise shape and length of the shoe-toe in Western fashion has undergone innumerable variations, as have those of the high heel. The pointed-toe effect, recurrently fashionable for women and sometimes shared by men as well, has been obtained in two ways. It is formed illusionistically by lengthening the shoe beyond the natural toes, and it has compressed the toes, eliminating the space between them.

The propensity of Western man and woman to force their feet into a pointed shape has been rhetorically dramatised by Bernard Rudofsky, who, unable to explain it, castigates it, Rousseau-like, as a sign of civilised degeneration. Yet the hierarchical symbolism is fairly clear. As observed above, the big, splayed-toe foot has been generally regarded as 'low'; anthropology has associated it with the Negro race; the hierarchical principle with the working class. Fashionable footwear has sought for centuries to produce 'bilateral symmetry', i.e. a foot longer and pointed in the middle, a shape anathema to nineteenth-century reformers, who cited the projecting big toe (not possessed by apes) 'as a mark of elevation in the scale of organised beings.' It was confusing, not to say embarrassing, that artists, following the ancient Greek canon, should show a preference for ideal figures with a second toe longer than the first, thus tending to justify the 'perverted aesthetic' of fashion.

In the postwar era, the donning of the first 'fashion shoe' has become a rite of passage. Insofar as infants' and schoolgirls' footwear is made with ample breath, the narrowing of the toe, like the raising of the heel, become symbols of sexual maturation. The distinction, moreover, between adults' 'sensible' or walking shoes, flat-heeled and broad-toed like children's wear, and the fashion shoe confirmed the latter in its aesthetic and ceremonial, as opposed to practical, role.

Extreme height and slenderness of heel, accompanied by an acutely pointed toe, serve to increase the wearer's sado-masochistic appeal, endowing her with predatory feet, much as long, pointed fingernails give her clawed hands. The term 'erect ankle', moreover (like 'erect torso'), appears to hold a special significance for fetishists. Extremists, not content with exaggerating the heel height to the point that the instep stands vertical, or even arches backwards into the shoe-vamp, have raised the foot on tiptoe in a shoe blocked in the manner of a ballet-slipper, but retaining an enormous foot-length heel. The 'tiptoe' or 'ballet' boot, often rising to the crotch, represents a 'classic' if extreme form of fetish footwear, one which in the fetishist mind reduces the whole leg to a huge hyper-erect, hyper-constricted or engorged 'phallic' unit. Likewise, the ballerina's leg has been called, by Susan Foster, a 'phallic pointe', making the whole body 'trembling, erect, responsive'.

In ballet, the tip toe stance has semi-contradictory associations with the ethereal, spiritual, airborne. The rising popularity of classical ballet and other forms of tip-toe dance in the nineteenth century represents a major public, artistically more-or-less sublimated manifestation of foot and leg fetishism. Some have seen an erectile phallic symbolism in the high-flailing leg of the can-can dance, also a product of the nineteenth century. The ballet-girl was the erotic priestess, a Terpsichorean hetaera, while the high heel gave to the woman of fashion the erotic lift of the dancer.

Just as certain parts of the body lend themselves by virtue of their shape, size, etc., to sexualisation, so certain movements of the body can suggest sexual action. Body-sculpture is designed to enhance and sexualise the movements of everyday life, as much as it is designed to enhance and sexualise the shape of the human form itself. Ultimately the two processes are inseparable. In the non-Western world, costume is movement, dance, theatre and sexual ritual. In the West, its role in the social rituals involving body-movement (including most obviously social dance), in 'body-language' as the current term goes, deserves further study. Costume historians have tended to view dress as a static agglomerate, outside its social-kinetic context.

Footwear alters not only the appearance of the foot, but also the action of the body as a whole. Significantly, the ordinary act of walking has become imbued with sexual connotations, which are reinforced by language, in equally ordinary words such as 'to come' and 'to go'. The more technical words, such as 'coition' (from Latin *coire*, to go together), 'congress', and 'intercourse', also mean sexual walk.

The intensity and ingenuity with which the West reinforces this association is unique. While the bound foot of China and the ankle-chains and high pattens of the Middle East suggest immobilisation and captivity, the Western shoe inhibits movement in order to increase it, at least in appearance. Standing in her high-heeled shoes, woman presents herself already half-walking, ready to go, ready for action. By reducing the length of the step, the high heel fosters the illusion of speed. It can even appear to increase step-capacity, lending some women the air of giants in seven-league boots. While there are women who walk more securely in high heels than their sisters in low or no heels, and there are those whose locomotion in high heels is an aggressive appropriation of space and time (which is why such heels are no enemy to feminism), the contrary and complementary associations are with precariousness and imbalance, the appeal for a supporting arm, the promise of imminent fall, surrender. High-heeled woman thus becomes, for man, a tantalising object of the chase, an incarnation of the restlessness of his own spirit and the socio-sexual contradictions with which it is fraught. The higher and more unstable-looking the heel, the more clearly these contradictions are expressed, and the more clearly is the duality exposed between woman immobilised, viewed as a passive sex-object, and woman elusive, (literally) *impeding* sexual fulfilment.

Since with the high and slender heel the points of support for the foot are drastically reduced (especially when the heel is also pitched forward), the ankle is obliged to undertake all sorts of compensatory actions, so that it, the instep and even the whole leg adopt a 'wobbling' or 'quivering', 'tottering' or 'teetering' action. Each word has its own associations, negative and positive. The lateral quiver of the ankle each time the foot hits the ground as the woman approaches the man, may be unconsciously interpreted by him, if he is at all susceptible, as sexual invitation.

The woman, moreover, experiences narcissistically a muscular provocation within herself, for the redistribution of muscular effort over the whole of her body serves to increase her sense of the body kinetic. As described to me by a habitual wearer of extreme stiletto heels, whose work in an office required constant movement: 'I feel I am in a constant and interesting state of tension; simply standing, I am on the go; turning round, bending to file a paper, is a balancing act; I am at rest only when I sit, which is never for long. I wear these heels because they make me feel in constant contact with my body.' Which distracted her, no doubt, from the mental boredom of her work.

Physicians assumed in the nineteenth century, as they still do, that this muscular adaptation would produce long-term adverse muscular and even organic changes in the body, but the physiology of these changes has been little studied. Objectively, a rather radical change in posture is involved, the exact character of which is problematical, and seems to vary according to the cultural epoch, as well as with the individual. Opponents of high heels have stressed the ungainly thrusting forward of the chin by the inexperienced high-heel wearer, supposedly as a counterweight. But the thrusting chin may be as much a psychological as a physical reaction, deriving from the fear of falling backwards and the instinctive search for some forward point of support. Little Chinese girls, learning to walk again after their feet were first bound, were explicitly warned against the bad habit of poking out their chin. In the 1870s, Western critics complained that high heels caused a pitching forward from the waist ('Grecian Bend') . . .; in the 1950s, on the other hand, such heels were accused of causing a slouched back and excessive bending at the knees. The defence has always claimed that they produced an upright carriage, head back, chest out. Clearly, there are many variables at play, the relative influence of which will depend upon the individual type of body, gait and psychology.

The way in which women walk has always varied from culture to culture, as has the socio-sexual symbolism. The Western high-heeled walk involves a quickening of leg and hip action that the Easterner would find unfeminine. The Chinese ideal gait was evidently a quiet, liquid waddle or shuffle, which binding, even more than the raised heel, was designed to induce. The walk of the Renaissance Venetian lady of fashion on her zoccoli was sometimes actually supported by servants on either side, and described as 'majestically deliberating of every step.' The nobility in some primitive cultures so shackle their feet with metal rings (connotive of wealth) that, on the ceremonial occasions when they wear them, they can barely move at all.

The hierarchical symbolism here is simple enough. In the West it operates in a contradictory manner. As exaggerated by the fetishist, footwear takes on powerful sado-masochistic associations, defining woman as submissive-aggressive, both predator and prey. To extrapolate from the fetishist literature: the modern Amazon shoots arrows into the ground with her feet, and strikes twofold pleasure-pain, imagined or real, into the fantasy of the male: that of her own fight against peculiar self-imposed shackles, and that of his own physical subjection, his body trodden (dented, even pierced) by the goddess before whom he secretly wishes to abase himself. A tight-lacer who works as a primary school teacher told me that one of her pupils, an 11-year-old, confessed to her his fantasy that he was a carpet over which she walked with her 5in stiletto heels.

We have started with the symbolism of the high heel because, as a 'fashion-fetish', it is still very much with us and appears less fraught with historical problems. Tight-lacing, however, historically the primary 'fashion-fetish' of the West, is imbued with the more potent hierarchical and sexual associations.

The most immediate visual effect of waist compression is to enhance the secondary female characteristics of comparative breadth of bust and hips, and at the same time increase the comparative slenderness of waist, with its evident connotations of youthfulness and physical leisure. The corset has also traditionally served to suggest firmness of the torso, and to raise the breasts, two other features associated with youth. Cultivation of the appearance and symbols of youth, which may be a characteristic of dynamic Western civilisations, has climaxed over the twentieth century, degenerating now into a pre-mammary, pre-pubescent ideal (Twiggy, etc.) that has paradoxically inhibited the return of the corset.

Waist or torso compression and breast-sculpture have been historically inseparable. The 'uplift' obtained by modern brassiére engineering was earlier achieved by the corset, the top of which pushed against the lower part of the breasts. Even the older and less well-endowed woman could thus produce an interesting and essentially juvenile swelling over the upper half of the breasts, and reverse the concave-convex shape which becomes more marked and pendulous with age. Thus are intimated the perfect hemispheres beloved of the poets and artists. Round and succulent-looking, these carnal apples (to use an age-old metaphor) are temptingly hidden and offered by the daughter of Eve, whose arms clasped over her bosom imitate or enhance the pressure of the stays (as in the Rubens portrait). At certain periods of history, which reach intermittently from the sixteenth to the eighteenth century, thoracic constriction was accompanied, not by the raising, but by the actual compression, of the breasts as a whole. Such breast-flattening served to emphasise breadth of hips, and suggest procreative power rather than sexual pleasure. Inconspicuous and flattened breasts have, however, never established themselves for long in the Western tradition, as they have in Asia.

The consciously modulated and aggressive forms of breast-sculpture which emerged in the post-Second-World-War era seem to correspond to a peculiarly Western sexual anxiety, which has taken positively phallic forms, or aggressive phallic associations. Manipulation of the breast by (male) fashion-designers has recently been castigated with feminist fervour: '[the female breasts] are a millstone around a woman's neck . . . they are not parts of a person but lures slung around her neck, to be kneaded and twisted like magic putty, or mumbled and mouthed like lolly-ices . . . Recent emphasis on the nipple, which was absent from the breast of popular pornography, is in women's favour, for the nipple is expressive and responsive.' The recent emergence into fashion of the natural nipple, the contour of which may be clearly delineated beneath an extra-light brassière (or, if the owner goes bra-less, under a clinging fabric), is indeed new, although the peaked bras of the 1950s may have been unconsciously intended to stylise erection of the nipple. These, like the male codpiece of the sixteenth century, served the illusion of a body in a permanent state of sexual excitation.

The constant reshaping, resizing and relocating of the bust by fashion in the course of the twentieth century may reflect the acute social instability of the era and embody very variable socio-sexual associations, which we cannot explore here.

The nurturance or fertility symbolism of the full, round breast is obvious and needs no further elucidation; the hierarchical symbolism is principally that of the sexual toy. The symbolism of the slender waist in itself, that is apart from its role in throwing breasts into higher relief, has many dimensions. Sylph-like delicacy of body and fragility of waist have exercised an almost archetypal attraction for man, for whom they connote both vulnerability and elusiveness. It is both foil and invocation to his superior socio-sexual power. The slender waist suggests the romantic and ethereal, the pure and virginal, all erotic qualities. The anti-maternalism (or – paternalism) that it also embodies, in so far as it denies, defies or even reverses the idea of pregnancy, is another matter, with far-reaching (and scandalous) social implications. Conversely, the small waist also says: obviously not pregnant now, I can be made so.

As with high heels, the corset may create a dynamic between restriction and movement. Compression in a relatively non-sexual area – the waist – induces movement in other, primarily sexual ones – bust and hips. The complementary character of high heels and tight-lacing, confirmed time and again in fetishism and in the history of costume, has its basis as far as body-dynamics are concerned in the fact (axiomatic with fetishists) that both enhance hip action, and that both mutually reinforce or complement each other in procuring 'erect' posture.

The correct posture of a lady since the eighteenth century has been erect; as with footwear, the 'erect' connotes social dignity and superiority. It distinguishes man from the animal: 'The erect human posture is an erogenous feature of its own. . . . The entire problem of posture is of deep-seated sexual significance.' It was the lower classes who went around with bowed backs, 'bad posture', because of the work they did and because they knew no better. Erect also means taller: posture can literally increase height, as can waist compression, which forces the lower ribs upwards and the pelvis downwards, stretching the spine ever so slightly and making it more comfortable to stand as tall as possible.

Erect posture and correct gait involved a degree of immobility in the upper half of the body. It is assumed today that in long, wide skirts that concealed her hips and legs woman 'floated' or progressed as if on wheels. While it is easy to understand how the stiff, tight-laced corset induced an erect posture, it is not clear that it would necessarily induce a floating walk. Indeed, the very opposite may be the case. The dress reformers' charge that tight-lacing induced a poor imitation of the correct walk, that is, a stiff 'parlour-tongue' gait, whether generally justified or not, may be based on the observation of a reaction *against* its movement-enhancing properties. It is self-evident that small movements about the pelvic girdle and ribcage will appear magnified if the area between is restricted. Additional movement may also be induced by certain compensatory actions, especially when walking, as a more or less unconscious, quasi-physiological response to intense local pressure, which may be relieved by changing the relative positions of pelvis and ribs. The tight-lacer may also seek to compensate for the relative immobility of the torso by exploiting the relative flexibility of hips and shoulders.

The swaying hips and flaunting bust can easily become overtly provocative. What is socially permissible in our own times, legitimised by the sex-goddesses of screen and stage, was, however, taboo to the Victorian lady, who, if she dared to tight-lace, may have felt (unconsciously) obliged to fight any body-expansive tendency induced by her corset that might overdetermine and betray a purpose hidden, as often as not, even from herself: that of sexual seduction.

In the late Victorian and Edwardian periods, on two distinct occasions, fashion discovered a further means of enhancing body-contour and movement, which, although not strictly sculptural, drastically modified body-action: binding of the legs by means of knee-tight skirts. The open-legged position has always been regarded as potentially indecent (one has only to think of the resistance to the idea of woman riding astride, and the fear of accidental breaking of the hymen in this position), and was totally prohibited to respectable women. It was even found suspect in its modified form of the crossed or slung leg, and acted, in art, as a metaphor for sexual intercourse. The close-pressed thighs and hobbled gait characteristic of fashion in the 1870s and 1910s are arguably connotive of chastity in an ambivalent, perverse, but by now not unfamiliar way. The tight skirt may be regarded as an even more provocative kind of hobbling than the high heel, especially in the 1870s, when tight-lacing was carried to new extremes, hips, thighs and buttocks were anatomically moulded, and locomotion depended upon vigorous agitation of the pelvic girdle. We have here a mutually reinforcing yet inherently contradictory cause-and-effect cycle: hips and breast swelling and agitated, legs tied together — thus sexual invitation and sexual denial simultaneously, the ultimate in provocation.

Tight-lacing also heightens sexuality by quickening the action of the lungs. It suppresses breathing over the belly and forces it upwards, momentarily and eventually permanently enlarging the thoracic cage. Many women experience inhibition of breathing, on a swing or by other means, as erotic, 'breathtaking'. Sexual experience is 'like when a swing goes too high. You feel you're cut in two, you swoop down, and you scream "Ha!" ' (This from Colette, who goes on to relate the mysticism of breathlessness, of 'losing all sense of existence, dying' to Polaire, the most famous wasp-waist of the age, whom she sets up as the young girl's ideal.) Elimination of abdominal in favour of pectoral breathing creates, moreover, movement about the breasts, which may be imagined constantly palpitating with desire. This sexualised change in breathing, this 'subclavicular enticement' and 'unnatural agitation' agitated fearful males.

The spasms to which the body is subject during orgasm involve, of course, an often violent quickening of breathing, sensations of breathlessness, heaving of the chest, and contraction of the belly, all of which may be erotically enhanced by manual pressure at the waist, and artificially induced by means of a corset. Similarly, the climactic response of spasmic twitching of the feet, stretching of the instep and curling up of the toes, is mimicked by the action and position of the feet in high heels.

[. . .]

Chapter 46

Valerie Steele

FASHION AND FETISHISM

THROUGHOUT THE NINETEENTH CENTURY, popular wisdom held that tight-lacing was foolish, pernicious, and all too common. "There is not one woman in a hundred" who does not suffer from "the wasp-waist mania," argued an American writer. Although physicians had denounced tight-lacing for centuries, they had failed to cure the "disease." Women's addiction to "the corset habit" was a "mystery" that "no man can understand," except by reference to "the proverbial feminine craze for emulating one another and arousing envy by excelling in some extravagance of dress, no matter at what cost."[1] Critics of tight-lacing attacked the practice on both "hygienic" and "aesthetic" grounds; it was dangerously unhealthy, and it was ugly and unnatural.[2] But by characterizing tight-lacing as a mania, a disease, and an addiction, it seems clear that critics perceived the real issue as the supposed immorality and depravity of the practice.

Girls and women who tight-laced were not merely vain and irrational. They were thought to be engaged in an evil habit, akin to masturbation. Their "perverted taste" and "criminal" behavior would necessarily result in "disease and pain."[3] "No young lady acknowledges herself to be laced too tight," warned Mrs. Sigourney. Mothers had to be aware of the symptoms of "hurtful practices" and "habits that shun the light." "Though the sufferer from tight-lacing may not own herself to be uncomfortable," though she may "throw an illusion over those who try to save her . . . and like the Spartan culprit, conceal the destroyer that feeds upon her vitals," the wise mother would know that "the laborious respiration, the constrained movement, perhaps the curved spine, bring different testimony."[4]

How tightly were corsets really laced? Significantly, there was no agreement about the precise definition of "tight-lacing." Women usually denied that they personally tight-laced. It was always someone else, such as an actress or a servant or a foolish young girl, who was accused of being a tight-lacer. This is hardly surprising, since, as we have seen, tight-lacers were frequently compared to suicides and infanticides, torturers and murderers. They were bad women, who solicited the lecherous gaze of "vulgar" men. Specifically, they were bad mothers – at a time in the late nineteenth century when motherhood was seen as women's sacred duty. As the English fashion writer Mrs. Haweis warned, "The sins of the mothers are . . . visited on the children . . . a deformed parent may create an idiot child . . . and many obscure horrors may spring from such a seed as a pinched waist."[5] Like "savages," tight-lacers deliberately deformed their God-given bodies until they resembled insects.

There were, however, some people who openly boasted about tight-lacing. From 1867 to 1874, *The Englishwoman's Domestic Magazine* (*EDM*) printed more than 150 letters on corsetry, many of which described tight-lacing to extreme tenuity (wasp waists of 16 inches or less). The letters included firsthand testimony of enforced tight-lacing at fashionable boarding schools, as well as fervent defenses of tight-lacing. The "corset correspondence" published in the magazine was revived occasionally thereafter in other periodicals, and it radically altered the discourse about tight-lacing in two ways. First, in its extreme claims and notoriety, it tended to overwhelm other contemporary discussions of tight-lacing. Secondly, it became retrospectively the primary source of "documentary" material on Victorian tight-lacing, skewing almost all later analyses of the subject.

Size is the first issue. How tightly did women lace? "Women ought to measure from 27 to 29 inches round the waist; but most females do not allow themselves to grow beyond 24; thousands are laced to 21, some to less than 20," declared *The Family Herald* (1848).[6] Although it is impossible to be certain, the evidence indicates that these figures seem plausible, at least for younger women. Yet the *EDM* correspondence focuses on much smaller waist sizes. The circumstances in which tight-lacing occurred also differ significantly. A great many young women probably did lace rather tightly on occasion, such as to attend a party that required clothing that was both formal and fashionable.

But the self-proclaimed "votaries of tight-lacing" emphasized dramatic reductions in waist size through rigorous "disciplinary" practices. "A Lady from Edinburgh," for example, wrote to the *EDM* in March 1867 to say that her daughter had been subjected at boarding school to a "merciless system of tight lacing." She and her fellow pupils had been "imprisoned in views of whalebone drawn tight by the muscular arms of sturdy waiting maids, till the fashionable standard of tenuity was attained." It was "torture," but "all entreaties were in vain," and "the lady principal . . . punished [her] severely for rebelling against the discipline of the school."[7] This was followed by many other letters, such as one from "Nora," who wrote to the *EDM* in May 1867, claiming to have attended "a fashionable school in London" where "it was the custom for the waists of the pupils to be reduced one inch per month . . . When I left school . . . my waist measured only thirteen inches."[8]

The *EDM* correspondence is fascinating to read, and it has frequently been cited as evidence of horrific tight-lacing during the Victorian era.[9] Correspondents such as "Alfred" expounded on the desirability of girls being "subjected to the strictest discipline of the corset." "Moralist" declared, "If you want a girl to grow up gentle and womanly in her ways and her feelings, lace her tight."[10] This does indeed sound like patriarchal abuse run mad, but there are serious problems with such a naive reading of this material.

To begin with, are these stories true? And are they typical of the behavior and attitudes of the period? Mainstream periodicals as diverse as *The Saturday Review*, *Punch*, and *The Lancet* heaped scorn on the *EDM* letters. The veracity of the letters was denied, while the opinions expressed were derided. Clearly, a nerve had been struck. In an article of 1869 on "The Elasticity of Young Ladies," *Punch* even compared the *EDM* correspondents with the notorious murderess Maria Manning (who killed her husband).[11] Some dress scholars, such as Doris Langley Moore in 1949, also characterized the *EDM* letters as "spurious" and simply the fantasies of a few "perverts," among whom she included the magazine's editor, Samuel Beeton.[12] This judgment seems to suggest that the letters should be dismissed altogether as evidence about nineteenth-century corsetry. Yet, at the very least, they provide valuable evidence of sexual fantasies about corsetry.

Other scholars, notably the art historian David Kunzle, have gone to the other extreme, arguing that the letters are largely authentic reports of personal experiences, accurately described. But whereas feminists have interpreted the letters as evidence that Victorian women were forced to submit to tight-lacing, either because fashion dictated a small waist or because male fetishists made women wear tight corsets, Kunzle argues that most tight-lacers who wrote to the *EDM* were sexually assertive female "fetishists," who were themselves erotically stimulated by tight corsets.[13] There are many problems with this idea, even apart from the reliability of the source material. For example, although he denies that women who wore tight corsets were masochists, the scenarios described tend to focus on bondage and discipline. It is doubtful, however, whether the reality of tight-lacing (whether fetishist or not) corresponded to the picture presented by the corset correspondents, let alone to Kunzle's edited and sanitized version, which omits or plays down references to "punishment corsets" and "fair flagellants."

Over the course of this chapter, it will become apparent that these letters need to be analyzed primarily as sexual fantasies, although they also reveal the existence of sexual subcultures involving fetishism, sadomasochism, and transvestism.[14] More importantly, it will become evident that fetishistic tight-lacing should not be confused with ordinary fashionable corsetry. Many women today wear high-heeled shoes, for example, but we recognize that there is a difference between ordinary fashionable shoes and the kind of fetish shoes with seven-inch heels worn by the professional dominatrix. Yet it is entirely possible that ordinarily fashionable women are also sometimes tight-laced. Indeed, as we shall see, this is quite likely, although the definitions of "tight-lacing," the circumstances under which tight-lacing occurred, and the significance it had may be quite different in the real world than in the literature of Victorian fetishists.

What is fetishism? The term is often used loosely to refer to the objectification of the female body. More precisely, fetishism is a type of variant sexuality involving the use of specific stimuli (such as corsets or high heels) for sexual arousal. There are degrees of fetishism, ranging from a preference for certain stimuli to the necessity for specific stimuli if sexual arousal and performance is to occur. In extreme cases, the fetish actually takes the place of a sex partner. For example, the fetishist might masturbate with a pair of shoes. Some psychiatrists believe that a degree of fetishizing is "the norm for males." Clinical studies also show that a higher level of fetishism frequently overlaps with sadomasochism and transvestism. As with all of the sexual "perversions," clinical cases of fetishism overwhelmingly involve males. The only (partial) exception is masochism, which is mainly a male characteristic but which is also found in a small but statistically significant number of women. Even so, by some estimates male masochists outnumber female masochists by a ratio of twenty to one; 99% of sexual fetishists are believed to be men.[15]

The question of female fetishism is important, nevertheless. In their book *Female Fetishism* (1994), Lorraine Gamman and Merja Makinen write: "Representations of women in corsets or high-heeled shoes may look fetishistic to some feminists, but whose is the fetishism under scrutiny, and what degree of fetishism are we talking about?"[16] The authors are attracted to the idea that fetishism is potentially sexually liberating for women, although they also suggest that eating disorders may constitute a type of fetishism. Moreover, despite Gamman and Makinen's characterization of some modern women as "active practitioners of fetishism,"[17] it seems improbable that there were more than a tiny number of Victorian female corset fetishists. On the contrary, the evidence indicates that the vast majority of corset fetishists were (and are) men. Among contemporary tight-lacers, men seem to outnumber women. Women who wear fetish clothing on a regular basis usually do so either because they are sex workers or because their male partners like these clothes. Cathy Jung, for example, says that she wears a tight corset because her husband finds it attractive.[18] With regard to the corset correspondences in Victorian magazines, it seems likely that men were the source of most stories about eroticized tight-lacing, and that most of these stories represented fantasies rather than actual experience. To distinguish among fashion, fetish, and fantasy, it is necessary to explore the specialized literature on tight-lacing.

"What is the smallest size waist known?" asked "Seraphine."[19] The year was 1862 and Samuel Beeton, editor of the *EDM*, only briefly quoted from the letter in which she claimed to have a waist measuring 15¾ inches. Later he actively solicited correspondence on the subject. Meanwhile, in 1863, "Constance" wrote to another fashion magazine, *The Queen*, also founded by Beeton, asking if tight-lacing was becoming fashionable and claiming to have a waist measurement of 16½ inches.[20] The next week, "Fanny" wrote to *The Queen* to say that yes, tight-lacing was fashionable; many women had waists of 16 inches or even less; and that she had personally attended a tight-lacing school outside Paris. Specifics of corset "discipline" and "bondage" were combined with a dream-like vagueness of narrative:

> Up to the age of fifteen, I was . . . suffered to run . . . wild . . . and grew stout, indifferent and careless as to personal appearance . . . Family circumstances and change of fortune . . . led my relatives to the conclusion that my education required a continental finish . . . I was . . . packed off to a highly genteel and fashionable establishment for young ladies, situated in the suburbs of Paris . . . [where] I was subjected to the strict and rigid system of lacing in force through the whole establishment, no relaxation of its discipline being allowed . . . and on taking my departure [three years later] I had grown from a clumsy girl to a very smart young lady, and my waist was exactly seven inches less than on the day of my arrival.[21]

Over the next few years, dozens of letters for and against tight-lacing were published in *The Queen*. "Eliza," for example, wrote several times in 1863 in favor of tight-lacing and claimed to have a 16-inch waist.[22]

A specialized literature in favor of tight-lacing was proliferating. In 1865, an unidentified person, using the nom de plume Madame de la Santé, wrote a pamphlet entitled *The Corset Defended*, which was approvingly reviewed in *The Queen*.[23] No sooner had the correspondence lapsed in *The Queen* than it flared up in the *EDM*. A number of the pro-tight-lacing letters were then reprinted in a book entitled *The Corset and the Crinoline* (1868), which also quoted La Santé's *The Corset Defended*: "Madame La Santé says – 'A waist may vary in circumference from seventeen to twenty-three inches' . . . We have abundant evidence before us, however, that seventeen inches is by no means the lowest standard of waist-measure to be met with in the fashionable circles of either London, New York, Paris, or Vienna. Numbers of corsets [measure] sixteen inches at the waist, and even less . . ."[24] Another book was published in 1871, entitled *Figure Training* by "E.D.M." Later it was reissued under the more pejorative title, *Freaks of Fashion*.

The corset correspondence in the *EDM* caused a sensation in Victorian England, because of what we now recognize as its sexually fetishistic and sadomasochistic nature. Correspondents argued that "half the charm in a small waist comes, not in spite of, but on account of, its being tight-laced"; "– the tighter the better"; "well-applied restraint is in itself attractive." Such opinions were, of course, diametrically opposed to the generally expressed belief that only "naturally small" waists were really attractive. Many of the tight-lacing letters have a pronounced sadomasochistic tone. References to "discipline," "confinement," "compulsion," "suffering," "torture," "agony," "submission," "martyrs," and "victims" abound – as do references to the "delightful," "delicious," "exquisite," "exciting," "pleasurable," and "superb" sensations experienced by tight-lacers. By contrast, the ordinary pro-corset literature, including corset advertisements, emphasized that well-made corsets provided "ease," "freedom," and "comfort." The anti-corset literature often described tight-lacing as "torture," but the only "victims" mentioned were unborn children. The *EDM* also published dozens of letters on flagellation, high heels, cross-dressing, and spurs for lady riders – all, needless to say, highly atypical of the ordinary discourse on fashion and corsetry.

The letters advocating enforced and painful tight-lacing of girls should really be read in conjunction with those on corporal punishment and cross-dressing. There were so many letters on whipping submitted to the *EDM* that the magazine published a special supplement devoted to them. There also developed an entire subgenre of letters advocating that boys and young men should be tight-laced at the hands of powerful women. The first and most famous of these was "Walter's" letter to the *EDM* of November 1867, which was still being quoted decades later in other fetishist correspondences:

> I was early sent to school in Austria, where lacing is not considered ridiculous in a gentleman as it is in England, and I objected in a thoroughly English way when the doctor's wife required me to be laced. . . . A sturdy *mädchen* was stoically deaf to my remonstrances, and speedily laced me up tightly . . . the daily lacing tighter and tighter produced

inconvenience and absolute pain. In a few months, however, I was . . . anxious . . . to have my corsets laced as tightly as a pair of strong arms could draw them.[25]

Over the years, many letters argued that disciplinary corsetry had "advantages, not only for girls, but also for boys."[26] Indeed, youths were said to need discipline more than their sisters, because they were rowdier and being corseted would make them "more tractable to the ladies having their management."[27]

In the 1880s, *The Family Doctor and People's Medical Advisor* picked up where the *EDM* had left off, publishing many articles and letters on tight-lacing, as well as letters on corporal punishment, high heels, underwear, and piercing. Not a professional medical journal, *The Family Doctor* was put out by the publishers of *The Illustrated Police News* and was sensationalistic. The "slaves of the stay lace" (as they called themselves) found bondage and waist confinement erotic in its own right. This was highly atypical of popular opinion, which praised "naturally" small waists, and complained that obvious compression was ugly as well as unhealthy. The correspondents for *The Family Doctor* also talked a lot about tight-lacing boarding schools.

An illustration from *The Family Doctor* of 1888 purports to show three young "martyrs" to tight-lacing: Mabel M who is described as having a waist of 12 inches; Bertha G, age 15, waist 11 inches; and Constance, waist 14½ inches."[28] Similar measurements were given in an article "Does Tight-Lacing Really Exist?" by Hygeia, which included [Table 46.1].[29]

Table 46.1

Name	Age	Size of waist	Reduce to	To wear corset
Nelly G.	15	20 inches	16 inches	Night and Day
Helen Vogler	12	21 inches	15 inches	Day
G. Van de M.	14	19 inches	13 inches	Night and Day
V.G.	13	22 inches	12 inches, if possible	Night and Day
Alice M.	17	16 inches	14 inches	Night and Day
Cora S.	16	18 inches	13 inches	Night and Day

Throughout the 1890s and into the twentieth century, other periodicals such as *Modern Society, Society,* and *London Life* published letters from advocates of tight-lacing, cross-dressing, and the rod.[30] Pornographic books, such as *Experiences of Flagellation* (1885) by "an amateur flagellant," also continued to cite the *EDM* while gloating about "FLOGGING SCHOOL."[31] Corporal punishment was, of course, a real feature of Victorian life, especially in boys' boarding schools, but other aspects of the tight-lacing scenarios seem more fantastic.

Certain foreign locales, especially Vienna, were said to be hotbeds of tight-lacing and crossdressing. In 1893, for example, V.S. wrote to say that he had been sent to Vienna, where "both sexes lace up tight." The school was run by a retired officer: "All his pupils were required to wear stays." Discipline was enforced by the principal's two tight-lacing daughters, one of whom was seventeen years old and had a 14-inch waist.[32] "An Upright Figure" was also sent to school in Vienna and quickly "found myself thoroughly under staylace *régime*," held "more and more erect" in an 18-inch corset.[33] Undisciplined and uncorseted for years, the boys are ultimately forced to submit – often at foreign boarding schools and almost always at the hands of a cruel but beautiful governess, principal, stepmother, French mistress, aided by various maids and daughters.

In a letter that recalls "Fanny's" 1863 missive to *The Queen*, "Stays" recounted how, "up to the age of sixteen I was allowed by my guardian unrestrained license to eat . . . and to slouch about." Then he was sent off to a school where all the boys were put into corsets, "which were laced each morning as firmly as possible by two maids when we came down to be inspected . . . by our principal's wife, who had herself the great advantage of going through the *régime* of an extremely fashionable finishing school in Paris."[34] "Admirer of Pretty Feet" (who clearly had several fetishes) also advocated "the compulsory wearing of . . . good, strongly-boned, stiff-busked, firm corsets," and claimed to have gone to a strict school, where he was tight-laced, slapped, and whipped by the "young lady" in charge:

> To be thoroughly well corseted . . . is an excellent reminder to any lad . . . that he can not have all his own way. The degree of tightness must vary, of course . . . but as a general rule it may be considered that in a moderate time any pupil, whether youth or girl, may be required to lace to two-thirds of the natural waist measurement. . . . As to the best persons to administer discipline, I have not a moment's hesitation in giving my voice in favour of the fair sex . . . it is one of the privileges of a pretty woman to be tyrannical.[35]

Contemporary pornography also frequently features dominant females, or what the Victorians liked to call "cruel ladies." Such representations of women should not, however, be taken at face value.

Another correspondent reported that when flogging failed to tame him, he was sent to a special tight-lacing boarding school:

> On my arrival I was immediately laced into an extremely tight, heavily-boned corset, fastened with a small padlock, and was securely locked in with a tiny key, which dangled among the jeweled charms fastened to the slender waist of the lady principal, a handsome widow, who was then about twenty-four. . . . The fair disciplinarian was . . . extremely strict. If she was displeased with us she would frequently tighten our corset with her own small, delicate white hands, and then, having made us prisoners with the dreaded key, would laughingly dismiss us with a smart slap on our cheek. . . . I went there a conceited, rough lad, and I left a perfectly obedient, polite youth.[36]

The theme of boarding schools, so popular in the corset correspondences, may well be related to the existence of specialized brothels, where male clients could engage in what today is known as role playing. There is no evidence that special tight-lacing boarding schools existed, either in England or in exotic foreign cities, such as Paris and Vienna. However, it is known that nineteenth-century brothels frequently did contain wardrobes of dress-up clothes, including nuns' habits, which recall pornographic fantasies of sexual misbehavior in convents.

It is also true that one occasionally finds advertisements for men's corsets, which seem to be aimed at a specialized client base. Madame Dowding, for example, in the late 1890s not only advertised a woman's corset called The Princess Wasp Waist, but also sold a variety of men's belts and stays – often with military names, such as the Carlton and the Marlboro.

The boarding school is also a class marker: many of the corset correspondents boast about their genteel families and aristocratic classmates. Anti-tight-lacing writers argue, in contrast, that the practice is seldom seen in good society, but only among servants and other lower-class women. The actual class background of correspondents is, of course, impossible to determine, although style, content, and production values of the *EDM* and *The Family Doctor* seem to indicate that both magazines had a predominantly middle- and/or lower-middle-class readership. Circulation figures are unknown, although these would not necessarily indicate the size of the "fetishist" readership, which was probably only a small percentage of total readers.

[. . .]

Notes

1   Henry T. Finck, *Romantic Love and Personal Beauty* (New York: Macmillan [1887], 1912), p. 379.
2   *Ibid.*, pp. 380–81.
3   "Tight Dressing – Corsets," *The Mother's Book* (August, 1838), p. 170.
4   Mrs. L. H. Sigourney, "On Health – To Mothers," ibid., p. 188.
5   Mrs. H. R. Haweis, *The Art of Dress* (London: Chatto & Windus, 1879), p. 35.
6   *The Family Herald* (March 4, 1848), p. 700, quoted in Peter Farrar, *Tight Lacing: A Bibliography of Articles and Letters Concerning Stays and Corsets for Men and Women* (Liverpool: Karn Publications Garston, 1999), p. 6.
7   A Lady from Edinburgh, *The English-woman's Domestic Magazine* [hereafter *EDM*] (March 1867), pp. 164–5. Reproduced in W. B. L. [William Barry Lord], *The Corset and the Crinoline* (London: Ward, Lock, and Tyler, n.d. [1868]), p. 193, p. 172.
8   Nora, *EDM* (May, 1867), p. 279.
9   Susan Faludi, *Backlash: The Undeclared War Against American Women* (New York: Crown, 1991), p. 173.
10 Alfred, *EDM* (January, 1871), p. 62; Moralist, *EDM* (February, 1871), p. 127.
11 "The Elasticity of Young Ladies," *Punch* (September 18, 1869), p. 111.
12 Doris Langley Moore, *The Woman in Fashion* (London: Batsford, 1949), pp. 17–18.
13 See David Kunzle, *Fashion and Fetishism: A Social History of the Corset, Tight Lacing, and Other Forms of Body Sculpture in the West* (Totowa, New Jersey: Rowman and Littlefield, 1982).
14 See Valerie Steele, *Fashion and Eroticism: Ideals of Feminine Beauty from the Victorian Era to the Jazz Age* (New York and Oxford: Oxford University Press, 1985), pp.

161–91; and Valerie Steele, *Fetish: Fashion, Sex, and Power* (New York and Oxford: Oxford University Press, 1996), pp. 57–90.

15   See Steele, *Fetish*, pp. 11–14.

16   Lorraine Gamman and Merja Makinen, *Female Fetishism* (New York University Press, 1994), p. 62.

17   *Ibid.*, p. 89.

18   See Steele, *Fetish*, p. 83.

19   Seraphine, *EDM* (July, 1862), p. 144.

20   Constance, *The Queen* (July 18, 1863), p. 44. Reproduced in W. B. L., *The Corset and the Crinoline*, p. 155.

21   Fanny, *The Queen* (July 25, 1863), p. 55. Reproduced in *ibid.*, p. 156.

22   Eliza, *The Queen* (August 1, 1863), p. 80. Reproduced in *ibid.*, p. 159. See also *The Queen* (December 5, 1863), p. 376 and (December 19, 1863), p. 411.

23   Madame de la Santé, *The Corset Defended* (London: T. E. Carler, 1865), reviewed in *The Queen* (February 25, 1865), p. 127. See Peter Farrar, *Tight-Lacing*, p. 34, as well as Peter Farrer, *The Regime of the Stay-Lace: A Further Selection of Letters from Victorian Newspapers* (Liverpool: Karn Publications Garston, 1995).

24   W. B. L., *The Corset and the Crinoline*, p. 193.

25   Walter, *EDM* (November, 1867), p. 613.

26   Medicus Parens, *The Family Doctor* (May 18, 1889), p. 184.

27   Experimentum Crucis, *The Family Doctor* (June 29, 1889), p. 281.

28   *The Family Doctor* (March 3, 1888).

29   Hygeia, "Does Tight-Lacing Really Exist?" *The Family Doctor* (September 3, 1887).

30   See Steele, *Fashion and Eroticism*, pp. 249–52.

31   An Amateur Flagellant, *Experiences of Flagellation* (London: Printed for Private Circulation, 1885), pp. 14, 80.

32   V. S., *The Family Doctor* (January 7, 1893), p. 300.

33   An Upright Figure, *The Family Doctor* (May 13, 1893), p. 172.

34   Stays, *ibid.*

35   Admirer of Pretty Feet, *The Family Doctor* (June 8, 1889), pp. 232–3.

36   R.D.B., *The Family Doctor* (June 29, 1889), pp. 281–2.

Chapter 47

Lorraine Gamman and Merja Makinen

FEMALE FETISHISM

[. . .]

Fashion and fetishism

THE RELATIONSHIP BETWEEN CLOTHES and fetishism is diverse and complex. Fetishism of clothing may include 'orthodox' sexual fetishism, that is orgasm from an article of clothing which becomes the fetish object. But clothes can also function as icons of commodity fetishism, because consumerism uses sexuality, or more particularly, codes of the sexual erotic, to give fashion *meaning*. Pleasure from over-emphasising parts of the body through dress – be it breasts, waist, thighs, etc. – may have a connection to visual pleasure, in that such images please the eye by fragmenting, sculpting or simply objectifying the body; but visual images are not always necessarily the same thing as fetish objects. As fetish objects, visual images rarely accommodate fourth degree sexual fetishism. Yet cultural practices that accommodate body modification – from corset-wearing to foot-binding – are commonly interpreted by fashion historians, like Laver, as 'fetishism', even though such practices rarely accommodate orgasm in *preference* to some other sexual stimulation or contact. We would argue that such images and practices should be looked at as mild forms of fetishism, or, as in the case of tight lacing associated with corset wearing, perhaps as forms of S&M practice, depending on the context under scrutiny.

There are so many myths about fashion and fetishism that it is no wonder that there is confusion. Fashion historians often use the term fetishism when they mean eroticism, and this slippage of terminology is very common to many discussions of fashion. Generally, fetishism of clothing is usually associated with men rather than women. Stereotoypes of men being fascinated with women's clothes (for example

DH Lawrence's obsession with Gudrun's stockings in *Women in Love* have been with us for a long time, as have the stereotypes of men secretly dressing themselves up in women's clothes. Then there are the stereotypes of men, out of control around the fetish item, 'stealing' women's underwear. These too have been with us at least since the nineteenth century when writers like Krafft Ebing connected all sexual diversity with deviance and actual criminality.

The narratives that accompany such stereotypes in books by sexologists often represent men as extreme cases and as 'out of control'. Women are usually seen as victims of male sexuality and it is argued that fashions such as corsets, or even suspenders and stockings are just designed to 'please' men. Linda Gordon and Ellen Dubois go so far as to suggest that women in the nineteenth century, who campaigned against prostitution for the social purity movement, simultaneously colluded with ideologies that underplayed the existence and intensity of female sexual desire.[1] Even today these attitudes are still with us and can be found in the sort of feminist criticism that connects women wearing 'fetish-fashions' – from corsets to thigh-length leather boots – with their oppression. Feminists have argued that such items require women to manipulate their bodies and to be uncomfortable, or to be unrealistically thin, in order to resemble caricatures found in comic books where women look like the American tv 'Wonder Woman' stereotype. Such fashions are often dismissed as accommodating male objectification of women's bodies. We take up these arguments again in chapter six when we explain why the corset had many meanings, even for Victorian women, and that it would be inappropriate for feminists to simply dismiss such clothing as a metaphor of patriarchal oppression, which literally 'restrains' women from becoming fully emancipated.

Freud may have argued that 'all women are clothing fetishists'[2] but most medical writers argue that orthodox clothing fetishism, for instance the fondling of undergarments leading to orgasm, is the province of 'deviant' men rather than women. But how can we avoid talking about clothing fetishism by women, when the fashion industry, one of the many homes of commodity fetishism, is aimed primarily at women rather than men? Even in the 1990s, when male narcissism is in evidence more than ever before, top fashion designers still design primarily for women because, overall, women still spend more money on fashion than men. All this activity of the female consumer cannot be explained in terms of women's desire to please men.

At the turn of the nineteenth century, Thorstein Veblen was one of the first to discuss women and clothing in relation to economic fetishism.[3] Writing after Marx he saw rich women in their corsets and finery as engaging in 'conspicuous consumption', a further development of the commodity fetishism which was originally described and defined by Marx.[4] Indeed, Veblen saw women's relationship to fashion as a sign of the fetishism of wealth. He saw women as decorative status symbols whose primary function, through the wearing of fashionable clothing, was to flaunt their men's accumulation of capital. Clearly in a context, as Ciciley Hamilton has pointed out, where many Victorian women viewed marriage as their 'trade',[5] there is validity in Veblen's thesis that women's bodies were often used as sites to flaunt their father's, husband's, or lover's wealth. In the Victorian period, more than ever before, both men and women used clothes, possessions and the other products they conspicuously consumed, to carve out class and gender identities for themselves.

This process of using clothes as fetish objects to differentiate changing social roles between the sexes was also examined by J C Flugel, who in the 1930s wrote a ground-breaking book on the subject called *The Psychology of Clothes*.[6] Flugel tried to explain the nineteenth century masculine renunciation of fashion in terms of economic shifts in the mode of production as well as changing psychology and social attitudes.[7] He argued that in the Victorian period women became constructed as *beautiful* 'Angels at the Hearth' while men renounced beauty to become *useful* 'Providers'. This was a shift from the eighteenth century when many Regency bucks wore make-up and fully enjoyed the pleasures of adornment and narcissism. It is only since the second half of the twentieth century that critics have really attempted to think about why in the Victorian period women's bodies became more eroticised than men's; explanations often point to the ramifications of the development of photography in the same period.

The objectification of women's appearance is now so central in Western culture that the relationship of women to fashion appears in itself to be fetishistic, or at least fixated on certain parts of the female body. Modern women often see themselves in fragments – a good pair of legs, tits or eyes, etc. Some women get fixated on emphasising their lips (by constantly putting on lipstick) or maintaining impractical ultra-long varnished nails at the expense of free movement. This behaviour appears to be linked to the overall effect of objectification of the female form. As John Berger has pointed out, to understand why women may enjoy commodifying themselves it is necessary to understand the effect of representation upon cultural definitions of masculinity and femininity. In essence Berger argues that women objectify themselves as a consequence of having internalised male ways of seeing the world. He says, 'from earliest childhood she has been persuaded to survey herself continually' and this surveillance is commodified by capitalism. In other words he locates the objectification of female appearance as a product of consumerism; commodity, not sexual, fetishism.

Across the cultures and the centuries fetishism has often been associated with perverse cultural codes which promote fashions that celebrate women 'suffering' to achieve beauty. Footbinding, or the wearing of corsets by women, are traditionally cited as evidence of masochism by vain or unthinking women. These fashions have also been seen as fetishistic in the sense of erotically over-emphasising parts of the female anatomy – a tiny foot or waist – to accommodate male pleasure. Strictly speaking, fashions which fragment the body constitute cultural eroticism or cultural fixation, not sexual fetishism in the orthodox sense. Fragmentation is related to objectification (and to fetishism), but over-emphasis of parts of the body is not the same thing as not wanting physical contact with the body at all. Fetishism involves the substitution of a part (the woman's handbag) for the whole (body of a woman) in order to achieve orgasm, as explained by Freud in his readings of orthodox sexual fetishism.

Representations of women in corsets or high-heeled shoes may look fetishistic to some feminists, but whose is the fetishism under scrutiny, and what degree of fetishism are we talking about? For example, discussion of images of powerful women which uses terms like 'phallic replacement' to describe how these images work, in our view confuses commodity fetishism of the erotic with orthodox sexual fetishism. This school of feminist criticism tends to describe 'women as spectacle' of the 'male gaze', and this has been equated with 'scopophilic' fetishism (ie, visual images become the fetish object of the voyeur). Because of the anxieties of the male unconscious, such discussion implies, these 'fetishised' images of powerful or fashionable women will never change, because men 'need' phallic replacement when they see representations of women, to cope with their castration anxiety. This is a 'universal' view we disagree with because we believe men *can* change. Over the last twenty years images of women (and men) have changed quite a lot. Indeed, we would find the concept of a commodity fetishism of masculinity (ie, powerful women are constructed as masculine) more helpful an analysis of phallic replacement issues. . . .

One of the reasons we find the 'woman as fetish' argument so misleading is because, as Caroline Evans and Minna Thornton have pointed out before us, 'fashion . . . is difficult to discuss . . . because its essence lies in its transitoriness.'[8] In the fashion system, bondage apparel or even cross-dressing (which have intrigued researchers on fetishism for so many years) may be worn as nothing more than as part of a season's 'new look'. The new look is, of course, an economic necessity for the fashion industry, an integral device used in order to persuade people to keep buying clothes; the proliferation of visual images of women is part of that marketing strategy, rather than a direct consequence of castration anxiety.

Female crossdressers

Another element of the 'season's new look' which may need to be addressed is the perennial woman in a man's suit. This is because for many years now the medical profession have connected dressing up in the clothes of the opposite sex with fetishism. Certain questions about female 'cross-dressing' should be re-considered, because male 'transvestism' is recognised as sometimes involving levels of fetishism, whereas women are rarely imagined to be clothing fetishists by the theoreticians on the subject.

When writing about transvestism, critics like Peter Ackroyd have found that some transvestite men achieve sexual gratification from wearing women's clothes: 'when I dress up it feels as if I have a continual orgasm'[9] Most medical writers agree with the view that fetishism and transvestism are often (but not always) connected[10] Explanations vary and there is no consensus about the motivation of either homosexual or heterosexual transvestites who achieve erotic pleasure from wearing clothes of the opposite sex. Nevertheless, the idea that some male transvestites may go on to have fetishistic relationships with women's clothes, rather than with sexual partners, is repeated throughout the medical literature on transvestism.[11]

Ackroyd is unsure exactly how to quantify this fetishistic behaviour. He points out, speculatively, that 'many transvestites, out of embarrassment or genuine disinterest, minimize the fetishistic elements of their cross dressing.'[12] He goes on to concur with the orthodox view that female transvestites are 'rare' and unlikely to become fetishists. Ackroyd suggests that this is because in our culture men's clothes are not emphasised as erotic as much as women's. Other critics have pointed out that 'men's clothing when worn by women only enhances the spectacle of femininity'.[13] But this latter point may be appropriate only to contemporary culture.

Historically, women cross-dressers may have simply been wearing the uniform for the job – like the black female slaves who in the early nineteenth century adopted trousers and other male attire because it helped them perform hard labour when doing work like digging trenches or even stage-coach driving.[14]

Since women have had easy access to wearing men's costume, perhaps it is logical to assume that it would be unlikely for them to find male garments dangerous or erotic. Some male transvestites (though clearly not all of them) seem to associate women's attire with illicit connotations that men's clothes, even undergarments, do not appear to offer to women.[15] Despite this gender gap, Ackroyd has speculated that 'men's clothes could become fetishes for women on the basis of the infantile female's belief in their own castration . . . on this basis it would be possible to construct a plausible etiology for female transvestism.[16]

The American psychiatrist Robert Stoller, well-known for his writings on 'perversion', would not agree with Ackroyd. He makes a clear distinction between cross-dressing and transvestism. He argues these terms should *not* be used as interchangeable concepts. He comments, 'the term transvestism should only be used to describe fetishistic cross-dressing, that is erotic excitement induced by garments of the opposite sex'.[17] He goes on to point out that female transvestism is 'rare', whereas female cross-dressing can be explained in terms of social factors.

This argument that female transvestism, and female fetishism associated with it, are rare, is further legitimated by feminist writing on the subject. Julie Wheelwright locates female cross-dressing as being primarily about social disguise.[18] For instance, in the past male disguise was often adopted by women who wanted to join the army, as a form of resistance to the social ideologies about femininity that said they could not be soldiers. Male attire gave women access to the greater social freedoms enjoyed by men.

Dutch writers Rudolf M. Dekker and Lotte C. van de Pol agree with this view. Despite their book title, which uses the words 'female transvestism', the authors say that evidence from the seventeenth and eighteenth centuries, when 119 cases of female cross-dressing were documented, shows that the cross-dressing was primarily about gender 'disguise'. They point out: 'We do not think the modern notion of transvestism contributes much to explain why women in the seventeenth and eighteenth centuries decided to cross dress'.[19]

Similarly, Annie Woodhouse, writing on the subject of female transvestism, concurs with the orthodox view and points out:

> there is no evidence, then or now, of fetishistic cross-dressing by women, the derivation of sexual pleasure from wearing certain garments or fabrics. Male dress was adopted for practical reasons . . . As Stoller (1982) points out female transvestism is largely a non issue as it is extremely rare'.[20]

Woodhouse goes on to align herself with Stoller and argue that 'the term transvestite should be taken to refer to men dressing as women'.[21]

We are sceptical about the certainty of the above comment, which writes women out of the entire account. We must confess, in addition, that despite the gender issue we haven't been completely persuaded by the dismantling of psychological distinctions between 'cross-dressing' and 'transvestism'. Cross-dressing appears to mean simply dressing up as a person of the opposite sex, whereas 'transvestism' implies there is an erotic charge connected with this behaviour (even though previously this has only been connected to male experience). In a recent book, Majorie Garber presents many new case studies of both men and women who have 'cross dressed'.[22] This material is exciting because so much of it documents new historical evidence about female activity. But again, it is difficult to know whether many of these cases involved fetishism because she uses the terms 'transvestism' and 'cross-dressing' interchangeably, ignoring the sexual distinction used by medical writers. This is because Garber reads cross-dressing as 'sign', as well as social behaviour. Her point in emphasising cross-dressing as sign is to argue that as a sign it is one that articulates a 'category crisis'.[23]

While we agree with Garber that in certain contexts (though not all), the figure of the transvestite or cross-dresser may destabilise gender boundaries, we are not convinced that this would always be so, or would necessarily articulate 'a crisis of category itself'. Underlying Garber's assertion about the radical potential of cross-dressing as sign is her idea that cross-dressing destabilises all social hierarchies:

> not only male and female but also gay and straight and sex and gender: This is the sense – the radical sense – in which transvestism is a third.[24]

Here, Garber suggests that cross-dressing is always a transgressive act. This is why she hints that the figure of the cross-dresser 'marks the space of desire'[25] and of a 'third' trans-gender term.

But how is cross-dressing transgressive, and what is it a third term of? While we can see that in some contexts the figure of the cross-dresser might be a transgressive one, we feel the transgression depends upon *context*. For example, at London nightclubs at the moment, such as 'Kinky Gerlinky, wearing drag is not about transgression or being risky, but is *de rigueur*. Additionally, as a sign it may serve to generate containment of sexual categories, by reinforcing sexual binary oppositions. This line of argument about the issue of 'containment' is one that Garber does not address or answer in her book, but 'containment' theorists such as Michel Foucault, who have written so eloquently about sexuality, would probably demand such an analysis.

Garber's most important contribution to this chapter is that she locates cross-dressing as something that women engage in in large numbers.[26] We were frustrated however, by her concurrence with the idea that women rarely fetishise. Garber discusses female theatrical performers, for example, who dress up as men and wear codpieces. Her analysis concerns only the public meaning of these events, in terms of the theatre of spectacle. She doesn't take the analysis of women any further to consider the differences of meaning provided by different contexts; for instance, differences between the public and private realms. She therefore doesn't discuss the question of female fetishism as an erotic reality for women, but instead dismisses feminist interest in this as another form of penis envy, which she calls 'fetish envy'.[27] . . . Yet wearing a codpiece by a woman and/or cross-dressing when she isn't being paid to do so, or being asked to do so, may involve unconscious or complex sexual desires and fantasies; Garber doesn't pay much attention to the female unconscious at all when discussing the question of fetishism in relationship to women. As Louise Kaplan, has commented about the erotic potential of cross-dressing: 'what distinguishes a female transvestite from other women who cross dress are her unconscious motives and the fantasy life that reveals these motives.'[28]

In the psychoanalytic literature there are case studies that analyse the female unconscious in more detail and reveal women engaging in cross-dressing for sexual pleasure. However, these cases of female transvestism involving fetishism in the orthodox sense are usually viewed as 'exceptional'. E. Guthiel writing in 1930, for instance, says his patient is a rarity when he describes a 34 year old female excited by wearing clothes of the opposite sex.

> I may say that simply putting on men's clothing gives me pleasure. The whole procedure is comparable to that tense anticipation of pleasure which subsides into relief and gratification as soon as the transvestism is complete. I even experience lustful satisfaction in dreams of this act.[29]

Clearly, the above comments locate Guthiel's case study as a 'transvestite' in the sense of Robert Stoller's definition of the term.

Stoller, himself, despite his contention that women are less likely to engage with the sexual perversions than men, cites three case studies of female transvestites who were all turned on by wearing male attire. He includes discussion of a 'divorced woman' who became aroused by Levi jeans. He quotes her as saying:

> when putting on the Levi's, I feel very excited immediately. I feel the texture, roughness of the material as I pull them over my feet, over the calves of my legs, onto my thighs . . . clitoris. It's a marvellous sensation but becomes close to painful if I am unable to relieve sexual tension.[30]

There are also case studies of women called 'transvestites' (in our view inappropriately) which turn up in the newspapers every now and again. In 1991 the *Sun* reported the case of eighteen year old Jennifer Saunders, who was prosecuted for her 'transvestism' and sentenced to six years imprisonment (she was released in 1992 after winning her appeal against her sentence). Evidently, this young woman dressed like a man, and like the fictional seventeenth century pickpocket Moll Cutpurse, passed herself off as a boy in order to date girls. The court alleged that Saunders seduced two seventeen year old girls whose parents said their daughters did not know about the disguise until it was 'too late'; other commentators have alleged that the girls did know Saunders was a girl but lied because they hadn't 'come out' as lesbians to their parents.

Although the above case of cross-dressing appears to have involved disguise rather than sexual fetishism, it does highlight, as does Garber's book, the importance of clothes in constructing sexual identities. Today, women are allowed to wear trousers with less comment than a man would provoke in a skirt; nevertheless it is still not acceptable for women to look too 'butch' or too 'mannish'.

[. . .]

Slenderness and eroticism

The thin erotic aesthetic is so central to the Western beauty ethos that for women, eating has become associated with sinning. As Shelley Bovey has pointed, out to many people 'being fat IS a sin'.[31] Recent medical surveys provide confirmation of female fears about fat and the oppressive nature of female psychological conditioning through compulsive weight control. They reveal that on any day 25 per cent of all American women are on diets. Although 40 per cent of men, compared to 32 per cent of women are overweight, almost 60 per cent of UK and US women in the sample group, compared to 10 per cent of men, had been on slimming diets in the twelve months previous to the date of survey.[32]

Obsessions with weight control contain so many other anxieties that it is common for women to fantasize that all their problems might be resolved if only they could lose a few more pounds[33] Even very young girls are identified as showing signs of being obsessed with dieting. Hilde Bruch in the 1970s found that 'concern with weight and feelings of fatness have been seen to be increasingly prominent among younger children, even as early as the age of 7'.[34] It seems that messages about slenderness are inscribed onto the female psyche at a young age – at the same time as the message about how to be 'feminine'.

While contemporary discourses about femininity have forged a direct association between sexual attractiveness and the 'thin' aesthetic, the development of the thin woman as cultural icon has a short history. Despite the nineteenth century penchant in Western Europe (and the USA) for small waists and tightly laced corsets, it was not until the beginning of the twentieth century that thinness became culturally emphasised in the West as an ideal for women.[35]

At the end of the nineteenth century historians like Veblen were noticing the slender wives of the wealthy.[36] By 1908, the Paris fashion correspondent for *Vogue* magazine was proclaiming that 'the fashionable figure is growing straighter and straighter, less bust, less hips more waist and a wonderfully, long slender suppleness about the limbs, . . . how slim, how graceful, how elegant women look.'[37]

It is fascinating to consider that the shape of the western female body appears to have significantly altered around the periods 1912–1919 and 1967–1974, periods which, as Juliet Mitchell has pointed out, were both characterised by mass movements of women as well as political and cultural rebellion.[38] Indeed, the boyish gamine first made her entrance in the 1920s with the arrival of the flapper who tightly bound her bosoms and created sexual ambiguity about the female form. The flapper's 'boyish androgynous body' was clearly a forerunner to the anti-maternal emaciated look that emerged in the 1960s.[39]

Models like Shrimpton (the 'Shrimp') and Twiggy took the fashion world by storm in 1965 when they arrived alongside of the pill and sexual liberation a little ahead of the second wave women's movement (but without any theoretical framework to explain the significance of this new female body ideal).[40] In retrospect, it is clear that the rounded icons of the 1950s post-war period – Monroe, Hayworth and Mansfield – went out of fashion at the same time as the emphasis on domesticity started to lose its allure. Into the spotlight came women with skinny 'hard' bodies, who looked more like adolescent boys than the softly curved female icons of the previous decade, and who were ready to take their place in a man's world.

It seems ironic that today, when western women have been undergoing such a vast change and expansion in their social roles, they should be represented as being 'less', that is, physically smaller. Elizabeth Wilson argues that technological inventions may have as much to do with the culture of slenderness as with patriarchal relations. She cites the influence of photography on fashion images as 'influencing and changing the actual appearance of the women in the street'.[41] She points out that photography accentuates width, and therefore makes the fashion industry over-conscious about fatness. She argues that because photography has come to dominate fashion journalism, 'it has contributed to the fashion for extreme thinness and length of leg'.[42] Although Wilson notes that photographic *illusion* may have come to change the appearance of real women, she is wary of oversimplifying:

> Foucault . . . puts the body back into the social sciences. As anyone who has tried to diet knows, it is rather difficult to radically alter the shape of one's body. Yet dress and adornment in all cultures has been used to do precisely this: from tattooing and neck rings, to the dyeing and curling of hair and the use of high heels, both women and men have worked hard to produce a 'different' body.[43]

Recent research by Silversteen *et al* would agree with Wilson about the difficulties of changing body shape, but nevertheless draws our attention to the contradictory effect of social change upon female identity. They argue that periods of female leanness correlate with periods where women's economic and social position improved.[44] After analysing photography of women from the nineteenth century to the present day, they argue that at the historical point when women start to achieve 'male status' they desire and start to look like men.

There is no denying that since the 1960s thinness in women has been celebrated. We can't simply 'blame' representations for 'causing' eating disorder but we note that even the average weight of the Playboy Playmate centrefold, has dropped.[45] Janine Cataldo has pointed out that 'in the last 20 years the current female body ideal has shown a decrease in weight, bust and hips and an increase in waist size'.[46] Less than 5 per cent of Western women are estimated to be born with the genetic predisposition to meet the modern ideal.[47] The thin 'ideal' remains despite the real conditions of female existence: at the same time, 'the weight of the average [American] woman has become steadily heavier than that of 20 years ago'.[48]

This recent Western phenomenon of eroticising images of underweight women has been the subject of many studies. Feminists like Shelley Bovey, Kim Chernin, Elizabeth Wilson and Naomi Wolf point out that thinness is a new fad even in the West. Previously, in portraits of women for example, 'various distributions of sexual fat were emphasised – big ripe bellies from the fifteenth to seventeenth centuries, plump faces and shoulders in the early nineteenth century . . . generous dimpled buttocks and thighs until the twentieth century'.[49]

[. . .]

Even books that take fetishism as their main topic of discussion, such as David Kunzle's *Fashion and Fetishism*,[50] have in our view been unable to make adequate distinctions between fetishism and *eroticism*. Descriptions of eroticism, inappropriately diagnosed as fetishism, are common to much of the literature we found under the subject index 'fetishism'. In what follows we consider Kunzle's book in detail because its problems are endemic to many other studies.

[. . .]

The empirical methodology of David Kunzle's book *Fashion and Fetishism* attempts to identify female fetishism by quoting journals and correspondence which describes the feelings of Victorian ladies who enjoyed tight-lacing of corsets. Kunzle's position is that corset-wearing wasn't just 'fashion' for many Victorian women of all classes, but often constituted sexual gratification because:

> Tight-lacing, like all forms of fetishism certainly exists . . . The capacity of modern woman for an active, rather than passive form of fetishism is confirmed by the practicing fetishist pairs personally known to me, amongst whom the female often assumes an active and sometimes leading role.[51]

Kunzle's argument is that a group of 'tight-lacers' – that is women who enjoyed the pleasures of constriction from wearing corsets as much the achievement of twelve inch waists – were sexually assertive women enjoying self-flagellation and thereby expressing female desire. (He uses the word 'fetishism' to categorise this behaviour but his descriptions are of S&M scenarios.)

Kunzle's book goes on to argue that those who saw the corset as simply 'oppressive', such as the dress reform movement or the physicians worried about women engaged in 'crushing' their ribs, were, not always in an objective position to understand or judge the behaviour they condemned. Critics of the corset were either socially conservative and/or sexually puritanical because:

> the rebellion/restraints of tight-lacing is not merely a masochistic reflection of socio-sexual subjection of women by man, but a submissive/aggressive protest against that role.[52]

Kunzle goes on to argue that his tight-lacers are women 'fetishists' and entirely different from fashion victims who endure discomfort to be fashionable.

Whatever we deduce about the activities of the 'tight-lacers' from the correspondence referred to by Kunzle, there is no denying there is much slippage in his terminology. Like other books on the subject of fetishism that try to read 'across' culture, Kunzle is unable to distinguish between the different types of fetishism he encounters in his case studies. Some cases of corset fixation may constitute sexual fetishism of clothing by women, but Kunzle's book makes so many generalisations, on subjects as diverse as starch linen fetishism, breast eroticism (which he inappropriately describes as 'breast fetishism'[53]) as well as 'Zoo fetishism',[54] that it is hard to be sure what he means at all. It is almost impossible to decide from Kunzle's accounts whether or not the men/women he describes choose the object to bring them to sexual orgasm in preference to any other sexual stimulation. If they did this would clearly constitute sexual fetishism in the fourth degree as outlined in chapter one when discussing Gebhard's model of the intensities of sexual fetishism. But Kunzle is not clear at all, either about the intensity of, or even the sexual nature of, the behaviour he is talking about.

His ideas about the sexual pleasure gained from 'constriction' or 'flagellation', for example, associated with women wearing corsets, more appropriately equate with bondage scenarios and the pscyhoanalytic concept of masochism than with fetishism. Yet Kunzle refutes the suggestion of masochism:

> The dependency which tight lacing might induce is both psychological and physical. One young woman described her feelings when she wanted to be tighter than the corset could make her as 'really hurting' and 'being out of touch with my body' . . . once the threshold of pain has been passed, it is experienced as pure pain, a condition the fetishist (as opposed to the masochist) does not seek.[55]

In the above quotation, fetishism is seen as pain that is not 'total', whereas masochism is associated with nothing but pain. Such an analysis ignores psycho-analytic theories of masochism and denies a notion of various intensities of gratifica-tion. This may be because Kunzle does not really address psychoanalytic concepts at all in his discussion of fetishism:

> the reduction by psychoanalysis of human personality to intra-psychic traits, and its elimination of social factors, has rendered it useless, if not actually harmful, when dealing with fetishism.[56]

Kunzle's dismisal of psychoanalysis is not as surprising as it might first appear, but is a political strategy. As Valerie Steele has pointed out:

> Kunzle deliberately eschews any attempt to analyze the possible unconscious significance of fetishism, presumably because such an analy-sis might make tight-lacing appear to be a sexual perversion rather than an orthodox but legitimate and sexually liberated form of behaviour . . . his work is a *defense* of fetishism.[57]

But by 'defending' fetishism Kunzle side-steps the issue of masochism and its pleasures and conflates ideas about eroticism and fetishism, a point we shall return to later.

How do we understand this apparent Victorian epidemic of female masochism in terms of female desire rather than women's oppression? Kunzle is of course right when he says it would be absurd to simply regard the corset as a metaphor of women's social restraints and subordination. As Elizabeth Wilson among other critics has pointed out, the corset has had so many different meanings in Victorian times as well as our own.

By focussing on corset 'fetishism' rather than on the issue of the 'masochism' of Victorian women, Kunzle implicitly refutes radical feminist arguments on corset-wearing: Mary Daly and Jane Caputi, among others, locate body modifications or uncomfortable fashions for women as further evidence of patriarchal oppression, and:

> a primary means by which phallocratic fixers fix, tame, and train women for their own designs; the bad magic by which fakers attempt to destroy female consciousness, embedding contagious anxieties and cravings trying to trap women in houses of correction/ houses of mirrors . . .[58]

Indeed, by implying that the meaning of the corset for women who derive sexual pleasure from tight-lacing was, and is, connected to ideas about social resistance, Kunzle is able to move away from a negative reading of female agency. But it should be borne in mind that only a simplistic understanding of 'masochism' would interpret such pleasure from tight-lacing as unproblematically equating with women's oppression; many feminists writing about cultural politics certainly would not take this line.[59]

So while we sympathise with Kunzle's dilemma, and his reluctance to accept the radical feminist argument that reads the corset as a metaphor of women's oppression, we feel his methodology is inappropriate. By refusing to engage with psychoanalysis he prevents himself from developing an informed analysis of the corset. A more sophisticated model of masochism and its pleasures would have served his argument much more appropriately than the concept of fetishism. In fact we found three main flaws to Kunzle's logic.

First, it must be noted that sexual pleasure derived from the tight-lacing of corsets by a small group of specific women – even if this interpretation could be proven – is unlikely to be representative of the meaning of the corset in the lives of the majority of nineteenth century women. (Kunzle's reading of Victorian journals and data, it should be noted, are by no means conclusive in their findings.) Secondly, the precise nature of the sexual pleasure Kunzle alludes to is not specified. It seems unlikely from the accounts found in Victorian journals that the corset, as an object in its own right, produced orgasm in women. It is more likely that it was the element of bondage and constriction that created sexual catharsis in women. Third, and finally, the gender gap between sexual pleasure gained by an individual from the process of achieving a tiny waist, and the widespread male erotic interest in tiny waists (and the erotic charge from binding and unbinding the waist and bosom) cannot be completely separated. Nor can it be over-stressed. Kunzle's logic suggests a compatibility between socially learned gender roles concerning who is laced and who isn't.

The tight-lacer may achieve pleasure from constriction (and release from it), associated with masochism; the viewer may achieve erotic pleasure from visual images of tiny waists and heaving bosoms and the fantasy of 'possessing' them, but Kunzle's gender equation implies that it is always the women who enjoy being tied up and the men who do the untying. This analysis, which to be fair may have only been meant to describe the tight-lacing pairs 'known' to Kunzle, nevertheless presents a restrictive and inaccurate analysis of S&M practice. Men as well as women are reported in great numbers to enjoy masochism. Despite the gender issues in the scenarios Kunzle describes, neither sex appears to be engaged in sexual fetishism, at the level that Gebhard described as the fourth degree.

This question of a *degree* of erotic charge seems to have escaped the curiosity of many fashion historians who connect fashion trends with fetishism. Laver, for example, suggested that 'fashion is the comparative of which fetishism is the superlative'.[60] He went on to talk about male appreciation of female fashion trends like 'frou frou fetishism' in a way that conflates terms. As Valerie Steele has pointed out 'fashion historians . . . jump to the conclusion that the incidence of fetishism was significantly higher in the nineteenth century than in the earlier or later periods – an hypothesis that the available evidence does not necessarily support.'[61]

What is positive about Kunzle's work, however flawed the analysis, is that he does recognise and try to theorise female agency. Not many critics have in fact looked at women as practitioners of fetishism. We see this focus as 'radical' because much writing which does appear at first glance to be about female fetishism, doesn't look at women as *practitioners* of fetishism at all. Instead it looks at the construction and representation of 'women as fetish'.

With one or two exceptions, most of the research on female fetishism that we found (written in the 1970s and 1980s) focussed on women as objects of fetishism, rather than as agents of fetishism, in order to explore women's oppression as a consequence of the male gaze. This work was important for feminism and opened up debates about women and representation. Questions about women's objectification are obviously relevant to debates about images of women in popular culture. But we feel that in such a changing cultural context, where images are often ironic and may be read differently by different groups anyway, feminists have to be careful about applying theoretical models too monolithically.

The image of 'Emma Peel' from the TV series *The Avengers*, for instance, may have given many women and men pleasure because of the energetic sexual spectacle she made in leather clothing, but this sort of active image is rarely discussed by critics as pleasurable at all.[62] Yet frequently feminist criticism has not talked about the *active pleasures* on offer to women from obviously fetishised images. This may be partly due to the rather generalised definition of 'fetishism' that has emerged in some feminist debates, which virtually dismiss all images of strong women as enacting 'phallic replacement'. Here, if the critic is Andrea Dworkin, ideas about the male gaze can become a crude metaphor which correlates with radical feminist readings of 'patriarchy'.[63]

Summary

In conclusion we argue that by looking at the issue of conflation in the different types of fetishisms employed in feminist theoretical discussion, we have highlighted the discursive formation contributing to the widespread critical conclusion that fetishism is 'rare' in women. We have pointed to the fact that the subject area has been neglected to some extent because the theoretical focus on 'Lack' has become a discursive practice. The Lacanian model has led to a feminist reading of images of women in the cinema as always 'objects' and 'victims' of male fetishism, obscuring questions about female agency. It has also ignored questions about shifts in representations as a result of change in social roles, and more recently through the emergence of post-modern aesthetics.

[. . .]

Notes

1   Linda Gordon and Ellen Dubois, 'Seeking Ecstasy on the Battlefield: Danger and Pleasure in Nineteenth Century Feminist Sexual Thought', *Feminist Review* 13, Spring 1983, pp42–54.

2   Louise Rose, 'Freud and Fetishism: Previously Unpublished Minutes of the Vienna Psychoanalytic Society', *Psychoanalytic Quarterly*, 57, 1988, pp147–160 (p 156).

3   Thorstein Bunde Veblen, *The Theory of the Leisure Class: An Economic Study in the Evolution of Institutions*, Macmillan Co, New York 1899.

4   See definition of 'Commodity Fetishism', pp29–38.

5   C. Hamilton, *Marriage as Trade*, Women's Press, London 1981.

6   J. Flugel, *The Psychology of Clothes*, L. & V. Woolf, Institute of Psychoanalysis, London 1930.

7   Ibid.

8   Caroline Evans and Minna Thornton, *Women and Fashion: A New Look*, Quartet, London 1989, p81.

9   Peter Ackroyd, *Dressing Up: Transvestism and Drag: the History of an Obsession*, Thames & Hudson, London 1979, p21.

10 Some medical writers note, however, that 'in a purely behavioural sense transvestism and fetishism are independent patterns'. Some qualification of this distinction is made by the comment that 'difficulty arises when we attempt to *interpret* these patterns'. H. Brierley, *Transvestism: A Handbook with Case Studies for Psychologists, Psychiatrists and Counsellors*, Pergamon, Oxford 1979, p224.

11 Many critics qualify that married male transvestites are able to have 'fulfilling' relationships with women. See Y. Sinclair's *Transvestism Within A Partnership of Marriage and Families*, The TV/TS Group, London 1984. The author stresses this point using case studies and quotes from wives.

12 P. Ackroyd, op. cit., 1979.

13 E. Apter, op. cit., 1991.

14 Lillian Faderman, *Odd Girls and Twilight Lovers: A History of Lesbian Life in 20th Century America*, Penguin, Harmondsworth 1992. An illustration opposite p86 shows a photograph 'of Mary Fields born a slave who often wore men's clothes as a stage-coach driver'.

15 We should qualify this point again by saying that not all male transvestites consciously find clothes erotic. When interviewed on ITV's 'Good Morning Britain' slot in 1990, some tvs invited on as guests said they didn't find wearing women's clothes erotic but it just made them feel good and/or that they enjoyed the element of disguise in passing as 'female'.

16 P. Ackroyd, op. cit., 1979.

17 Robert Stoller, *Observing The Erotic Imagination*, Yale University Press, New Haven, London 1985, p176.

18 J. Wheelwright, *Amazons and Military Maids: women who dressed as men in the pursuit of life, liberty and happiness*, Pandora, London 1989.

19   *The Tradition of Female Transvestism in Early Modern Europe*, Rudolf M. Dekker and Lotte C. van de Pol, Macmillan, London 1989, p55.

20   Annie Woodhouse, *Fantastic Women: Sex, Gender and Transvestism*, Macmillan, London 1989, p18.

21   Ibid., p18–20.

22   Marjorie Garber, *Vested Interests: Cross-Dressing and Cultural Anxiety*, Routledge, London 1991.

23   Ibid., p16.

24   Ibid., p133.

25   Ibid., p133.

26   Margorie Garber, p44, cites references we hadn't heard of before like the 1985 publication, *Information for the Female to Male Crossdress or Transsexual*, in a way we haven't been able to find in British books.

27   M. Garber, op. cit., p118, does talk about 'fetish envy' but this relates only to her analysis of the wearing of cod pieces by female performers in the theatre, discussion of which is critically assessed in chapter six of this book.

28   L. Kaplan, op. cit., 1991, p244.

29   E. Guthiel, 1930, 'Analysis of a Case of Female Transvestism', in W. Stekel, *Sexual Aberrations*, Vision, London 1953.

30   R. Stoller, op. cit., p143.

31   Shelley Bovey, *Being Fat is not a Sin*, Pandora, London 1989.

32   Naomi Wolf, *The Beauty Myth*, Chatto & Windus, London 1990, p151.

33   R.A. Gordon, op. cit., p48.

34   Richard A. Gordon *Anorexia and Bulimia: Anatomy of a Social Epidemic*, Blackwell, London 1990, p71.

35   Ibid., p77.

36   T. Veblen, *The Theory of the Leisure Class*, Macmillan, London 1899, pp148–9.

37   V. Steele, *Fashion and Eroticism*, Oxford University Press, Oxford 1985, p227.

38   Juliet Mitchell, 'Feminist Theory and Feminist Movements: The Past Before us', in *What is Feminism*', Juliet Mitchell and Ann Oakley (eds), Blackwell, London 1986, p58.

39   William Bonnet and Joel Gurin, *The Dieter's Dilemma*, Harper Row, New York 1982, chapter 7.

40   Twiggy was initially received with a certain amount of amusement by the popular press, as the deliberately ironic name suggests. We are indebted to Ian Birchall for reminding us of the popular joke of the time, 'Forget Oxfam: feed Twiggy'.

41   Wilson, op. cit. p116.

42   Ibid., p116.

43   Julie Ash and Elizabeth Wilson, *Chic Thrills: A Fashion Reader*, Pandora, London 1992, p10.

44   Cited in R.A. Gordon, *Anorexia and Bulimia: Anatomy of a Social Epidemic*, Blackwell, London 1990, p7.

45   Researchers found the body size of the *Playboy* centre fold decreased from 11 per cent below the national average in 1970 to 17 per cent eight years later. Gardener *et al.*, 'Cultural Expectations of Thinness in Women', *Psychological Reports*, 47 (1980), pp483–9.

46   Janine Cataldo, 'Obesity: A New Perspective on An Old Problem', *Health Education Journal*, Vol 44 (1985), p213.

47   K. Chernin, *Womansize: The Tyranny of Slenderness*, Women's Press, London 1981.

48   R.A. Gordon, *Anorexia and Bulimia, op cit*, p69.

49   Wolf, op. cit., p150.

50   D. Kunzle, *Fashion and Fetishism: A Social History of the Corset, Tight-lacing and Other Forms of Body Sculpture in the West*, New York: Rowman & Littlefield, 1982.

51   Ibid., p36.

52   Ibid., p250.

53   Ibid., p16.

54   Ibid., p9.

55   Ibid., p39.

56   Ibid., p14.

57   V. Steele, *Fashion and Eroticism: Ideals of Feminine Beauty From the Victorian Era to the Jazz Age*, Oxford University Press, Oxford 1985, p30.

58   Mary Daly (with Jane Caputo), *Websters' First New Integalactic Wickedary of the English Language*, Beacon Press, Boston, 1987, p198.

59   'See definition of masochism by Ellie Rayland-Sullivan in *Feminism and Psychoanalysis*, discussed in E. Wright, (ed), *Feminism and Psychoanalysis: A Critical Dictionary*, Blackwell, Oxford', 1992.

60   V. Steele, 1985, op. cit., p30.

61   Ibid., p30.

62   L. Gamman and M. Marshment (eds), *The Female Gaze: Women as Viewers of Popular Culture*, Women's Press, London, 1988, p10.

63   This argument about fetishised images of women has become so general that Andrea Dworkin, known for her biological essentialism and sweeping radical feminist statements, applies wholesale ideas about 'fetishised' images of women and argues: 'men look at women in an abstracting or fetishizing way; the voyeurism, the displaced excitement (displaced to the mind), puts the physical reality . . . into a dimension of numbed abstraction', Andrea Dworkin, *Intercourse*, Martin & Secker, 1987, London, p33.

Chapter 48

Roland Barthes

'WHERE THE GARMENT GAPES'

[. . .]

IS NOT THE MOST EROTIC PORTION of a body *where the garment gapes?* In perversion (which is the realm of textual pleasure) there are no "erogenous zones" (a foolish expression, besides); it is intermittence, as psycho-analysis has so rightly stated, which is erotic: the intermittence of skin flashing between two articles of clothing (trousers and sweater), between two edges (the open-necked shirt, the glove and the sleeve); it is this flash itself which seduces, or rather: the staging of an appearance-as-disappearance.

The pleasure of the text is not the pleasure of the corporeal striptease or of narrative suspense. In these cases, there is no tear, no edges: a gradual unveiling: the entire excitation takes refuge in the *hope* of seeing the sexual organ (schoolboy's dream) or in knowing the end of the story (novelistic satisfaction). Paradoxically (since it is mass-consumed), this is a far more intellectual pleasure than the other: an Oedipal pleasure (to denude, to know, to learn the origin and the end), if it is true that every narrative (every unveiling of the truth) is a staging of the (absent, hidden, or hypostatized) father — which would explain the solidarity of narrative forms, of family structures, and of prohibitions of nudity, all collected in our culture in the myth of Noah's sons covering his nakedness.

[. . .]

Index